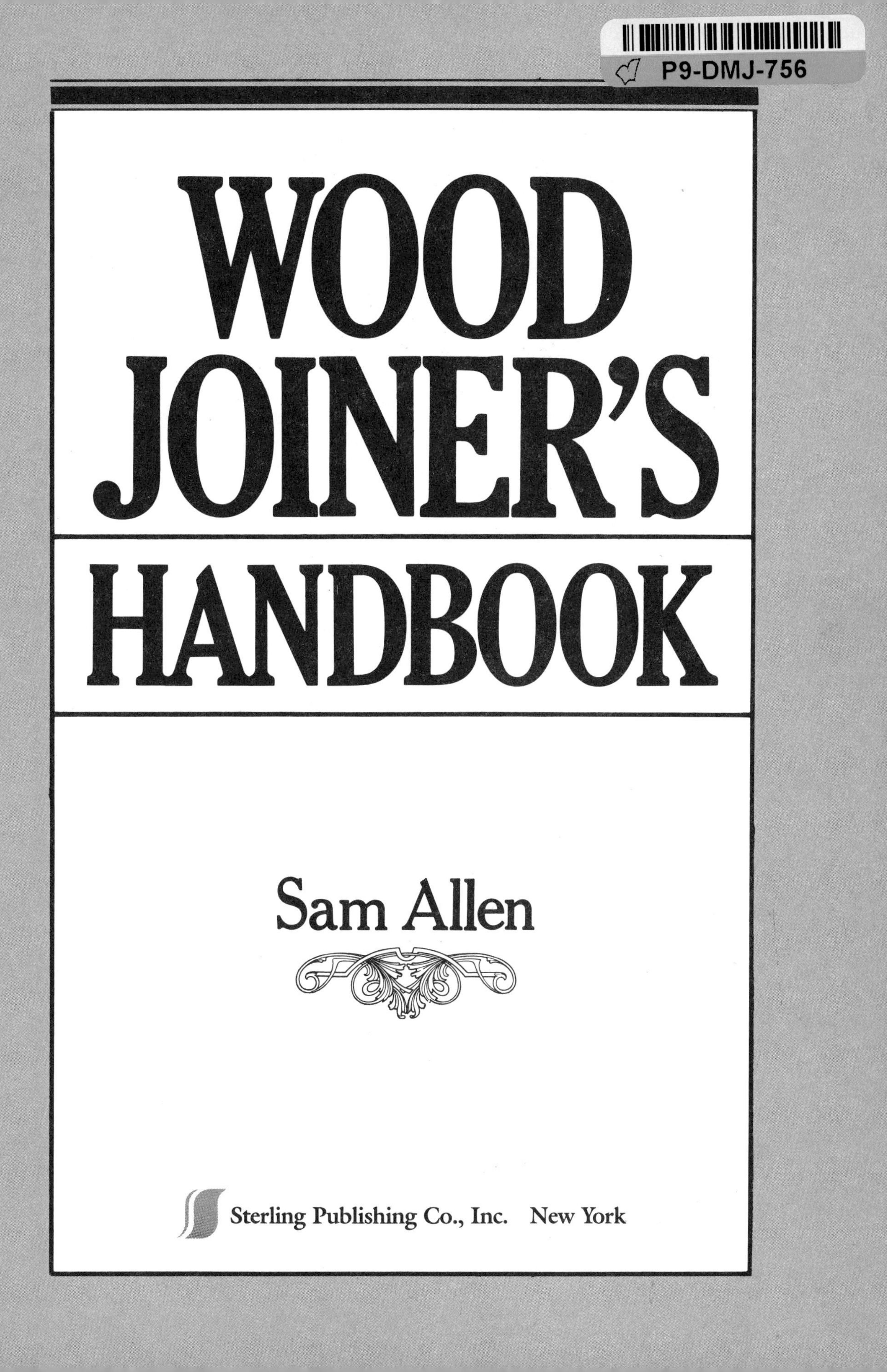

WOOD JOINER'S HANDBOOK

Sam Allen

Sterling Publishing Co., Inc. New York

DEDICATION

This book is dedicated to the memory of my uncle, Dr. Elbert Stevenson. Before his untimely death in 1987, he contributed several ideas for this book. His shop appears in some of the photos throughout the book.

ACKNOWLEDGMENTS

I would like to thank the following people for their help in the preparation of this book: Mark Johnson, for allowing me access to his antique furniture collection; Elaine Evans, for allowing me access to her collection of Oriental furniture; Wayne Ruth, for allowing me access to his collection of antique tools; Rick Newcombe, Sales and Marketing Manager for Leigh Industries Ltd., for providing illustrations and information about the Leigh dovetail jig and a sample jig for testing and evaluation; David A. Keller, President Keller and Co., for providing information about the Keller dovetail jig and a sample jig for testing and evaluation; my Dad, Samuel M. Allen, M.D., for his help with research and photography of Japanese joints; Marie Stevenson for allowing me to photograph the timber framing used in her barn. I would also like to thank my wife, Virginia, for her help in preparing the manuscript.

Edited by Rodman Neumann

Library of Congress Cataloging-in-Publication Data

Allen, Sam.
Wood joiner's handbook / Sam Allen.
p. cm.
ISBN 0-8069-6999-7
1. Joinery. I. Title.
TH5662.A45 1990
694'.6—dc20 89-26189
CIP

Published by Sterling Publishing Co., Inc.
387 Park Avenue South, New York, N.Y. 10016
Distributed in Canada by Sterling Publishing
℅ Canadian Manda Group, P.O. Box 920, Station U
Toronto, Ontario, Canada M8Z 5P9
Distributed in Great Britain and Europe by Cassell PLC
Artillery House, Artillery Row, London SW1P 1RT, England
Distributed in Australia by Capricorn Ltd.
P.O. Box 665, Lane Cove, NSW 2066
Manufactured in the United States of America

Library of Congress Catalog Card No.: 89-26189
Sterling ISBN 0-8069-6999-7 Paper

Contents

Introduction

For as long as people have worked with wood, there has been some form of joinery. Many of the joints developed at the dawn of woodworking are still in use. A few years ago, I visited an exhibit of Egyptian artifacts from the tomb of Ramses II. I felt a closeness to these ancient woodworkers when I recognized the same joints that I frequently use. I saw evidence of mortise-and-tenon joints, splines, and dovetails.

Egyptian woodwork survives because of the dry climate. We can't say what the earliest joints were, but it's likely that they were notched logs for shelters. Some examples from A.D. 800 survive in Scandinavia. The log cabin of the Old West of the United States is a descendant of these (Illus. 1).

Timber framing developed subsequently, and uses wood more economically than log structures. The mortise-and-tenon joint, in particular, made timber framing possible.

As early as the fifteenth century woodworking had developed such that one person could barely master all phases of the craft. Specialized trades developed allowing individual craftsmen to master a specific aspect of woodworking. In its strictest definition the title "joiner" belongs to a specialized craft within the broad range of woodworking. A joiner is a woodworker specializing in doors, windows, panelled walls, decorative trim, cupboards, etc. (Illus. 2). However, in a broader sense all woodworkers are joiners since the basis of woodwork is joining several boards into a product. The carpenter uses joints to bear the weight of a building; the cooper must join wood into a water-tight container; and the cabinetmaker joins boards to form the carcass, doors, and drawers of a cabinet.

Before the development of reliable glue, wood joints had to hold even if the glue failed. This led to the development of many complex self-locking joints (Illus. 3). Today glues are usually so strong that you really don't need to use these complex joints for strength. But there are still many instances where such joints are useful. For example, teakwood contains a latex-like substance that can contaminate the glue line, causing it to fail. If you choose to use a self-locking joint you

Illus. 1. The joints used to make log cabins are direct descendents of some of the earliest-known wood joints.

Illus. 2. This panelled door is an example of what would traditionally be considered joiner's work.

can ensure against such glue failure. In other cases you may choose to use a complex joint for purely aesthetic reasons.

While many things in wood joinery stay the same, many things change. New joints are developed to accommodate new materials; some joints are better suited to machine work while others remain best done by hand. In this book I have sought to strike a balance between the old and the new. Many old techniques are worth preserving, but because they require a lot of hand labor, commercial shops can't afford to use them. These techniques are presented nevertheless for the serious amateur who wants to exercise skill in advanced joinery. For those interested in less labor-intensive joints and perhaps mass production, some of the newest methods are included.

While working in a furniture repair shop for several years, I had a wonderful opportunity to observe firsthand the strengths and weaknesses of various joints. I learned much more about joints by repairing rather than building furniture. When you build a piece and sell it, you don't get to see how it stands up to the test of time. But, when you are repairing furniture, you see how the joints perform after years of use. I found out that many times a joint had been used inappropriately, resulting in a weakness in the piece of furniture that would not exist if a different joint had been used. This is true par-

Illus. 3. Complex self-locking joints like this Japanese gooseneck joint were developed in part to compensate for the lack of reliable glues.

ticularly when a joint developed for use with hardwood is applied to a manmade material such as plywood or particleboard. Throughout the book I will point out typical joint failures and weaknesses and how to avoid the failure (Illus. 4).

Illus. 4. A short stub tenon was used at the corner joint of a panelled door. Notice how the joint has failed along the grain of the stile. In this application, a longer tenon would have been more appropriate.

Every woodworker has a favorite way of making a particular joint. I will give several methods for each joint; you can discover the one you like best. There are many specialized tools used in joinery, but you can make any of the joints in this book with a few basic hand tools or with common power equipment such as a table saw and router. I will explain how to make the joint using the more common tools, but I will also discuss some of the specialized equipment so that you will know what is available.

Scope of the Work

The full range of joinery is so diverse that I couldn't cover every conceivable joint; therefore, I picked the ones that I found interesting or particularly useful for the general woodworker. Most of the joints have applications in cabinetmaking, but I have included from other specialties some joints that I felt would be useful in more general woodworking. My intention is that this book be as useful as possible equally to the novice and the advanced woodworker. The book is divided into three sections. Part One, Joinery Fundamentals, will give you a basic understanding of joinery. Chapter 1 covers the elements of how joints work along with gluing technique, some time-tested rules of thumb, and joinery tools. In Chapter 2 you will learn how to make six basic joints with hand tools. Chapter 3 covers joint reinforcement.

Once you have the basics, you are ready for the in-depth exposition of Part Two: Joinery Techniques. In this section, each chapter is devoted to a particular type of joint. You will learn about variations on the design of the basic joint and various techniques for making the joint. Part Two begins with Chapter 4: Mitre Variations. The other joints covered in Part Two are: rabbets, dadoes, and grooves in Chapter 5; mortise-and-tenon, Chapter 6; dovetails, Chapter 7; box joints and multiple splines, Chapter 8; and lap joints, Chapter 9.

Part Three, Joinery Applications, shows how joints are used in real-world applications and introduces some joints that are adapted specifically to a particular application. This section begins with frame-and-panel joinery in Chapter 10, and cabinetmaking applications in Chapter 11. The specific advantages and problems of plywood and particleboard joints are covered in Chapter 12. Chapter 13 contains material on a variety of specialty joints. These are joints that, although they were developed to fit the needs of a particular woodworking specialty, have applications in general woodworking. Some of the specialty joints included are: moulding joints, coopering joints, mechanical joints, sash joints, and timber-framing joints.

Part Three concludes with decorative joints in Chapter 14 and with the opportunity to further your understanding of the nature of wood by studying its transcultural applications in joints from China and Japan in Chapter 15.

Safety

In joinery as with all aspects of woodworking, keep safety in mind at all times. Keep your tools sharp and in good condition. Clamp the workpiece securely to the bench when working and keep your hands behind the cutting edge of the tools. Wear protective equipment such as safety glasses, hearing protectors, and dust masks (Illus. 5). Avoid loose clothing and jewelry, and

Illus. 5. Protective equipment such as safety glasses, hearing protectors, and dust masks should be worn when necessary for your personal safety. (Drawing courtesy Leigh Industries, Ltd.)

tie back long hair when operating power equipment. Use the guards provided with power equipment (Illus. 6). *In some photos in this book, guards had to be removed to clearly show the operation, but you should use the guard whenever possible.* If the operation can't be performed with the guard in place, use extreme caution. Read and follow the manufacturer's instructions before operating any piece of equipment. Always keep your hands well clear of the cutting part of any tool. Use push sticks, scrap or manufactured, whenever necessary (Illus. 7).

Don't work while under the influence of drugs or alcohol; don't work if you are taking medications that will make you drowsy while working. Think through each operation with an eye towards safety. Use an alternate technique if the one you plan on using will put you at risk of an accident. Be aware of what the risks are for any operation you attempt.

Illus. 6. Use the guards provided with power equipment. In some photos later in this book, guards have been removed to show the operation more clearly, but you should make sure to use the guard whenever possible.

Illus. 7. Use push sticks to keep your hands away from the blade.

PART I
JOINERY FUNDAMENTALS

1
The Elements of Joinery

There are a number of things you need to know about the way joints work in order to understand thoroughly the rest of this book. An understanding of the types of stress to which joints are subject will help you find the right joint for the job. Glue is also an important factor in overall joint strength. Proper gluing technique is needed for achieving the maximum strength.

Over the years a number of traditional rules of thumb have been developed and passed down. Most of these are tried and true for most joinery situations. Occasionally bending the rules will result in a better joint for a specific application. I will present a few basic rules of thumb in this chapter. Others as they apply to specific joints will be included in the appropriate chapter.

I am assuming that you are familiar with basic woodworking tools as well as their maintenance and operation, so I won't go into a lot of detail about tools. There are a few specific tools that I will discuss at some length because of their importance in joinery.

Types of Stress

Wood joints are subjected to several types of stress (Illus. 8). Different joints will hold up to certain types of stress better than others. To select the appropriate joint intelligently, you need to understand the types of stress to which the joint will be subjected.

Compressional stress results when most of the force is pushing the joint together. To counteract compression you need to provide a large surface area of contact at a right angle to the stress. Compressional stress is the easiest for a joint to handle since the force applied is directed into the joint, so many joints are designed to convert the various forces acting within the pieces into compressional stress.

Shear stress results when most of the force tends to cause two sides to slide relative to each other in a direction parallel to their contact, as might be found on the joint between a shelf and the side of a cabinet. The weight of the shelf and anything on it is acting to push the shelf down the side. In a simple butt joint, the glue line would be subjected to the total effect of the shear stress. To counteract this shear in a butt joint, some type of reinforcement is needed. If dowels are placed across the joint line then the shear stress would have to be great enough to snap the dowels before the joint would fail (Illus. 9). Another method of counteracting shear is to con-

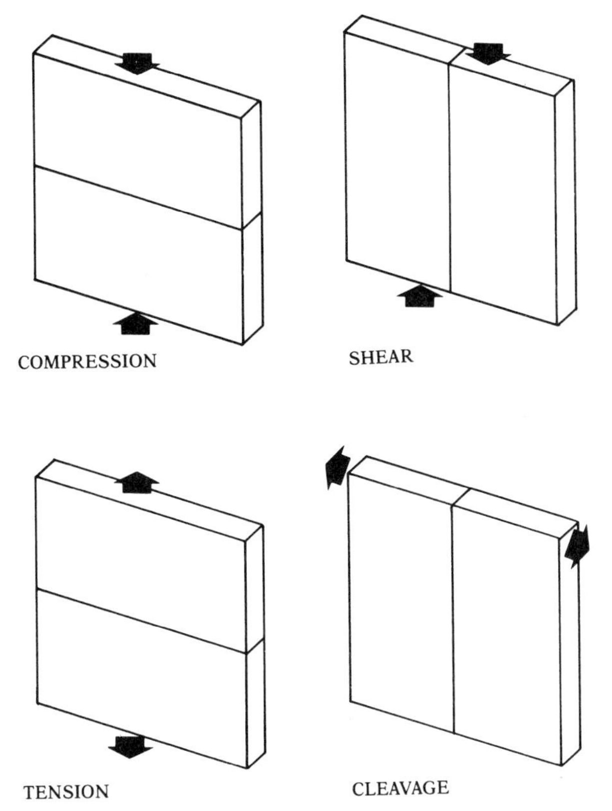

Illus. 8. Types of stress.

Illus. 9. Shear stress can be counteracted in the joint with reinforcements such as dowels or by providing a shoulder to convert the shear into compression as with the dado joint on the left.

vert much of it into compression. If the shelf is joined to the side with a dado, then the downward component is a compressional force against the shoulder of the dado.

Tensional stress results when most of the force is tending to pull a joint apart. For example, if the bottom shelf of a wall-hung cabinet is attached with a butt joint, and the joint is arranged so that the face of the shelf is against the ends of the sides (i.e., attached beneath), then any weight on the shelf will result in tension at the joint. Another example is a stretcher between the legs of a table or chair. Downward pressure on the legs would tend to force them apart, thus producing, in effect, tension at the joints between the legs and the stretcher. To effectively counteract tension, the joint must provide for either a good glue bond or mechanical locking. The dovetail joint is one example of mechanical locking. Tension on the joint is converted into compression against the sides of the dovetail. When the shelf at the bottom of a wall-hung cabinet is attached with dovetail joints, its tensile strength is much greater (Illus. 10).

Illus. 10. Tension is largely converted into compression in a dovetail joint by the wedging action between the pins and tail.

The mortise-and-tenon joint is an example of a joint that resists tension by providing a good glue bond (Illus. 11). If a tenon on a stretcher is glued into a mortise in the leg of a chair, the tensile strength of the joint will be greater due to the good glue bond between the sides of the mortise and the tenon cheeks.

Illus. 11. The mortise-and-tenon joint resists tension by providing a large glue-surface area.

Cleavage stress refers to a particular instance in which a tensional stress is concentrated on one end of a joint line, tending to produce a split. A wood joint is often least able to resist cleavage stress. Even a joint with good tensile strength may fail due to cleavage. In a well-designed joint, ideally the stresses are distributed evenly over the entire joint line so that one section isn't placed under cleavage stress.

Combined stresses are at work in most joints. It is rare for a joint to experience only one type of stress. For example, the mortise-and-tenon joint used in the example above would certainly face more than just tension. When you lean back on the rear legs of a chair, the stress changes; lateral force is tending to twist the joint, parts of the joint are under compression, and parts of the joint are subjected to shear. The tensile strength of the joint comes mostly from the glue bond between the mortise and the tenon cheeks, but other stresses are counteracted by the design of the joint. The mortise-and-tenon in Illus. 12 is a well-designed joint because it converts much of the force into compression. The lateral force tending to twist the joint apart is converted into compression between contact areas inside the joint. Notice that the shoulder takes part of the stress. A shoulder on a joint is one of the principal ways of converting many types of stress into compression.

The ability of the joint to withstand stress is determined by how well the joint fits and by the strength of the glue bond. A joint that is made to close tolerances is better able to transfer the stress from one part to the other. A loose-fitting joint won't be able to convert the stress into compression, placing additional stress on the glue line and, perhaps, causing it to fail.

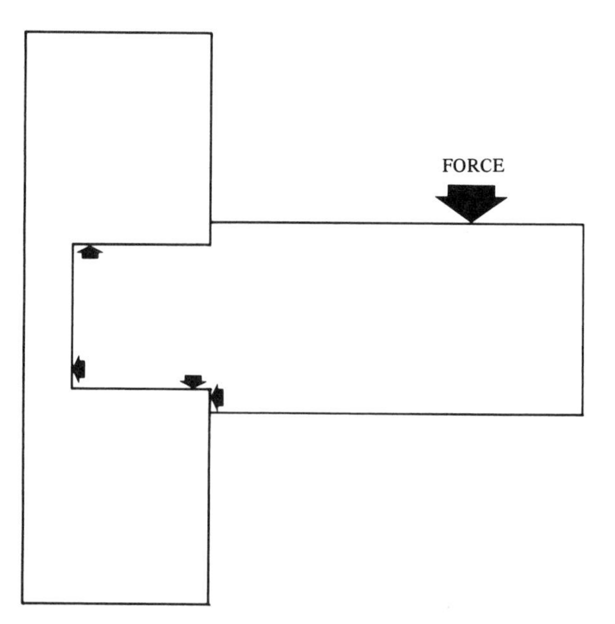

Illus. 12. In most applications, the joint must resist a combination of stresses. In this cross section of a mortise-and-tenon joint, the large arrow represents a downward force. The smaller arrows represent compression points inside the joint that tend to counteract the force.

Gluing Technique

To provide for a good glue bond, a joint requires two things: a large gluing surface area and a significant proportion of long-grain contact. Other factors are involved in determining the total strength of a joint, such as mechanical locking and reinforcement, so gluing surface area and the proportion of long-grain contact should not be the sole basis for your decision. However, they are very important considerations. When long grain is glued to long grain, the bond is stronger than the surrounding wood. In other words, the wood around the joint will split before the joint will. When glue is applied to end grain, the bond with any other grain is much weaker. End grain contains many open cell cavities, which tend to pull the glue away from the glue line, weakening the joint. The strongest bond occurs when the cell walls are in close contact. In end grain this occurs in only about one tenth of the total joint area.

If you want the maximum strength from a glued joint, you need to use proper gluing technique. First, make sure the joint surfaces when cut are actually smooth. The old practice of roughening up a joint to give it a "tooth" is no longer recommended. Tests show that a smooth surface glues better than a rough one (Illus. 13). This is because the best glue bond occurs when there is a thin layer of glue between the cell walls of the mating parts; a rough surface creates a lot of little pockets that keep the cell walls farther apart, and the loose fibers that do come in close contact are not firmly attached. On the other hand, you should also avoid burned or burnished joint surfaces that result from using dull tools. A glossy, glazed surface doesn't glue well either. The best surface is the result of a sharp cutting tool; usually no further smoothing is necessary.

The glue should be spread evenly over all mating surfaces of the joint. A brush is useful for applying the glue. The small stiff brush used to apply soldering flux makes an ideal glue applicator for small areas. It also has the advantage of being cheap enough to make it disposable after several uses. It is better to apply a thin coat of glue to both mating surfaces than to apply a heavy coat to only one surface. Brushing the glue on creates a wet surface for the glue to flow over, avoiding voids. If the glue is applied only to one surface, the glue must then flow over a dry surface, making the possibility of voids much greater (Illus. 14).

Illus. 13. The rough surface is the result of band sawing. The other wood has been planed smooth. The many loose fibres on the rough piece interfere with good adhesion.

Illus. 14. Apply glue to both mating surfaces of the joint to prevent the uneven glue transfer pattern that results when glue is applied only to one surface. In the other example, the even coating of glue results when glue is applied to both surfaces before joining.

During assembly, joints should be clamped to assure a good glue bond, but avoid overtightening the clamps. Tighten the clamps until all surfaces are making good contact. If you tighten the clamps past this point, you run the risk of squeezing out too much glue, resulting in a weak glue-starved joint. Try to gauge the amount of glue you apply so that when the joint is pulled tight just a small bead of glue oozes out of the joint. This indicates that there is enough glue to prevent a glue-starved joint, but it doesn't leave a mess of squeezed-out glue on the joint. Too much glue can even keep a well-fitting joint from pulling in tight, or it may cause the wood to split due to the hydraulic pressure exerted by the glue on the sides of the joint.

Long after the glue has cured, the joints expand and contract with seasonal changes in humidity. This is responsible for a process called glue-line ageing. A tenon may shrink or swell as much as 1/16" in width due to these seasonal humidity changes. This not only affects the fit of the joint, but it also places a shear stress on the glue line. Glues that remain flexible after curing tend to age better than glues that become brittle. The common white glue (PVA or polyvinyl acetate) stays flexible so ageing is not a big factor. On the other hand, plastic resin glue (UF or urea formaldehyde) is very brittle, particularly if the joint line is not tight. Ageing can decrease significantly the strength of a joint made with UF glue. After two years, the glue line may be 35 percent weaker than it was initially. To minimize the effects of ageing, joints should fit well and be clamped during curing.

Since the fit of the joint is so important for the overall strength, try to cut the parts to close tolerance. The moisture content of the wood can produce difficulties in achieving a tight fit unless you take it into account. If the two boards to be joined have different moisture contents at the time the joint is cut, the fit of the joint will be adversely affected. For best results, all of the wood should be in equilibrium with the atmosphere (i.e., temperature and humidity) so that dimensional change will be minimized. It's also a good idea to assemble the joints soon after they are cut. If the parts are set aside for several months before assembly, shrinkage may make the fit too loose for a good glue bond. This is particularly a problem for joints in which the grain of one part runs at a right angle to the grain of the other mating part. For example, in a mortise-and-tenon joint the length of the mortise runs with the grain; this dimension won't change much no matter what the moisture content of the wood. The corresponding dimension on the tenon is its width. (The terminology is discussed in Chapter 2, page 21, under the mortise-and-tenon heading and in relation to Illus. 51.) This dimension can change considerably due to shrinkage across the grain. The result is a loose fit at the ends of the mortise.

Joinery Rules of Thumb

In joinery, many rules of thumb have been developed over the years. These rules give proportions and methods of joint layout as well as procedures for cutting the joint. Throughout this book, I will give the applicable rule of thumb for a particular joint. Don't become too rigid in using these rules. They give good results in many applications, but you can modify the rules to fit an unusual situation once you have a thorough understanding of how joints work.

Here are a few general rules of thumb that apply to all joints:

Rule 1: Make all measurements from a common starting point. When you lay out a joint, pick one face as the reference. This reference face should be the most important face, usually the front, so that all errors show up on the back. Always place the marking gauge against this face. This eliminates errors caused by variation in stock thickness (Illus. 15).

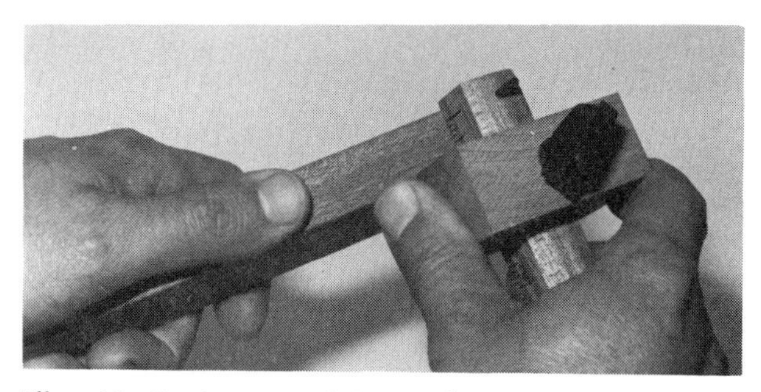

Illus. 15. Laying out a joint: Rule 1.

Rule 2: Use the mating part as layout tool. Instead of transferring the layout from one part to another by repeated measurement, place the mating part in its proper orientation, and scribe around it. This helps eliminate the possibility of errors in measurement (Illus. 16).

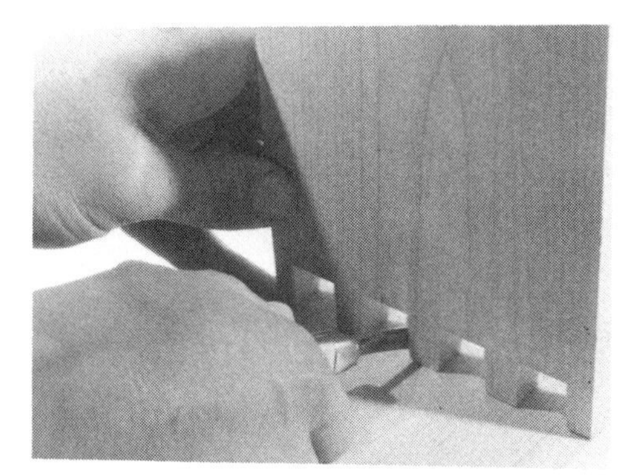

Illus. 16. Laying out the mating part: Rule 2.

Rule 3: Do most of the sanding before laying out the joint. Sanding reduces the thickness of the board. If you cut the joint before sanding, you may finish up with a loose fit. This is most important in joints such as the dado, in which the thickness of the board is critical to the fit of the joint (Illus. 17). Joints such as the mortise-and-tenon are not affected by sanding.

Illus. 17. Sanding before cutting prevents a loose-fitting joint: Rule 3.

Rule 4: Always take grain direction into account, and allow for wood movement. Grain orientation is very important in joint design. Wood can withstand much more stress at a right angle to the grain than it can in line with the grain. To compensate for this in-line weakness, the joint design needs to allow more wood backup along the grain than across the grain. If insufficient backup wood is available, the term "short grain" is used. If the grain is oriented improperly, short-grain problems will result. Short-grain failures are common in joints such as the mortise-and-tenon, for instance, if the mortise is cut too close to the end of the board (Illus. 18). Wood moves as

Illus. 18. Orienting grain direction properly prevents short-grain failure: Rule 4.

moisture content changes. A good joint design will allow for some movement in larger parts to avoid splits in the wood.

Rule 5: Joints should be balanced. A joint is only as strong as its weakest part. For maximum strength, the individual members should be approximately equal in strength. In a mortise-and-tenon, for example, if the tenon is too large, then the wood surrounding the mortise will be weak. Since the wood is stronger across the grain, the section between the end of the mortise and the end of the board is usually the weak link. (For clarity, please refer to Illus. 51, page 31.) To balance the joint, make this area larger and the tenon smaller.

Tools

Most tools used in joinery are standard woodworking tools, so I won't go into a lot of detail about them; however, there are a few specialized tools that need a bit of explanation along with some points about a variety of standard tools that have intrinsic significance in joinery. If you aren't familiar with the operation and maintenance of woodworking tools, a book on basic woodworking will give you some background information.

LAYOUT TOOLS

Layout is a very important aspect of joinery. The tools you use must be accurate if you expect to get tight-fitting joints (Illus. 19).

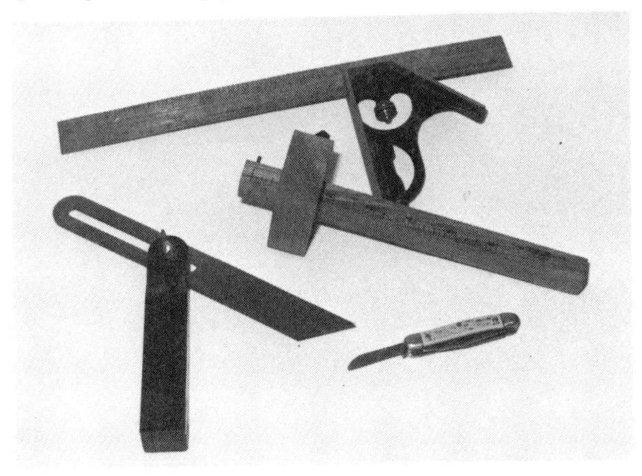

Illus. 19. The four most common layout tools used in joinery are the square, the marking gauge, a sliding T-bevel, and a pocketknife.

Knives are good for striking lines on the board; a knife gives a sharper line than a pencil. It also has the advantage of severing the top layer of wood fibres; this minimizes splintering on the face as the cut is made. The knife blade must be able to rest flat against the blade of a square; however, most knives have a double bevel that prevents this. A special marking knife is available commercially that has a single bevel so that the flat side can rest against the square. You can buy one of these or regrind the edge of your own knife to a single bevel. A pocketknife reground to a single bevel is especially handy because you can keep it in your pocket at all times.

Squares are necessary to make accurate layout lines. Either a try square or a combination square can be used for most joinery layout. Occasionally, a framing square may be needed. The important thing is that the square must be accurate. Test your squares occasionally to make sure that they are maintaining their accuracy. To test a square, hold it against the edge of a board and make a line on the face of the board. Then flip the square over and place it against the same edge as used to make the line. The blade should line up exactly with the line made previously. If the blade doesn't match the line exactly, then the angle formed will represent twice the error in the square (Illus. 20).

Illus. 20. Check the accuracy of your square.

The marking gauge is another important layout tool. Using a marking gauge eliminates errors caused by multiple measurements. The gauge can be set directly from a reference point and then used to transfer that measurement to all other parts. There are a variety of marking gauges available. The style you choose is a matter of personal preference. All marking gauges have three main parts: the stock, the fence, and the spur or blade. The fence is held in position on the stock by a thumb screw or a wedge. The standard type of marking gauge has a steel pin, called a spur, sharpened to a point to make the mark. This works fine with the grain, but across the grain the line is fuzzy. A cutting gauge uses a blade instead of a point to make the mark. It will cut a well-defined line across the grain. It is a very good tool to use for striking shoulder lines. The clean line made by the blade scores the wood, eliminating splinters on the face of the work.

The mortise gauge has two spurs. One is fixed to the stock, and the other is adjustable. The distance between the spurs can be set to the width of the mortise and the fence set to the desired position, then the gauge can be used to lay out both the mortise and the tenon.

An important point to remember when using any marking gauge is to use one face or edge of the board as a reference, and always place the fence against it. Usually you want to choose the most visible face as the reference point. By using this technique you ensure that the faces will line up flush in the finished joint and that any variation in the thickness of the boards won't affect the fit of the joint.

Bevels are used to mark angles other than 90° and 45°. The blade of the bevel can be adjusted to any angle and locked in position. There are a number of types of bevels. The sliding T-bevel is one of the most common. You use a bevel just like a try square. Once the blade is set to the correct angle, place the handle against the edge of the board, and use the blade to guide the marking knife. The angle can be set directly from a drawing, taken from a mating part, or set using a protractor or framing square. Many times an angle will be specified as a slope ratio instead of in degrees. For example, a dovetail may be described as having a slope of 1:7. To set the bevel to this slope, place it on a framing square. Hold the handle of the bevel against the blade of the square. Adjust the blade on the bevel until it lines up with the 1″ mark on the blade of the square and the 7″ mark on the tongue.

PLANES

Until recent times a well-equipped joiner's shop needed a large number of specialized planes (Illus. 21 and 22). Today many of the functions once performed with planes are done with power equipment; however, a few specialized planes are particularly useful in a number of situations. If you want to make joints by hand, then you will find the following planes very useful.

Illus. 21. Before the advent of power tools, a well-equipped joiner's shop needed a shelf full of specialized planes.

Illus. 22. Many specialized planes performed operations that are done with the router or shaper in a modern shop.

The rabbet plane makes cutting rabbets by hand easy, and it is also useful in making other joints. It is a specialty plane that is made so that the plane iron extends completely across the sole (Illus. 23). Some types have a fence to control the width of cut and a stop to control the depth of cut. Planes that incorporate these features are called fillister. An adjustable spur, called a nicker, is included on some models. The nicker severs the wood fibres along the edge of the cut for making rabbets across the grain. In some models the iron can be placed near the front in what is called the bull-nose position. This makes it easier to make stopped rabbets.

The plow plane is used to cut grooves. It has an adjustable fence to guide the cut. A depth stop sets the depth of the groove. When you plow a groove, work on one small section at a time, starting at the far end of the board and working away from you. When you reach full depth in that section, move back and complete another small section, working into the one just finished. Traditionally a *groove* refers to a cut with the grain, whereas the cut across the grain is distinguished as the *dado*. Thus, naturally a variation on the plow plane is the dado plane. This plane incorporates nickers on both sides to sever the cross-grain fibres of the board. It doesn't have a fence; a board clamped to the work is used instead.

A universal plane combines the functions of several specialty planes. By inserting various irons you can make joints such as the tongue-and-groove.

The router plane is the hand-tool equivalent of the power router. It has a wide base and a small cutter that projects below the base. It is useful in making dadoes by hand. The shoulders are first sawn and most of the waste chiselled out, then the router plane is used to smooth up and make the cut a constant depth. You can also use the router plane any time you need to create any recess of constant depth.

Illus. 23. The plane iron of a rabbet plane extends all the way across the sole, permitting the plane to cut right up to the shoulder of the rabbet.

DADO BLADES

Dado blades are used on the power table saw or radial-arm saw. They can be used to make rabbets, dadoes, and grooves. They are also useful for making a number of other joints. There are two basic types of dado blades: the stack dado blade and the wobbler dado blade.

The stack dado blade consists of two blades and several chippers of various sizes (Illus. 24).

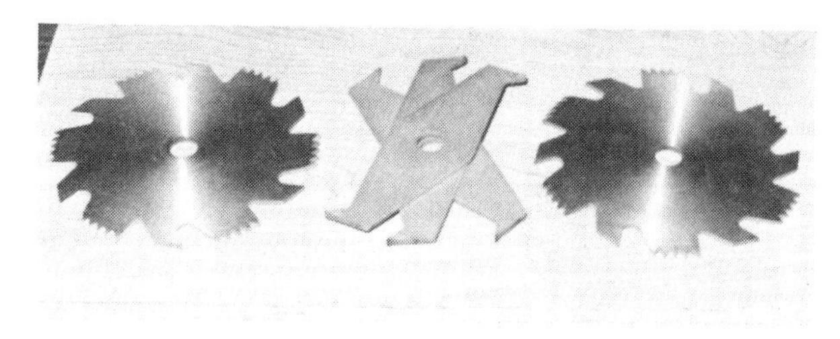

Illus. 24. The stack dado blade uses two blades in combination with chippers of various sizes.

The saw blades make shoulder cuts, and the chippers remove the material between the cuts. To set the width of the cut you assemble several different chippers between the blades. The chippers come in various thicknesses, so with particular combinations you can select one of many widths. Small adjustments in width can be made by placing paper shims or thin aluminum or brass washers between the chippers. Rotate the chippers to space them around the blade so that they won't interfere with each other or with the teeth on the saw blades (Illus. 25). The stack dado blade makes a cut that is flat on the bottom, and the sides are square with the face of the board.

Illus. 25. Arrange the chippers so that they won't interfere with each other or with the blades.

The wobbler dado blade has a single blade mounted in an assembly of tapered washers. This assembly can vary the angle of the blade with respect to the arbor (Illus. 26). This produces a wobble in the blade. As the blade wobbles back and forth, it makes a cut wider than the blade; the more wobble there is, the wider the cut will be. The width is continuously adjustable through its range. The washers have index marks that indicate where to set them for various widths. Most blades of this type can be adjusted from ⅛" to about 1". The main advantage of the wobbler blade is that it can be adjusted without removing it from the arbor. You simply loosen the nut and twist the adjustment, then retighten the nut. Also, since it can adjust to any size within its range, there is no need for shimming.

Because the blade travels in an arc from side to side, the bottom of the cut is slightly rounded, but this is usually not a problem. This deviation gets smaller as the blade diameter is increased,

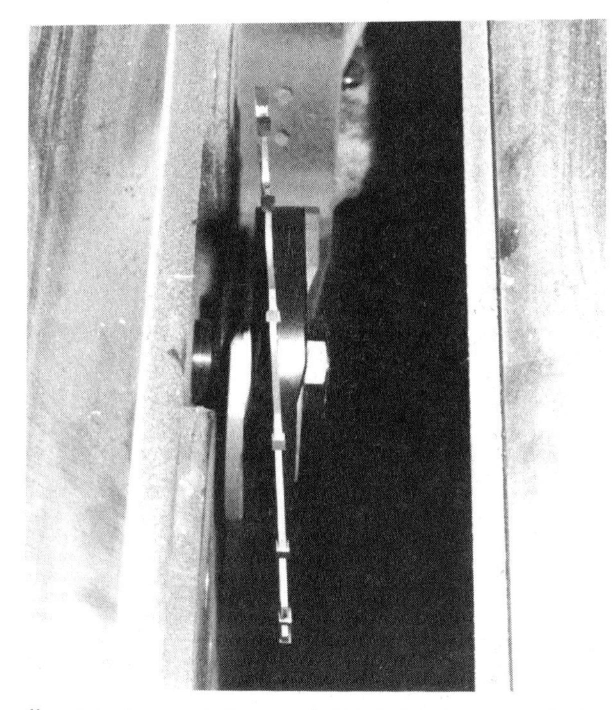

Illus. 26. The wobbler type of dado blade uses a single blade mounted into an assembly of tapered washers. Varying the angle of the blade changes the width of the cut.

so a large wobbler blade can make a cut that is almost as flat bottomed as the cut made with a stack dado blade.

Both types of dado blades are available with carbide tips. The carbide-tip blade will stay sharp much longer, and a sharp blade makes a smoother cut with fewer tearouts and chips along the edge. If you will be using the blade frequently, the carbide tips are a very good investment.

THE JOINTER

The jointer is essentially a stationary power version of the hand plane, but faster, more accurate, and more dangerous. A smooth and true joint surface is one of the most important factors in achieving a good glue joint. The jointer can be used to prepare the stock for gluing (Illus. 27).

The jointer can be used to square and true an edge. If the edge is high on the ends, take a pass over both ends before running the board all the way through. If the edge is high in the middle, rock the board until there is a small gap between the end and the table, then take a cut from the middle. After the edge is fairly straight, make a complete pass over the jointer. After about 6″ of the board have passed onto the outfeed table, put most of the downward pressure on this portion on the outfeed table, and let up on the infeed portion. This will keep the board from rocking on any irregularities along the unjointed edge.

When jointing a board in preparation for gluing, take a cut of 1/16″ or less. Run the board through with the grain to get the smoothest possible cut. If, when you feed the stock slow enough to avoid washboarding, the edge is burnished, then the blades need to be resharpened.

When you are jointing edges to be glued into a panel, first lay out the panel. Then, decide which face to put up before actually jointing the edges. Mark the faces, then joint them; but, alternate the way you place the boards on the jointer so that one is jointed with the front face against the fence and the other is jointed with the back face against the fence. When the boards are assembled, this will compensate for any slight out of square on the fence. Even though you can compensate for out of square in this way, try to get the fence as square as possible. If the edges are badly out of square, you may have trouble clamping them because they will tend to slip out of position.

The jointer has a couple of features that make it useful for making several other types of joints. First, the fence can be adjusted at an angle. This makes it possible to cut edge mitres with a jointer. The other feature found on most jointers is the rabbeting ledge (Illus. 28). The guard must be removed when using the rabbeting ledge, so exercise extreme caution when you use this feature. On some jointers you can place the guard behind the fence. This is useful when the fence is moved close to the edge because it at least covers the exposed cutting head that is still behind the fence. If you won't be able to guide the board without getting your fingers near the knives, use a push stick that will hold the board against the table as well as push it.

Illus. 27. The jointer is used to produce a smooth and true joint surface.

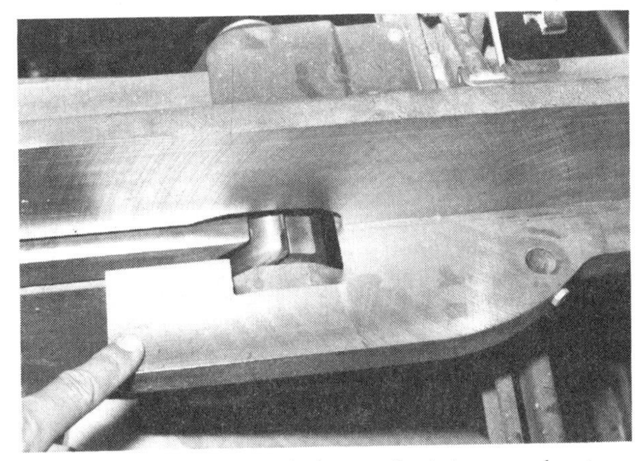

Illus. 28. The rabbeting ledge on the jointer makes it possible to cut rabbets, tenons, and laps.

The rabbeting ledge permits you to cut rabbets, tenons, and laps on the jointer. The fence controls the width of the cut, and the infeed-table setting controls the depth of cut. If the cut is deep, it is best to make more than one pass, lowering the infeed table to the desired depth for the final cut.

THE ROUTER

The router is a very versatile tool for making joints. The plunge type is especially useful because it permits you to make stopped cuts easily (Illus. 29). The router can be guided with a fence attached to the base, or with a board or jig

Illus. 29. A plunge router makes it easy to make stopped cuts. The base stays in contact with the work while the bit is raised or lowered.

clamped to the work. Template-following collars are also very useful in joinery. The collar fits into the base and surrounds the bit (Illus. 30). The collar rubs against a template to guide the router. You can use the collars with commercial jigs, or you can cut your own templates from hardboard. The opening in the template must always be larger than the finished size of the routed joint. This is to allow for the thickness of the collar and for the space between the collar and the bit. Template-following collars, however, have one shortcoming; because they attach to the base of the router, they may not always be concentric with the bit. This means that the bit may be a little closer to one side of the collar than to the other, which can create an inaccuracy in the joint. The problem can be eliminated by keeping the router in the same position while making the cut; if you rotate the base any more than 10° to 15° during the operation, inaccuracies may result.

Illus. 30. A template-following collar fits into the router base and surrounds the bit. The collar rubs against a template to guide the cut.

A ball-bearing pilot on the bit eliminates the problems caused by a nonconcentric collar. Another advantage of this pilot is that the template can be made exactly the same size as the desired finished size of the joint. The ball bearing rides against the template and guides the router. It can be mounted on the end of the bit or on the shank. Generally, the shank-mounted pilot is the most useful for joinery (Illus. 31).

Illus. 31. A shank-mounted ball-bearing pilot can also be used to follow a template. The cut will be more accurate, because the bearing is mounted directly on the bit.

A number of special bits are also available to make different types of joints. They will be described as is appropriate in following chapters where the various joints are discussed.

A router table is an accessory that allows the router to operate more like a shaper. The router mounts under the table, and the bit extends through a hole in the tabletop. A fence or mitre gauge can then be used to guide the work just as you would with a tablesaw (Illus. 32).

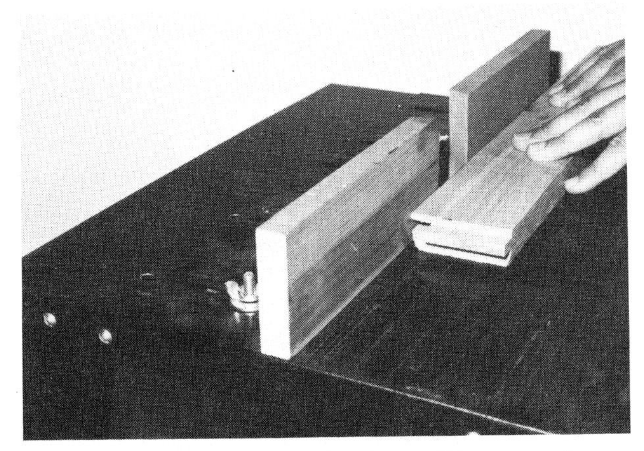

Illus. 32. A router table makes it possible to use the router in a manner similar to a shaper.

Dovetail jigs can be used to guide the router. These jigs are, of course, specifically designed to cut dovetail joints, but they also have other uses. They are used, in fact, in several types of joints, so I will briefly describe them here. You can find more information in Chapter 7, page 109, on dovetails. Before using any of these jigs, you should study the owner's manual. The instructions given in this book are meant only to supplement those provided by the manufacturer.

There are basically three types of dovetail jigs. The oldest is the half-blind dovetail jig (Illus. 33). Several different sizes of template for the jig are available. This type cuts both pins and tails of a half-blind dovetail in a single operation. It uses a finger template with fixed spacing; a template-following collar guides the router. A single dovetail bit makes both the pins and the tails. When used with a straight bit, this jig can be used to cut the grooves for multiple-spline joints.

Until recently, the half-blind dovetail jig was the only type available. Now there are two other types capable of cutting through dovetails. The Keller jig consists of two aluminum templates and a set of special router bits that have shank-mounted ball-bearing pilots (Illus. 34). The jig is available in three sizes; the smallest is suitable for use in constructing small boxes and drawers, and the largest can be used to make large carcass joints. All three sizes are capable of making joints of unlimited length since they can be repositioned on the boards. Because of the shank-mounted pilots, the bit follows the template very accurately, resulting in close joint tolerances. The pins and tails are cut in two separate operations that use different templates and bits; a dovetail bit is used to cut the tails, and a straight bit is used for the pins. The Keller jig offers accurate joints with fast setup and a minimum of adjustments.

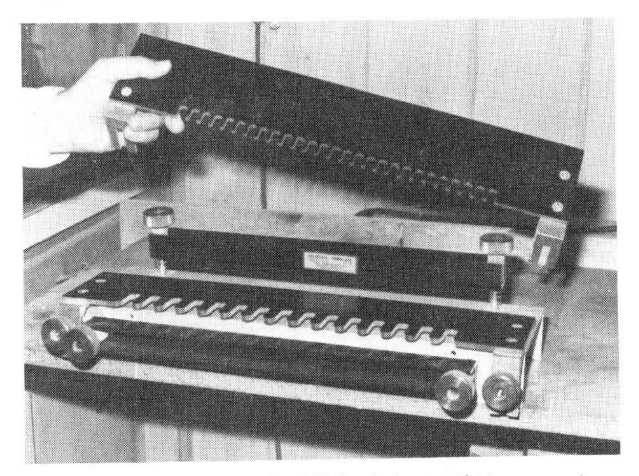

Illus. 33. This type of half-blind dovetail jig cuts pins and tails in a single operation. The pins and tails are equal in size and spacing, but the size can be changed by using a different template.

Illus. 34. The Keller dovetail jig is an efficient way to make through dovetails. Bits with shaft-mounted bearings are used to follow the aluminum templates.

The third type of dovetail jig is the Leigh jig, which is fully adjustable (Illus. 35). It can be used to make both half-blind and through dovetails with variable size pins and tails. The initial setup is more complex than the other jigs, but this is an extremely versatile tool. A template-following collar is used to guide the cut. The size and spacing of the pins and tails is determined by the placement of adjustable guide fingers. Similar to the Keller jig, the pins and tails are cut separately using a straight bit for the pins and a dovetail bit for the tails.

The adjustable guides of the Leigh dovetail jig are the distinguishing feature that make it useful for cutting several other types of joint. For instance, it can be used to make the grooves for multiple splines; or a crosscut bar can be used to make straight cuts. The crosscut bar feature can be used to make rabbets, dadoes, grooves, and sliding dovetails (Illus. 36).

Illus. 35. The Leigh dovetail jig is very versatile. It can be used to make variably spaced through dovetails and half-blind dovetails along with several other types of joints.

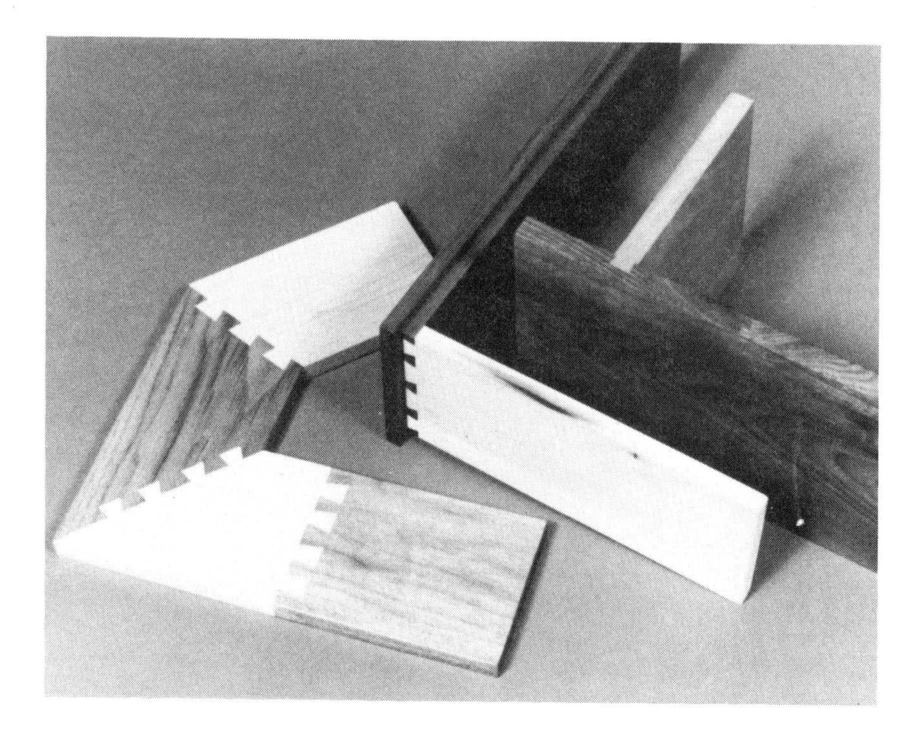

Illus. 36. These are just a few types of joints that can be made with the Leigh dovetail jig.

2

Basic Joints—Hand-Tool Techniques

Although there are hundreds of joints, only a few are used with enough regularity to be called basic joints. This chapter deals with six joints: the butt, mitre, rabbet, dado and groove, mortise-and-tenon, and dovetail. Most other joints are related to these basic joints in some way. This may be by some slight or major variation of a basic joint or by some combination of two or more basic joints.

The joints covered in this chapter are purposely the most basic form of each type, and only hand-tool techniques are given. I don't think that there is only one correct way to make a particular joint. I have worked with several experienced woodworkers and each has had his own way of doing things. I found that by learning their methods, I was better prepared for any unusual situations because I could then choose the method that best suited that particular situation. Throughout this handbook I present a number of methods; discover the ones you like and keep the others in mind for that unusual situation. Understanding the material in this chapter will give you a firm foundation for the chapters that follow. These later chapters will include advanced techniques and variations on these joints along with power-tool methods and joint reinforcement. The mortise-and-tenon and dovetail are such strong joints that they rarely need reinforcement. The rest of the joints covered in this chapter, however, frequently need some form of reinforcement, such as dowels or splines. Chapter 3 covers joint reinforcement in some depth, so reinforcement is only mentioned briefly in this chapter.

Butt Joints

The butt joint is perhaps the oldest and probably the simplest type of joint. When used appropriately, it can be a very strong joint; but, when used inappropriately, it is very weak. Advances in glues and reinforcements have allowed the butt joint to become increasingly popular. Many factory-built pieces of furniture use butt joints, particularly when reconstituted wood is used in panel construction. The butt joint is very strong in compression because it offers the maximum surface area.

When butt joints are glued, the grain direction has a large effect on the joint strength. A butt joint that involves end grain is relatively weak. As explained in Chapter 1, the actual glue surface of end grain is only about one tenth of the area of the joint because the open cell cavities don't contribute to the effective glue-surface area. When end grain is glued to long grain, there is the additional problem of unequal expansion rates between the two boards, setting up internal stress in the glue line that may eventually cause the joint to fail. For these reasons practically all butt joints involving end grain must be reinforced.

A butt joint that joins two long-grain surfaces is one of the strongest types of joints. Considering strength, this joint usually needs no reinforcement, but in considering ease of assembly, dowels or splines are often used to help align the parts.

Because there is no mechanical locking in a butt joint, all of the strength comes from the glue line. This means that careful fitting is crucial to achieving a strong joint.

There are four basic types of butt joint. The panel butt and the edge butt join long grain to long grain and are, therefore, strong without reinforcement. The frame butt and case butt usually involve end grain and, thus, require reinforcement.

PANEL BUTT

To join smaller boards into a larger panel, the panel-butt joint is most frequently used (Illus. 37). This joint can be assembled without reinforcement since the joint is long grain to long grain. The most important factor is achieving a good fit between the boards. The edges should be jointed square and true before assembly. To joint the edges with a hand plane, a long plane such as the jointer plane is best because it will make the edges true. Shorter planes will follow the bumps and curves of the edge rather than cut them off. If you don't have a jointer plane, however, on short boards you can use a jack plane. When jointing by hand, it is a good idea to plane the mating surfaces together. This way any deviation from square will be compensated for by a complementary angle in the other board. But, this will only work when the boards are clamped with their faces opposite to each other; otherwise the error will be doubled.

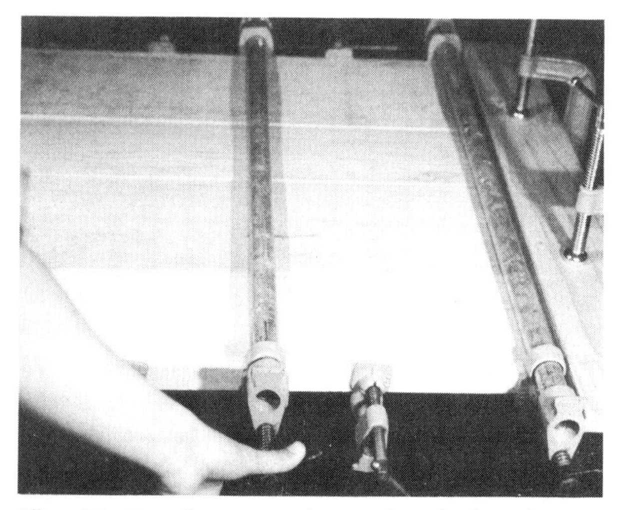

Illus. 37. Bar clamps are the usual method used to apply pressure to the panel-butt joint. If the joints don't stay in alignment, you can clamp a board across the end using C-clamps.

Another way to joint the edges is to use a shooting board, which is a guide for the plane that keeps it square with the edge of the board. Rubbing paraffin along the surface on which the plane rides will make it glide more easily.

End grain loses (and absorbs) moisture to the air faster than the long-grain area of the board. This means that the section from the end of the board inward about 6″ tends to shrink more rapidly than the rest of the board. The result can be a cracked panel. To counteract this, some woodworkers add what they call "spring" to the joint. A thin shaving is taken 6″ from one end to 6″ from the other end. When the joint is clamped, the additional pressure on the ends compresses them slightly. As the ends shrink faster than the rest of the panel, there is a little leeway built in allowing the rest of the panel to catch up, thus avoiding splits. This technique can be used only when the joints will be clamped. Rubbed joints, using hot hide glue without clamps, should be perfectly flat.

The way that the grain of the individual boards is aligned can affect the stability of the finished panel. This is particularly true when working with plain-sawn lumber, which is cut so that the faces of the board are tangent to the rings. Boards cut this way are more apt to cup and change dimension across their width. Examine the end grain to determine the direction of the annular rings for each board. Glue up the panel with the rings reversed in every other board. This combination will help keep the panel flat because the cupping tendency of each board will be effectively cancelled out by the adjoining board. When the boards are wide, however, this technique can lead to a wavy surface. In this case, some woodworkers prefer to glue the boards together with all of the rings oriented in the same direction, bark side out, and then they secure the panel with screws to a supporting frame. If you use this method, be sure to allow for dimensional change in the panel by slotting the screw holes, or the panel may split as it shrinks.

Quarter-sawn lumber, which is cut so that the face forms a 90° angle with the rings, doesn't usually cup, so grain alignment isn't as important. There is a small difference in the shrinkage between young wood (i.e., wood near the outside of the tree) and old wood (i.e., wood near the heart). This is particularly true in pieces thicker than one inch. You can compensate for this by gluing young wood to young wood and old wood to old wood. Shrinkage across each joint is effectively equalized.

Once you have decided on the way the boards will be placed, mark them so that you can assemble the panel in the same orientation after jointing the edges and applying glue. The traditional method for marking the boards is to draw a triangle or *V* across them. You can simply number them if you prefer.

Gluing and Clamping

After you have jointed the boards on the edges, you are ready to clamp them. A couple of saw horses make a good gluing stand. If you do a lot of this type of gluing, you may want to make a gluing table similar to one a large shop uses. This is a table with a rack on top that has notches to fit the bar clamps.

Place the boards on the saw horses in the proper order; then, tip them up on one edge and spread the glue on the edges. First run a bead of glue along the middle of the edge, then spread it out to cover the entire edge. On a joint like this, you can easily spread the glue with your finger. If you don't like the mess, use a small brush or a scrap of wood or a small piece of cardboard as a spreader. When you have a lot of joints to glue, a small paint roller actually makes a good glue spreader. Many woodworkers simply apply glue to one edge; but, for maximum strength, it is better to apply a thin coat of glue to both edges. This will ensure uniform wetting of both surfaces so that the glue will flow evenly throughout the joint as the clamps are applied.

While I was repairing furniture for a living, I saw many failed panel-butt joints. Almost all of these failures could be traced to two causes. In many, the joint was glue starved because the glue hadn't been spread evenly or not enough glue had been used. Most of the other failures were caused by moisture weakening the glue line. As simple precautions to avoid these failures, be sure to use enough glue and to spread it evenly, and use a moisture-resistant glue if the joint will be in a wet or very humid environment.

Place a bar clamp over the middle first, and tighten it until the joints are snug but not completely tight. Use strips of scrap wood to protect the edges from denting by the bar-clamp jaws. If the boards are not properly aligned, tap them with a hammer using a block of wood to cushion the work. Next, apply two more bar clamps on the underside at each end. After tightening them, retighten the middle clamp. All of the clamps should be only as tight as you can get them by hand; don't use a wrench for added leverage or the clamp will be too tight, causing the joint to be glue starved.

If you applied the correct amount of glue, you will see a small bead of glue squeeze out of the joint as the pressure is applied. Too much glue and the squeezed-out glue will run all over in big drips. If no glue oozes out, then you didn't apply enough glue, and the joint will be weak.

When the edges have been properly jointed, three clamps are usually sufficient for boards up to about three feet long. Longer boards require more clamps. Try to place them no more than one foot apart, and alternate them so that one is on top and the next is on the bottom. This will equalize the pressure and keep the board from bowing as it is clamped. If you allow a space of about ½" from the bar of each clamp to the board, the clamp will also help keep the board flat. This puts the clamp screw directly in line with the middle of the edge. Keeping the bar off the face of the board also makes sure that you won't get black marks where the bar touches the wet glue, which causes a chemical reaction between the steel and the tannin in the wood.

Ordinarily you won't have any problems with the panel bowing as long as you alternate the clamps and the edges have been jointed correctly. But, once in a while, you will have a panel that refuses to stay flat as you tighten the clamps.

To solve this, clamp wood blocks on both sides of the panel in the problem area. Place wax paper between the blocks and the panel to keep them from being glued to the panel by squeezed-out glue. If you frequently need clamp blocks, make a set and rub paraffin on the surfaces; this eliminates the need for wax paper and keeps the blocks from sticking to the glue.

When there are only a few joints in a panel, you usually won't have problems keeping it flat; but, when there are many joints, any tiny error is augmented. Panels with many joints are also hard to glue up because the glue may begin to dry out on the first joint before you can spread it on the last joint. If you think that you will have problems assembling a panel from many small boards, assemble smaller sections first, and glue the sections together later into the panel. This is probably only necessary when the panel is large and the boards are small as in constructing a butcher block or a workbench top.

When the glue begins to gel but before it sets hard, shave the excess from the surface of the panel with a chisel or scraper. Don't wipe it off with a wet rag or you will actually be forcing the glue into the wood, thus sealing the wood and marring any later finish.

Clamping is the best way to ensure a strong joint; but, if you don't have clamps available, you can use the time-honored method called the rubbed joint. To use this method you must have hot glue available. To rub a joint, the edges must be planed true so that there are no gaps in the joint; hide glue has very poor gap-filling properties. Place one of the boards in a vise—hand-hold the other board—with the edge to be joined facing up, and apply glue to both of them. If you hold the other board up against the one in the vise, you can run a wide brush across both edges at once. Work quickly so that the joint won't cool before it is assembled. Hold the loose board by the ends, close to the bottom edge. Place it on top of the board in the vise, and rub it back and forth three or four times; then, slide it into the proper alignment, and hold it steady for a few seconds as the joint cools and the glue grabs. Although the joint won't reach full strength for several hours, the initial tack of the glue is strong enough to hold the boards in place.

If you are only gluing a single panel, simply leave it in the vise to set. If you are gluing up several panels, lean a couple of sturdy strips of scrap against the wall; then, carefully remove the panel from the vise, and lean it so that it is supported by the strips along its entire width. Glue up the next panel, and lean it against the first one. For wide panels, rub small sections together first, then assemble the sections only after the joints are thoroughly set.

EDGE BUTT

The edge butt typically is used to apply trim or face frames (Illus. 38). It is a long-grain-to-long-grain joint that is just as strong as a panel-butt joint. Reinforcement is not necessary, but dowels or splines are often used for alignment. Just as for panel butts, the strength of the joint depends on careful fitting and gluing. Joint the edge of the board that will be attached to the flat face of the other board. Before gluing, hold the board in place, and trace a line along the inside edge so that you will know where the glue should stop. If the inside corner won't be visible, you don't need to mark in advance; just spread the glue wide enough so that you will be sure to cover the joint. Spread glue on both surfaces.

Illus. 38. The edge butt joins long grain to long grain, so no reinforcement is necessary when it is properly glued and clamped.

Clamp the joint with hand screws or C-clamps if the boards are small enough; use bar clamps when the boards are wider. You can also assemble this joint without clamps by using fasteners such as nails or screws through the face of one board into the edge of the other. The strength of the joint will come primarily from the glue bond, so you need to use only enough fasteners to hold the boards in place while the glue sets.

FRAME BUTT

The frame butt is used to make corners by joining the end of one board to the edge of another. It is used most frequently in making face frames, drawer-guide frames, etc. Left unreinforced, the joint is very weak because, although the jointing edge of one board is long grain, the glue joint is bonded with the end grain of the other (Illus. 39). The frame butt is almost always reinforced except in small or decorative applications.

The type of glue used makes a big difference in the strength of a frame-butt joint. The glue should have good gap-filling properties to stop up the porous end grain, but it should be heavy bodied enough to keep the joint from becoming glue starved by too much soaking into the end grain.

For the joint to be successful, the end of the board must be cut exactly square. A mitre box can be used to guide the saw. If you want to make a slight adjustment to the end, use a block plane, and place the board on a shooting board to guide the plane and keep it square. The mating edge should be jointed so that it is square and smooth. If the mating end and edge are out of square in either direction, then the frame will be out of square or there will be a gap in the joint. Accuracy at this stage determines the final success of the project.

Bar clamps are used ordinarily to apply pressure to the joint. When using this joint to make a frame, immediately check with a framing square, or by measuring the diagonals, whether the frame is out of square. If so, rack it into square before the glue has a chance to set. If the frame is stubbornly out of square, place a bar clamp across the corners that have the longest diagonal and gently tighten the clamp until the frame is square.

CASE BUTT

The case-butt joint attaches the square end of one board to the flat face of another board (Illus. 40). This joint is commonly used for boxes, cabinet carcasses, shelves, etc. As with all butt joints, the ends of the boards must be square for the joint to be successful. Special reinforcement techniques are usually needed, because while they are very strong under compression, case-butt joints aren't able to resist tension, shear stress, or lateral forces very well. Plan the joint layout to take advantage of the compressional strength of the case-butt joint. Consider a cabinet top joined to the sides using a case butt. With the top over the sides, any weight placed on top will be supported by the sides in compression. If the top is joined between the sides, all of the weight on the top will be experienced as a shear stress on the joint.

The simplest method of reinforcing a case butt is by means of nails or screws. Drive nails through the joint at an angle towards the middle of the board to improve the holding power. When

Illus. 39. The frame-butt joint joins end grain to long grain. This results in a very weak joint unless reinforcement is used.

Illus. 40. The case butt joins one board's end grain to the face of another. Reinforcement must be used to resist tension, shear or lateral stress.

appearance isn't of primary importance, use box nails because the large heads are unlikely to pull through the wood. For improved appearance, use finishing nails; set the heads below the surface, and putty the holes. In commercial work, power-driven staples frequently are used to reinforce butt joints. While nails improve the shear strength of the joint, they don't help it to withstand lateral forces to any significant degree. Nail spacing is a trade-off between strength and appearance. In most cases, the closer the nails are spaced, the stronger the joint will be, but only up to a point. After that, spacing the nails any closer will weaken the joint by creating a break line in the board, possibly causing it to split. As a rough rule of thumb, for ¾″ lumber the minimum distance between nails is abut 1″.

End grain doesn't hold screws as well as face or edge grain, so this isn't the best application for screws; but they are stronger than nails. Screws resist tensional stresses better than nails and tend to improve resistance to lateral forces a little more than nails. It is usually a good idea to drill pilot holes for the screws. Even if you are using drywall or face-frame screws, which in many applications don't require a separate clearance hole, drilling a pilot hole will help to prevent splitting. Be sure to drill a shank-clearance hole, not just the thread-clearance hole, if you want the screws to pull the joint tight. The screws can be concealed with buttons or dowels.

For entirely concealed reinforcement, use dowels or splines as described in Chapter 3.

Mitre Joints

The mitre is an attractive-looking joint that is often used when appearance is more important than strength. Since it can hide the end grain of both of the boards, it is particularly useful for plywood. Typically a mitre is used to join boards at a right angle; however, the mitre can be used to join boards at any angle. The mitre cut is always one-half of the desired angle; for a right angle the mitre angle is 45°. I will cover 45° mitres here; the range of other angles will be discussed in Part Two, Chapter 4, page 56.

There are two basic types of mitres: the face mitre and the edge mitre. The face mitre always joins end grain; however, the edge mitre can also join long grain, in which case it is sometimes called a rip mitre. Any mitre that involves end grain must be reinforced. Practically every failed mitre I've seen was due to insufficient reinforcement. Refer to Chapter 3, page 43, for details on reinforcement.

Accuracy is especially important in making a successful mitre. Make sure your tools are sharp; a saw that is dull or incorrectly set will tend to wander off the line. Check the accuracy of setups before making a cut, and make a test cut before beginning the actual work.

There's one technique that will help you compensate for minor inaccuracies in the setup. Make the cuts so that mating sides are cut on opposite sides of the saw. This ensures that the angles will be complementary even if they are not exactly 45°, thus cancelling out errors. This procedure isn't applicable in all cases, so try to keep your tools and adjustments precisely accurate.

FACE MITRES

A face mitre is the type that you would use to make a picture frame or to frame around an opening. You can cut a face mitre freehand after making a 45° mark with a combination square; but usually you'd do best with a mitre box. The simplest type of mitre box is made from three boards, with slots cut in the side boards to guide the saw. Commercially available mitre boxes use metal guides and can be adjusted to various angles. To use the mitre box, mark the location of the cut, and place the board in the box. Use a backsaw, cutting across the entire face of the board (Illus. 41). If you cut the first board face up

Illus. 41. Face mitres can be cut accurately by using a mitre box.

and the second face down, the angles will be complementary. However, this method will only work with flat boards, not irregularly shaped pieces such as mouldings. At the back and bottom of a saw cut, there is always a little rag (rough fibres). Plan the way you position the cut so that this can be easily removed with a chisel or sandpaper. For instance, mouldings should be cut face up with the outside edge at the back.

After you have cut the mitres, dry-assemble the joint. The parts should make equal contact along the entire joint line. If they don't meet perfectly, mark the needed correction and trim to fit. You can trim the joints with a block plane by cutting to the correction line. Plane from the inside corner to the outside corner of the joint to avoid splitting the edge. You can use a 45° shooting board to guide the plane. Professional picture framers often use a knife-edge trimming machine with a sliding or guillotine action. This produces a smooth accurate mitre with no rag.

Whether or not you will be reinforcing the joint, it should be glued. Use a glue with a good gap-filling ability to get the best bond on end grain; the type referred to as yellow woodworker's or carpenter's glue (aliphatic resin) works well in most applications. A special mitre clamp is usually required when clamping mitres (Illus. 42); but you can use a regular clamp if you attach temporary clamp blocks to the pieces of the joint. Use a hot-melt-glue gun to attach the blocks. After the glue is dry, you can remove the blocks carefully with a chisel.

Illus. 42. A mitre clamp is useful especially when assembling face mitres. Adjust the parts in the clamp until the best fit is achieved, then drill pilot holes for nails or screws.

For most applications, you will need to reinforce a face mitre. Even in picture framing and similar work, some type of reinforcement is necessary; nails are most frequently used. When using softwood, you can drive nails without drilling pilot holes; however, I prefer to drill pilot holes in all mitre joints because it not only prevents splitting but also keeps the nails from following the grain and thus pulling the joint out of alignment. I like to place the joint in a mitre clamp before nailing. To do it this way, you must line up the joint accurately in the clamp because it will never get any tighter. Some woodworkers prefer to clamp one part in a vise and to hold the other in place while they nail the joint. This way the nails will pull the joint tight. If the frame members are wider than about 1", then you need two or more nails in each joint. For wide boards, use different size nails, a long one near the inside corner, a shorter one near the outside corner to compensate for the greater distance between the joint line and the edge. You can lock a joint by nailing from both edges, but be sure to offset the nails slightly or they may hit each other and split the frame. Don't place nails close to the outside edge where the parts narrow because the heads will likely go right through the first part when you set them, leaving the joint without reinforcement. When making a frame, assemble the two opposite corners separately, and nail each so that you have two completed *L*'s; then join the *L*'s to make the frame.

Nails give enough strength for light work such as picture frames, but when you need more strength, dowels or splines, covered in Chapter 3, are much better.

EDGE MITRES

Edge mitres are used to join the ends or edges of boards (Illus. 43). When used to join end grain, they are very weak and need reinforcement. Long-grain joints are also often reinforced to help align the parts during assembly, but they don't require reinforcement for added strength.

Short edge mitres can be cut in a mitre box. Longer ones are more difficult to cut by hand. One way to cut long edges is to use a panel saw guided by an angle block. You can also use a block plane to make an edge mitre. This works best on edge grain where the joint runs with the grain, but you can use the plane on end grain if

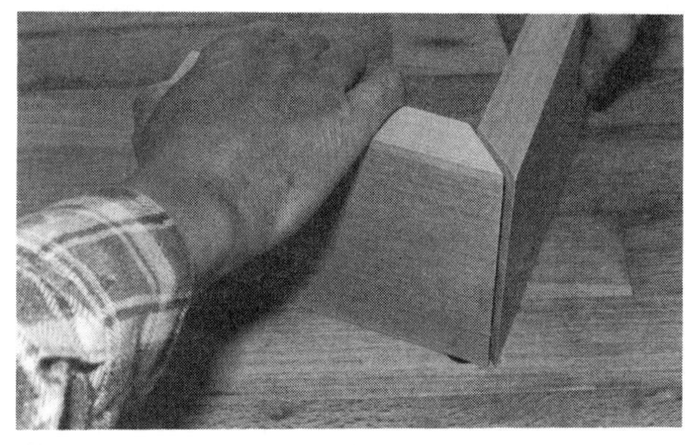

Illus. 43. Edge mitres can be used to join the ends or sides of boards. They can also be used to join long grain, as in joining the sides to the top of a piece of cabinetry, and need no reinforcement. When used to join end grain, as shown here, reinforcement is necessary.

you work from both sides towards the middle. Start by gauging a line on the inside face of the board that is exactly the same distance from the edge as the width of the mating board. Hold the plane at approximately 45° to the surface of the board and start planing off the edge. Continue to remove wood until the plane iron is touching both the front edge and the line. This should result in a 45° mitre. Use a combination square to check its accuracy. Make any adjustments with light planing strokes. You might want to consider using a shooting board, provided you make 45° angle blocks to hold the work. This will result in a more accurate angle. You can also temporarily glue 45° angle blocks to the boards to make clamping any edge mitre easier (Illus. 44). After the joint is dry, the blocks can be removed with a chisel.

Illus. 44. Clamping blocks temporarily glued to the boards can make clamping an edge mitre easier.

Rabbet Joints

A rabbet is an L-shaped recess made on the end or edge of a board (Illus. 45). This joint is stronger than a butt joint in many applications. Because the shoulder forms a ledge on which the mating part rests, stresses that would be shear in a butt joint are experienced as compression. When a rabbet is cut in end grain, there is no long-grain contact area, which is better than a butt joint; but, a rabbet cut into the edge of a board has good long-grain contact on both surfaces of the joint and will provide a strong glue bond. Some type of reinforcement is needed with an end-grain rabbet. (Refer to Chapter 3, page 43, for various means of reinforcement.)

Illus. 45. The L-shaped cutout on the end of this board is a rabbet. The shoulder gives added support, making the rabbet stronger than a butt joint.

Rabbets are often used to join the corners of boxes or cabinets. It is the joint most frequently used to attach the back of a cabinet to the sides and top. It can also be used in drawer construction as well as many other applications.

The width of a rabbet is simply equal to the thickness of the mating board; however, you can make the rabbet wider than the mating board, if you like, and trim the joint flush after assembly. When used to attach the back of a built-in cabinet, the rabbet is usually made 1/8" to 1/4" wider than the back. This leaves room to scribe the cabinet to an irregular wall so that the cabinet will nevertheless be flush. You can make the rabbet even wider if you anticipate a great deal of scribing.

As a general rule of thumb, the depth of a rabbet equals one-half the thickness of the board being cut. You can vary the depth for special applications. In thick stock, it may not be necessary to make the rabbet that deep; when appearance is especially important, you may want to make the rabbet deep enough so that as little end grain shows as possible.

RABBETING WITH HAND TOOLS

Short rabbets can be made with a backsaw. Make a shoulder cut in the face of the board, then cut in from the end to remove the waste. Although you can make the cuts freehand, you will obtain more accurate results if you use guide boards clamped to the work to help keep the saw square and in the proper position, making the cut straighter. If the boards will fit in your mitre box, you can use it to guide the shoulder cut. You can also make a simple jig for cutting rabbets by attaching a board that is one-half the thickness of the work to a scrap of plywood or particleboard. Place the work on the jig with the outside face down and the end to be cut against the spacer block. Clamp a guide board on top of the work to guide the saw for the shoulder cut (Illus. 46). After making the shoulder cut, turn the saw on its side, and rest it on the spacer block. Cut into the end of the board to remove the waste (Illus. 47). If you prefer, make the shoulder cut with the saw, but then use a chisel to remove the waste. You can use the same jig; the spacer block is still used to indicate the depth of the cut.

Illus. 46. This simple jig can be used to guide a backsaw while cutting a rabbet. Make the shoulder cut first, using the board clamped on top as a guide.

Illus. 47. To complete the rabbet, rest the saw on the spacer block at the end of the jig and saw into the end of the board.

To make longer rabbets by hand, the best method is to use a rabbet plane (Illus. 48). The plane removes only a thin shaving of wood with each pass, so it may take quite a few passes to complete the rabbet. Hold the plane square; don't let it rock on the edge. To plane a rabbet across the grain of the board, you need a plane that has a spur to sever the fibres. Keep the spur sharp, and adjust so that the spur will make a cut that is as deep as the plane-iron setting. The spur rides in front of the plane iron to sever the fibres; then, the plane iron lifts them without tearing into the good face of the board.

Illus. 48. You can guide a rabbet plane by placing a finger under the sole and rubbing against the edge of the board, or by using a guide board clamped to the work. If you use a fillister plane, you can set the fence and depth stop to the size of the rabbet.

Dado and Groove Joints

Dadoes and grooves are especially suited for attaching shelves to the sides of a cabinet, since any shear stress is inherently eliminated because the board is supported by a shoulder on both sides. The shoulders also help to hold the part in alignment during assembly, and they help to prevent boards from cupping afterwards. When a dado or groove joint fails, it is usually due to poor design that in some way places tension on the joint, effectively pulling it apart. Essentially the one weakness of these joints is under tension; under compression or shear, they are very strong. Your best precaution is to analyze the project; see if there will be tensional forces pulling the joint apart. If you find that the joint will have to resist tension, consider using a variation on the dado or groove called a sliding dovetail, which is covered under Rabbet, Dado, and Groove Variations in Chapter 5, page 73.

Traditionally, the distinction between these joints has been that a groove runs with the grain and a dado runs across the grain (Illus. 49). For a generation of woodworkers raised on plywood and power tools, this distinction has become obscure. When there is no discernible grain direction, as in plywood or particleboard, it is common practice to call this type of joint a dado when it is cut in the face of a board and a groove when it is cut on an edge.

Illus. 49. The dado runs across the grain and the groove runs with the grain. This distinction can be obscure when working with power tools or man-made materials, but it is obvious when working with lumber and especially with hand tools.

When you use hand tools, you soon discover why woodworkers in earlier times distinguished between the dado and the groove. Going with the grain, you can easily plow a groove using a plane, but to cut across the grain to make a dado, you need spurs on the plane to sever the fibres before the plane iron lifts them; or you may want to use a saw and chisel or router plane as described below to cut the dado. A dado or groove is usually cut to a depth one-half the thickness of the board; so, for ¾″ stock the cut is ⅜″ deep. When the intrinsic strength of the part in which the joint is cut is more important than the strength that might be achieved with more of a shoulder to support the mating part, then the cuts can be shallower. A ⅜″-deep joint is usually sufficient even for stock thicker than ¾″. In its usual application, the dado is primarily an end-grain joint, so you can't rely solely on glue to hold the joint. On the other hand, connecting long grain to long grain with a groove provides a good glue bond.

Planes can be used to make either dadoes or grooves. A groove can be cut by hand using a plow plane, which can be equipped with different size irons for cutting grooves of various widths. It has an adjustable fence to guide the plane and a depth stop. To plow a groove, first install the correct size iron. Then set the fence to position the groove, and set the depth stop. Start at the far end of the board, working only on a small section; cut down a little at a time until you reach the depth stop. Then move on to the next section. When you have completed all of the sections, run the plane along the entire length of the groove once or twice.

To cut a dado by hand with a plane, a special dado plane is needed. It has cutting spurs called nickers on both sides to sever the wood fibres. A dado is typically far enough in from the end to make using a fence attached to the plane impractical; you need to clamp a board to the work to guide the plane. Set the depth stop on the plane; the width of the dado is determined by the size of the plane. Make a pass across the entire length of the dado so that the nickers will score the shoulders; then, start shaving down the dado. If the dado isn't too long, you might be able to make passes across the entire length, cutting it all at once. For a longer dado, shave down one section at a time just as described above for cutting a groove; start at the far side so that as you move back you will be working into the previously cut section. Make one or two passes across the entire length at the end.

As mentioned above, you can also cut a dado by hand without a dado plane by using a saw and chisel or router plane. Use a backsaw to make shoulder cuts at each side of the joint, stopping at the desired depth for the dado. You can clamp a guide board to the work to help you keep the saw straight and square with the face. For sufficiently narrow boards, you can use your mitre box to guide the saw. Some woodworkers like to make several saw kerfs between the two side cuts to help remove the waste, whereas others go straight to chiselling. To remove most of the waste, hold the chisel bevel side down and take deep cuts (Illus. 50). As you get close to the desired depth, start taking light cuts to smooth the rough surface left by the heavy cuts. If the chisel is long enough, turn it bevel side up and pare the surface smooth.

Instead of a chisel, you may prefer to use a router plane to finish the cut. The router plane will make a smooth surface that is of uniform depth. Usually, you will find that it's best to remove most of the waste with a chisel, then switch to the router plane just to smooth the bottom of the cut.

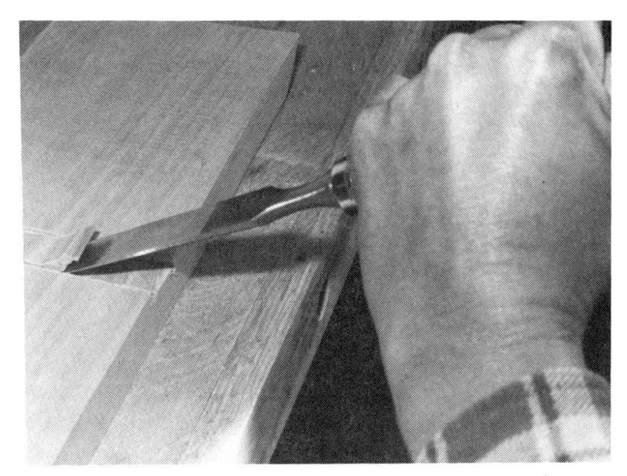

Illus. 50. You can use a chisel to remove the waste between saw cuts when cutting a dado by hand.

Mortise-and-Tenon

The mortise-and-tenon is a real workhorse joint: it is strong and versatile. The tenon is a projection on one board that fits into the mortise or hole in the mating board (Illus. 51). There are surviving examples of mortise-and-tenon joints from ancient Egypt, and they were probably in use for some time before that. The mortise-and-tenon makes a strong glue joint primarily because of its large long-grain contact area; yet it

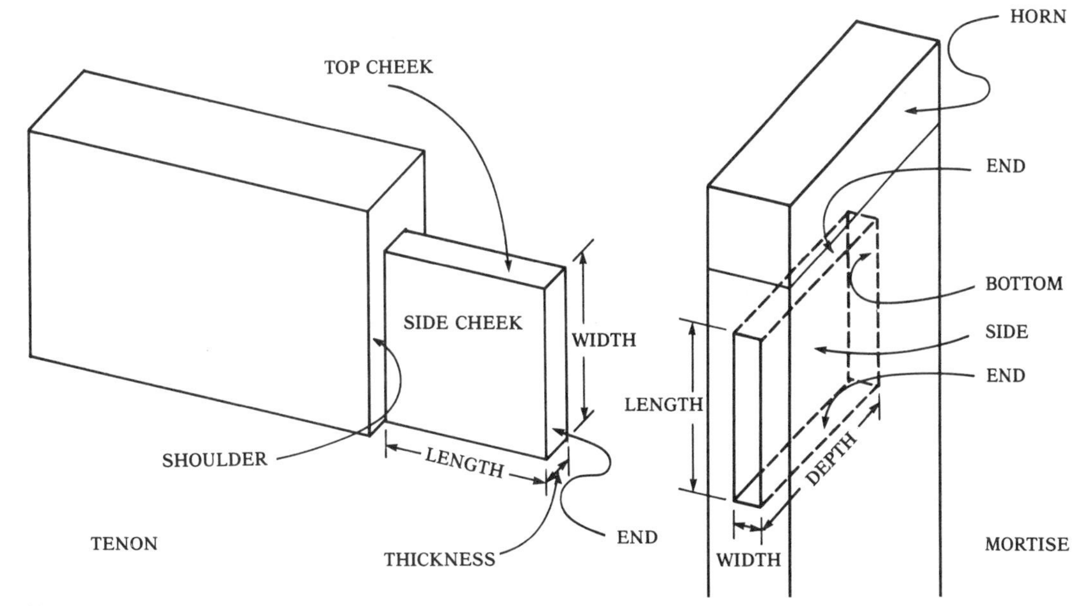

Illus. 51. Mortise-and-tenon joints are very useful when great strength is required.

can be used without glue when necessary to allow for dimensional changes in the wood. It has been used in nearly all phases of woodworking from timber framing for houses to shipbuilding to cabinetmaking. Because the mortise-and-tenon is used in such diverse applications, numerous methods exist for making the joint. I don't use the same method for a backyard fence's mortise-and-tenon joints as I use for a panel door's corner joints. Personal preference is also a factor in deciding which method you will use.

But first, to make the following directions clear, you need some basics. Illus. 51 labels the parts of a mortise-and-tenon. Notice the way dimensions are designated differently on the tenon and on the mortise; this is a little confusing, but it is standard practice so you do need to become quite familiar with it. The thickness of the tenon corresponds to the width of the mortise; the width of the tenon corresponds to the length of the mortise; and the length of the tenon corresponds to the depth of the mortise.

There are some traditional rules for the proportions of a mortise-and-tenon. They work fairly well in most cases; later for specific applications, I'll tell you how to bend the rules to make the joint stronger, but for now let's use these four rules of thumb:

Rule 1: The tenon thickness should be about one-third the thickness of the stock that will be mortised. Notice that this is specifically not one-third the thickness of the part with the tenon. This is to ensure that cutting the mortise doesn't weaken its part too much. When the parts are of equal thickness, then, the tenon will also be one-third the thickness of the part with the tenon; but when the part with the mortise is thicker—say, for example, when a rail is joined to a leg—the tenon can be thicker, preferably close to one-third the thickness of the part being mortised. This gives a stronger joint because the tenon is less likely to break the thicker it is.

Rule 2: The tenon width should be no more than five times its thickness—with a maximum width of about four inches. When the planned tenon width-to-thickness ratio is more than 5:1, it should be divided into two tenons. There are several practical reasons for this rule. A single long mortise can weaken the board. Wide tenons are dimensionally unstable; seasonal changes in humidity can lead to a loose joint or a split board. If you wedge a wide, thin tenon, it can buckle. In serious cases, a buckled tenon can even split the wood around the mortise.

Rule 3: When a blind mortise is used—the mortise doesn't go all the way through the stock—the depth of the mortise should be two-thirds of the width of the board in which it is cut. The strength of the joint is proportional to the length of the tenon. A longer tenon means a stronger joint. With a blind mortise, you want to make it as deep as is feasible without leaving a weak section between the bottom of the mortise and the edge of the stock. Generally, this rule gives the appropriate depth; however, later I'll give some exceptions.

Rule 4: Leave a horn that is about equal to the thickness of the board (refer again to Illus. 51). The horn is an extra length of board left on the end of the piece being mortised. The horn reinforces the mortise during chopping and assembly, after which it is trimmed off. The exact length of the horn isn't critical as long as it keeps the wood from splitting or breaking out as you work. Leaving a horn isn't as necessary when you are using power tools to make the mortise; but a horn is still useful to reinforce the joint as it is assembled.

MAKING A MORTISE-AND-TENON BY HAND

There are many methods for making a mortise-and-tenon joint. The first method I'll describe produces good results for many applications. In Part Two, Chapter 6, page 89, I'll describe variations on this technique.

Tools

A knife is good for making marks because it gives you a notch in which to place the chisel. If you plan to make many mortise-and-tenon joints by hand, a mortise gauge is a good investment. It has two spurs that can be set to the width of the mortise. It is also very helpful when you want to offset the mortise in a thick board because you can change the fence setting while leaving the distance between the spurs undisturbed.

A good mortising chisel is one of the most important requirements for making an accurate mortise by hand. The mortising chisel—with a somewhat longer, thicker blade, and a heavy-duty handle—is stronger than other chisels. Once you have started chopping a mortise with the mortising chisel, the sides of the chisel will follow the previous cut, making it easier to keep the sides of the mortise straight and square with the face. Because of this, it is important that the sides of the chisel are accurately ground.

Strike the chisel with a cabinetmaker's mallet (Illus. 52). It has a heavy wooden head with a flat face that is slightly angled. The angle and flat face make it easy to hit direct blows and to avoid glancing strokes.

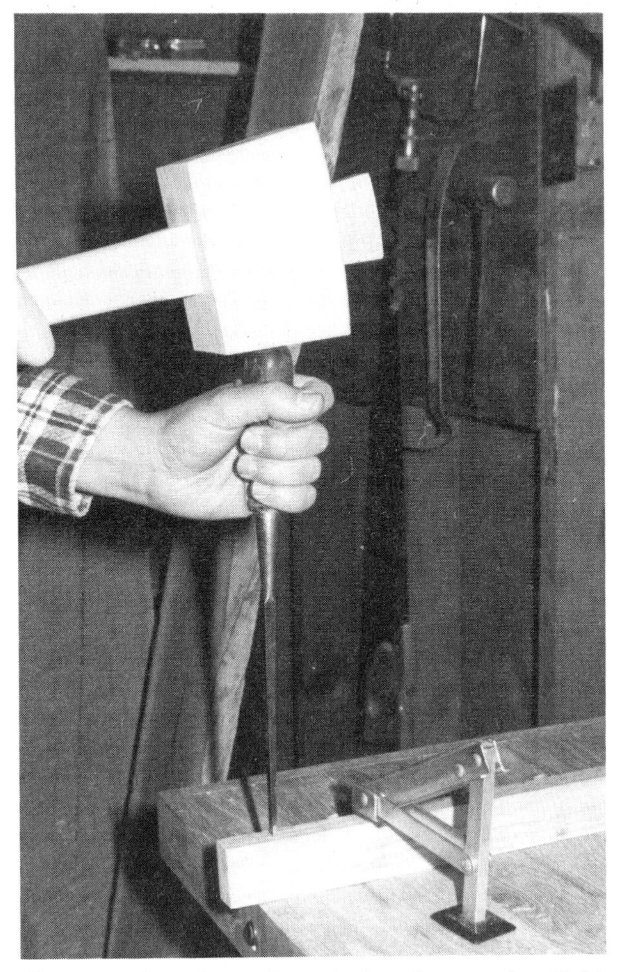

Illus. 52. Place the work on the bench over a leg. Hold the chisel far enough away from your body to sight along it and strike it with a cabinetmaker's mallet.

The saw you use is also important. A backsaw or tenoning saw is a good choice. You can also use a bow saw. The important thing is that the saw is sharpened and set correctly so that it will cut straight. It is also important that the saw be stiff enough not to whip as you make the cut.

Layout

The mortise-and-tenon is a matched set; mark the boards so that you can identify the front faces and which parts go together. Allow for a horn; then, mark the location of the top and the bottom of the mortise. When several identical parts are being made, you can place the parts together and square across all the boards at once. When the boards are the same thickness, a knife is the best marking tool; but when the mortise is cut into a board that is wider than the one with the tenon, you may want to use a pencil since the marks left by a knife will show, and they can be difficult to remove. Next, mark the shoulder cuts for the tenon. Use a knife to mark and make a fairly deep cut. The knife's marking cut will help you have a sharp line for sawing the shoulder. You can use a chisel to deepen this shoulder mark. Draw the corner of the chisel along the line with the bevel facing the waste. Then, hold the chisel at an angle, and cut a slope on the waste side. This scores the shoulder and provides a notch in which the saw can rest. The ultimately visible shoulder line will be sharp and free from rag if you follow this method.

One important rule to abide by when laying out the joint is to gauge all lines from the front face. That way any variations in thickness won't keep the front faces from being aligned. Use rule-of-thumb number one, above, to determine the thickness of the tenon and from that the width of the mortise, then find the closest-size chisel you have. Typically, for ¾" stock a ¼" chisel is used. Set the spurs of the mortise gauge to the width of the chisel; hold the chisel so that the points of the spurs just touch the corners of the chisel. Next, set the fence for the distance between the side of the mortise and the front face of the board; place the fence against the front face of the board, and mark the sides of the mortise. With the same gauge setting, lay out the cheeks of the tenon; place the fence against the front face, and mark on both edges and across the end of the board.

If you don't have a mortising gauge, set a regular marking gauge for one side of the mortise, and mark on all of the parts; then, line up the chisel with a mortise line, and give it a light tap.

Set the gauge to the other end of the mark left by the chisel. Use this setting to make the balance of the marks.

Chopping the Mortise

Tradition dictates that you chop the mortise first. This has a certain logic in that once you make one part you need to make the second to fit it. The main reason for chopping the mortise first is that the size is fixed by the size of the mortising chisel, while you can easily adjust the size of the tenon when you go to saw it. However, I know of woodworkers who prefer to make the tenons first; they can come up with just as good an argument for their method as the argument for chopping the mortise first. So the choice is really up to you.

Place the board on the bench directly over a leg, as shown in Illus. 52. You don't want to waste any energy bouncing the bench as you chop. The area directly over the leg is the most solid part of the bench. Don't put the board in a vise; it will absorb a lot of the power of each blow, and you will end up loosening the vise.

The chisel must be held square in all directions to make a good mortise. When you drive a chisel into wood, the bevel tends to force the chisel towards the opposite side. This creates a slightly curved cut, which you can use later to scoop out the bottom of the cut. Hold the chisel square and far enough away from your body so that you can sight along it to keep it vertical, counteracting the tendency to curve. Place the chisel inside the layout lines; the back of the chisel should be parallel with the end of the mortise. Start the cut about ⅛" inside the layout line. Strike the chisel hard with the mallet; you should be able to drive it about ½" into the wood. Reposition the chisel about ⅜" past the first cut and make another (Illus. 53). Continue in this way until you are about ⅛" away from the other end. The scooping action of the chisel tends to sever the fibres at the bottom of the cut so that you can easily remove the waste by levering it out with the chisel (Illus. 54).

Now start the chopping process over again, and make the mortise deeper. Continue in this way until the mortise is halfway through the board, then—providing it is not a blind mortise—turn the board over and chop from the opposite side until you chop through. When making a blind mortise, work from one side only. You can wrap a piece of tape around the chisel blade as a depth stop. When you have chopped the mortise to full depth, pare the remaining ⅛" from the ends to the layout lines (Illus. 55).

Illus. 53. Start chopping about ⅛" inside the end layout line. Make repeated cuts inward until you get close to the other end.

Illus. 54. Lever out the waste with the chisel.

Illus. 55. After chopping to full depth, pare the ends of the mortise to the layout lines.

Illus. 56. To cut the tenons, first place the board in the vise at about a 45° angle. Start a kerf with the saw teeth flat against the end of the board; then start to angle the cut until you reach the shoulder mark.

Illus. 57. The second step in cutting the tenons is to turn the board around in the vise and saw down to the other shoulder mark.

Illus. 58. To complete the cheek cuts, place the board straight up in the vise and saw down to the shoulder marks.

Cutting the Tenon

Once you have chopped all of the mortises, check the layout of each tenon against the corresponding mortise, and make any adjustments. Make all cuts on the waste side of the layout lines. To cut the tenon, start by making the cheek cuts. Since you can only see two of the three lines at once—the end and one edge of the board—you need to make the cut in a way that will keep the saw aligned on all three lines. The following three-step approach accomplishes this because you follow each line separately while using the previous cut to help guide the saw.

Make the cuts on both sides of the tenon in each of the three steps to avoid repeated repositioning of the work. Place the board in a vise at about 45° with the end with the layout lines pointing up. As a first step, start a kerf with the saw teeth flat against the end of the board. Cut straight down about 1/8"; then lower the handle of the saw to about level, and cut at an angle to the board until you reach the shoulder mark that is facing you (Illus. 56). For the second step, turn the board around in the vise—bottom edge up—but keep it at about 45°. Put the saw in the kerf on the end; then lower the handle and angle the saw down while you cut until you reach the shoulder mark (Illus. 57). For the third step, reposition the board so that it is straight up. Then saw straight down to each of the shoulder marks (Illus. 58).

You can hold the board against a bench hook to cut the shoulders or use your mitre box. Place the work in the mitre box, and line up the shoulder mark. The outside teeth of the saw should come right up to the knifed line but not cross it. Saw straight down to the cheek (Illus. 59).

Illus. 59. Put the board in a mitre box to saw the shoulders, as shown here, or hold the board against a bench hook.

When the tenon is complete, test it in its mortise. It should be a snug fit; but, it shouldn't take more than hand pressure to push it in. A tenon that is too tight may split the wood around the mortise, while one that is too loose will result in a poor glue joint. The front faces should be flush and the boards should be square with each other. Make any adjustments by paring across the grain on the tenon cheek. If the shoulder doesn't fit snug against the edge of the mortised board, make a saw kerf along the joint. Keep the saw completely on the tenon side of the line. Make the kerf just about ⅛" deep; then disassemble the parts, and pare the shoulder down to the kerf with a chisel. Remember that this will slightly shorten the part; if you are making a frame, take an equal amount off the opposite board to keep the frame square.

Alternate Methods

The techniques described above aren't the only ones that can produce good results. There are several other techniques for chopping the mortise and cutting the tenon. Let's look at the mortise again first. One alternative approach is to chop as described above; then, when you reach the far end, turn the chisel around and work your way back. When you reach the near end again, remove the waste. This will deepen the cuts and loosen the waste.

After levering out the waste, you can tap the chisel blade horizontally straight ahead while you hold the chisel in a vertical position. Place the point of the chisel at one end of the cut with the bevel facing that end. Strike the bevel side with the mallet. This scrapes the point of the chisel along the bottom of the cut, removing the waste and smoothing the bottom.

Another alternative is that, instead of starting at one end of the mortise and progressing to the other, you can start chopping in the middle. Make all of the cuts with the flat back of the chisel blade facing the middle. Make one cut, then reverse the chisel and make another cut, progressing outward from the middle in both directions. Finally, turn the flat back of the blade parallel to each end and pare the ends to the line.

One alternate method for cutting the tenon is particularly applicable when the wood is straight grained for then you can use a chisel to cut the tenon cheeks. First, make the shoulder cuts; then, place a wide chisel on the end of the tenon and split away the waste. Pare across the grain to smooth the cheek and bring it to the desired final size.

Some woodworkers use a two-step approach to cutting the cheeks instead of the three-step technique. The first step is just like the one described earlier; with the board at 45° in the vise, cut a ⅛" kerf parallel to the end, lower the handle and cut at an angle down to the shoulder. Next, put the board straight up in the vise and turn it around so that the uncut line faces you. Saw straight down the line to the shoulder. The previous cut will help guide the saw.

You can also make a tenon using a rabbet plane or a fillister plane. Using a plane is particularly practicable for wide tenons because they are harder to saw. Set the fence on the plane to the length of the tenon, and set the depth stop for the shoulder width. Plane across the end of the board until you reach the depth stop; then, flip the board over, and plane the other side.

Another planing method is especially useful for long tenons. Use a plow plane to make a dado at the shoulder. Then use a bench plane or a block plane to remove the waste on the cheek.

Both of these planing methods are fast, and they produce a much smoother surface on the tenon than sawing or chiselling. This smooth surface can lead to a better glue joint than could be achieved with other methods. Planing also gives you a very fine control over the thickness of the tenon.

Dovetails

Well-made dovetails have long been considered to be the mark of true craftsmanship. Dovetails have proven through centuries of use to form strong, interlocking joints particularly suited for joining two boards at a corner. The interlocking pins and tails provide both mechanical locking and long-grain contact for gluing (Illus. 60).

A dovetail joint should always start and end in a half-pin. The half-pins are so named because they are angled only on one side; the faces of half-pins are quite often the same size as the faces of the rest of the pins, but they can be any size. The dovetails get their name from their shape mimicking that of a dove's tail. When speaking about the individual parts of a dovetail joint, many woodworkers call the dovetails simply *tails*; this eliminates some confusion, since the entire joint is referred to as a dovetail.

A dovetail joint is stronger in one direction—parallel to the tail board—than the other—parallel to the pin board. For this reason, you need to decide which part will take the most stress. In a drawer, for example, the pins are placed on the drawer front and the tails on the side. This locks the front so that it won't pull off. Dovetails are really only suited for use in solid wood; nevertheless, you often see them used with particleboard or plywood, especially in commercial items. But this use, or misuse, just isn't very satisfactory; I saw a lot of them in the furniture repair shop, broken to pieces. Particleboard pins tend to crumble; plywood works a little better, but the half-blind dovetails usually used in drawer construction tend to break off at one of the joints between plies.

The through dovetail is the most basic type of dovetail; it is also the strongest. Since the tails and pins both extend all the way through the mating board, there is visible end grain on both faces. Half-blind and full-blind dovetails that hide the end grain are described in Chapter 7, page 109. Through dovetails are often used as design elements.

CUTTING THROUGH DOVETAILS BY HAND

There are a couple of rules of thumb to use in laying out dovetails; I'll use them in this chapter, then in the appropriate chapter I'll explain ways to vary the proportions. First, the widest part of the pin should equal the thickness of the stock. Second, the narrowest point of the tails should be twice the width of the widest part of the pins. With these rules in mind, measure the thickness of the stock and begin working out how many tails and pins will fit on the board. Remember that the joint must begin and end with a half-pin. Make sure the half-pins will be equal in width to the full-pins at their widest point. You can vary the width of the tails to make an adjustment so the half-pins come out right.

Once you have decided on the number of pins, you are ready to lay out the pin board. The best way to start is to mark the middle line of both half-pins. Then, angle a rule with any convenient

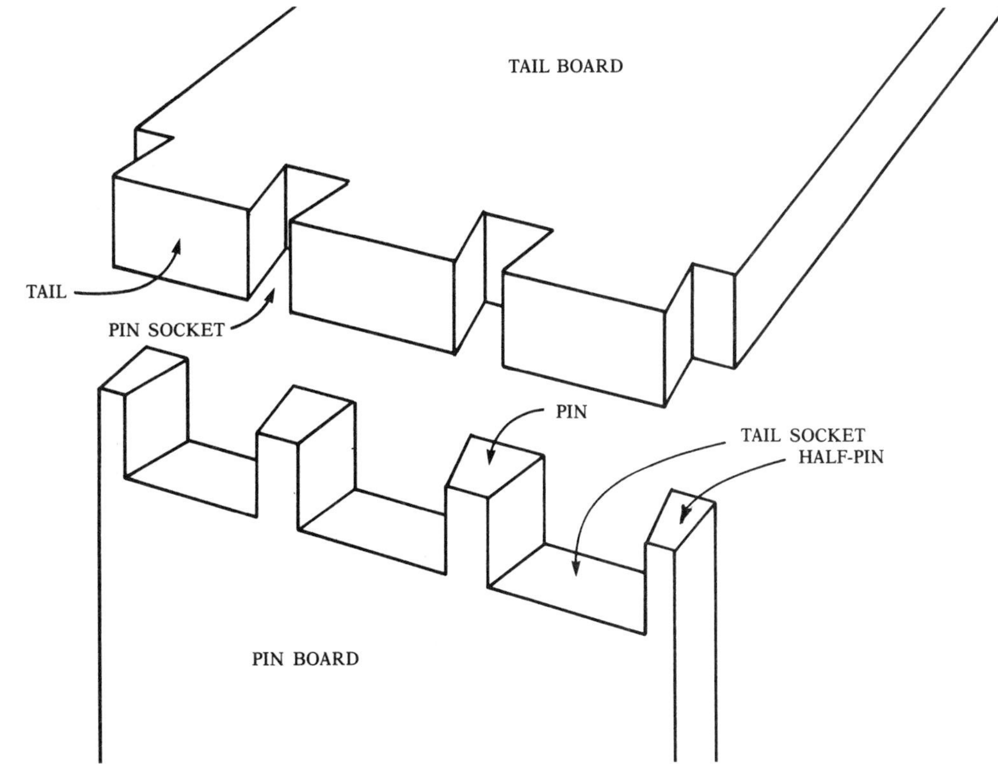

Illus. 60. Parts of a dovetail joint.

units across the board with "0" units lined up on one of the half-pin middle lines and a number of units that is easily divisible by the number of pins lined up on the other half-pin middle line. Make a mark with a pencil for the middle of each pin across the board. For example, if there are to be five pins, angle the rule until fifteen units line

Illus. 61. Gauge a line on both faces of the pin board after setting the marking gauge. The setting is only slightly more than the thickness of the tail board.

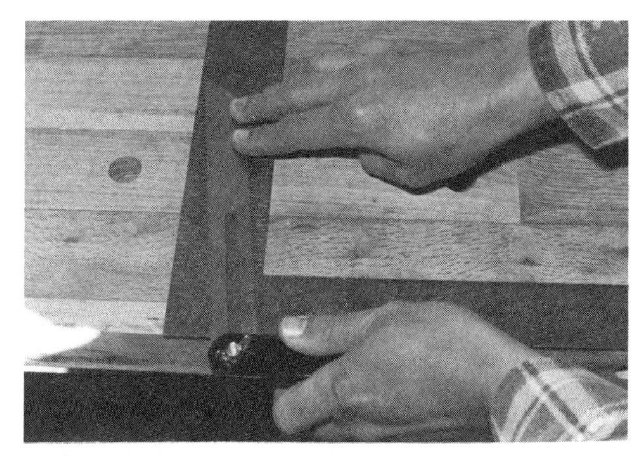

Illus. 62. Set the bevel to a 1:7 slope.

Illus. 63. Use the bevel to lay out the pins on the end of the pin board.

up with the half-pin middle line, then make a mark every three units. Use a square to transfer each mark to the end of the board. Then measure from each side of the mark one-half of the width of the pin. These marks are made with a pencil so that they'll be easy to remove; the rest of the layout should be done with a sharp knife or marking gauge.

Set a marking gauge for a hair more than the thickness of the tail board. This is so that the pins—and later the tails—are left slightly high for trimming with a plane or belt sander after assembly. With the fence against the end grain, gauge a line on both faces of the board (Illus. 61). Set a bevel to a 1 in 7 slope (Illus. 62). With the bevel and a knife, lay out the pins on the end of the board (Illus. 63). Use a square to carry the bevel lines down the face to the gauged line. Mark the waste area with an *X* to avoid any confusion while cutting.

Place the board end up in a vise. Use a dovetail saw, a fine-toothed backsaw or bow saw to make the cuts. It's a good idea to get in the habit of making the cuts precisely to the line right from the start. If you leave the pins large to trim later, you will just add more work, and you'll wind up not enjoying making dovetails. Place the saw so that the kerf will be in the waste area and will leave half the layout line (Illus. 64). Work across

Illus. 64. Saw straight down along the layout lines to cut the pins. I find it easiest to hold the saw at the same angle and make every other cut across the board first.

the board, stopping exactly at the gauged line with each cut. Work across the board, making every other cut so that the saw stays at the same angle; then work back, cutting the other angle (Illus. 65).

Saw the pins on all of the boards; then chop out the waste. The waste is removed using a chisel. Place the work on a solid part of the bench, preferably over a leg; clamp it down, outside face up. Draw the corner of the chisel over the line made by the marking gauge in the areas to be removed (Illus. 66). This will deepen the cut. Then place the chisel on the face of the pin board about ⅛" away from the line, and make a sloping cut into the shoulder (Illus. 67). You have now established what will be the visible shoulder line of the finished joint; don't alter this line during any of the subsequent steps. Place the chisel in the *V* with the flat of the blade against the shoulder. Drive the chisel into the wood with a mallet (Illus. 68). Hold the chisel at an ever so slight angle so that the shoulder will be just barely undercut. This undercutting is really very subtle, almost imperceptible. When finished, the cross section is a very flat *V*. This ensures a tight fit at the visible shoulder line; it doesn't weaken the joint because the end grain won't really contribute to the glue area anyway.

Once you have driven the chisel about ⅛" deep along all of the shoulders on this side, place the chisel on the end grain with the bevel down, and split out a chip of waste about ⅛" thick. When you have removed a sliver from each of the waste

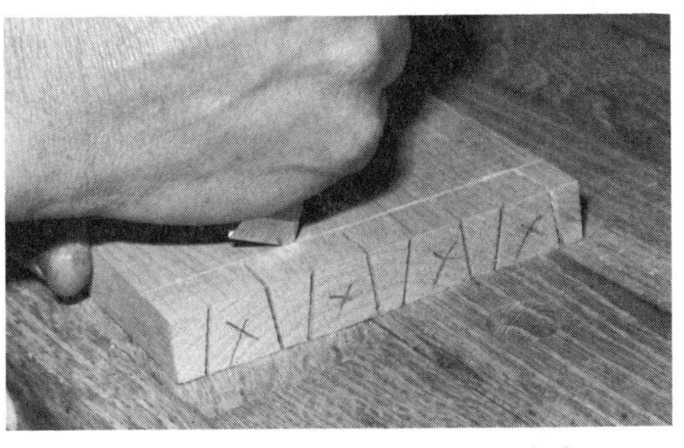

Illus. 66. Score along the shoulder line with the corner of a chisel.

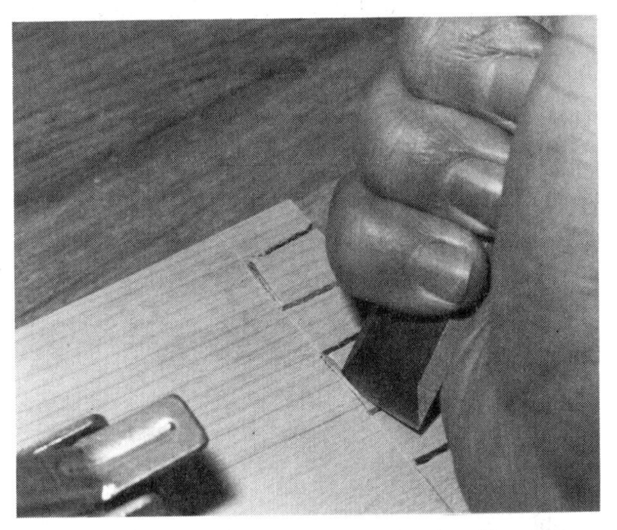

Illus. 67. Make a sloping cut into the shoulder with the corner of the chisel. This produces a sharp shoulder line.

Illus. 65. After making the first series of cuts, hold the saw at the other angle and finish cutting the pins.

Illus. 68. Place the chisel in the V-notch *previously cut at the shoulder and chop down about ⅛".*

areas between pins, chop the shoulder again, and remove another sliver. When you reach the middle, turn the board over and repeat the same procedure on the other side (Illus. 69). When removing the waste with the inside face up, you may find that the edges of the pins are getting torn because each waste chip gets wider as you work down. To avoid this problem, angle the chisel one way while removing one chip, then angle it the other way while removing the next; this will lift one side of the chip out first so it won't wedge between the pins. Clean up any pieces left in the corners, and you are ready to lay out the tails.

The pins are used to lay out the tails. Start by gauging a shoulder line all around the end of the tail board. Set the marking gauge to a hair more than the thickness of the pin board. Lay the board with its inside face up on the bench. Next, place the mating pin board on top of this board, and line it up with the shoulder line and the edges. With a marking knife, reach into the space between pins and trace the pin locations onto the tail board. Start the mark at the narrow part of the pin, and pull towards the inside. This lessens the chance of the knife being pulled away from the pin by the grain of the wood (Illus. 70). Use a square to carry the lines across the end grain.

Place the tail board end up in a vise and saw down these lines. Keep the kerf in the waste while leaving half of the layout line. Stop exactly at the shoulder line. If you cut the tails in this way, they should require a little or no additional fitting (Illus. 71).

Remove the waste in the half-pin's sockets with the saw by cutting straight along the gauge lines (Illus. 72). The waste in the rest of the sockets is removed with a chisel. The technique is

Illus. 69. After driving the chisel into the wood at the shoulder, split out the waste from the end.

Illus. 70. Place the pin board on top of the tail board, and line it up with the shoulder line. Scribe around the pins to mark the tail locations.

Illus. 71. Hold the saw at the proper angle, and saw along the layout lines down to the shoulder to cut out the tails.

Illus. 72. Remove the waste in the half-pin socket by sawing down the shoulder line.

about the same as described for the pins; start by making the shoulder cut by deepening the gauged line with the chisel. Chop down about ⅛", undercutting very slightly. Use a small chisel on the end grain with the bevel down to split out a chip (Illus. 73). Work down to the middle; then turn the board over and remove the waste from the other side. Once you've cleaned up any waste left in the corners, the joint is ready to dry-assemble.

Illus. 73. Split out the waste between the tails with the chisel.

Dry-assemble the joints to check the fit; but don't drive them all the way home (Illus. 74). A well-made joint will fit quite snugly, and disassembling it after it has been driven tight can cause damage. If you're satisfied with the fit in partial assembly, apply glue to the joint, and make the final assembly. If the joint doesn't seem to fit right, you still may be able to salvage it; refer to the section on correcting defects that appears later in Chapter 7, page 109.

Illus. 74. Check the fit of the joint by partially assembling it. Don't drive the joint tight during the dry assembly, because it may be difficult to disassemble without causing damage.

Use a block of wood to cushion the joint as you drive the tail board and the pin board together with a mallet. If they fit well enough, you may not even need to clamp the joint. If you do use clamps, you will need special clamp blocks to apply pressure to the tails and pins because they have been made slightly proud for trimming after assembly. Such clamp blocks have dadoes cut in them to clear the slightly projecting parts of the joint.

HAND-CUTTING VARIATIONS

It seems as if every experienced woodworker has a favorite technique for making dovetails. Here are a few methods that you may want to try. In one approach, you can cut the tails first if you prefer. This works best when making coarse dovetails because it is difficult to transfer the layout to the pin board if the pins will be very small. The advantage of cutting the tails first is that you can gang up several boards and cut all of the tails at once. In that case, place them together in a vise and make the saw cuts. Then lay the stack on the bench and stagger the ends before you clamp it. In this way, you can remove the waste on all of the boards at once, repositioning them only when you need to turn them over to chop on the other side. When the tails are finished, transfer the layout to the pin board using a layout knife. Then cut the pins as described above.

In another approach, you can use a coping saw to help remove the waste. This is most useful when the waste areas are particularly large, as would be the case with very coarse dovetails or when working with softwood. When you chop out the waste in softwood, you may find that there is a considerable tendency for the fibers to break off behind the shoulder line. You can minimize this problem by keeping the chisel sharp, but even then you may still have problems. Here is where the coping saw can be so useful; removing most of the waste with the coping saw eliminates the fibre breakage problem. After making the cuts with the dovetail saw, slip the blade of the coping saw down one kerf, cut a small radius to get the blade parallel to the shoulder line; then cut across to the other kerf, staying slightly above the gauged line. This will remove most of the waste; use a chisel to pare to the line, and remove any waste left in the corners.

When you use a chisel to remove the waste in softwood, a different technique may help avoid the problem of the fibres breaking behind the shoulder line. Start on the front face and angle the chisel into the shoulder, leaving the waste full width at the end. Work halfway down, then flip the board over and work down on the other side normally. The full-width end of the waste will rest on the bench to provide support, so chopping the shoulder won't snap off the waste before it is cut.

In the first dovetail method described above, the marking gauge is set a hair more than the width of the mating board; this leaves the ends of the tails and pins projecting slightly from the joint. After assembly, the ends are trimmed down to the faces of the boards with a plane or belt sander. This produces a very nicely finished joint, but if clamps are used, as discussed above, special clamp blocks are needed. Rather than have to make or work with these clamp blocks, some woodworkers prefer to make the gauged line a hair *less* than the thickness of the mating board. This leaves the ends slightly below the surface, so no special clamp blocks are needed. If you use this method, however, you then need to sand or plane the entire surface of each board until the ends of the pins and tails are flush with the faces. If the boards aren't too large, though, this isn't too big a job. If they are large, on the other hand, be prepared to sand or plane awhile.

3
Joint Reinforcement

When a joint is unlikely to be strong enough on its own to accommodate the stress that will be placed on it, you can strengthen the joint with some form of reinforcement. Butt joints and mitres are the types of joints that most frequently need reinforcing. Because of the clean uncluttered lines that butt and mitre joints provide, some custom cabinetmakers use them almost exclusively in their designs, reinforcing them with dowels or splines. In general, the most common types of joint reinforcement include not only dowels and splines but also plate or biscuit splines, reinforcement blocks, screws and nails, and specialized fasteners. You are probably already familiar with screws and nails, so I will concentrate on some of the other types of reinforcement in this chapter. Since specialized fasteners are most useful with plywood and particleboard, they are specifically covered in the discussion of plywood and particleboard joints of Chapter 12.

Dowels

Dowels can greatly improve the shear strength of a joint, and they are useful for aligning joints that will need to withstand compressional forces; but they are not as well suited for resisting tensional forces. Because they are easy to make and adapt well to mass production, dowel-reinforced butt joints are often found in commercial furniture (Illus. 75). When dowels are used in conjunction with other joints, the result can be very strong. Using a dowel to peg a mortise-and-

Illus. 75. Dowels are one of the most popular ways to reinforce a butt joint.

tenon joint, for example, locks the joint together, making it extremely resistant to tensional forces. See Chapter 6 for a detailed discussion of this joint.

DOWEL PINS

Dowels come in three-foot lengths or as ready-made pins. When selecting dowelling or dowel pins, check their moisture content to make sure that they are thoroughly dry. Otherwise they can shrink after assembly, weakening the joint. Pick straight-grained dowels. If the grain angles across the dowel, it will have less tensile strength. When I was repairing furniture, it was common to see a broken dowel joint expressly caused by angled grain in the dowel.

As a rule of thumb, the dowel diameter should be one-third to one-half the thickness of the board. So for ¾"-thick stock, a ¼"- or ⅜"-diameter dowel is just right. Ready-made pins come in ¼", 5⁄16", ⅜", and ½" diameters. They are usually available in lengths of 1½", 2", 2½", and 3". Ready-made dowel pins have chamfered ends and grooves or flutes to allow the glue and air to escape from the hole as the joint is assembled (Illus. 76). Some types have spiral grooves while others have straight flutes. You can make your own pins, of course, from the three-foot lengths of dowelling.

First cut the dowelling to the desired pin length. Then make one or more grooves in the side of the pin; you can do this by scratching with an awl or the point of a knife. The grooves don't need to spiral; straight grooves will be fine. In theory, the cabinetmaker would expect to achieve the strongest joint from a dowel with a single groove, because the smooth surface of the dowel theoretically should offer the best gluing surface. In practice this doesn't hold true; with the single-grooved dowel, a lot of the surface is in fact glue starved because the glue scrapes off during assembly. Slight variations in dowel size can also lead to a loose fit. The best overall performance comes from a multiflute dowel, both because the glue spreads more evenly over the surface and because the dowel can be slightly oversize. As the dowel is inserted in the hole, the multiple grooves allow the dowel to compress, ensuring a tight hold.

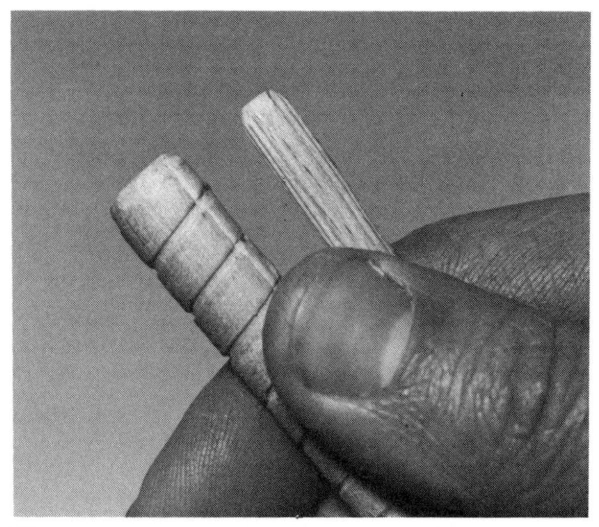

Illus. 76. Dowels are commercially available with either spiral grooves or straight flutes.

After making the grooves, chamfer the ends. This bevelling makes it easier to insert the dowels in the holes. By folding a piece of 100 grit medium sandpaper into a pad and placing it in the palm of your hand, you can twist the end of the dowel in the pad to make a chamfer. A couple of other methods make use of an electric drill. Chuck the dowel in the electric drill, and secure a piece of sandpaper on a hard surface. Turn on the drill, and place the end of the spinning dowel pin against the sandpaper at about a 45° angle to make the chamfer. You can also buy a commercial dowel-end former that fits into a drill. It is a cone-shaped cutter; the dowel fits into the center of the cone and the end is chamfered as the cutter turns. Another approach is to use a pencil sharpener in a similar fashion. For ¼" dowels, any pencil sharpener from a small handheld one to a large electric model will work; for dowels of larger sizes, you will need the type that has the multiple-size guide holes. Put the dowel in the sharpener for a moment just until a small chamfer has been formed on the end. Don't overdo the chamfering because it takes away from the effective glue-surface area.

Having a set of test dowel pins is a good idea to let you dry-assemble a joint to test the fit. To make the test points, cut a slot all the way through from one end of the pin to slightly more than halfway down; then, turn the pin over and cut another slot in the opposite end at the right angle to the first (Illus. 77). This gives the dowel some spring so you can easily dry-assemble and disassemble the joints for testing. For final as-

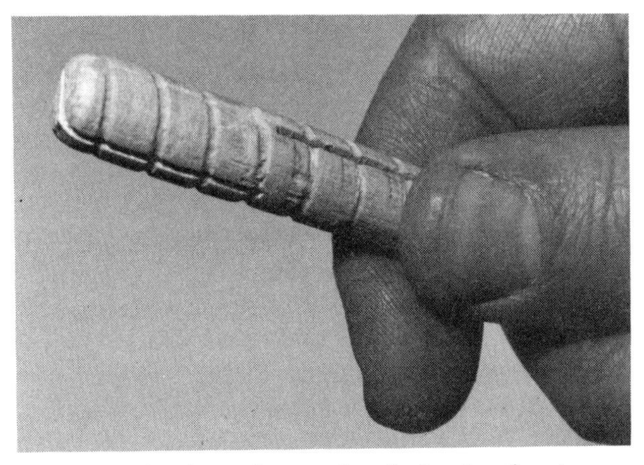

Illus. 77. The slots of a test dowel pin give the pin enough spring to make the joint easy to dry-assemble and disassemble for a test fitting.

sembly, of course, substitute the standard dowel pins, ready-made or homemade, that you used in designing the joint.

PEGGED JOINTS

There are several methods for positioning dowels. The simplest is called a pegged joint (Illus. 78). Even though pegged joints are simple to make, they are probably the strongest type of dowel joint because they give the most dowel penetration into both parts. To make a pegged joint, assemble the joint just as if there were going to be no pegs; then, after assembly, drill the dowel holes. The dowels are then inserted into the holes and trimmed flush. When you apply this method, the dowel ends show. This can be used quite agreeably for decorative effect. In the pegged joint shown in Illus. 78, notice that the middle dowel is straight while the two outside ones are angled slightly. This improves the joint's ability to withstand tensional forces. Joints with all straight dowels are much easier to pull apart. When used to reinforce a mitre joint, the dowel placement can be alternated from one side to the other, effectively locking the joint in both directions.

Locating the holes for a pegged joint is uncomplicated. Simply lay out the desired location of the holes on the outside of the board; then, drill the holes once the joint is assembled. Just be sure to carefully guide the drill so that it doesn't angle off to the side and break through the surface of the adjoining board. After the dowels have been inserted, trim off the ends until they are flush with the surface.

BLIND DOWEL JOINTS

When you want to hide the dowels you can use blind dowels (Illus. 79). Blind dowels can't be

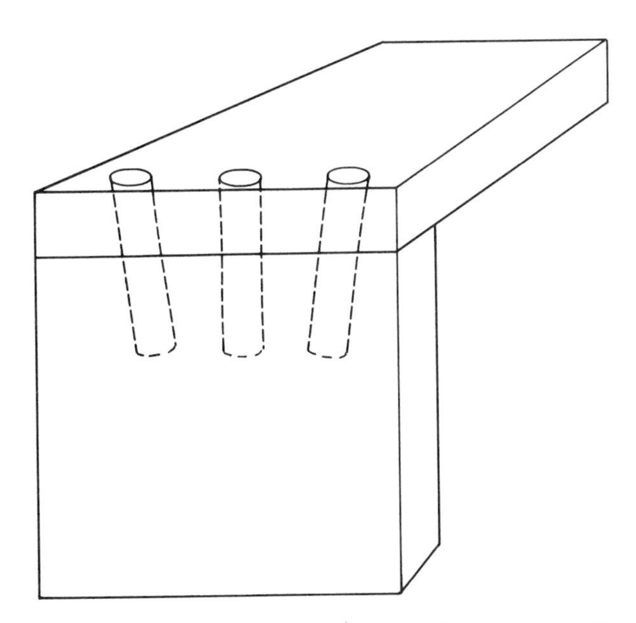

Illus. 78. In a pegged joint, the dowel pins extend all the way to the face of one of the boards. Angling the pins increases the strength of the joint.

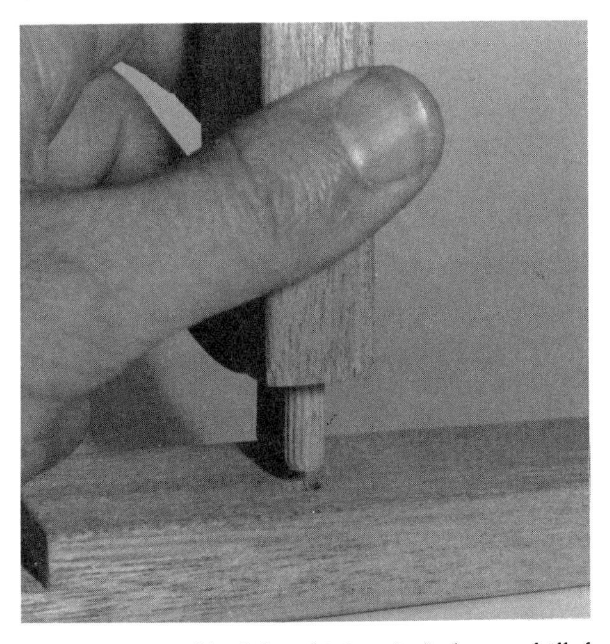

Illus. 79. For a blind-dowel joint, the holes are drilled only partway through the board. The result is a completely invisible reinforcement.

angled, so the joint can't resist tension as well as when the dowels are used to make a pegged joint. The penetration of the blind dowel is also quite limited. In ¾" stock, the penetration can't be much more than ½". A typical defect in this type of joint is the failure to use enough dowels. When there aren't enough dowels in the joint, stress on the joint can snap the dowels or pull them out of their holes. For maximum strength, the distance between the middle point of each dowel should be about three times the dowel diameter. For ¼" dowels, the spacing is ¾".

Blind dowels, however, are a good way to improve the shear strength of a joint, provided there are enough. They also help to align a joint during assembly, so even when a joint doesn't actually need reinforcement, a few dowels may be added to align the joint. In this case the dowels can be spaced farther apart.

Blind dowels are more difficult to lay out because holes drilled in both boards before assembly must line up accurately. To lay out blind dowels, position the boards as shown in Illus. 80, side by side but in their proper position. The face of each of the boards should be to the outside. Set a marking gauge for one-half the thickness of the board and mark a line down the middle of each board. Hold the marking gauge against the face of each board as you make each of the marks. This will ensure that the holes will line up even if the line isn't exactly in the middle.

Illus. 80. To lay out the location of blind dowels, hold the boards side by side in their proper position; then, use a marking gauge to make a line down the middle of each board, and scribe a line as shown across both boards.

Next, use a square to make a mark across both boards at each of the desired dowel locations. Use the point of an awl to indent the wood at each hole location, and you'll find it easier to start the hole without drifting off the mark.

You can also make a simple jig, or gauge, for marking the locations of dowel holes by gluing a piece of ⅛" hardboard into a dado cut in the side of a hardwood block (Illus. 81). Drill small holes at the correct dowel locations. Mark a 1 on one side of the gauge and a 2 on the other. Next, place the gauge so that the 1 is face up on the first board, and mark the holes by pushing the point of an awl through each hole in the gauge. Then, place the gauge so that the 2 is face up on the second board and mark the holes.

Now drill the holes. A brad point or bullet point drill works best because the spur keeps the drill from wandering off the mark (Illus. 82).

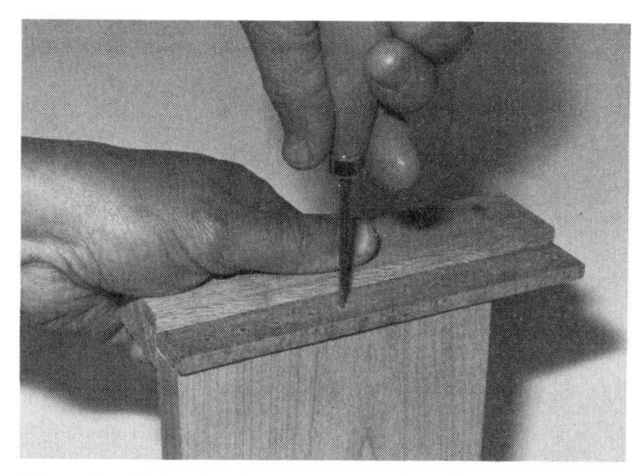

Illus. 81. This simple jig can speed up blind-dowel layout. The point of the awl is pushed through holes drilled in the hardboard to mark the dowel locations.

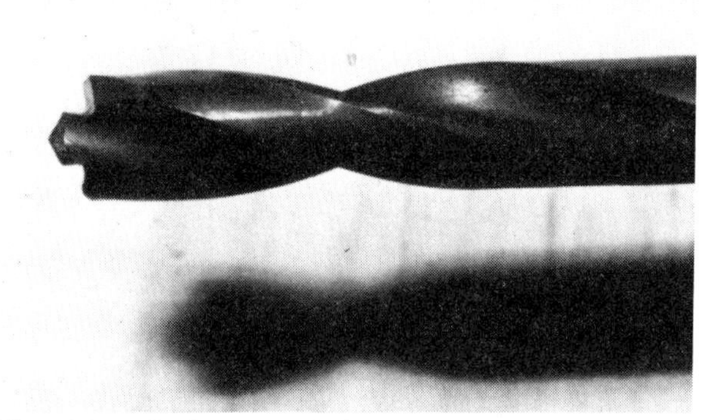

Illus. 82. A bullet-point drill is useful for drilling dowel holes, because it won't wander off the mark.

Make the holes as deep as possible; the strength of the joint will increase with increased dowel penetration. In most cases, however, a penetration of about 1" for each part gives close to the maximum strength. Make sure that the hole is a little deeper than is strictly necessary for the dowel pin to allow clearance for excess glue; but be careful that it is not too deep because the dowel can slip too far into one board during assembly, leaving a weak joint. About ⅛" deeper than one-half the dowel length is about right. Use a depth gauge on the drill bit to mark the desired depth of the hole. You can use a commercial drill stop to gauge the depth or simply wrap a piece of tape around the drill to form a flag. Always use a sharp drill bit when drilling dowel holes because, when the interior of the hole is rough with loose fibres, or if it is burned or burnished, the glue joint between the dowel and the sides of the hole will be weak.

By using a countersink, you can remove the fuzz from around the mouth of the hole. Countersinking the hole also makes it easier to insert the dowel pins, and it forms a small depression for any excess glue that squeezes out of the hole as the joint is clamped.

DOWEL CENTERS

The layout method described in the previous section works well on boards of equal thickness as are used typically for making corner joints and edge joining, but there are many situations where it is difficult to lay out the hole locations accurately. Dowel centers are an easy way to mark the hole locations in these situations.

Dowel centers are metal plugs that come in several sizes to fit into the dowel holes. At the middle of each plug there is a small point (Illus. 83). To use dowel centers, lay out the hole location on one of the boards and drill the holes. Insert the dowel centers into the holes. Next, place the mating board over the joint in position and push or tap it in place. The points on the dowel centers will leave a mark where the holes should be drilled (Illus. 84). When using dowel centers, it is important to carefully position the mating board accurately as you make the marks. A framing square can help with this alignment. Lay the square on the bench, and place the part that has the dowel centers against the inside corner. Place the mating part against the blade of the square and slide it into place. When the dowel holes aren't at the edge of the board, a different method must be used. When attaching a shelf with dowels, for example, lay out the hole locations on the side, drill the holes, and insert the dowel centers. Then, clamp a board to the side to guide the shelf. Rest the shelf against the guide board, and slide it down onto the dowel centers.

When you are using dowels to join a leg to the rails on a table, lay out and drill the holes in the

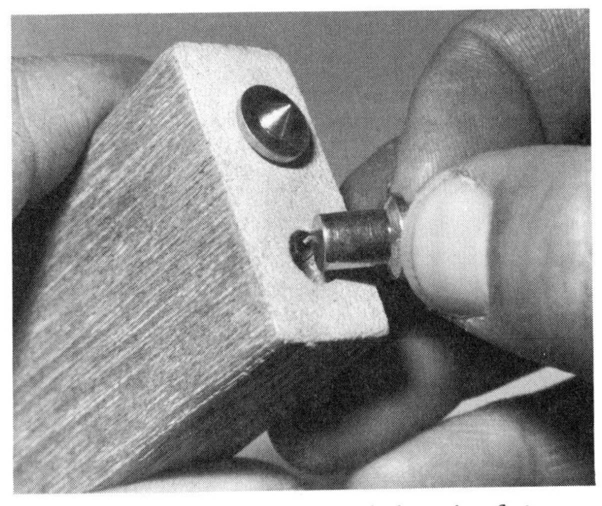

Illus. 83. Dowel centers are metal plugs that fit into the dowel holes. The points mark the locations of the holes on the mating part.

Illus. 84. With the dowel centers in place, press the board against the mating part, making sure that they are in proper alignment. The points leave small indentations indicating the locations of the holes.

leg first. Then, tack guide boards to the bench or to a scrap of plywood; use them to guide the rails as you mark the hole locations.

You can also use small brads to locate the dowel holes in a similar manner. Drive the brads into one board at the hole locations. Leave the heads protruding, then snip them off with wire cutters. Press the parts together. The snipped off ends will be sharp enough to leave an impression on the mating part. Pull out the brads with pliers and drill the holes (Illus. 85).

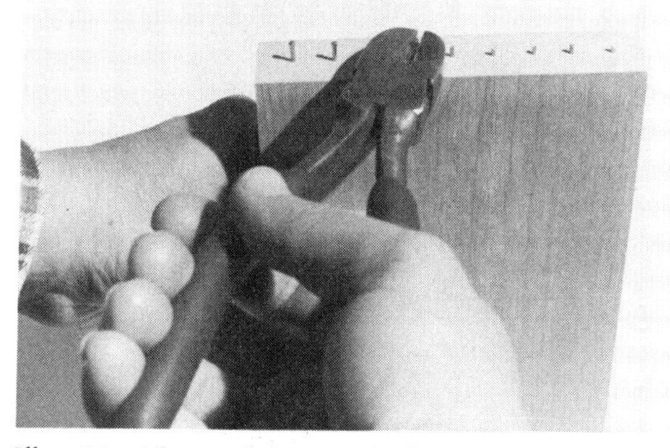

Illus. 85. After you've snipped off the heads with wire cutters, the sharp ends of the brads will leave dents in the mating board when you press them together. Then pull out the brads with pliers, and drill the holes in both boards.

HORIZONTAL BORING

If you have a multipurpose woodworking machine, you can use its horizontal-boring capabilities to good advantage for drilling dowel holes. Rest the work on the table face up. Set the fence so that the edge of the board rests against it. Set the depth stop to the desired depth. Adjust the table height to position the holes along the middle of the edge of the board. Place the two boards together while marking the hole locations, and make a mark across both edges using a square as a guide. When you bore the holes, make sure that both boards are face up. This helps to compensate for any error in the table height adjustment.

DOWELLING JIGS

Dowelling jigs come in a wide variety of styles. Their main function is to guide the drill bit so that the hole is perfectly square with the joint face, not angled off to one direction or another (Illus. 86). They are mainly designed to help when you are using a hand drill. So, if you use a drill press or a horizontal-boring machine, you won't need a dowelling jig. Besides keeping the bit straight, a jig keeps it from wandering off the mark; some types even have a self-centering feature. Even though a jig automatically compensates for various thicknesses of wood, most of the ones that I've used still have a little error. It's always best to place the jig on each board with the same side against the face to compensate for errors in centering.

Sometimes, however, you want the hole actually to be off center; for example, when you join a rail to a leg, you usually put the rail closer to the outside of the leg. The dowel holes are centered on the rail, but they are offset on the leg. Some types of dowelling jigs will allow you to offset the holes. Even if you have the type that always centers itself, you can manage effectively to offset the holes by adding a spacer block between the jaw of the jig and the work.

Some dowelling jigs have special extension rods that allow you to use them far in from the edge of the board. A typical case where this might be useful is in attaching a shelf. You can make a simple guide yourself to accomplish this same function. Use a piece of hardwood about 2″ wide and ¾″ thick. Make the guide long enough for your needs. Use a dowelling jig or a drill

Illus. 86. A dowelling jig positions the hole and guides the bit. This particular jig incorporates a guide that fits over a dowel placed in the first hole to automatically position the mating hole.

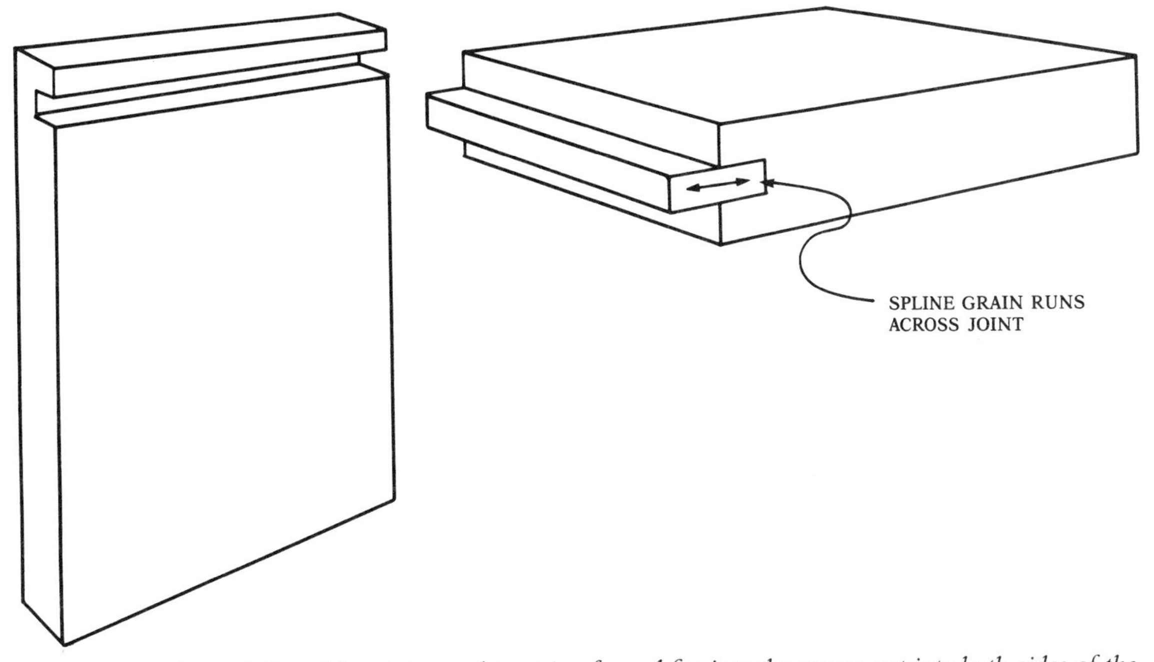

Illus. 87. In a spline-reinforced butt joint, a thin strip of wood fits into the groove cut into both sides of the joint for greater shear strength. Align the grain in the spline across the joint.

press to drill holes through the guide at the proper locations. Take care that the holes are perpendicular and accurately laid out because they will be the guide for all of the holes you drill in the work. Now clamp the guide to the work and insert the drill bit in the predrilled holes of the guide. The guide will function similarly to a dowelling jig to keep the bit aligned correctly while the holes are drilled.

Splines

Another type of joint reinforcement is a spline. A spline is a thin strip of wood that fits into a groove cut in the two mating surfaces of the joint (Illus. 87). In most cases a spline will be stronger than a dowel. A spline can greatly increase the long-grain contact of a joint and also provide greater shear strength.

Splines can be made from hardwood, hardboard, or plywood. When joining solid-lumber end grain, a hardwood spline should be used. The grain in the spline should run in the same direction as the boards being joined. For an end-grain joint, this means that the grain in the spline will run across the width of the spline.

This is the opposite of the normal convention of running the grain with the length of a part, but under shear forces the spline would be likely to split along the grain if the grain were running parallel to the joint line. If you don't align the grain in the spline with the boards being joined, the spline and the boards will also expand and contract at different rates, leading to the eventual failure of the joint. Don't use a plywood or hardboard spline in an end-grain joint because then the spline won't follow the wood movement in the beneficial way that a solid-wood spline will.

In a long-grain joint, however, the grain of the spline should run along its length; although this will result in a weak spline since it can split along the grain, the spline is only used for alignment in the long-grain joint so that this is not a problem. Since a long-grain joint is dimensionally stable, you can also use plywood or hardboard for the spline. Hardboard can be an ideal spline material; the tempered variety is particularly strong.

The groove for the spline can be cut with a handsaw, a table saw, a router, or a shaper. To cut the groove with a handsaw, make two parallel cuts, and then clean out the middle with a chisel. Using a dado blade on the table saw is a very efficient way to make the spline grooves (Illus. 88). You can set the fence for the correct distance and make a series of spline grooves rapidly. Blind grooves can be cut on the table saw by lowering the work onto the blade and being careful to lift it off before the cut reaches the end. One method is to make marks on the fence to indicate both where the end of the board should be when it is lowered onto the blade and second, where the other end should be just when you are to lift the board off of the blade. Once the fence is marked, the procedure involves placing and releasing the board while keeping it tight against the fence. With the saw running, place the board against the fence and press down on the free end. This will raise the other end off the table. Position it over the blade and align that end with the mark on the fence. Now raise the free end to lower the other end onto the blade. Advance the board until this end aligns with the other mark on the fence. Release your downward pressure on the board, but keep it tight against the fence. Simply guide the board as the weight of the outfeed end tips it up off the blade. You now have a blind groove. For maximum strength, the spline should extend as close to the edge of the board as possible. When you use the table saw to cut blind grooves, cut the ends of the spline to fit the radius left by the blade.

A router is also a good tool for cutting blind spline grooves because the spline can stay its full width right to the end of the groove.

A shaper with a slotting cutter also can be used to cut the spline groove. The shaper is particularly good for production work because it is very fast. Blind grooves can be made in the same way as they are on the table saw. The radius left by the cutter will be a lot smaller than what is left by the table saw, so the joints will be stronger at the ends.

The splines themselves are usually about one-third the board thickness and generally not any thicker. Using too wide a spline can weaken the surrounding wood. For 3/4″ thick boards, 1/8″ and 1/4″ splines are commonly used. For thicker boards, you can use a thicker spline; but you will actually get more strength by using multiple 1/4″ thick splines, with a spacing of at least 1/4″ between the spline grooves. The width of the spline depends on the application. If you are cutting the groove in the face of the board, don't cut any deeper than halfway through the board; half of the board's thickness limits the width of the spline to the width of the board. When the groove is placed in the edge, however, the spline can be wider. A wider spline gives you more long-grain contact for a better glue joint, but making the spline too wide can also lead to problems. About twice the thickness of the boards being joined is usually a good estimate for the maximum-width spline you can consider using.

Illus. 88. To make spline grooves with the table saw, you can use the dado blade to make a wide groove in a single pass. You can also use a standard blade by readjusting the fence after the first pass and making a second cut.

For maximum strength the spline should fit snugly in the groove; leave just enough clearance for the glue. When the ends of the groove are open, the excess glue can run out the ends; but, in blind grooves, you should leave a little clearance between the ends of the spline and the ends of the groove to allow the glue to escape. The spline should otherwise fill the groove as closely as possible.

To assemble a spline-reinforced joint, use a small stiff brush to spread the glue evenly inside the groove. Be sure the sides are well coated because most of the strength comes from the glue bond between the sides of the spline and the sides of the groove. Don't apply any glue directly to the spline; if you do, the spline will absorb moisture from the glue and expand before you're able to insert it in the groove. You do want the spline to expand slightly *after* it is inserted in the groove to make a tight joint. Try to judge the amount of glue you apply to the joint so that there isn't a lot of excess. If there is too much glue in the groove, it will also be difficult to clamp the joint tight. You may have to wait for the glue to ooze out of the ends. If you have to wait too long, the glue will start to grab on the spline, and you will be stuck with an open joint.

USING SPLINES FOR ALIGNMENT

The panel-butt joint and long-grain edge mitres don't usually need reinforcement; however, a spline is sometimes useful for aligning the boards during assembly. A ⅛"-thick spline is sufficient for this purpose; use a saw blade that makes a ⅛" kerf. Set the table-saw fence so that the kerf will be right in the middle of the edge of the board. Run each board through with the same face against the fence. Set the blade for a ⅜"-deep cut. If you don't mind having the ends of the spline show, then cut the grooves all the way through. If you want to hide the splines, then cut blind grooves.

Hardboard makes a good spline for this application. Cut a piece into ¾"-wide splines. Use a file to remove the fuzz from the edges, and bevel them slightly. The splines can be trimmed after they are in place. For blind grooves, cut the splines to the exact length. In using splines to add strength to a joint, as discussed earlier, it is important to shape the ends to fit the curvature of the end of a blind groove; but since the splines are used primarily for alignment, you can just cut them square for their blind groove.

By using a thin ⅛" spline, the groove doesn't remove too much surface area from the joint itself, so you can get by without having to carefully apply glue to the spline groove. The spline, in this case, is just for alignment. When you use a thicker spline, the groove removes a lot of the gluing surface on the edges, so you do have to carefully brush glue in the groove. But with the thin spline, just apply glue to the edges as usual. Any glue that drips into the groove will hold the spline stationary, but you don't have to do anything in particular to ensure an even application of glue throughout the groove. Put the spline in the groove in one of the boards; then align the other board's groove with the spline, and slip the spline into that groove. Apply pressure with bar clamps in the usual manner.

SPLINED EDGE MITRES

One of the most popular methods for reinforcing edge mitres is to use a spline. A spline usually involves less work than dowels because, with dowels, you need to drill many holes to get the required strength, whereas with a spline it only takes a short time to make the grooves following the initial set up. You can usually use a spline that is as wide as the thickness of the boards being joined. For ¾"-thick stock, a spline that is ¾" wide and ⅛" thick is about right. Keep the spline groove closer to the inside edge; for ¾" stock, the groove can be about 1/16" from the inside edge. In the standard-type spline joint, the spline must be perpendicular to the mitre face.

You can cut the grooves by hand using a backsaw or a plow plane; but usually a table saw is used to make the grooves. Set the blade angle to 45° and position the fence as shown in Illus. 89. The work is placed with the inside face on the table, and the cut is made.

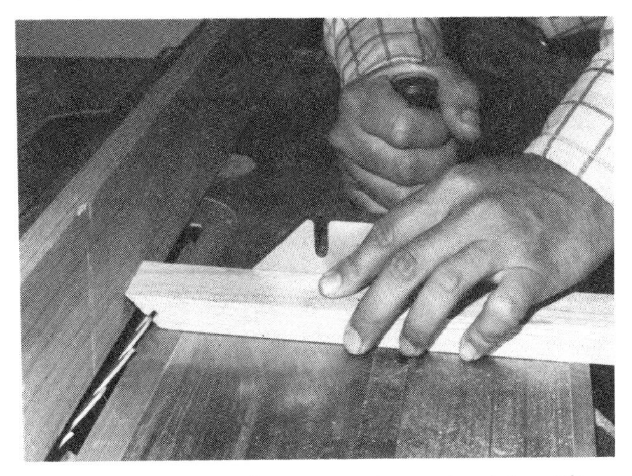

Illus. 89. To cut a spline groove in a mitre joint, tilt the saw blade to 45°.

Because the spline is on an angle to the faces of the parts, special assembly procedures are needed. If all four corners are mitred, assemble two opposite corners to form *L*'s, then assemble the *L*'s to form the box. The joint must be clamped in both directions.

Making a blind groove on the table saw is difficult when the blade is set at an angle. If you want to conceal the joint, you might do best to simply add edging after the parts are assembled. Before making the groove, you can rip the edging directly from the part to which it will be applied;

this way the grain and color will match perfectly, and the joint will be difficult to see. If you use this method, be sure to allow for the width of the saw kerf when you cut the boards to width.

RIGHT-ANGLE SPLINE

You can make a very strong right-angle spline for an edge mitre by dovetailing two spline-width boards together. The boards should be ¼″ thick for ¾″-thick lumber (Illus. 90). This spline isn't practical for thinner lumber, but you can make thicker splines for heavier stock. Make the spline about one-third of the thickness of the board. The fastest way to make the spline is to use a dovetail jig and a router. For wide joints, make several shorter splines that will fit into your dovetail jig, and then place them end to end in the joint. Box joints, which use equally spaced and equal-size rectangular pins, can be used in place of dovetails if you prefer (see Chapter 8).

The most efficient approach is to cut the spline groove before cutting the mitre. Clamp a wide auxiliary fence to the rip fence of your table saw to help support the board. Use a dado blade set to the thickness of the spline. Position the cut on the middle of the end of the board. After cutting the mitres and you're satisfied with the fit, apply glue to the mating surfaces and to the spline grooves. Insert the splines first into one side of the joint, then slide the other side in place. Since the parts can be slid together straight on rather than at an angle, the right-angle spline is especially suited to situations in which it would be difficult to assemble using an angled spline. This joint also is suitable for either solid lumber or plywood.

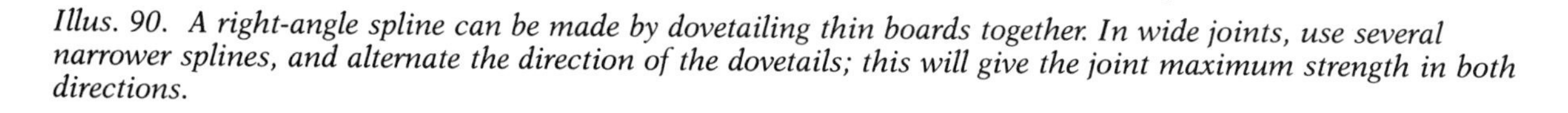

Illus. 90. A right-angle spline can be made by dovetailing thin boards together. In wide joints, use several narrower splines, and alternate the direction of the dovetails; this will give the joint maximum strength in both directions.

Illus. 91. Plate splines are often called biscuits because of their shape and embossed pattern.

PLATE (BISCUIT) SPLINES

The plate or biscuit spline is a type of manufactured spline of compressed wood that combines the strength of splines with the easy application of dowels. They are increasingly popular with commercial shops; many shops have switched entirely from using dowels to using plate splines.

The splines are made of beech wood with the grain running diagonally to the length; this gives the joint increased shear strength because the grain runs across the joint line. The shape and embossed pattern of plate splines make them resemble a biscuit or cracker, so they are often simply called biscuits (Illus. 91). Since the wood is compressed in manufacture, the splines expand as they absorb moisture from the glue, creating an extremely tight-fitting joint. Some specialized equipment is needed, however, to use plate splines; it can be as simple as a special bit for a router, or as specialized as production machines expressly designed for cutting the pockets for the plates (Illus. 92). The plate-joining tool is basically a plunge-cutting circular saw with a 4"-diameter blade (Illus. 93).

To get the full benefit from the use of plate splines, you would do best to have access to one of the specialized machines, because it allows you to cut a pocket anywhere in the face or edge of a board and to align it easily and accurately. But, if you don't have one available or don't want to invest in your own plate-joint tool, you can still use the splines. Use a 5/32" slotting cutter in a router. Use a ball-bearing pilot on the cutter to make a 1/2"-deep cut. The slotter's diameter is too small to make the pocket in a single plunge cut as is possible with the plate-joining tool; instead you must make a plunge cut at one end of the pocket, and then guide the router to the other end.

Illus. 92. A specialized plate-joining tool makes it possible to cut the pockets quickly and accurately.

Illus. 93. A 4"-diameter saw blade is used to make the blind cuts for the pockets.

Illus. 94. A depth adjustment on the plate-joining machine controls the depth of the pocket.

The plates are available in three sizes, but they are all 5/32" thick; No. 0 is 5/8" × 1 3/4", No. 10 is 3/4" × 2 1/8", and No. 20 is 1" × 2 1/2". An adjustment on the machine sets the depth of cut for each size of plate (Illus. 94). For long joints, several plates should be used, spaced every four to six inches. For maximum strength, the plates can be spaced as closely as 2½″ from the middle of one to the middle of the next. Two rows of plates will give added strength for boards ¾″ thick or thicker (Illus. 95).

Since the pockets are slightly longer than the plates, you can slide the parts into alignment during assembly. There is about ⅛″ of lengthwise adjustment in the joint.

To lay out the joint, place the parts side by side, and make a pencil line across both parts at the middle of the pocket location (Illus. 96). The exact procedure for aligning the machine differs from one manufacturer to another, but the joiners usually can be guided either by a fence or by resting the base on the bench top. For joints such as frame butts and face mitres, place the part on a flat working surface, and rest the base of the plate-joining machine on the same surface. Align the locating mark on the machine with the mark on the joint, and make the cut. Make sure that you have the same face against the bench for each part of the joint. Case butts, however, require a pocket in the end of one board and in the face of the other. When the joint is far from an edge, to guide the cut you can clamp a board to the face of the part.

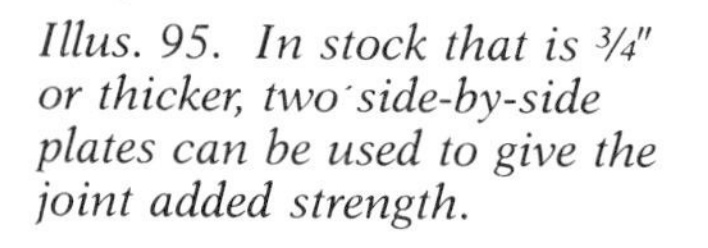

Illus. 95. In stock that is ¾″ or thicker, two side-by-side plates can be used to give the joint added strength.

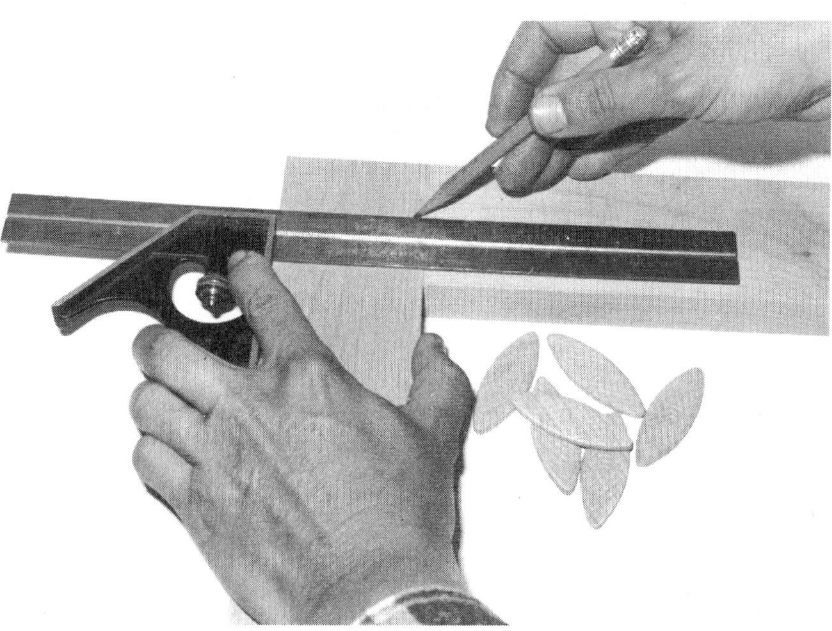

Illus. 96. To lay out the joint, place the parts in their proper alignment, and make a pencil mark at the middle of the pocket location.

A 45° fence attaches to the base of the machine to make the pockets in an edge-mitre joint (Illus. 97). In this joint, the parts are placed on the bench with the inside face up. The fence on the plate-joining machine rests on the bench and will guide the cut perpendicular to the joint face (Illus. 98).

Illus. 97. A 45° fence can be attached to the plate-joining machine for use with mitres.

Apply glue to the pockets and insert the plate splines. Assemble the joint and clamp. Manufacturers typically recommend clamping until the glue is set; but, you can sometimes remove the clamps after only about ten minutes because the splines expand and hold the joint tight.

REINFORCEMENT BLOCKS

When the inside of a joint won't show, a reinforcement block can be used to give the joint added strength. The simplest type of reinforcement block is the glue block. This is a small block with a triangular cross section. It is glued in the inside corner of any type of joint. The glue block increases the long-grain contact area and also helps the joint to resist twisting forces. Glue blocks are usually rubbed into place to avoid clamping. Although hide glue is best for rubbing, aliphatic resin glue works for these small blocks. For greater strength, the blocks can be made larger and screws added.

Glue blocks, however, can create problems if used incorrectly. While working in the furniture repair shop, I saw instances where glue blocks caused parts to split. When the grain of the glue block runs perpendicular to the grain of the boards being joined, cross-grain problems can result. Over time the blocks may come loose or cause the boards to split. When using small triangular glue blocks, you can run the grain perpendicular to the boards if you keep the blocks under about 2″ long and separate them by at least 1″.

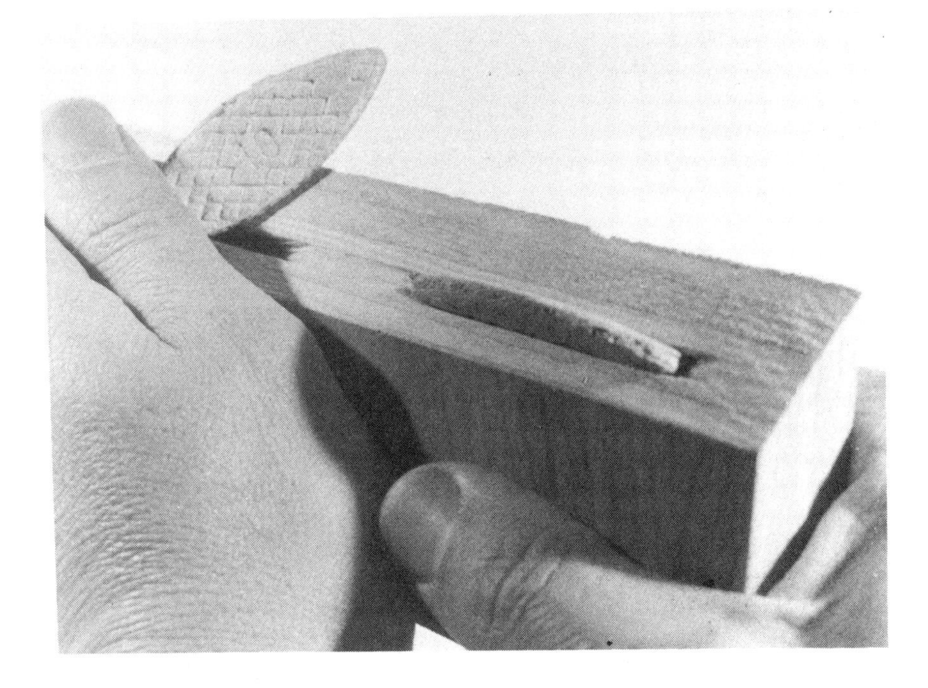

Illus. 98. In a mitre joint, the plates are perpendicular to the joint face. Keep the pocket closer to the inside of the joint for maximum strength.

PART II
JOINERY TECHNIQUES

4
Mitre Variations

Mitre joints are attractive looking, but the basic mitre is a weak joint. Variations on the mitre joint can give the finished appearance of a mitre but have greater strength. Mitre joints aren't always at 45°; other angles can be used to produce polygons, and compound mitres can be used to joint boards that are tilted. Mitres can be cut with power equipment such as the power mitre box, radial-arm saw, and table saw.

Power-Tool Methods

A power mitre box works just as an adjustable mitre box, but it has a built-in circular saw. It works best for face mitres. Some models have an adjustable-tilt capability for making compound-angle cuts (Illus. 99). The radial-arm saw is also a convenient tool for making face mitres. The arm can be set to the correct angle, and a stop block can be clamped to the fence. It is particularly useful when you have a number of identical cuts to make. The radial-arm saw is also suited to making edge mitres on the ends of boards. Because the board remains stationary on the table and it is the saw that moves, long boards are easier to handle. Set the blade tilt to the desired angle. Make the cut with the inside face of the board up (Illus. 100).

You can make face mitres on the table saw using the mitre gauge or a special jig. Before using the mitre gauge, check the accuracy of its angle indicator. With the saw turned off, place a

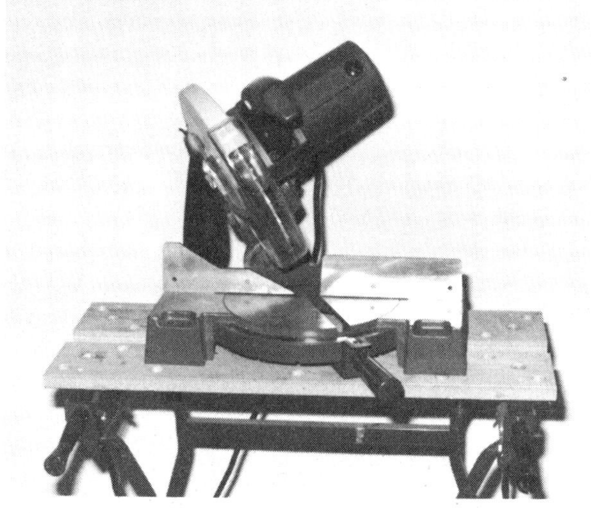

Illus. 99. A power mitre box works in a similar way to an adjustable mitre box with a built-in circular saw. This particular model has an adjustable tilt to make compound angle cuts.

Illus. 100. The radial-arm saw can be used to make edge mitres by tilting the blade.

square against the blade and the mitre gauge (Illus. 101). Adjust the pointer until it reads 90°. Then, with the gauge set to 45°, make a test joint. Use a square to make sure the cut is accurate. You'll probably find that it is difficult to keep a board from slipping slightly when you make a mitre with a standard mitre gauge. One solution is to get a commercial model that has a holding clamp, or you can add a wood extension to the standard fence. Glue 100 grit medium sandpaper to the face of the extension to help it grip the work. In addition to gripping the work, the extension has the advantage that you can make it long enough to back up the board during the cut; this will help to avoid split outs on the back edge of the work (Illus. 102). When working with flat boards, usually you can make all of the cuts with the same mitre gauge setting; but, when working with mouldings, you will need to change the mitre gauge to the opposite slot and to readjust the angle for half of the cuts. This means that having an accurate indicator on the gauge is even that much more important.

A sliding mitre table is not hard to make, and it will help you to cut accurate mitres time after time, without adjustment. For maximum versatility, I like to have both the inside- and the outside-corner types (Illus. 103). The inside-corner type makes a better cut because the rag is on the outside; but, the parts must be precut to length. The outside-corner type can be used to cut the parts to length; but, it puts the rag on the inside of the joint where it is harder to remove, particularly if the face of the board is moulded rather than flat.

Constructing the sliding tables is relatively simple, but take care to make them accurately. Start with a piece of plywood or particleboard for the base of the jig. Attach boards across the front and back to reinforce the base. Cut two hardwood strips for guides to fit into the mitre gauge slots in your saw table. Place the strips in the slots. Lower the blade below the table. Place the base on the saw table, and tack the guide strips in place. Remove the jig from the table top, and attach the strips more firmly. Next,

Illus. 101. Occasionally check the accuracy of the mitre-gauge angle indicator by placing a framing square against the blade and the mitre gauge. If the pointer doesn't read 90°, readjust it.

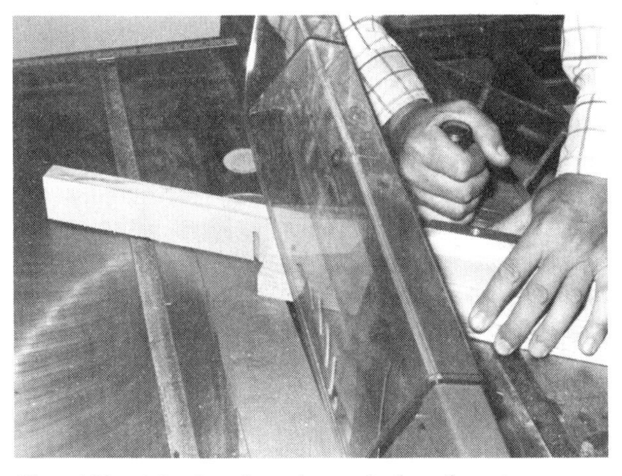

Illus. 102. A backup board attached to the mitre gauge is useful when making mitres. Sandpaper glued to the board keeps the part from slipping during the cut.

Illus. 103. *A sliding mitre table makes it easy to cut accurate mitres. Make the table out of plywood or particleboard. Keys on the underside of the table fit in the mitre gauge slots. The outside-corner type (shown on the saw table) can be used to cut the parts to length while the mitre is being made. The inside-corner type makes a cleaner cut, but parts must be precut to length.*

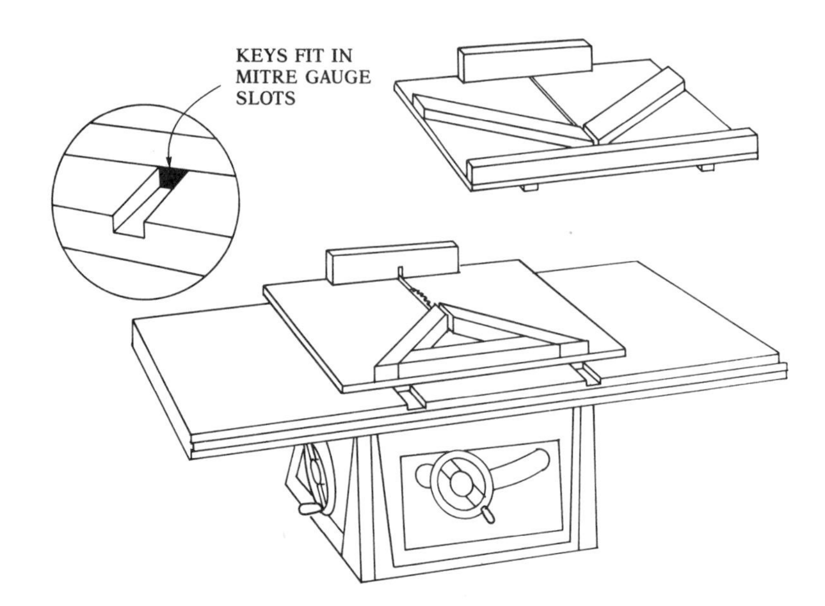

place the jig again on the saw table, turn on the saw, and slowly raise the blade through the base of the sliding-table jig. Then cut a kerf, stopping before you reach the other end of the base. Next, lay out the 45° marks for the fences; make sure that the two fences will form a precise 90° angle and that they are each 45° in relation to the saw kerf. Attach the fences to the base, and apply 100 grit medium sandpaper to their front edges. When you use the jig, make the first cut with the work against one fence, then cut the mating part against the other fence. This will make the angles complementary, effectively cancelling any error.

To cut an edge mitre on the table saw, set the blade tilt to the desired angle. Make the cut with the outside face of the board up; this will minimize chipping on the face, and, if the board lifts from the table during the cut, the joint won't be ruined. If you place the board outside face down and the board lifts during the cut, the blade will dig into the work.

The mitre gauge can be used to guide the board while making mitres on the ends of boards that aren't too wide (Illus. 104). For wider boards, and to make mitres along the sides, use the rip fence. The safest way is to position the board against the fence so that the waste will be on the outside of the blade (Illus. 105). This isn't always possible; sometimes you will also have to

Illus. 104. The mitre gauge can be used to guide narrow boards while cutting an edge mitre on the end.

Illus. 105. To make an edge mitre on the side of a board, use the rip fence as a guide.

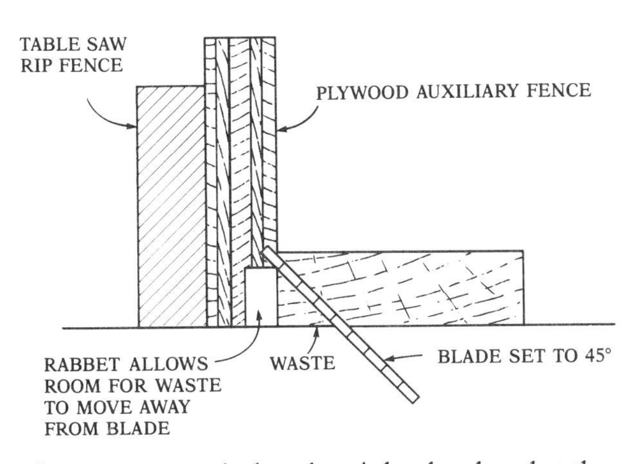

Illus. 106. When the board can't be placed so that the waste piece will be on the outside of the blade, use this setup. The rabbet in the auxiliary fence gives the waste some room to move away from the blade.

Illus. 107. You can use the jointer to cut mitres by setting the fence to the desired angle.

make cuts for which the waste will be on the inside, between the fence and the blade. This can lead to kickbacks, so don't stand in line with the blade. An auxiliary wood fence is necessary when making this type of cut. Attach the wood fence to the rip fence. Set the blade angle, and lower the blade below the table. Move the fence into position, and turn on the saw. Raise the blade until it just starts to cut into the wood fence. You can now cut a mitre at the very edge of the board. Keep most of the pressure against the fence on the uncut section because the section that is already cut is only guided by the pointed edge of the mitre. You can improve the safety of this setup by making a rabbet at the bottom of the wood fence before you install it. Make the rabbet as wide as the thickness of the work minus the blade width measured across the vertical plane (Illus. 106). This will provide some clearance for the waste piece, but you still need to be cautious and watch out for kickback.

You can also use a jointer to make edge mitres. It works best with long-grain joints. Set the fence to the desired angle. Hold the work firmly against the fence and make a pass over the blades. Keep making passes until the mitre is fully cut (Illus. 107).

A disc sander is very useful for fitting face mitres. Make sure that the table is square with the disc. Hold the board so that the entire face of the joint is against the disc and carefully apply pressure to the side that needs to be trimmed.

Face-Mitre Variations

By combining a face mitre with other types of joints, you can get a stronger joint that doesn't need additional reinforcement. I discussed reinforcement in Chapter 3, and, in particular, splines, but there is one additional type of spline that I will cover here called the feather spline. Then I will discuss the many variations on the basic face-mitre joint.

FEATHER SPLINE

The feather spline is installed after the mitre joint is assembled (Illus. 108). First, glue the joint together. Remember that if you use hot hide glue, you can hold the joint as it grabs, so no clamps are needed. Next, place the joint in a *V*-block jig on the table saw, and cut a groove through the joint. Adjust the blade height so that the blade is just low enough to avoid cutting through the inside corner of the joint. Glue and clamp an oversized spline into the groove. After the glue is dry, trim the spline flush with the sides. You can use a contrasting wood for the spline decoration, or you can use the same wood throughout to conceal the spline.

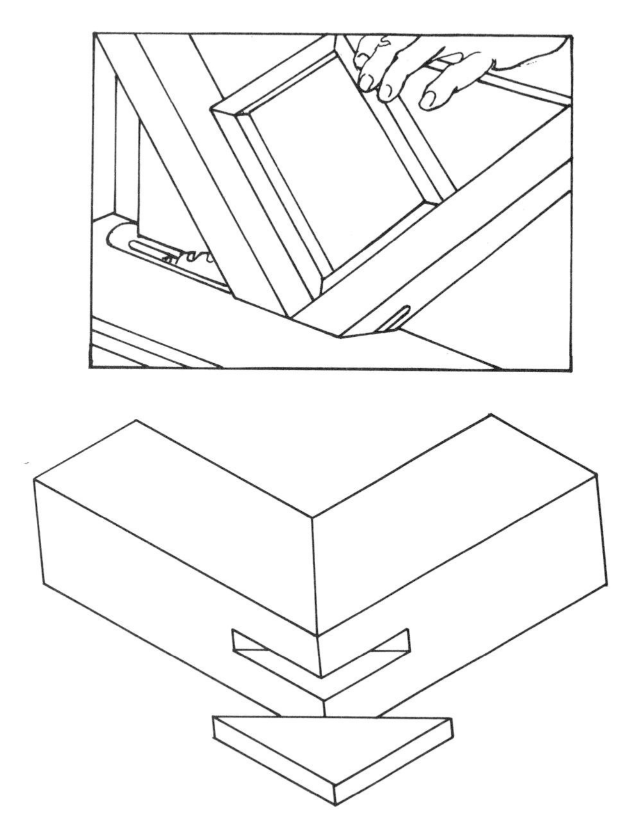

MITRED HALF-LAP

Cut a normal half-lap on Part A (Illus. 109). (Refer to Chapter 9 for the discussion of lap joints.) Then mitre the end. Part B is cut differently. First, cut the piece longer than necessary, and mitre the end. Place the mitred end on the saw table, and clamp the work in a tenoning jig. Make the cheek cut. Then, set the mitre gauge to 45°, and make the shoulder cut. Next, reset the mitre gauge to 90°, and trim the end square to 45° (Illus. 110). Place the work with the front face

Illus. 108. The feather spline is installed after the mitres are assembled. Use a V-block jig on the table saw to cut the groove. The jig consists of two boards attached to a piece of plywood or particleboard. Use the rip fence to guide the jig.

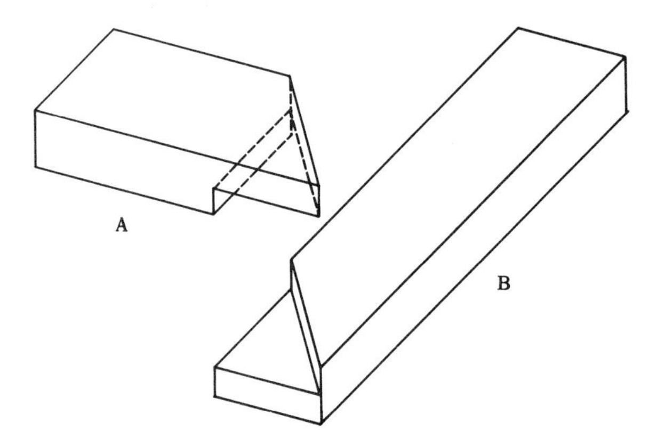

Illus. 109. The mitred half-lap is stronger than a mitre joint because of the long-grain contact. Part A is a normal half-lap that is then mitred. Part B is cut longer and cut differently.

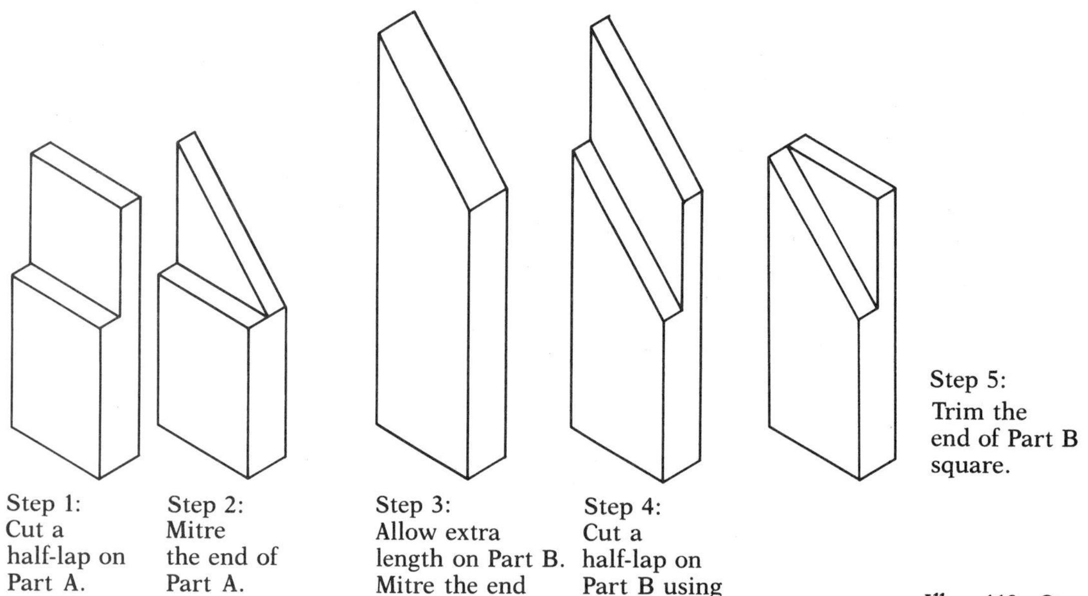

Illus. 110. Steps in cutting the mitred half-lap Parts A and B.

down on the saw table. Make the shoulder cut first, then clean out the waste with multiple passes over the dado blade. Glue and clamp the joint. After the glue is dry, trim the overhang flush with the side.

OPEN-MORTISE MITRE

The open-mortise mitre has the finished appearance of the mitre while taking advantage of the strength of the mortise-and-tenon (Illus. 111). Start with the square end of Part A. Clamp it in a tenoning jig and cut a mortise with a dado blade. Leave Part B longer than the joint requires (Illus. 112). Mitre the ends of both boards. Cut a tenon on the end of Part B using one of the methods described in Chapter 6. If you use a tenoning jig, place the mitred end against the saw table. If you use the dado blade method, set the mitre gauge to 45°. Assemble the joint with glue and clamps; place an additional clamp directly over the joint to press the cheeks of the mortise-and-tenon together. After the glue is dry, trim the tenon flush with the side.

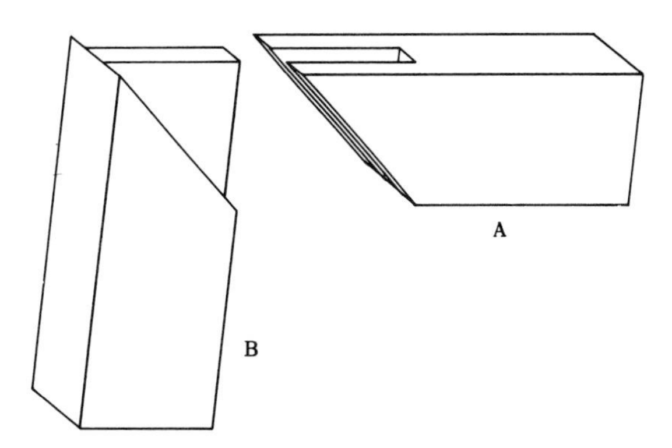

Illus. 111. Part A and Part B of the open-mortise mitre combine to give the strength of a mortise-and-tenon but the finished appearance of a mitre.

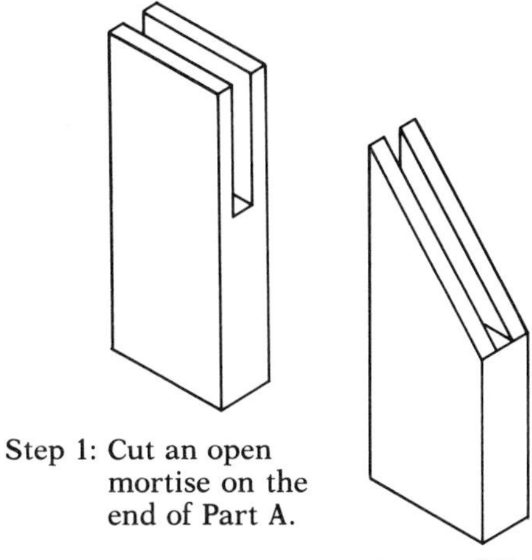

Step 1: Cut an open mortise on the end of Part A.

Step 2: Mitre the end of Part A.

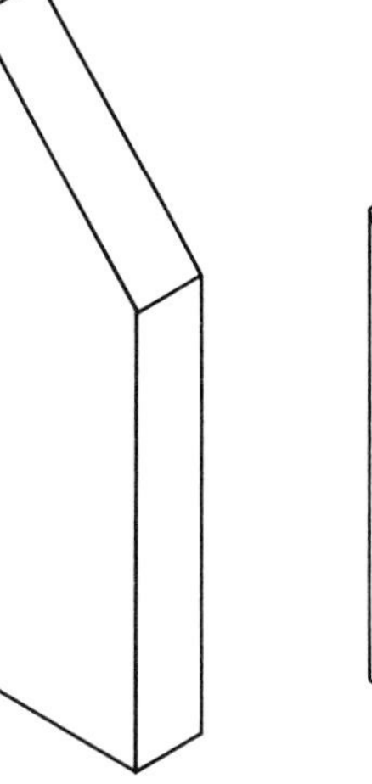

Step 3: Allow extra length on Part B. Mitre the end of Part B.

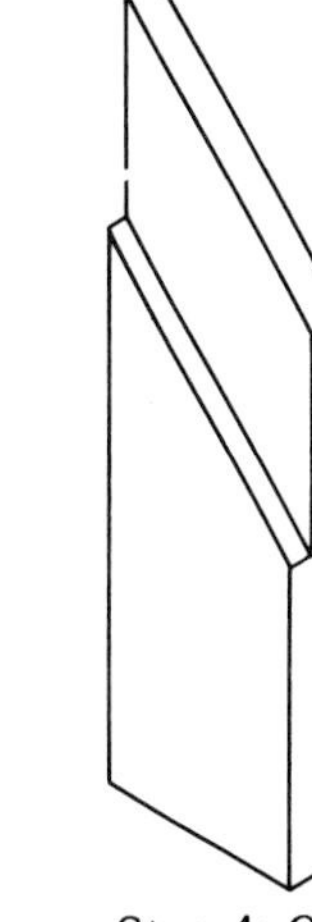

Step 4: Cut a tenon on the end of Part B using mitred end as a guide.

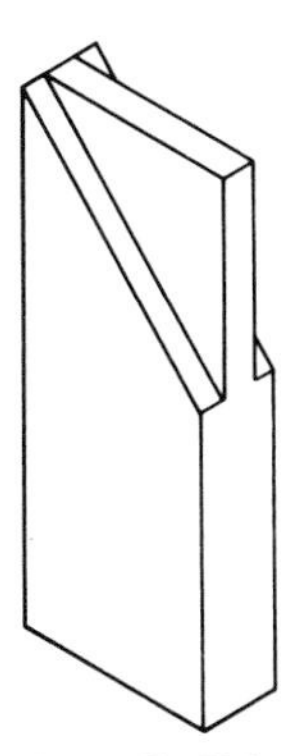

Step 5: Trim the end of Part B square.

Illus. 112. Steps in cutting both Part A and Part B for an open-mortise mitre.

BLIND MORTISE-AND-TENON MITRE

You can also make a completely concealed mitred mortise-and-tenon (Illus. 113). Begin by mitring both boards. The board that will have a

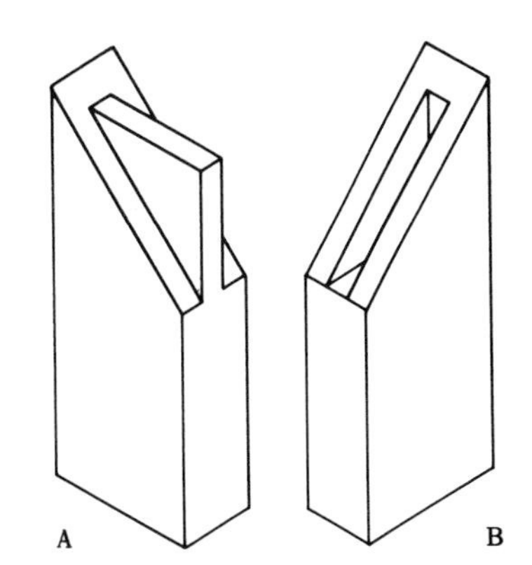

Illus. 113. When Part A is properly oriented and inserted into Part B, the blind mortise-and-tenon mitre completely conceals the tenon.

tenon (Part A) should be left long. Cut the tenon in the same way as described above for the open-mortise mitre. Next, trim the tenon so that the end of the tenon is square and set back from the part's end. Cut a mortise into Part B. It is difficult to cut this mortise with power tools unless you have a square chisel mortising machine, but it's fairly simple to cut by hand with a chisel. Place the piece on its side, and chop across the grain.

DOVETAIL MORTISE-AND-TENON MITRE

This joint is simply a variation of the blind mortise-and-tenon mitre in which the tenon is made self-locking by being shaped into a dovetail (Illus. 114). In this case, most of the work is done by hand with a chisel. Start by mitring the ends, leaving the tenon end (Part A) long. Make a standard tenon as described above. Next, use a chisel to shape the tenon into a dovetail. Use a chisel to then cut a matching mortise in Part B.

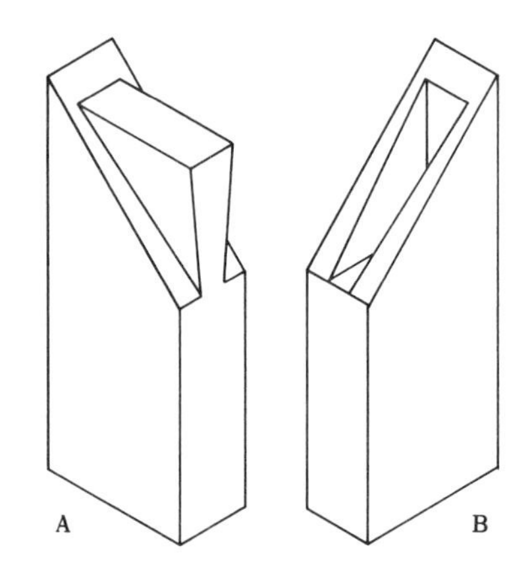

Illus. 114. The dovetail mortise-and-tenon mitre adds mechanical locking to the joint when Part A is slid into Part B.

ROUTER-MITRED MORTISE-AND-TENON

This joint is easier than the above joints to make with power equipment; but, since the tenon isn't as long, this joint is not quite as strong as the hand-cut variations (Illus. 115). Start by mitring both boards. Leave the tenon end (Part A) long to allow for the tenon. Clamp Part B in a router mortising jig or set up the router table to make the mortise. Use a straight bit, and cut a mortise as deep as possible without breaking through the side of the work. Next, cut the tenon in Part A. You can use any of the methods described in Chapter 6. The router-table method is handy since you just used it to make the mortise. Set the fence so that the bit will cut along the side of the board. Make a cut on each side of the board with the mitred end against the table; this will cut the cheeks of the tenon. Then, trim the ends of the tenon to get the correct tenon width.

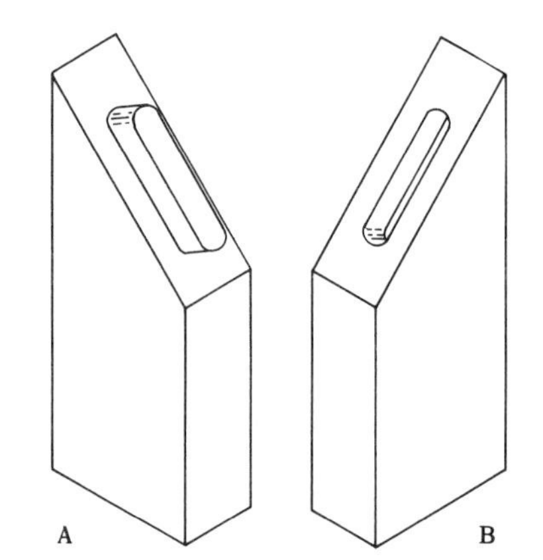

Illus. 115. In this variation of the mitred mortise-and-tenon, both Part A and Part B can be cut using a router.

FOUR-WAY MITRE

When four pieces meet to form a cross, the ends can be mitred (Illus. 116). Before making any mitre cuts, make an open mortise on the ends of all four parts. It takes two 45° cuts on each of the four ends to make the joint. Make sure that the

Illus. 116. A four-way mitre can be used when four pieces meet at a single point to form a cross.

point is right along the middle of the board's width. Cut a square spline from plywood or hardboard. Apply glue to the spline and to all of the mating surfaces; then assemble the joint.

MITRING BOARDS OF DIFFERING WIDTHS

When it is necessary to mitre the joint between boards of different widths, the angle will not be 45° (Illus. 117). An easy way to determine the angle is to lay the narrower board on top of the wider one, and line it up to form a square corner.

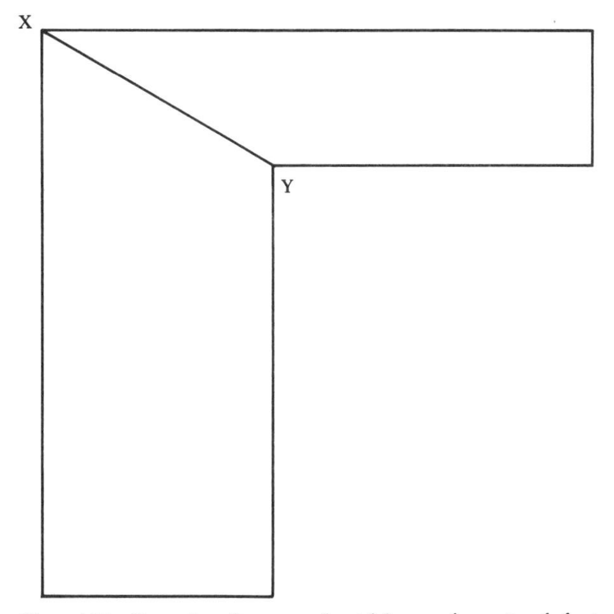

Illus. 117. Boards of unequal width can be mitred, but the angle will not be 45°. To find the angle, place the narrower board on top of the wider one and mark point Y. *Connect point* Y *and the corner* X *with a straight line.*

Mark the point at which the inside edge of the narrow board crosses the inside edge of the wide board beneath. Separate the boards, and mark a line between the outside corner of the wide board and the mark on the inside edge. Cut along this line, then use it to mark the cut on the second board.

COMPOUND FACE MITRES

At one time I made custom picture frames, and one of the most popular types used a compound mitre and looked difficult; but it was really very simple to make. The best way to cut a compound face mitre is to make an angle block that will fit in your mitre box or attach to the mitre gauge or sliding table (Illus. 118). If you expect to make a lot, as I did, you can make a special sliding table with built-in angle blocks. Place the moulding on the block, and make a standard mitre. The compound angle will automatically be formed.

There's a trick, however, to nailing the frame together. It won't fit in a clamp, so place one part in a vise with padded jaws. Apply glue to the mating surfaces, then hold the other board in place while you drill pilot holes in the back of the frame (Illus. 119). Angle the holes so that they will go straight into the other part. Keep the

Illus. 118. A compound face mitre can be cut using an angled auxiliary fence attached to the saw. The angle on the fence should equal the desired side slope angle. Hold the board against the angled fence, and make the mitre cut as usual. The compound angle will automatically be formed.

Illus. 119. To nail a compound mitre, place one part in the vise, and hold the other part in position while you drill pilot holes for the nails.

holes as far back from the corner as you can; otherwise, there won't be enough wood for the nail head to grab. Now nail the joint. Don't set the nails very deep. Make two *L*'s first, then connect them.

Variations on the Edge Mitre

There are two problems with the standard edge mitre that make variations desirable. First it is hard to assemble, slipping under clamping pressure. Second end-grain mitres are weak and need reinforcement. By combining the edge mitre with other joints, you get a joint that is self-aligning during assembly with self-locking features. One variation not covered here is the blind dovetail (see Chapter 7, page 109).

RABBET MITRE

By adding the flat surface of a rabbet to a mitre joint, you can make the edge-mitre joint easier to align during assembly (Illus. 120). This joint doesn't add any long-grain contact area to an end-grain joint. But, in addition to the advantage of ease of alignment, the rabbet mitre can be used to join boards of unequal thickness.

First, cut a normal rabbet on Part A. The width is equal to the full stock thickness, and the depth is equal to one-half the stock thickness. Next, cut a rabbet on Part B; its width is equal to one-half the stock thickness, and its depth is equal to one-half the stock thickness.

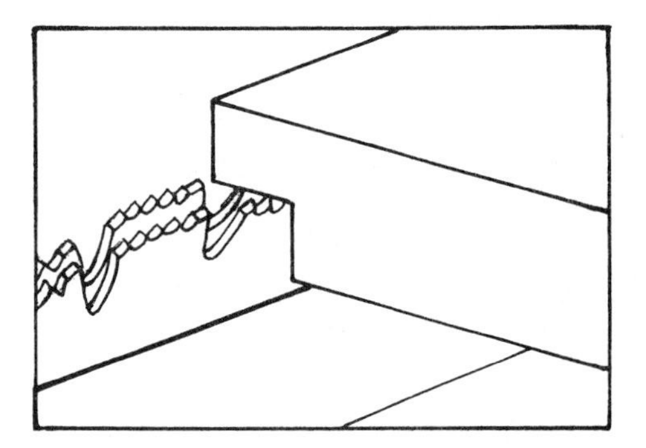

1. Cut a rabbet on Part A. The width should equal the stock thickness and the depth is ½ the stock thickness.

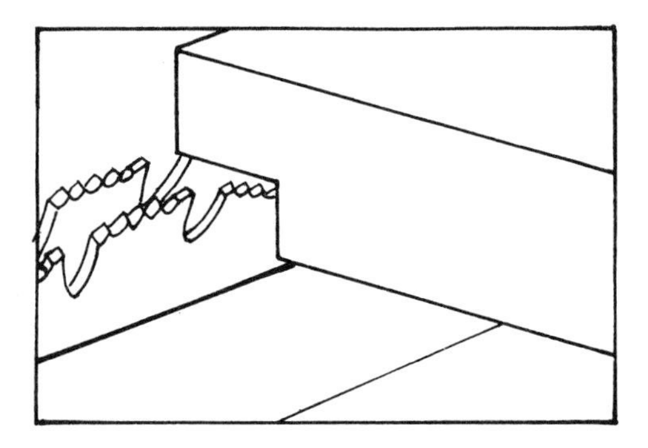

2. Cut a rabbet on Part B. Both the width and depth should equal ½ the stock thickness.

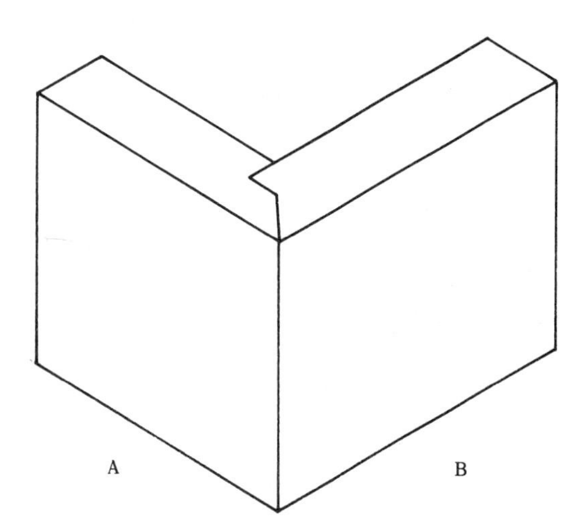

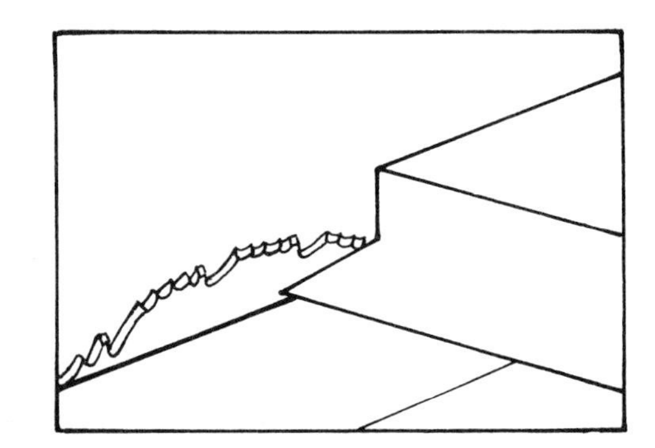

3. Mitre the ends.

Illus. 120. Steps for cutting a rabbet mitre.

Set the blade angle to 45°. Mitre the end of Part A, making sure that the cut begins exactly at the corner. The blade height will be especially critical when you make the mitre on Part B; the blade should just barely touch the corner of the rabbet.

When the parts are unequal in thickness, the joint is even simpler to make. Cut a standard edge mitre on the thinner part. Place this part on the edge of the thicker part, and trace its outline. Adjust the blade height and the fence location to make the shoulder cut. Then mitre the end, making sure that the blade height is adjusted so that the blade just barely touches the shoulder.

Since the rabbet mitre doesn't actually add any long-grain contact area to the basic mitre joint, it still needs to be reinforced. The rabbeted area does give you a good, flat surface, however, for nails, screws, or dowels. When dowels are used, they can be pegged in or blind.

LOCK MITRE

By adding a tongue-and-groove to the rabbet mitre, you can create a locked joint (Illus. 121). The lock mitre still doesn't add any long-grain contact area to an end-grain joint, but the tongue-and-groove adds considerable strength to the joint. Some additional benefits are that this joint is self-aligning during assembly and requires clamping in only one direction.

Begin by raising the table-saw blade to one-quarter of the stock thickness; then set the fence so that the distance to the far side of the blade is equal to the stock thickness. Cut the groove in Part A with the end against the fence and with the inside face against the table. If the board is particularly narrow, use the mitre gauge to help guide it.

Next, set the dado blade to one-half the stock thickness. Place Part B in a tenoning jig with the end against the table. Adjust the jig until the cut will leave a tongue that will fit into the groove on Part A. Cut the groove on Part B.

Now cut a rabbet on the end of Part A. This rabbet should be as wide as the thickness of the outside tongue on Part B; and it should be as deep as the stock thickness minus the thickness of the outside tongue on Part B.

Trim the inside tongue on Part B to fit the depth of the groove in Part A.

Attach an auxiliary wood fence to the rip fence. Raise the fence off the table until the bottom is separated from the table by three-quarters of the stock thickness. Tilt the blade to 45°. Adjust the fence so that, when the inside tongue on Part B is resting against it, the blade will cut a mitre beginning exactly at the end of the outside tongue. Cut the mitre with the outside face of Part B against the table and with the end of the inside tongue resting against the fence.

To complete the joint, place Part A with the outside face on the table and the shoulder of the rabbet against the auxiliary fence. Adjust the fence to cut a mitre that will start at the corner. Adjust the blade height so that the blade will just barely touch the rabbet, and then make the final cut.

When the boards are unequal in thickness, you will want to follow the same basic procedure with some specific guidelines. The thinner piece should be used as Part A. Make the groove in Part A with the fence set so that the distance between it and the far side of the blade is equal to the thickness of Part B. The depth of the groove in Part B should be equal to the thickness of Part A.

SHAPER LOCK MITRE

A similar locked-mitre joint can be cut on the shaper (Illus. 122). This is probably the best way to make a lock mitre for mass production. Once the cutter height and the fence position are set, you can cut both parts of the joint without further adjustment. The first part is cut with the face against the table and the second cut is made with the face of the board against the fence (Illus. 123 and 124).

Similar cutters are available for the router. It is easiest to use if you mount the router in a router table. This shaping bit removes a lot of wood, so a heavy-duty router that will accept a ½"-shank bit is needed.

Mitres for Regular Polygons

Mitre joints can be used to join shapes with other than four sides (Illus. 125). The mitre angle will be one-half the joint angle. To figure the mitre angle for any regular polygon, divide 180°

by the number of sides. The mitre angle chart has the angles figured for you (Illus. 126). To use this chart, find the desired number of sides and read across to the mitre angle. If you are using a table saw to make edge mitres, the mitre angle corresponds to the blade tilt. When using the mitre gauge to cut a face mitre, use the setting listed under mitre gauge.

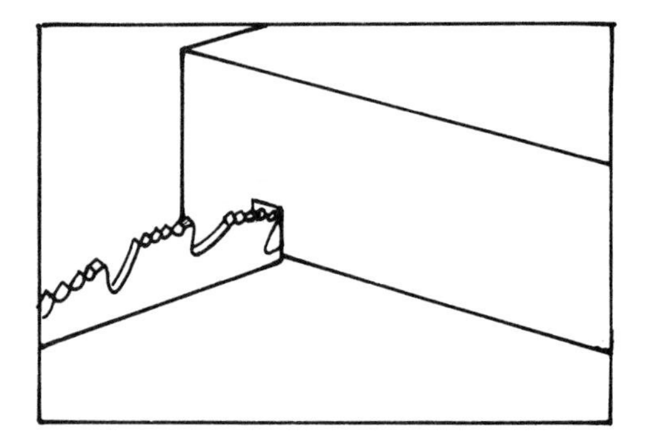

1. Cut a groove in Part A. The distance from the far side of the blade to the fence should equal the stock thickness.

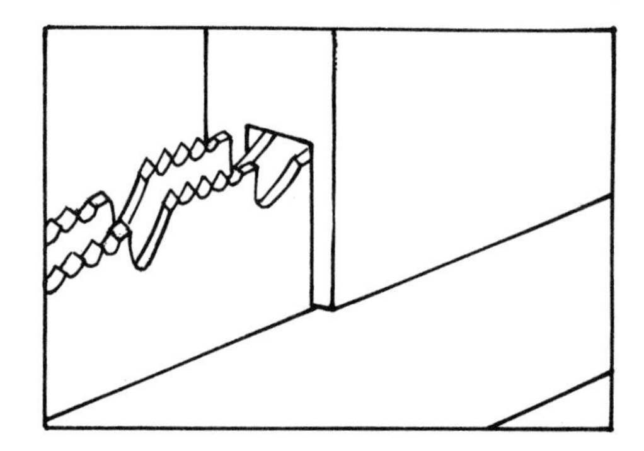

2. Cut a groove in Part B. Set the dado blade to ½ the stock thickness. Leave a tongue that will fit in Part A.

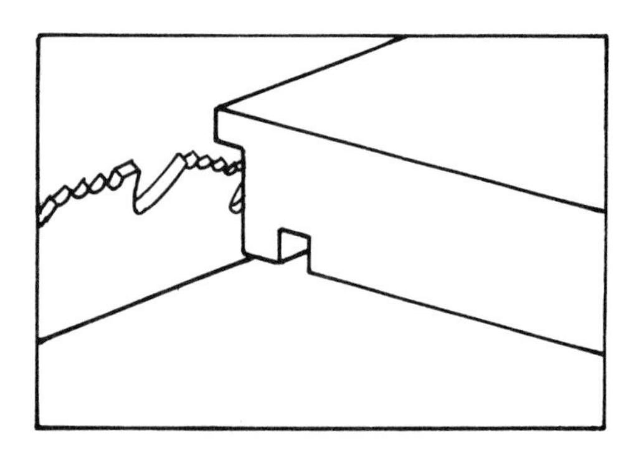

3. Cut a rabbet on Part A. The width should equal the outside tongue on Part B.

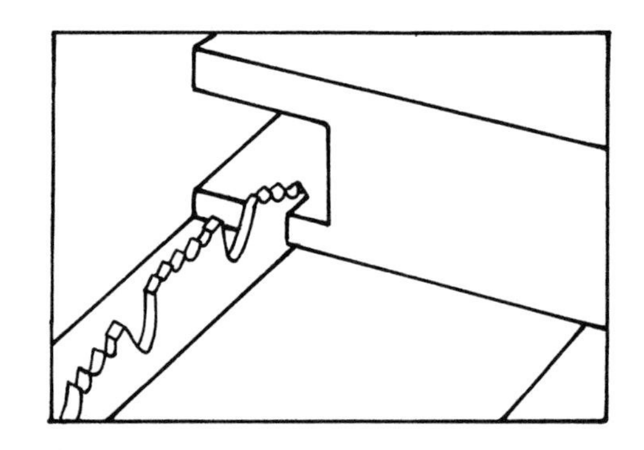

4. Trim the inside tongue on Part B to length.

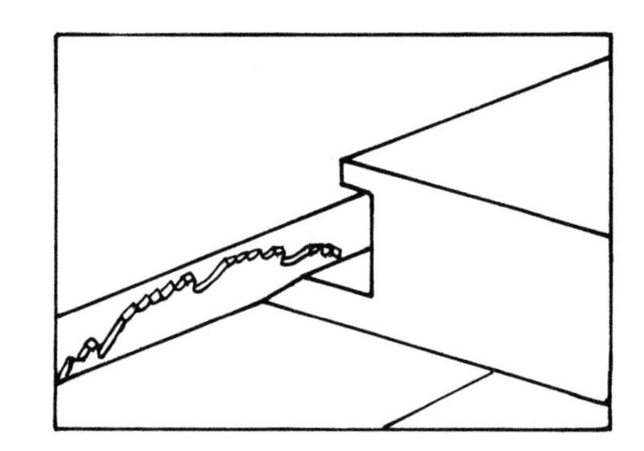

5. Mitre the ends. Use an auxiliary wood fence raised off of the table.

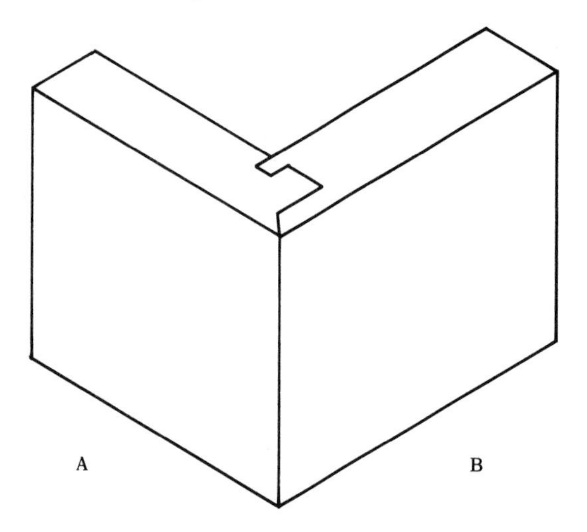

Illus. 121. Steps for cutting a lock mitre.

Illus. 122. A special shaper cutter can be used to make this type of lock mitre.

Illus. 123. Step 1. To make a locked mitre using the shaper cutter, place the first part inside face down on the table and make a cut.

Illus. 124. Step 2. The second part is cut with the inside face of the board against the fence. Add a wide auxiliary fence to help support the work.

Illus. 125. This octagonal barometer is an example of how mitres can be used to join shapes with other than four sides.

MITRE ANGLE CHART

sides	mitre angle	mitre gauge
3	60.000	30.000
4	45.000	45.000
5	36.000	54.000
6	30.000	60.000
7	25.714	64.285
8	22.500	67.500
11	16.363	73.636
12	15.000	75.000
13	13.846	76.153
14	12.857	77.142
15	12.000	78.000
16	11.250	78.750
17	10.588	79.411
18	10.000	80.000
19	9.473	80.526
20	9.000	81.000
21	8.571	81.428
22	8.181	81.818
23	7.826	82.173
24	7.500	82.500
25	7.200	82.800
26	6.923	83.076
27	6.666	83.333
28	6.428	83.571
29	6.206	83.793
30	6.000	84.000
31	5.806	84.193
32	5.625	84.375
33	5.454	84.545
34	5.294	84.705
35	5.142	84.857
36	5.000	85.000
37	4.864	85.135
38	4.736	85.263
39	4.165	85.384
40	4.500	85.500
41	4.390	85.609
42	4.285	85.714
43	4.186	85.813
44	4.090	85.909
45	4.000	86.000
46	3.913	86.086
47	3.829	86.170
48	3.750	86.250
49	3.673	86.326
50	3.600	86.400

Illus. 126. Mitre angle chart.

FACE MITRES

It's a good idea to plan out the cuts at full size on a piece of paper. Draw a circle that circumscribes the size of the finished part. Draw a line through the middle point of the circle. Then use a protractor to mark out the mitre angles. The length of the parts can be measured from the full-size drawing.

To cut the joint on a table saw, set the mitre gauge to the mitre-gauge angle listed in the chart. Because of the way the mitre gauge is laid out, this angle is the complementary angle of the actual mitre angle. You could also use a radial-arm saw or a power mitre box. Before you cut the actual parts, cut a mock-up from scrap. Assemble the mock-up to make sure that the angle is set correctly. The more joints there are, the more likely that a small error will be multiplied. When you are satisfied that the angle is correct, cut the finished pieces. The joints, however, should be reinforced with splines or dowels. A web clamp is the easiest way to clamp the joints as the glue dries.

EDGE MITRES

When the angle of an edge mitre is less than 45°, the joint is often called a coopered joint because it is the same joint used by coopers to make barrels. Each segment of a coopered joint is therefore called a stave. When many staves are used, you can make cylindrical objects similar to a barrel. When fewer staves are used, the result is a polygon with flat sides. Chapter 13 covers other aspects of barrel-making.

The coopered joint is a good way to make large pedestals and columns because the hollow middle saves material and decreases the weight; the jointed construction also eliminates checking and splitting that would occur if the part were solid. If the diameter is small enough to fit on a lathe, you can plug the ends and then turn the jointed object as well.

Coopered joints can also be used to make larger curved parts such as a barrel door or the curved end for a cabinet. You can often use coopered joints to make a curved part that would otherwise require steam-bending or form lamination. To make a smooth curve, plane or belt-sand the surface to a uniform curvature after the joints are assembled. You can then apply veneer to the finished part to completely hide the coopered joints, making it appear to be a single bent piece of wood.

Illus. 127. The blade-tilt gauge reads from 0 to 45, so the mitre angle can be set directly.

You can use the mitre angle chart to determine the mitre angle of the coopered joint. The mitre is usually cut on a table saw, but the jointer can also be used. Make the cuts just as you would for any other edge mitre, but set the blade angle to the mitre angle shown in the chart. The blade-angle gauge starts at 0° and goes to 45°, so you don't need to use the complementary angle as you would with the mitre gauge (Illus. 127).

When you are making a project with a large number of coopered staves, you usually won't care about what the exact number of staves will be; but you may want them to be a certain width. An easy way to figure the angle is to draw one-quarter of the circle at full size on paper or on a scrap of board. Start by using a square to draw two lines at a right angle. Next, use a compass, or use a string with a nail at one end and a pencil at the other end, to swing an arc. Put the point of the compass or the nail at the end of the string at the corner of the right angle. Set the compass or pencil end of the string for one-half the desired diameter of the project. Swing an arc between the two lines. Now set a compass or divider to the desired width of the staves. Mark off this distance along the arc from one of the lines. Draw a line from this mark down to the center where the lines meet. This is the angle to make the joint. Set a sliding T-bevel directly from the drawing. For the problem of figuring out the number of staves, use the divider to mark off the width of the staves all along the quarter arc. Multiply by four and you have the number of staves to cut. When using this method, you will probably have to adjust the width and angle on the final staves after a trial assembly.

Make the trial assembly, and pull the joints tight with a web clamp. When you use many staves, you are sure to find that it's practically impossible to eliminate all error because even a tiny error is multiplied by the number of staves. You can easily correct the error nevertheless by aligning all of the joints so that only one is left with any error. This will be the sum of all the errors in every joint. Hold a straight edge parallel to the mating joint, and mark the correction on the joint that has the error. Disassemble the object, and plane the one joint to the corrected angle. When you reassemble the object, all of the joints will be tight.

Whether the object is a cylindrical body or a regular polygon, it can be assembled without glue. Bands around the outside will hold it together like a barrel. I once had to repair some wooden irrigation pipe that was made in exactly this fashion. The pipe was made of redwood and was about one foot in diameter. Heavy wire spiralled around the outside. It was all that had held the staves together successfully for over one hundred years.

When you want to glue a coopered joint, you can use hot hide glue to eliminate the need for clamps (Illus. 128). Work in small sections, first rubbing together two staves into a set; then, rub together two sets of two staves into a set of four, and so forth, until you have two halves. Support one half on the bench with a couple of blocks, and place the other half on top; rub the two remaining joints simultaneously.

As mentioned, web clamps are the most convenient way to clamp a coopered joint if the project makes a full circle. When the object is only part of a cylinder, such as a barrel door, web clamps can't be used. A solution for the partial cylinder is to temporarily attach clamp blocks on either side of the joints. The clamp blocks can be attached with a hot glue gun or any other type of glue. If you place a piece of paper in the joint between the block and the work, you can knock it off easily after the clamping is finished. To avoid using clamp blocks, you can use hot hide glue and rub the joints.

Usually, when you are using solid wood, you will not need to use reinforcement in a coopered joint because the joint will be long grain to long grain. But, you may want to add splines to help align the joints during assembly. With plywood, however, you must use reinforcement; splines are the most practical. The groove for the spline should be cut perpendicular to the face of the mitre.

Illus. 128. Coopered joints can be glued with hot hide glue to eliminate the need for clamping. Assemble small sections, and then rub the sections together.

Compound Mitres for Polygons

You can make face-mitre compound angles using the angle-block method. Place the work on an angle block as you cut the mitre (Illus. 129). You can also cut compound angles on the table saw using the mitre gauge and blade tilt in combination (Illus. 130). The compound mitre-angle chart gives the angles to use (Illus. 131). The radial-arm saw or the power mitre box can be set as well to the angles listed in the chart for cutting compound angles.

Edge mitres can also be cut on a compound angle. This results in the type of joint used in objects that taper such as buckets or a butter churn. Compound angles can also be used in creating objects that are shaped like pyramids or in other cases where two boards meet at an angle.

Illus. 129. Compound face mitres can be cut using the angle-block method. Attach an angled auxiliary fence to the mitre gauge. The angle of the fence should equal the desired side slope. Set the mitre gauge to the angle shown in the mitre angle chart (Illus. 126).

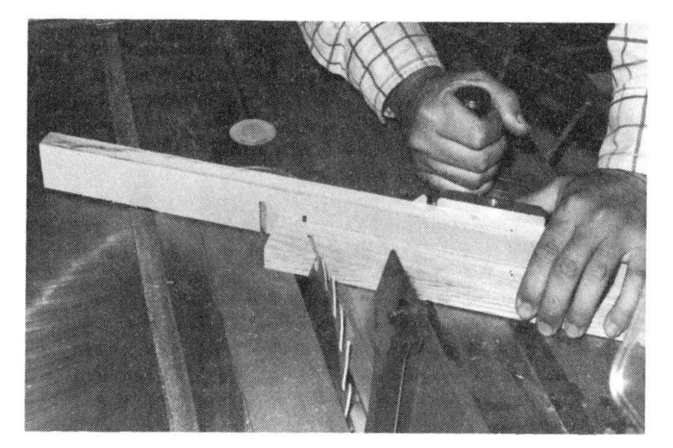

Illus. 130. Compound angles can also be cut by setting the blade tilt and the mitre gauge to the angles listed in the compound mitre angle chart (Illus. 131).

The cuts are usually made on a table saw; however, when the parts are small enough, a radial-arm saw can be used. The jointer can also be used provided that the parts are first tapered on the saw, and then the jointer fence is set to the angle shown in the chart.

For small parts, you can use the mitre gauge to guide the work. Set the mitre gauge to the angle listed in the chart, and tilt the blade to the required angle. Make a test cut before proceeding to check the accuracy of the setup. You will have to either reset the angle of the mitre gauge or move it to the other side of the blade to make the cuts on the opposite edges.

When the parts are too long for the mitre gauge, use a taper jig with the rip fence to guide the work. You can use a commercial taper jig if you only need to make the cut on one edge of the board (Illus. 132). The problem with the type shown in the illustration is that you can't reverse

Illus. 132. A commercial taper jig can be used when a compound mitre is cut on only one edge of a board.

COMPOUND MITRE ANGLES
Side Slope

		5°	10°	15°	20°	25°	30°	35°	40°	45°	50°	55°	60°
Square	Mitre gauge	85°	80.25°	75.5°	71.25°	67°	63.5°	60.25°	57.25°	54.75°	52.5°	50.5°	49°
	Blade tilt	44.75°	44.25°	43.25°	41.75°	40°	37.75°	35.25°	32.5°	30°	27°	24°	21°
Hexagon	Mitre gauge	87.5°	84.5°	81.75°	79°	76.5°	74°	71.75°	69.75°	67.75°	66.25°	64.75°	63.5°
	Blade tilt	29.75°	29.5°	29°	28.25°	27.25°	26°	24.5°	22.75°	21°	19°	16.75°	14.5°
Octagon	Mitre gauge	88°	86°	84°	82°	80°	78.25°	76.75°	75°	73.75°	72.5°	71.25°	70.25°
	Blade tilt	22.25°	22°	21.5°	21°	20.25°	19.5°	18.25°	17°	15.75°	14.25°	12.5°	11°

Illus. 131. Compound mitre angle chart. To use this chart, find the desired side slope along the top, then read down to get the mitre gauge and blade tilt for a square, hexagon, or octagon.

it to make the compound mitre cut on the opposite edge. When you need both edges cut to the compound angle, make a jig by cutting a notch at the correct angle in a piece of plywood. Place the jig on the saw table with the straight edge against the fence and with the open end of the notch facing away from the blade (Illus. 133). Make all of the cuts on one side of each board. Save one of the waste pieces. After all of the parts have been cut on one edge, place one of the waste pieces in the jig. Tack it in place by putting another board or a couple of hardboard strips over the joint and nailing into the jig and the waste piece. The jig is now ready to use to make the cut on the opposite side. This time place the jig on the saw with the open end facing the blade. Put one of the boards in the jig so that the previous cut matches up with the cut side on the waste piece that is tacked to the jig, then make the second cut.

If you want to add splines, leave the blade set to the same angle. Place the board with the outside face against the fence, and cut the spline groove.

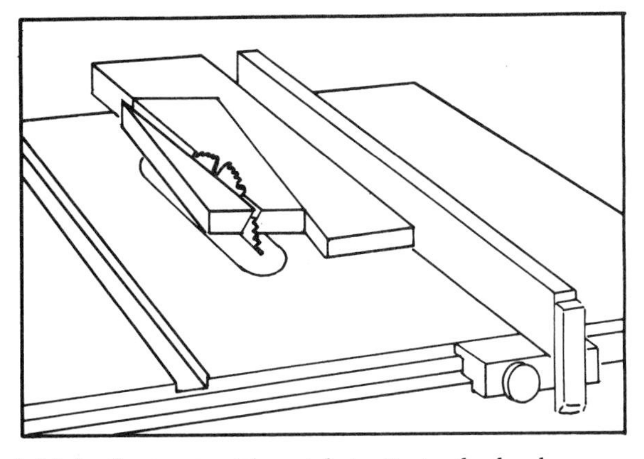

1. Make first cut with notch in jig to the back.

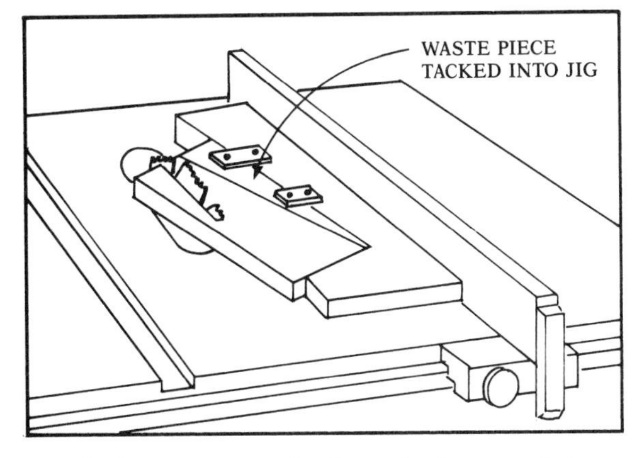

2. Tack the waste into the jig and place notch to front to cut the other side.

Illus. 133. To make a compound mitre cut on both sides of a board, use a homemade plywood jig with an angled notch.

Finding Angles Step by Step Without a Chart

You can use trigonometry to figure the angles for any number of sides with any slope angle you want. Don't worry, you don't need to be a math whiz; you just need a calculator that has trigonometric keys and then follow the procedure listed here. I'll give the formulas first for those interested, then I'll show you step by step how to enter the numbers into a calculator.

To figure the angles, you first need to know the mitre gauge angle listed in the chart in Illus. 126. You can use the number from the chart or figure it yourself with equation (1) by dividing 180 by the number of sides and subtracting the answer from 90. This number is labelled *A* in the following equations.

$$A = 90 - \frac{180}{\text{sides}} \qquad (1)$$

You will also need to determine the side slope you want. The slope angle is measured off of vertical. The side slope is labelled *B* in the following equations.

$$B = \text{side slope} \qquad (2)$$

Use equation (3) below to find the angle that you would set the arm of a radial-arm saw or a taper jig. This angle is labelled *C*.

$$\tan^{-1}(C) = \frac{1}{\tan(A)} \times \sin(B) \qquad (3)$$

If you are using a table-saw mitre gauge, you can get the setting with equation (4) by subtracting *C* from 90.

$$\text{Mitre-gauge angle} = 90 - C \qquad (4)$$

The blade-tilt angle, labelled *D*, is found using equation (5).

$$\sin^{-1}(D) = \cos(A) \times \cos(B) \qquad (5)$$

If you're confused, don't worry; all you really need to do is follow the step-by-step directions below to enter the numbers into your calculator. The directions tell you the keys to press and indicate what the display should show. Note that I have only listed the display to two decimal places; you may see a lot more numbers after the decimal in the actual display, but such precision is only useful up to a point. The calculator must have keys labelled with the following trigonometric functions: sin, cos, tan, $\sin^{-1}$, $\tan^{-1}$.

For this example, I'll figure the angles for a five-sided object with a slope angle of 30°.

First find *A* in the chart or figure it with equation (1) in this sequence of steps:

KEYPAD	**DISPLAY**
enter 90	90
press −	90
enter 180	180
press ÷	180
enter 5 (no. of sides)	5
press =	54

Now I know that $A = 54$, so I can use 54 whenever *A* appears in an equation. The side slope is 30°, so I also know with equation (2) that $B = 30$. To find angle *C* for a radial-arm saw arm or taper jig, use equation (3) by following this procedure:

KEYPAD	**DISPLAY**
enter 1	1
press ÷	1
enter 54 (angle *A*)	54
press tan	1.37
press ×	0.72
enter 30 (angle *B*)	30
press sin	0.5
press =	0.36
press $\tan^{-1}$	19.96

Now I know that angle *C* is 19.96°. I can use this to set a radial-arm saw or taper jig. To get the setting for a mitre gauge, use equation (4) to subtract 19.96 from 90 with this sequence of steps.

KEYPAD	**DISPLAY**
enter 90	90
press −	90
enter 19.96	19.96
press =	70.04

The mitre-gauge angle is thus 70.04°. I can use this for setting the table-saw mitre gauge. The blade-tilt angle is the same for a table saw or radial-arm saw. To find the blade-tilt angle (*D*), use equation (5) by following this procedure:

KEYPAD	**DISPLAY**
enter 54 (angle *A*)	54
press cos	0.58
press ×	0.58
enter 30 (angle *B*)	30
press cos	0.86
press =	0.50
press $\sin^{-1}$	30.59

Now I know that the blade-tilt angle is 30.59°. Run through this example on your calculator to make sure that you get the same results. Then, practice with a few examples from Illus. 131. If you get the same answers as the chart shows, you can be confident that you are performing the calculations correctly; then, you can go ahead and figure any other combination of sides and slope angles.

5

Rabbets, Dadoes, and Grooves: Power-Tool Methods and Variations

Rabbets, dadoes, and grooves are particularly well-suited for power-tool work. There are several ways to make them using common power tools. Variations on these joints can be used to improve the appearance or strength of the finished joint. The rabbet, the dado, and the groove are very versatile; each can be adapted to a variety of applications.

Power-Tool Methods

The table saw and the router are the power tools most commonly used to make rabbets, dadoes, and grooves. Other tools, including the radial-arm saw, the jointer, and the shaper, sometimes used as well. Each of these tools has certain advantages that can make the job easier for particular applications, but you don't need a shop full of tools to make these joints. The router is possibly the most versatile method, and the table saw is probably the fastest method.

TABLE SAW

There are several methods for making a rabbet with a table saw, using either the standard blade or a dado blade. Just using the standard blade, there are three different ways to cut a rabbet; each has advantages and disadvantages.

The first method is the safest way to cut the rabbet while using a standard blade (Illus. 134 and 135). When you make the second cut, the waste piece should fall away with little chance of kickback. The principal disadvantage of this method is that the size of the board is limited by the maximum setting of the fence; also, if the edge drifts away from the fence during the cutting, the rabbet will become too wide at that point. The fence must be readjusted each time a different-width board is used. To cut a rabbet on the end of a long board using this method, make the second cut without the fence; use the mitre gauge instead. You can clamp a stop block to the mitre gauge to hold the end of the board in place. Position the stop block so that the end is above the top of the waste piece; this clearance ensures that the waste won't get wedged when the cut is complete.

The second method can handle any size board without changing the fence settings (Illus. 136 and 137). To use this method safely, you need to make a zero-clearance insert for the blade throat of the saw. Lower the blade below the table. Cut a piece of plywood or hardboard to fit the throat of the saw without the blade. Place the insert in the throat, and secure it with screws or clamp it down. Start the saw. Slowly raise the blade until it has neatly cut a slot through the insert.

Illus. 134. To begin a rabbet using the first method, set the blade height to the width of the rabbet. Set the fence so that the distance between it and the far side of the blade is equal to the depth of the rabbet. Make the cut with the edge of the board on the table and with the inside face against the fence.

Illus. 135. To complete the rabbet using the first method, readjust the fence so that the distance from the inside edge of the blade to the fence is equal to the width of the board minus the width of the rabbet. Adjust the blade height, and make the cut with the inside face of the board against the table.

To make the first cut, set the blade height to the depth of the rabbet. Set the fence so that the distance between it and the far side of the blade is equal to the width of the rabbet. Make the first cut with the inside face of the board against the table and with the end or edge against the fence. Next, set the blade height equal to the width of the rabbet, and set the fence so that the distance between it and the near side of the blade equals the thickness of the board minus the depth of the rabbet. Make the second cut with the end or edge of the board on the table and with the outside face against the fence. As mentioned previously, be careful not to let the board drift away from the fence or, in this case, the rabbet will be too deep.

Illus. 136. In the second method, the shoulder cut is made first.

Illus. 137. Make the second cut with the outside face against the fence. Use a zero-clearance insert to support the edge of the board.

The third method is considered more dangerous than the previous two because the waste piece is likely to become wedged between the blade and the fence (Illus. 138). This can lead to a brisk kickback, sending the waste piece backwards at high speed. And certainly, no matter what operation you are performing, you should make a practice of standing out of direct line with the saw blade; but, when using this method, be especially careful. The advantage of this method is that if the board drifts away from the fence, the rabbet is not ruined; instead of being too large or too deep, it is only too small, so you can simply make another pass to correct the error.

Make the first cut with the blade height set to the width of the rabbet and with the fence set so that the distance between it and the far side of the blade is equal to the depth of the rabbet just as at the start of the first method. Place the end or edge of the board on the table with the inside face against the fence.

You can help to alleviate the possibility of kickback by attaching an auxiliary fence before you make the second cut. Position the auxiliary fence so that its bottom edge is above the table a little more than the depth of the rabbet. Set the blade height to the depth of the rabbet, and set the fence so that the distance between the side of the auxiliary fence and the far side of the blade is equal to the width of the rabbet. Make the second cut with the end or edge of the board against the auxiliary fence and with the inside fence against the table.

When using any of these methods, you don't need to change the setup for each board. Make the first cut on all of the boards in the project; then, set up the saw for the second cut, and make this cut on all of the boards. A board with a bow in it may lift off the table as you make the cut. This will result in a piece of wood being left in the corner of the rabbet. If you can't flatten the bow by simply pressing down on the board as you make the cut, you can remove the piece left in the corner with a chisel or sharp knife.

A dado blade can be used to make rabbets on the table saw (Illus. 139). Adjust the dado blade to make a cut that is wider than the desired width of the rabbet. For rabbets on the ends of narrow boards, you can guide the work with the mitre gauge. If what you need is a rabbet that is wider than the capacity of your dado blade, you can make more than one pass over the blade. Set the blade height to the depth of the rabbet. Attach a wood extension to the mitre gauge, and clamp a stop block to the extension for positioning the end of the board. Make the cut with the inside face of the board against the table.

Illus. 138. The third method for making a rabbet begins the same as the first step in method one (Illus. 134). In the second step, the board is placed with the face on the table. The distance between the fence and the far side of the blade is equal to the width of the rabbet. To help avoid kickback, attach an auxiliary fence with a space underneath to allow the waste to move away from the blade.

Illus. 139. To make a rabbet using a dado blade, set the blade a little wider than the desired width of the rabbet. Attach a wood auxiliary fence, and raise the blade into the auxiliary fence to cut a pocket. Adjust the fence position to get a rabbet of the desired size.

You can use the table-saw fence to guide the work when you are making a rabbet, but you must first attach an auxiliary fence made of wood. After the auxiliary fence is in place, lower the dado blade below the table, and position the auxiliary fence so that part of it juts over the blade. Start the saw and slowly raise the blade to cut a pocket in the side of the fence. Turn off the saw, then readjust the fence so that the distance between the far side of the blade and the auxiliary fence is equal to the width of the rabbet. Set the blade height to the depth of the rabbet. Run the board through with the inside face on the table and with the edge or end against the fence.

To cut a dado or groove on the table saw, set the dado blade for the width. Set the blade height equal to the desired depth. You can use the fence or the mitre gauge to guide the cut (Illus. 140 and 141). For dadoes, you'll find that the mitre gauge works well; whereas for grooves, you will usually use the fence. If the board is wide enough so that you can safely use the fence without risk of kickback, then you can use the fence when making dadoes. Be sure to keep the board pressed flat against the table; if the board is cupped, the dado may be too shallow in the middle.

Illus. 140. Dadoes can be cut in narrow boards using the mitre gauge as a guide.

Illus. 141. Use the rip fence as a guide for cutting grooves.

Dado blades have a tendency to chip the face veneer off plywood. You can help to prevent this chipping by applying masking tape to the face before making the cut. Rub the tape down hard so that it sticks to the fibres. If the chipping is particularly severe, you can score along the sides of the cut with a sharp knife.

RADIAL-ARM SAW

The radial-arm saw can be used to make dadoes and rabbets across the grain in boards that are too long to handle easily on the table saw. If you adjust this saw to the rip position, you can also cut longer joints, but I prefer to use the table saw for this operation. Use a dado blade for both rabbets and dadoes.

To make a rabbet on the radial-arm saw, set the dado blade to make a cut wider than the rabbet (Illus. 142). Raise the arm until the distance between the blade and the table is equal to the thickness of the board minus the depth of the rabbet. Make a mark on the inside face of the board indicating the width of the rabbet. Make the cut with the inside face of the board up and with the board supported by the table.

Illus. 142. To make a rabbet on the radial-arm saw, use a dado blade. Raise the saw to the proper position for making a rabbet of the desired size.

The radial-arm saw also makes it easy to cut dadoes in long boards because the table supports the board. You can clamp a stop to the fence, to make it much easier to dado many identical parts. The dado is cut with the inside face of the board up just as was done for cutting the rabbet. Set the dado blade for the desired width, and adjust the arm height to set the depth. Keep the board pressed flat against the table; if it lifts up, the cut will be too deep. The radial-arm saw is also a good tool to use when you need to make back-to-back dadoes such as you might have in the middle divider of a shelf unit (Illus. 143). With a stop set on the fence, you can cut a dado in one side; then, flip the board over, and cut the other side.

Illus. 143. Stops placed on the fence of the radial-arm saw make it easy to align back-to-back dadoes.

ROUTER

The router is handy for making rabbets, dadoes, and grooves. With the router, handling large parts is easier because you move the tool instead of the board. Straight router bits are available in several sizes up to ¾″. For cuts wider than ¾″, you can make more than one pass. If the cut is near an edge, you can use a router fence as a guide (Illus. 144). When the cut is beyond the extension capacity of the router fence, you can clamp a guide board to the work.

Illus. 144. A router fence can be used to guide the router when making rabbets, dadoes, or grooves, especially when close to an edge.

To set up a guide board, measure the distance between the cutting edge of the bit and the edge of the router base; place the guide board this distance away from the location of the cut. Make sure that the base of the router doesn't drift away from the guide board or the cut will be crooked. You can eliminate this problem of the router wandering away from the guide board by using a jig similar to the one shown in Illus. 145.

The jig is simple to make, and it speeds up the process of making rabbets and dadoes with the router considerably. You can make the jig any length you want. Start by measuring the diameter of your router base; use this measurement to space the side guides. You want the router base to slide freely between the two side guides. Using this spacing measurement, attach the two end fences to the underside of the side guides; install screws through the side guides into the fences. Make sure that the fences are square with the side guides.

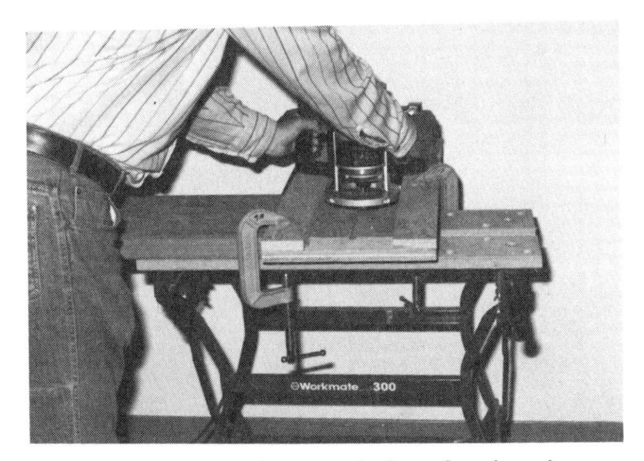

Illus. 145. This simple jig made from four boards can be used to guide the router when making dadoes, grooves, or rabbets.

When you have the jig assembled, use the router to make a short cut into one of the end fences using the same bit that you will use to make the dadoes. You will then have a slot that is the exact width and in the desired location of the dadoes that will be cut with the jig.

To use the jig, mark the location of the dado or rabbet on the face of the board. Line up the slot with the marks, and press the slotted end fence against the edge. Clamp the jig to the work. When making a rabbet, place a scrap of the same thickness next to the board to help support the jig. Place the router in the jig past the edge of the board, and start the router. Make the cut while keeping the router base rubbing against one of the side guides. To make a wide dado, you can reposition the jig and make another pass. You can clamp the jig to the board in any position, so it can be used to make diagonal cuts that would be difficult using other methods (Illus. 146).

Illus. 146. The jig can be made any size and angled if necessary.

The Leigh dovetail jig can also be used to cut rabbets and dadoes (Illus. 147). Attach the crosscut bar to the finger assembly. Clamp the work face up in the top clamp. Use a straight bit and a template-following collar. Make a test cut in a scrap. Note the position of the scale indicator on the finger assembly. Then, readjust the assembly so that the crosscut bar lines up with the edge of the cut. Look at the scale again, and note the difference in readings. This gives you the clearance needed for the collar. As long as you use the same bit and collar, you can use this setting to position the work. Adjust the scale to the second setting; then, place the work in the top clamp, and align the layout line with the crosscut bar. Tighten the clamp, then readjust the scale setting to the first reading. Place the router on the finger assembly, and rest the collar against the crosscut bar. Start the router, and make the cut. Be sure to keep the collar against the bar. If it wanders away while you're making a rabbet, you can take another pass to correct it; but, when you're making a dado, the joint will be ruined.

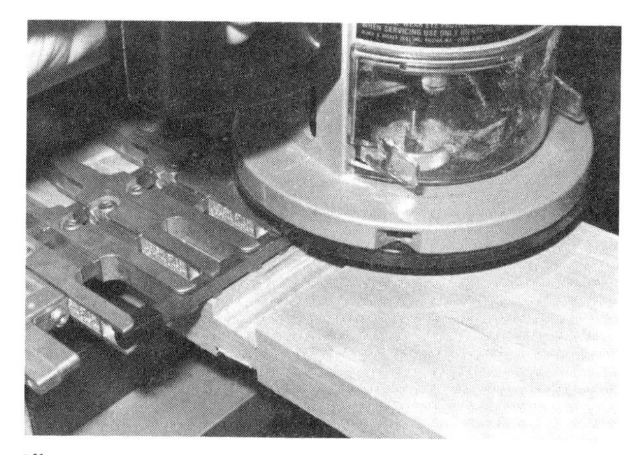

Illus. 147. The Leigh dovetail jig has a crosscut bar that can be used to cut rabbets and dadoes.

One further option you have is to use a special rabbeting bit that has a ball-bearing pilot (Illus. 148). The distance between the bearing and the cutting edge is fixed, so one dimension of the rabbet is determined by the size of the bit. You can adjust the other dimension by raising or lowering the depth-of-cut adjustment on the router. Usually, the bit pilot runs against the edge of the board, and the router base rests on

Illus. 148. This rabbeting bit has a pilot that guides it along the edge of the work.

the face. If the situation calls for it, you can run the pilot on the face and rest the base on the end. In such a case, it is a good idea to clamp a support block to the work to provide a wider resting area for the router base. One of the main advantages of this type of bit is that it will follow any contour on the edge of a board, so you can make a rabbet that follows exactly a curve that has been cut in the edge of the board. Say, for example, that you are making an arched-top door and you want to rabbet it to allow for a pane of glass. The pilot bit will follow the curve of the arched top. In fact, you can assemble the door frame completely before making the rabbet; then, run the router all around the inside edge to cut the rabbet for the glass. The corners will be round, so you will have to square them up using a chisel.

It is also possible to set up a router table to make rabbets (Illus. 149). Use the fence to guide the work. If you are running the boards through with the face against the fence instead of against the table, you may want to add a wider auxiliary fence. The wider fence will help keep the boards steady as you run them through. You can use the pilot bit in the router table as well. When using it to follow a curve, you will need to remove the fence.

JOINTER

A jointer can be used to make rabbets if it has a rabbeting ledge. Set the fence to the desired width of the rabbet, and lower the infeed table to set the desired depth of the rabbet (Illus. 150). When cutting deep rabbets, it is advisable to make two or more passes to cut the rabbet to depth. In the case of two passes, set the depth to a comfortable cut, and run all of the rabbets through; then, set the final depth, and run them through again. *The guard must be removed to rabbet on the jointer, so use caution.* Place the guard in back of the fence if your jointer has a mount for it on that side; this, at least, will cover the exposed cutter in back of the fence. A push stick with which you can hold the board against the table as well as advance it along the tabletop should be used, as needed, to keep both hands away from the cutter. When you are cutting the rabbet across the grain, advance the board more slowly than you would when you are cutting with the grain. If chipping on the face of the board is a problem when you cut a rabbet across

Illus. 149. A straight bit mounted in a router table can be used to cut rabbets. Set the fence to guide the work.

the grain, you can make a clean edge by cutting with the table saw first. Set the blade height to the desired depth of the rabbet, and set the saw fence so that the distance between the far side of the blade and the fence is equal to the width of the rabbet. Run the boards through the saw with the inside face down. After making this cut, you can remove the rest of the wood cleanly on the jointer.

When cutting rabbets in the ends of boards, it is best to have the face of the board against the table as described above; however, you can cut a

Illus. 150. A jointer equipped with a rabbeting ledge can be used to cut rabbets.

rabbet in the edge of a board with the face against the fence instead. This is actually a more comfortable way to make the cut because it is similar to the procedure for jointing an edge. Set the fence for the depth of the rabbet, and lower the infeed table to the width of the rabbet. This method is typically best for rabbets that aren't too wide; it is particularly useful, for instance, for making ¼" rabbets in cabinet sides to accept the back.

SHAPER

A shaper can be used in a similar manner to the router for making rabbets (Illus. 151). The size of the rabbet, however, is limited by both the size of the cutter and the distance between the cutting edge and the spindle. The fence is set so that the infeed and the outfeed sides are in line. To make the cut with the face of the board on the table, set the fence for the width of the rabbet, and raise the cutter to the depth of the rabbet. You can also make the cut with the face of the board against the fence; in this case, set the fence for the depth instead, and raise the cutter for the width.

Illus. 151. The shaper can be used to cut a rabbet. Use a straight cutter, and guide the work with the fence.

Rabbet, Dado, and Groove Variations

Rabbets, dadoes, and grooves can be varied to make them less visible or to improve the strength of the joint. They can be stopped so that the visible joint line looks like a simple butt joint. The tensile strength of a particular joint can be improved, for instance, by combining with a dovetail to form a sliding dovetail. For a fine adaptation of the basic joints, the tongue-and-groove joint is a very useful hybrid.

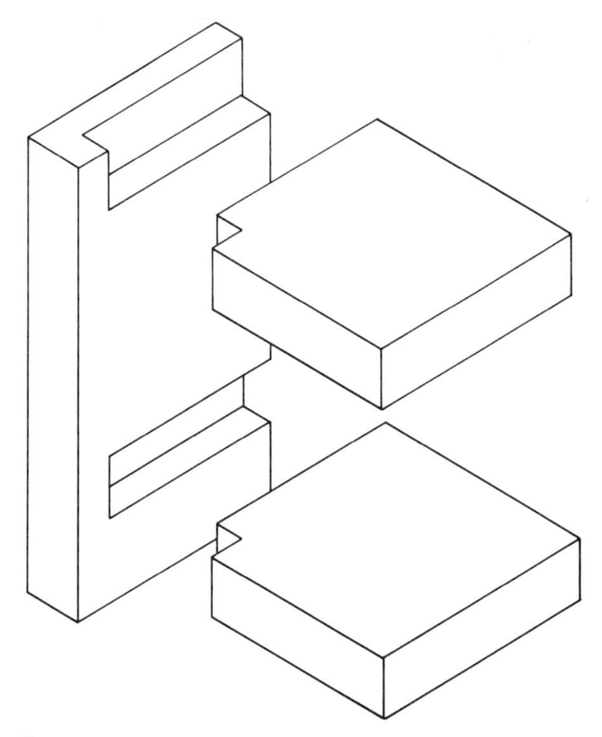

Illus. 152. Stopped rabbets and dadoes end before the front edge of the board.

STOPPED RABBETS, DADOES, AND GROOVES

When you don't want the joints to show from the front of the project, you can use stopped joints (Illus. 152). To make a stopped rabbet, dado, or groove with hand tools, first cut a mortise at the stopped end (Illus. 153). This gives clearance for cutting with the saw or plane. When using a plane, start next to the mortise; work down a small section aligned with the mortise, then move back and proceed normally. When using a backsaw, place the heel of the saw in the mortise for clearance while sawing the shoulders.

It's especially easy to make stopped joints using the router; just turn it off at the desired stopping point, and lift it from the work. A plunge router makes the job even simpler. Since you can see the layout while you cut, a mark at

Illus. 153. To cut a stopped dado, first make a mortise at the stopped end. Then place the heel of the handsaw in the mortise and saw both of the shoulders of the dado.

Illus. 154. To make a stopped joint on the table saw, you need a reference mark on the fence. A piece of masking tape can be applied to the fence so that you can draw the mark. When the edge of the board is in alignment with the mark on the fence, lift the board from the saw.

the correct location is all that is necessary. After routing, use a chisel to square up the corner at the stopped end.

To make a stopped joint using the table saw, the mark you need to make is on the fence; make a reference mark that indicates where the edge of the board should be at the moment you need to stop the cut (Illus. 154). Measure from the point where the front of the blade turns below the table to make a mark that is the same distance away as the distance from the end of the dado to the edge of the board. When you cut the dado, stop cutting when the edge of the board aligns with this mark. You can square up the cut with a chisel, or you can leave it as is and instead cut the end of the mating board to fit the curved contour. It is important that the mating board fill the dado as far as possible to achieve the maximum strength.

It's easier to make a stopped dado on the radial-arm saw because you can see the dado as you cut it. Simply make a mark on the work to indicate the end of the cut.

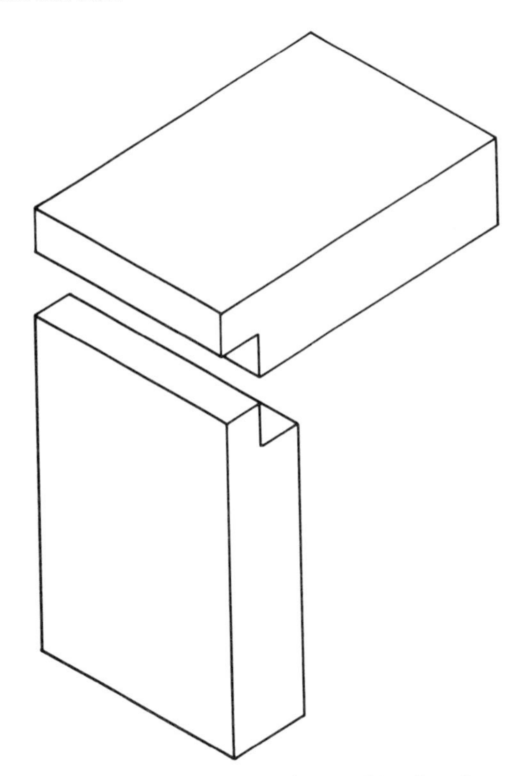

Illus. 155. Two rabbets can be combined to form a double-rabbet joint.

DOUBLE RABBET

You can use two rabbets in combination to form a double-rabbet joint (Illus. 155). The advantage is that less end grain shows without weakening the joint. You can use this joint, for instance, to hide plywood edges; make one of the rabbets deep enough so that only the face ply remains. The rabbet in the mating board provides the strength, while the first rabbet hides the plywood edge.

SHIPLAP

A shiplap joint is made by cutting a rabbet in the edge of two boards and assembling them end on end to make a flush joint as shown in Illus. 156. This joint is frequently used for sliding. Since plywood can't be edge-joined using a panel butt with much success, if you do need to join two pieces of plywood into a larger panel, you can use two rabbet joints to form the shiplap joint.

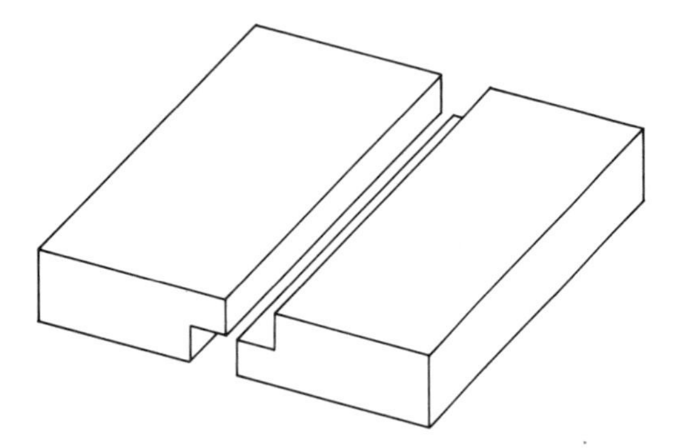

Illus. 156. Two rabbets used together in this manner are called a shiplap joint.

SELF-WEDGING DADO

The weak point of a dado joint is in tension pulling it apart. Consequently, the standard dado can't be relied on to hold the sides of a cabinet together without some form of reinforcement. There are two variations on the dado that increase its resistance to tension. (The first is discussed here; the second in the following section.) The first is the self-wedging dado (Illus. 157). To cut a self-wedging dado, you actually cut two smaller dadoes side by side. Set the tilt arbor on the table saw about two degrees to the left, and cut the first dado; then set it two degrees to the right, and cut the second dado, leaving a narrow wedge in the center. Even though most saws are only made to tilt in one direction, there is usually enough slack in the mechanism to get the needed two-degree tilt in the opposite direction. On some saws you will need to readjust the depth of cut after reversing the tilt.

Be particularly careful with the wedge because it can break off easily. Next, in the end of the mating board, cut a groove in which the wedge will be inserted. Make the groove only as wide as the narrowest part of the wedge. Apply glue to all of the joint surfaces, including the wedge. As you assemble the joint, make sure that the wedge is lining up with the groove. As you clamp the joint, the self-wedging dado earns its name and gains its strength as the wedge forces the sides of the board out into the angled sides of the dado. This locks the joint and produces its greater tensile strength.

SLIDING DOVETAIL

The sliding dovetail is another way to give the dado greater tensile strength. The sides of the dado are angled so that it is wider at the bottom than at the top. The end of the mating board is then cut to fit into the dovetailed dado. The sliding dovetail can be cut by hand or with a router.

I developed a bad impression of this joint, however, when I had to repair about fifty commercially made drawers that used sliding dovetails to attach the sides to the front. The fronts were all coming loose. But, the problem was not that this is an inherently weak joint; it isn't. It was just used inappropriately. The fronts were made of oak whereas the sides were ½″ pine. The sides were simply too thin and too soft for this type of joint; the dovetailed ends just broke off. As a general rule, the sliding-dovetail joint should really be used only in hardwoods unless the parts are thicker than usual. The sliding dovetail is particularly useful for attaching shelves or drawer guides to cabinet sides as well as for drawer construction. Another interesting use is for attaching legs to a pedestal base.

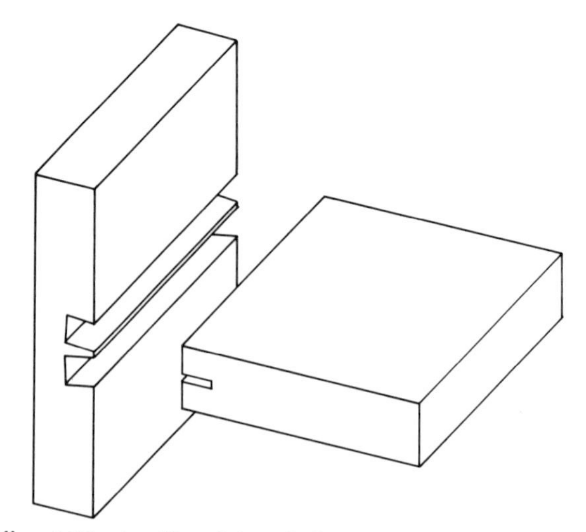

Illus. 157. A self-wedging dado can be cut on the table saw.

Since you have to slide the joint together, friction makes it hard to assemble a straight sliding dovetail that is longer than about 8". There are two alternatives for longer joints. First, you can make a standard dado for most of the length, then make a sliding dovetail on the last two or three inches. The other alternative is to make a tapered sliding dovetail. This joint is wider at the back than at the front, so you can easily slide it in place until it wedges tight.

When cutting the joint by hand, it is just as easy to make a tapered joint as a straight one, so it is almost always made tapered. The hand-cut version is usually barefaced (Illus. 158). Start by

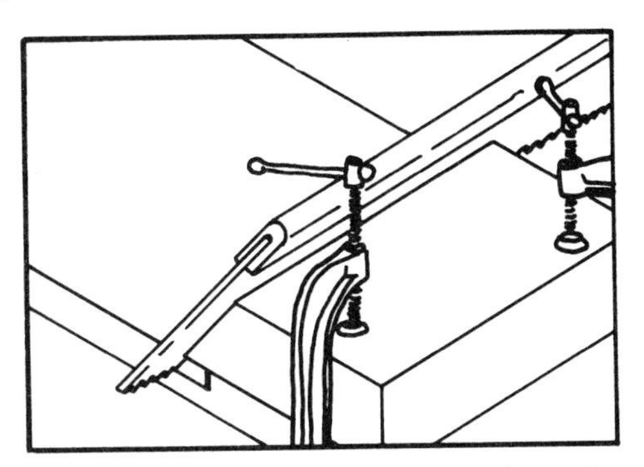

1. Clamp a block that is cut to a 10° angle to the work. Guide the saw against the block to make the angled shoulder.

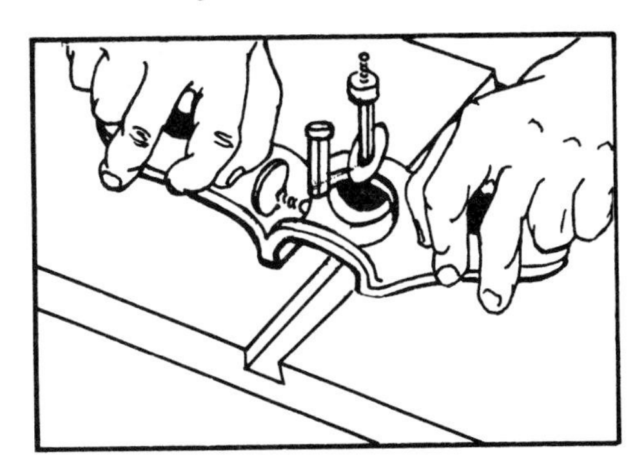

2. Remove the waste between saw cuts with a chisel or router plane.

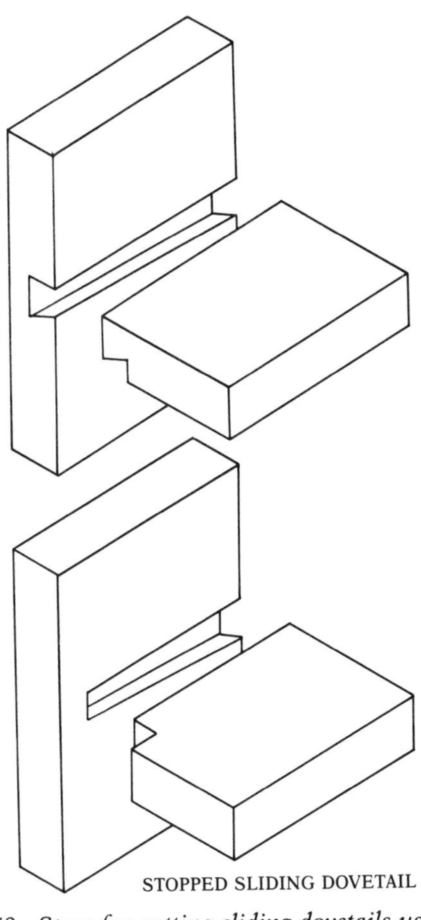

STOPPED SLIDING DOVETAIL

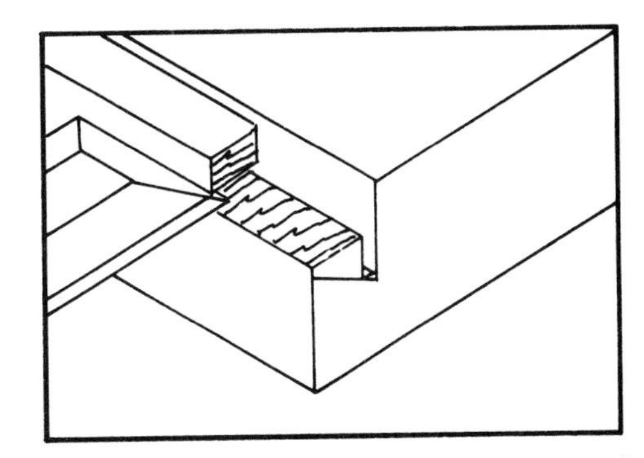

3. Saw the shoulder cut for the dovetail; then chisel straight in from the end to remove most of the waste.

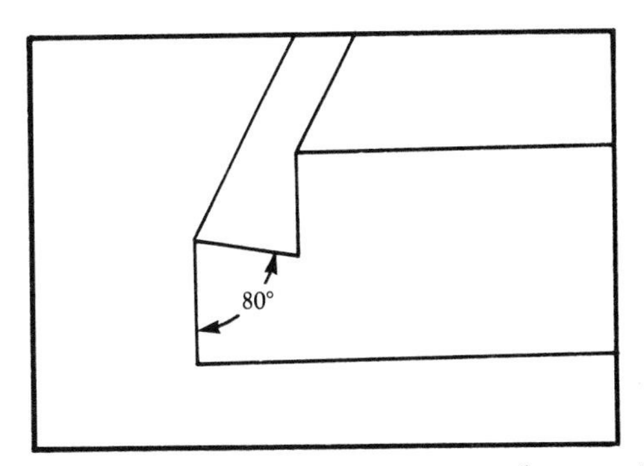

4. Hold the chisel at 10° and pare away the remaining waste to form the dovetail. This creates a dovetail angle of 80°.

Illus. 158. Steps for cutting sliding dovetails using hand tools.

laying out the joint on the face of the board. The top shoulder is square with the face and edge of the board. The lower shoulder forms the taper and is the only shoulder dovetailed. The taper should be about one-half the thickness of the board at its narrowest point. The angle is about 10° off the vertical. A guide block that is cut at 10° on its edge and clamped along the taper will help to guide the saw, keeping it properly oriented. Score the lines with the corner of a chisel to sever the fibers and to make a clean shoulder line. After making the saw cuts, remove the waste with a chisel or router plane. The tapered dado can be stopped if you first cut a mortise at the stopped end with a chisel.

To form the dovetail on the end of the mating board, lay out the cut on the board so that you can see the depth of the shoulder cut on both edges. Use a backsaw to cut the shoulder, stopping at the correct depth on both edges to form the taper. Mark the taper on the end of the board. Chisel straight in from the end along the taper line, and break out the waste. Then, hold the chisel at the proper angle, and slice off shavings until the corner of the blade is at the bottom of the shoulder cut.

Another method is to make a straight standard dado for most of the length, then cut a short, tapered sliding dovetail that stops about 2″ from the edge. It is easiest to cut the short dovetail dado entirely with a chisel (Illus. 159).

A straight sliding dovetail can be cut with a router. Use a guide or router fence, and cut the dado in much the same way you would cut a standard dado. First, use a straight bit that is slightly smaller than the narrowest part of the dovetail. Make a dado that is also a fraction less than the finished depth (Illus. 160). This will remove most of the waste and make it easier to cut with the dovetail bit; switch to the dovetail bit, and finish the cut (Illus. 161). If the dado is stopped, beware; you can't lift the router from the work at the stopping point. You have to slide it back to the beginning of the cut.

To form the dovetail on the end of the mating board, mount the router in the router table. Set the fence so that the bit will cut into the side of the board to the proper depth. Run the board through with the face against the fence; then turn it around, and make another cut on the other face (Illus. 162). Test the setup on a scrap first, and adjust the fence position until the scrap dovetail is a tight fit in the dado. To assemble the joint, apply glue to all surfaces, then slide the dovetail into the dado. As pointed out, this will work for joints up to about 8″, then it will be too hard to slide the parts together. Wider boards will usually need a tapered dado.

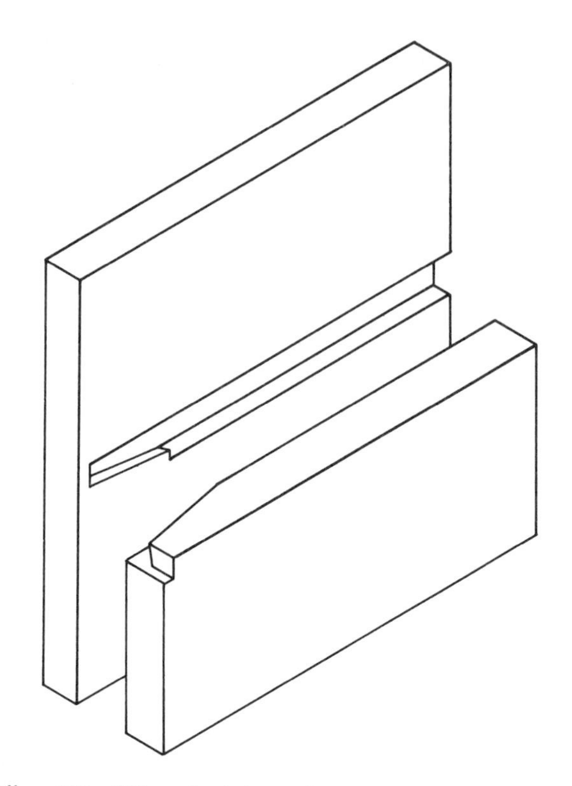

Illus. 159. When the joint is long, a standard dado can be used for most of the length, and a short sliding dovetail can be cut near the end.

Illus. 160. The first step in making a sliding dovetail with the router is to cut a straight dado that is slightly smaller than the finished size of the sliding dovetail.

Illus. 161. Switch to a dovetail bit, and make the finished cut. In small joints, you can eliminate the first step and make the entire cut using the dovetail bit; but when a large amount of wood must be removed, making the straight cut first takes some strain off the dovetail bit.

Illus. 162. Use the dovetail bit in a router table to form the dovetail end on the mating board.

Illus. 163. The Leigh dovetail jig can be used to cut a tapered sliding dovetail. Make a straight dado; then readjust the scale to angle the crosscut bar. Switch to a dovetail bit, and cut along one side of the dado.

Illus. 164. With the jig set to the same angle, cut a dovetail along the bottom edge of the mating board.

To make a tapered sliding dovetail with the router, use one of the dado jigs described earlier or the Leigh dovetail jig with the crosscut bar (Illus. 163). Start with a straight bit that is smaller than the finished size of the narrowest part of the dado. Use a router guide to make a straight dado along the top of the joint. Then, switch to a dovetail bit, and place the router guide on an angle to match the desired taper. If you are using the Leigh jig, you can adjust the finger assembly for a slight taper by setting the two scales to different settings; a 1/16" offset is usually sufficient. Make the second cut using the dovetail bit to form the lower shoulder of the joint.

To cut the dovetail on the end of the mating board, place it in the front clamp of the Leigh jig. Adjust the finger assembly, in or out, to position the cut, but keep the same angle. It's best to make a test cut on a scrap to make sure that the joint will fit correctly. Use the dovetail bit to cut along the bottom edge of the board (Illus. 164).

The router table can also be used to cut the dovetailed end on the board. Make a jig that corresponds to the taper angle, and clamp it to the board. Rest the jig against the fence, and adjust the fence until the proper depth of cut is set. Run the board through using the jig against the fence as a guide.

Another option is that, instead of a tapered joint, you can simply make a standard dado for most of the length, stopping it two or three inches from the edge. Then switch to a dovetail bit, and complete the dado. Use the same router-table setup as described for the straight sliding dovetail; but only dovetail the end that will fit into the dovetailed dado (Illus. 165).

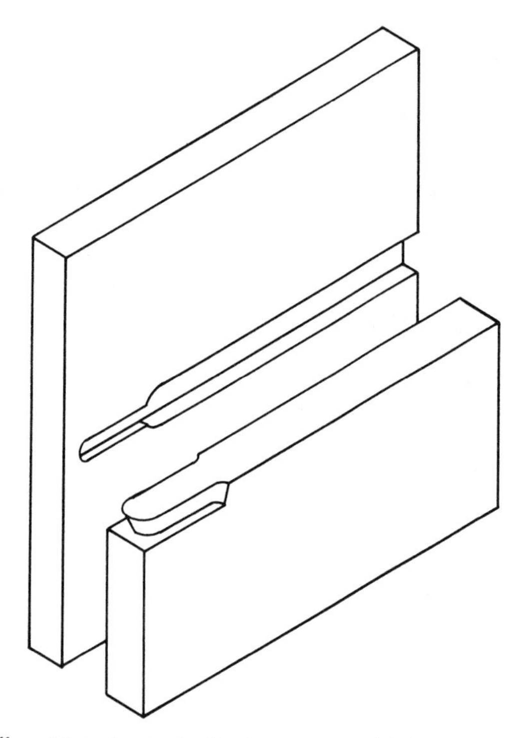

Illus. 165. Instead of using a tapered joint, you can cut a standard dado for most of the length, and then cut a short sliding dovetail near the front edge.

Finally, another particular use of sliding dovetails is for attaching drawer blades (the rail between drawers in a cabinet). A blind dado is cut behind the stopped sliding dovetail. To install the drawer blades, first place the dovetail ends of the drawer blade in the blind dado, then slide them forward into the dovetailed dado (Illus. 166).

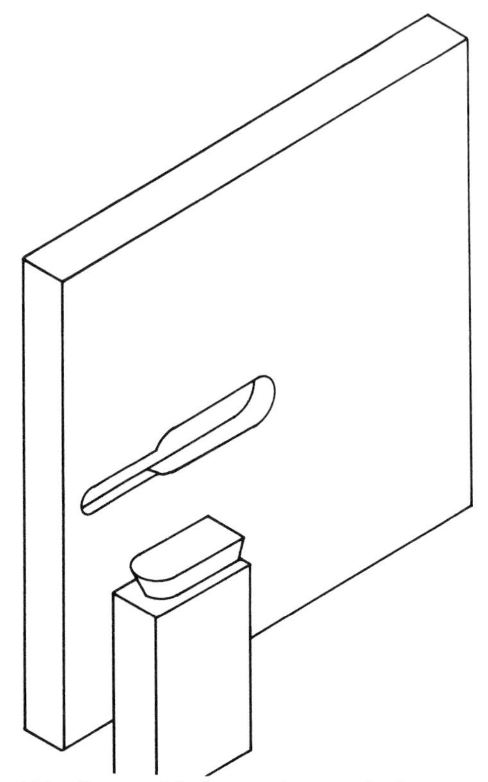

Illus. 166. Drawer blades can be attached using a sliding dovetail, if you cut a short dado to the rear to allow installation.

DOVETAIL RABBET

You can improve the tensile strength of a rabbet joint by dovetailing (Illus. 167). The dovetail can be placed in two ways depending on the direction that needs the most strength. The joint is cut in much the same way as a sliding dovetail. You

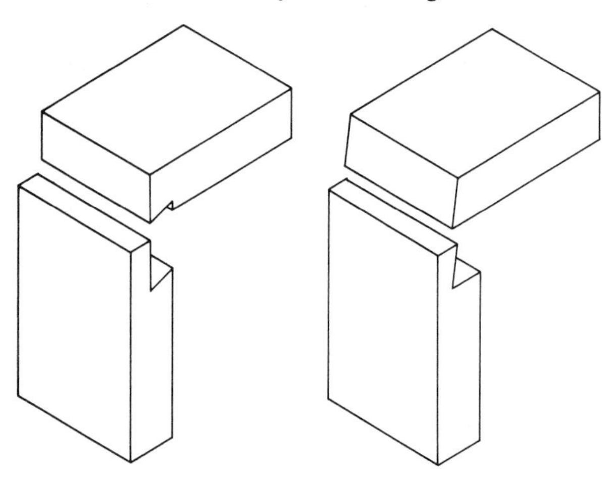

Illus. 167. Dovetailing can be used to add some tensile strength to rabbet joints.

can use a router and a jig; or you can use the table saw. Cut the joint as you would normally, except the blade is tilted 10° when you cut the dovetail shoulder. The slope on the mating board can be cut on the table saw or use a router and jig as just described for sliding dovetails.

TONGUE-AND-GROOVE

If you cut a rabbet on both sides of a board, you have formed a tongue. The tongue-and-groove joint is useful in a wide range of applications (Illus. 168). One of the main advantages of this joint is that you can edge-join boards without glue, allowing them to move independently. The free movement helps make dimensional change less of a problem. Tongue-and-groove lumber is often used as wall panelling or when a solid lumber back is needed for a cabinet. Each board is nailed or screwed to the support only at its middle or at one edge. The tongue-and-groove joints allow each board to expand or contract without splitting or breaking the joints. When the boards are attached at the middle, they don't change position; all of the movement is taken up in the joints. If the particular boards you are using have a tendency to cup, it is better to attach them near the edge; this will keep the edges from lifting away from the supports. A bevel or decorative bead can be used to conceal the gap in the joints.

Illus. 168. The tongue-and-groove joint can be used to allow boards to move independently at the joint. The bevel helps conceal the gap in the joint.

The width of the groove should be one-third the thickness of the board. The depth of the groove is one-half the board thickness. The groove can be made using any of the techniques previously described. The tongue can be formed, as mentioned, by cutting a rabbet on both sides of the board and using any of the techniques for cutting rabbets. There are several options in addition to these methods; you can obtain a special matched set of planes that will cut a tongue and a matching groove. You can cut a tongue-and-groove on the shaper using a matched set of cutters (Illus. 169). You can use tongue-and-groove bits that are also available for the router.

Illus. 169. A matched set of cutters for the shaper can be used to cut tongue-and-groove joints.

You can also cut a tongue-and-groove with a straight router bit with the router mounted in a router table. To cut the groove, set the fence so that the bit is right in the middle of the edge of the board, and raise the bit to the desired depth of cut. The tongue is made in two passes. Set the fence so that the bit will make a rabbet on the side of a test board. Adjust the fence until the tongue left between the two rabbets is the correct size.

The procedure for using the table saw is similar, only a dado blade is used. Make the groove with the fence set to place the cut in the middle of the board edge. Form the tongue by making two rabbets on either side of the mating board.

The tongue-and-groove joint can be used instead of a dado to attach shelves or other parts of a cabinet carcass (Illus. 170). One advantage is that the joint is hidden by the shoulders, so any splintering around the groove is hidden. Another is that the shoulders give the joint more lateral strength. Also, it lets you sand the boards after the joints are cut. If you sand the board that fits into a dado after the dado is cut, the joint will be loose. This joint is fine for solid lumber and plywood, but don't use it with particleboard; the tongue will break off too easily.

First, make a dado in the normal way. I like to make the tongue about one-half the thickness of the stock, so I make the dado to match. Next, cut a tongue on the mating board. You can use a router or table saw. If you find that you use this

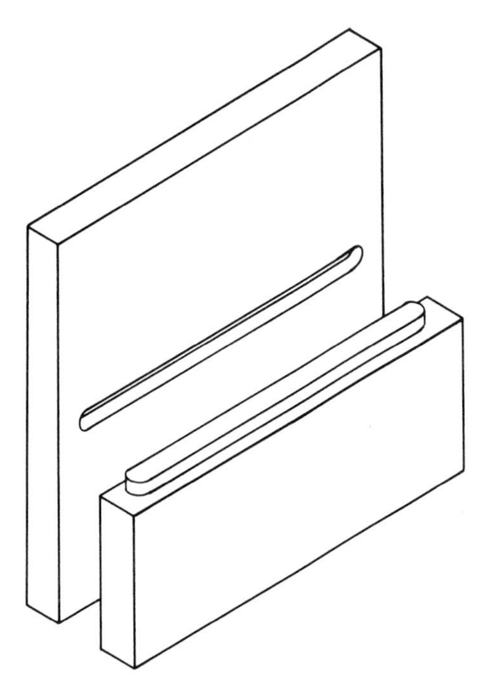

Illus. 170. A tongue-and-groove joint can be used instead of a dado with the advantage that any splintering around the groove will be hidden. The shoulders also give the joint more lateral strength.

joint frequently, you may want to set up the table saw with two identical blades that are separated by a washer equal to the thickness of the tongue (Illus. 171). The advantage of this setup is that the tongue will be the correct size even if the thickness varies from board to board. Make the washer out of hardboard to fit over the saw arbor between the blades.

You can make a blind groove using the router when you want to conceal the joint. Stop the groove about ½" away from the edge. After forming the tongue, cut away ½" from the end. You

Illus. 171. Two identical saw blades separated by a washer that is the desired thickness of the tongue can be used to cut both cheeks on the tongue in a single pass. Use a zero-clearance insert to support the board.

can either round the end of the tongue or square up the end of the groove with a chisel if you prefer. However, the round end of the groove left by the router is actually small enough that it won't weaken the joint appreciably, if you prefer to leave the end of the tongue square; just make sure to cut it back enough to clear the round end of the groove.

BAREFACED TONGUE-AND-GROOVE

If a dado is cut too close to the end of a board, it will be weak because the narrow section between the end of the board and the side of the dado tends to break off. When you do need a dado near the end of a board, however, you can combine it with a rabbet to form a barefaced tongue-and-groove (Illus. 172). Even though it is usually called a tongue-and-groove, it can be either a dado or a groove. The tongue is formed by cutting a rabbet on the end of the board. The barefaced tongue-and-groove enables you to make a flush corner and still get the advantages of a dado. The joint will be stronger if you can recess it a little from the edge. This joint is often used in drawer construction. When used to attach the back of a cabinet, it can be recessed. The barefaced tongue-and-groove is also a good way to attach a thin panel to a thicker frame when you want a flush face.

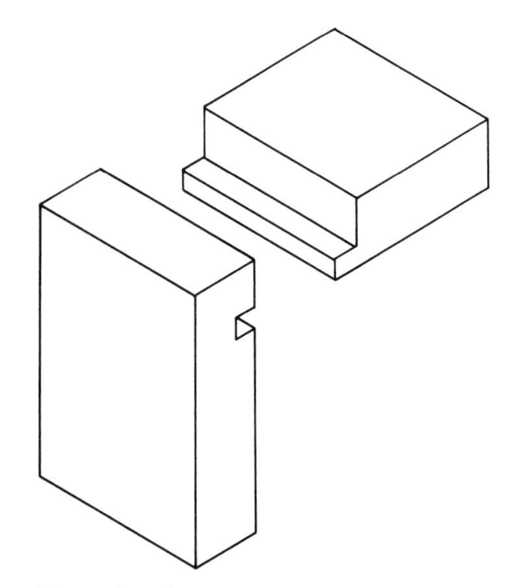

Illus. 172. A barefaced tongue-and-groove can be used when a dado is desirable close to the end of a board.

6

Advanced Mortise-and-Tenon

The basic mortise-and-tenon joint described in Chapter 2 can be used in a variety of applications, but there are some variations on the joint that make it stronger or better suited for a particular application (Illus. 173). In some circumstances, you will get a stronger joint by varying

Illus. 173. The haunched mortise-and-tenon is a traditional joint that can be used when added strength is needed.

the proportions of the joint. Other factors, however, such as joint tolerances and dimensional change also affect the strength of the joint.

Power tools can be used very effectively for making mortise-and-tenon joints. There are specialized tools that are used for mass production, but standard shop equipment can be used in several ways to make the joint. Power-tool methods are addressed specifically in the final section of this chapter.

Increasing the Strength of a Mortise-and-Tenon

A mortise-and-tenon has both mechanical strength and strength that comes from the large glue-surface area. The mechanical strength of the mortise-and-tenon joint comes from the way in which it converts the various stresses into compression. The strength of the glue line comes from the large long-grain contact area between the side cheeks of the tenon and the sides of the mortise.

A mortise-and-tenon joint can fail in any of three typical ways. The failure can be due to improper joint tolerance, poor gluing technique, or the wood breaking as a result of joint proportions that are inadequate to provide sufficient strength (Illus. 174).

The most common failures that I saw in the furniture repair shop were glue failures. Joint tolerance, though, plays an important role in the strength of the glue line. Most glues require a tight fit to create a strong bond. If the tenon doesn't fit snugly into the mortise, the glue line will not be strong. The most important glue surfaces are the side cheeks of the tenon and the sides of the mortise. The glue line on the side cheeks should be about 0.05 mm. The next most important surfaces are the top and bottom cheeks. They are compression points that contribute to the strength of the joint. The clearance between them and the ends of the mortise should not exceed 0.5 mm. This means that if you use one of the power tool techniques that makes a round end mortise, you will need to either square up the ends of the mortise or round the tenon to fit. If you put a square tenon in a mortise with round ends, the gap will be too large.

The end of the tenon doesn't actually contribute much strength to the glue joint because it is end grain, so the clearance is not as important. You can leave a little space there for excess glue. However, the length of the tenon does contribute proportionally to the overall strength of the joint, so you should try to fill the mortise as completely as possible. In fact, even the practice of chamfering the end of the tenon to make insertion easier can decrease the strength of the joint, because it decreases the effective length of the side cheeks. If you chamfer the ends, keep the bevel small. If you cut a ⅛" chamfer on a tenon that is ¾" long, you have decreased the strength proportionally by about 16 percent.

The moisture content can affect the joint tolerance. If the parts are cut with high moisture content, the clearances will be too large once the wood dries. The moisture content shouldn't be more than 10 to 12 percent. Kiln-dried lumber at 6 to 9 percent is best.

The particular gluing technique used at the time of assembly is a very important factor in the final strength of the joint. It is common practice to drip some glue into the mortise and to assume that, as the clamps are applied, it will squeeze evenly throughout the joint; but, I have seen many glue-starved joints come through the repair shop because of this practice. Sometimes

Illus. 174. The joint on the left failed because of a poor fit between the tenon and the mortise. Notice that only a few fibres from the mortise adhered to the tenon. The middle joint failed because the glue was not spread evenly throughout the joint; only the end grain and a small section of side cheek received glue. The joint on the right failed because the tenon was too thin to support the applied load.

the joints were being held together by glue only on the end grain of the tenon at the bottom of the mortise. To ensure that the joint will have the full strength offered by the glue area available, you should apply the glue evenly to both the mortise and the tenon. One very successful method is to use a small stiff brush to spread the glue evenly over all of the surfaces.

The type of glue is also important. Mortise-and-tenon joints will be stronger if you use a glue with some gap-filling capability and flexibility. This usually means aliphatic resin or PVA white glue. PVA isn't as strong for a joint that is placed under constant tension, but its greater flexibility can be an asset when you expect the joint to have to deal with dimensional change. Seasonal changes in moisture content can cause dimensional change to create stress in the joint; a glue that is flexible can cope with the seasonal change better than one that is brittle. Urea formaldehyde (UF) glue is popular in production shops because of its rapid curing time, but it is brittle and doesn't age as well as a more flexible glue. UF glue is particularly intolerant of a poor fit in the joint; the glue will crystallize when the glue line is too wide. I have seen many mortise-and-tenon joints fail that were glued using UF glue. When I would disassemble such a joint, I'd find a light brown powder. This was the crystallized glue. It indicates that the joint did not fit properly when assembled.

The strength of the wood surrounding the mortise and comprising the tenon is another factor in determining the strength of a mortise-and-tenon joint. The strength of the wood varies with species and density; but, since this will be proportional in the entire part, it is not a major factor in joint design. What is particularly important is how much wood is left after the joint is cut. The basic mortise-and-tenon joint is relatively simple but quite strong when it is made according to the traditional rules; under certain circumstances, however, you can alter the proportions to strengthen one aspect of the joint.

Tradition calls for the mortise to be one-third the width of the part that is mortised. This leaves an equal amount of wood on either side of the mortise so that the part is not weakened too much by the mortise. With this proportioning, the tenon is usually the weak link. The tenon must take all of the stress placed on the joint, yet it is usually also only one-third of the thickness of the board. Increasing the thickness of the tenon will increase its strength, but it will decrease the strength of the mortised member. Usually, though, the stress placed on the mortised member is not as great as the stress on the tenon, so you can increase the width of the tenon to about one-half the thickness. When lateral forces that may tend to split the mortised member are likely to be present, don't exceed the one-third rule. In many cases, the mortised member is actually thicker than the part with the tenon; this is the case in which a rail is joined to a leg. In this instance, it is completely safe to increase the thickness of the tenon.

The length and width of the tenon also play a role in the strength of the joint. Increasing these dimensions increases the strength of the joint proportionally. If you increase the length of the tenon from ⅝" to ⅞", the strength of the joint would increase by about 30 percent. In a blind mortise, you can usually increase the tenon length until the bottom of the mortise is about ¼" from the edge. When the width of the tenon is increased from one-half the total width of the part to three-fourths the width, the joint will be strengthened by about 20 percent. When the mortise is near the end of the board, however, the width of the tenon is limited because the short grain between the end of the mortise and the end of the board is weak. Stress on the joint can cause the grain to fail. (Please refer to Chapter 1 and the failed mortise shown in Illus. 18, page 13.) The traditional solution to this dilemma is the haunched tenon described in the section on variations.

Mechanical Locking

The mortise-and-tenon joint is strong under all types of stress, but it is at its weakest point under tensional stress. A standard mortise-and-tenon relies solely on the shear strength of the glue to counteract tensional stress. The large glue-surface area makes it fairly strong, but you can add mechanical locking specifically to increase the tensile strength. The locking methods can be used in conjunction with glue, or the joint can be left dry. Using mechanical locking without glue can have advantages, particularly when dealing with dimensional change, which is described below in the next main section. Until recently with the development of reliable glues, mortise-and-tenon joints were almost always wedged or pegged.

WEDGES

By driving wedges into the end of the tenon, it becomes dovetail shaped and locked into the mortise. The easiest type of joint to wedge is the through mortise (Illus. 175). Chop the mortise with the ends tapering slightly with the largest dimension to the outside. The taper can be varied depending on the type of wood and the size of the tenon, but a good average is ¹⁄₁₆" in 1". This

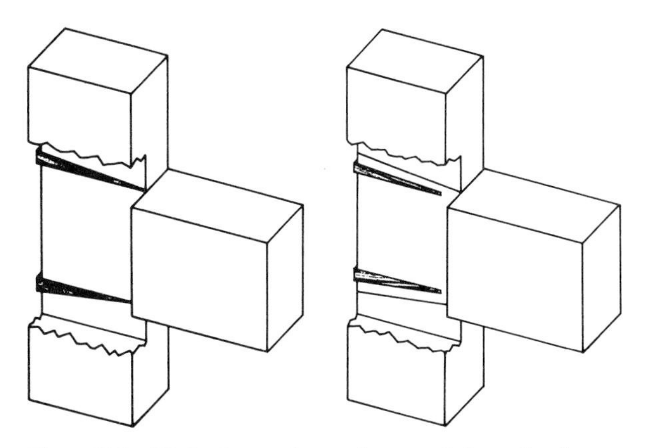

Illus. 175. Wedged mortise-and-tenon joints. In the joint on the left, the wedges clamp the tenon tight. In the joint on the right, the wedges are placed in kerfs cut in the tenon; this gives the tenon a dovetail shape.

means that a mortise cut in 2″-wide stock would be ¼″ longer at the outside than on the inside edge of the board. It is especially important to make the wedges correctly. They should not taper too much, and they should have a square end instead of coming completely to a point. The wedges can be made of the same wood to conceal them or of a contrasting wood to make them a design element. Mill out a block of wood from which to cut the wedges. Make the block as thick as the tenon. Make it longer and wider than necessary for easier handling. Lay out the wedges on the board alternating between square and angled cuts (Illus. 176).

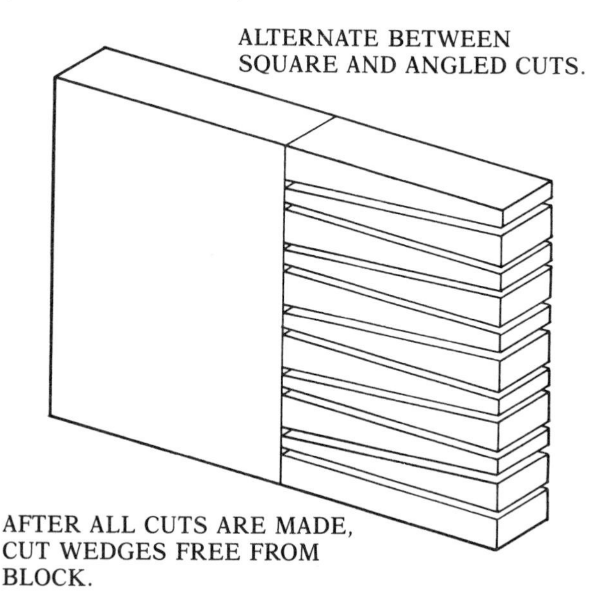

Illus. 176. Several wedges can be cut at once by laying them out as shown here.

The wedges can be inserted in two ways. They can be placed on the outside of the tenon in the ends of the mortise, or they can be placed in kerfs cut into the tenon. Placing them in the ends of the mortise is the method favored by many old-time woodworkers because it won't split the wood, and it doesn't involve cutting a kerf. This method clamps the tenon tightly in the mortise, but it doesn't give the tenon a dovetail shape. To do that, saw kerfs in the tenon. The kerfs should be between 1/16″ and ⅛″ in from the top and bottom cheeks for the typical mortise size used in cabinetry. In larger mortises, separate the kerf from the cheek by the width of the widest end of the wedge. Stop the kerf about ⅛″ to ¼″ from the shoulder.

Drive the wedges into the kerfs, and the tenon will expand to fill the mortise and give the tenon the dovetail shape. The disadvantage of this method is that the wood can split past the shoulder, and the crack will show. If the tenon is a close fit in the mortise near the shoulder, splitting usually isn't a problem; but, some woods tend to split more than others. Use a steel hammer to drive the wedges rather than the wooden mallet. The hammer will ring with each blow; you can tell when you have reached the bottom of the kerf by the change in pitch. Alternate blows between the two wedges so that you drive them in evenly. If you are having a problem with splitting, drill a hole at the end of the kerf with a small bit. The hole will help to stop the split.

When you are using a blind mortise, you can still wedge the joint by using foxtail wedges (Illus. 177). Cut kerfs in the tenon as before, but

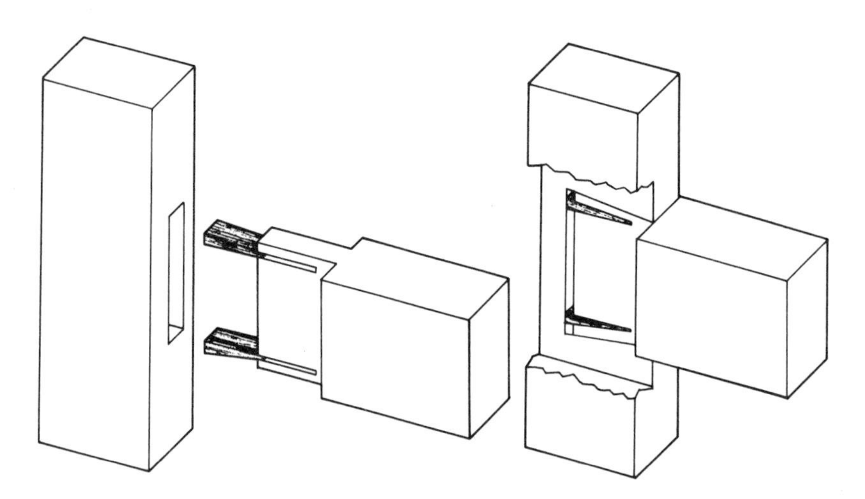

Illus. 177. Foxtail wedges are used to wedge a blind joint.

insert the wedges part way into the kerf before inserting the tenon into the mortise. As you clamp the joint, the wedges will hit the bottom of the mortise and be forced into the kerfs. Leave a little more wood than usual between the bottom of the mortise and the edge of the board. The wedges can break through if the wood at the bottom of the mortise is too thin. Place a backup board behind the mortise as you clamp to keep the wedges from breaking through. The size of the wedge is very important. If it is too long, the joint won't pull up tight to the shoulder. If it is too short, the joint will be loose. It pays to experiment with a sample joint, because once you assemble a foxtail joint, it can't be disassembled.

PEGS

You can also lock the mortise-and-tenon joint using pegs (Illus. 178). If you can clamp the joint tight, the peg holes can be drilled after the joint is assembled. One advantage of pegging, however, is that you can pull a joint tight without clamps by using the method called *draw boring*, in which the holes are bored with a slight offset so that inserting the peg actually draws the joint tight. When the tenon width is less than 1½", use only one peg; larger tenons can have two pegs. Usually it is best to locate both pegs close to the shoulder; if the pegs are too close to the end of the tenon, the short grain may fail, and the tenon will slip out of the mortise. Placing the pegs near the end also presents some problems with dimensional change which are discussed further below.

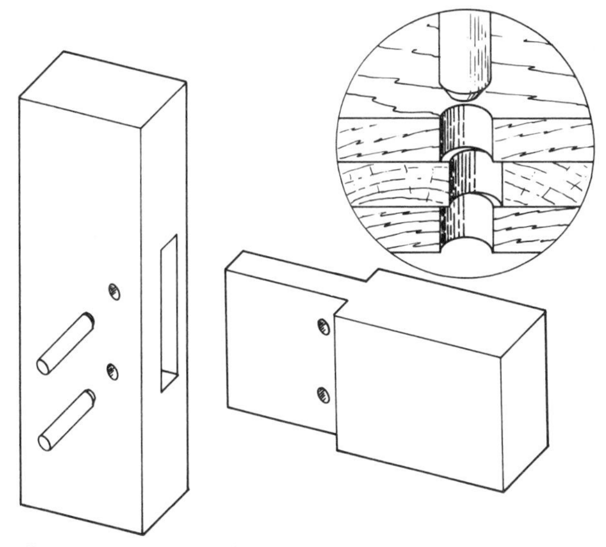

Illus. 178. Pegs can be used to lock a mortise-and-tenon. Draw boring is the technique of slightly offsetting the holes so that the peg will draw the joint tight as it is inserted.

Drill the hole in the mortised member first, then insert the tenon. Mark the hole location by inserting the drill bit and pressing the point into the tenon. Now remove the tenon, and find the mark. Make a new mark closer to the shoulder; the distance to move the mark depends on the size of the peg and of the tenon as well as the strength of the wood. Usually it is 1⁄32" to 1⁄16". In any case, as a rule of thumb, don't exceed one-third the bit diameter. Drill the hole using the new mark that is closer to the shoulder. Assemble the joint. Make sure to taper the end of the peg, and then drive it into the hole. As the peg is driven home, it will pull the joint tight. If you have trouble getting the peg started, insert an awl in the hole first to pull the holes closer into alignment.

If you examine antiques, you may notice that the pegs are square or octagonal in many cases. That's because these woodworkers didn't use manufactured dowels for the pegs; instead, the woodworker made the pegs by splitting them from a block of wood with a chisel. If you are making an antique reproduction, you may want to use the same method to add authenticity. Often the end of such a peg is left proud, that is, above the surface.

Dealing with Dimensional Change

When a mortise-and-tenon joint is used on large stock, dimensional change can become a significant factor. If a tenon is wider than 4", it can shrink enough to loosen the joint. When making a tenon on wide stock, divide the tenon into two or more parts (Illus. 179). Each part should not be wider than five times its thickness. The parts of the divided tenon are connected with a haunch. Once you have decided on the size of the tenons, chop the mortises. Connect the mortises with a groove for the haunch.

The divided tenon has another advantage. A long mortise can be difficult to glue properly because the sides tend to pull away from the cheeks

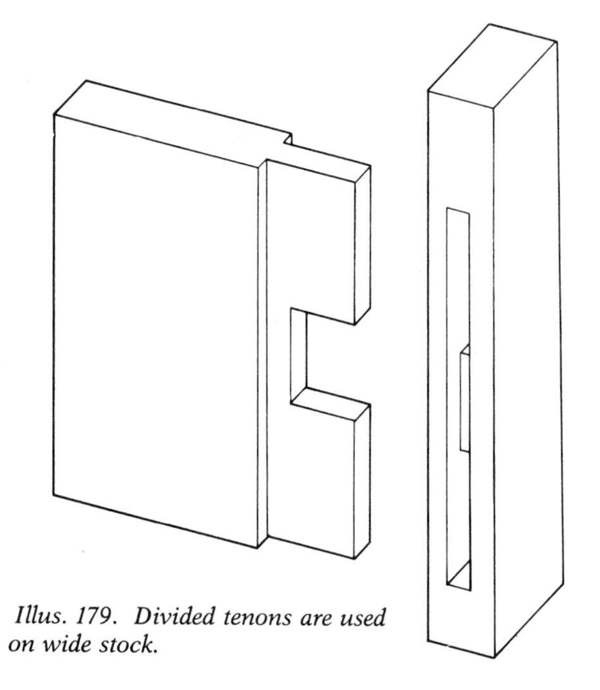

Illus. 179. Divided tenons are used on wide stock.

of the tenon. When the mortise is long, you will have to place a clamp across the joint to press the sides of the mortise firmly against the tenon cheeks. The divided tenon has the advantage of keeping the mortise short enough to avoid using this extra clamp.

Dividing the tenons will help to keep them from loosening in the mortise, but you may still have a problem with the board splitting. When a wide board is firmly attached to another board that has the grain running at a right angle to the grain of the wide board, the movement of the adjoining board will be constrained. This can result in splits. There are several techniques that you can use to allow for the movement and to keep the board from splitting. One method is to glue only one section of the divided tenon. Chop the other mortise a little long so that the tenon can slide up and down in it. If the tenon is divided in two parts, glue the one closest to the end; if it is divided into three parts, glue the middle section. This way the joint won't be as strong as it perhaps might be because of the decreased glue-surface area; but in most cases it will be strong enough, and it will completely alleviate any splitting caused by cross-grain gluing.

If you are convinced that you need the maximum strength, you can use wedges to help solve dimensional-change problems in divided tenons. When wedging a through tenon, start all of the wedges, then drive the outside wedges home before driving in the inside wedges. This will compress the board across its width so that if it shrinks later there will be less chance of the board splitting. Foxtail wedges can also be used to compress the board. In that case, use only one wedge per tenon, and place it near the outside edge.

You can also compress the wood without wedges. When you lay out the tenon, offset the sections so that they extend past the outside ends of the mortises about 1/32" to 1/16". Don't increase the width of the tenon sections, however, just offset them. Slightly taper the ends of the mortise so that you can insert the tenon. As you clamp the joint tight, the wood will be compressed. Compressing the wood is helpful, but it is not as reliable a way to prevent splits as allowing for full movement.

Long tenons present another problem: shrinkage in the mortised member can cause it to split or pull away from the tenon shoulder (Illus. 180). To prevent this problem, only apply glue to the part of the tenon closest to the shoulder. This way the shoulder joint will remain tight while allowing the mortised member freedom to move.

Fastening with pegs by draw boring is another way to remedy the problem. Draw boring compresses the wood so that there is some spring in it to take up the slack from shrinkage. Place the pegs only in the area close to the shoulder; this leaves the end free to slide back and forth as the mortised member expands and contracts.

When using wedges in a long tenon, cut the taper of the wedge so that the joint will be tighter in the shoulder area. This will keep the shoulders tight against the mortised member and allow the joint some freedom of movement at the outside.

Mortise-and-Tenon Variations

Because the mortise-and-tenon is used in so many applications, there are many variations, each suited to a particular use. I won't try to cover every variation, but I will show you some

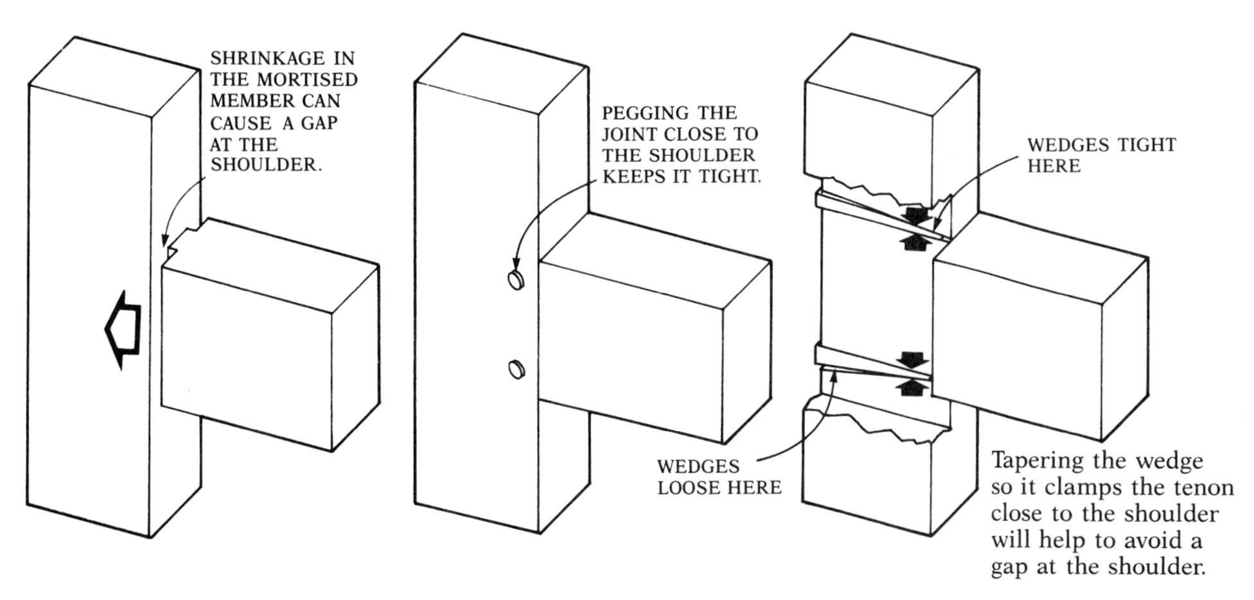

Illus. 180. Shrinkage in the mortised member (left) can cause it to split or pull away from the tenon shoulder. To prevent this, secure the tenon close to the shoulder with pegs (middle) or wedges (right).

of the ones that are most commonly used (Illus. 181, this page and next). Once you understand how the joint can be modified, you can use it in other applications that are not covered here. Some other specialized variations that are used in sash joinery, timber framing, and panel-frame making will be covered in later chapters (Chapters 13, 13, and 10, respectively).

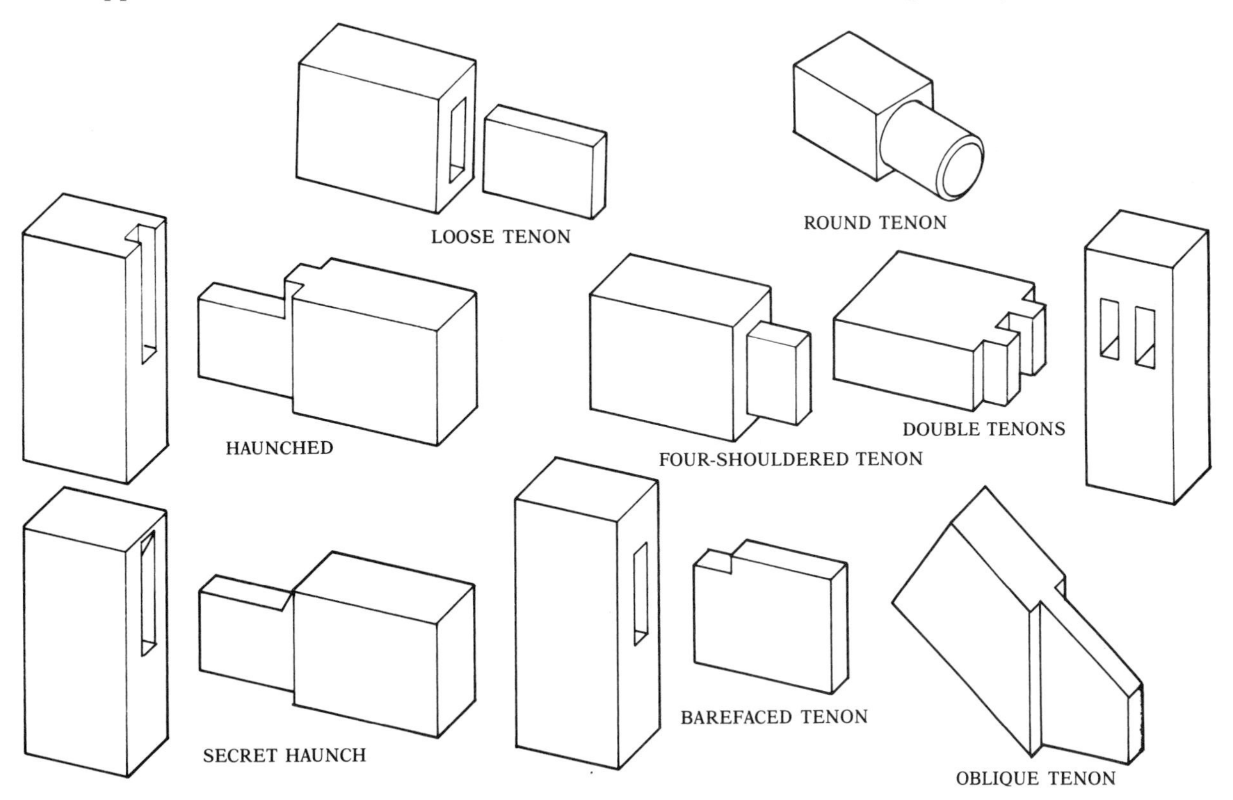

Illus. 181. Mortise-and-tenon variations. (Continued on next page.)

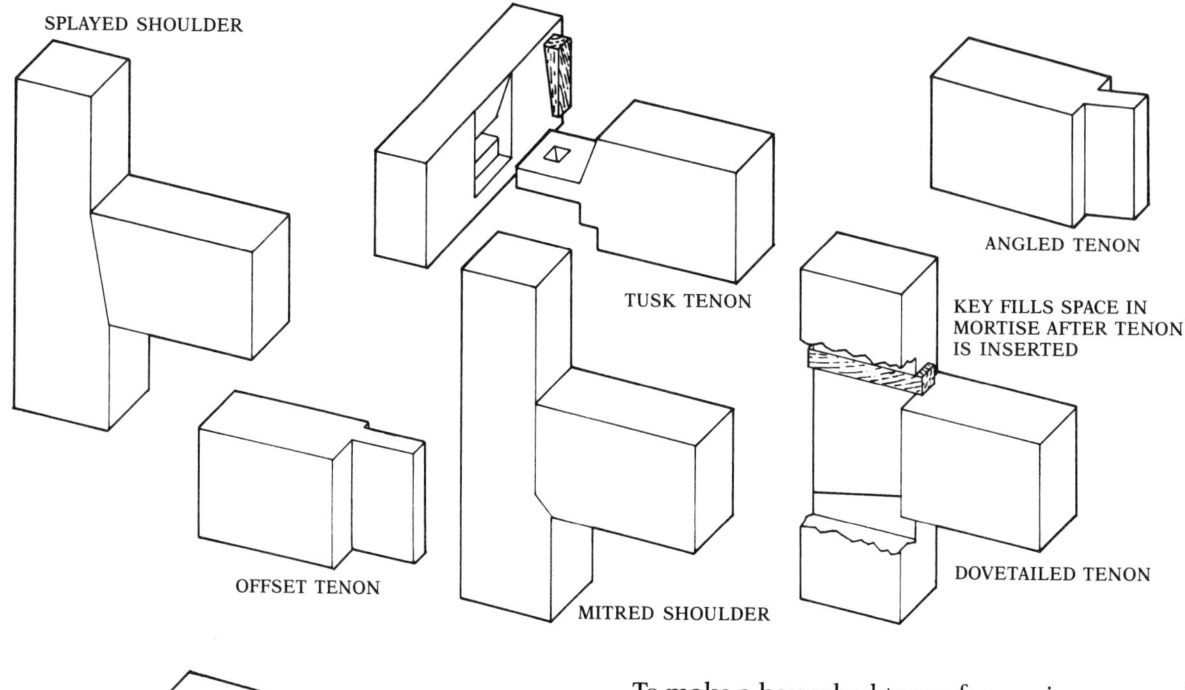

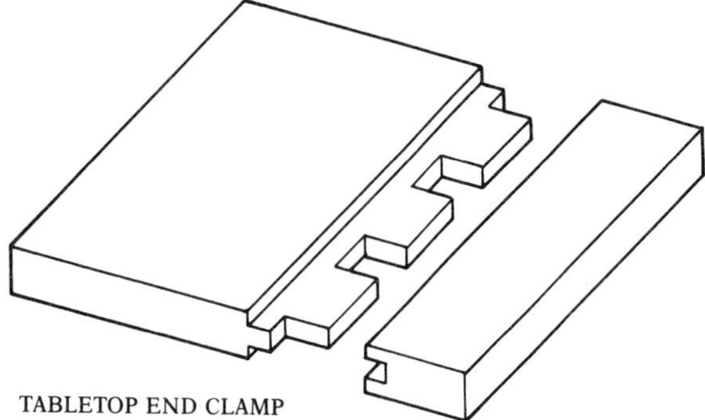

Illus. 181. (Continued.) Mortise-and-tenon variations.

HAUNCHED TENON

The haunched tenon has a notch cut on the top cheek. This creates a short stub tenon that extends to the end of the board. It strengthens the joint by adding support in this area that would otherwise be left unsupported. The haunched tenon is well suited for use in panel-frame construction because the tenon will fill the same groove that has to be made for the panel. If a haunched tenon is not used for the panel frame, then the groove must be stopped. The standard haunched tenon can be used as well in parts that are not grooved for panels, but you can also use a secret haunch that will not show on the end.

To make a haunched tenon for use in a grooved panel frame, start by cutting the groove for the panel. Be sure to leave the mortised member long enough to allow for the horn (refer to Chapter 2, page 31, Illus. 51). Chop the mortise inside the groove. Make the width of the mortise equal to the width of the groove. The length of the mortise should be about the same as you would make it if you weren't using a haunched tenon. Illus. 182 shows the proportions for several variations of the haunched tenon. If the joint won't be wedged, the haunch can be smaller. Wedged joints should have a larger haunch to avoid short-grain problems between the end of the mortise and the end of the board.

Cut the haunch after laying out the tenon; if you cut the cheeks of the tenon first, you will lose the layout lines for the haunch. If you prefer to cut the tenons before you chop the mortise, you can make a full-size tenon, then cut it down to make the haunch. The width of the haunch can be eyeballed provided that you make the mortise to match. Hold the completed tenon in place to mark the length of the mortise.

When the parts aren't grooved, a short groove must be cut on the end of the mortised board. Chop the mortise first, then use a dovetail saw or a backsaw to cut the sides of the groove. Clean out the waste with a chisel.

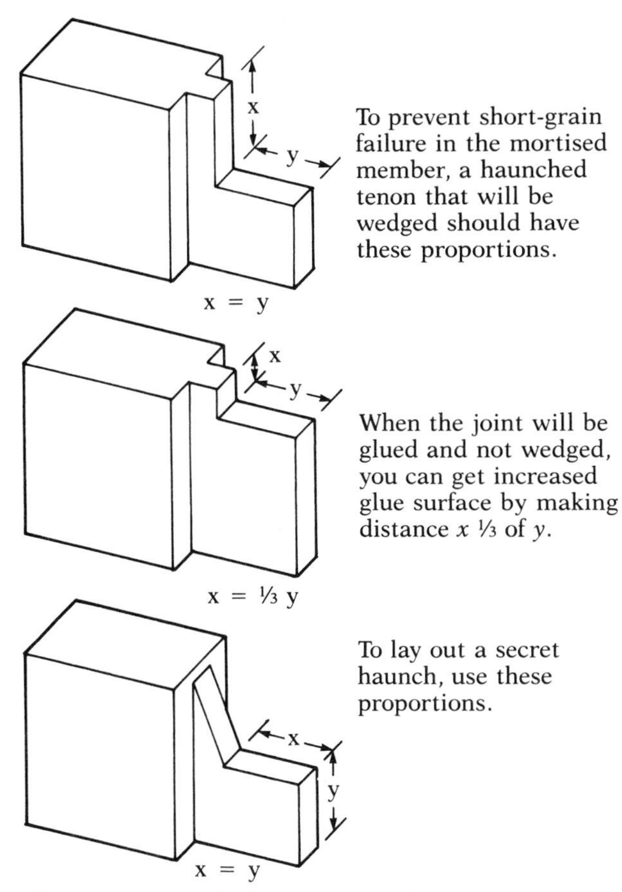

Illus. 182. Haunched-tenon proportions.

The secret haunch can be used when the appearance on the end is important enough that you don't want it to show. The secret haunch isn't quite as strong as the standard type, so only use it when appearance is absolutely a prime consideration. To make the secret haunch, chop the mortise as usual; then, make a sloping cut with a chisel between the end of the mortise and the end of the board. Actually, it's best to stop the cut about ⅛″ from the finished end of the board. This will keep the tenon completely concealed and allows a little space for trimming after assembly.

Lay out the tenon, and cut the haunch first. After the tenon is complete, dry-assemble the joint, and make any adjustments to the angle that are necessary.

FOUR-SHOULDERED TENON

The shoulder on the tenon not only improves the strength of the joint, but also it improves the appearance. The shoulder hides any slight imperfections in the mortise and gives the joint a sharp, clean joint line. In the traditional tenon, there is no shoulder on the bottom. By making a small shoulder on the bottom to make a four-shouldered tenon, the last remaining area that can show the mortise is covered.

BAREFACED TENON

The opposite extreme from the four-shouldered tenon is the barefaced tenon. A barefaced tenon might not have any shoulders at all, or it may have only one or two shoulders (Illus. 183). A barefaced tenon is typically used when joining a thin piece of wood to a thicker one; the ladder-back chair is a good example. Shoulderless barefaced tenons present a problem in assembly precisely because there is no shoulder to serve as a positive depth stop. If the mortise is a little deep, the tenon can slide in too far; this may throw other parts out of alignment. One solution is to cut shoulders on two of the parts to fix the separation. The other solution is to use a spreader board inserted between the parts during assembly. After the glue is set, the spreader can be removed. A single-shouldered barefaced tenon can be used when joining a thin board to a thicker one. If you want one of the faces to be flush, cut a shoulder on that face, and leave the other cheek barefaced. This will allow enough room between the side of the mortise and the face of the board.

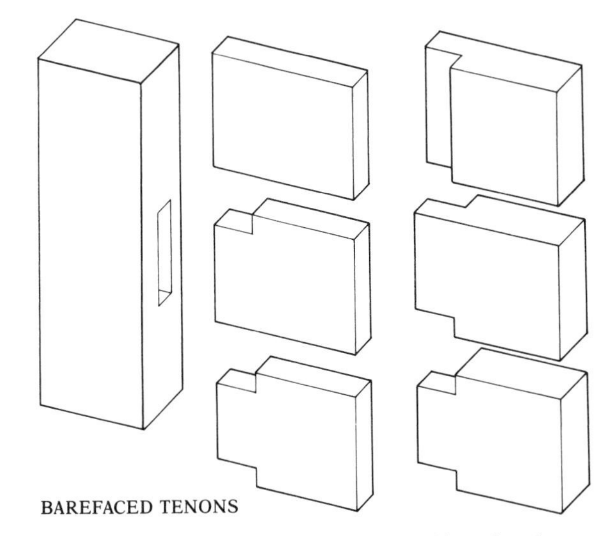

Illus. 183. There are many varieties of barefaced tenons. A tenon is usually considered barefaced if it doesn't have a shoulder on both sides.

DOUBLE TENONS

When a mortise is cut so that the sides are end grain, the glue joint will be weak. It is better to orient the mortise so that the grain running along the sides will be long grain. Sometimes the size and shape of the parts make this desirable orientation impossible while still using a standard tenon. The solution is to use two or more tenons cut side by side; this increases the long-grain contact area. Double tenons, in particular, are often used to join the drawer blades to the posts in post-and-panel cabinet construction.

Double tenons can also be used when the boards are arranged in the normal orientation, but the stock is very thick. This can produce a joint that, in fact, will resist lateral forces better because the tenons can be closer to the faces without weakening the mortised member with an unusually large mortise. It also avoids large shoulders; this is desirable since the shoulder is end grain, and thus it will not glue well. Large shoulders also have a tendency to separate from the mortised member after a while, leaving a visible gap. Placing the tenons closer to the face prevents this. If you find that you have to use a single tenon with large shoulders, you can prevent a gap at the shoulder joint by adding splines in the shoulder. Adding splines, incidentally, also improves the lateral strength of the joint.

OBLIQUE TENONS

When the boards to be joined meet at an angle, oblique tenons are called for. A straight tenon cut at an angle to the grain would have short-grain areas that are too likely to break off easily. And a mortise cut at an angle to the grain includes an undercut area that introduces problems. The oblique tenon is designed to eliminate both the undercut area of the mortise and the short-grain section of the tenon.

ANGLED TENONS

When the angle is in the other plane, that is, not in the plane that the joining pieces define but perpendicular to it, as is the case when a side rail of a chair meets the leg, then the tenons can be angled. This will only work when the angle is slight. If the angle is too great, the tenon will be weak because of the short grain angled across its thickness.

SPLAYED SHOULDERS

When the mortised member becomes narrower at the joint, you have two options. The splayed shoulder can be used to make a smooth transition from one width to the other; the shoulder is angled between the two widths. The other option is to mitre just the corner where the shoulder meets the wider section to make a mitred shoulder; most of the shoulder is then straight except for the abrupt transition to the wider width at the mitred corner.

OFFSET TENONS

The tenon doesn't necessarily need to be positioned right in the middle of the end of the board. In some cases it is better to offset the tenon. When you are joining a thin part to a thicker one, for example, and you want one face to be flush, you can offset the tenon to keep the mortise from being too close to the face of the thicker part.

Offset tenons can increase the effective length of the tenons, for instance, when two rail tenons meet at a corner leg. Offsetting the tenons towards the outside of the rail gives you more length for the tenons in the leg before their mortises run into each other.

TUSK TENONS

Another way to wedge a tenon is to make it longer than the depth of the mortise and to insert a wedge in the part that extends past the mortise. Originally, the term tusk tenon applied only to the type that is shown above in Illus. 181. This is a joint that was developed for use in house framing. You can see that it does look a little like an elephant's tusk. In general usage today, any tenon that extends past the mortise and is wedged is called a tusk tenon (Illus. 184).

The framing type of tusk tenon has a step cut on the bottom. The tenon itself is much smaller than the width of the board; this is because the joint was originally used for floor joists. It can carry a lot of weight because the step resists shear stress. The tenon doesn't need to be as strong because its only purpose is to hold the joist into the beam.

When you don't need the extra shear strength, you can use a simpler type of tusk tenon. These joints are often used as knockdown joints in projects that need to be disassembled occasionally. You will typically see them used to attach the stretcher to the legs of a trestle table.

In any type of tusk tenon, there are a few points to observe. First, make the tenon long enough; the part that extends past the mortise should be at least four times the size of the wedge. This is to prevent short-grain failure when the wedge is driven home. Second, the wedge should be at least twice as long as the width of the tenon. This is to provide a good bearing surface against the mortised member. The wedge should be angled on the outside edge and flat on the inside edge; the taper should be about 1:6. You can vary this somewhat, but if it tapers too much, the wedge will work itself loose. If it doesn't taper enough, you won't be able to tighten the joint later if the joint loosens due to shrinkage. Make the hole for the wedge to match the angle on the wedge. The wedge hole should start about ⅛" inside the area that is inside the mortise. If you were to make the back of the hole flush with the outside of the mortised member, the wedge would bottom out before it could pull the parts tight.

Folding wedges can be used if you want to make a square hole for the wedges. Folding wedges are two similar wedges that are placed with their flat sides out and their tapered sides facing each other. Drive them in evenly from both directions.

Dowels can also be used as the wedges. Drill the wedge hole so that it is partially inside the mortise. Flatten one side of the dowel, and give it a slight taper; you can do this with a saw or by planing. A simple jig can be easily made by drilling a hole for the dowel through the edge of a board. Drill the hole at the taper angle. Next, saw a kerf down through the edge of the board, and, finally, cut the end of the board off so that part of the dowel will be exposed. Put a dowel in the jig and clamp the jig in a vise. Plane the edge of the dowel flush with the end of the jig, and it will be correctly tapered.

DOVETAILED TENONS

At first thought, a dovetailed tenon may seem to be impossible; but the secret is that the mortise is made large enough for the dovetail to be in-

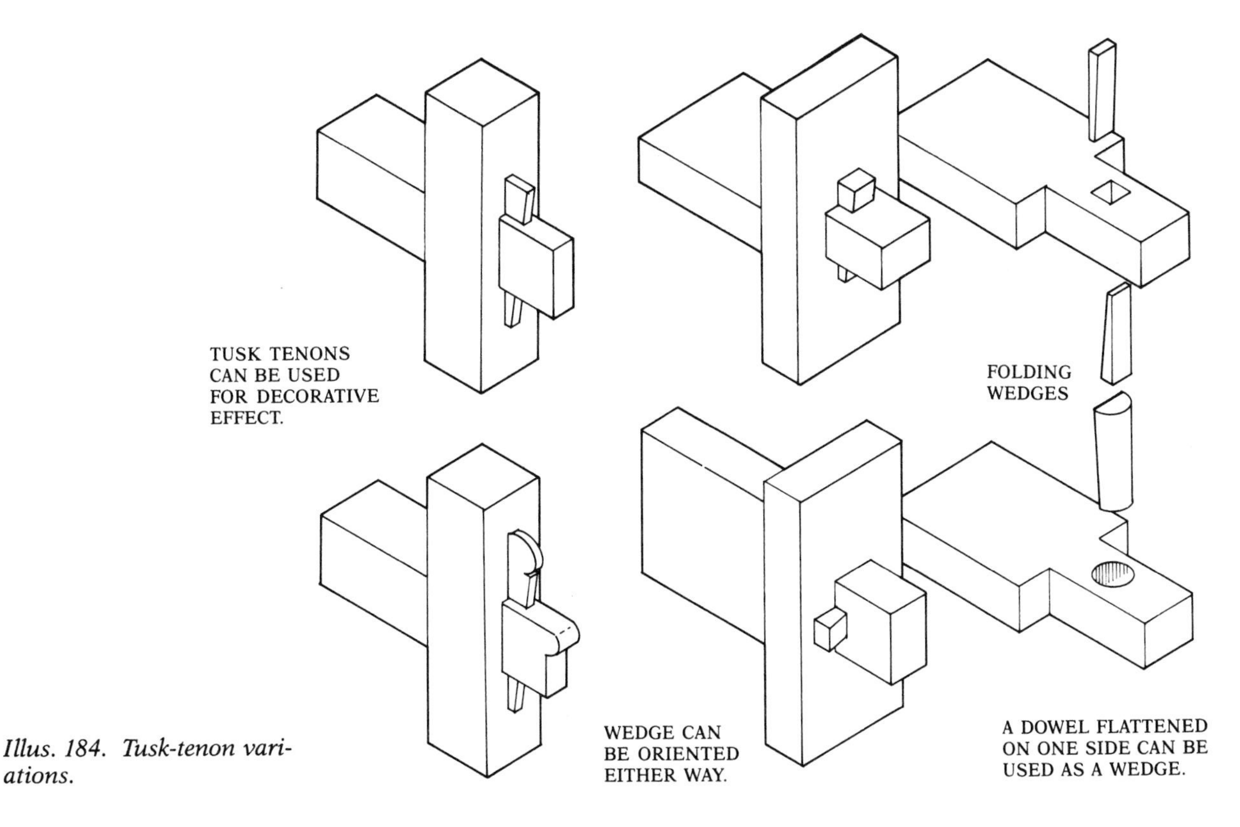

Illus. 184. Tusk-tenon variations.

serted, and then a separate key is inserted to fill up the space. Cut the dovetail first, then cut the tenon in the normal manner. Chop the mortise with a corresponding angle on one end, and make it long enough for the tenon to be inserted. This type is typically used with a through mortise, but it can be made blind. In the blind version, the key is inserted from the inside rather than the outside as is done for the through mortise. A wedge can be used instead of a straight key.

LOOSE TENONS

The loose tenon is really a spline, but, because it is inserted in a deep mortise, it is as strong as a standard mortise-and-tenon. The grain in the tenon should run in the same direction it would if you were making a standard tenon. Mortises are chopped in both parts, and the tenon is slipped into the mortise. A mortise chisel isn't designed to chop into end grain, so you will need to use another method to make the mortise in the end grain. One method you can use is to drill a series of holes, and clean up the mortise with a chisel. The loose-tenon joint is especially suited to power-tool work because you can easily make the end-grain mortises, and you can use the same machine for all the parts, so a separate setup for the tenon is unnecessary.

TABLETOP END CLAMP

You may see a type of mortise-and-tenon joint used on old tabletops. The end clamp is mortised to receive multiple tenons cut on the end of the tabletop. The clamp helps to keep the boards from cupping, and it used to help hold the joints together in the days before reliable glue. The problem with the end clamp is that it introduces a cross-grain member that can lead to splits in the top. One way to alleviate the problem is to make all of the mortises except the middle one slightly long. Don't use any glue. Instead attach the clamp with pegs. Make slotted holes in the outside tenons. This method gives the tops some room to move, but the clamp will still keep the boards from cupping.

Because the top is typically too wide to use a saw for making the tenons, a plane used with one of the various planing methods is usually best.

ROUND TENONS

A tenon doesn't have to be rectangular. One place that round tenons are particularly used is in chair construction. When the parts are turned on a lathe, the tenons can be turned at the same time. A round tenon can be cut on square stock using a tenon cutter. This is a special type of drill bit. It is similar to a plug cutter; the hollow center of the bit is the diameter of the tenon. The rest of the stock is cut away by the cutter. You can also cut a round tenon by hand. Lay out the circle on the end. Saw around the shoulder, then split off the waste with a chisel. Finish up with a knife. The mortise is simply a round hole bored with a bit.

Round tenons are typically used when making chairs from green wood. Using green wood is a traditional way of making chairs because the shrinkage can be used to lock the joints. When using green wood to make round tenons, the parts with the tenons should be drier than the parts with the mortise; that way the mortise will shrink onto the tenon (Illus. 185). You can whittle the tenons with a knife. Make them slightly oval with the wide part aligned with the grain of the mortised member. This helps to keep the mortised member from splitting as it dries because the stress is in line with the grain. Also make the tenon larger at the end than at the shoulder; this creates a dovetail effect as the wood shrinks. Working with green wood is an art that must be practiced to be perfected, so make some trial joints to get the hang of it.

Power-Tool Methods

When I worked in a large shop, we made mortises using a step mortiser. This is a specialized piece of equipment that is designed expressly for the job. It has a square, hollow chisel with a drill bit inside. A foot pedal lowers the chisel when you step on it; hence the name step mortiser, (Illus. 186, 187, and 188). Unless you work in a production shop, you are unlikely to use this type of machine; but, there are other ways to make a mortise using power tools.

You can get an attachment for the drill press that adapts it to use the same hollow chisels that a step mortiser uses. This method produces a finished mortise with square corners without re-

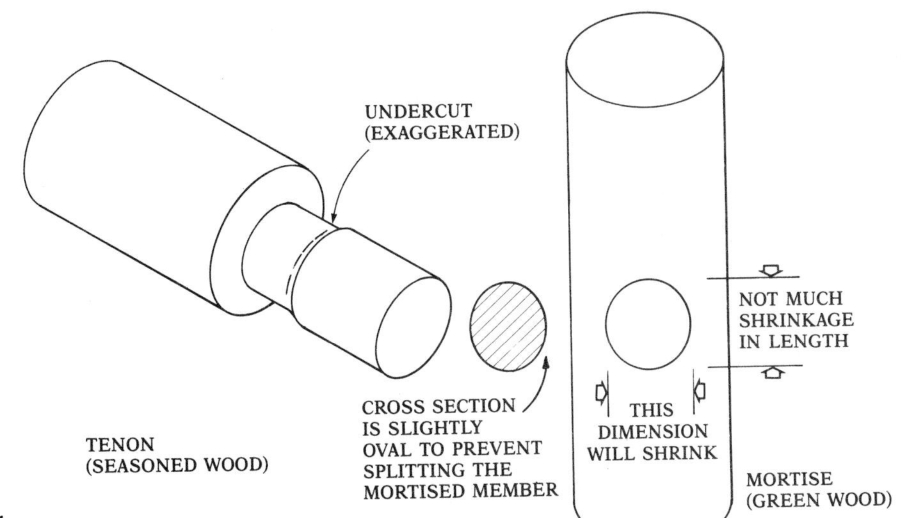

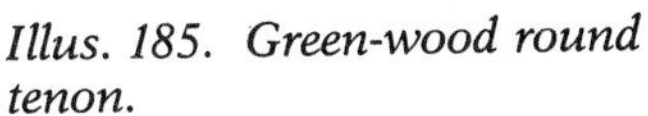

Illus. 185. Green-wood round tenon.

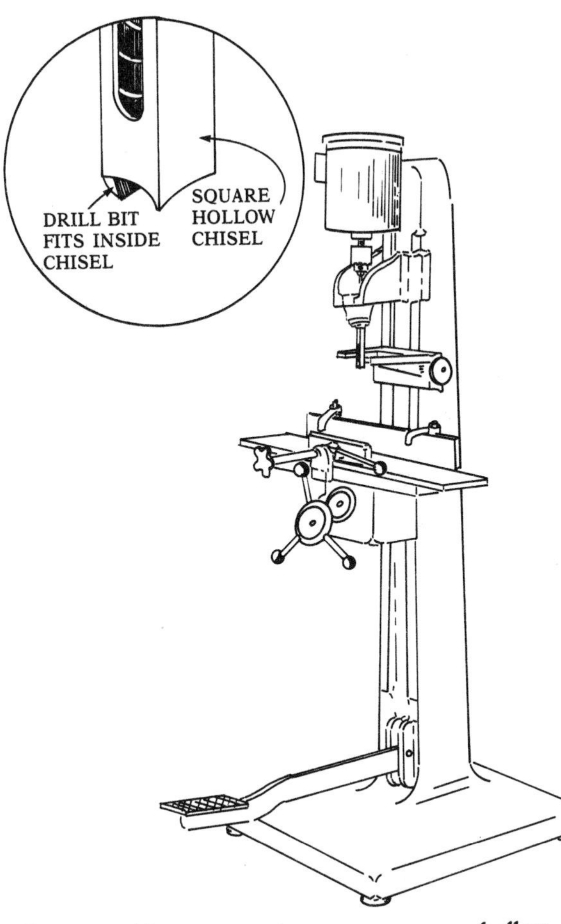

Illus. 186. The step mortiser uses a square, hollow chisel to make a mortise. Quick-release clamps and positioning stops make this an ideal machine for mass production.

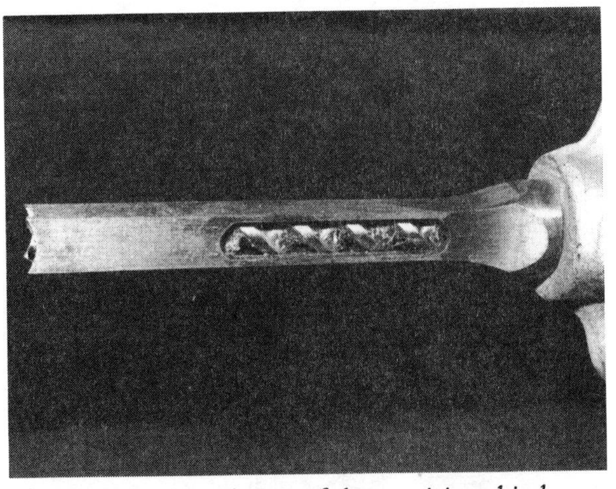

Illus. 187. In this closeup of the mortising chisel, you can see the slot where the waste is ejected.

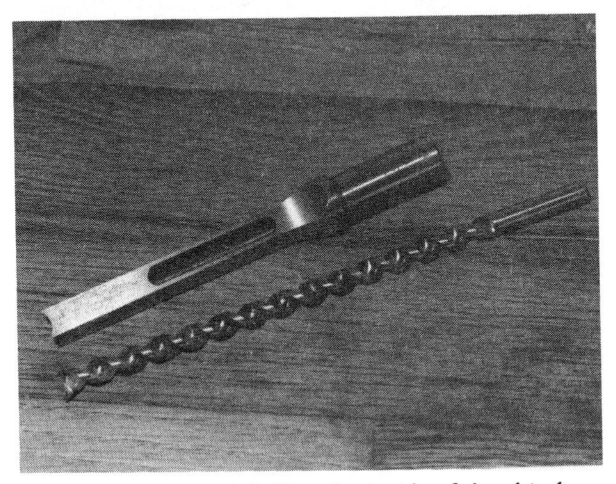

Illus. 188. A special drill bit fits inside of the chisel.

quiring any hand-tool steps. When you set up the drill and chisel, allow a small amount of clearance between the bit and the chisel. I found that my thumb nail was just the right thickness for gauging the clearance. When setting up the step mortiser, I would adjust the bit until my thumb nail just slipped between the bit and the chisel.

You will need to add some type of fence to the drill press. It can be as simple as a board clamped to the table; or, you may want to incorporate adjustable stops to position the mortise. Set the depth stop on the drill press. Make a hole at each end of the mortise first (Illus. 189). I found that the square chisel bound in the hole

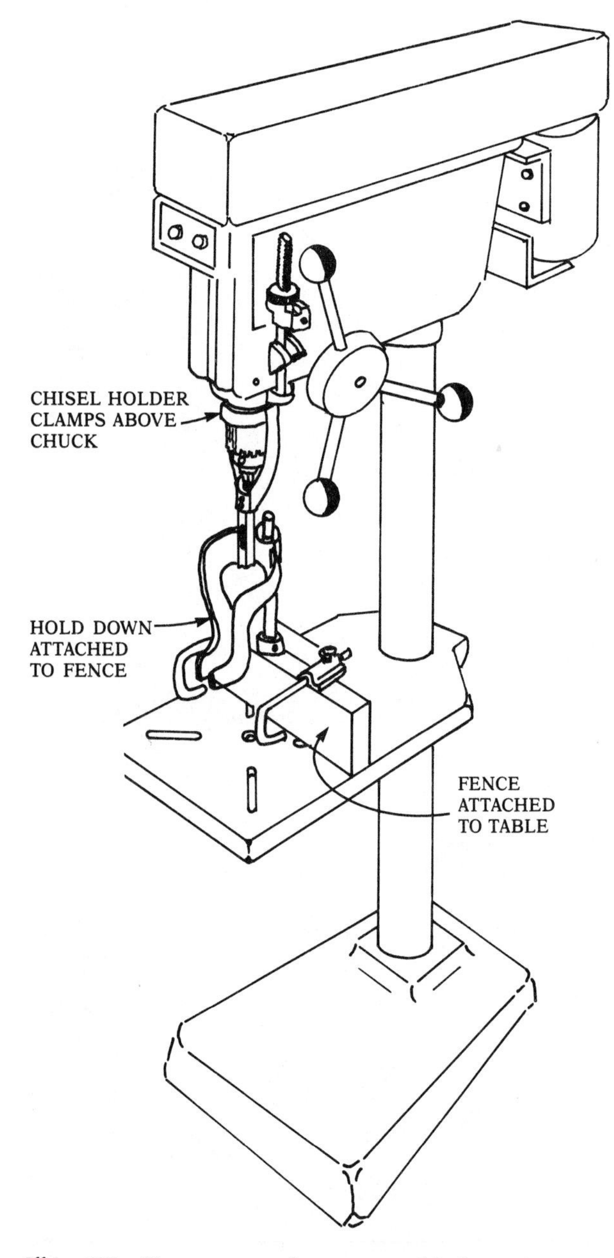

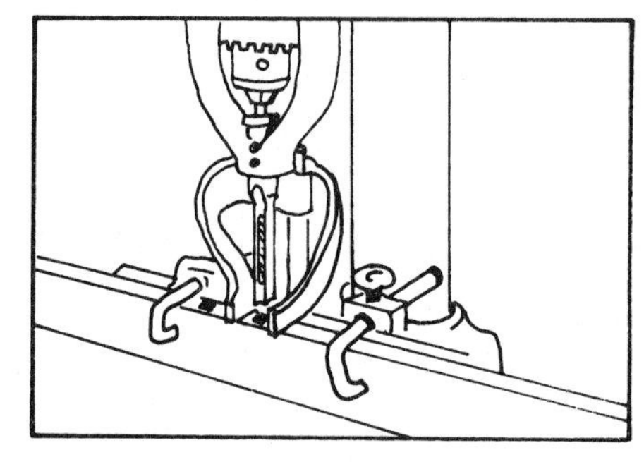

1. Make a hole at each end of the mortise first, then make the end cuts.

2. If the chisel sticks when making the end cuts, make a relief cut next to the first cut after cutting partway down.

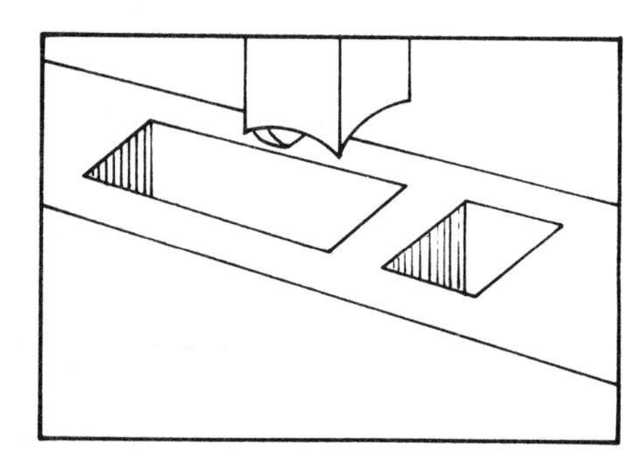

3. Remove the waste between the end cuts by moving the chisel about 3/4 of its width for each new bite.

Illus. 189. You can attach a square chisel mortiser to a drill press with an adaptor kit.

when I made a deep cut right at first. So I would cut part way down, then I'd move the board slightly and make another cut next to the first one. Don't make this relief cut deeper than the original hole because the chisel can drift if it isn't cutting on all four sides. When you reach the depth of the first cut, withdraw the chisel, and reposition the work to cut the first hole to the final depth. When you have made the end cuts, slide the board along the fence about three-fourths of the width of the chisel, and make a cut; continue in this manner until all of the waste is removed.

Another type of specialized tool for making mortises is the horizontal long-hole-boring machine. This is sometimes available as an accessory on a table saw. It has a movable table with stops and clamps. A special bit is used to drill into the wood and then to cut sideways. Just as with square-chisel mortising, you should first make the end cuts, and then clean out the waste. Advance the work into the cutter at each end; then, move the table sideways to clean out the waste.

This horizontal boring-matching method and all of those that follow produce a mortise with rounded ends. You have two choices; you can use a chisel to square up the ends of the mortise by hand, or you can round the tenon to fit (Illus. 190). Don't use a square tenon, however, in a mortise with round ends. The resulting gap will be too big for a good glue bond, and there won't be enough contact area to transfer the compressional stress.

My late uncle, Elbert Stevenson, used a metalworking milling machine to make mortises. It operates much like a long-hole-boring machine; but it is much more accurate because it is designed for the close tolerances needed in metalwork. If you have access to a milling machine, you might want to try this method. Clamp the work in the jaws of the milling machine (Illus. 191). If the machine has been set up level, you can use a spirit level to line up the board. Advance the work into the cutter, and make a cut. Keep the cuts shallow for the greatest accuracy.

Even if you don't have any of this specialized equipment, you can still make mortises with power tools. You can use a drill press, or a portable drill and a dowelling jig, to partially make a mortise; but, you will need to finish the mortise by hand with a chisel.

In this process, you drill a series of holes to remove most of the waste before finishing the mortise by hand. The holes must be accurately placed or they can cause the chisel to wander and make the sides of the mortise out of shape. When you're using the drill press, attach a fence to the table. Use a bit that is the same diameter as the desired width of the mortise. Adjust the drill-press depth stop, and set the fence to align

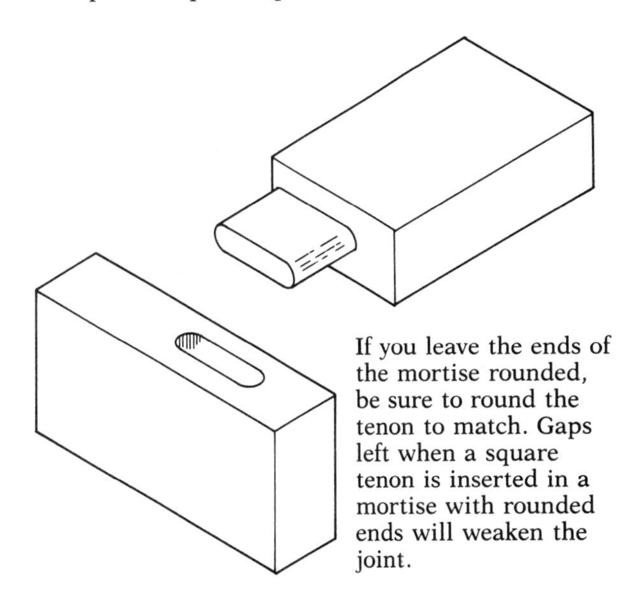

Illus. 190. Mortise-and-tenon joint with rounded ends.

Illus. 191. A metalworking milling machine can be used to cut accurate mortises.

the board into the proper relationship with the bit (Illus. 192). Make the end holes first, then drill holes side by side to clean out the waste. This is where it is critically important that the holes be perfectly in line since they will guide the chisel. If you use a portable drill instead, make the holes using a dowelling jig. The jig will keep the holes in alignment.

Illus. 192. Use this setup to drill out most of the waste in the mortise. A fence attached to the drill-press table keeps the holes in line.

Now square up the mortise using chisels. A wide chisel is used on the sides. Place the chisel so that it removes the remaining waste and just skims the sides of the holes. If you used a small bit and then try to enlarge the mortise with the wide chisel, the chisel will wander, and the sides will be out of square. By skimming down the sides of the holes, the chisel will be guided square (Illus. 193). After removing the waste from the sides, use a smaller chisel to square up the ends. If you can't use a drill bit that is the correct size, use a mortising chisel to clean out the waste. Follow the same procedure given in the section for chopping the mortises by hand in Chapter 2. The drill will remove most of the waste, so the chopping will be easier, particularly if the mortise is large.

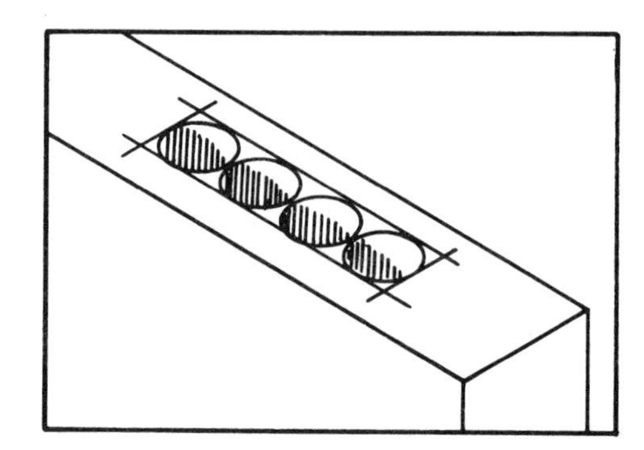

1. Drill a series of holes. Make sure they are in line, because they will guide the chisel.

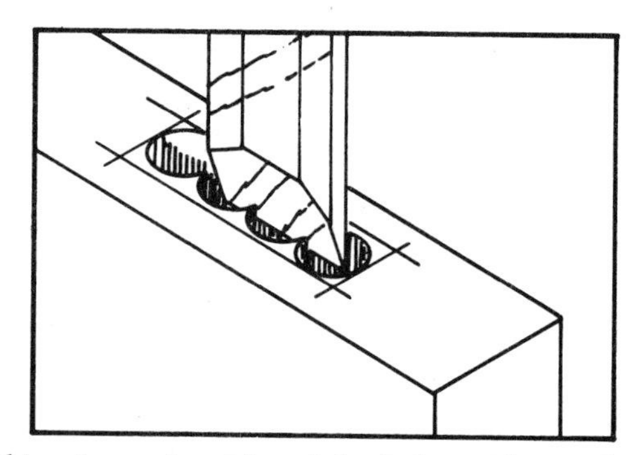

2. Skim down the sides of the holes with a wide chisel to remove the waste in between the holes.

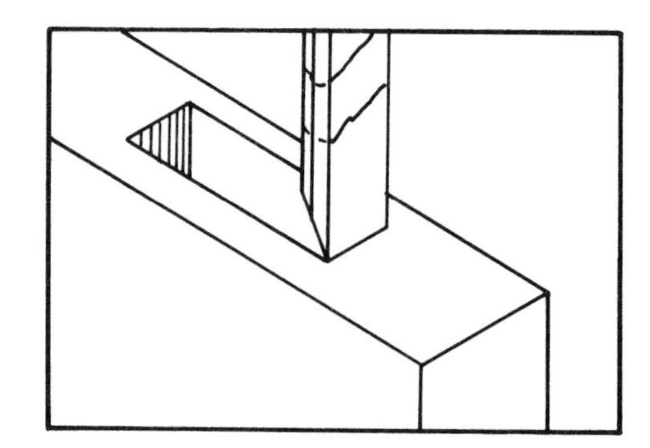

3. Square up the ends of the mortise with a small chisel.

Illus. 193. After drilling the holes using the drill press, or using a portable drill and a dowelling jig, use chisels to square up the mortise.

The router is another very good tool for making mortises. The best type to use is the plunge router (Illus. 194). It can be placed on the work with the bit above the base; then, the bit is advanced into the work by lowering until it reaches a preset stop. Because the base is in contact with the work before cutting begins, the plunge cut is guided more accurately. If you don't have access to a plunge router, you can use a regular router. The plunge cut must be made carefully to keep the bit from wandering.

Illus. 194. A plunge router is useful when making a mortise, because the base and fence stay in contact with the work while the bit is lowered or raised.

Use a straight bit that is the desired size of the mortise. When the mortise is going to be deep, it is best to make two or more shallow cuts instead of trying to cut the full depth in one pass. If the mortise is going to be wider than ½", use a smaller bit, and make two parallel cuts; then, clean out the waste between the cuts.

There are several ways to guide the router. You can simply use a router fence. Place the work in a vise, and put another board next to it in the vise to give more bearing surface for the router base. Place the fence against the face of the work, and make the plunge cut; then, guide the router along the work to the other end, and lift it from the board. If you aren't using a plunge router, it's best to let the bit stop turning before you lift the router so that you don't enlarge the hole inadvertently. If you attach a wide auxiliary fence to the router fence, you will find it much easier to guide the plunge cut when you're using a standard router.

The tenoning machine is a piece of equipment used in large shops to make tenons; but, like the step mortiser, it is such a specialized piece of equipment that most woodworkers don't use it. There are several more common types of power tools that you can use to make tenons.

The table saw is probably the most widely used tool for making tenons. To do the job safely, you need a tenoning jig. You can use a commercial type or one like the shopmade jig shown in Illus. 195. This jig slips over the rip fence; the fence is used to adjust the jig.

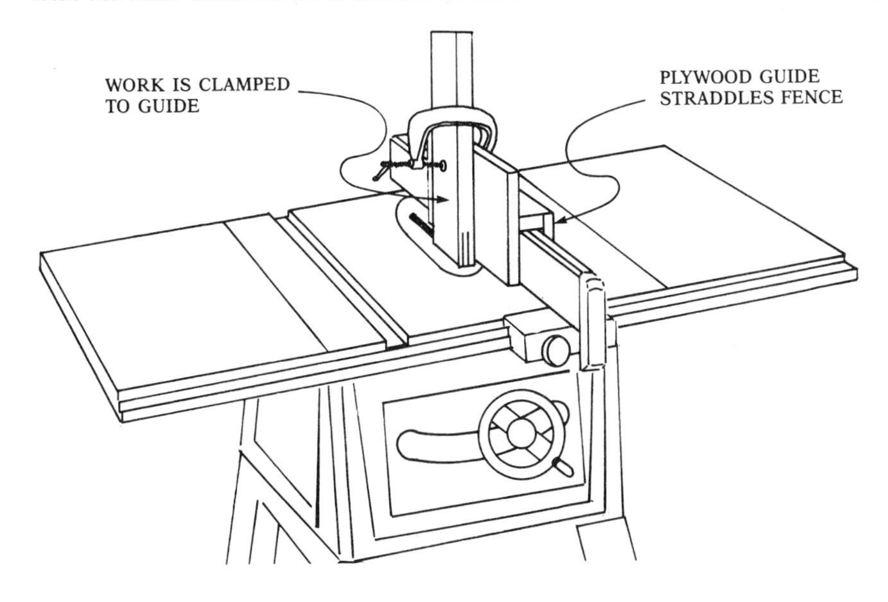

Illus. 195. To use this shopmade jig to cut tenons, clamp the work to the tall board on the blade side of the fence. The jig straddles the fence so that it can't wander during the cut. Adjust the fence position to line up the blade with the layout lines on the work, and then make the cut.

For the greatest accuracy, both cheeks should be cut with the same face of the board remaining in place against the tenoning jig. This means that you must make two separate setups. You can get around this by using two blades; you will need two identical blades. Make a spacer out of hardboard that is the same thickness as that desired for the tenon. Drill a hole in the spacer for the saw arbor. Put both blades on the arbor, with the spacer in the middle. Make a zero-clearance wood insert for the saw throat. Lower the blades and install the insert; attach it with screws or clamp it down. Turn on the saw, and raise the blades to cut through the insert. Turn off the saw, and adjust the blade height to the length of the tenon. Adjust the tenoning jig to place the tenon in the desired position. Then, clamp the board in the jig, and cut; this makes both cheek cuts in a single pass.

When you have cut the cheeks on all of the tenons, change back to a single blade, and make the shoulder cuts. Use the mitre gauge to guide the board; but, clamp a stop block to the fence to position the board on the mitre gauge. Press the end of the tenon against the stop block, and hold the board firmly against the mitre gauge. As you move the gauge towards the blade, however, the end of the tenon should clear the stop block before the blade begins to cut (Illus. 196). Using the stop block in this way helps to prevent kickback that might be caused by the waste piece becoming trapped between the fence and the blade.

The twin-blade setup can also be used to make angled tenons. In such a case, after installing the throat insert but before cutting through, first set the blade tilt at the desired angle; then, raise the blades to cut through the insert. Guide the work with a tenoning jig as before. The shoulders are cut using a single blade set to the same angle. Use the mitre gauge to guide the cut. The first cut is made with the gauge to one side of the blade, and the second cut is made with the gauge in the opposite slot.

The dado blade can also be used on the table saw to cut tenons. Set the blade for the widest cut. Raise the blade to the desired depth of the shoulder. Hold the board against the mitre gauge with the face against the saw table. You can use a stop block on the fence, as above, to position the board on the mitre gauge. Adjust it so that the first cut will form the shoulder. Then slide the board about three-fourths of the width of the dado blade, and make another pass. Continue in this manner until you reach the end of the tenon. Flip the board over, and repeat the operation for the other side (Illus. 197). This method is not as accurate as the twin-blade setup because you are using both faces to gauge from; in addition, the surface of the tenon will be rougher, so it may not glue as well.

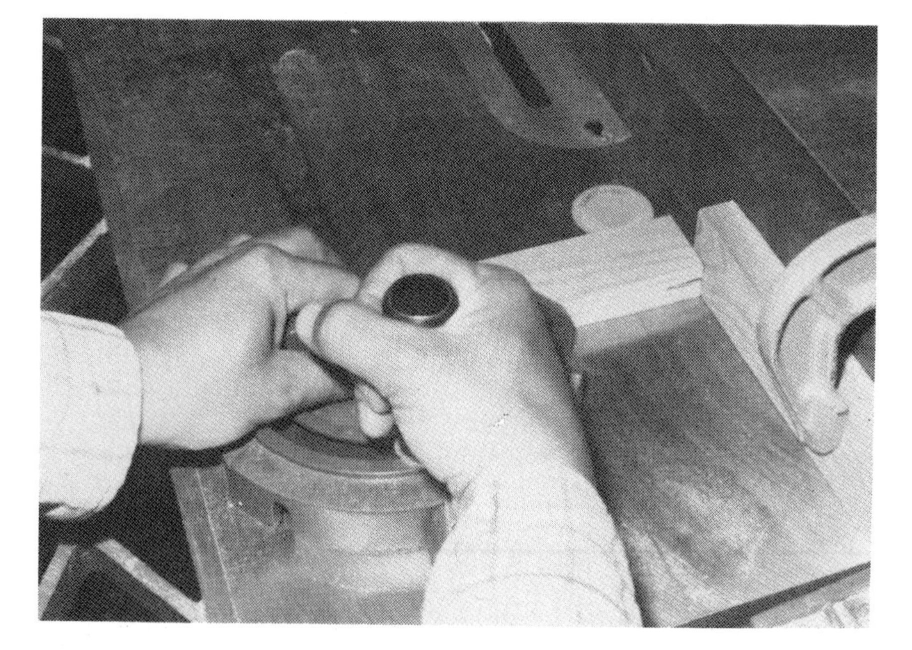

Illus. 196. Here, a shoulder is being cut for a barefaced tenon. The same procedure is used for tenons with shoulders on both sides; simply flip the work over to cut the other shoulder. Use a stop block clamped to the rip fence to position the work when cutting shoulders on the table saw. Once the work has been positioned, hold it tightly against the mitre gauge, and advance it into the blade.

Illus. 197. A dado blade on the table saw can also be used to cut the tenon. Use a stop block to position the work for the shoulder cut; then, take additional passes as necessary to remove the waste.

The radial-arm saw can be used to cut tenons. You will need an auxiliary table, though, to raise the work when making the cheek cuts. Turn the saw head so that the blade is parallel to the table, and adjust the height so that the saw will clear the fence. Make an auxiliary table from a piece of plywood and some wood blocks. Attach a fence to the back of the table. Place the board on the auxiliary table, and adjust the saw height to the position of the cheek cut. The length of the tenon is governed by how far the tenon extends past the edge of the auxiliary table. Make a mark on the edge of the board to line up with the edge of the auxiliary table. *Use extreme caution when performing this operation because the blade is very exposed*. Push the saw back against the stop, and position the board on the auxiliary table. Turn on the saw, and slowly pull it through the board to make the first cheek cut (Illus. 198). You can make both cheek cuts using the same setup; but, it is more accurate to readjust the saw for the second cut so that you can always keep the same face against the table. When the cheeks are all cut, return the saw to the normal vertical position, and remove the auxiliary table. Adjust the blade height to make the shoulder cuts. Hold the board against the fence, and cut the shoulder.

You can also make tenons using the dado blade on the radial-arm saw. In this case, the saw is set in the normal position. The process is similar to the one used on the table saw. Use a stop on the fence to position the board for the shoulder cut. Adjust the blade height to get the proper depth of cut. Make the shoulder cut; then, move the board, and make another cut closer to the end. Keep moving the board until the cheek is completely free of waste.

The band saw can be used to cut tenons as well. Use the widest blade you can; the wide blade will help to keep the cuts straight. Lay out the tenons on the board as if you were cutting them by hand. You can use a fence to guide the cut, but the band saw has a tendency to wander when using a fence; I prefer to clamp a board in line with the blade (Illus. 199). This will guide the work, but it gives you the freedom to move the board and to keep the cut straight. Use this setup to cut the cheeks. You can use the mitre-gauge to guide the board as you cut the shoulders on the band saw, or you might prefer to use a backsaw and a mitre box to cut the shoulders.

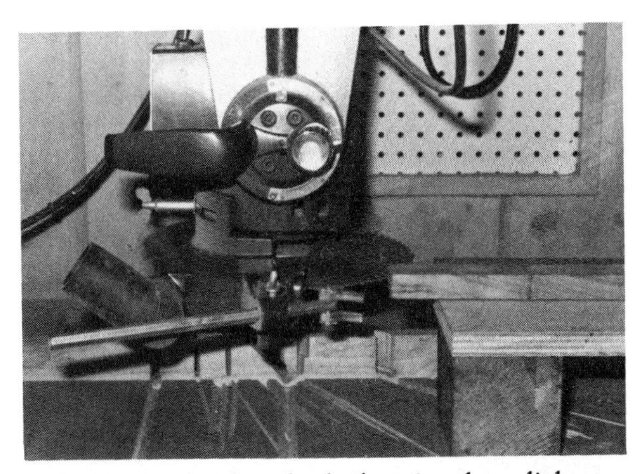

Illus. 198. To cut the side cheeks using the radial-arm saw, turn the blade parallel to the table; an auxiliary table is also necessary. Use extreme caution because the blade is very exposed.

Illus. 199. A board clamped in line with the blade can be used to guide the work when cutting tenons on a band saw.

Tenons can also be cut on a jointer that is equipped with a rabbeting ledge. Set the fence to the length of the tenon, and lower the infeed table to make a cut that is equal to the desired depth of the shoulder. If this will result in too deep a cut to make all at once, then make the cut in two or more passes. *Use caution because this operation must be performed with the guard removed.* Place the board on the table face down with the end against the fence. Feed the board through, keeping your fingers well away from the cutting head. Use a push stick if necessary.

And one last power-tool option that can be used to cut tenons is the router. The maximum length of the tenon is determined by the length of the router bit. You will need some type of jig to guide the router; a router table can be used. Set the fence to guide the board. An L-shaped support block clamped to the work will make it more stable (Illus. 200).

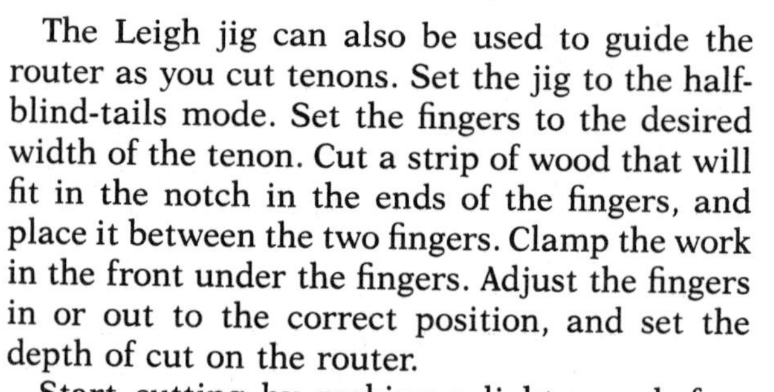

The Leigh jig can also be used to guide the router as you cut tenons. Set the jig to the half-blind-tails mode. Set the fingers to the desired width of the tenon. Cut a strip of wood that will fit in the notch in the ends of the fingers, and place it between the two fingers. Clamp the work in the front under the fingers. Adjust the fingers in or out to the correct position, and set the depth of cut on the router.

Start cutting by making a light pass before putting the collar all the way against the fingers. This will help to prevent splintering at the shoulder. Turn the board around, and make the other cut (Illus. 201). The fingers are rounded on the ends. This will make a tenon that will fit into a round-end mortise, so you don't need to use a chisel to square up the mortise.

The finger assembly can further be adjusted in and out to accommodate variations in the board thickness or to make offset tenons.

Illus. 200. Tenons can be cut using a router table. Clamp the work to an L-shaped support block, and set the fence to guide the cut.

Illus. 201. The Leigh jig can be used to cut tenons with rounded ends. This eliminates the need for squaring up a mortise that was also cut with a router. A small block of wood placed between the fingers guides the router while cutting the side cheeks.

7

Dovetails: Variations and Power-Tool Techniques

Because of its strength and reliability, the dovetail has been adapted for use in many applications. The through dovetail described in Chapter 2 is the most basic type of dovetail; however, it can be laid out in a variety of ways. When the strength of the dovetail is desirable but the joint needs to be hidden, a half-blind or full-blind version can be used.

The dovetail can be made using power tools. There are several methods that range from what amounts to power-assisted hand cutting to a cut that is fully controlled by a jig (Illus. 202). Cutting dovetails is truly exacting work: occasionally everyone makes a mistake. In acknowledging as much, this chapter contains a concluding section on correcting defects in dovetail joints.

Illus. 202. This bench made with a Leigh jig illustrates that variable spacing can be achieved by machine. (Photo courtesy Leigh Industries Ltd.)

Layout Variations

The rules of thumb given for layout are not hard-and-fast rules; they are meant just to give the beginner someplace to start while still producing a well-proportioned joint. With experience, you can vary the proportions depending on the wood used and on the use that the part will receive. Pin spacing, for instance, can be varied to create interesting visual effects. The dovetail slope can vary as well from 1:4 to 1:8 (Illus. 203).

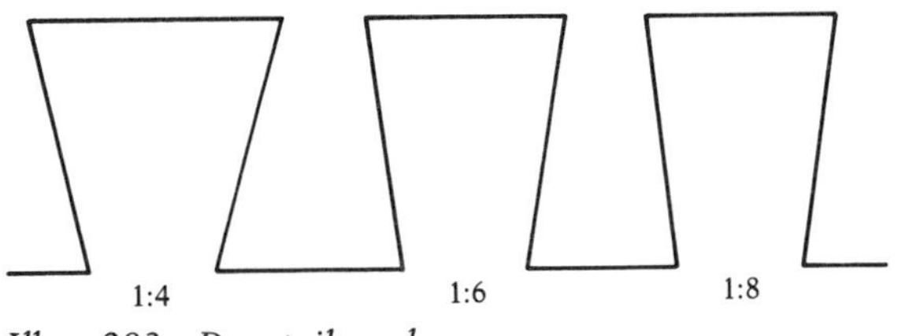

Illus. 203. Dovetail angles.

For softwood you can use a 1:6 to get more strength; whereas, the slope can be as shallow as 1:8 for hardwoods. The size of the pins can be changed to increase strength or to create a visual effect (Illus. 204). The strongest joint results when the pins and tails are of equal size. When appearance is most important, the pins can be made very small; in the extreme, they come to a sharp point (Illus. 205). Pins this small are considered to be very stylish; however, they aren't as strong as wider ones.

When using small pins, you won't be able to get a chisel into the pin socket to split out a chip. Instead, use the chisel to shave down the face side of the waste, angling down to the shoulder. Hold the chisel on an angle so that it cuts deeper on the outside edge; then, reverse the angle, and take another cut from the opposite side. This will result in a pyramid-shaped piece of waste being

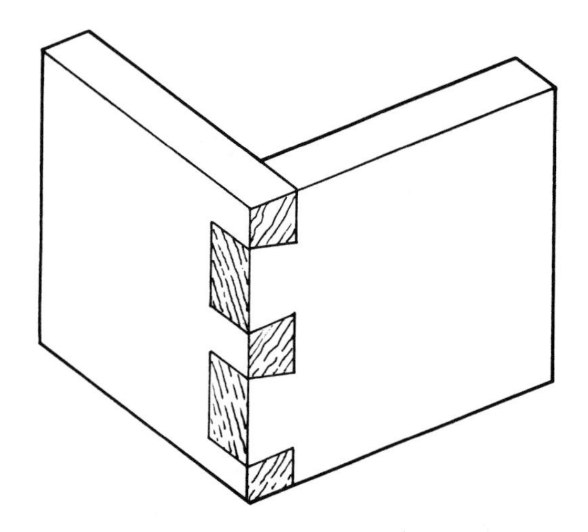

Using the traditional rule of thumb, the widest part of the pin is equal to the thickness of the stock, and the narrowest part of the tail is equal to two times the thickness of the stock.

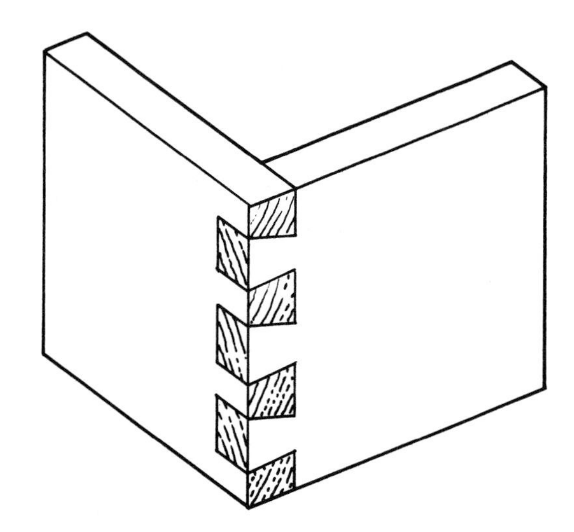

Equal-size pins and tails offer the greatest strength.

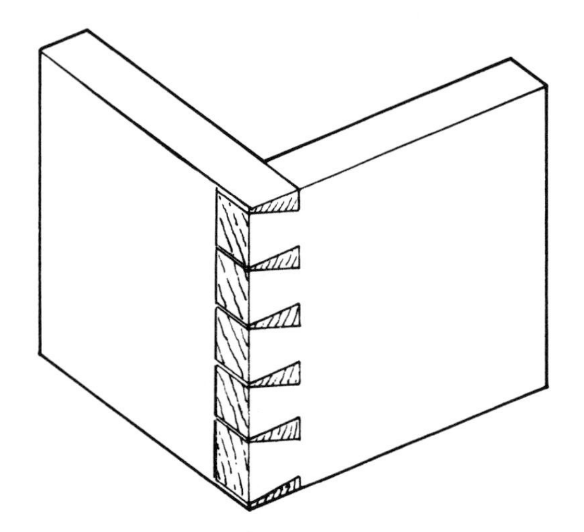

Very small pins can be stylish but they aren't as strong.

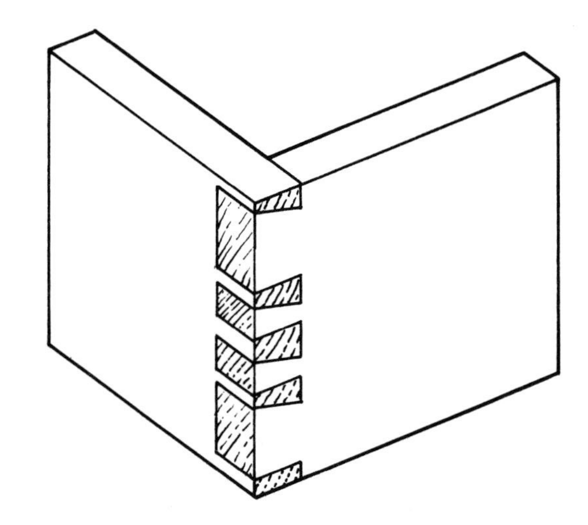

Varying the size and spacing of the pins can produce interesting visual effects.

Illus. 204. The size and spacing of the pins and tails can be varied for visual effect or greater strength.

Illus. 205. Very small pins are used when style and appearance are the foremost consideration.

left in the center. When you have cut down halfway, turn the board over, and repeat the procedure from the opposite side. When the two cuts meet, the waste will be free, and a little diamond-shaped piece will fall out (Illus. 206).

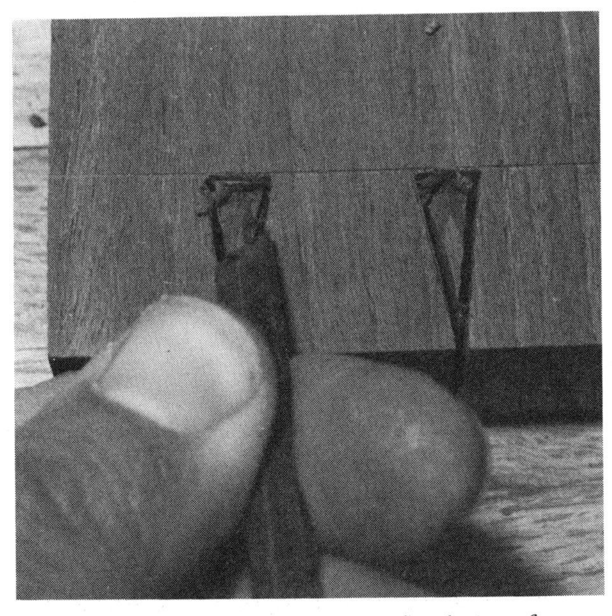

Illus. 206. You can't use the normal technique for splitting out the waste in very small pin sockets. Instead, the chisel is held on an angle.

LAYOUT TOOLS

When you expect to be doing a lot of hand layout, it pays to make a few simple layout tools to speed up the work. If you find that you use a particular angle for most of your work, you may want a dovetail gauge instead of a sliding T-bevel. You can get several commercial varieties, or you can make your own from wood or metal (Illus. 207). The advantage of using a dovetail gauge is that there is no blade that could by chance slip out of adjustment.

Illus. 207. A shopmade dovetail-angle jig such as this can help make dovetail layout faster and more accurate.

If you are making a large number of identical dovetails, you may want to make a layout template. Use the sheet aluminum that hardware stores sell for roof flashing. Use thin snips to cut it to the width of the board. Lay out the pins on the aluminum. Use the tin snips to make the side cuts, then break out the waste by bending it back and forth with a pair of pliers. Use a triangular file to smooth up everything. Once the edges are smoothed, you can use the template to lay out the pins on all of the boards. Place the template on the end of the board, and line it up carefully. Use a knife to make the marks. You will still need to use a marking gauge for the shoulder and a square to carry the lines onto the face; but, the template eliminates measuring and laying out the angle over and over again.

Another tool that you can make is a pin-spacing story stick from a scrap of wood. Lay out the stick with the proportions that you prefer. The same stick can be used for various board widths. Angle the stick so that the end marks line up with the edges of the board. Clamp a hand screw to the stick to hold the angle; then, slide the stick towards the end of the board. As each mark on the stick meets the end of the board, transfer its location to the work (Illus. 208).

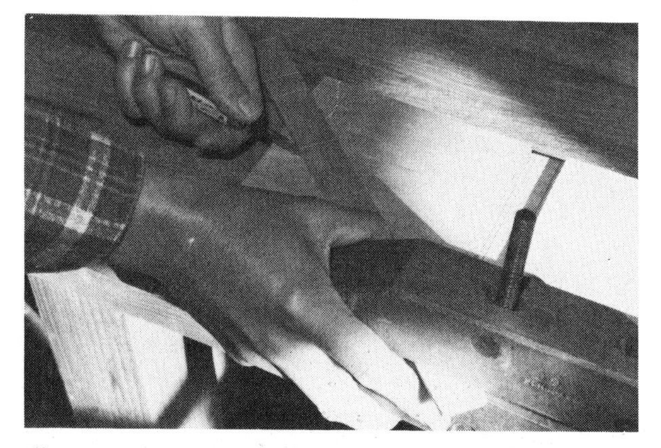

Illus. 208. A story stick can be used to mark the pin spacing. Clamping the stick at an angle permits you to use the same stick for a variety of widths. Slide the clamp along the edge of the board until the mark reaches the end; then, transfer its location to the board, and slide the stick up farther for the next mark.

Typically you would use a knife to transfer the layout, but instead you can use the saw. In this case the layout is transferred before the waste is removed. After making the first set of cuts in the tail board, place the board on its mate. Put the saw back in the kerf, and pull it backwards to make a scratch on the pin board. Repeat this in all of the kerfs. When you remove and separate the boards, the layout lines on the pin board should be clearly visible. The trick to this method is that when you cut the second set of kerfs, you can't place the saw directly on the line scratched with the saw. That would place the kerf in the good part instead of the waste, not allowing the pieces to match properly. You have to place the saw so that the kerf will be in the waste and just touching the edge of the mark left by the saw. It may help clarify this if you think of the very edge of the saw mark as the equivalent of the transfer line that you would make with a knife.

The prevailing tendency today is to lay out the dovetail joint as accurately as possible, but this was not always the case. Many early joiners preferred to eyeball the joint; they simply cut the joint with minimal layout as accurately as they could judge by eye. This was particularly true when the work needed the strength of a dovetail but didn't justify the cost of a lot of labor. An example is what is known as a rough box. When you are making a reproduction of one of these "country" pieces, you may want to use the eyeball method to make the work look more authentic. These joints aren't poorly fitting joints; they simply have variations in the size and spacing of the pins and tails. They are not wildly out of proportion either; in fact, the trained eye of an experienced joiner can produce a joint that is more aesthetically pleasing than the mechanical look of a perfect layout.

You only need to gauge a shoulder line to lay out a board for making freehand dovetails. Clamp the board that will be cut for the pins end up in a vise. Picture in your mind how you want the joint to look; then, place the saw on the end in the position that you want the first half-pin. Adjust the angle until it looks right, then saw straight down until you reach the gauged line. Repeat the process for the other half-pin.

When cutting freehand dovetails, it is a good idea to have an odd number of pins. That way you will have a pin in the middle, and it's much easier to judge the middle by eye than it is to judge an arbitrary distance. Cut the middle pin making the angles parallel to the two cuts you have already made. If there are more than three pins, then split the distance between the pins you have already cut, and cut two more pins. Continue in this manner until all of the pins are cut. The rest of the operation is just like the procedure already described. Use a chisel to remove the waste between the pins, then use the pins to lay out the tails.

Through Dovetail—Machine Techniques

Several pieces of power equipment can be used to make through dovetails or to assist in hand cutting. The band saw or the jigsaw can be used to speed up the process of cutting dovetails by hand. The result looks just like a hand-cut dovetail because you lay it out exactly as you would were you making it completely by hand. The difference is that you use the power saw to make the cuts. The table saw can be used to make dovetails with machine precision and minimal layout that can still look hand cut. The router can cut dovetails using a jig or template.

BAND SAW

To cut through dovetails on a band saw, lay out the work exactly as you would for cutting them by hand (Illus. 209). If your band-saw table will tilt in both directions, you can cut the pins without any additional equipment; but, since most band-saw tables will only tilt in one direction, you will probably need to make an auxiliary table. Make the table from plywood or particleboard. Set the saw table so it is 90° to the blade (0° on the scale); the auxiliary table will tilt 10° opposite to the table tilt. Make all of the cuts at that angle, then set the table to 20°. Make the rest of the cuts at this angle.

You can do this totally freehand or you can install a stop and fence (Illus. 210). The stop is attached to the table behind the blade. Set it so that when the end of the board butts into it, the kerf is at the correct depth. Attach the fence in the location to make the half-pin cuts; then, make spacer blocks that rest against the fence for the subsequent cuts. If you use the fence-and-stop method, you can make the cuts without layout lines.

You can use a chisel to remove the waste just as you would normally, or you can cut out the waste on the saw. To remove the waste on the saw, set the table to 90°. Place the pin board with the inside face up, and make straight cuts alongside the angled cut. Then curve in the opposite corner to remove most of the waste. Turn the board so that the blade can cut along the shoulder, and square up the cut. This will leave a small wedge of wood alongside of the pin; you can nibble it out with the saw or simply remove it with a chisel.

Lay out the tails from the pins as usual. Set the table to 90° to cut the tails. You can make the cuts freehand or you can use an angle jig. Make the jig from plywood or particleboard. The jig is a sliding auxiliary table with a key that fits in the

Illus. 209. It's hard to tell these dovetails that were cut on a band saw from similar ones cut by hand.

mitre-gauge slot. Attach a fence to the sliding table at the desired angle. You can cut out most of the waste by nibbling it out with the saw blade; if necessary you can clean up the shoulder with a chisel.

JIGSAW

The jigsaw can be used in much the same way as the band saw to power-assist in hand cutting dovetails. The difference is that the jigsaw can cut tighter into the corners, so it is easier to remove the waste. You can angle the table to cut the pins as described above for the band saw. It is more likely that the jigsaw table can tilt in both directions, so you probably won't need an auxiliary tilt table.

Another method is to leave the table square and to cut out most of the waste. Then use a chisel to pare the pins to the correct angle (Illus. 211). This method can be used on the band saw as well to avoid using the auxiliary tilt table.

TABLE SAW

The table saw can be used to make dovetails that look like they are hand cut (Illus. 212). The initial layout is done in the same manner as for hand-cut dovetails, but you only need to lay out one pin board and to transfer the layout to one tail board. This method has the precision necessary for making interchangeable parts in a production run. The technique requires an auxiliary wood fence attached to the mitre gauge. Make the fence at least 3″ tall and long enough to handle the widest board that you will be dovetailing.

Lay out one pin board just as you would for hand-cut dovetails. Set the mitre gauge to the desired angle; in this example, I'll use 80°, but it can be varied. Raise the blade to the desired shoulder depth of the pins. Place the pin board against the mitre gauge with the end against the table. With the saw turned off, line up the blade with the first cut, and clamp a stop to the mitre-gauge fence. Then, turn on the saw, and make this cut on all of the boards that need it. Turn off the saw and reposition the stop and clamp to make cuts on the next pin. With the stop clamped in this position, make the cut on all of the boards. Continue in this manner until you have cut one side of all of the pins. Then place the mitre gauge in the opposite slot. Reverse the angle setting so that it is set at 80° on the other side of the scale. Then repeat the same procedure to cut the other side of all of the pins.

You can chop out the waste between pins with a chisel or remove it on the table saw. If the space between pins is small, use the same blade, and make multiple passes between each pin to re-

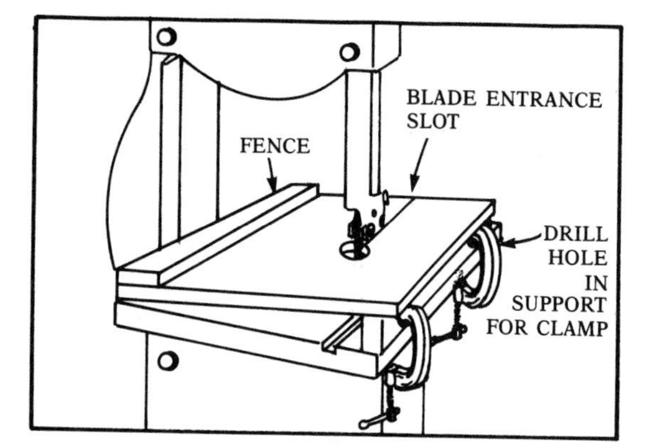

1. Make an auxiliary table for the saw to tilt 10° opposite the normal table tilt.

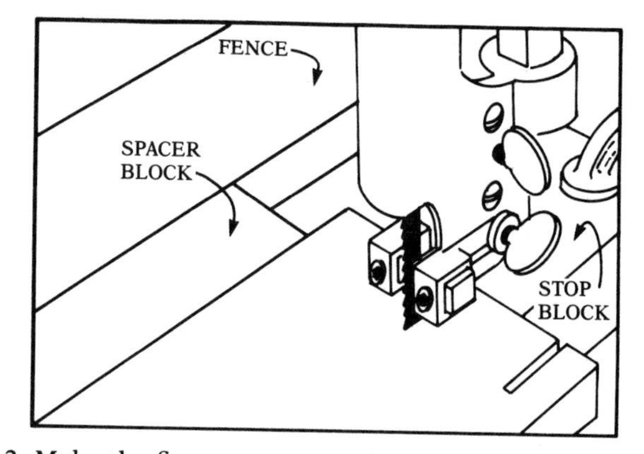

2. Make the first cut against the fence; then add spacer blocks for the next cuts. A stop block behind the blade keeps the shoulder depth constant.

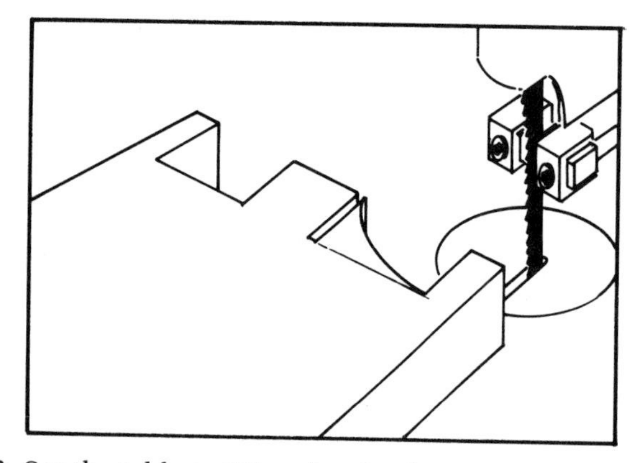

3. Set the table to 20° and make the opposite cuts; then remove the waste by making curved cuts into the corners and a straight cut along the shoulder line.

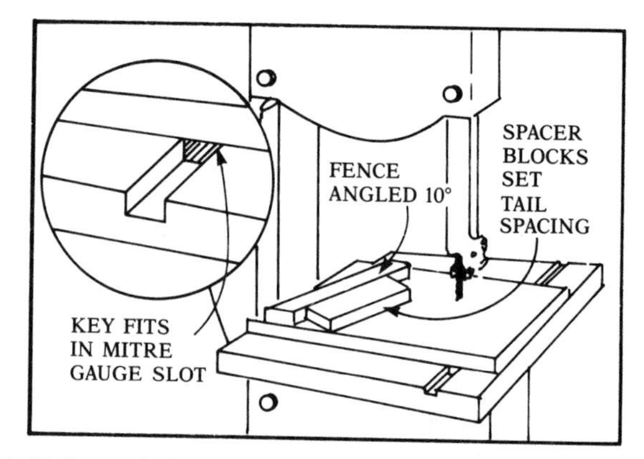

4. Make a sliding table with an angled fence to cut tails. Use spacer blocks between the fence and the work to set the tail spacing. Make half of the cuts with the work face up; then turn the board face down to cut the opposite angles.

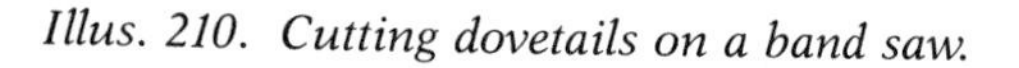

Illus. 210. Cutting dovetails on a band saw.

move the waste. It works best if you set the mitre gauge to 90° and lower the blade slightly. Then use a chisel to pare to the shoulder line. When the socket is large, use a dado blade.

After the pins are cut, transfer the layout from the pin board to the tail board in the same way that you would for hand-cut dovetails. Set the saw tilt to make the same angle cut as used for the pins. Since the tilt gauge is arranged differently from the mitre gauge, the complementary angle is used, which is 10° in this example (90 − 80 = 10). Raise the blade to the shoulder line. Clamp a stop on the mitre gauge for the first cut. Make sure that the kerf is in the waste and that you just split the layout line with the very edge of the kerf. Make all of the cuts that you can with this stop position; then, turn off the saw, and reposition the stop. Since most saws will tilt only in one direction, you may have to reverse the board to make half of the cuts.

If you use this method frequently to make dovetails of the same size, you may want to make a set of spacer blocks. Set the stop on the fence to make the cut farthest from the stop. Then add one spacer block, and make the second cut. Add the second spacer block to make the third cut, and so forth. The same set of blocks can be used to make both the pins and the tails. You can adjust the fit of the joint by placing paper shims between the blocks, if necessary.

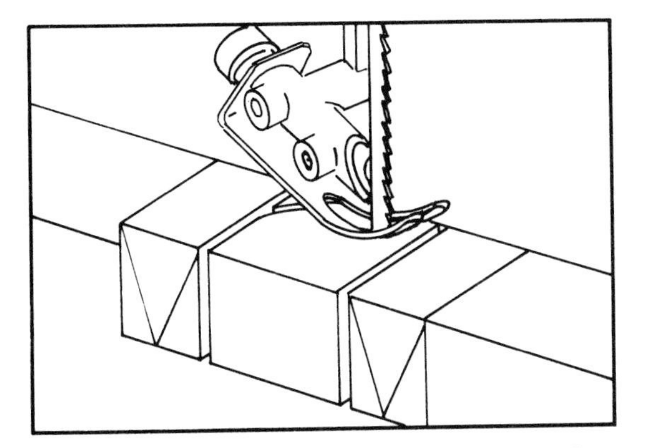

1. Remove most of the waste between pins on the jigsaw.

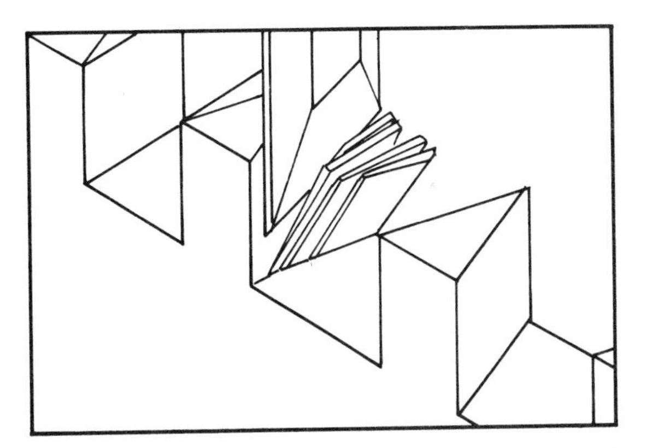

2. Use a chisel to pare the pins to the correct angle.

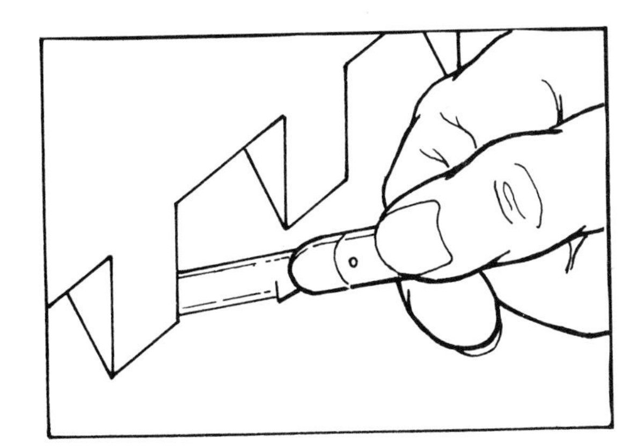

3. Mark the pin locations on the tail board.

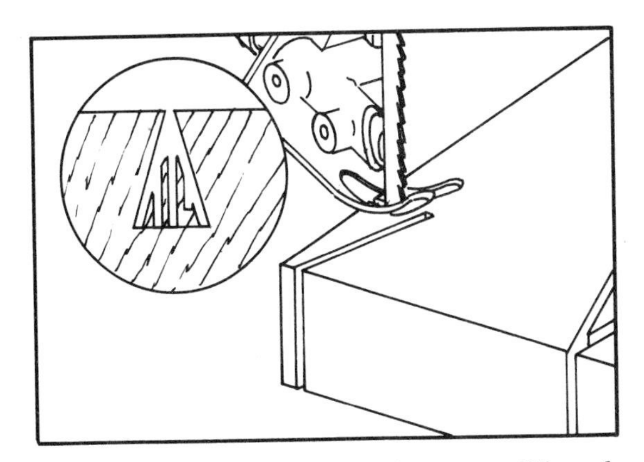

4. Cut out the tails entirely on the jigsaw. When the pin socket is small, you may need to nibble out the waste with several straight cuts.

Illus. 211. Cutting dovetails on a jigsaw.

ROUTER

The router can be used to make a variety of dovetail types. Usually a commercial template is used to guide the router. Most templates are designed to make half-blind dovetails and are typically used in drawer construction; but, there are two types that are capable of making through dovetails. Both of these jigs are fairly expensive, but they can really speed up a production run. I recommend that you make sure you have a full-face shield when you are using a router to make dovetails; chips will fly all over, and there is always the possibility that the bit may break or come out of the chuck. If the router tips or lifts, the joint will be loose, and the bit could catch and cause the router to become uncontrollable. *Exercise caution; use the full-face shield, and beware of catching the router bit. Be sure to study the owner's manuals that come with the jigs before using them.* The descriptions given here are meant to supplement the instructions provided by the manufacturer and to give you an idea of how the jigs operate before you purchase one.

The Keller jig is a set of two aluminum templates and special bits with ballbearing guides on the shaft. There are three models: the smallest one uses ¼″-shank bits; the other two are designed for heavy duty use, so the bits provided have ⅜″ or ½″ shanks. You will need a router capable of taking ½″-shank bits to use them. The

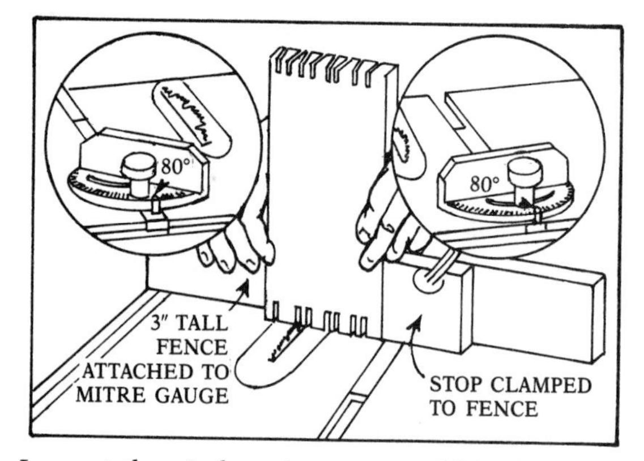

1. Lay out the pin board as you would for hand-cut dovetails. Set the mitre gauge to 80°. Attach a 3″-tall fence and clamp on a stop. Make first series of cuts; then reverse the angle on the mitre gauge and place it in the opposite slot.

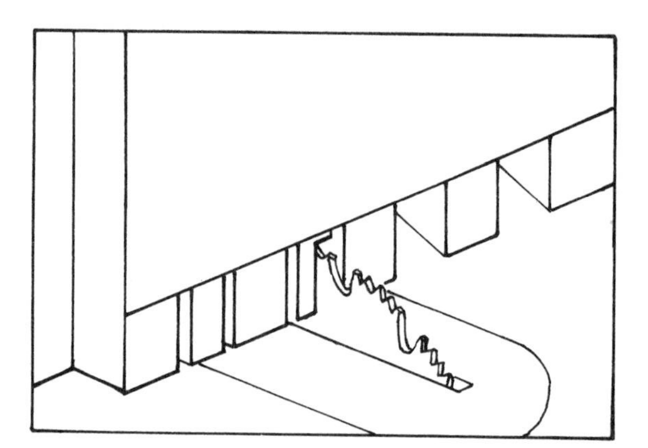

2. Set mitre gauge to 90° to remove the waste between pins.

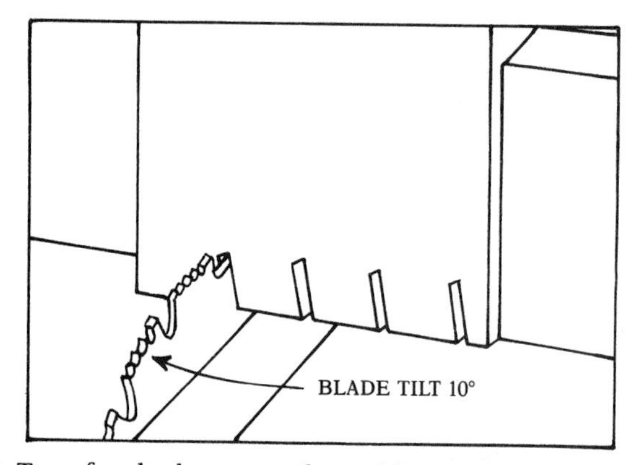

3. Transfer the layout to the tail board. Set the blade tilt to 10°. Use the 3″-tall fence attached to the mitre gauge and clamp on a stop for the tail cuts. Set mitre gauge to 90°. Reverse the board to make the second series of cuts.

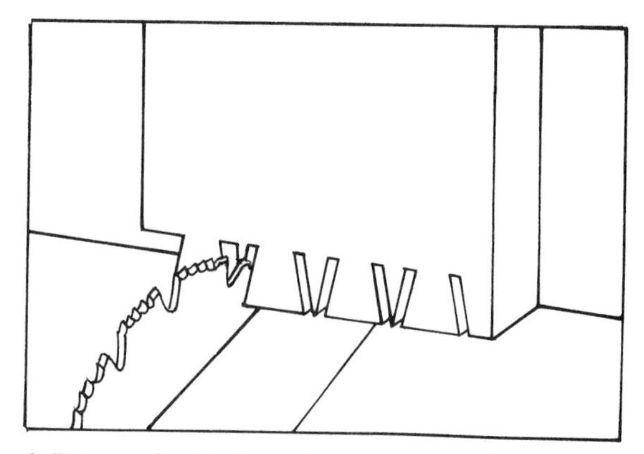

4. Return the blade to 90° to remove the waste between tails.

Illus. 212. Cutting dovetails on a table saw.

small template cuts 7° dovetails with 1⅛" pin spacing. The medium-sized jig cuts 7° dovetails with 1¾" pin spacing. The third template is designed to cut large 14° dovetails with 1" pins that are spaced 3" apart. The stock can be up to ⅞" thick. The largest jig can make a joint 36" long without repositioning. In particular, this is a good size for carcass joints, and, naturally, that is the main application of this jig. It can be used for making boxes, trunks, cabinet carcasses, etc. The smaller jigs can be used for drawers, small boxes, etc. Each of these jigs must be mounted to a wood fence before it can be used. The bit can damage the template and could break, possibly causing personal injury, if it comes in contact with the template; so, keep the router base flat against the template at all times.

The size of the tails is determined both by the bit and by the jig. The fit of the joint is adjusted on the pin template. The initial adjustment is determined by making a test joint and by moving the pin template in or out on the backing board until the desired fit is achieved. Once the template screws are tightened, you can use the same setting over and over without readjustment; this is one of the virtues of the Keller jig. After the initial setup, there is practically no setup required; just clamp the template to the board, and go to work.

The tails are cut first using the template with straight slots. Clamp it to the tail board, and align it so that you will get a half-pin at each end; this may require making the half-pins larger than the rest of the pins (Illus. 213). Chuck the dovetail bit into the router. The bit has a ballbearing collar on the shaft; this collar rides against the template and guides the cut. Adjust the depth of cut for the thickness of the stock, and make sure that the collar is lined up with the template. Align the bit with the first slot, and then start the router. Be sure to keep the router flat against the jig, and don't try to feed too fast (Illus. 214).

To cut the pins, transfer the pin locations from the tail board. You don't need to mark them all, just one or two at each end. Clamp the template that has the dovetail-shaped openings to the pin board (Illus. 215). Insert the straight bit in the router chuck, and make sure that it is tight. Set the depth of cut for the stock thickness, and

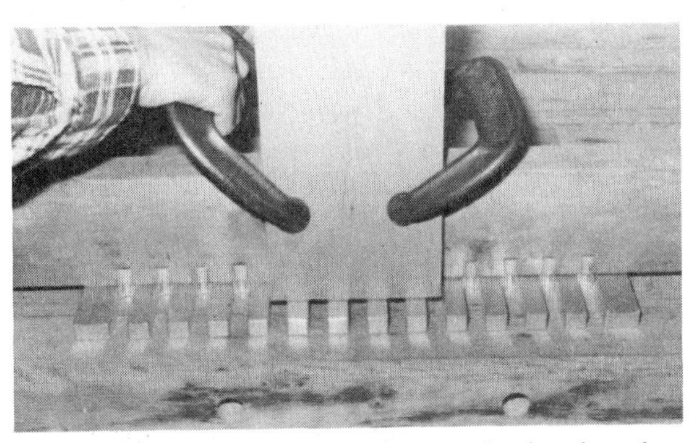

Illus. 213. The Keller jig attaches to a backup board. The backup board is clamped to the work.

Illus. 214. The straight slot template and dovetail bit are used to cut the tails. Notice how the ball-bearing collar on the bit follows the template.

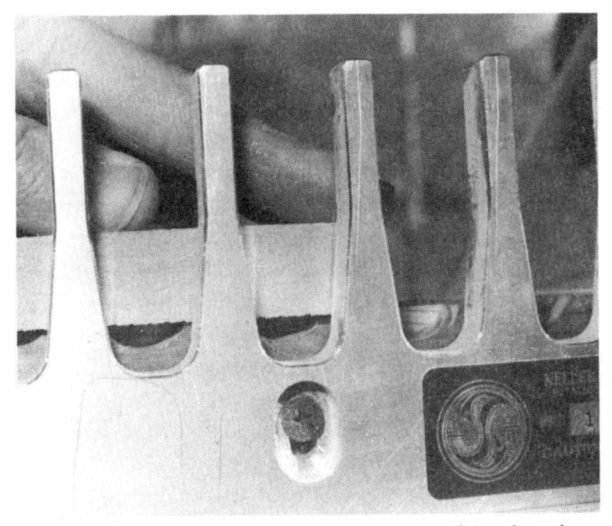

Illus. 215. Line up the marks on the pin board with the pin template, and clamp in place.

make sure that the ballbearing collar rides against the jig. Place the bit in the first opening, and then start the router. Keep the base of the router flat on the template as you remove the waste between the pins. Cut all of the pins using the same method (Illus. 216).

You can make the joint tighter or looser by adjusting the pin template fence. If you set the fence to make a tight joint, you can still loosen the fit when necessary by applying masking tape to the fence to shim it away from the pin board. Thicker stock up to 1½" thick can be joined using this template if you cut a rabbet on the pin board. When you are going to be dovetailing several boards that are the same size, you can attach a stop to the fence on the templates to align with the edge of the board; that way you don't need to transfer the pin locations. The wood fences act as backup boards to keep the wood from chipping as the bit exits. After awhile, the fence may need to be replaced to provide a good backup because the cuts in the fence will become enlarged with use. This jig is at its best when used for mass-producing uniform dovetails. It can be used to achieve variable spacing by shifting the template between cuts; but, you then lose the speed and positive alignment that makes this jig so convenient to use.

The Leigh dovetail jig has the advantage of being completely adjustable (Illus. 217). You can have the same degree of control over pin size and spacing that you have with hand-cut dovetails. The initial setup can be time consuming, however, because you adjust a separate finger for each cut; but, once set up, you can mass-produce parts quickly. Like the Keller jig, two bits are used, and the pins and tails are cut independently. The Leigh jig automatically aligns the pins and tails, so there is no layout necessary.

The Leigh jig is available in two models: the 12" model is designed for smaller work such as drawers and small boxes; the 24" model is the most versatile. The 24" jig can be used for small and large work. The Leigh jigs can also be used to cut other joints besides dovetails. Both ¼"-shank and ½"-shank bits are available. An instructional video is also available from Leigh Industries Ltd. to supplement the printed instructions. This makes it that much easier to learn the operation of the jig.

Once you have made the initial setup, clamp

Illus. 216. The straight bit is used to cut the pins.

the tail board to the front of the jig. Set the fingers to the TD (through dovetail) tail setting; this puts the straight fingers over the end of the board. Install the template-following collar on the router base, and chuck the dovetail bit into the router (Illus. 218). Adjust the depth of cut to allow about a 1/64" cleanup allowance. After cutting the tails, replace the dovetail bit with the straight bit. Clamp the pin board to the front of the jig. Rotate the finger assembly to the TD pin setting; this places the tapered fingers over the end of the board. Follow the fingers with the collar on the base of the router (Illus. 219).

When you are making the initial setup, use scrap wood to make a test joint. Some trial-and-

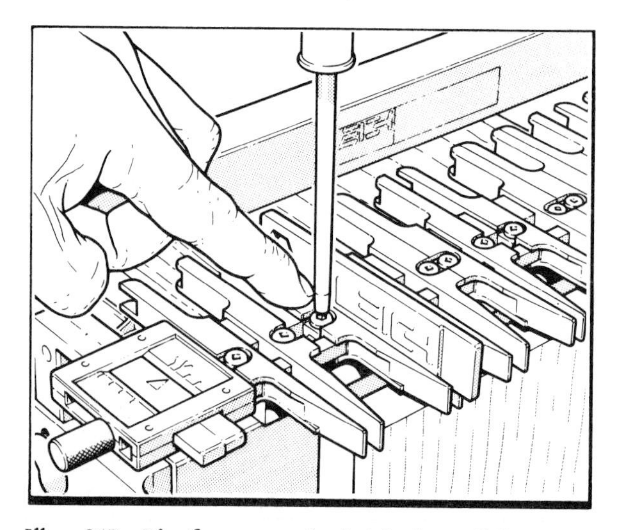

Illus. 217. The fingers on the Leigh dovetail jig are adjustable, so you can vary the size and spacing however you want. (Drawing courtesy Leigh Industries Ltd.)

Illus. 218. The tails are cut using a dovetail bit together with the straight fingers.

error adjustments are usually necessary to get a good fit. If you have trouble with splintering when the bit exits the wood, try a procedure called back routing. Back routing reverses the normal feed direction of the router. Because the bit can grab and jerk the router out of control, care must be used when back routing; keep the cut light, and never back rout on end grain, as would be the case in cutting half-blind dovetails. Begin back routing by making a light cut from right to left across the front of the board between the two guide fingers. Then, cut through the board with the collar against the right guide finger. With the cutter behind the board, take a light cut from left to right. Cut out to the front again with the collar against the left guide finger. Then, remove the waste by working the router back and forth.

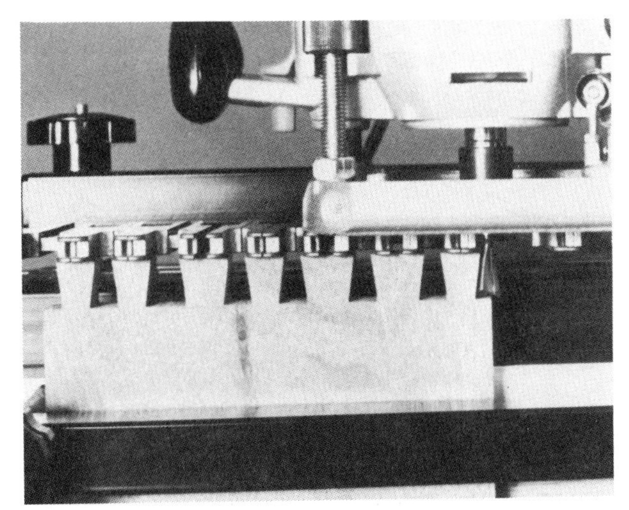

Illus. 219. To cut the pins, rotate the finger assembly so that the angled fingers face out, and use a straight bit.

The router table can be used to make through dovetail joints (Illus. 220). Chuck a dovetail bit in the router, and attach the router to the router table.

The pins are cut with the pin board outside faceup on the table. Adjust the fence to act as a depth stop. Clamp an auxiliary fence to the table at a right angle to the standard fence. This auxiliary fence is used to set the spacing for the pins. Cut a set of spacer blocks that are the width of the desired pin spacing. With the pin board

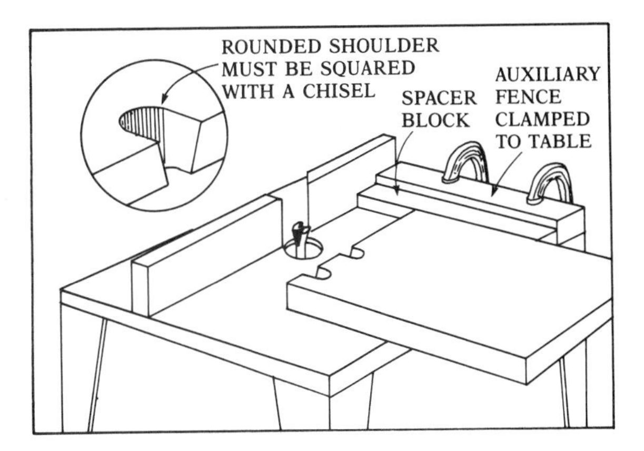

1. To cut the pins, attach an auxiliary fence at a right angle to the original fence. Use spacer blocks between the fence and the work to space the cuts. Place the pin board outside face up on the table.

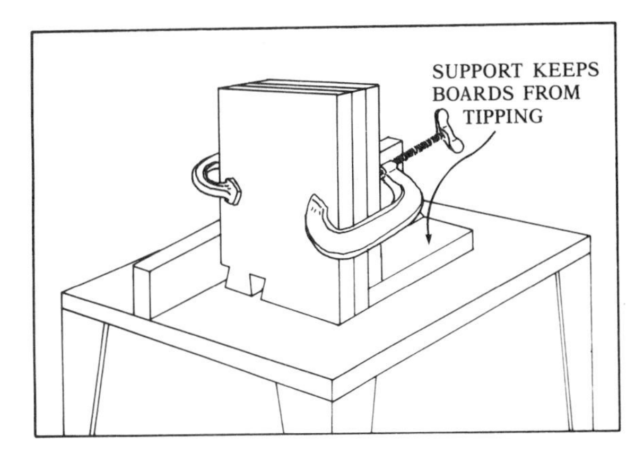

2. Several tail boards can be cut at once. Clamp them to an L-shaped support. Use the fence to position the cut.

Illus. 220. Cutting dovetails using a router table.

faceup on the table, align the edge with the auxiliary fence, and make the first cut, pushing the board into the bit until you reach the fence in back of the bit. Make all of the cuts that require this setup; then, place the first spacer block against the auxiliary fence, and make the next cut. Proceed in this manner until all of the pins are cut. The shoulder will need to be squared up with a chisel, of course, because the router leaves a round cut.

Transfer the layout of the pins to one of the tail boards. This board will be used to position the fence for cutting the tails. You can actually clamp several tail boards together, and cut all of the tails at once. Clamp a backup board behind the last board to prevent splintering. Make an L-shaped support block to keep the boards square with the table, and clamp it to the backup board. Set the fence on the router table to position the first cut, and place the tail boards with their ends against the table and the edges against the fence. Use the L-shaped support to push the boards, and make the cut. Reposition the fence, and make the next cut. If the pins are wide, you may need to make an additional pass to clean out the waste between cuts.

Dealing with Rabbets and Grooves

Special procedures are needed when the parts being dovetailed are rabbeted or grooved (Illus. 221). If you make the dovetails in the normal way, the end of the rabbet or groove will show. The simplest solution for rabbets is not to cut the rabbet first, but to wait until the parts are assembled, and then make the rabbet with a router and rabbeting bit. This method won't work for grooves, however, and it's difficult if you are using only hand tools. One solution is to make a square finger on the tail board that will fill the rabbet or groove. You don't need to do anything special to the pin board. If you would rather have the square finger be the same length as the tails, then cut a notch in the pin board.

MITRED HALF-PIN

A mitred half-pin can be used to conceal the rabbet or groove. It also makes an attractive edge finish even if there isn't a rabbet or groove. If you want to shape the edge, the mitred half-pin eliminates end grain in the shaped edge (Illus. 222).

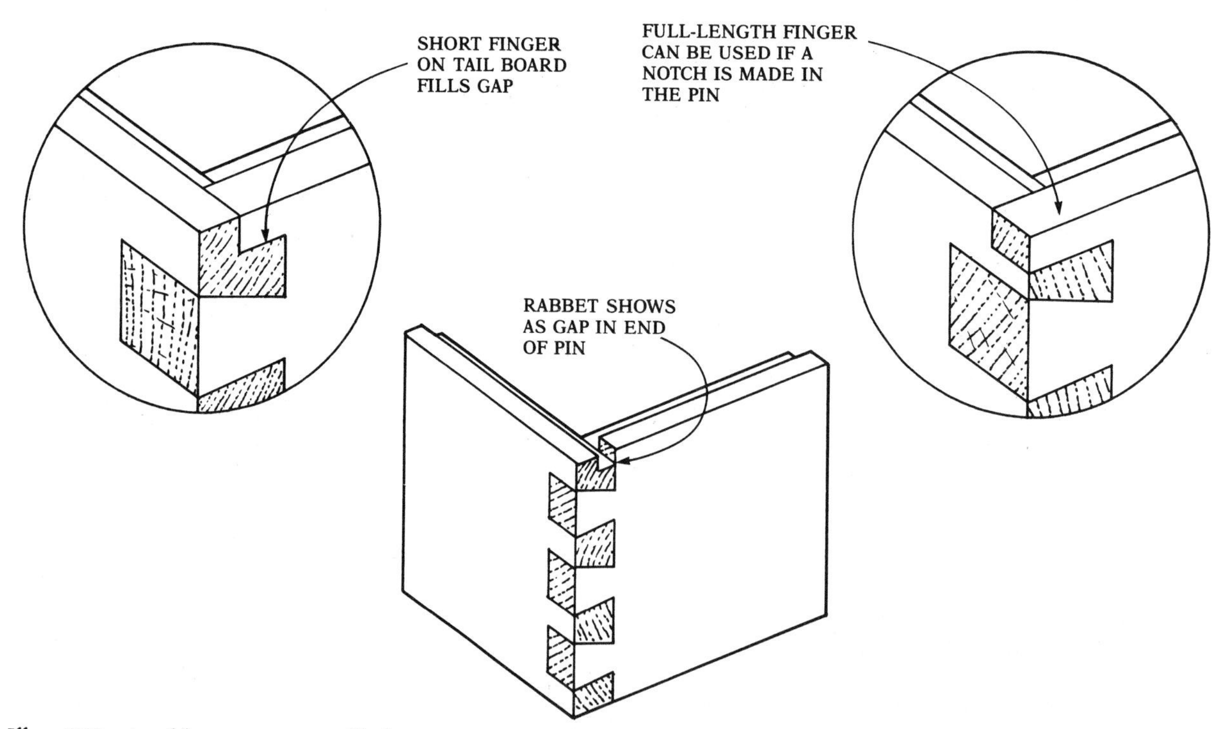

Illus. 221. A rabbet or groove will show as a gap in the end of the pin unless special procedures are used.

To make the joint, lay out and cut the pins as usual. Next, transfer the layout to the tail board as usual; then, make a mitre cut in the socket for the half-pin. Cut the tails as usual except for the one next to the half-pin socket. Hold the saw at a 45° angle, and stop the cut when you reach the mitre cut. Finally, cut the end of the half-pin off at a 45° angle.

You can mitre one or both half-pins. You can use the alternate joint in Illus. 223. In this case, the half-pin is cut straight instead of angled. The rest of the procedure is the same.

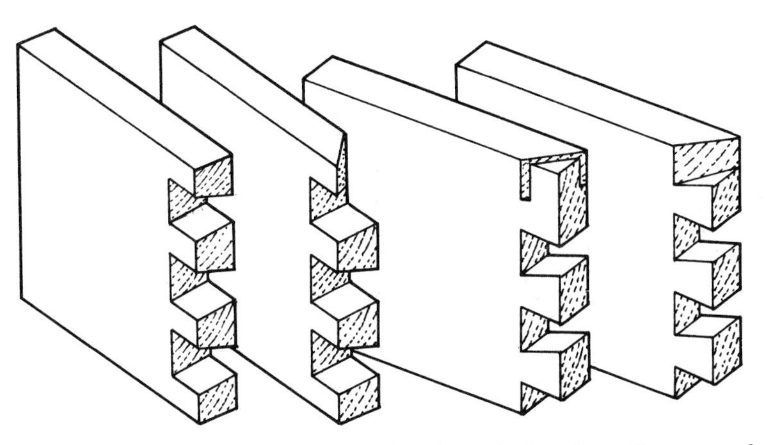

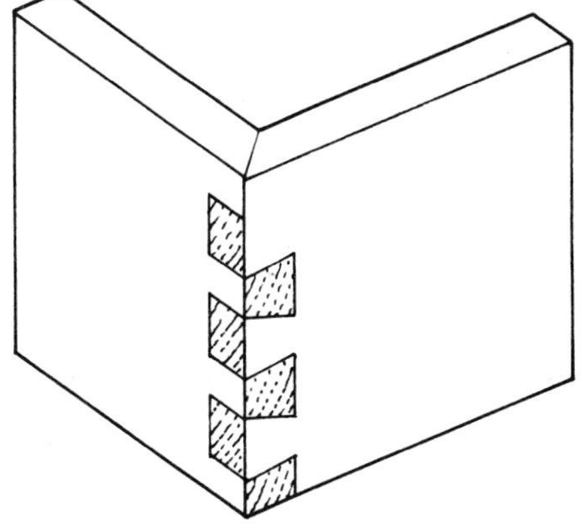

Step 1. Cut the pin board as usual and use it to lay out the tail board; then cut off the half-pin at 45°.

Step 2. Cut the tails as usual except for the half-pin socket. First make a mitre cut down to the layout lines of the tail. Next, saw in from the corner to remove the waste.

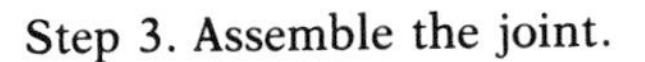

Step 3. Assemble the joint.

Illus. 222. Mitred half-pin step by step.

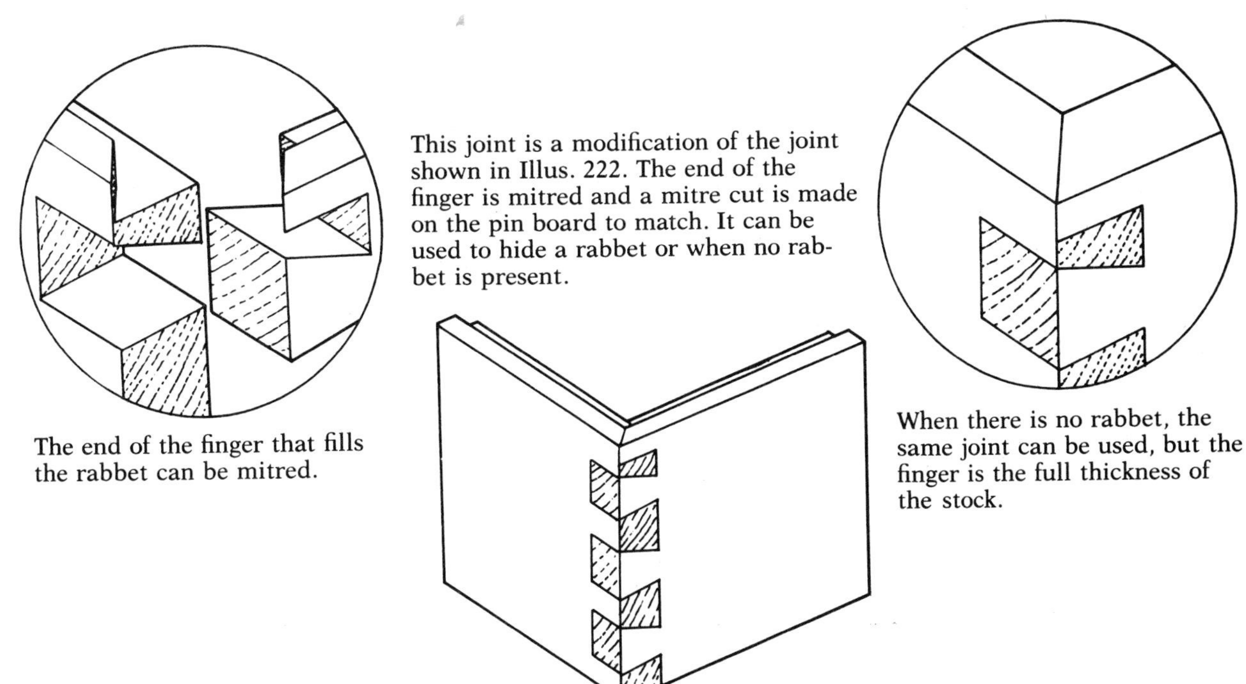

The end of the finger that fills the rabbet can be mitred.

This joint is a modification of the joint shown in Illus. 222. The end of the finger is mitred and a mitre cut is made on the pin board to match. It can be used to hide a rabbet or when no rabbet is present.

When there is no rabbet, the same joint can be used, but the finger is the full thickness of the stock.

Illus. 223. Mitred half-pin variations.

Half-Blind Dovetails

When you don't want the end grain of the tails to show, you can use a half-blind dovetail (Illus. 224). This joint is also called a lapped dovetail. They are often used in drawer construction and are also useful in carcass construction. Half-blind dovetails can be used to join boards that are of different thicknesses; this is usually the case in the construction of a drawer where the front will be thicker than the sides.

Illus. 224. The half-blind or lapped dovetail is used to hide the end grain of the tails.

HAND-CUT HALF-BLIND DOVETAILS

The layout for hand-cut half-blind dovetails is very similar to the layout for through dovetails (Illus. 225). Set the marking gauge to two-thirds of the thickness of the pin board. Gauge a line on the end of the pin board with the gauge fence against the inside face. With the same setting, gauge the shoulder lines on the tail board. Next, set the marking gauge to the thickness of the tail board, and mark the shoulder on the pin board. Lay out the joint as described above for through dovetails. If the sockets between the tails will be large enough for you to get a marking knife between the tails, you can cut the tails first; but, if the pins are going to be small, it is still easier to make the pins first, and mark the tails from them.

Once you've laid out the pins, the first step is to make the saw kerfs. To avoid leaving a kerf in the face of the board, the saw must be held at an angle. This leaves the lower part of the pin uncut, but you take care of that with a chisel. The process is similar to making a through dovetail, but you only work from one side. Cut along the shoulder line with the edge of the chisel. Then chop out the waste with the chisel, stopping at the gauged line. Carefully pare to the line to make the final cut.

Next, place the pin board on the tail board, and mark the location of the tails with a knife. The tails are cut exactly as described in Chapter 2 for through dovetails.

The procedure is basically the same when you cut the tails first; just transfer the layout from the tail board to the pin board with a knife, then cut the pins as described above.

Drawer fronts are often rabbeted on the edges to make a lip that overhangs the face frame. Dovetailing a rabbeted drawer is similar to the procedure already described, but make the rabbet first. The pins are then laid out and cut as before.

HALF-BLIND DOVETAILS WITH A ROUTER

The router can assist in making hand-cut-style half-blind dovetails, or can be used to make machine-style half-blind dovetails, by utilizing a template guide. The router can remove most of the waste between the pins for a hand-cut-style joint. The layout is the same, but the router is used instead of a saw and chisel for removing the waste. Clamp the pin board in a vise with a wide backup board. The board will help support the router base. Set the router depth to the shoulder depth of the pins. Attach a stop block to the backup board so that the router base will hit it just when the cut should stop. Use the router to cut out most of the waste; but leave a little around the pins to allow you to pare away the waste, bringing the pins to final size.

The router jig most commonly used for half-blind dovetails uses interchangeable finger templates to make several styles of joints (Illus. 226). The pins and tails are cut in a single operation, and all alignment is automatically taken care of by the jig. This is by far the fastest way to make dovetail joints. Most jigs can handle flush, offset, and rabbeted joints (Illus. 227). The initial setup and adjustment can vary depending on the manufacturer, but they all operate essentially in the same way. The pin board is placed under the finger template, on top of the jig, with the inside face of the pin board up. The tail board is placed on the front of the jig with its inside face out. Adjustable guides offset the tail board so that the tails and pins line up for the cut. A template-following collar is used on the router base, and a dovetail bit makes the cut. Since the pin board acts as a backup to the tail board, there is very little splintering.

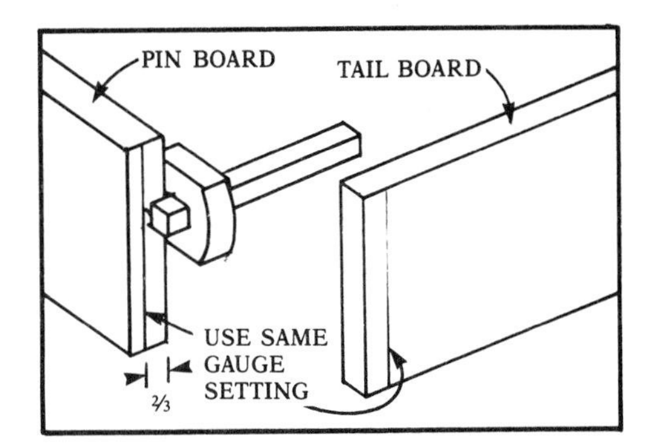

1. To lay out the joint, set the marking gauge to ⅔ of the thickness of the pin board. Use this to mark the stop cut on the pin board and the shoulder of the tails.

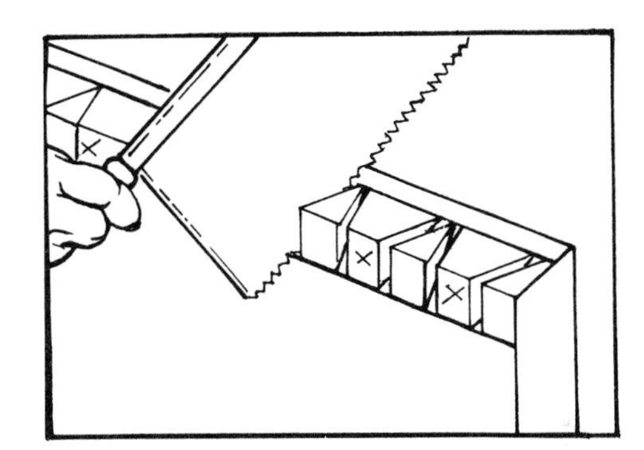

2. Hold the saw at an angle and cut in from the corner until you reach the layout lines.

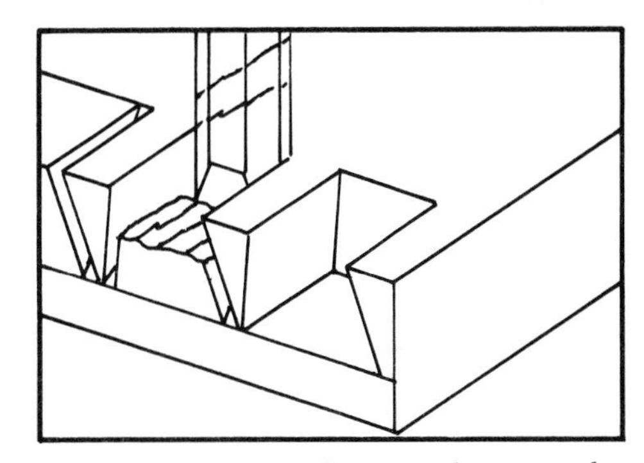

3. Use a chisel to remove the waste between the pins.

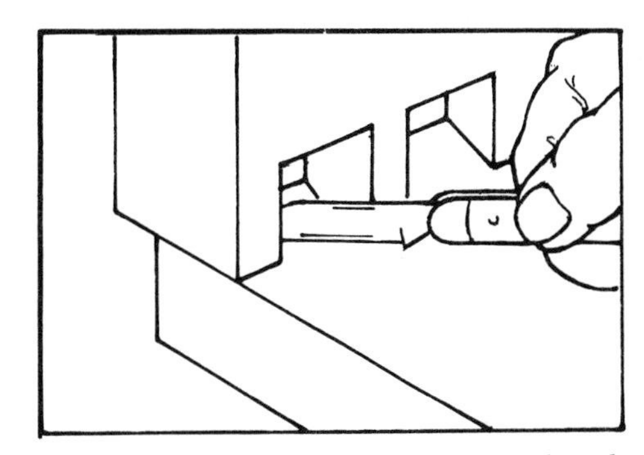

4. Line up the inside edge of the pin board with the shoulder line on the tail board to mark the tails. Cut the tails as usual.

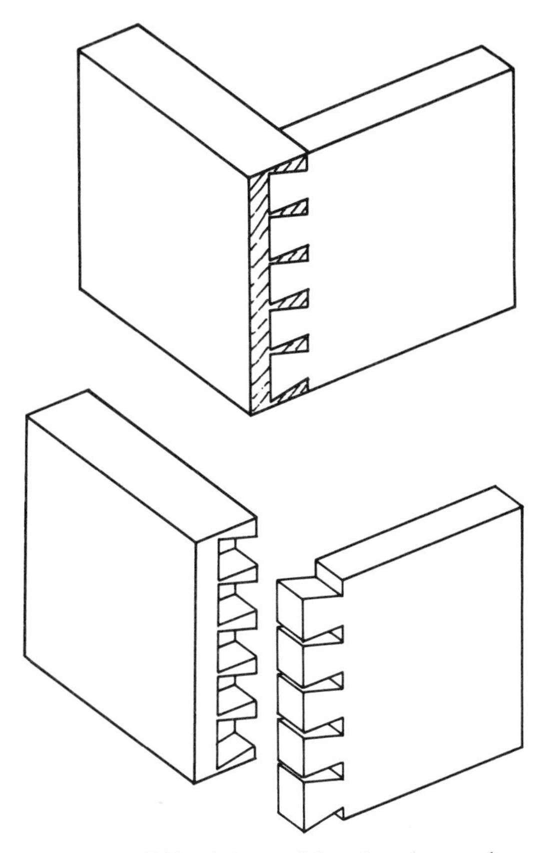

Illus. 225. Half-blind dovetail hand-tool procedure.

Place the router base on the template before turning on the router. The base must be flat against the template throughout the cut or the joint will not fit correctly. You will get a smoother cut with even less splintering if you make a very shallow cut across the board, just touching the ends of the fingers on the template, before you begin following the template. Next, guide the router into the first slot. A reminder once again: keep the base flat against the template, and also make sure that the bushing rubs against the template as you clean out the waste. Follow around the rounded end of the template finger and into the next slot. Never lift the router while it is on the template because the bit will cut into the template and ruin it. Before removing the boards, inspect the joint; if wood chips were collecting in the template as you worked, some of the sockets may be too shallow. If you find a socket that needs to be deeper, remove the dust and chips from the template, and cut that socket again.

The fit of the joint is controlled by the depth setting on the router. Lowering the bit tightens the joint, and raising the bit loosens the joint. Make a test joint and adjust the bit until you are satisfied with the fit; then, make a gauge block so that you can easily set the router depth each time you use the jig. The gauge block is simply a scrap of wood with a rabbet cut in the edge. The guide bushing on the router will prevent the bit from making the rabbet, so make a shallow rabbet on the board first. Then, deepen the rabbet with the dovetail bit set at the final depth setting from the test joint. Now you can return the router to the correct depth setting every time you use it by placing the gauge block on the router base and then adjusting the depth of cut setting until the bit just touches the bottom of the rabbet.

Illus. 226. This type of router jig cuts pins and tails in a single operation.

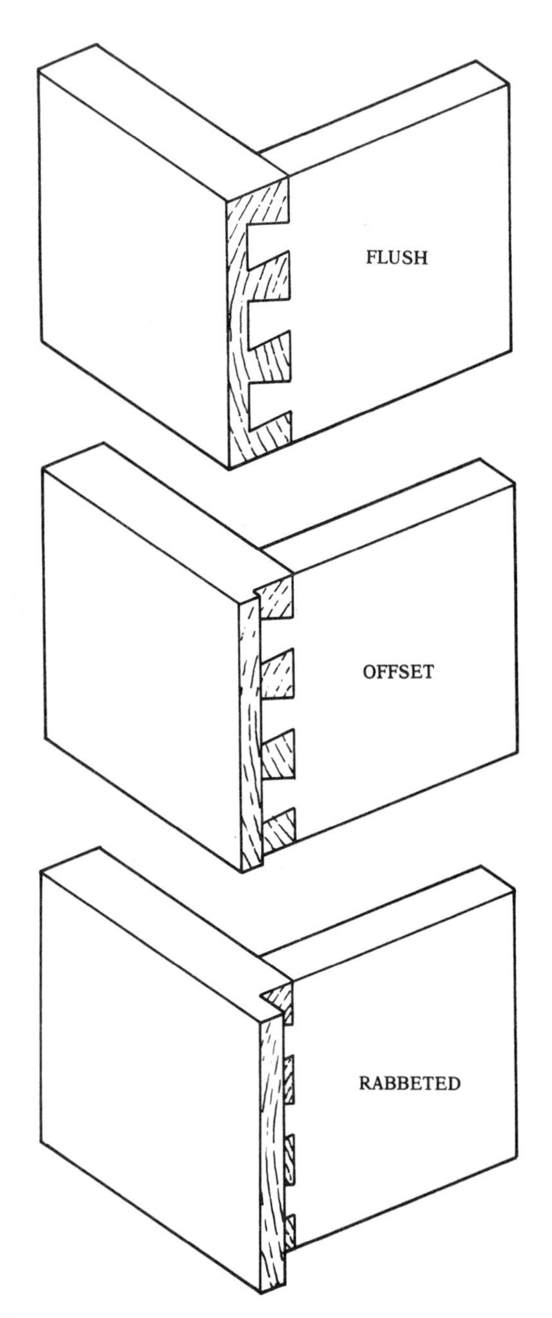

Illus. 227. Drawer fronts can be flush, offset, or rabbeted.

If the face of the tail board isn't flush with the end of the pin board, adjust the depth setting on the jig. This may take some trial and error; but, once it is set, you won't need to change the depth setting as long as you use boards of the same thickness.

The joint produced has the unmistakable look of a machine-cut dovetail (Illus. 228). If you would like the joint to look more like a hand-cut dovetail, for some jigs you can get a special template. This template will produce a joint that has the approximate proportions of a hand-cut dovetail, except that they are reversed: the tails are narrow, and the pins are wide (Illus. 229 and 230). The procedure is similar to that just described above. The joint looks better if it is symmetrical about the middle. The template has positioning marks to help you align the pin board in relation to the middle of the joint. A locating bracket is then positioned next to the edge of the pin board to align the tail board. A special technique is helpful for removing the large waste area on the tail board; follow the pattern shown in Illus. 231. You can minimize splintering by making a light cut across the front before you follow the template.

Illus. 228. The equal size and spacing of this joint have the unmistakable look of a machine-cut dovetail.

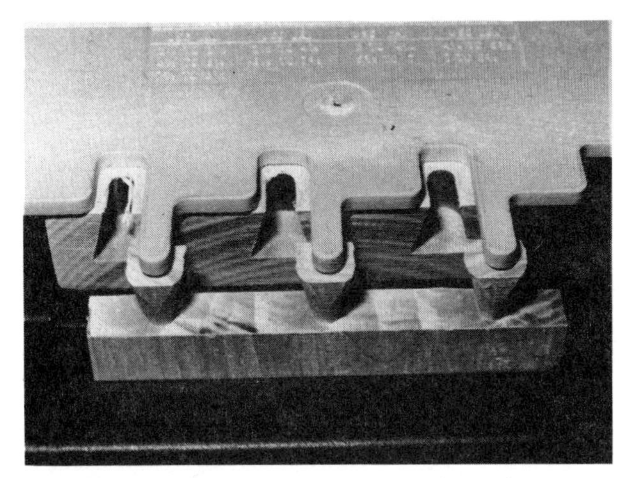

Illus. 229. This jig, sold by Sears, produces the approximate proportions of a hand-cut joint; but, the tails are narrow, and the pins are wide.

Illus. 230. To the casual observer, this joint will appear more like a hand-cut joint than the type traditionally made with a half-blind dovetail template.

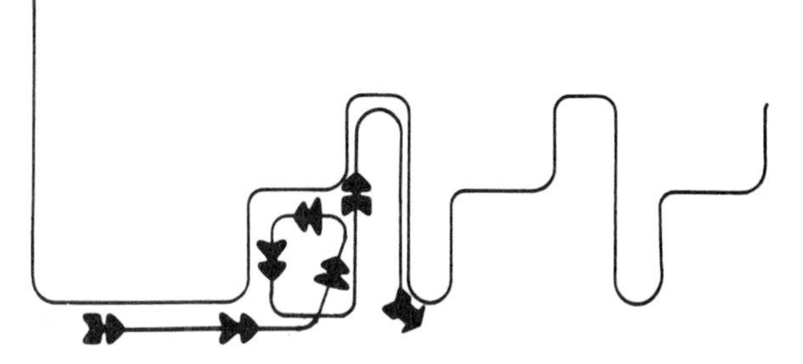

Illus. 231. Move the router in the direction indicated by the arrows to get a clean splinter-free cut.

The Leigh jig can also be used to make half-blind dovetails. The procedure is more time consuming than the jig above, but you can set the pin size and spacing in any way that you want (Illus. 232 and 233).

Illus. 232. The Leigh jig can be used to make half-blind dovetails that closely resemble a hand-cut joint.

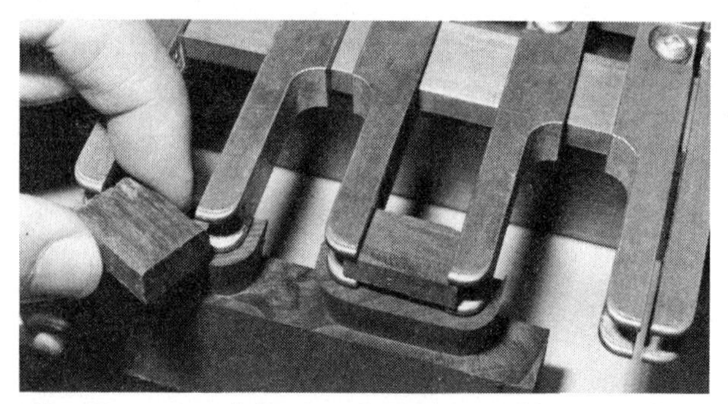

Illus. 233. Small blocks of wood placed between the fingers of the Leigh jig guide the router for the cut along the inside of the tails; this is necessary when making half-blind joints with the router.

Full-Blind Dovetails

When you need the strength of a dovetail but you don't want the joint to show, you can use a full-blind dovetail. They are also called secret dovetails, or, simply, blind dovetails. There are two types of blind dovetails, double-lap and mitred. Both are similar in construction.

The double-lap blind dovetail can have the projecting lap on either the tail board or the pin board (Illus. 234). Begin by cutting a rabbet on the end of the board with the projecting lap. For this example, let's make it the pin board. Next, lay out the pins on the board. Make the pins a little larger than usual; this will make the job of cutting the tails easier. If you prefer, the pins and tails can be about the same size; the main reason for making small pins is appearance, and since this is a blind joint, you might as well design it for maximum strength. Since the rabbet will interfere with the blade of the sliding T-bevel, it is easier to use a template to mark the pins. You can use a commercial type or make one from wood or sheet metal. Butt the end of the template up against the rabbet, and use a knife to make the marks.

The procedure for cutting the pins is the same as it is for making a half-blind dovetail on a rabbeted drawer front. When the pins are complete, transfer the layout to the tail board with a knife. The main difference from the half-blind dovetail procedure comes when cutting the tails; you can cut them in the same way as you cut the pins, by holding the saw on an angle and then by chopping out the waste with a chisel. If you made the pins large, you won't have any trouble removing

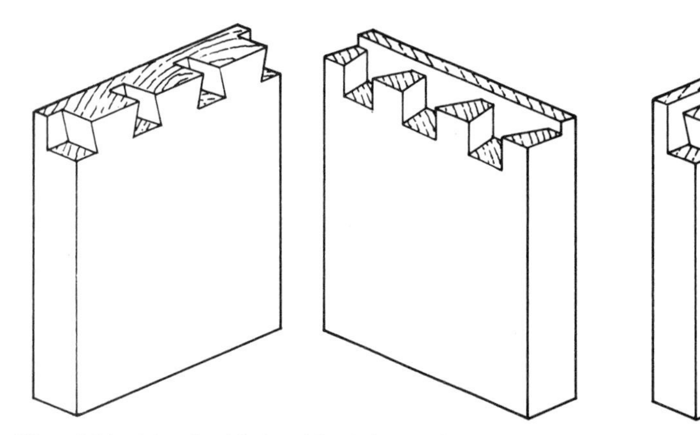

Illus. 234. The double-lap blind dovetail can have the projecting lap on either the tail board or the pin board.

the waste from between the tails. Dry-assemble the joint, and drive it all the way home. In this case, you need to know that the joint will pull tight before you apply the glue.

The mitred blind dovetail completely hides the end grain. It is made in much the same way as the lapped version (Illus. 235). Start by cutting a rabbet on the ends of both boards. Next, cut mitres on the edges. Cut down about ¼"; then, cut in from the corner, and remove the waste. Lay out and cut the pins as described above. Mark the tails using the pin board and cut them also in the same manner as described for the lapped blind dovetail. Finally, the end of the rabbet is cut off at 45°. You can use a chisel to cut this mitre or you can plane it off. In either case, work from both edges toward the middle to avoid splitting off a chip at the edge.

You can use power equipment to assist in making both types of blind dovetail. The table saw can be used both to cut the rabbets and to mitre the end of the rabbet. A router can be used to clean out the waste between pins and tails. Clamp the board in a vise with a wide board behind it to support the router base. Attach a stop block to the backup board to stop the router base when you reach the end of the cut. Clean out most, but not all, of the waste with the router; then, pare to the line with a chisel.

Correcting Defects in Dovetail Joints

No matter how hard you try for perfection, occasionally you will come up with a joint that just doesn't fit right. There are a few tricks that you can use short of starting over.

A joint that is too tight is the easiest to correct because you can pare off a little bit with the chisel or file, but be sure that you carefully mark where to remove the wood; if the pins and tails are properly aligned but just tight, take small but equal amounts off each side. Sometimes all

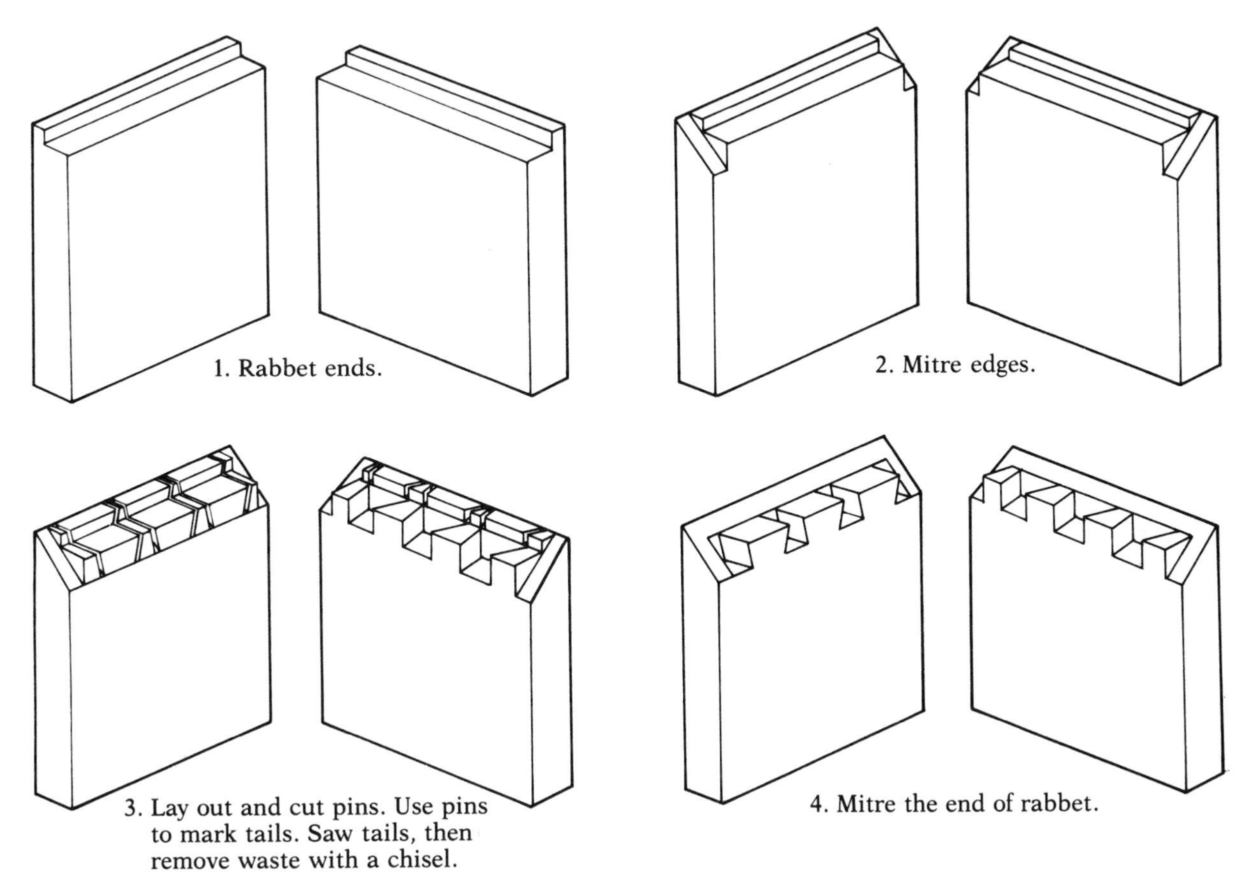

Illus. 235. Mitred blind dovetail step by step.

of the pins and tails line up except one; then, you will need to do all of your paring on one side of that particular part. If you get confused, however, about where to remove the wood, you can end up making the problem worse instead of better; if the parts are badly out of alignment, you can end up with a gap in the joint after you meant to pare them to fit.

Gaps in the joint will detract from the strength as well as the appearance. When the gap is small, try tapping the end grain with a steel hammer while the glue is still wet. This will make the end mushroom and fill the gap if it works. The hammer marks are removed when the ends are trimmed flush with the sides. If the gap is too large to fix with a hammer, insert a piece of veneer (Illus. 236). If you carefully choose the veneer to match the wood, this repair can be almost invisible. For a perfect match, take a plane shaving off the part you are repairing. Cut the veneer in a triangular shape so that the grain will run the same way as the pin when the triangular piece is inserted. If the gap is a little thinner than the veneer, place the veneer on the steel anvil of a vise, and pound it with a steel hammer; this will thin the veneer by compressing the fibres. When the glue soaks into the veneer, the veneer will expand to make a very tight joint. Slip the veneer into the gap while the glue in the joint is still wet, but don't apply any glue to the veneer itself, or it will swell before you can get it into the joint. When the veneer is too thick to slip into the gap, you can widen the gap by sawing a kerf along the joint line; then, insert the veneer. Trim off the excess veneer after the glue is dry, and sand the joint flush.

Sometimes one board will have a slight cup that makes it difficult to transfer the marks from the pin board to the tail board. To correct this, first clamp the board to a straight board while you complete the marking. Then, when you assemble the joint, it will also allow you to pull the cupping out of the board with clamps.

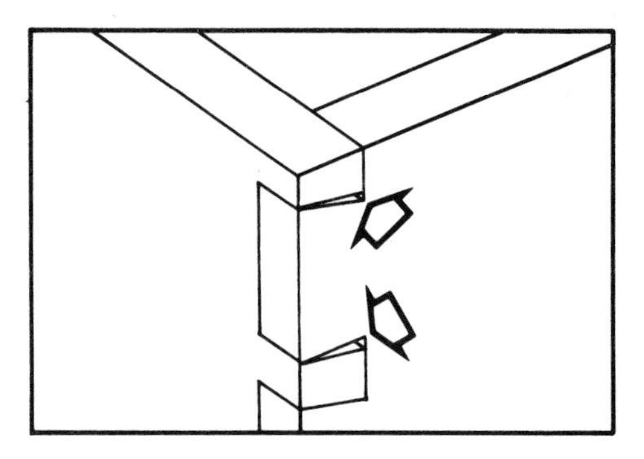

1. This joint has gaps caused by a variation in angle between the pin and tail.

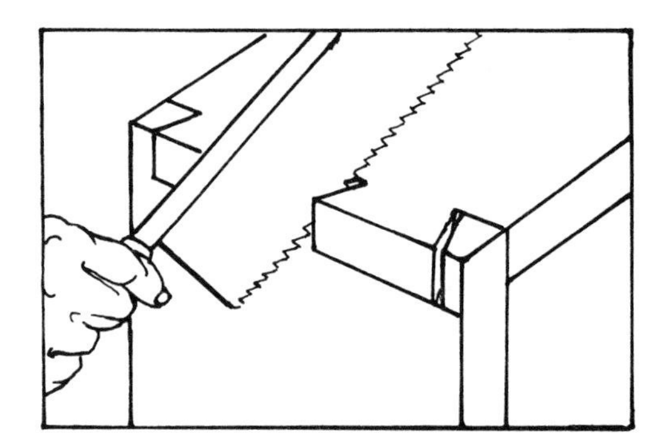

2. First saw a kerf along the join line. This makes an even opening to insert the veneer.

3. Glue in a triangular piece of matching veneer to fill the gap.

Illus. 236. Pieces of veneer can be used to fill gaps in a dovetail joint.

8

Box Joints and Multiple Splines

Box joints are also called finger joints. The joint consists of many interlocking fingers (Illus. 237). The long-grain contact area is high because each finger contributes to the glue area. Although box joints can be cut by hand, the joint is inherently a machine joint. Box joints were used extensively in mass-produced products of the nineteenth and early twentieth centuries. Products such as coffee grinders, telephones, scientific instruments, and packing boxes from this period almost always used box joints (Illus. 238 and 239). Special machines are typically used for mass production, but box joints can be cut using the table saw.

The box joint lacks the mechanical locking of a dovetail, so it derives its tensile strength solely from the glue. The only box-joint failures I have seen have been due to glue failure. For a strong joint, the glue must be spread evenly on all of the mating surfaces of both parts. You can do this with a small stiff brush or with a strip of wood. Hold the board end up, and drip a little glue in the notches, or sockets, between the fingers. Then use the brush or strip of wood to spread the glue evenly over the inside surfaces of the socket. Actually dipping the end of the board into the glue is faster, but it is a little messy. Usually the pins are left proud and sanded flush after assembly, so you can sand off the excess glue at the same time.

All of the fingers of a box joint are also referred to as pins; as indicated above, the notches be-

Illus. 237. Box joints consist of many interlocking fingers.

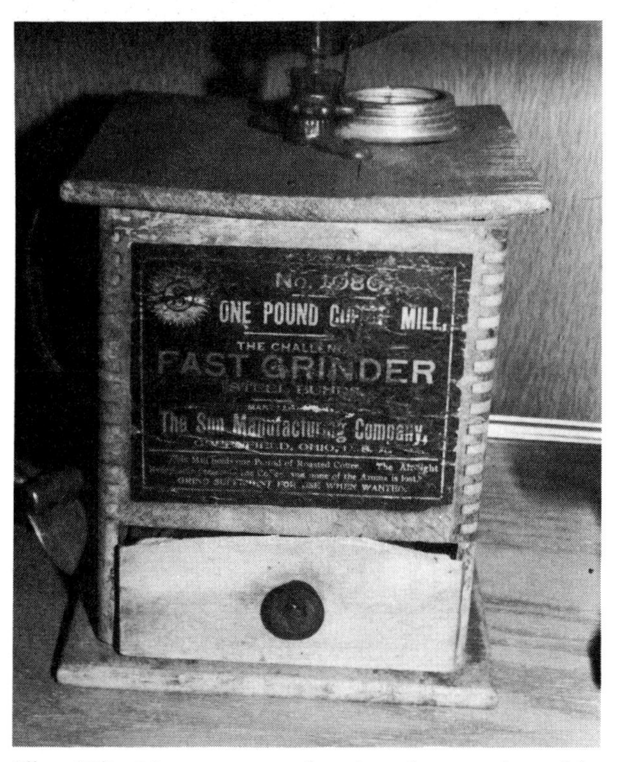

Illus. 238. Many mass-produced products such as this coffee grinder from the 1800s used box joints in their construction.

Illus. 239. This reproduction of an antique telephone uses box joints for authenticity.

tween the fingers are commonly called sockets. Pin size and spacing is a matter of personal preference; but, as a rule of thumb, the pins can be made one-half or one-fourth the stock thickness (Illus. 240 and 241). The sockets are always the same size as the pins.

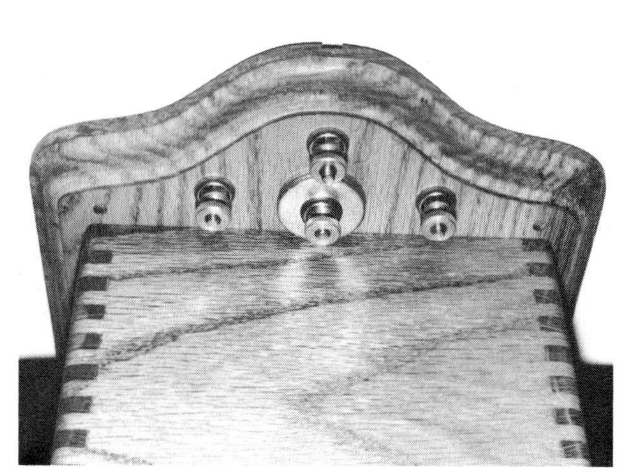

Illus. 240. The pins in this box joint are one-half the stock thickness.

Illus. 241. These pins are one-fourth the stock thickness.

Box Joints on the Table Saw

To cut a box joint on the table saw, you need a simple jig. The directions that follow are for making ¼" pins on ½" stock, but you can use the same procedure for other pin sizes simply by changing the dimensions. *The blade guard must be removed to use this jig, so use caution; be sure to keep your fingers away from the blade.*

Mount a dado blade on the saw arbor. The stack type of dado blade is best for this operation. Set up the dado blade to make a cut equal to the pin size; in this case, that is ¼". The blade height should be about 1/32" greater than the stock thickness to allow for trimming the pins after assembly. But, before using the dado blade to cut the sockets, you will use it to cut a notch in the jig that will assist in making the joint. For this cut, the dado blade height should actually be less than the setting that will be used to cut the sockets. Set the blade height to ⅜". This will allow some clearance between the positioning key and the bottom of the socket.

For the jig, make an extension fence out of plywood to be attached to the mitre gauge, but don't attach it with screws at this time; instead, clamp it in place. Make a notch in this fence by advancing the mitre gauge past the dado blade. A key made from hardwood fits into the notch (Illus. 242). In this example, the size of the key is ¼" × ⅜" × ½". Glue the key into the notch with the key projecting from the front of the fence. After the glue is dry, round the top of the key, and remove a little from the sides using sandpaper or a file. This will make it easier to slip the ¼"-wide socket over the key. Don't remove too much from the sides or you will have a poor-fitting joint. The one problem with this method of making box joints using this jig is that errors do tend to build up as the joint gets longer. Each succeeding socket is gauged from the previous one, so any slight inaccuracy is multiplied.

Reposition the fence on the mitre gauge with the key ¼" away from the far side of the blade. Make a test cut with the fence clamped in position; if the spacing is correct, then you can finally attach the fence with screws.

To begin making the joint, butt the edge of one of the boards against the key and cut a socket (Illus. 243). Now pull the mitre gauge back, and place this first socket over the key. Make another cut, and then reposition the board so that the second socket is on the key. Continue in this manner until you have cut sockets all the way across the board. To position the first socket on the second board, place the first socket on the first board over the key. Butt the edge of the second board against the edge of the first board. Using this setup, the first socket on the second board will be positioned right on the edge of the board (Illus. 244). Then, remove the first board, and place the first socket on the second board over

Illus. 242. This simple jig is used to make box joints on the table saw.

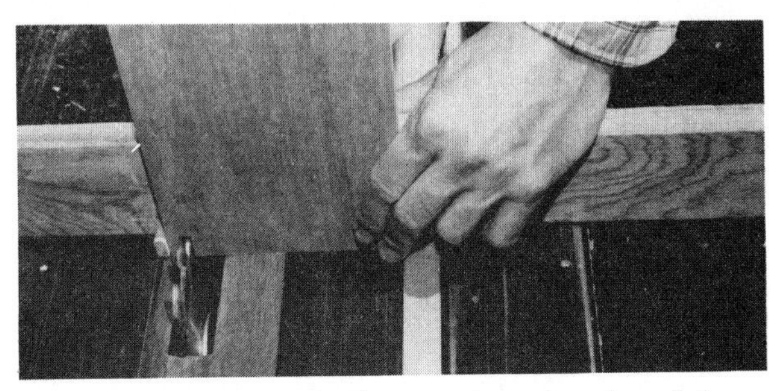

Illus. 243. To make the first cut, butt the edge of the work against the side of the key.

Illus. 244. To position the cut in the mating board, place the first socket on the first board over the key and butt the edge of the second board against the edge of the first board.

the key. Proceed to cut all of the sockets just as you did on the first board.

You can cut the sockets in both boards in one operation if you clamp them together. Make sure to offset one board by the pin width; then, cut the sockets as described for the first board above.

It's important that the sockets are all the same depth. The blade-height adjustment should be firmly locked to prevent creeping during the cut; but, the biggest problem comes from sawdust and chips building up in the sockets or on the key. If the board is held slightly above the table by this buildup, the socket will be too shallow. That the key was made slightly smaller than the socket does help some, but you still need to keep an eye out for buildup.

If you're not particularly careful, you can end up with joints that don't line up with each other—pin opposing pin, socket opposing socket—on opposite ends of the board. While this doesn't cause any problems with assembly or strength, it can be aesthetically disturbing. If you want the joints to match on all four corners of a box, follow this procedure. The corner joints are numbered, and sides labelled, in Illus. 245 to make the procedure easier to describe. Place Side A with the outside face against the jig and with the end marked 1 against the table. Butt the edge against the key, and use the procedure described previously to cut joint 1 for the first board.

Use Side A to position the first cut in Side B. Turn Side A so that the inside face is against the jig and the first socket is over the key. Butt the edge of Side B against the edge of Side A. The inside face of Side B should be against the jig and the end marked 1 against the table. Follow the procedure described above for the second board.

The corner labelled joint 2 is diagonally opposite joint 1. It is cut in the same manner as joint 1.

Joint 3 is cut with the inside face of its Part A against the jig and with the end marked 3 against the table. Butt the edge against the key, and follow the procedure described earlier for the first board. Next, position Part B for joint 3. Part A is placed with the outside face against the jig and the first socket over the key. Place B on the jig with the outside face against the jig. Butt the edge of Part B against the edge of Part A, and

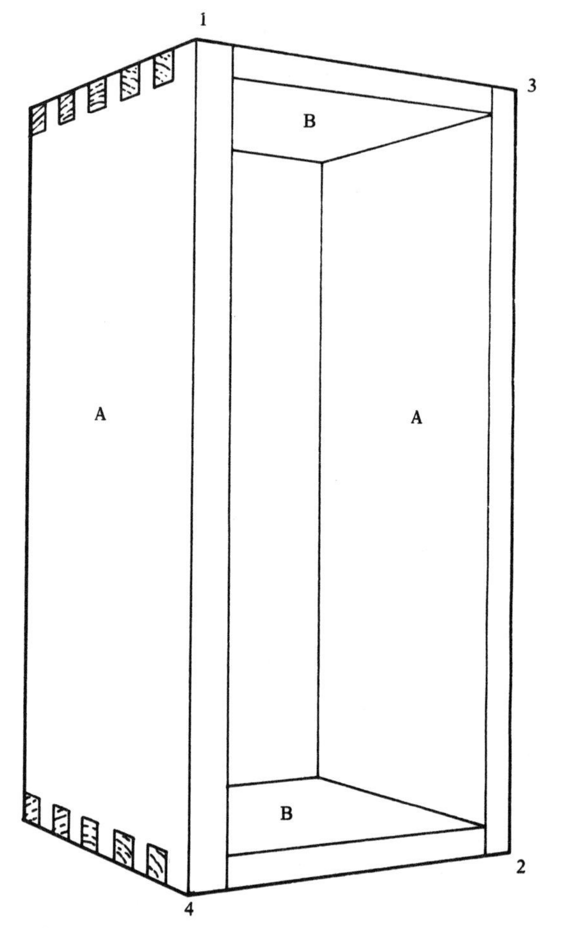

Illus. 245. Use the labels on this drawing to follow the accompanying text for cutting the joints so that they will correspond on both ends.

cut the sockets using the procedure described earlier for the second board. The diagonally opposite corner, joint 4, is cut using the same procedure.

You can avoid any confusion and eliminate the need for the procedure above by planning the joint so that there will be a full pin on both edges on the sides. The joint can be cut with either face against the jig and still come out even. Alternately, you can make the parts wider than necessary; then, cut them to final width after the joint is cut. This will enable you to trim the sides so that you have equally sized half-pins on each edge.

Use 100 grit sandpaper to remove splinters from the joint, and then dry-assemble. You can correct small errors with a file. If the dado blade leaves an irregular cut at the bottom of the socket, use the file to square it up; but, be careful not to deepen the socket. When you are satisfied with the fit, glue and clamp the joint. Gaps can be filled with strips of veneer in the same way as described in Chapter 7 on dovetails.

Locking a Box Joint

Dowel pegs can be used to mechanically lock a box joint. The pegs can be inserted in two ways: concealed and exposed. For a concealed lock, drill a hole through the edge of the joint after assembly. Drive a peg into the hole, and trim it flush (Illus. 246). The diameter of the peg must not be greater than one-half the stock thickness or the joint will be weakened.

Exposed pegs can be used both to lock the joint and to add visual interest. In this case, the pins must be made larger than usual. Pins that are the same size as the stock thickness work well. After assembly, drill a hole in the center of each pin, and insert a peg. Use pegs of contrasting color for a most striking visual effect. You can achieve other effects, for instance, by making the pins wider, by using several pegs per pin, or by using square pegs.

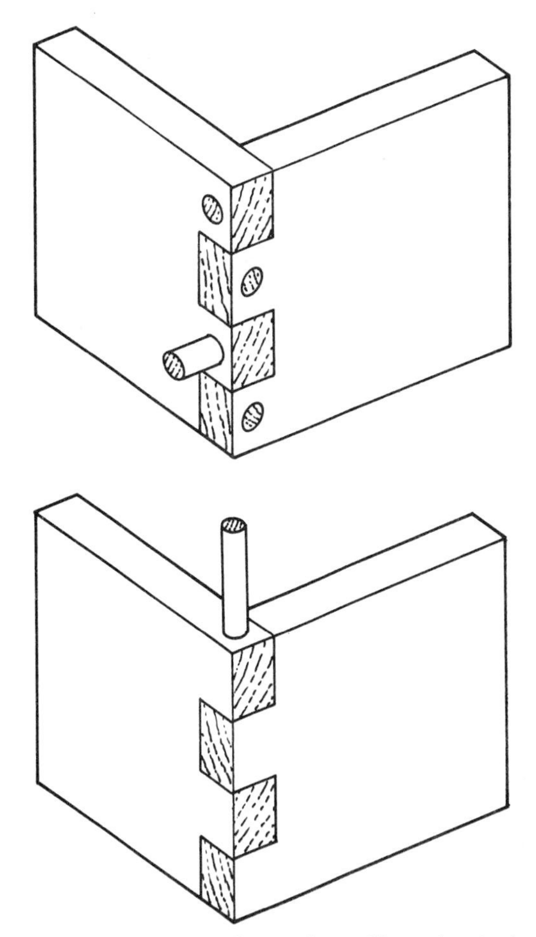

Illus. 246. Dowels can be used to add mechanical locking to a box joint. The dowels can be concealed (bottom) or exposed (top).

Box Joint Variations

The pin size can be varied in the joint to create other visual effects. Variably spaced wide pins can be cut effectively by hand. The layout and procedure is similar to hand-cut dovetails. Start by gauging a shoulder line. Then, use a square to lay out the pin locations on one board. Use a backsaw or dovetail saw to cut down the sides of the pins. The waste can be chopped out with a chisel using the same method described for dovetails, or you can saw it out with a coping saw, and then use the chisel to square up the shoulder. Once you have one board cut, use it to mark the other.

Box joints can be used when the boards meet at an angle other than 90° (Illus. 247). The procedure is basically the same, but the jig is a little different. The extension fence attached to the mitre gauge must be cut on an angle. Use a thick piece of lumber such as a two-by-four. Set the tilt arbor on the saw to the joint angle, and rip the extension fence. Cut a notch in the fence, and insert a key to complete the jig as described

Illus. 247. An angled jig can be used to cut box joints when the boards meet at an odd angle.

above. Before cutting the pins, cut the ends of the board to the correct angle for the joint. Then, place the board against the jig so that the angled end rests flat on the table. The rest of the procedure is the same as described above for cutting box joints on the table saw.

MITRED END PINS

The end pins of a box joint can be mitred just as the half-pins of a dovetail were mitred (Illus. 248). Cut the first board as usual. Then cut the second board omitting the first socket. Cut the end pin off at a 45° angle; then, cut a mitred socket in the second board to receive it. You can cut this socket by hand or use the technique described below for half-blind box joints.

HALF-BLIND BOX JOINTS

In the half-blind box joint, the pins are visible only on one side of the joint (refer again to Illus. 248). To cut the joint, make the first set of cuts as usual; then, set the table saw blade tilt to 45°, and cut off the ends of the pins. To make the second set of pins, you need a different type of jig; the face of the jig needs to be on a 45° angle. You can use a piece of two-by-four ripped with the saw set to 45°. Attach it to the mitre gauge, and cut a key slot as described earlier. Insert the key, and position the jig on the mitre gauge. When the square-ended board is placed on the jig, one corner of the end will rest on the table. Adjust the blade height so that the cut won't cut into the face past the other square corner. Cut the second set of pins using this jig, and make a trial assembly.

Multiple-Spline Joints

Multiple-spline joints are similar to box joints in strength and finished appearance. The difference is that, in the case of the multiple spline, the two jointing boards each have sockets or kerfs cut in them for splines; but, there are no projecting pins on either board.

The simplest type of multiple-spline joint is the multiple feather spline (Illus. 249). To cut the kerfs, you will need a V-shaped jig. Two types can be used. The first type in Illus. 249 works best for short joints such as are in a picture frame. The second jig in Illus. 249 works best on longer joints such as are needed for a box. Both jigs are used in the same way. Set the dado blade for the width of the splines. Make a kerf at one end of the jig with the dado blade. Next, cut a piece of spline to fit in the kerf. The splines are made by ripping a piece off the edge of a board, and then cutting the piece into triangular sections or to the shape needed for the jig. This spline in the jig acts as a key. Reposition the jig so that the key is separated from the blade by the desired space

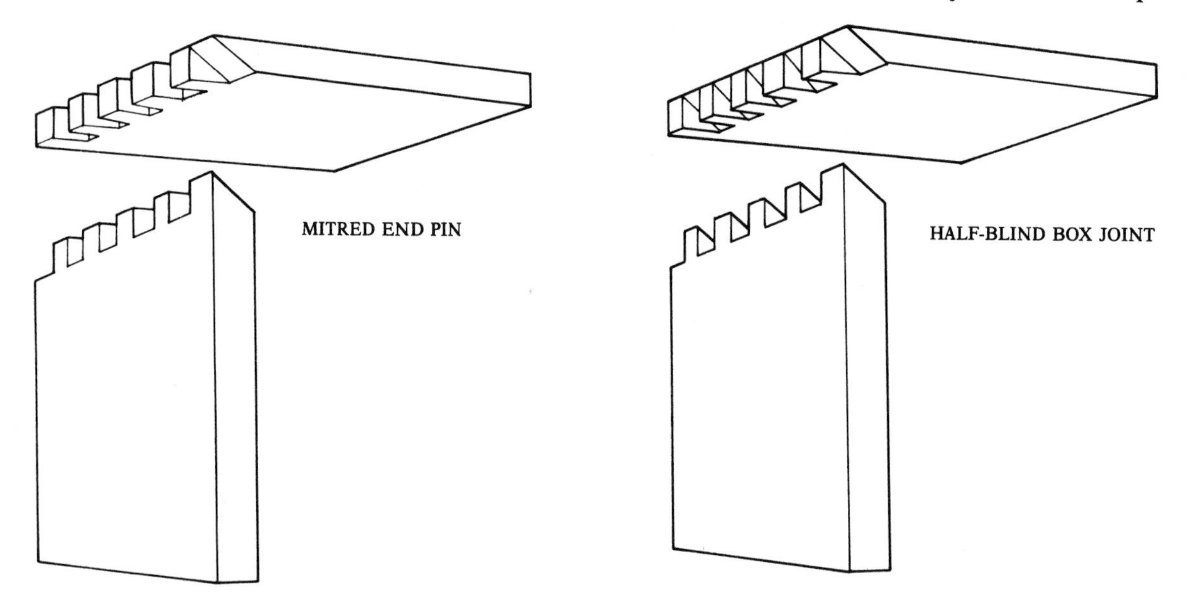

Illus. 248. The mitred end pin and half-blind box joint are variations on the standard box joint.

between kerfs in the joint. Attach the jig to the mitre gauge, or, for the first type in Illus. 249, set the rip fence, with an auxiliary fence to guide the jig.

First, cut a standard mitre joint, and assemble the parts with glue. Then, make the spline kerfs after the glue is set. Since you will need to handle the fully assembled article on the table saw, naturally it is best to keep the project small. Place one corner in the jig, and butt the edge against the key. Make a kerf through the corner with the blade set as high as is possible without actually cutting through the inside of the corner. Then, reposition the work so that the first kerf is

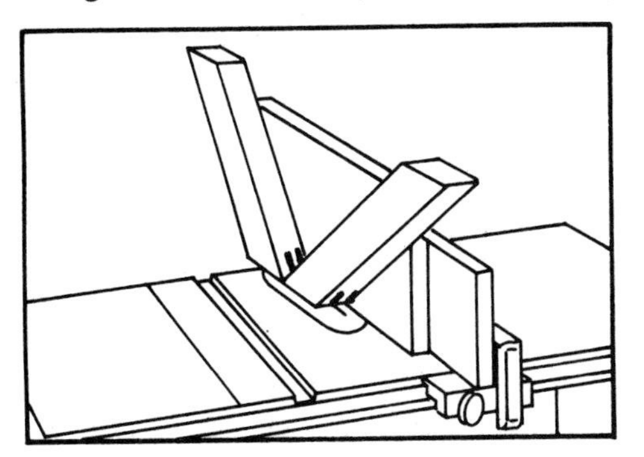

1. Narrow objects like picture frames can be handled on this jig. A wide auxiliary fence attached to the rip fence guides the jig.

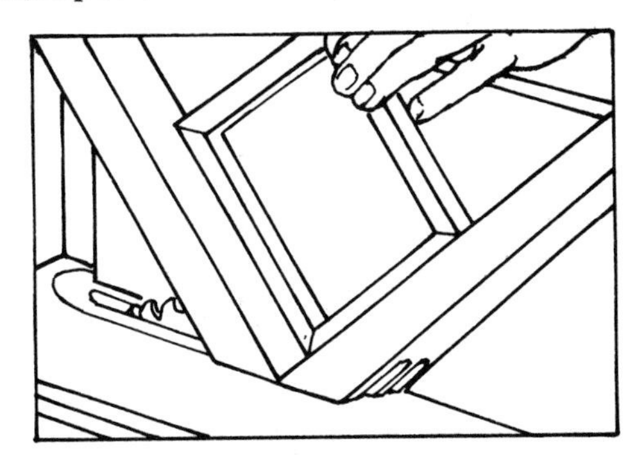

2. Place the assembled frame in the jig and raise the blade enough to make the groove for the spline. Spacing can be controlled by moving the fence or by using a key like the jig below.

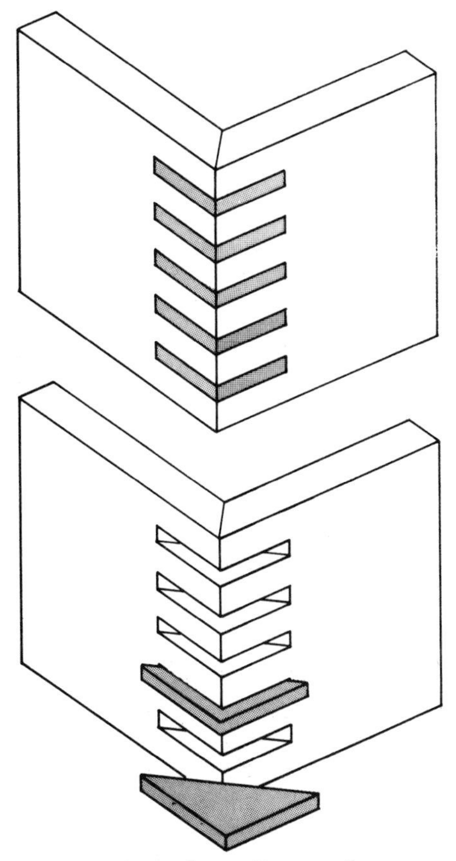

Illus. 249. Multiple feather spline step by step.

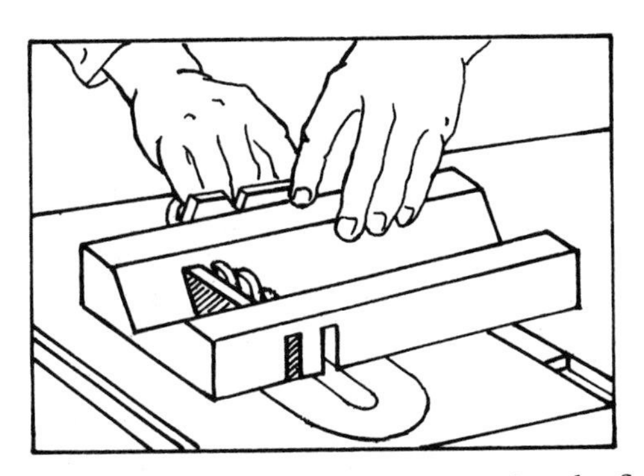

3. This jig attaches to the mitre gauge. Cut the first slot and insert a key. Move the jig the desired spacing and cut a second slot.

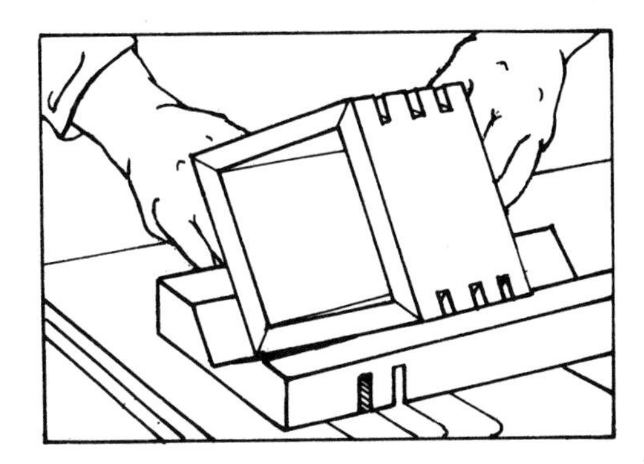

4. Attach the jig to the mitre gauge and cut the slots for the splines. The key makes spacing automatic.

over the key, and make the second cut. Reposition the work again, and continue in this manner until you have made as many cuts as are needed. Place the next corner in the jig, and start the procedure again.

When all of the kerfs are made, insert the splines. Apply glue to the inside of the kerfs, but don't put any glue on the splines themselves. The glue will cause the splines to swell. Insert the splines in the kerfs, and let the glue set. If the splines are tight, no clamps are needed; but, if they seem loose in the kerf after they have had a minute or two to swell, then apply a clamp.

You can also use veneer as the spline. In this case, of course, the kerf needs to be very thin, so you will need to use a handsaw. Lay out the spline locations, and saw down from the corner (Illus. 250). Cut the splines from veneer, and compress them by placing them on the anvil of an iron vise and hitting the veneer with a steel hammer. Then, apply glue inside the kerf using a thin strip of cardboard. Insert the splines, and let the moisture in the glue cause them to swell. The thinning with the hammer ensures that the veneer will swell enough to make a tight joint.

You can use the same types of jig as described above to cut the spline grooves using a router table. Chuck a straight bit into the router. Use it to make the cut in the jig for the key; then, use the jig in exactly the same way as described for the table saw.

This setup can also be used to cut a multiple-dovetail-spline joint (Illus. 251). Use the same jig. Make the cut for the key using a straight bit; then, reposition the jig, and make the second cut. The size of the straight bit should equal the narrowest point of the dovetail bit. Then, replace the straight bit with a dovetail bit, and make another pass through the second cut in the jig. Set the router depth so that the dovetail section of the bit will extend through the jig, just clearing the bottom of the V. The cut made with the straight bit, if done with the proper size bit, will allow clearance for the dovetail-bit shaft.

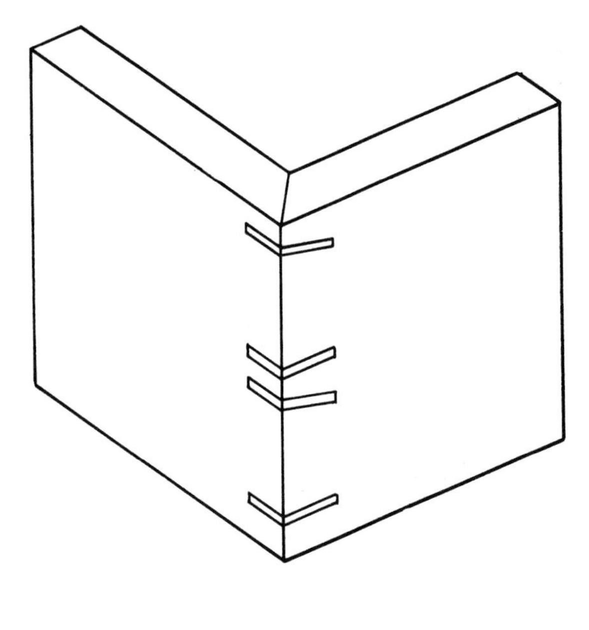

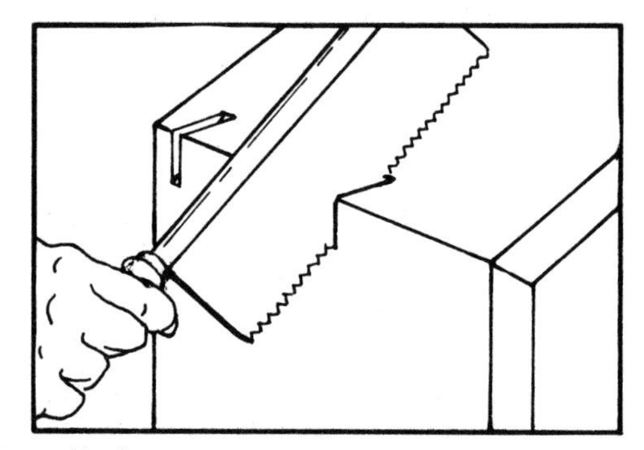

1. Use a backsaw or tenon saw to make the kerfs. Angling the cut gives the joint a dovetail effect.

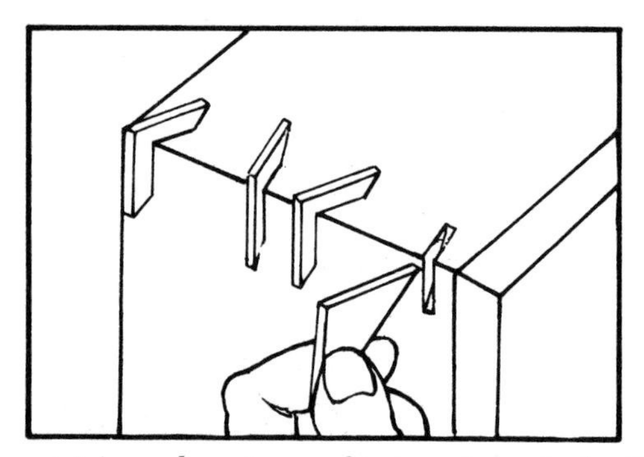

2. Insert triangular pieces of veneer into the kerfs.

Illus. 250. Pieces of veneer placed in saw kerfs can be used to spline a mitre joint.

The joint is mitred and assembled just as for the straight multiple spline. After the glue has set, place one corner in the jig with the edge butted against the key. Make a pass across the dovetail bit, and the cut will give you a dovetail-shaped groove in the corner. Reposition the work so that the first groove sits on the key; the key should fill the narrowest part of the groove so that there is no movement. Make another pass over the bit, and reposition the work again. Continue in this way until all of the grooves are cut; then, start on another corner.

The dovetail spline itself is ripped on the table saw with the blade tilt set to the angle of the dovetail bit. Cut the piece of spline into short sections that are a little longer than needed to fill

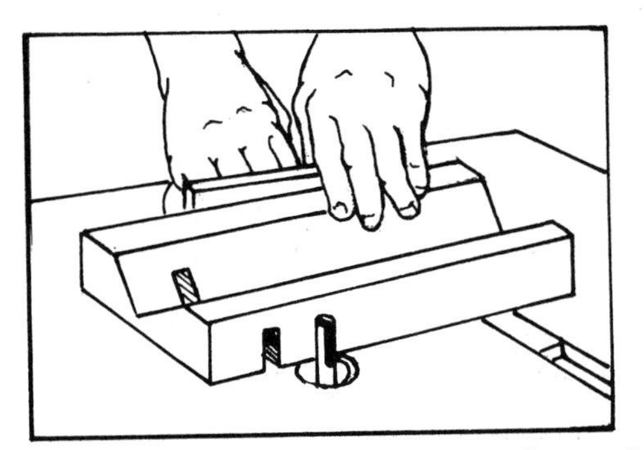

1. To prepare the jig for the router table, first make a straight cut for the bit and the key.

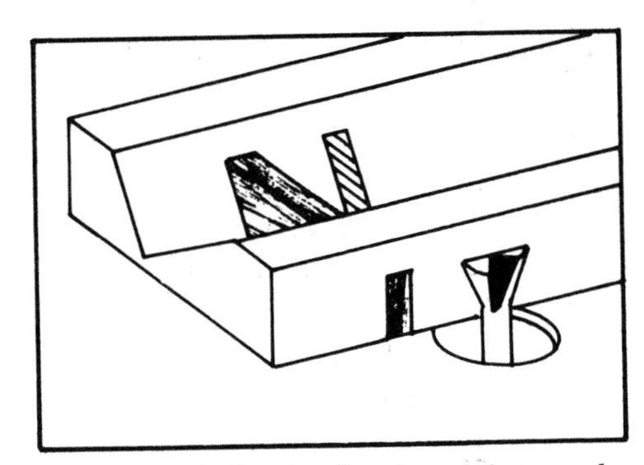

2. Insert a straight key in the slot and use a dovetail bit to widen the bit slot.

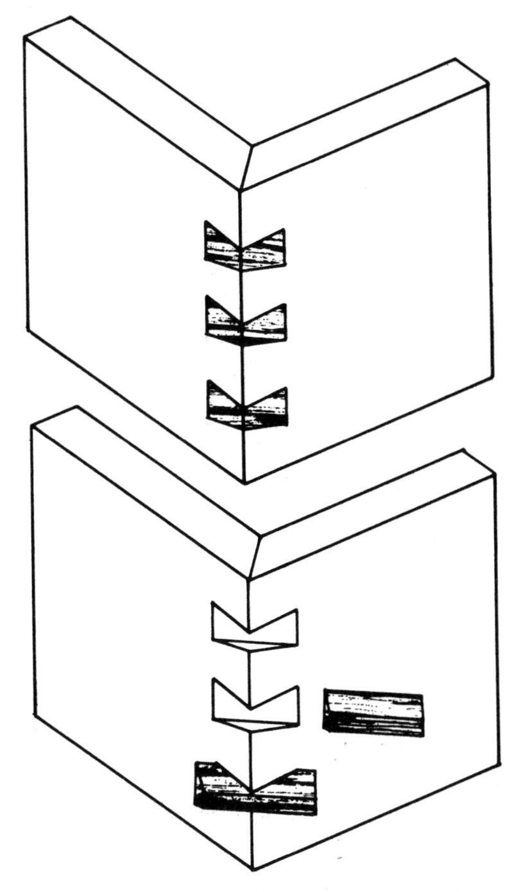

3. Place the corner of the project in the jig with the end against the key and make a cut.

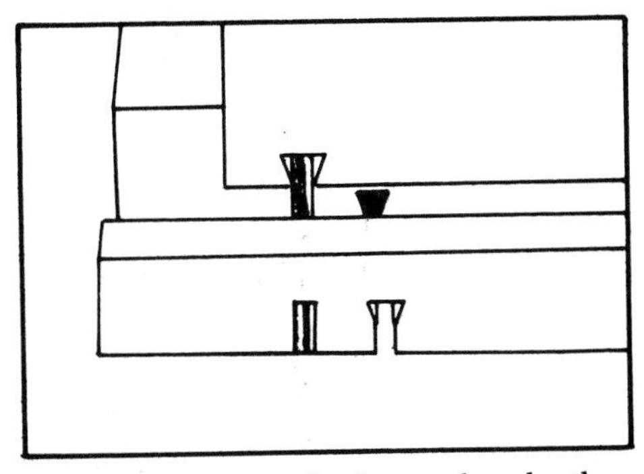

4. Place the first cut over the key and make the next cut.

Illus. 251. A router table can be used to cut the grooves for dovetail splines.

the grooves. Spread glue inside the grooves, and then slip the dovetail splines into the grooves. After the glue is set, the spline can be trimmed and sanded flush.

If you prefer, the splines can be wider than a standard dovetail bit. The jig will need an extra groove and key. Don't glue the keys in place, because you will need to remove and replace them during the process. Start by cutting the first groove on all four corners. Remove the original key and insert one that is spaced away from it by the distance needed to achieve the desired width of the dovetail. Butt the edge of the work against the key. When all four corners are done, remove the key, and replace the original one. Place the previously cut groove over the key, and make the next cut. If the two cuts are close together, the waste piece will easily break out; if not, remove the key and position the work so that an additional pass over the bit will cut out the waste. Then, with the key in place, position the work over the key with one side of the groove touching the key. Make a pass over the bit; then, slide the work over a little, and make another pass to make the groove continuously smooth. Keep moving the work and making passes over the bit until the other edge of the groove hits the key. Then, reposition the work so that the latest groove is over the key, and make another groove. Repeat the process for all of the subsequent grooves. Rip splines to fit the grooves, and glue them in place.

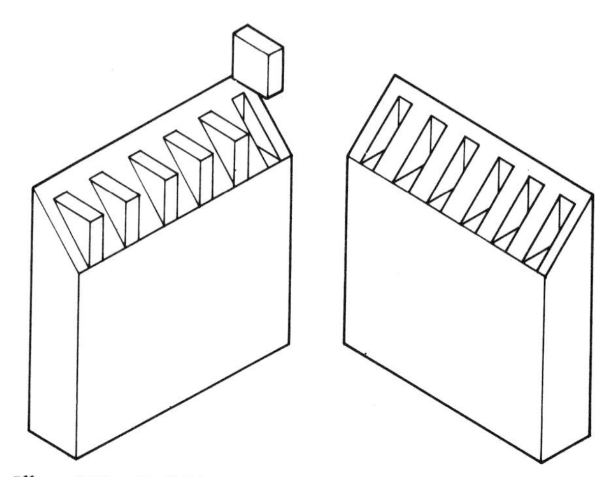

Illus. 252. Full-blind multiple-spline joint.

Illus. 253. A dovetail jig can be used to guide the router when making the spline grooves in a full-blind multiple-spline joint.

FULL-BLIND MULTIPLE SPLINES

Full-blind multiple splines are a very strong type of reinforcement for a mitre joint (Illus. 252). Begin by cutting a standard mitre. The grooves for the splines are cut using the router dovetail jig. Place one of the parts in the top clamp of the dovetail jig with the inside face out. Instead of using the same positioning pin that is used for dovetail joints, line up the edge of the board with the outside edge of one of the fingers on the template. Adjust the template so that the rear stop will keep the bit from cutting past the inside edge of the mitre. Then, cut the grooves using a straight bit in the router and the template-following collar. The mating board is cut in the same manner, but the opposite edge is aligned with a finger on the template (Illus. 253).

You don't absolutely have to square up the grooves with a chisel; but, to get the largest splines possible, it is a good idea. Cut the splines to fit in the grooves, and dry-assemble the joint. Make sure that the splines aren't too large, or they will hold the joint open. When the joint fits properly, apply glue to the joint and assemble. Clamps are necessary to keep the joint tight as the glue sets.

9
Lap Joints

Lap joints can be used whenever two frame members meet at a corner or cross each other (Illus. 254). The main advantage of the lap joint is that it is one of the simplest frame joints to offer good long-grain contact. Lap joints are strong enough so that reinforcement is usually unnecessary. In order to achieve the optimum strength, the joint must be clamped so that the two cheeks are pressed tightly together. Sometimes a few nails or staples are driven through the joint, but just to hold it together while the glue sets.

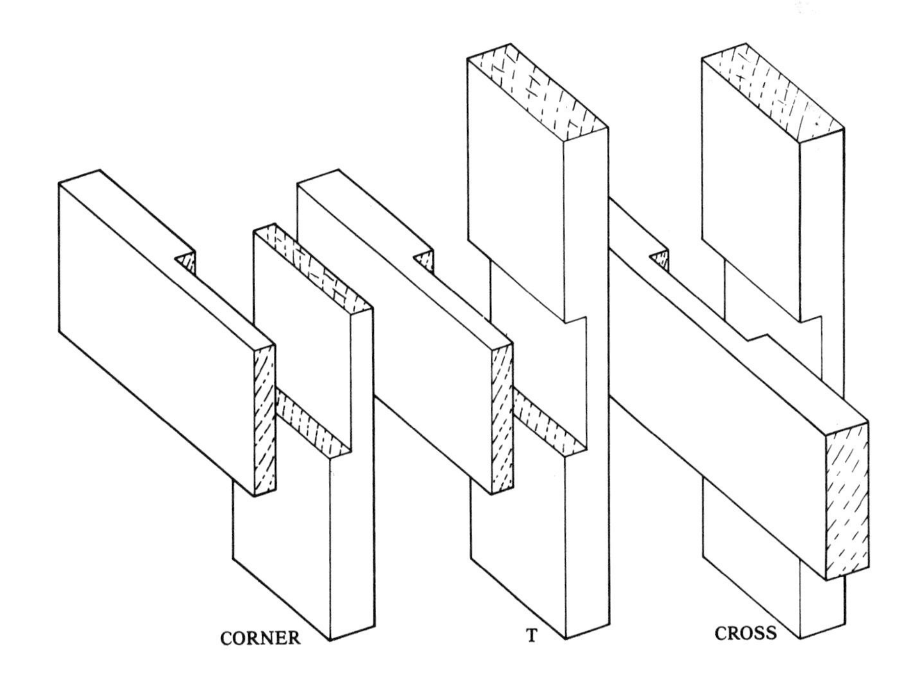

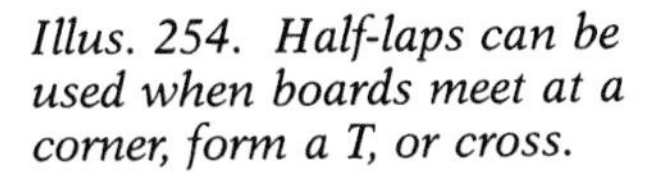

Illus. 254. Half-laps can be used when boards meet at a corner, form a T, or cross.

Half-Laps

One of the most frequently used lap joints is the half-lap. It can be used at a frame corner when one board meets the other, in a T-shaped junction, or where two boards cross. You can cut half-laps with a backsaw and chisel, the table saw, a radial-arm saw, the router, or a band saw.

To cut half-laps by hand, first lay out the cuts on the ends of the boards. The corner joint can be cut entirely with a backsaw (Illus. 255). Make the shoulder cut first; then, cut the cheek. The technique used is exactly the same as for hand-cut tenons. Refer to Chapter 2 for details. To cut a T-type joint, make the shoulder cuts with a backsaw; then, remove the waste with a chisel (Illus. 256). If the joint is wide, you can cut a few extra saw kerfs inside the waste so that achieving a uniform depth will be easier as you chisel out the waste. A router plane can be used to smooth up the bottom.

Table Saw

You can cut lap joints on the table saw in two ways: a standard table-saw blade can be used, or you can use a dado blade. In using the standard blade, you make two cuts. You need to use a tenoning jig to hold the board as you make the cheek cut. Use the mitre gauge as you make the shoulder cut. Don't place the end of the board directly against the fence, or the waste will kick back. Instead, clamp a block of wood to the front of the fence, and use it to position the board on the mitre gauge. Then, advance the gauge forward past the block, and make the shoulder cut. This way the waste will be freed, not trapped between the fence and the blade.

The other way to cut a half-lap on the table saw is to use the dado blade. Make the shoulder cut; then, make passes to remove the waste (Illus. 257). The dado blade is suited to making the T-type and cross-type joint. Cut the shoulders before removing the waste.

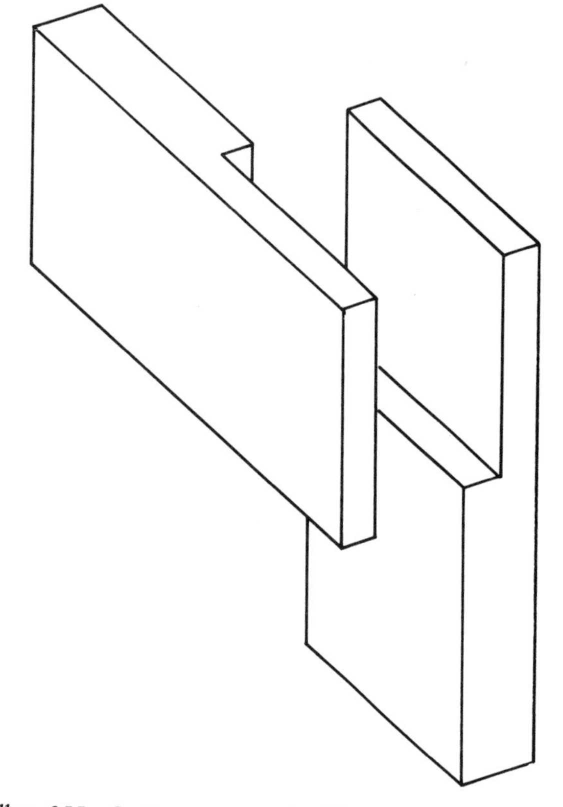

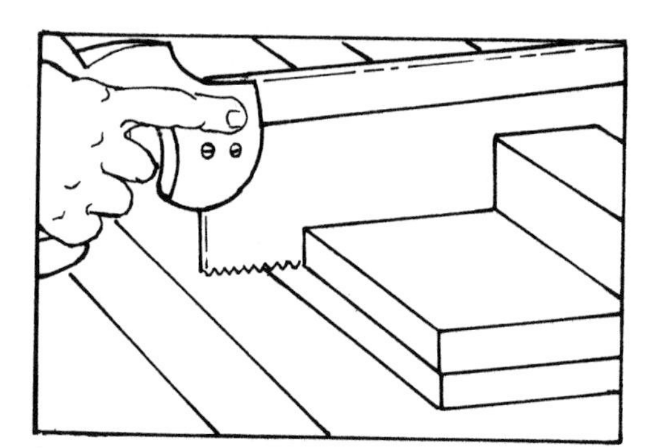

1. Make the shoulder cut first.

2. Cut the cheek using the same technique described for cutting tenons.

Illus. 255. Cutting a corner half-lap.

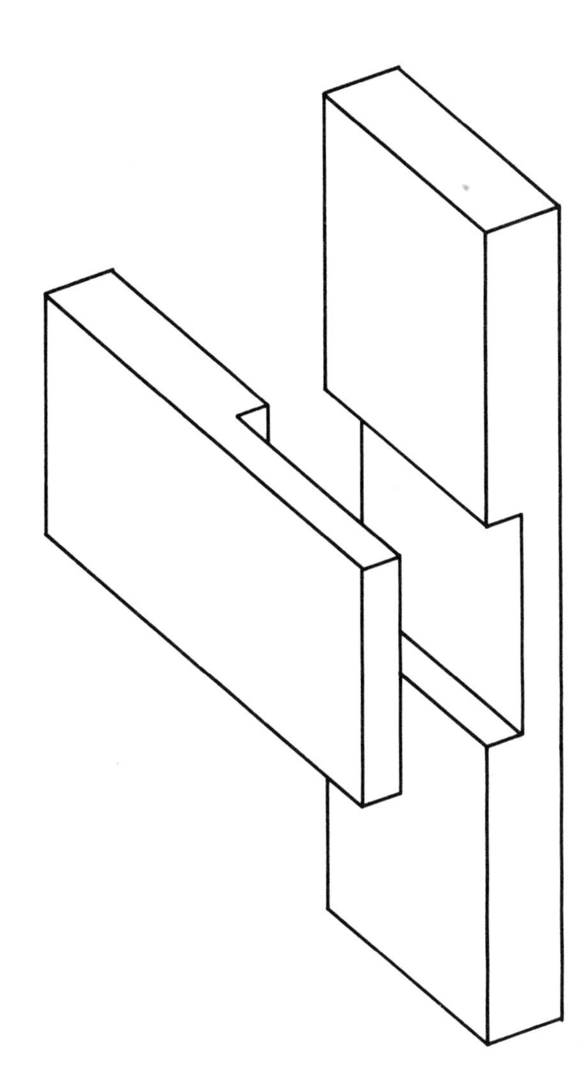

Illus. 256. *Cutting a T-type half-lap.*

1. Make several saw kerfs in the waste area.

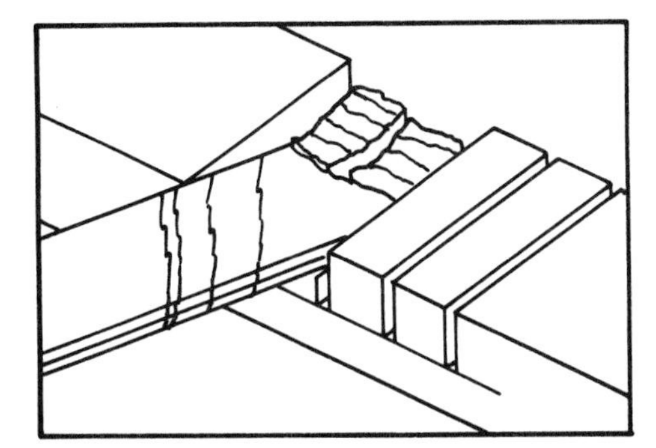

2. Remove most of the waste with a chisel.

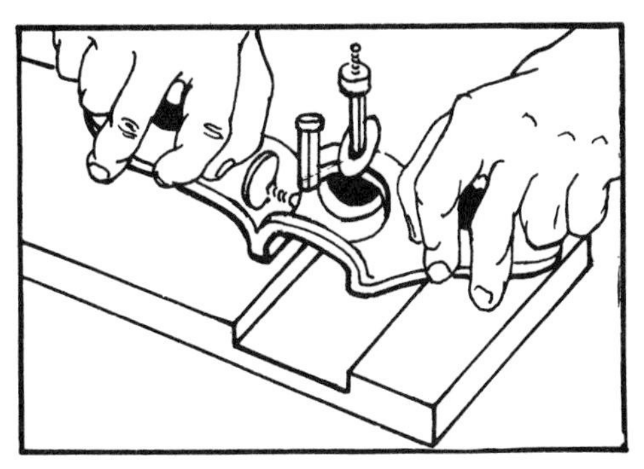

3. Smooth up the cut with a chisel or a router plane.

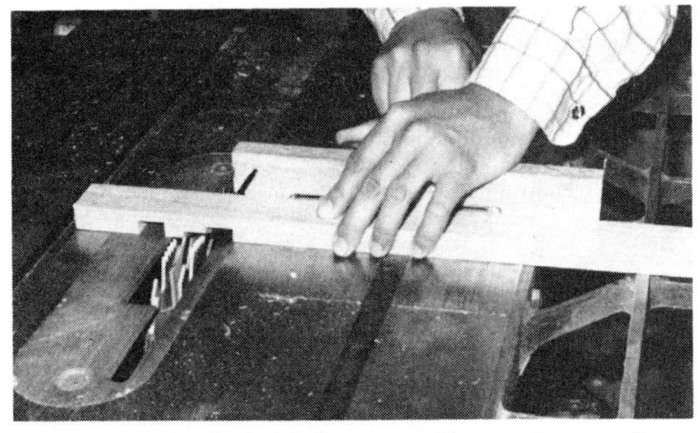

Illus. 257. The dado blade on a table saw is a good way to cut T-type and cross half-laps.

You can also use the dado blade in a radial-arm saw to perform this operation. Since the work will be face up, it is easier to see as you cut the joint.

Router

The router can also be used to make half-lap joints. It is particularly useful for half-blind joints. This is usually used for the T-type joint, but you can use a half-blind joint at a corner as well. You can make a simple jig that allows clearance for the template-following collar to cut half-blind lap joints from a piece of ¼" hardboard (Illus. 258).

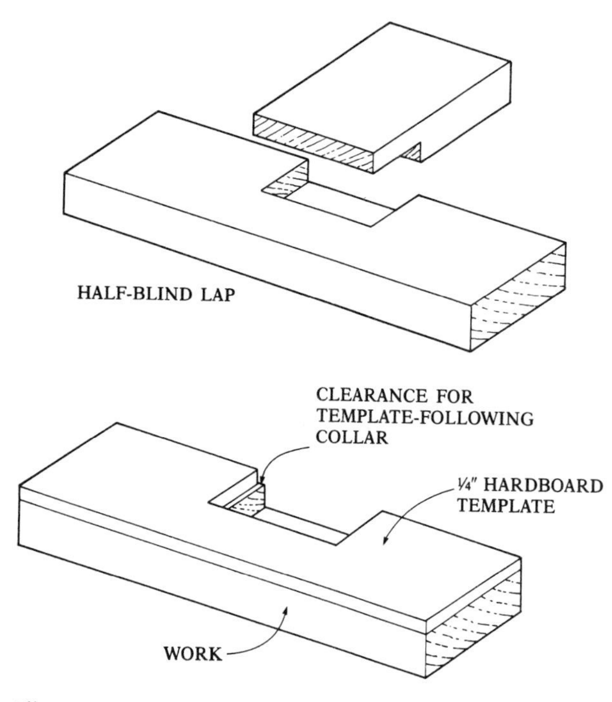

Illus. 258. A router can be used to cut a half-blind lap. Make a template from hardboard, and use a template-following collar on the router.

Band Saw

A band saw can be used to cut lap joints; but, use a wide blade to get a straight cut. Make the shoulder cut first using the mitre gauge. Then, set the fence or clamp a board to the table to guide the work for the cheek cut.

VARIATIONS

Half-laps don't necessarily need to be at right angles; you can use them to join parts—whether at a corner, a cross, or an angled T—at various angles other than 90° (Illus. 259). First, cut the ends of the board to the desired angle. Place the board in the tenoning jig with the angled end flat on the table, and make the cheek cut. With the mitre gauge set to the correct angle, make the shoulder cut.

You can add some locking to a joint by bevelling the lap. The dovetailed half-lap adds even more locking to the joint (Illus. 260). When the joint is at a corner, only the inside shoulder is dovetailed. In a T-type joint, one or both shoulders can be cut on an angle.

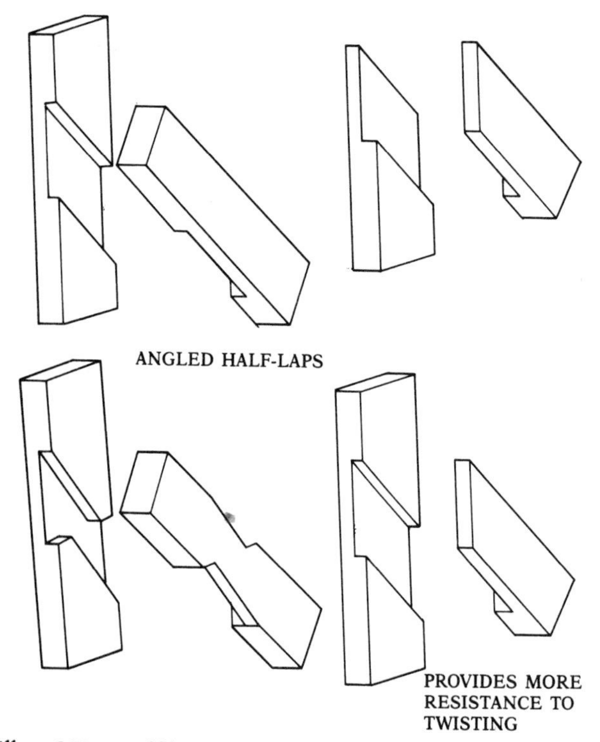

Illus. 259. Half-laps can be used when the parts meet at angles other than 90°.

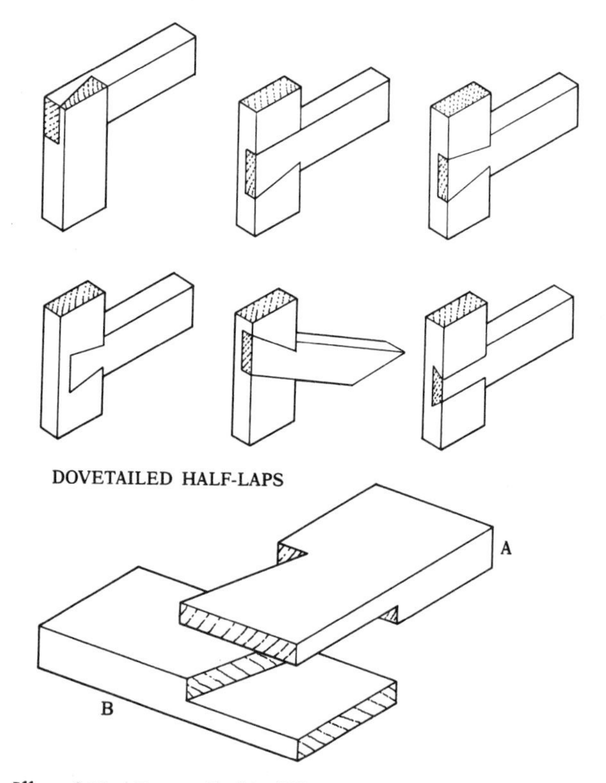

Illus. 260. Dovetailed half-laps add mechanical locking to the joint. Parts A and B are referred to in the text.

To make a dovetailed half-lap, cut Part A first. Make a standard half-lap, then cut the dovetail. Next, use Part A to make the angle(s) on Part B. Make the shoulder cuts, then remove the waste. You can also make a half-blind dovetailed lap. The easiest way to cut the socket is with a router. Make a jig out of ¼" hardboard to guide the router; use a template-following collar around the bit. The cutout in the jig needs to be a little bigger than the actual desired size for the socket to allow for the collar. Square up the corners afterwards with a chisel.

To make the sliding dovetailed half-lap shown on the middle right of Illus. 260, cut a standard half-lap on Part A; then, cut the sides away at a 10° angle. Cut the shoulders on Part B in at the same 10° angle so that the parts will match. This can be done with a router and a dovetail bit or with a backsaw. You can also set the blade tilt on a table saw to make the shoulder cuts.

Edge Half-Laps

Half-laps can be made on the edge of a board as well as on the face. In this case, the long-grain contact area is not as large so that the edge joint isn't as strong as the face half-lap. Under stress, solid lumber tends to split along the grain at the bottom of the notch (Illus. 261). When the boards are wide, this joint is more suited to plywood than solid lumber because plywood doesn't have a weakness along the grain. (See Chapter 12, page 178, for a discussion of plywood joints.)

Solid lumber tends to break at the bottom of the notch because the sides of the notched portion are left unsupported in the standard version of this joint. The joint will be stronger if you provide support for the entire width of the board by using one of the following methods. The simplest method is to first cut a shallow dado on both sides of both boards at the joint location, and then cut the notches (Illus. 262). Make the notches to fit over the thickness between the two dadoes, not the board thickness. Don't cut the dadoes very deep or you will weaken the joint, eliminating the purpose of the support.

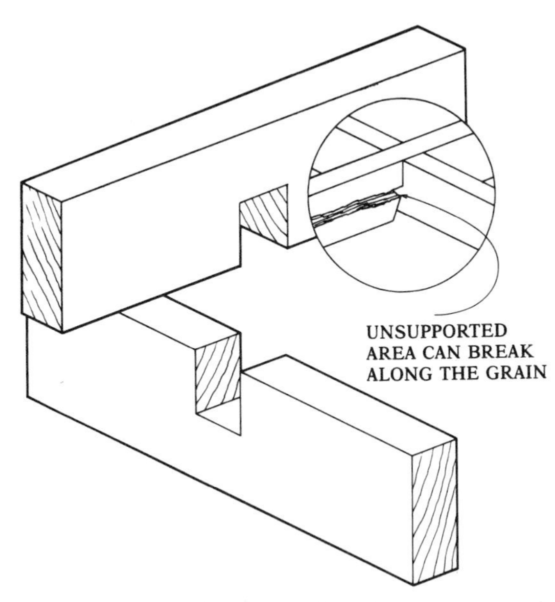

Illus. 261. When used with solid lumber, unsupported edge half-laps have a tendency to break along the grain.

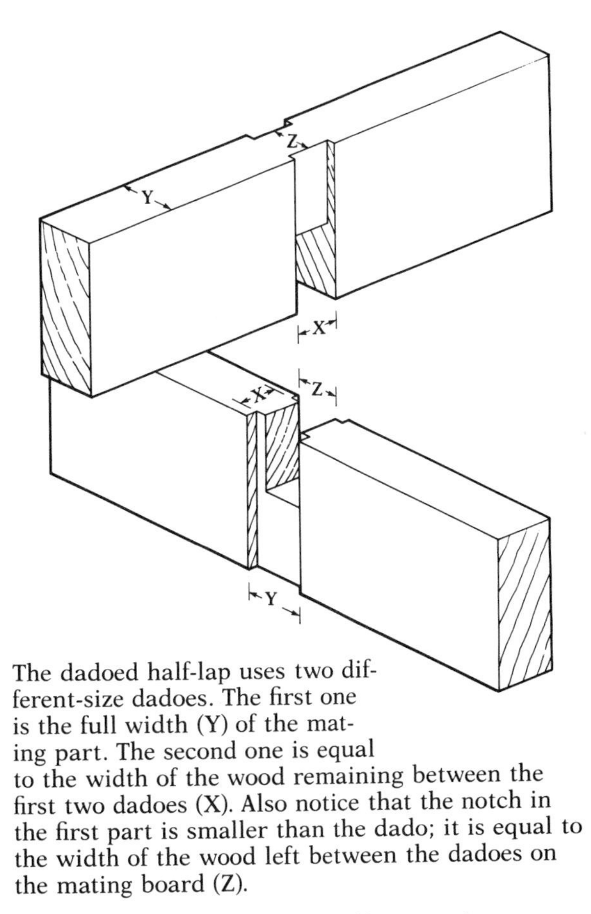

The dadoed half-lap uses two different-size dadoes. The first one is the full width (Y) of the mating part. The second one is equal to the width of the wood remaining between the first two dadoes (X). Also notice that the notch in the first part is smaller than the dado; it is equal to the width of the wood left between the dadoes on the mating board (Z).

Illus. 262. The dadoed edge half-lap provides support for the full width of the board, making failure along the grain less likely.

The next alternative provides support without removing as much wood from the sides, so the resulting joint will be stronger (Illus. 263). This is a hand-cut joint, and it is not easily adaptable to machine work. Start by marking the board thickness at the joint location on each board. Then, mark a line half-way across the width of the board to indicate the bottom of the notch. Measure in from the side marks 1/8", and mark on the middle line. Mark the angle lines by connecting these marks with the point where the side lines meet the edges. Saw out the notch along these angle lines. Inside the notch on the bottom, make marks 1/8" in from each face. Then, chisel out the slope so that it starts at the edge of the board and ends at this line. Finally, cut away the area between the side lines and the notch and slope so that the angle intersects the slope. Test fit the joint, and use the chisel to make any adjustments.

For the ultimate edge half-lap, combine it with a sliding dovetail to make a double-dovetail half-lap (Illus. 264). You can use power tools for most of the work; but, some hand work is necessary. Start by making a dovetailed dado on both faces of both boards at the joint location. You can do it with a backsaw and chisel; but, a router with a dovetail bit will be faster. Next, cut the notch halfway through each board; make the notch as wide as the thickness of the board between the two dadoes. Finally, use a chisel to cut the dovetailed ends on the sides of the notch.

The cogged joint can be used to join boards of unequal width or thickness or to join a board on edge to the face of another (Illus. 265). It is also useful when the joint must carry a lot of weight. To make the simplest cogged joint, cut two blind sockets in the first board; then, cut the notch in the other board to fit. This joint is not flush. If you want a flush joint, cut a dado in the first

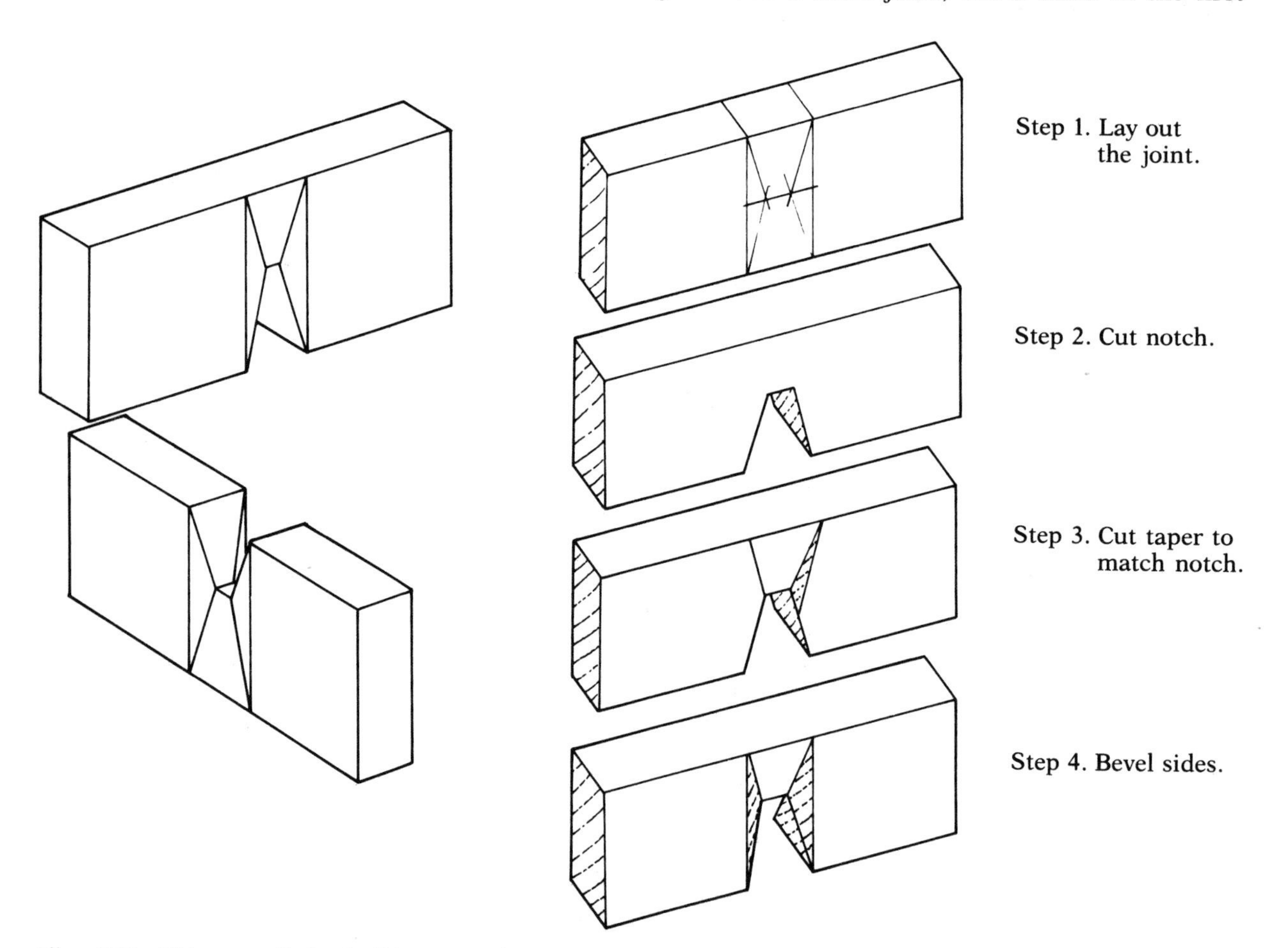

Illus. 263. This type of edge half-lap is good to use when you are working with hand tools.

board to a depth equal to one-half the width of the second board. Then, cut the blind sockets in the bottom of the dado. Finally, notch the second board to fit.

Bridle Joint

The bridle joint an be made by using many of the same techniques as for a half-lap. This joint is a

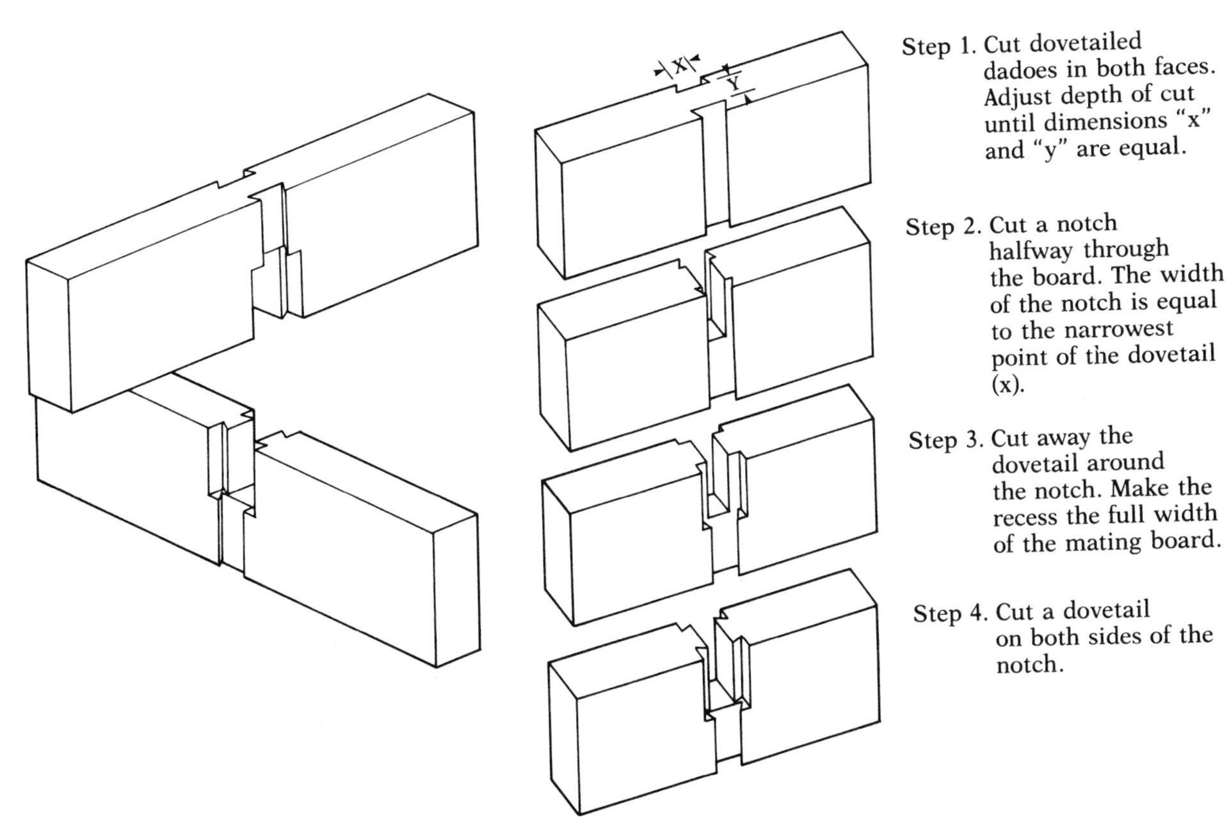

Illus. 264. Double-dovetail half-lap step by step.

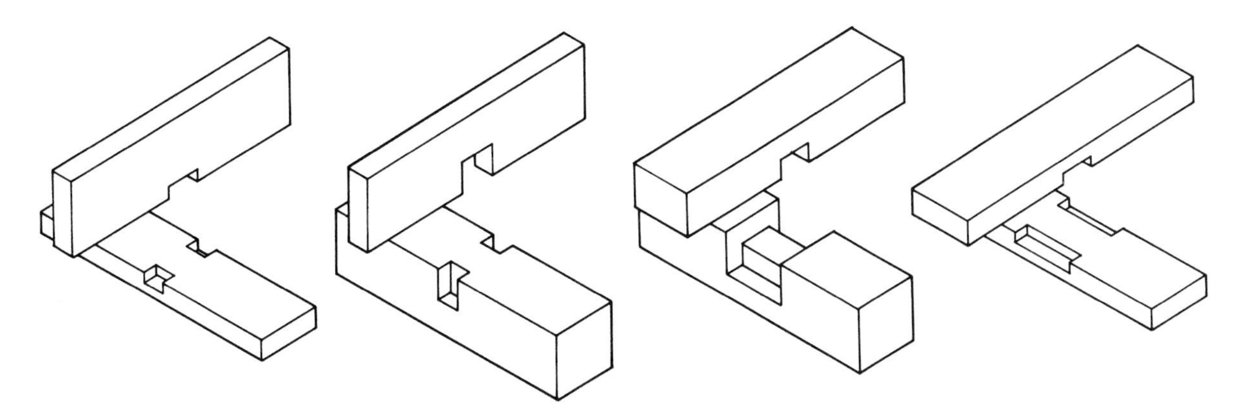

COGGED JOINTS

Illus. 265. Cogged joints can be stronger than half-laps in certain situations, because the upper member is supported more effectively.

T-type joint. Since it laps over both faces, it resists side-to-side force better than a half-lap (Illus. 266). The long-grain contact area is double that of the half-lap. Just as with the half-lap, clamps must be applied to the face of the joint to press the cheeks together while the glue dries. The bridle joint is typically used to connect a leg to a rail when the leg isn't located at a corner. It can also be used to attach a leg to a base or a rocking chair leg to the rocker (Illus. 267). When the leg is thicker than the rail, a barefaced bridle can be used. In this case, no dadoes are made in the rail. The barefaced version doesn't provide as much lateral strength as the standard bridle.

To make a standard bridal joint, begin by cutting dadoes on both sides of Part A. Next, cut the notch in Part B. You can use a dado blade and a tenoning jig to cut the notch as long as the notch isn't too deep. You can also cut the notch by hand with a backsaw. Use a mortising chisel to cut the bottom. Chisel halfway from one side, then flip the board over and complete the cut.

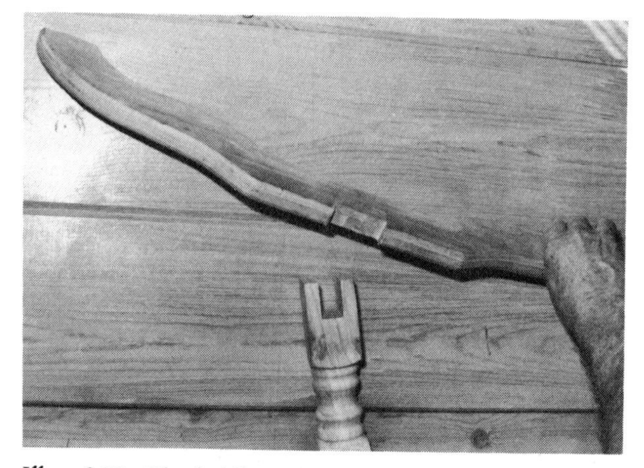

Illus. 267. The bridle joint is often used to attach this type of base to a leg.

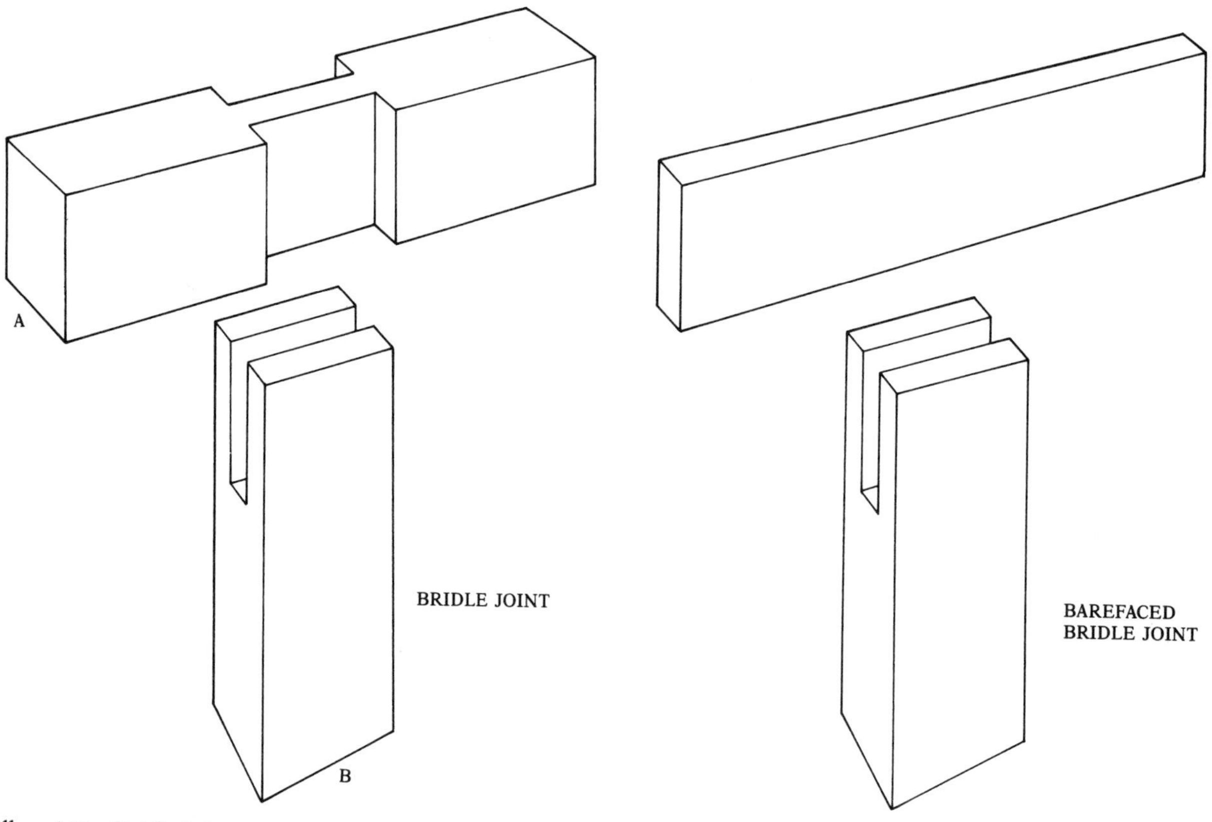

Illus. 266. Bridle joints.

PART III
JOINERY APPLICATIONS

10
Frame-and-Panel Joinery

Frame-and-panel joinery is used in cabinetmaking, door making, and interior finish work (Illus. 268). It reached its pinnacle in the eighteenth century when raised panels were used extensively in wainscot as well as entire walls. Intricate joints and beautiful proportions characterized this period. Changing styles didn't feature the framed panel as prominently; but, the frame-and-panel system survives today because it is one of the most reliable methods for dealing with dimensional change in solid lumber.

In a living tree, the cell walls are saturated with fluid. The life processes of the tree keep the fluid level constant, but once the tree is cut the cells begin to dry out. From that moment on, the wood is dimensionally unstable. Changes in size will occur with changes in moisture content; even after the wood is cut into lumber and dried, changes in atmospheric humidity will cause the wood to shrink or swell. It is this dimensional change that causes joints to open and boards to split. Early woodworkers recognized the problem and developed the frame and panel system to compensate for it. The system works so well that it has remained unchanged for centuries.

Dimensional change in wood can be traced to the cellular level. Wood is composed of bundles of elongated cells. As the moisture content

Illus. 268. Frame-and-panel joinery is often used in cabinetmaking, door making, and interior finish work.

changes, the cells expand or contract. Each cell changes only slightly, but the combined effect of all of the cells adds up to a significant change in dimension. As a result of the cell structure, most of the change occurs in the cell diameter and not in length. The consequence is that the longitudinal grain (long grain) is practically stable. There is some small change in length; but, unless you are dealing with very long spans, the effect is negligible. However, the width and the thickness of a board—perpendicular to the longitudinal grain—do change considerably with variations in moisture content.

Since the effect is cumulative, the wider a board is, the greater dimensional change will be. While a 6″-wide board may change only ⅛″ in width during an extreme change in humidity, a similar board that is 12″ wide may vary as much as ¼″ in width. For the same boards, the thickness also changes; but, that effect is essentially minimal when the board thickness is less than about 2″.

The cell structure has another effect on the tendency of wood to adjust dimensionally to moisture content. More change occurs tangent to the rings than occurs in the radial direction, perpendicular to the rings (Illus. 269). This means that the way the wood is cut affects the dimensional stability. In quarter-sawn lumber the grain across the width is essentially radial grain since the saw blade cuts at a right angle to the rings and the board only contains a small segment of each of the many rings. The grain in plain-sawn lumber is closer to tangential grain since the board contains larger segments of a relatively few rings. In the quarter-sawn board, most of the dimensional change takes place across its thickness; whereas for the plain-sawn board, most of the shrinkage and swelling takes place across its width. This means that the width of plain-sawn lumber will change almost twice as much as that of quarter-sawn lumber.

Frame-and-panel construction allows the wood to move without causing damage or changing the overall dimensions of the project.

Like most traditional crafts, frame-and-panel joinery has its own vocabulary. The long, narrow piece of wood used to make the frame members is called a *stick*. The edge of the stick is often moulded; traditionally this was done with a special plane. Moulding the edge with a plane is called *sticking*. The resulting moulded edge is also called sticking (Illus. 270).

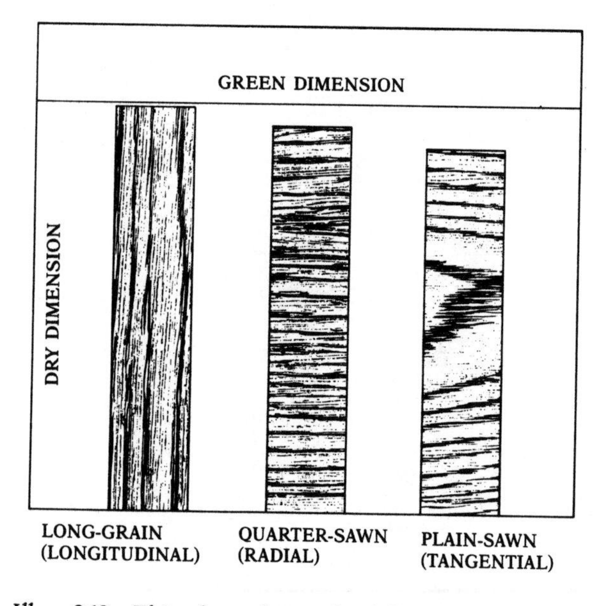

Illus. 269. This chart shows the difference in shrinkage between long-grain, quarter-sawn, and plain-sawn lumber.

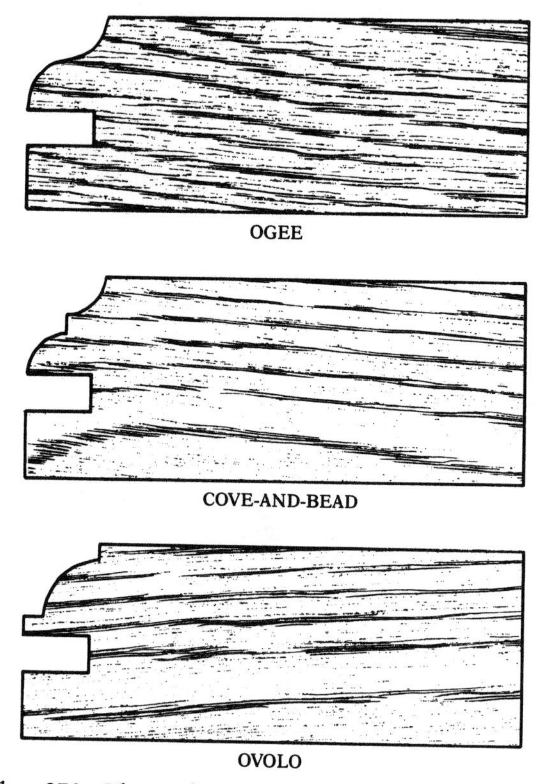

Illus. 270. The ovolo, cove and bead, and ogee are three popular types of sticking.

The stick is cut into several types of frame members. The vertical members on the outside of the frame are called *stiles*. The horizontal members are called *rails*. A vertical member inside the framework is called a *mullion* (Illus. 271). The large board that fits inside the frame is a *panel*. A *raised panel* has a bevel cut around the edges. The flat area in the center of a raised panel is called the *field*.

The simplest type of frame-and-panel consists of a single, flat panel surrounded by a frame without sticking. The mortise-and-tenon is the joint that has been traditionally preferred for joining the frame. Mortises are chopped in the stiles, and the rails acquire the tenons. A groove is cut on the inside edge of the rails and stiles to accept the panel. A haunched tenon is used on the rail to fill the exposed end of the groove.

Because the frame members are relatively narrow, their dimensions won't change much as the moisture content varies. This makes the outside dimension of the frame stable. The wide panel inside the frame, however, is subject to dimensional change. To allow for this movement, the grooves are made deeper than the expected amount of change. The panel can be cut to fill the groove at the top and bottom because the length of the panel won't change appreciably. It is the width of the panel that will change the most, so the panel is cut to leave a space between the panel edge and the bottom of the groove. The panel floats in the frame; no glue or fasteners constrain its movement. The only place that you can attach the panel to the frame is in the middle of the top and bottom rails. It is not always done, but attaching the panel at these points will help

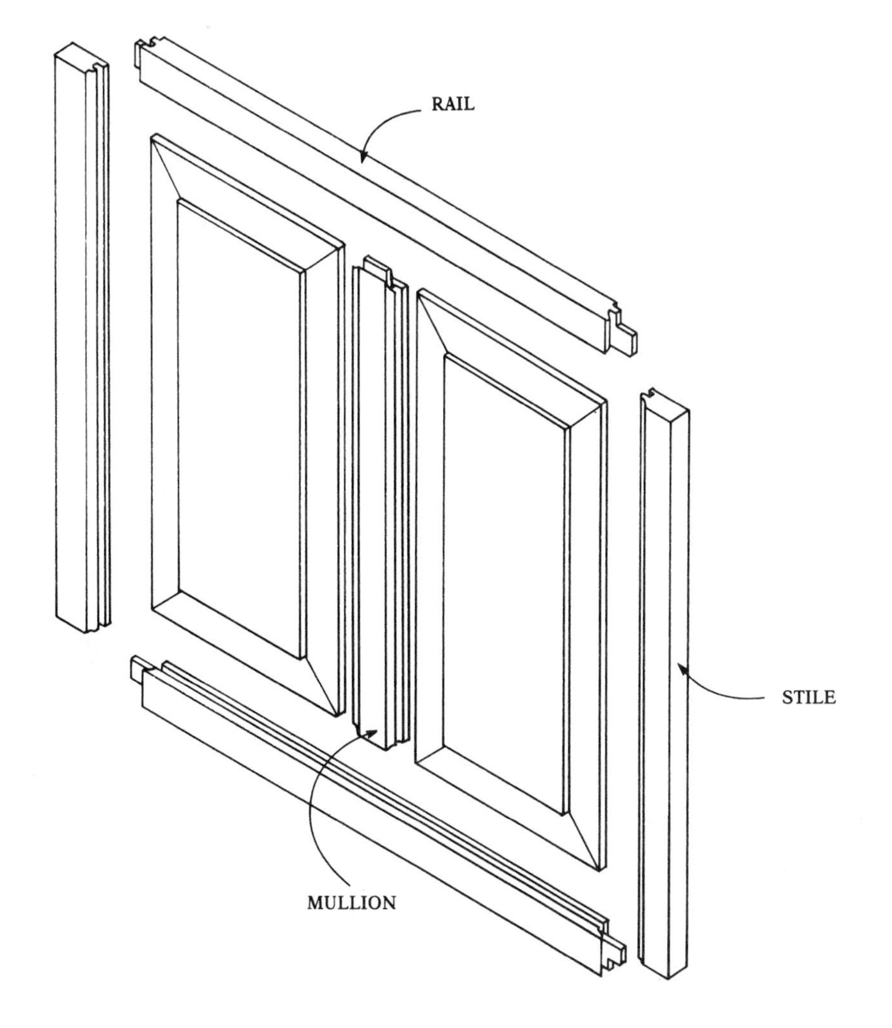

Illus. 271. Frame-and-panel terminology.

to keep it in alignment. You can use a nail or dowel driven from the rear or a daub of glue. Silicone rubber glue works especially well in this application because it remains flexible.

In earlier times it was difficult to make a thin panel, so the raised panel was developed. The edges of the panel are bevelled so that the outer edge is thin enough to fit into the groove in the frame. It is interesting to note that the bevel was commonly put to the back to show a flat panel on the front. Today the raised panel is thought of as both decoration and the traditional look, and always placed to the front. Nowadays, when a flat panel is desirable, plywood is typically used.

When the frame is too large for a single panel, a mullion is used to divide the frame. The mullion-to-rail joint doesn't take as much stress as the corner joints, so a simple stub tenon that fits into the groove is often used.

The addition of sticking complicates the joinery. If the sticking runs the full length of the parts, it must be mitred, scribed, or coped at the joints.

Making the Frame

The size of the frame members is largely a matter of personal taste and depends on the size and proportions of the project. For cabinetwork, the stiles are usually in the 1½" to 2½" range; for wall panelling and doors, the stiles may be as wide as 6". As the frame members become wider, they can present dimensional change problems. Generally, 6" is the safe limit on stile width, unless provision is made for dimensional change of the frame. All of the frame members can be of equal width or of any proportions that you choose. A traditional rule of thumb is to make the stiles three-fourths the width of the top rail and the top rail two-thirds the width of the bottom rail.

Cut the stiles to the full height of the frame, and cut the rails to the full width. Some woodworkers prefer to cut the panel groove next, while others prefer to chop the mortise first. Each method has its virtues. If you cut the groove first, you can use it to position the mortise; however, cutting the groove removes your layout lines, and, unless the mortising chisel is exactly the width of the groove, it is hard to chop the mortise accurately. In these directions, I'll chop the mortise first.

Lay out the mortise as described in Chapter 2. You need to take the size of the groove into consideration, since the joint is easiest to make when the mortise is approximately the same width as the groove. Chop the mortise with a mortising chisel, then plow the groove. Next, lay out a haunched tenon on the rail; the haunch is sized to fill the end of the groove. Following the traditional practice the joint is still often assembled without glue; peg or wedges secure the joint. Assembling the joint without glue has the advantage of eliminating any possibility of glue from the joint getting into the panel groove and inadvertently gluing the panel in place. However, in many modern applications, glue is used to secure the corner joints.

The joinery in the example above uses standard mortise-and-tenon techniques. Other joints can be used (Illus. 272). When decorative sticking is added, as I said, the joinery becomes more complex. One way to get around the problem is to assemble the frame before sticking (Illus. 273). Use a router with a pilot-guided bit to do the sticking. This can leave a rounded corner that may or may not be desirable, depending on the style of the project. One way to avoid the round corner is to stop the sticking a short distance before reaching the corner. This leaves the corner square and produces its own decorative effect. The mason's mitre is another solution; after the sticking is done, use a chisel to square up the corner. The mason's mitre works best ordinarily when a simple bevel is used; but, if you are adept at carving, you may be able to use this method with more complicated designs.

MITRED STICKING

A mitre can be used at the point where the sticking on the rail and stile meet (Illus. 274). A chisel is used to cut the mitre on the stile; use a 45° guide block to guide the chisel. After making the mitre, use the chisel or a fine-toothed saw to remove the waste portion of the sticking between the mitre cut and the end of the stile. This area must be flat because the shoulder on the rail will butt against it to form the visible joint line.

Note that when making the tenon, the rear shoulder is cut back farther than the front shoulder. The difference between the positions of the

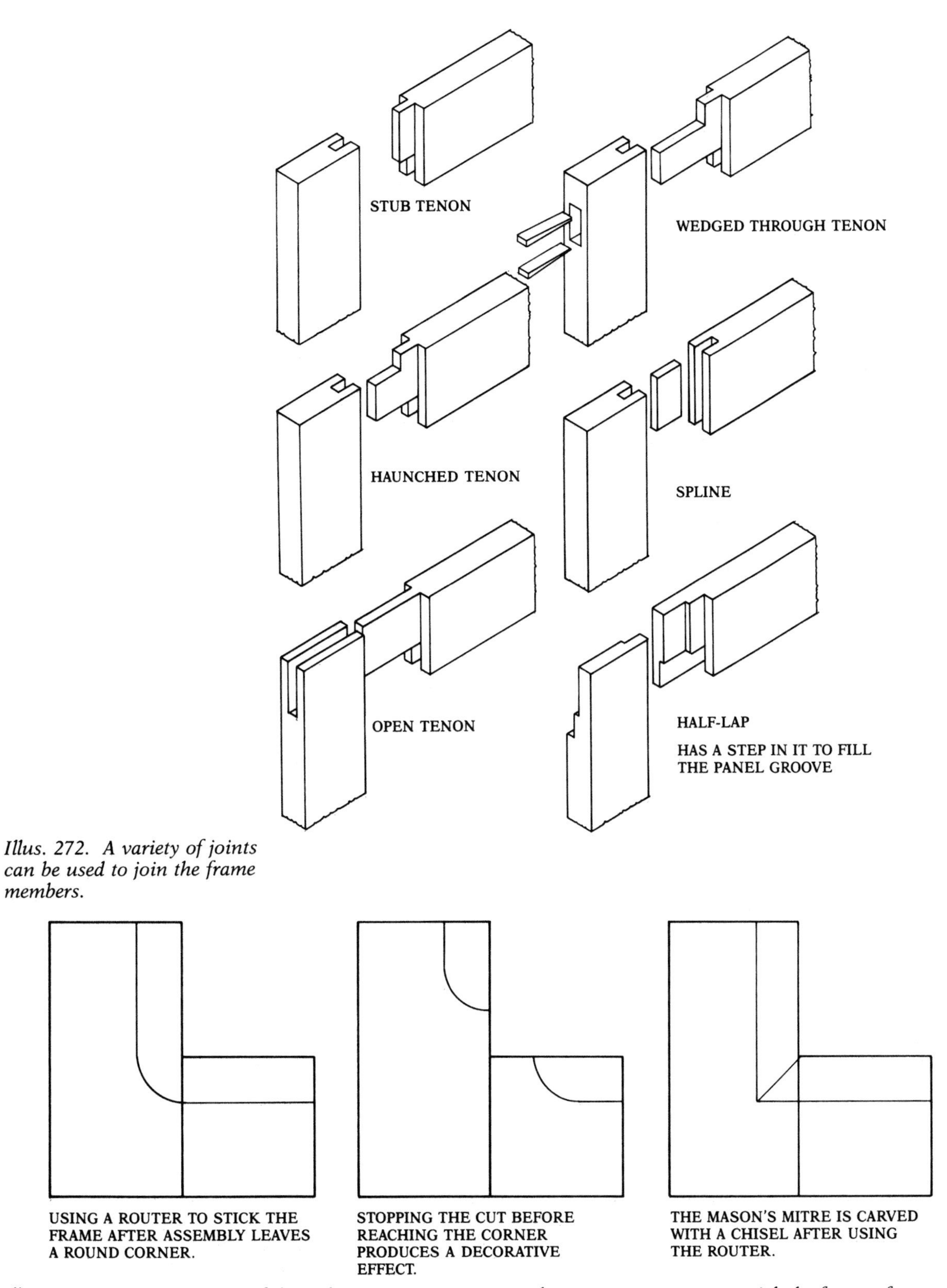

Illus. 272. A variety of joints can be used to join the frame members.

Illus. 273. You can use one of these three corner treatments when you use a router to stick the frame after assembly.

front shoulder and the rear shoulder is exactly the width of the sticking.

Next, mitre the end of the sticking on the rail. Dry-assemble the joint, and make any necessary adjustments.

When a mullion meets a rail, the joint must be mitred on both edges. The procedure is basically the same, except that you can't use a saw to remove the waste. All of the work is done with a chisel.

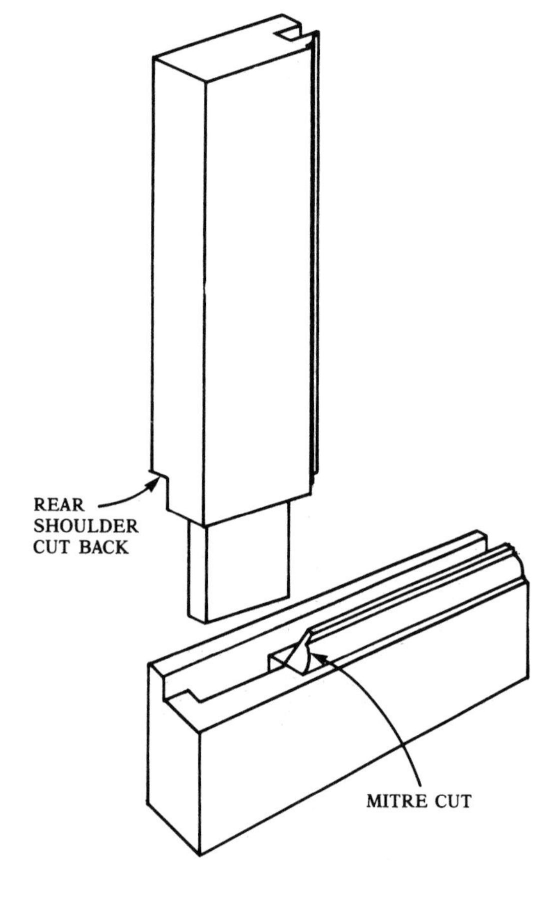

Illus. 274. Mitred sticking step by step.

SCRIBED JOINTS

The mitre joint is fairly easy to make and looks good, but there is one problem with it; shrinkage in the stile or rail can cause the joint to open. This isn't too much of a problem when the frame members are relatively narrow, but the wide frame members found in wall panelling and in entry doors can shrink enough to create a noticeable gap in the joint. One solution to this shrinkage-gap problem is the scribed joint. In a

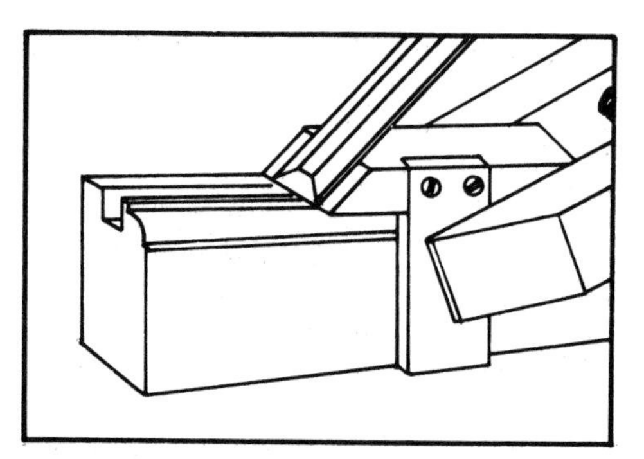

1. Use a 45° guide block to guide the chisel as you make the mitre cut on the stile.

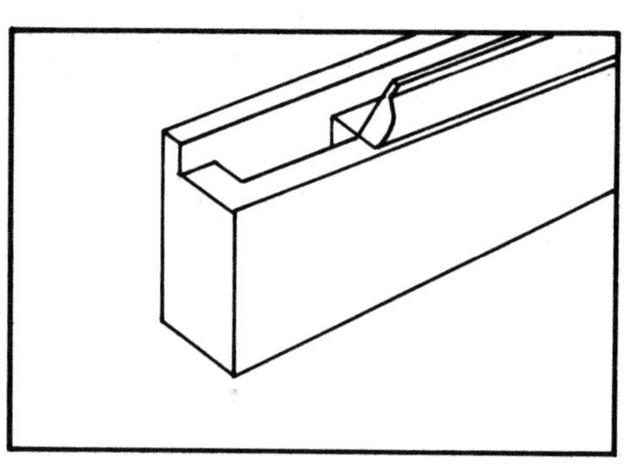

2. Remove the waste down to the joint line.

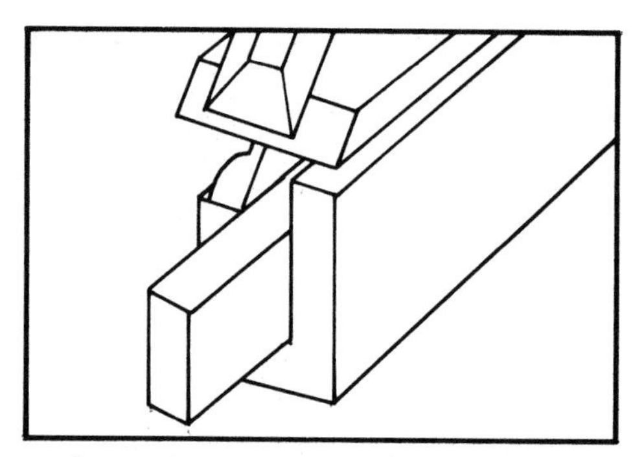

3. Mitre the sticking on the rail.

scribed joint, the end of the sticking on the rail is cut to the reverse profile of the sticking on the stile. The sticking on the stile is cut off square; the scribed end on the rail fits over the sticking on the stile. The rail is usually the larger part and therefore has a greater chance of moving. As the rail shrinks or swells, the scribed end of the sticking slides over the sticking on the stile, and the joint remains tight.

The scribed joint is easiest to make if the sticking is simple, but it can be done with any sticking profile except those that are undercut. In this example, ovolo sticking is used (Illus. 275). The procedure is similar to the one described above,

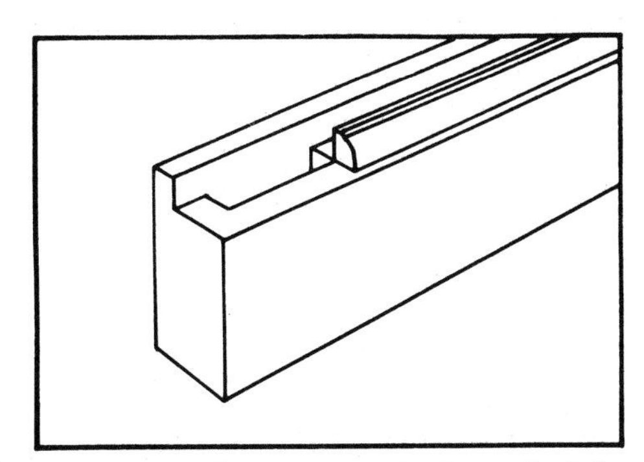

1. Make a square cut in line with the end of the mortise on the stile. Remove the waste down to the joint line.

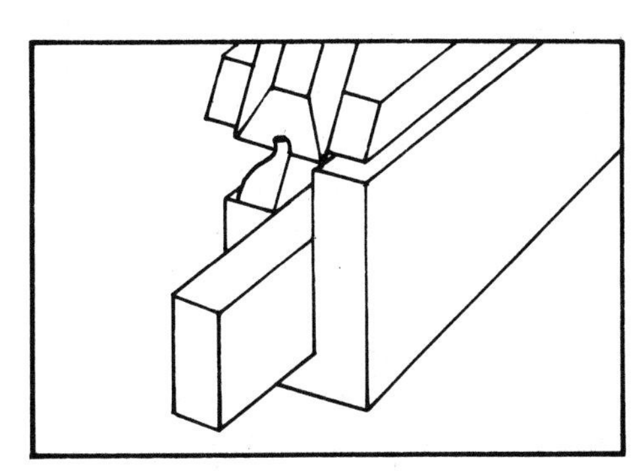

2. Mitre the sticking on the rail.

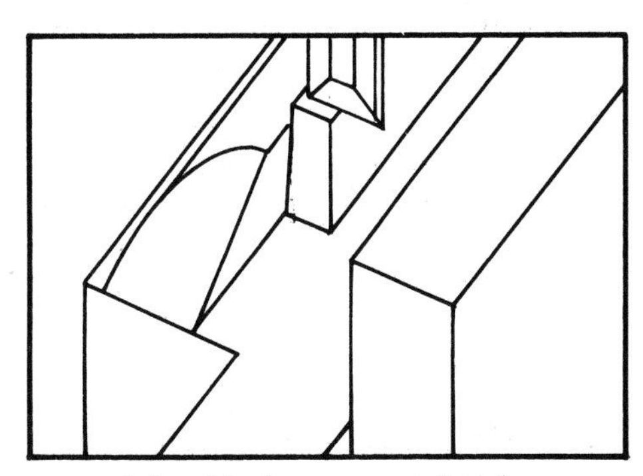

3. Use a straight chisel to cut out listel area.

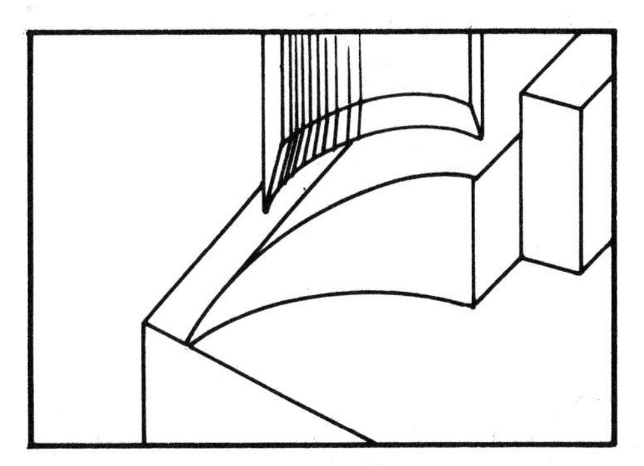

4. Use an incannelled gouge to cope the end of the sticking. Use the profile of the mitre as a guide.

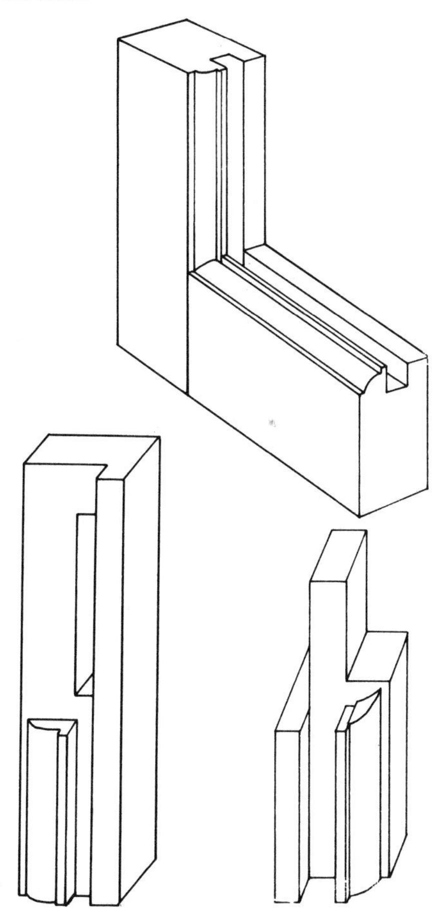

Illus. 275. Scribed joint step by step.

but a square cut is made on the stile instead of a mitre cut. Make the cut directly in line with the end of the mortise. Next, cut a mitre on the rail. Align the guide block so that the mitre will end exactly at the shoulder of the tenon. This mitre serves as a guide to make the scribed cut. Next, you will need chisels to match the sticking. For the ovolo, a straight chisel and an incannelled gouge with a radius that matches the sticking are needed. The line, or profile, formed by the intersection of the mitre and the face of the sticking is your guide. Use the chisels to carve away the waste to leave a contoured cut that is essentially parallel to the tenon shoulder.

In a standard scribed joint, there is a weak area of short grain on the scribed sticking that may break off. The scribed mitre has the advantages of a scribed joint and eliminates the short-grain problem (Illus. 276).

COPED JOINTS

The two previous methods are basically hand-tool techniques. When you are using power equipment to do the sticking, the coped joint is the most efficient. In a coped mortise-and-tenon joint, the sticking runs uninterrupted along the stile; a reverse profile cut along the tenon shoulder fits over the stile (Illus. 277). This joint has the same advantages as the scribed joint, but it is easier to make with power equipment. Special cutters for your shaper or router are available to make this joint. Large shops use a tenoner equipped with cope heads to make the joint. The advantage of using the tenoner is that full-length tenons can be used. The shaper or router can only produce stub tenons.

The shaper cutters usually are designed so that one cutter cuts the sticking and the groove, and the other cutter makes the cope cut and the stub tenon. There are some router bit sets that are similar. They must be used, however, with a heavy-duty router capable of handling ½"-shank bits. For use in smaller routers, there are sets that make the joint in several passes. Illus. 278 shows the steps involved for one particular set. Other sets may require different procedures, but the idea is the same. The router must be mounted in a table to perform the operation. Follow the manufacturer's safety precautions when using these sets.

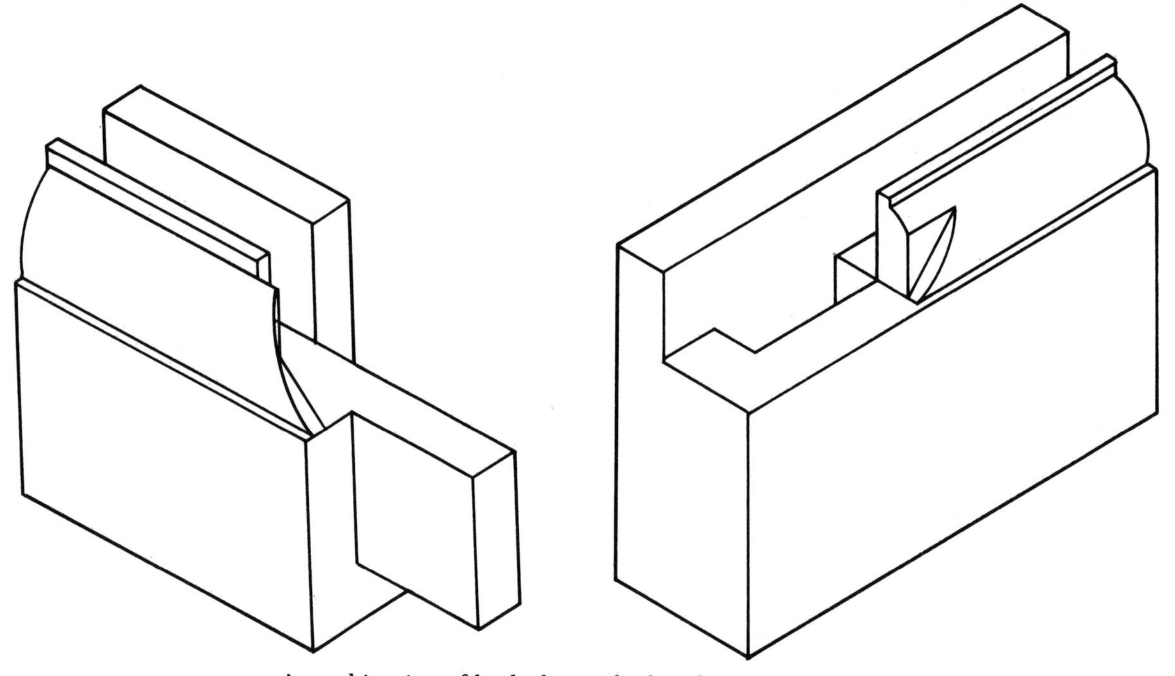

A combination of both the scribed and mitre joints. It eliminates the fragile short-grain area on the scribed sticking.

Illus. 276. Scribed mitre.

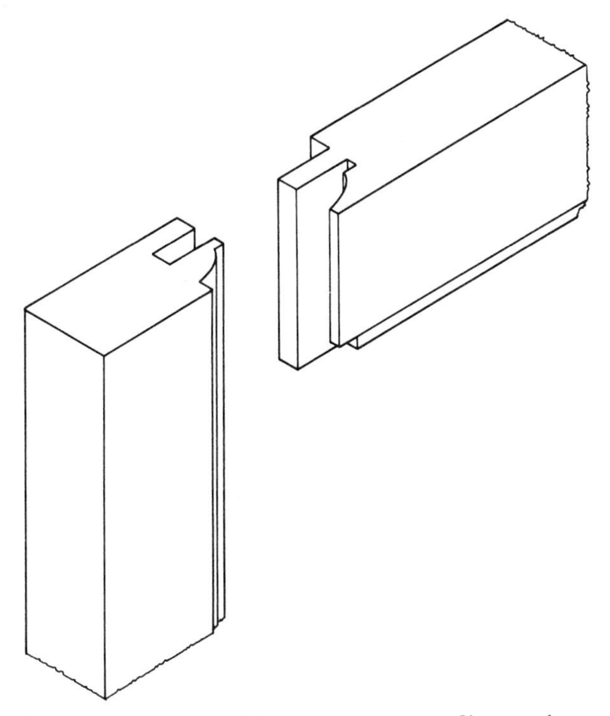

Illus. 277. In a coped joint, a reverse profile cut along the tenon shoulder fits over the sticking on the stile.

Whether using the shaper or the router, it is standard procedure to make the end-grain cuts first, since the end grain is likely to split out at the completion of the cut (Illus. 279). The split-out area will be cleaned up when the sticking is cut.

The router sets have a ball-bearing pilot that guides the cutter. This makes them especially well suited for making arched top frames (Illus. 280). The top rail is cut to the desired shape before routing. The pilot on the bit will follow the contour of the rail exactly. Illus. 281 shows the completed router-cut joint.

DOWEL-REINFORCED TENON

The stub tenon made with the bit sets on the shaper or router fits into the groove, so no mortise is needed. Large doors such as entry doors often use a coped stub-tenon joint, but they are reinforced with dowels. The top joint on the hinge side of a door must be capable of handling stress equal to about five times the weight of the door. The dowel reinforced tenon has proven to

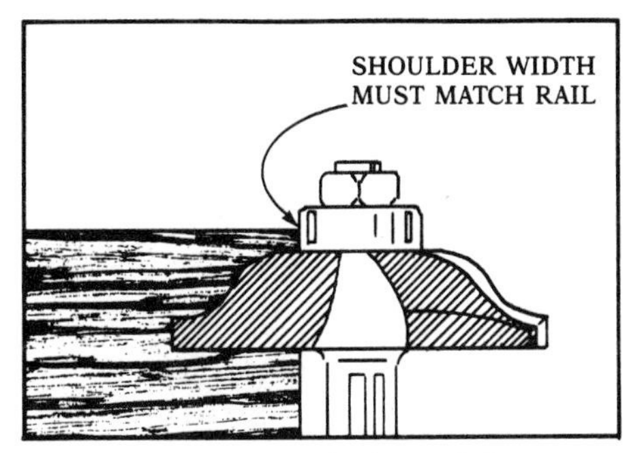

1. The cope cut is made with the rail face up on the router table.

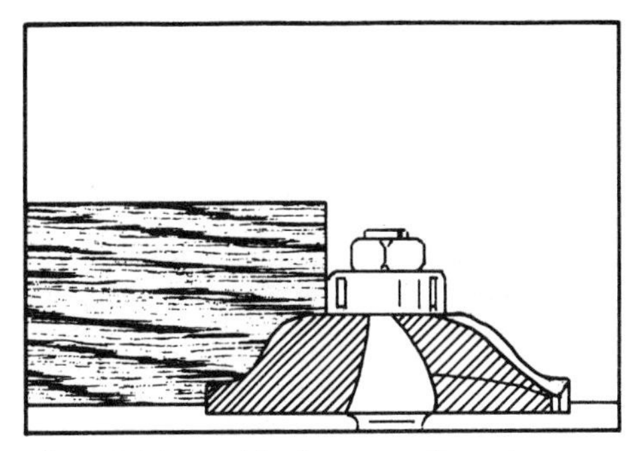

2. Cut the sticking with the parts face down on the router table. Make sure that the shoulder width matches the cope cut.

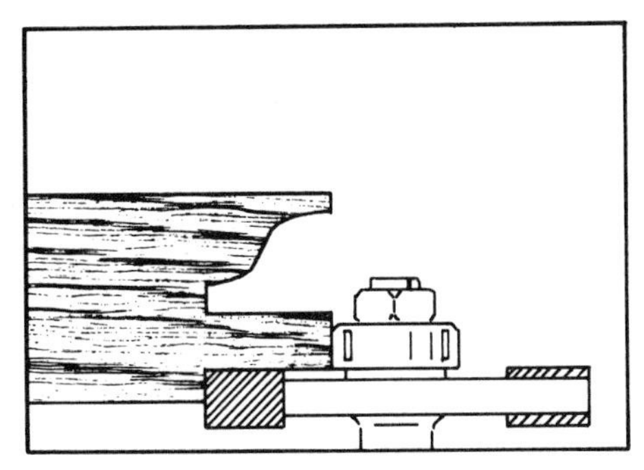

3. The stub tenon is formed by making a cut on the back of the rail. The tenon width should equal the width of the cutter.

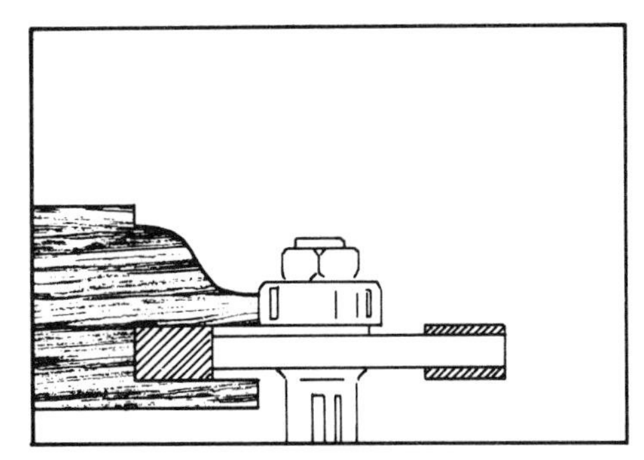

4. The groove is cut with the parts face up. Make sure that it is positioned to line up with stub tenon.

Illus. 278. Router-made coped joint step by step.

Illus. 279. An L-shaped support block clamped to the work makes it more stable during the end-grain cuts.

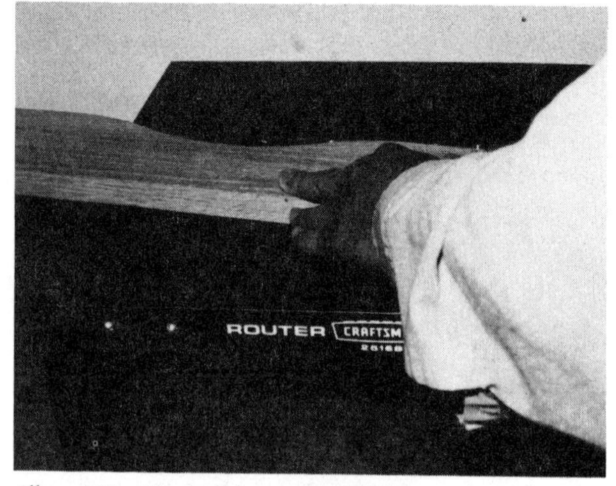

Illus. 280. The ball-bearing pilot that guides the cutter makes it easy to stick arched-top frames.

Illus. 281. When all the steps on the router table are complete, the completed joint looks like this.

be the strongest joint for this application. It is stronger than either the pinned tenon or the wedged tenon.

The unreinforced stub-tenon joint is strong enough for parts that won't receive a lot of stress, such as wall panelling that is supported by the wall, for example. Because the stub tenon is easy to mass-produce, you will frequently see it used inappropriately. It is the standard joint used for panel doors in most factory-made kitchen cabinets. In the repair shop, I learned that the unreinforced stub tenon isn't really strong enough for use on doors. The hinge-side joint often breaks. Following the inspiration of entry-door construction, we repaired the joints using dowels. I recommend that you reinforce the stub tenon with dowels in the first place and thus avoid later repair (Illus. 282). It is easiest if you drill the holes before you shape the tenon. On most cabinet doors, the tenon is ¼" thick, so it is difficult to drill a ¼"-diameter hole after the tenon is cut. Drill the holes deep enough so that the dowels will get a good bite in the rail.

Illus. 282. Dowels give added strength to the stub tenon.

SPLINE JOINTS

Spline joints provide a quick, simple way to make frames. The resulting joint is at least as strong as a stub tenon. This joint is most useful, however, when no sticking is present. Set up the table saw to cut the panel groove. After cutting the panel groove, cut the parts to length. The length of the rails will be equal to the overall width minus two times the width of the stile, just as if this were a simple butt frame. Next, use a tenoning jig to cut grooves for the splines in the ends of the rails. Each spline fits into the groove on one end of the rail and the panel groove on the stile. Make the spline short enough so that it won't interfere with the panel. This joint is particularly good when you will be using a plywood panel. Since the plywood doesn't have the same dimensional-change problem as the plain-sawn lumber, the panel can be glued in the groove, and it will give added strength.

APPLIED MOULDINGS

If you examine antique frame-and-panel construction closely, as I have, you will notice that many times the moulding was actually added after the frame had been assembled; it is applied moulding rather than sticking done at an earlier step. This greatly simplifies the frame construction and can be very aesthetically pleasing. Illus. 283 shows several ways to use these applied mouldings.

Instead of using an applied moulding on both sides, you can cut a rabbet in the frame. The panel is placed in the rabbet, and a moulding attached to the frame holds it in place. Other variations include moulding with a tongue-and-groove or a large groove that accepts the full thickness of the frame.

Making Panels

The panel can play an important visual role in the design. Flat panels can be used for a simple look or to display highly figured wood. Raised panels are the traditional favorite. By varying the size and shape of the field, you can create a different look; but, most people opt for what they consider the traditional design.

Wide panels usually will need to be glued up from smaller boards. A panel butt with no reinforcement is all that is needed (see Chapter 2). To show off a highly figured piece of wood, you can resaw it into two thinner pieces and glue them

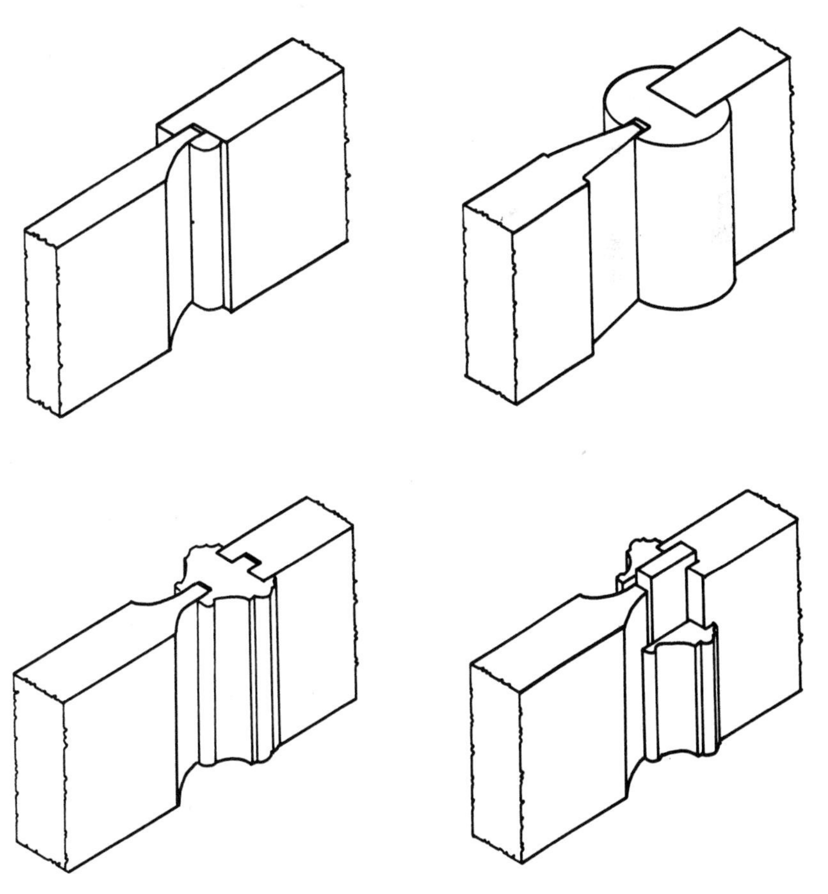

Illus. 283. Applied mouldings can be used for a bold appearance or to simplify frame construction.

up in a book-match pattern. Veneered panels can be highly decorative using a variety of patterns.

FLAT PANELS

Usually a flat panel is made from thin stock and fits into a groove in the frame; but, this is not the only way that a flat panel can be used. You can rabbet the edge of the panel and bring the face flush with the frame. A bead around the edge of the panel can be used to delineate it.

The flat panel is usually recessed below the frame; but, it can also overlap the frame. Cut a groove in the edge of the panel. The tongue formed on the back of the panel fits into the groove in the frame. The edge of the panel can be left square, or a number of different decorative edges can be used. This same method can be used to show a recessed panel on the front. In this case, the overlap is placed to the back of the frame. By overlapping the panel in the back, you can use thicker stock for the panel.

RAISED PANELS

The raised panel is another method for using thicker stock. The bevelled edge allows the panel to fit into a groove in the frame. Even though the original purpose was to allow thicker panels to be used, the effect is so visually pleasing that it is usually used today for its decorative aspect.

In most cases, the field of the panel should not extend above the frame. If the panel is bevelled on one side only, then the panel must be thinner than the frame. Bevelling the panel on both sides permits the use of a panel that is the same thickness as the frame (Illus. 284).

Using planes, you can cut the bevel by hand. You can make a simple bevel, with no shoulder, using a standard plane. Lay out the desired thickness on the edge, and make a line where the bevel should stop. Hold the plane on the approximate angle, and begin planing. Plane the ends first, working from both sides to the middle; then, plane the sides. As the sole of the plane gets close to the layout lines, adjust the angle with each pass until the final pass just touches both lines. This method produces a panel that works, but lacks sharp visual definition as the bevel has no shoulder.

You can cut a shoulder using a fillister, then you can use a block plane to cut the bevel. The ultimate way to cut bevels with a plane is to use a proper panel-raising plane. These are speciality planes that are expressly designed for the job. The shoulder and the bevel are cut in one step. The plane iron is set skew to cut across the grain. Some of these planes incorporate a nicker to score the shoulder and to prevent tearouts. While some panel-raising planes produce a straight bevel similar to that produced with the fillister and block plane, others make a concave or double-angle bevel. The advantage of both the concave and the double angle bevel is that the part of the panel that fits into the groove is not as wedge shaped as it is when made with a flat-soled plane. By making the edge of the panel better match the groove dimension, the panel has more freedom of movement. With the straight bevel, the panel may wedge too tight as it expands or become loose and rattle in the groove when it shrinks.

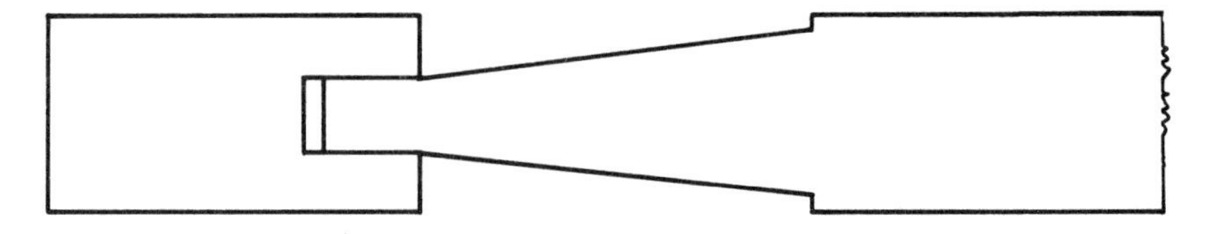

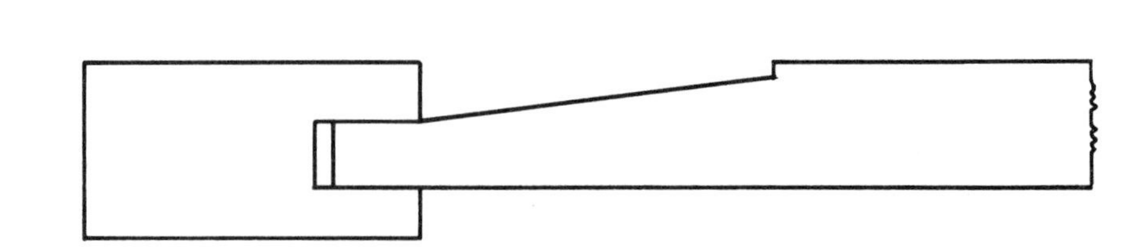

Illus. 284. The bevel on a panel permits you to use thicker stock and still have it fit the groove in the frame. A bevel on both sides permits you to use stock that is the same thickness as the frame.

The shoulder angle produced by a panel-raising plane is usually greater than 90°. This permits the plane to be used with various panel thicknesses and also without making an undercut shoulder.

The shaper and router are often used to raise panels. Special cutters are available; they are designed to produce a concave or double-angle bevel, so you get the same type of smooth-fitting panel produced by a panel-raising plane. By using a ball-bearing pilot, arched-top panels are easy to produce. The router must be mounted in a router table for the operation. Cut across the top and bottom first so that any tearouts can be removed as the sides are bevelled. Because each cutter has its own characteristics, be sure to follow the manufacturer's recommendations when using it. Since the cutter must remove a significant amount of wood, proper adjustment of the feed rate is important. If you have trouble making the cut in a single pass, adjust the cutter to take a lighter cut, and run all of the panels through; then, readjust the cutter to the final setting, and make another pass.

The table saw can also be used to make the bevels. A two-step approach is best. Begin by lowering the blade until it is projecting above the table just the height of the shoulder. Set the rip fence for the width of the bevel. Place the panel face down on the table, and make all four shoulder cuts. When all of the shoulder cuts are complete on all of the panels for the project, set the saw to make the bevel. Place a panel on its edge next to the blade, and raise the blade to the height of the shoulder. Next, make a mark on the edge of the panel indicating the thickness at the edge. Since this will be a straight bevel, mark the thickness so that the panel will be snug in the groove at a point about ¼" in from the edge. Mark a line connecting the bottom of the shoulder cut to the mark on the edge: this is the bevel angle.

Then, hold the panel against the fence and behind the blade so that you can sight across the blade. Adjust the blade tilt until it matches the angle on the panel.

Make a wooden zero-clearance insert for the saw throat to prevent the edge of the panel from getting snagged on the lip. Lower the blade, and install the zero-clearance insert. Attach the insert with screws, or clamp it down; then, turn on the saw, and slowly raise the blade to make the slot in the insert. Attach a high auxiliary fence to the rip fence to help support the panel. The height of the auxiliary fence depends on what size the panels are, but it should be at least 10". Adjust the fence so that the blade will line up with the mark on the panel. The panel should be positioned with the bevel side away from the fence; that way the waste piece can fall free and not get trapped between the fence and the blade. Make the cuts across the grain first, then cut the sides.

You can produce a double-angle bevel on the table saw that will have a better fit in the groove. After completing the above procedure, set the blade to make a square cut, and lower it to a little more than the depth of the panel groove in the frame. Adjust the fence so that a flat tongue will be cut around the edge of the panel. Run the panels through the saw again using the auxiliary fence for support.

The cut left by the saw will be too rough to use as is; you can plane it smooth or use sandpaper. One efficient way to smooth up the cut is to mount a disc sanding attachment on the table saw. Use the type that has a 2° bevel on the face; this type will leave straight sanding marks instead of semicircular ones. Set up the saw just as you did for cutting the bevels, and run the panels through again. The sanding disc will remove the saw marks and leave a smooth surface.

The radial-arm saw can be used in a similar manner to make raised panels. You will need to use an auxiliary table to lift the work high enough to get the proper tilt on the saw. Rather than tilt the saw, you can build an angle table. Then, set the saw to the horizontal position. *Be sure to use some type of blade guard when using the saw in this operation. Keep your hands well away from the blade.*

PLYWOOD PANELS

Even though the frame-and-panel system was developed for use with solid lumber, nevertheless plywood panels are often used today. Plywood is easier to handle in relatively thin sheets than solid lumber, so it is ideal for flat panels. Raised panels can be made from plywood, but the plies will show; you can use wood-veneer tape to hide the plies. Plywood panels can be glued directly to the frame because there is no problem with dimensional change. This stiffens the frame so there is less stress on the frame joints.

Wall Panelling Joints

Since a panelled wall involves a large area that may contain inside corners, outside corners, windows, doors, and a fireplace, it is not practical to make a single frame for the entire wall (Illus. 285). Individual frames for sections of the wall are used, and the frames are joined together. The joinery is actually fairly simple. The joints are typically designed more for appearance than for strength, since the panelling will be supported by a softwood ground.

SOFTWOOD GROUNDS

The softwood ground is a framework of softwood strips attached to the structure of the building. In new construction, the ground is usually applied early in the interior finish work before plastering. Design the ground so that it can be firmly attached to the studs and so that it will provide adequate mounting surfaces for the panels at appropriate locations. By using a ground, the design of the frames for the panels is not limited by the stud locations. Joinery for the ground can be simple; half-lap or mortise-and-tenon joints will give strength where members cross. Use shims between the studs and the ground as necessary to make the ground plumb and straight. An accurate ground makes the job of installing the panels that much easier. If portions of the wall will be plastered, the ground should be the same thickness as the finished plaster.

The panels are attached to the ground last, after all the other finish work is done, to avoid damage to the panels. There are several ways to attach the panels to the softwood ground (Illus.

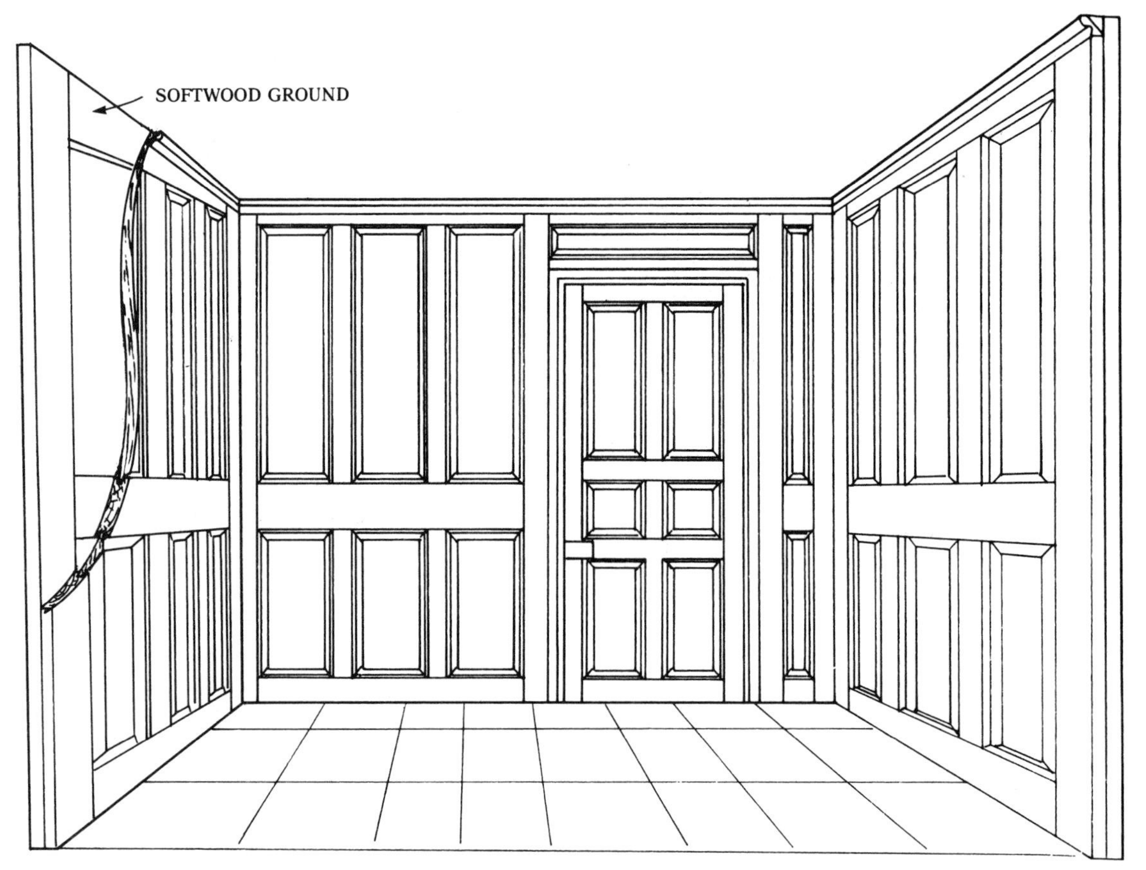

Illus. 285. Panelled walls are usually made in sections and applied to a softwood ground that is firmly attached to the wall studs.

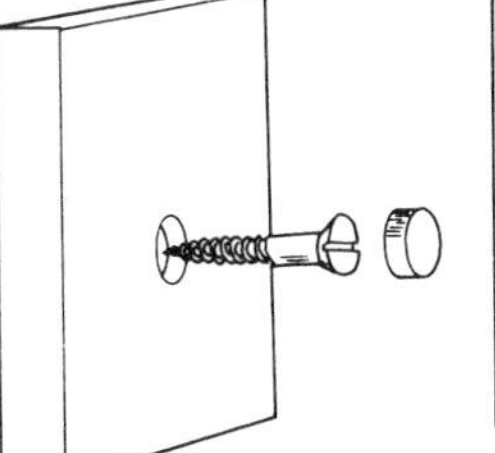

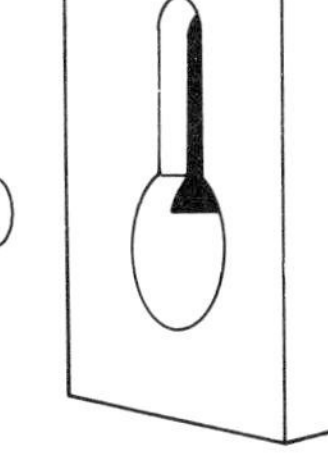

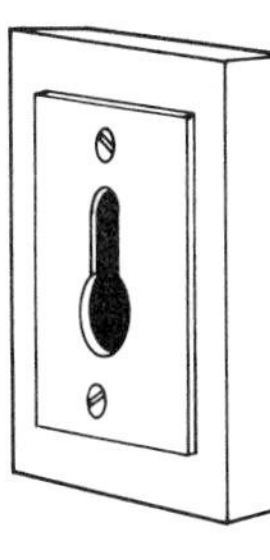

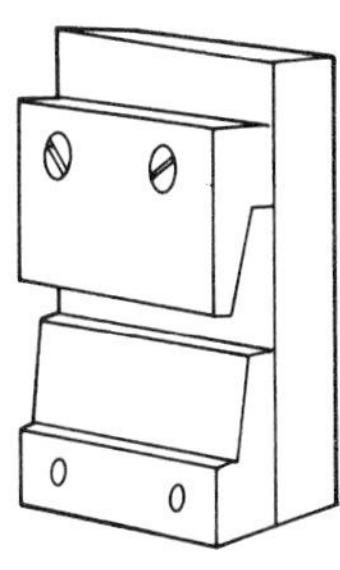

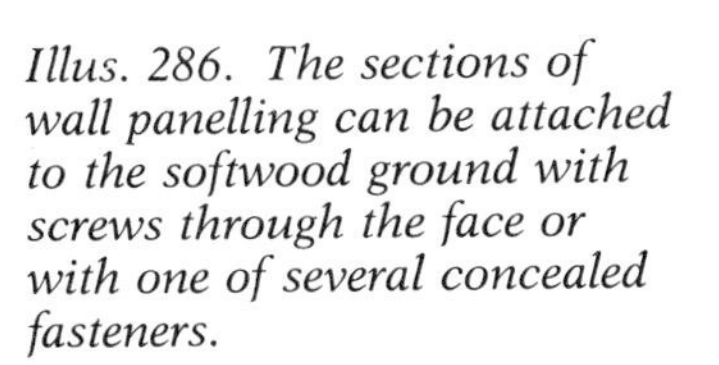

Illus. 286. The sections of wall panelling can be attached to the softwood ground with screws through the face or with one of several concealed fasteners.

286). Keyhole-slotted screw holes on the back of the panel frames provide a completely concealed attachment. You can use a special router bit to make the slot or use metal plates that have a keyhole slot. The difficulty is that the screws must be placed accurately to line up with the slots. Interlocking wood blocks or metal hangers also provide concealed attachment, but the alignment is easier. Screws driven through the face of the frame can be concealed with cover fillets or with dowel buttons.

MAKING THE PANELS

The panels and frames are usually not made on-site. It is much easier to make them in a shop, and then assemble them on the wall after they are done. Take careful measurements of the area to be panelled. Story sticks will be very helpful. Make a stick for each section of wall and lay it on the floor in front of the wall. Mark all openings and corners on the stick. This will give you a full-size reference to use at the shop. The frames and panels are made using the same methods described earlier. When the panels are large, plywood and applied mouldings are sometimes used (Illus. 287).

ASSEMBLY

The frame sections must be small enough to be carried into the building. They are assembled in place on the softwood ground. Joinery between sections is fairly simple (Illus. 288). A butt joint is often used and reinforced with nails or screws. The heads can be set and puttied, or dowel buttons can be used in the case of screw heads. If the work will be painted, the nail or screw heads won't be visible. A spline can be added for alignment, but a few nails or screws will still be necessary to pull the joint tight. The return bead-and-butt joint conceals the joint line.

Rabbets can also be used at the corner. They are easier to align than a butt, and there is less exposed edge. Shaping the edge will help conceal the joint. A barefaced tongue-and-groove is a good joint at an outside corner; a bead or ovolo can then be used to conceal the joint line.

A standard mitre can be hard to align when working with large frames; the rabbet mitre provides a ledge to aid in alignment. When the angle is greater than 90°, a double-tongue mitre joint provides a very secure joint that resists opening.

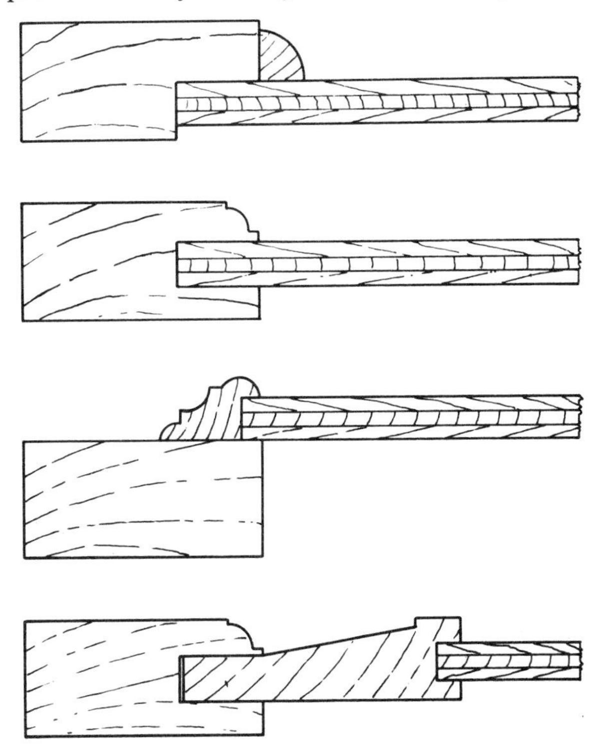

Illus. 287. Plywood panels can be used in conjunction with solid-wood frames and mouldings.

A simpler way to make an odd-angled joint is the double rabbet; this joint relies on nails to hold it tight. A bead can be used at the joint line on either of these joints.

Pilasters can be used for decorative effects at the corners (Illus. 289). A barefaced tongue-and-groove joins the panel frames to the pilaster. Inside corners can be treated in a similar fashion; the barefaced tongue-and-groove can be used. When you just want a rounded corner with no projections, you can use the standard tongue-and-groove joint.

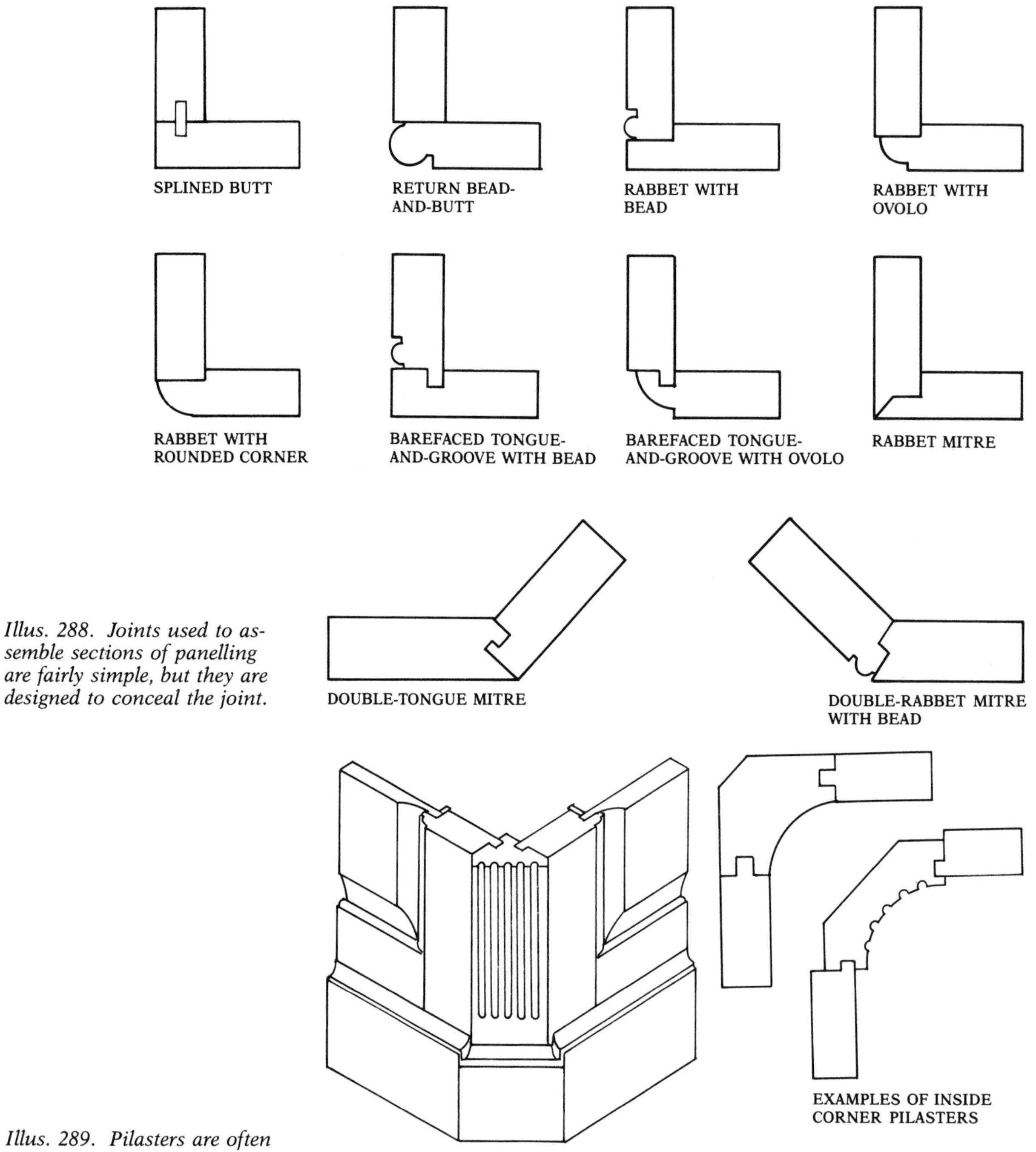

Illus. 288. Joints used to assemble sections of panelling are fairly simple, but they are designed to conceal the joint.

Illus. 289. Pilasters are often used at the corner.

11

Cabinetmaking Applications

Practically all of the joints I have described have an application in cabinetmaking, but this chapter will deal with some joints, in particular, that are closely associated with cabinetmaking. Cabinetmaking applications for some joints that I have already covered to some extent will be included along with some joints that I haven't covered yet.

Carcass Joints

The main body of any cabinet is called the carcass. The joints used in building the carcass determine the overall strength of the cabinet. Carcasses can be built in several ways, and each method uses a variety of joints.

Case construction is a method of making carcasses that uses wide boards as structural members (Illus. 290). It is particularly well suited for use with plywood and particleboard (see Chapter 12, page 178); but, it also works well with solid lumber, if you take care to avoid cross-grain joints. Keep the grain in the same orientation for all of the parts so that mating parts will shrink and swell together. That way dimensional change won't stress the joints.

The simplest joint for case construction is the reinforced butt. Dowels, splines, or mechanical fasteners can be used as reinforcement. Dadoes, grooves, and rabbets are also frequently used in case construction. When used with plywood, the joints can be cut through to the edge because the

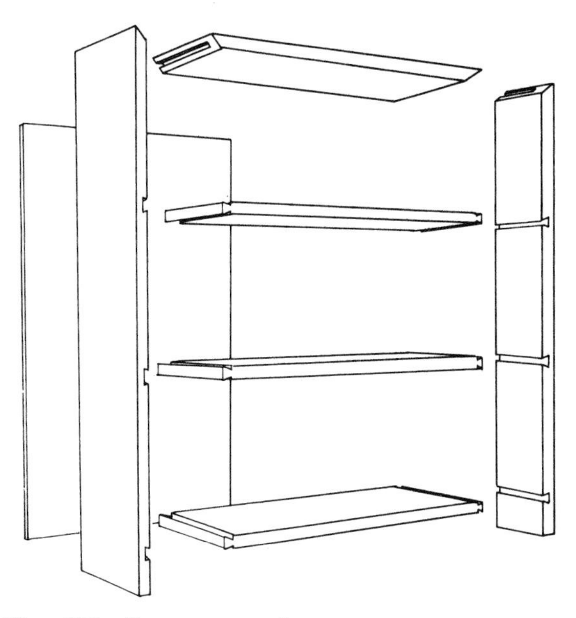

Illus. 290. Case construction.

edging added after assembly will hide the joint. When it is desirable to hide the joint in solid lumber, use stopped dadoes and grooves. The dovetail dado will add strength to the carcass because it prevents the parts from pulling apart.

Mitres are often used when appearance is particularly important. The mitres must be reinforced, however, for the joint to contribute to the strength of the carcass.

A type of mortise-and-tenon joint called carcass pinning adds considerably to the strength of case construction. Multiple small tenons called pins fit into mortises in the mating part (Illus. 291). This joint is most frequently used to attach vertical partitions inside a carcass. In its simplest form, the pins extend all the way through the other part. Wedges are used to secure the pins in the mortises. Unless the shoulders between the pins fit perfectly against the inside face of the mating part, the joint will be visible

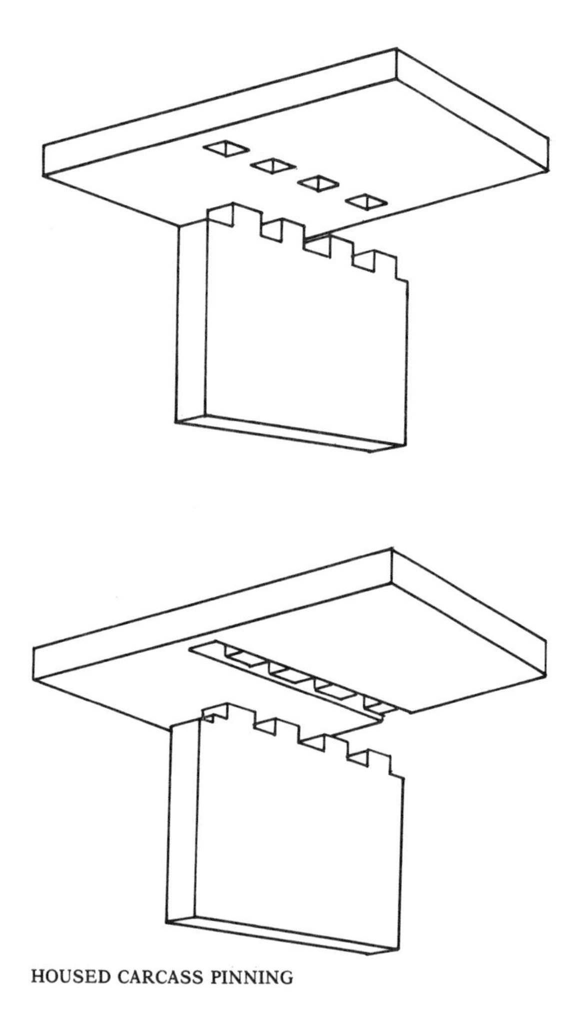

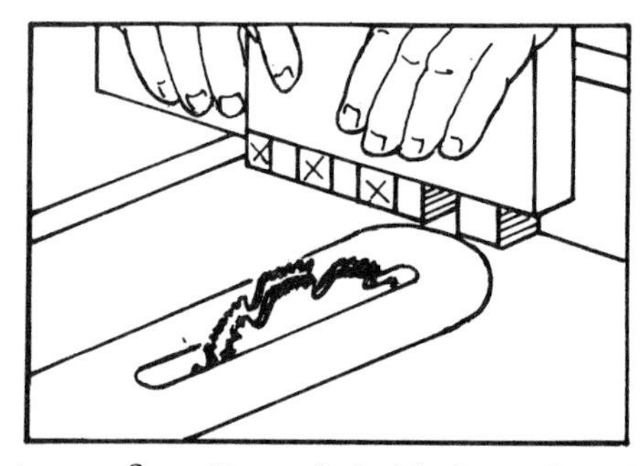

1. Cut tenons first. Use a dado blade or the table saw, or cut by hand with a backsaw and chisel.

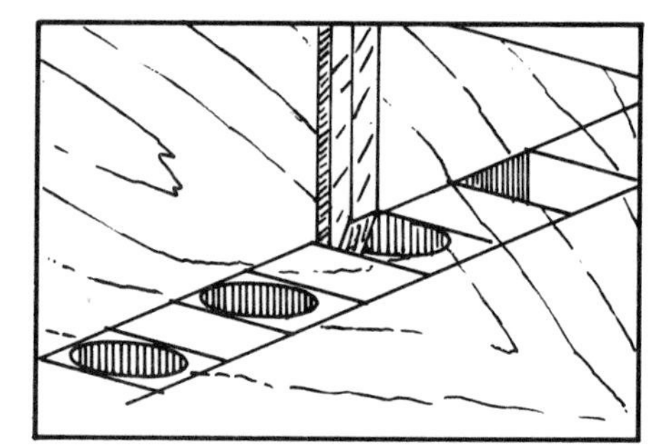

2. Use tenons to lay out mortise positions. Drill a hole to remove most of the waste. Square up the mortise with a chisel.

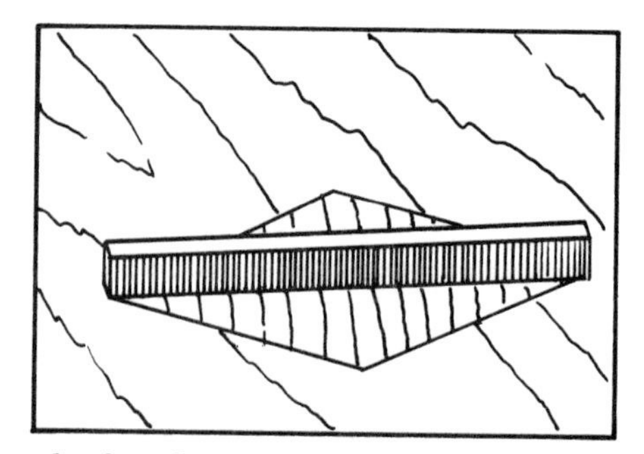

3. Cut a kerf in the tenons before assembly. Drive a wedge into the kerf to tighten the tenon in the mortise.

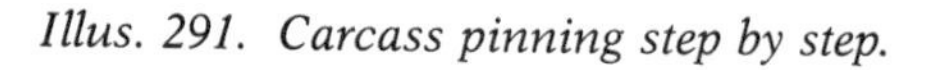

Illus. 291. Carcass pinning step by step.

from the interior of the cabinet. The housed version of this joint makes the joint less visible from the inside. For the housed carcass-pinning joint, cut a shallow dado before chopping the mortises. The dado will hide the shoulders between the pins, so slight imperfections in fit won't be visible.

Dovetails can be used to get a very strong corner joint. Through dovetails are typically used when the joinery is featured as a design element. Half-blind or full-blind dovetails can be used when it is desirable to hide the joint. Dovetails can be used in a variety of ways in case construction (Illus. 292).

The dovetails can be hand cut or machine made. The Keller dovetail jig is specifically designed to make carcass dovetails. The large Leigh dovetail jig will handle parts up to 24″ wide, so it can also be used to make carcass dovetails. It also has the advantage of being fully adjustable so that you can alter the spacing and size of the pins and tails to suit the project. Any

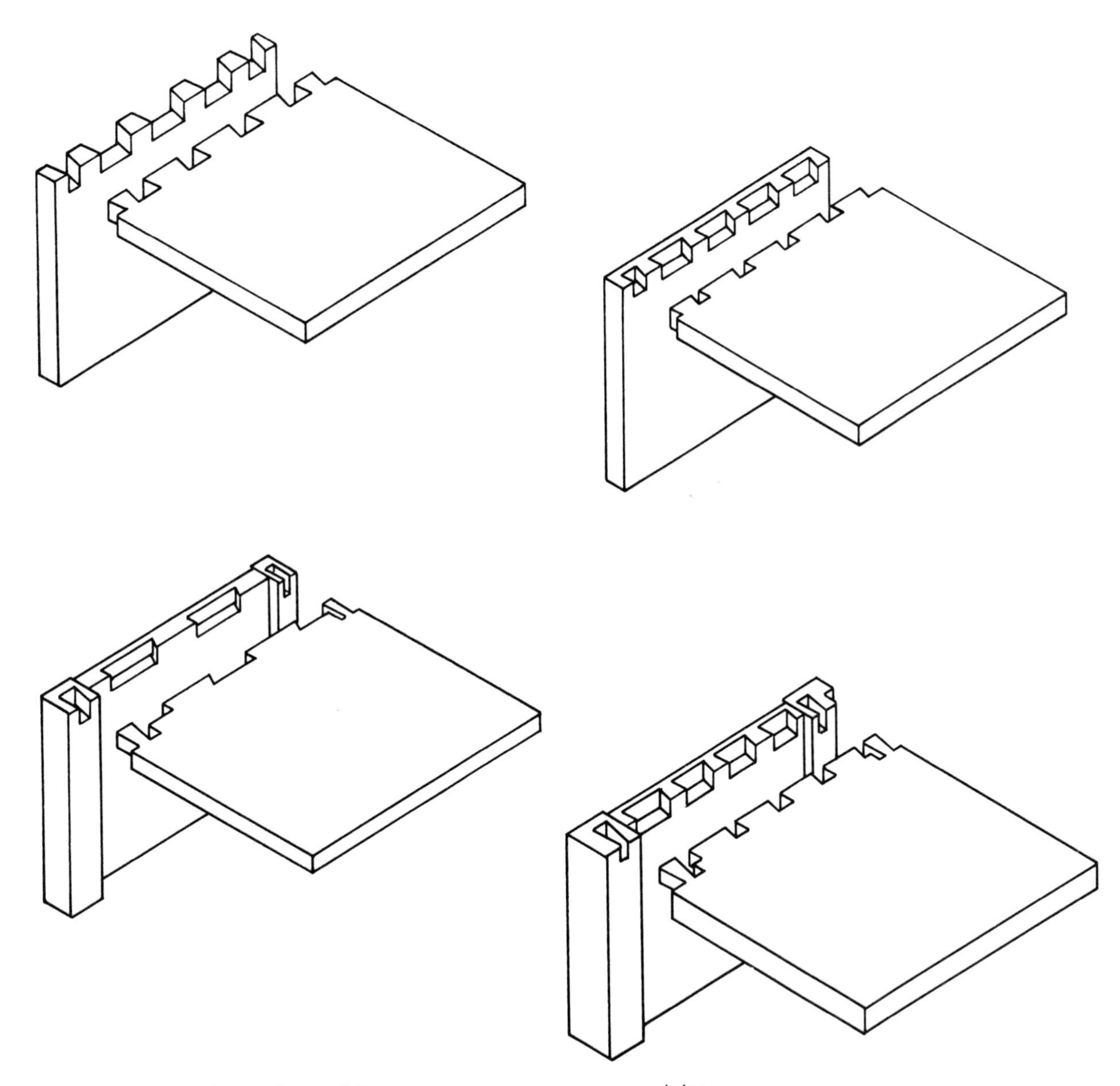

Illus. 292. Dovetails can be used for a very strong carcass corner joint.

of the other dovetail techniques described earlier can be used to make carcass dovetails.

Skeleton-frame construction uses a skeleton framework for structural strength and a thin skin over the framework for appearance (Illus. 293). Since the skin will hide the joints in the skeleton frame, you can design the joints for maximum strength without regard to appearance. Mortise-and-tenon joints or half-laps are commonly used to assemble frames. Drawer blades, or guides, can be attached using double or triple through tenons. Through dovetails can be used at the corners.

The skin is applied after the skeleton is assembled. The skin is usually made from thin plywood, and it is attached with glue. Simple joints are used where pieces of the skin meet: typically butt or mitre joints. While the skin adds rigidity to the skeleton, the skin's corner joints don't make an important contribution to the strength of the carcass, so they don't need to be reinforced.

Panel construction is similar in some respects to skeleton-frame construction except that the framework is visible from the outside (Illus. 294). Panel construction was developed to deal with the dimensional changes caused by fluctua-

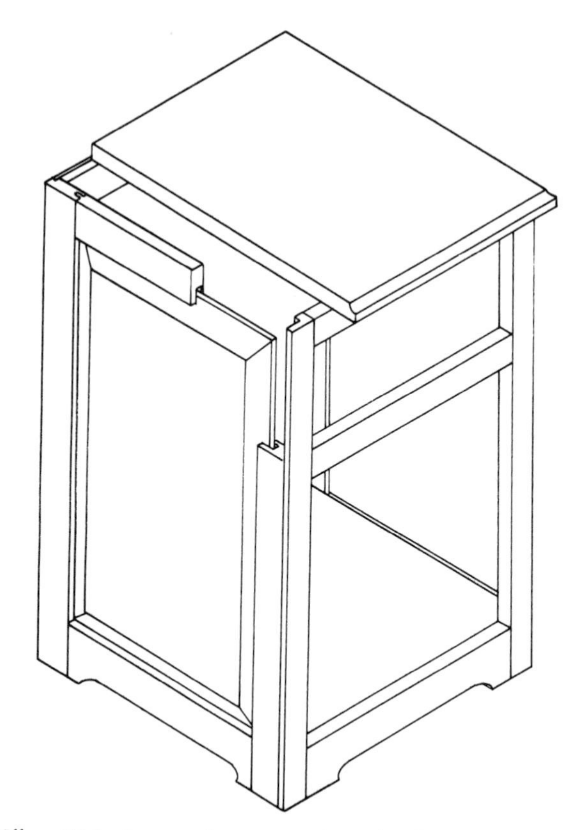

Illus. 294. In panel construction, the framework is visible on the outside of the project.

Illus. 293. Skeleton-frame construction uses a framework of narrow boards for strength and a thin skin for appearance.

tions in humidity. The framework is composed of relatively narrow parts that effectively remain dimensionally stable. Large panels float in grooves in the frame. The panels are free to shrink and swell inside the frames without affecting the overall carcass dimensions. Refer to Chapter 10 for complete details on making the panels and frames; in this section, I discuss how to use them in carcass construction.

There are two methods for using panel construction in making a carcass. In the first method, the frames and panels are assembled individually and then put together using case-construction techniques. Each frame and panel is treated as if it were a solid board. When you are using this method, make sure that all of the joints are made between frame members. The panels must be free to float and should not be used for structural attachment.

The other method is called post-and-panel construction (Illus. 295). In this method, large posts are used at the corners; they ordinarily extend down to form the legs of the cabinet. Rails attach to the posts with mortise-and-tenon joints. The panels rest in grooves cut in the posts and in the rails. Drawer blades, or guides, are attached to the posts with tenons.

A modified type of dovetail can be used with post-and-panel construction. Since the post is wider than the side rail, the dovetail on the front rail will have two different shoulder depths to match the differing widths. The haunch on the side rail tenon must be large enough to allow for the dovetail.

Cross-grain difficulties arise when attaching a solid-lumber top to a carcass that uses panel or skeleton-frame construction. The framework will remain relatively stable, but the top will shrink and swell considerably across its width. To prevent splits in the top, you must attach it in a way that provides for movement (Illus. 296). Metal or wood clips can be used to attach the top directly to the sides. When a subframe for the

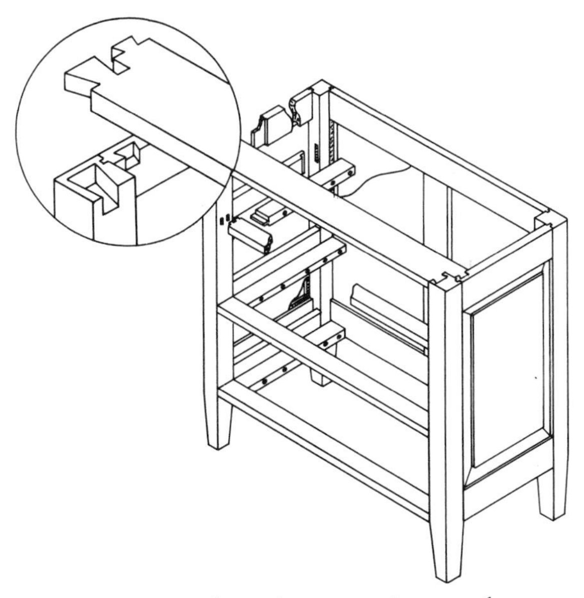

Illus. 295. Post-and-panel construction uses large corner posts for added strength. A modified type of dovetail for use with post-and-panel construction compensates for the variation in width between the post and the side rail.

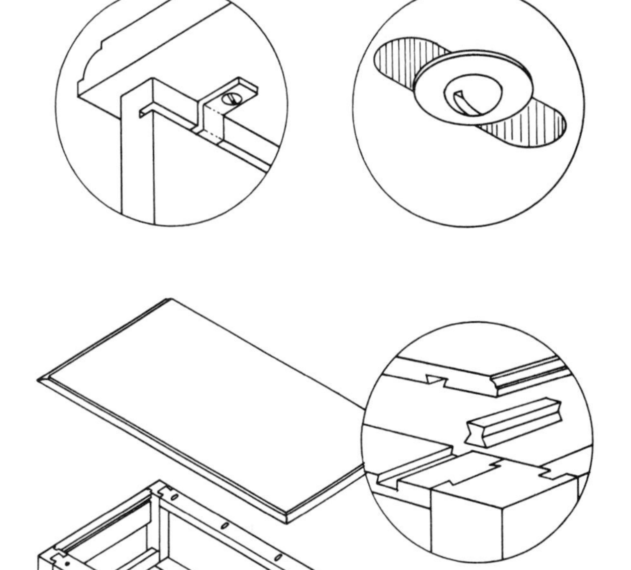

Illus. 296. When you are using a solid-wood top, the method of fastening must allow for shrinkage or swelling. Metal clips or slotted screw holes are two methods that are often used. A butterfly key is a traditional way to allow movement.

top is used, you can attach the top using slotted screw holes in the subframe; the holes along the front, however, are not slotted so that the front will remain in proper alignment. All of the rest of the holes should be slotted to allow the top to expand or shrink across the width. Use round-head screws with washers so that the screws won't jam in the slots. Another method is to use wooden butterfly keys in matching slots; this is a traditional way to overcome the movement problem. Cut matching dovetail dadoes in the top of the rear frame member and in the underside of the top. Put the top in place and attach it securely to the front frame member. Insert the butterfly keys into the dovetail dadoes. Leave the keys loose; don't glue them.

When using solid lumber, care must be taken in choosing the joints for the drawer blades and dust panels. When the sides are made from a dimensionally stable material such as plywood, you can use the type of frame and dust panel construction shown in Illus. 297 in the drawing labelled A. If you use this type of construction with a carcass made of solid wood, the sides may eventually split due to the cross-grain joint between the side and the dust panel frame. In Illus. 297, the drawing labelled B shows an alternate type of dust panel that eliminates the cross-grain joint. The drawer blade is firmly attached to both of the sides with dovetail dadoes or with tenons.

Drawer Joints

Drawers are subjected to a lot of stress as they are opened and closed. Strong joints are necessary if you expect the drawers to last. The type of drawer front plays a role in determining the joints used. Drawer fronts are classified as flush, overlay, and lipped (Illus. 298). Flush drawer fronts fit inside the face frame of the cabinet, and the front is flush with the frame. Overlay drawer fronts are larger than the drawer opening; they extend past the face frame the full thickness of the front. Lipped drawer fronts have a rabbet cut around the edge; they lip over the face frame.

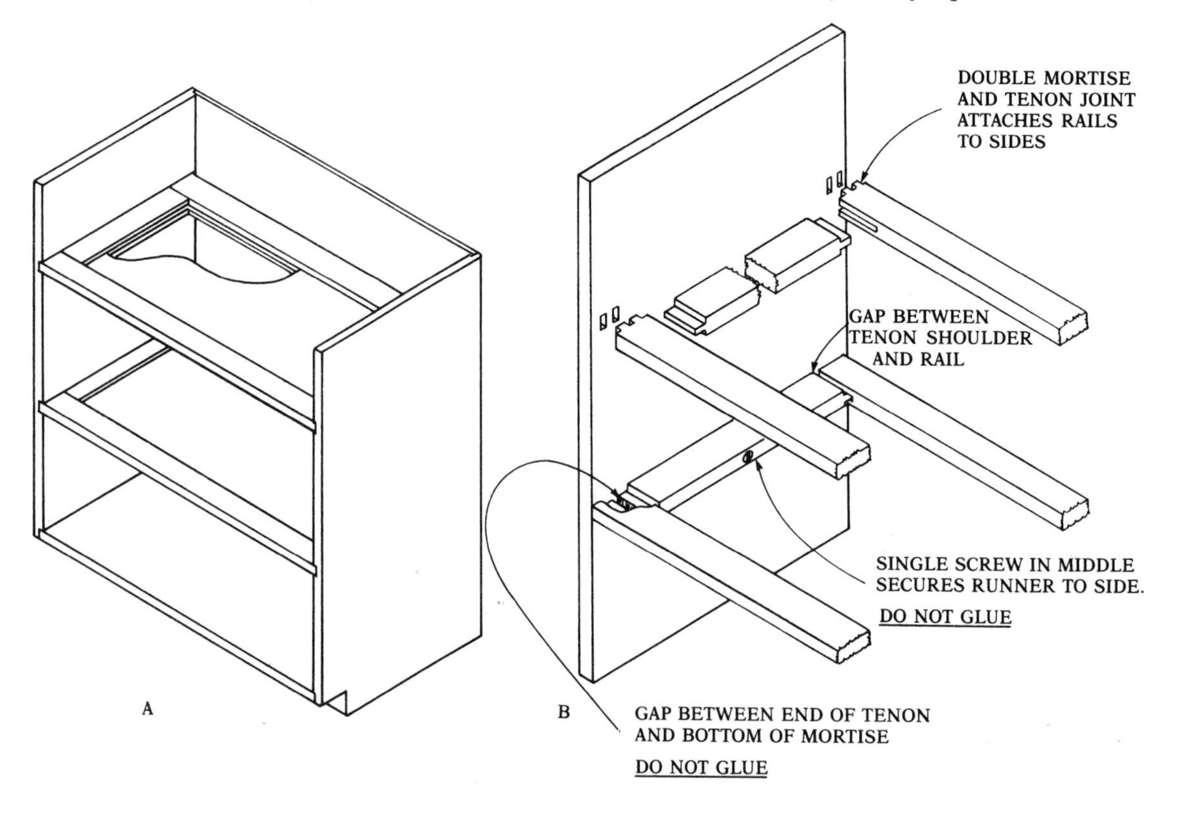

Illus. 297. The type of drawer guide and dust panel shown in A can be used with plywood; but, it introduces cross-grain problems when used with solid lumber. To overcome this, use the alternate construction in B.

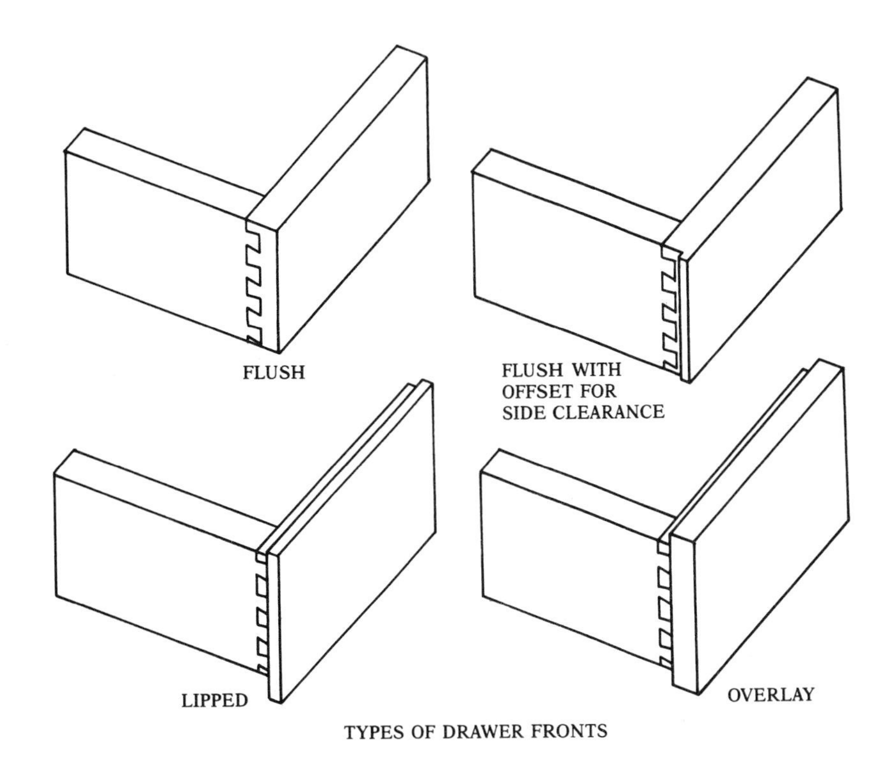

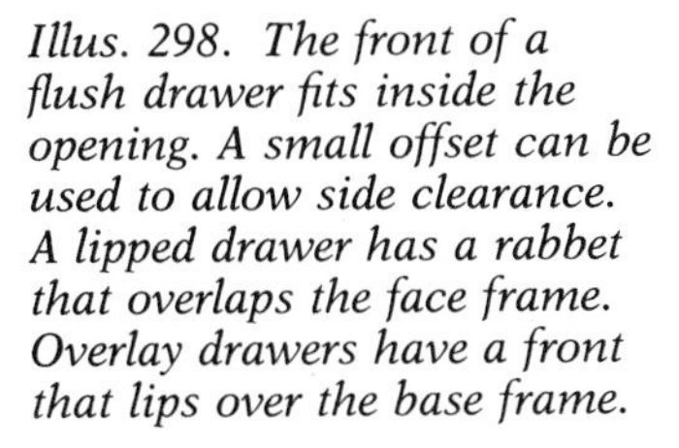

Illus. 298. The front of a flush drawer fits inside the opening. A small offset can be used to allow side clearance. A lipped drawer has a rabbet that overlaps the face frame. Overlay drawers have a front that lips over the base frame.

The front can be an integral part of the drawer, or a false front can be used. When a false front is used, the drawer is simply constructed like a box, and the front is added after assembly.

Dovetail joints are the traditional favorite for drawer construction (Illus. 299). Refer to Chapter 7, page 109, where I cover dovetails in detail. In most cases, half-blind dovetails are used to attach the front to the sides of a drawer. In fine cabinetry using hardwoods, the pins are typically made very small, almost coming to a point. The back can be attached using half-blind dovetails or through dovetails; the pins can be a little coarser in the back joint. You also have a choice for orienting the dovetails in the back joint; you can align them to withstand the force of objects hitting the back as the drawer is pulled out or pushed in, or you can align the dovetails to hold the sides together. A well-glued dovetail is strong in both directions, so ordinarily either way is sufficiently strong. The back isn't subjected to as much stress as the drawer front, so you can actually substitute a simpler joint for the dovetails at the back.

Dovetails aren't suitable for use with particleboard, and they don't work too well in plywood either, so an alternate construction of the drawer is needed for these materials. Some projects don't justify the work involved in making dovetails; for these instances, you can use simpler joints as long as they still give adequate strength.

Illus. 299. Half-blind dovetail joints are the traditional favorite for drawer construction. This end table was made using the Leigh dovetail jig. Notice the through dovetails used at the corners of the carcass. (Photo courtesy Leigh Industries Ltd.)

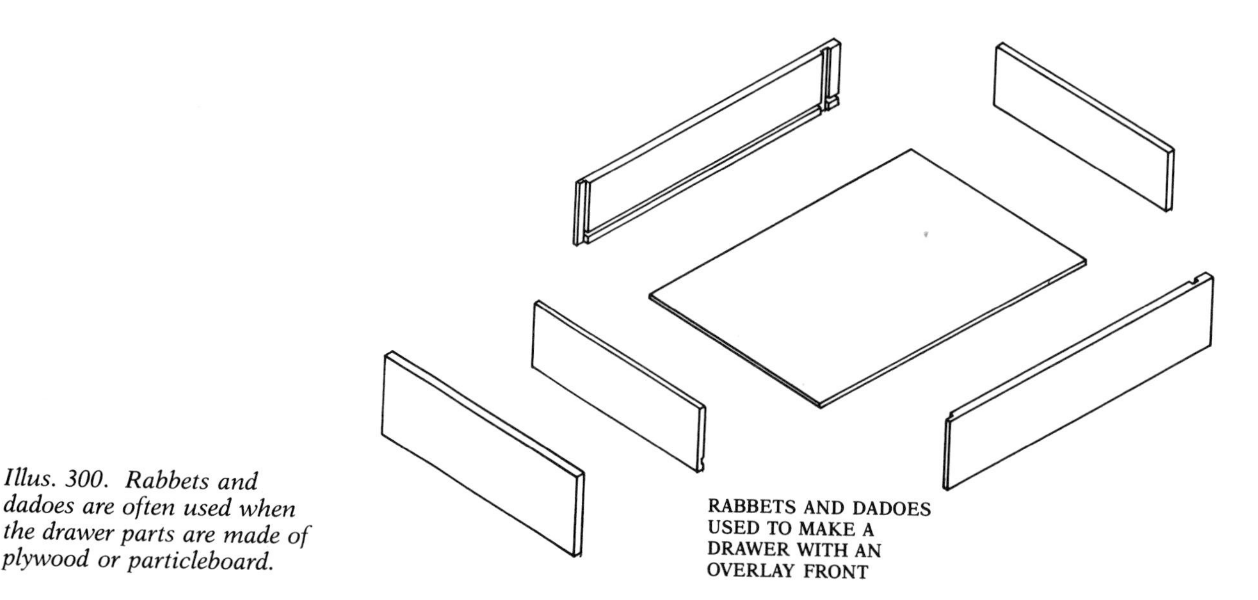

Illus. 300. Rabbets and dadoes are often used when the drawer parts are made of plywood or particleboard.

Rabbets and dadoes are often used in drawer construction that is relatively simple (Illus. 300). A rabbet can be used to join the sides to the front. For flush drawers, the rabbet is made as wide as the width of the side. In lipped drawers, the rabbet is made as wide as the width of the side and the lip combined. The rabbet joint doesn't work too well, however, for overlay fronts, unless a false front is used. Rabbets can also be used to attach the back to the sides, but a dado is stronger. By making a dado about ½″ from the end, the back is locked in position. When a false front is used, you can also use a dado to attach the front; the dado is placed ½″ from the front end of the sides. This makes the sides reversible, so you can mass-produce them without regard for left or right sides. Make stopped dadoes in the false front so that, when the false front is attached with screws, a stopped dado fits over the end of each side. This locks the joint. Using a router is one of the easiest ways to make stopped dadoes.

Sliding dovetails are particularly well suited in drawer construction for attaching the sides to an overlay front (Illus. 301). Make sure that you use hardwood for the front and sides if you use this joint. My experience has been that with use soft wood will compress and pull out of the joint eventually as the drawer is slammed shut. Make the sliding dovetail using a router with a dovetail bit. You can make the cut easier if you make a smaller standard dado on the table saw first. Use the router mounted in a router table to make the dovetail on the sides, or use a table saw. Refer to Chapter 5 where I discuss sliding dovetails in detail. When the drawer front extends past the top of the sides, use a stopped joint. A sliding dovetail can also be used to attach the back to the sides; this is a very good joint for this application because it withstands force in both.directions. Make the dovetail dado in the sides about ½″ from the ends. The back is prevented from pushing out the rear just as it is with a standard dado, but the dovetailing holds the sides together.

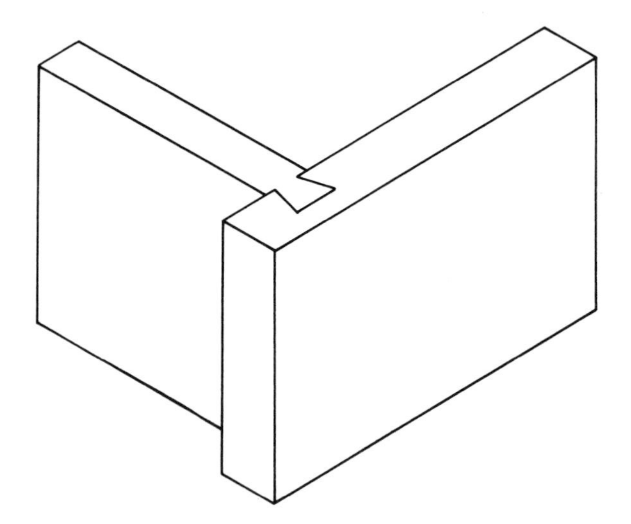

Illus. 301. Sliding dovetails can be used to join drawer sides to the front.

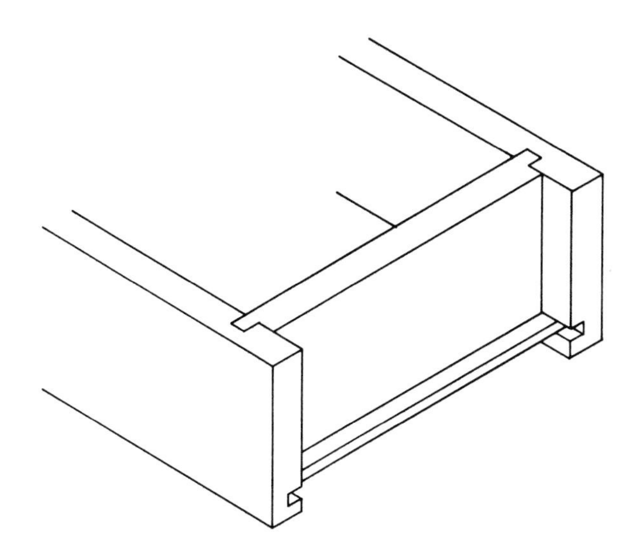

Illus. 302. The tongue-and-dado joint is often used to join the back of a drawer to the sides.

Tongue-and-dado joints can be used to attach the back of the drawer or front to the sides (Illus. 302). To attach the back, cut barefaced tongues on the ends, and cut a matching dado in the sides. Place the dado at least ½″ from the end of each side. The advantage of this joint is that it provides a little more room inside the drawer than the standard dado. This joint can be used as well to attach the front to the sides when a false front is used on the drawer. In this case, the dado should be positioned so that the front will be flush with the sides. If the space between the side of the dado and the end of the side is too small, the joint may fail when the short-grain breaks. Make the tongue smaller than usual to keep the dado set back from the end. The tongue can be as small as ⅛″ and still provide adequate strength.

Drawer-lock joints are also called double-dado joints or tongue-and-lap joints. This is an interlocking type of joint that can be used to attach the front to the sides of a drawer. Illus. 303 gives step-by-step directions for making this joint on the table saw. You can also get a special router bit or shaper cutter to make this joint in a single pass. The same bit or cutter is used for both parts. One part is cut face against the table, and the other part is cut face against the fence. Be-

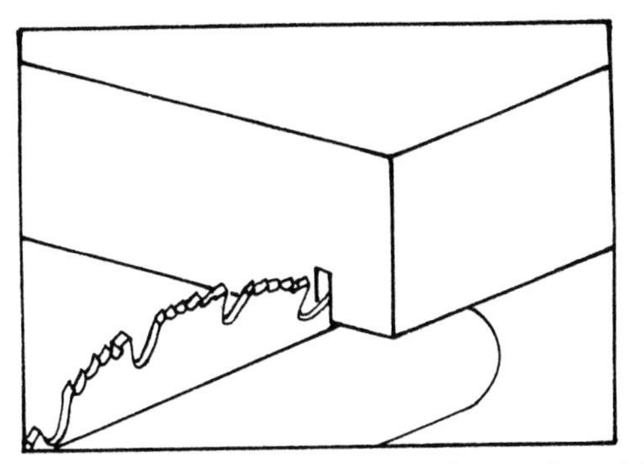

1. Make a dado in the drawer side that is the width of the saw blade and one-third as deep as the side.

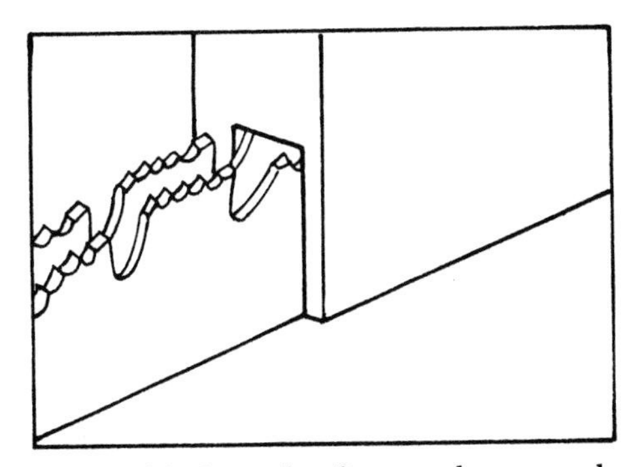

2. Set a dado blade to the distance between the end of the side and the dado. Use a tenoning jig to guide the front for this cut.

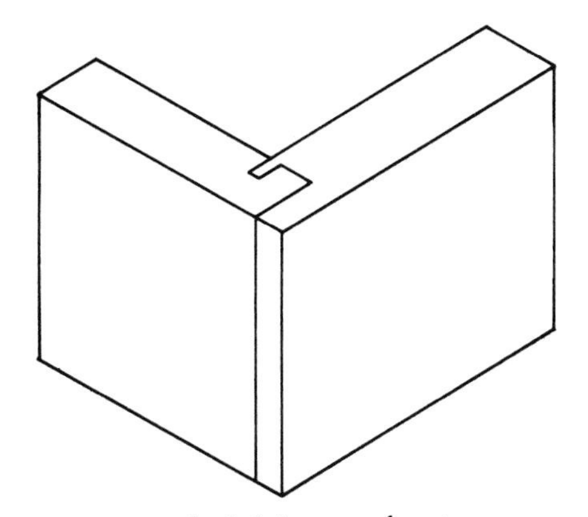

Illus. 303. Drawer-lock joint step by step.

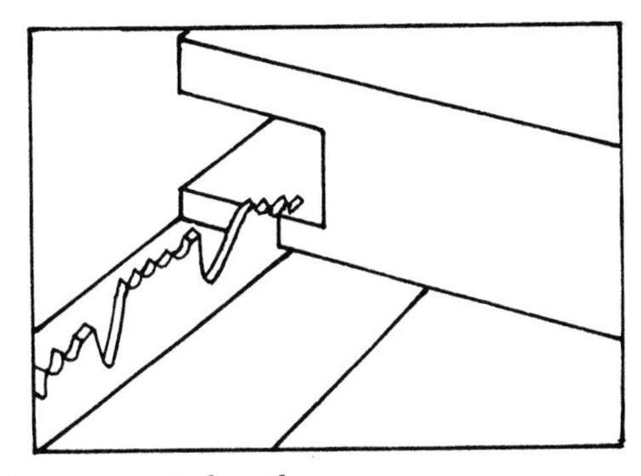

3. Trim tongue to length.

cause the tongue is thin, it can easily break when a lot of stress is placed on the drawer front. It is a good idea to add a stop block at the rear of the drawer so that the front doesn't take all of the stress when the drawer is slammed shut.

The double-lock corner adds another tongue to lock the joint in both directions (Illus. 304). The joint must slide together, so its applications are limited to boards less than about 8" wide.

Box joints provide strength comparable to dovetails. For a decorative effect, leave the joint exposed on the front. A false front can hide the joint. See Chapter 8, page 129, for details on cutting box joints.

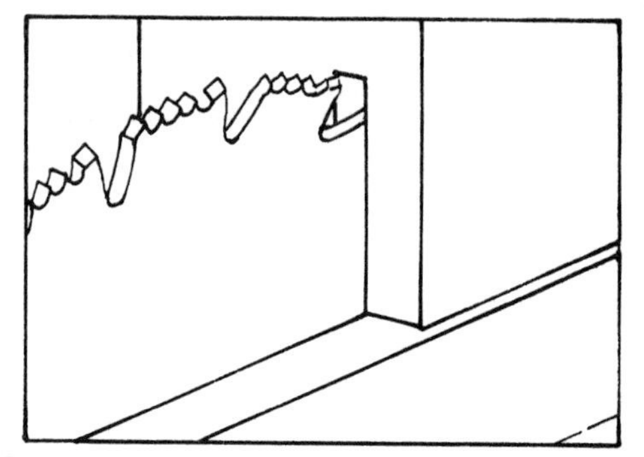

1. Make the first cut on the front with the blade height equal to the width of the side. The end is against the table. Use a tenoning jig to guide the cut.

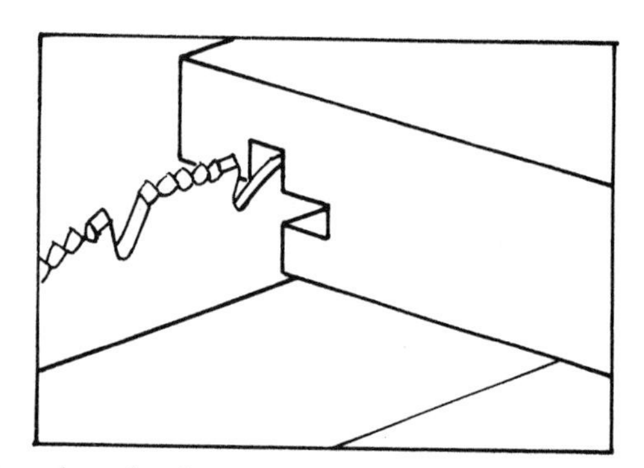

2. Complete the front part of the joint by placing the front with the inside face against the table. Set the blade height to ¾ of the thickness of the front.

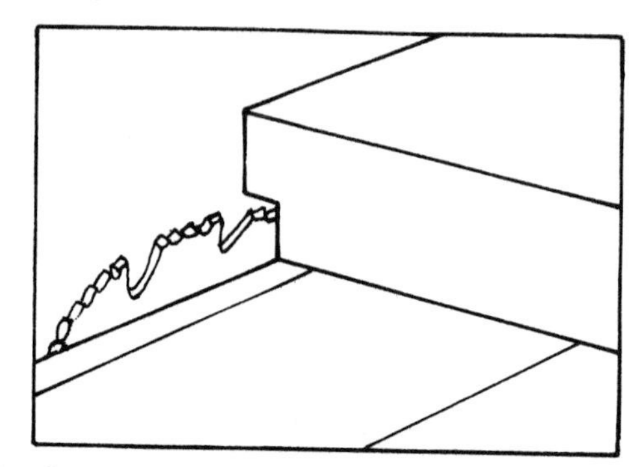

3. The first cut on the side is made with the inside face against the table. Set the blade height to the length of the tongue on the front.

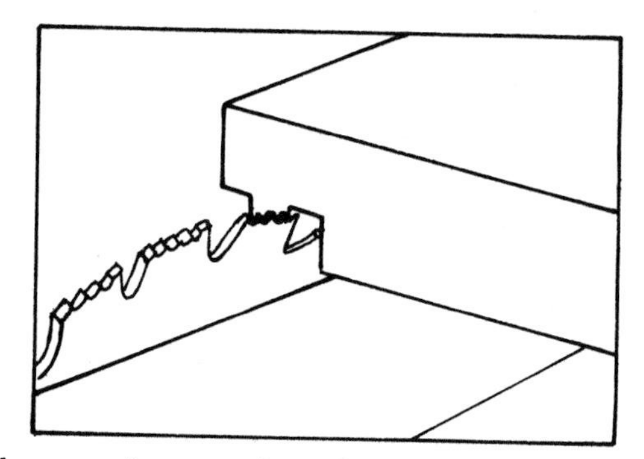

4. The second cut on the side uses the same blade height. Move the board over by the width of the saw blade.

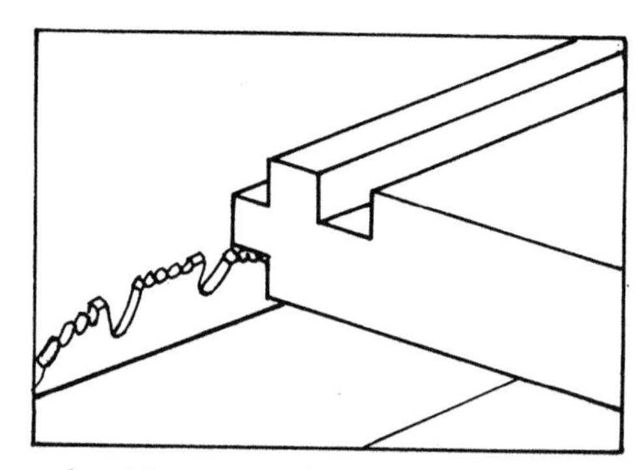

5. Turn the side over so that the outside face is against the table for the final cut.

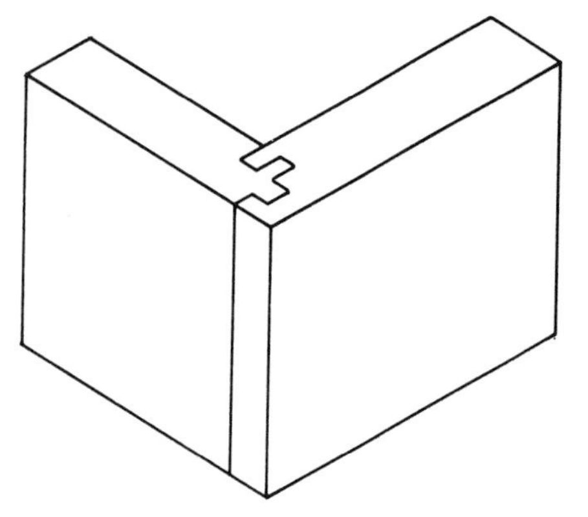

Illus. 304. Double-lock corner step by step.

Scallop-and-pin joints were frequently used on factory-made furniture about a hundred years ago (Illus. 305). It was developed as an easily mass-produced alternative to dovetail joints. The joint is very decorative, so you may want to use it even if you aren't specifically concerned with reproducing one of these old pieces. The original joints were made with the Knapp Dovetailing Machine; but, you can reproduce them without special equipment. The round tenons are cut in the end of the drawer front using a tenon cutter; this is a special type of drill bit that has a hollow center. It is similar to a plug cutter, but the outside diameter is larger in relation to the hole at the middle. Cutting the tenons leaves the scalloped edge on the drawer front. Cut the end of the drawer front to match using a band saw or jigsaw. Then, drill holes in the side for the tenons. If you don't want to use a tenon cutter, you can get a similar effect with dowels. Use a flat bottomed drill bit, such as a Forstner bit, to make the cuts in the end of the front. You can also use a router. Make a template out of hardboard and use a template-following collar on the router. Prepare the sides as described above. Put the side in place, and drill through the holes into the front. Glue dowels into the holes, and then trim them flush with the sides.

Drawer bottoms are usually made from ⅛″ or ¼″ plywood or particleboard. Before the widespread use of these materials, of course, solid wood was used. If you choose to use solid wood, you will need to take precautions to allow for the expansion and shrinking of the wood. The bottom is usually placed in a groove cut in the sides and front of the drawer. Typically the drawer back is cut narrower than the sides so that the bottom can be slipped in after assembly. Screws or nails are used to attach the bottom to the back. This type of construction is, in fact, a holdover from the days when the bottoms were made of solid wood. When solid wood is used for the bottom, it is not glued into the grooves. The grain in the bottom is oriented so that shrinkage will cause the bottom to pull away from the front and not the sides. The drawer front is usually thicker, so a deeper groove can be used, allowing more room for movement. If the bottom shrinks enough to pull out of the groove in the front, it can be unscrewed at the back, pushed forward, and then reattached. When you use plywood, particleboard or hardboard, you don't need to allow for movement, so you can use a groove in the back if you want. The bottom can be glued in when dimensionally stable materials such as these as used; this helps to keep the drawer square.

Illus. 305. Scallop-and-pin joints provide strength and decoration. They were frequently used on factory-made furniture from the late nineteenth century.

When the sides are thinner than ½″, grooving for the bottom will weaken them, and they may split at the groove, letting the bottom drop out. To strengthen the bottom attachment on thin sides, grooved slips are sometimes used. The slips are glued to the sides; then, the bottom is installed as usual.

The groove in the front may need to be stopped. It depends on the joint used and whether or not having the groove show on the edge is objectionable. When using half-blind dovetails, plan the joint so that the groove will fall between two pins. That way the groove will be hidden by the dovetail on the side. If you are using a nonadjustable router jig to make the joint, you can make the groove after the joint is cut, and then position it so that it is between the last two pins.

Leg Joints

There are many ways to attach legs to cabinets. The joint you choose depends on the type of leg, on whether or not the leg joins to a rail, and on the strength needed. Dowel-reinforced butt joints and mortise-and-tenon joints are the most commonly used joints when a leg joins to rails. Refer to Chapter 3 where I cover dowel-reinforced butts and to Chapter 6 where I cover the mortise-and-tenon. This section covers some variations that can be used specifically for leg-to-rail joints.

BUTT JOINTS

When they are properly reinforced, butt joints are suitable for attaching legs to rails (Illus. 306). Dowels are the most frequently used reinforcement. The placement of the dowels is important for maximum strength. The joint strength is increased when the dowels are placed closer to the edges of the rail; but if they are too close, the dowels may cause the rail to split under stress. A good compromise is to place the dowels about 3/8" to 1/2" from the edge. If the space between the two dowels will be greater than 1¼", add a third dowel in the center.

Additional strength can be achieved by using a metal reinforcing plate or a wood corner block behind the leg. Metal plates are commercially available for this purpose; the ends of the plate fit into saw kerfs in the rails, and a bolt is driven into the leg at an angle to secure the leg to the plate. In commercial furniture, you may see this type of plate used to secure a leg with an unreinforced butt. I have found that this type of joint is unsatisfactory. I've had to repair many piano benches that used this type of joint. The saw kerf creates a break line, and the resulting short grain in the rail then fails under stress. If you do use this type of plate, be sure to reinforce the joint with dowels. A wood corner block can be used for the same purpose, and in at least one respect it is superior to the metal plate; no saw kerfs are needed, so you can avoid the short-grain problem. A finger joint can be used to provide a better glue bond between the corner block and the rails. The best way to make the joint is with a special shaper cutter.

Special techniques are needed to join a round leg to rails using dowels (Illus. 307). Often, turned legs are left square at the top for attachment to the rails; but, when it is desirable for the legs to be turned the entire length, it is easier to drill the dowel holes before turning the leg. Lay out the dowel locations on the square stock, and drill the holes. Then, turn the legs on the lathe. The ends of the rails also need to be contoured to fit the curvature of the leg. Use a band saw to cut away the waste; then, choose a drum sander that is close to the diameter of the leg. Clamp a guide block to the drill-press table to guide the rail, and sand the end of the rail to the final contour. The joint can then be assembled as usual.

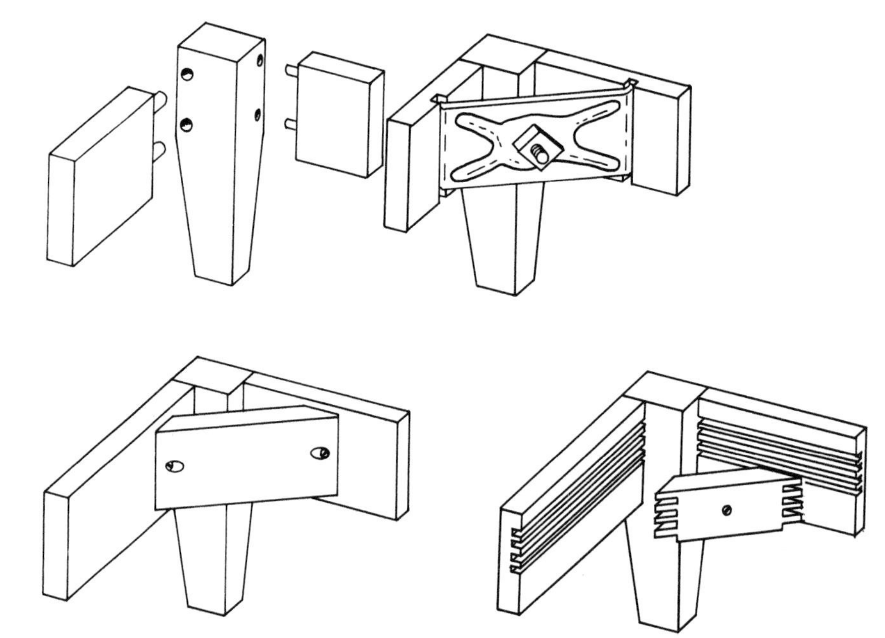

Illus. 306. A dowel-reinforced butt joint can be used to attach legs to rails. A reinforcing plate or corner block gives added strength.

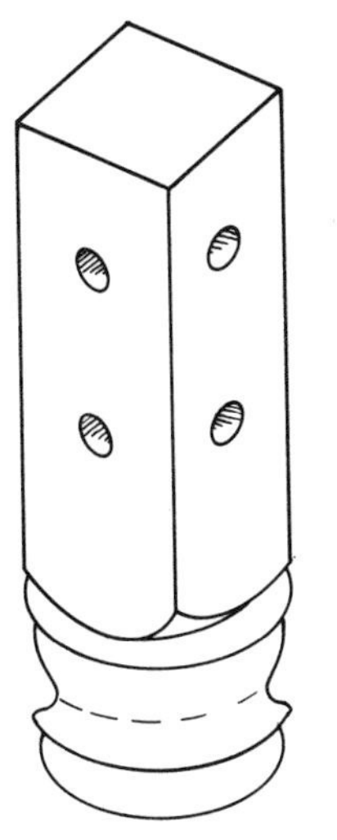

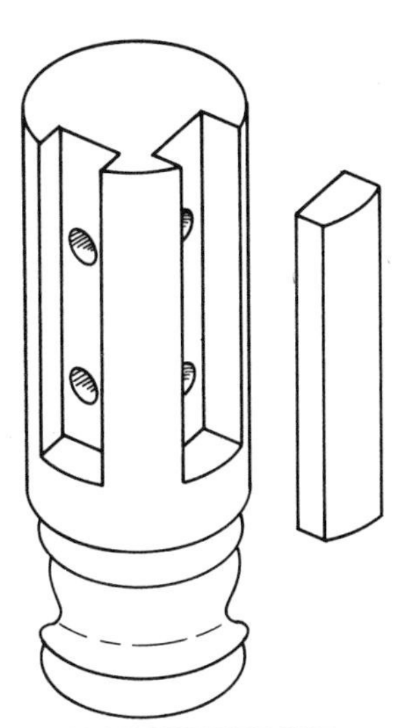

Illus. 307. Dowelling techniques for round legs.

Another method uses shallow mortises in conjunction with the dowels. This procedure is also easier if you make the joint before turning the leg. Lay out and drill the dowel holes while the stock is still square; then, in the leg cut mortises that will accept the full size of each rail. Next, cut temporary filler blocks to fit in the mortises. Put a couple of small drops of glue in the mortise, and press the filler blocks in place. You will remove the blocks later, so make sure you don't glue them too securely. When the glue is dry, you can turn the legs. The filler blocks will keep the lathe chisels from getting caught in the mortises as you turn the leg.

After the legs are turned, use a hand chisel to remove the filler blocks; and then assemble the joint. This method for joining a round leg to rails is stronger than the previous one, and the ends of the rails don't need to be contoured to fit the leg.

MORTISE-AND-TENON

A mortise-and-tenon joint will be approximately 15 to 40 percent stronger than the equivalent dowel joint when used to attach legs to rails.

When a mortise-and-tenon joint is used to attach a leg to the rails, usually there will be two mortises cut into the leg. For maximum length, the tenons should be as long as possible; this means, however, that the two mortises will end up running into each other. When this occurs, there are several ways to treat the joint between the two tenons (Illus. 308).

Mitred tenons can be used when two mortises meet. The two ends shouldn't actually touch because they may prevent the shoulders from pulling up tight. Instead, leave a small amount (1/32") of clearance between the ends of the tenons.

Half-lap tenons are another solution to the problem. Cut a notch in the ends of the tenons so that they will overlap. It is also a good idea to leave a little clearance in this joint so that the shoulders will pull in tight.

Interlocking tenons can be used with an open mortise. The visible ends of the rails can be used as a decorative element in the design. The tenons are barefaced which means that no shoulders are cut on the rail. The mortises can be cut easily on a table saw using a tenoning jig. You can use a dado blade or make multiple passes with a stan-

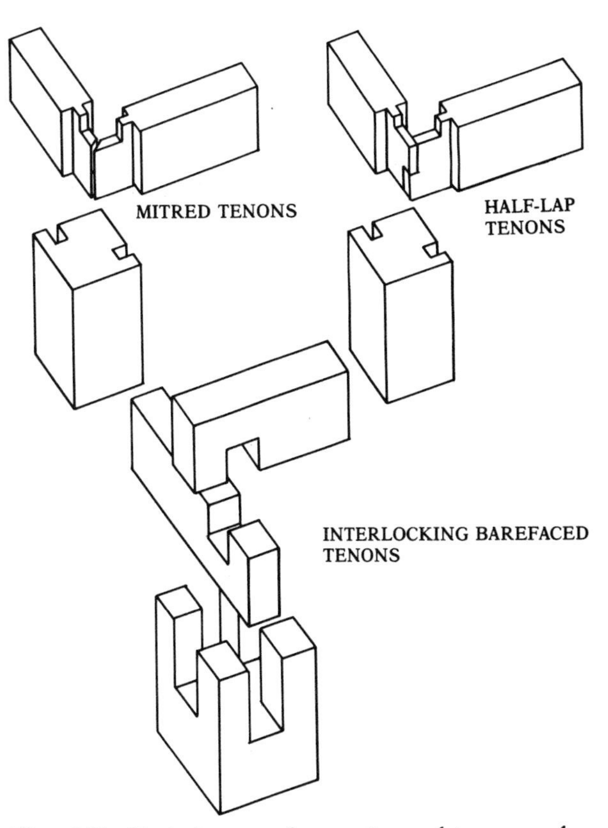

Illus. 308. Variations on the mortise-and-tenon used to attach legs and rails.

dard blade. Next, cut a half-lap in the rails. The ends of the rails can be set flush with the sides of the leg or left proud as part of the design. To assemble the joint, put the half-lap joint together first, then slide the rails into the mortises in the leg.

Mortising a round leg can present problems similar to those encountered when dowelling a round leg (Illus. 309). A flat is cut on the leg in the area around where the mortise will be. The flat can be carried to the top of the leg, or the rail can be contoured to fit the curvature of the leg.

If you use a barefaced tenon, you can cut the mortises before turning the leg, and you can use filler blocks as described above at the beginning of this section on leg joints where dowelling is discussed. If this method would weaken the leg too much, you can cut a shallow mortise the full size of the rail, and then make a smaller mortise inside the first one.

Round tenons can also be used to attach round legs directly to the bottom of a cabinet or chair without rails. The strongest joint will result if the tenon projects all the way through and is wedged. Be sure to orient the wedge at a 90° angle to the grain of the mortised member so that the wedging action won't split the grain. The leg itself can be placed on an angle by boring the hole at the appropriate angle and direction.

BRIDLE JOINTS

When a leg joins to a rail at a point other than the corner, a bridle joint can be used (Illus. 310). Make the joint by cutting an open mortise in the end of the leg and dadoes on both sides of the rail.

When the rail is lying flat, a combination bridle and mortise is needed. Cut a dado in the front of the rail and a mortise behind it. The leg is cut in the same way as before except that a shoulder is cut on the back.

Another type of bridle joint can be used at a corner. This joint is useful when the design calls for the leg to be at a 45° angle to each of the rails. Assemble the rails using dovetails, box joints or dowels; then, cut the corner off at a 45° angle so that the resulting flat is equal to the leg width.

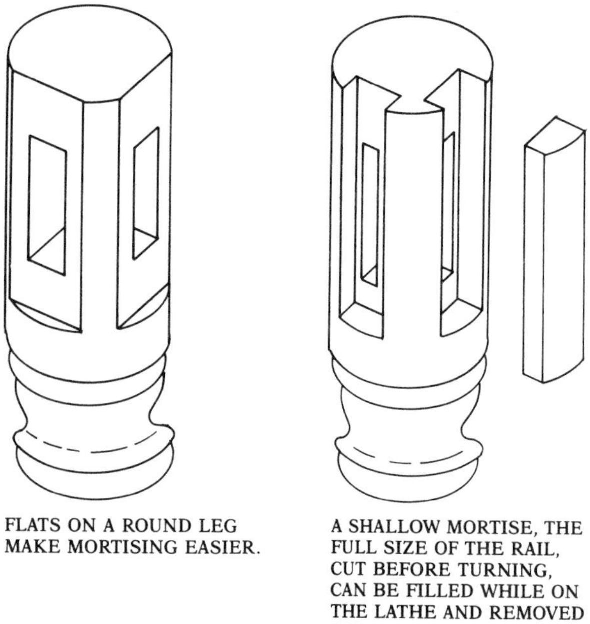

FLATS ON A ROUND LEG MAKE MORTISING EASIER.

A SHALLOW MORTISE, THE FULL SIZE OF THE RAIL, CUT BEFORE TURNING, CAN BE FILLED WHILE ON THE LATHE AND REMOVED FOR ASSEMBLY. A SMALLER MORTISE INSIDE ACCOMMODATES A FULL-LENGTH TENON.

Illus. 309. Techniques for mortising round legs.

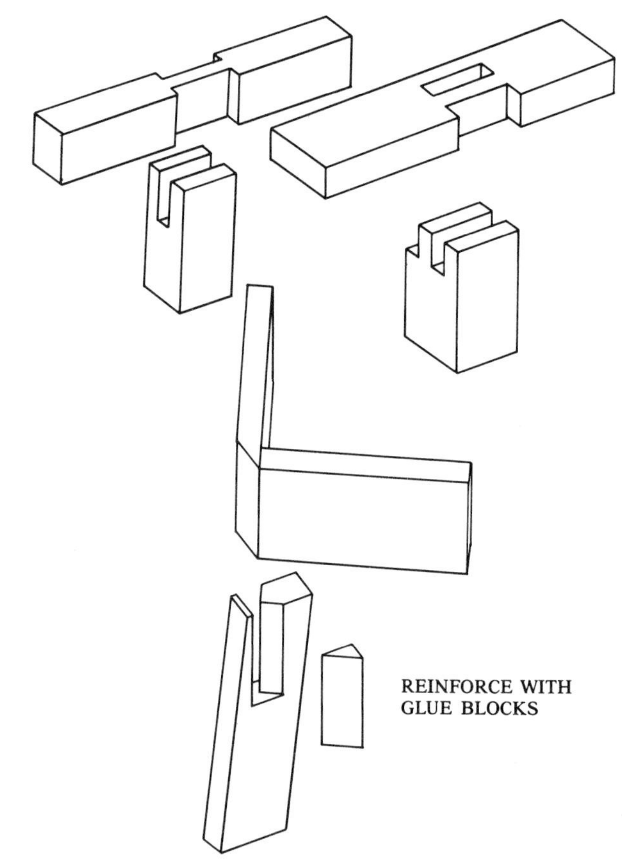

Illus. 310. Bridle joints used to attach legs to rails.

Cut an open mortise in the end of the leg; then, bevel the inside edges of the mortise to 45°. Next, assemble the joint by sliding the leg over the rails. Add glue blocks on the inside of the joint to provide additional strength.

SLIDING DOVETAIL

The sliding dovetail, or dovetailed dado, can be used in several ways to attach legs. It can be used to attach rails to a leg. A router and a dovetail bit can be used to make the dovetailed groove, or you can cut it by hand. In either case, it is easier if you first cut a slightly smaller square groove using a dado blade on the table saw. Dovetail the ends of the rails using one of the methods described in Chapter 5 under the heading Sliding Dovetail, page 82.

The sliding dovetail can also be used to attach legs to a pedestal. In this case, the dovetail grooves are cut in the pedestal, and the ends of the legs are dovetailed.

An angled sliding dovetail can be used to attach a leg directly to the top (Illus. 311). The dovetailed dado starts with the widest part at the surface, and then it angles down. A dovetail cut on the leg slides into the dado. To cut the dado with a router, you need to make a wedge-shaped jig. The jig is placed on the work, and the router rests on the jig. As you slide the router down the incline of the jig, it will make an angled sliding dovetail.

BRACKET FEET

When both sides of a bracket foot will show, as is usually the case for the front two feet, a mitre joint is used (Illus. 312). The joint can be reinforced with a spline or dowels. For the maximum-strength joint, use a full-blind dovetail. The rear feet are usually joined with a half-blind dovetail. A glue block adds considerably to the strength of a bracket foot, and usually it is the glue block that actually carries the weight of the cabinet. The glue block, however, can introduce a cross-grain problem that may lead to a split in the foot. To avoid this, use a laminated glue block that is built up from smaller pieces of wood with the grain in each piece turned 90° to the previous one. This lamination provides a long-grain glue surface between every other glue-block segment and the inside face of one of the legs; the grain direction of the alternating segments is the same as one of the legs.

Illus. 311. An angled sliding dovetail attaches this leg to the tabletop.

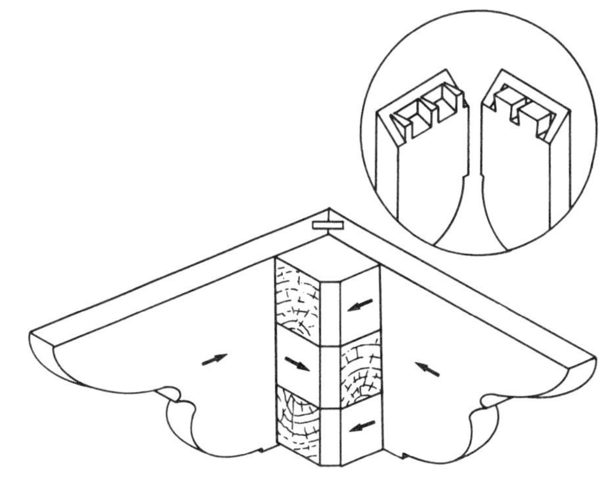

Illus. 312. A laminated glue block can be used to reinforce a bracket foot. Aligning the grain as shown prevents cross-grain problems. A full-blind dovetail can be used instead of the spline joint.

12 Plywood and Particleboard Joints

Most woodworking joints have a long history. They were developed long before the development of materials such as plywood and particleboard. Some of these joints are unsuitable for use with the new materials and others need to be modified. Plywood and particleboard also have distinctive properties that make some new joints possible. As a general rule, joints used with plywood and particleboard are simpler and coarser than those used with solid lumber. Because edging is usually applied after assembly, blind joints are not ordinarily necessary.

Plywood

Plywood is made by laminating wood veneer; each layer of veneer is called a ply. The grain direction of each ply is at a 90° angle to the grain of the plies directly above and below. There is always an odd number of plies so that the grain of the face veneers will run in the same direction.

Because of the alternating grain direction, changes in moisture content don't cause large changes in size, so plywood is essentially considered to be dimensionally stable. This means that in making the joints you don't need to allow for panel movement. The alternating plies also eliminate the problem of weakness along the grain, so the joint doesn't need to provide as much support in this area. Plywood has two main disadvantages. First the plies form a break line that can cause intricate joints to fail. Second fasteners such as nails and screws can cause the plies to split apart. In addition, the plywood edges contain exposed end grain, so they won't glue very well.

The strongest type of plywood joint results when face is glued to face with a large contact area; however, this is not usually practical. In most applications, you will need to attach an edge to a face or an edge to an edge. To do this, you need joint reinforcement of some kind. Screws and nails will hold much better when driven into the face rather than into an edge, so whenever possible the reinforcement should be designed to take advantage of the greater holding power.

It seems that face veneers are actually getting thinner, particularly on hardwood plywood. I first noticed this a while ago when I was remodelling some 30-year-old cabinets. It seemed that I wasn't having as much of a problem with face-veneer chipping when I cut the joints in the old plywood as I did when I was using new plywood. On close comparison, I noticed that the new plywood has a much thinner face veneer. This means that you need to take extra precautions when you cut joints in plywood. Dado blades are particularly troublesome; while some are better than others, practically all of them will chip the face veneer as you cut across the grain.

To minimize the chipping, try putting masking tape over the joint area before cutting. Press the tape down hard, then make the cut. The tape holds the veneer in place as it's cut and can eliminate chipping in many cases. Sometimes, however, even the masking tape won't eliminate all of the chipping. In that case, first score along the joint line with a sharp knife; make the cut deep enough to cut completely through the face ply. Then, when you cut the joint, keep the saw completely on the waste side of the scored line. Cutting dadoes with a router can help alleviate the chipping problem, but you still may need to use masking tape or score the line.

MITRE

Mitre joints are used extensively with plywood because they hide the plywood edge. Most of the mitre-reinforcement methods described in Chapter 4 work with plywood. Plate splines are especially good because the grooves don't form a continuous break line (Illus. 313).

Illus. 313. Plate splines are especially good in plywood joints, because the pockets don't form a continuous break line that would weaken the joint.

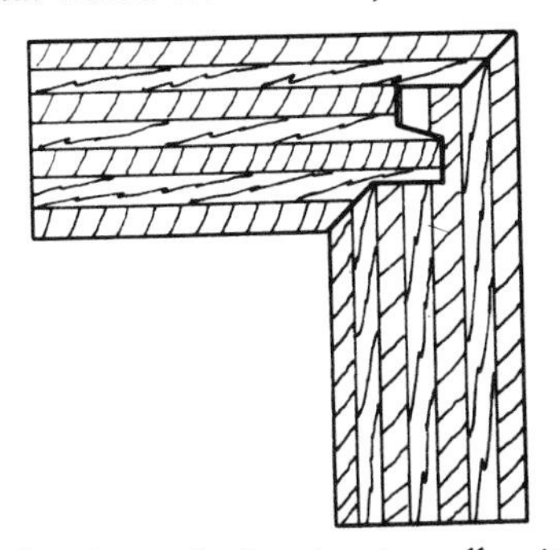

Illus. 314. The shaper lock mitre is well suited to plywood because the short tapered tongues won't break off.

The shaper lock mitre is also a good plywood joint. The locking tongues are short and tapered so they won't break off (Illus. 314).

When splining a mitre in plywood, keep the spline close to the inside edge. If the groove gets too close to the face, it will cut through too many plies and weaken the corner. You may want to use a different method of splining in plywood; instead of angling the groove so that it is perpendicular to the joint, cut it square with the face of the board (Illus. 315). This joint will only work in

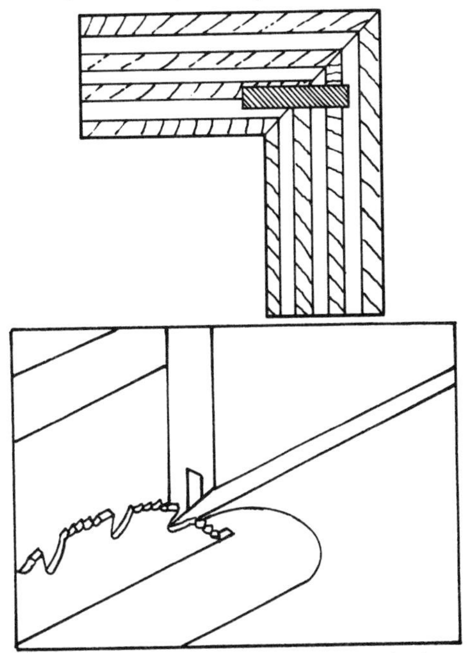

1. Make the groove in the first board with the outside face against the fence or tenon jig. Add a wide auxiliary fence for added support.

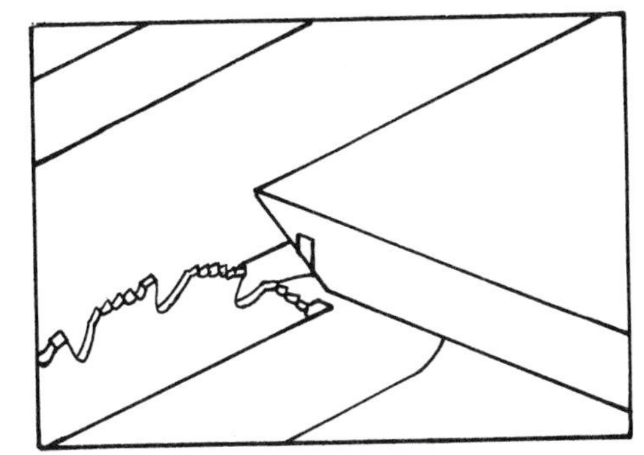

2. The groove in the second board is made with the inside face against the saw table. Offset the groove slightly to the outside corner so that clamping pressure will pull the corner tight.

Illus. 315. This method of splining a mitre joint makes assembly and clamping easier.

plywood; it can't be used with solid lumber or particleboard because the wood will crumble off at the short-grain point. The major advantage of orienting the spline in this way is that the joint then needs to be clamped in only one direction; assembly is simplified as well because the parts can be pushed together straight. If you offset the grooves slightly (1/32"), then one side of the joint will be a little higher than the other as you assemble. Put the clamps on this higher side. The sliding action on the joint will wedge the spline and pull the corner tight.

RABBETS AND DADOES

Rabbets and dadoes are generally good plywood joints. When all of the stress on the rabbet joint will be against the shoulder, you can simply use the rabbet as a way to hide the plywood edge (Illus. 316). Cut the rabbet so that only the face veneer is left. When the joint is assembled, there won't be any exposed edge. A stronger version of this joint uses a double rabbet. Cut a rabbet in the end of each board; make one rabbet in the normal way, and cut the other so that only the face veneer remains. This joint gives the added strength of the standard rabbet while still hiding the edge. You can even use a triple rabbet. The joint has a stair-step look. The final rabbet is cut to the face veneer to hide the edge.

Two rabbets forming a shiplap joint can be used to edge-join plywood. Make the rabbets large enough to get a good glue joint on the face of the exposed plies. This joint is useful mostly when it is necessary to join thin plywood (Illus. 317). Thicker plywood can be edge-joined with a tongue-and-groove or spline joint.

Dado joints in plywood should not be deeper than halfway through the plywood. Deep dadoes tend to weaken the parts too much.

TONGUE-AND-GROOVE

Because of the problem of chipping associated with making dadoes in plywood, tongue-and-groove joints are often used in their place. The tongue-and-groove will hide the joint better and cover small chip outs (Illus. 318). The tongue-and-groove can also be used to edge-join

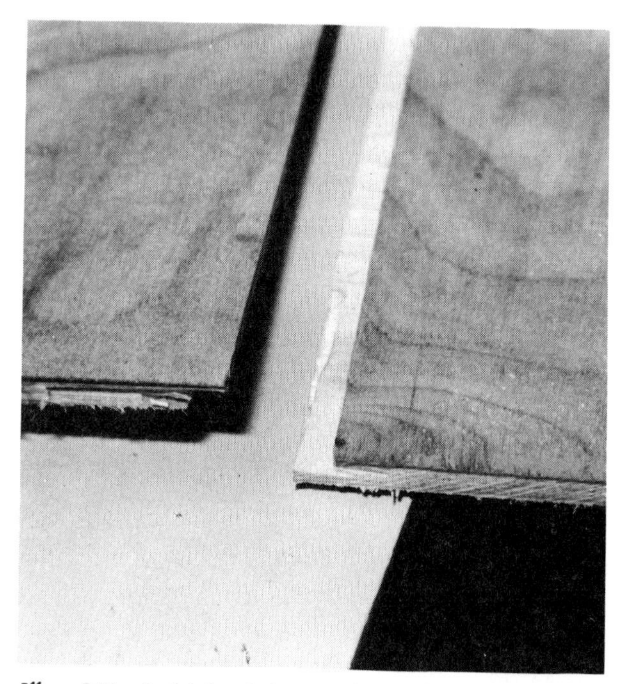

Illus. 317. A shiplap joint can be used to edge-join thin plywood.

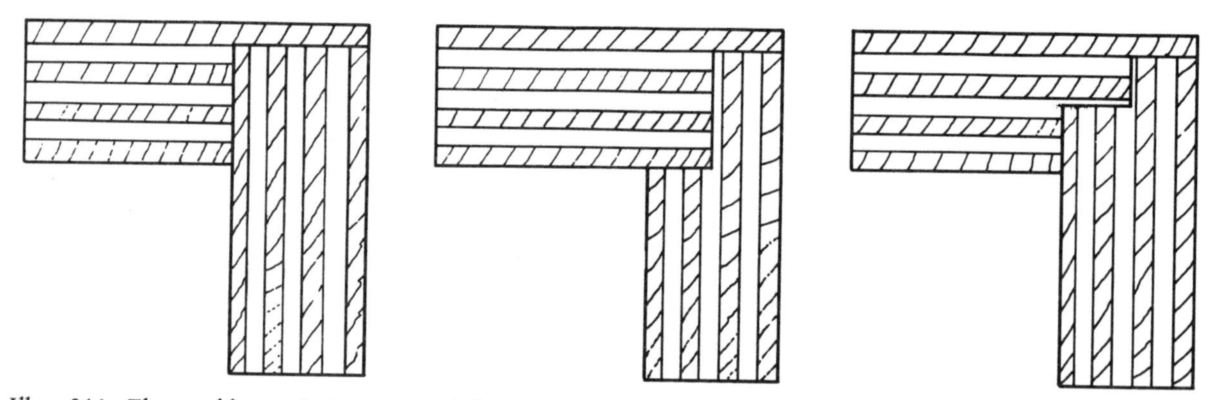

Illus. 316. These rabbet variations conceal the plywood edge: a face-veneer rabbet (left), the double-rabbet version (middle), and a triple-rabbet version (right).

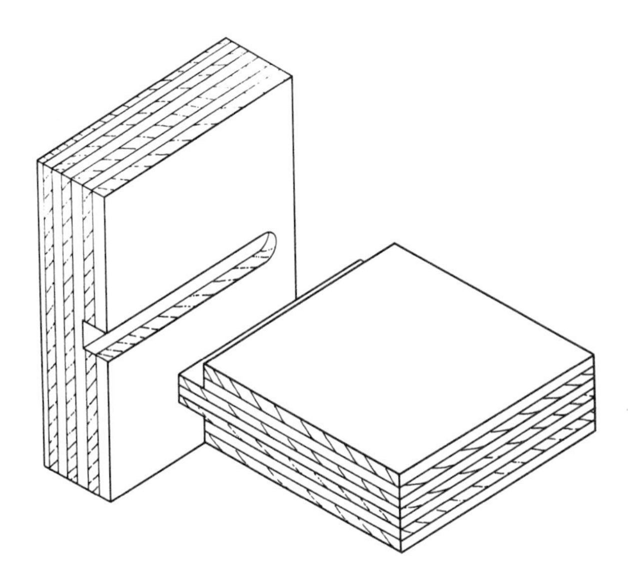

Illus. 318. The tongue-and-groove joint is used in place of a dado to help hide tear outs along the groove. It can be blind as shown here, but when edge trim will be added after assembly, a blind joint is not necessary.

plywood. Whenever possible, it is a good idea to have the tongue composed of at least three plies. This is not always practical; in five-ply sheets, for instance, you could only make the shoulder as deep as the face veneer. If you end up with a tongue that is only the size of the core ply, make sure that the grain of the core ply runs across the joint.

SPLINE JOINTS

Sometimes with plywood it is impossible to get a tongue that is good enough. If the tongue is only one-ply thick and the grain of the core ply runs along the joint, it will break off. In this case, a spline joint will be superior. Splines can be used to join the plywood parts at right angles or edge to edge.

Plate splines are well suited to plywood. The pockets don't form a continuous groove, so they can be used close to the edge. When you make a continuous groove close to a plywood edge, you run the risk of having shear failure occur along the ply line (Illus. 319).

Standard splines can be used when the joint is not close to the corner; in a shelf, for example. They can also be used to edge-join plywood. The splines should be made of plywood or hardboard. Solid-lumber splines aren't suitable because they will expand and contract whereas the

Illus. 319. When a spline groove is cut close to an edge, the joint can fail as shown in the top example. Since the pockets for plate splines don't form a continuous break line, the joint will be stronger.

plywood will remain dimensionally stable. The solid-lumber splines will introduce stress into the joint that can eventually lead to glue failure. When the spline is in the edge, the groove can be deep; but, don't cut a groove in the face any deeper than halfway through the plywood.

DOVETAILS

Dovetails can be used with plywood if you make the pins and tails large and approximately equal in size (Illus. 320). Small pins will break off easily. The standard type of router-made half-blind dovetail, however, is not well suited to plywood; the pins and tails are too small, so the plies form a natural break line. Instead, use an adjustable dovetail jig, or cut the dovetails by hand, to get larger dimensions. Through dovetails are better for plywood than the half-blind variety. In both types, the narrowest part of the pin or tail should not be less than the thickness of the plywood.

SOLID CORNER BLOCKS

Solid-lumber corner blocks are often used with plywood construction. In some cases, the corner block is extended to form the leg. The corner block provides a good face-gluing surface and

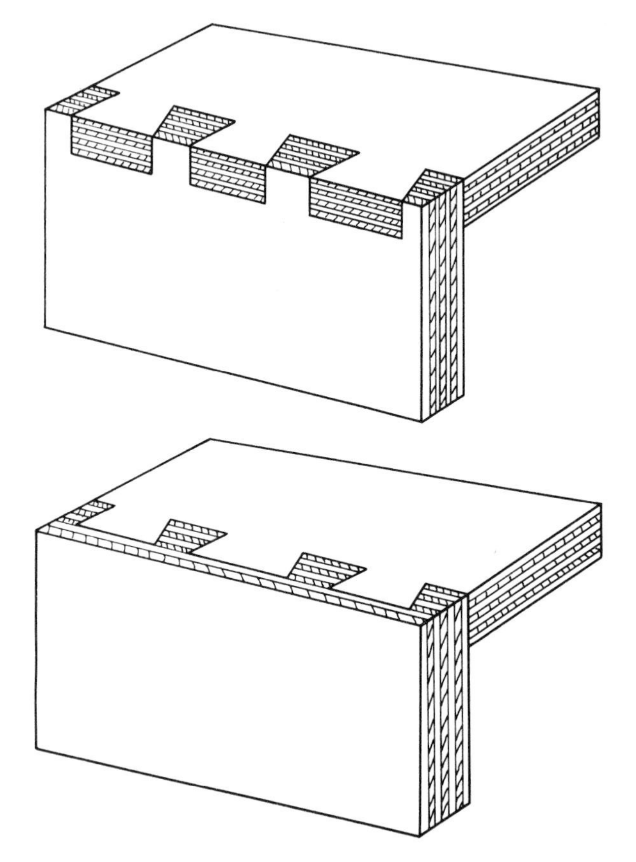

Illus. 320. *Plywood dovetails. Use coarse dovetails in plywood. The narrow part of both pins and tails should not be less than the thickness of the plywood.*

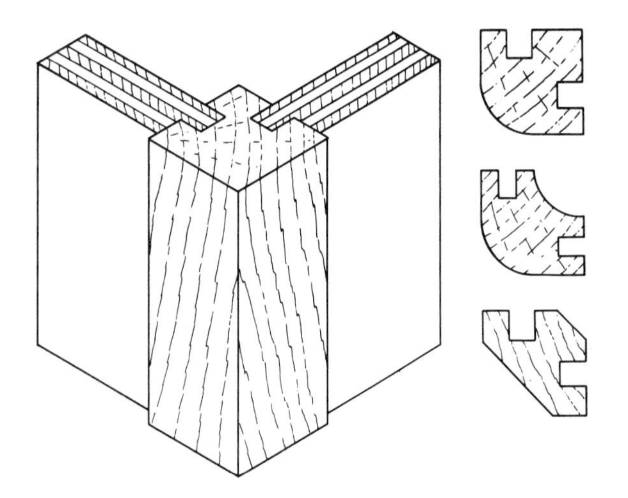

Illus. 321. *A solid-lumber corner block is joined to the plywood with a barefaced tongue-and-groove. The corner block can be left square or shaped for decorative effect.*

can be used to hide the plywood edge. The inside and outside corners of the block can be rounded, chamfered, or shaped to complement the style of the project (Illus. 321).

When the interior appearance of the project is not important, you can add corner bracing. This can be a simple block, glued and screwed in the corner, or a more sophisticated corner brace in which two boards are joined with dovetailing (Illus. 322). Box joints can be substituted for the dovetail joint. In either case, recess the ends of the pins and tails slightly. That way, if the thickness of the brace shrinks, the ends won't protrude and push open the joint. For greatest strength, alternate the bracket direction along the joint so that you have the dovetails facing both ways.

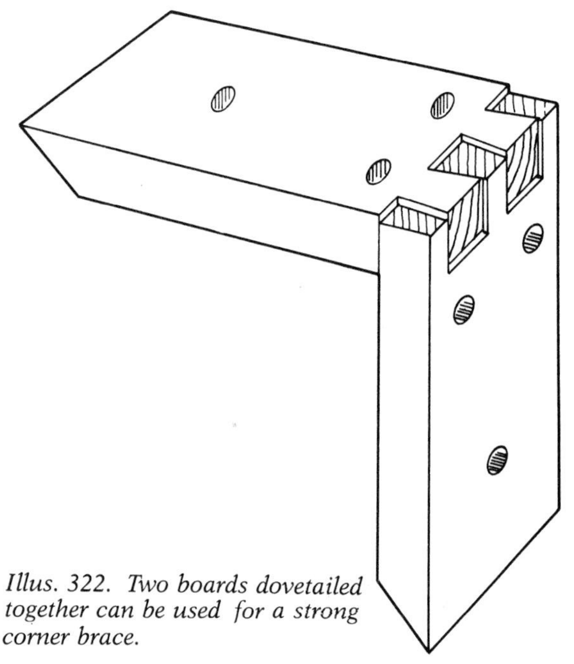

Illus. 322. *Two boards dovetailed together can be used for a strong corner brace.*

EDGING

Solid lumber is often attached to the edge of plywood to hide the plywood edges and to provide an area that can be shaped. When the purpose is only to hide the edge, thin strips of veneer, or special paper-backed veneer tape, can be attached with contact cement. When the edging is going to be shaped or used for decorative effect, thicker pieces are needed. There are several methods for attaching the edging (Illus. 323). The tongue-and-groove or spline joints

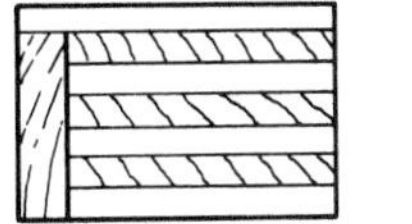

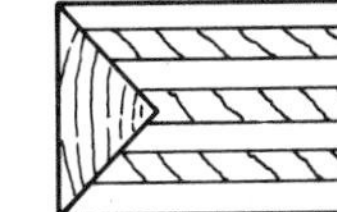

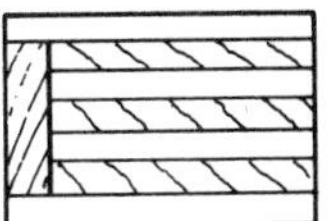

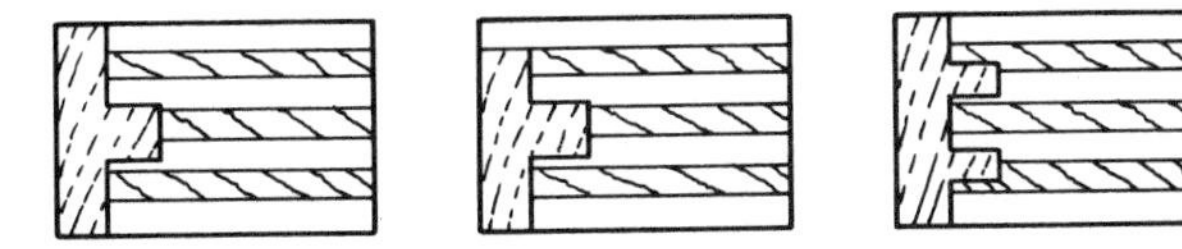

Illus. 323. *A variety of joints can be used when solid lumber is applied as plywood edging. The edging can be concealed by cutting the joint so that the face ply will extend over the edging.*

should be used when the edging is large or will be subjected to a lot of stress.

UNSUPPORTED LAP

Because of the alternating grain direction of the plies, plywood won't break along the grain in the way that solid lumber will. This makes it possible to use large, unsupported lap joints that would be impossible with solid lumber (Illus. 324). These joints are often used to make knock-down furniture. The parts slide together and can be disassembled and reassembled repeatedly (Illus. 325). The unsupported lap can be used to

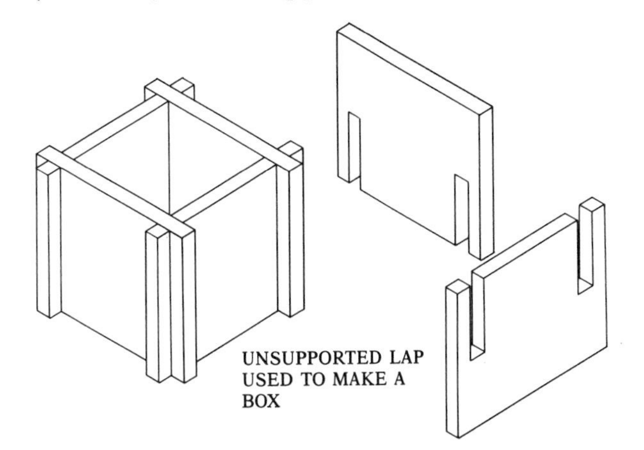

Illus. 324. *Unsupported lap joints can be used with plywood in situations that would be impossible with solid lumber.*

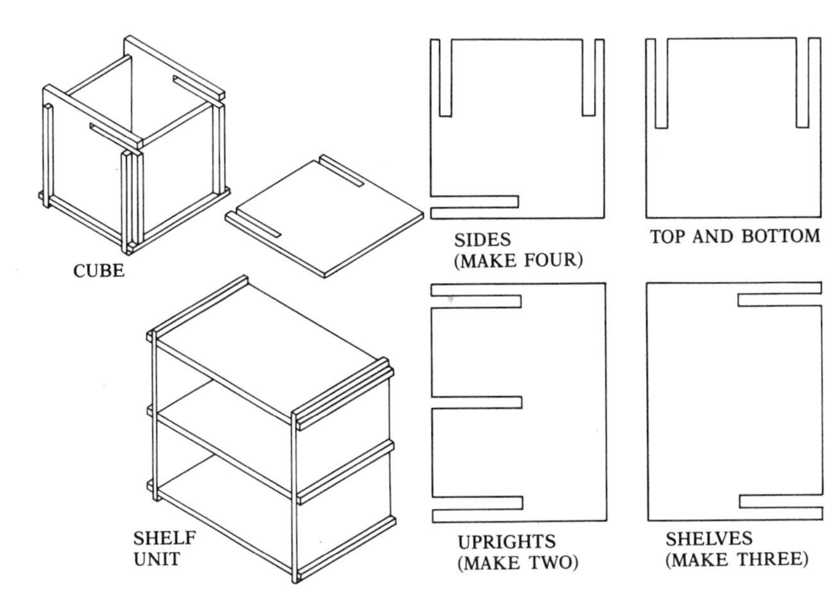

Illus. 325. *Unsupported laps can be used to make a variety of useful objects out of plywood. The joints can be left unglued so that the objects can be disassembled whenever necessary.*

make legs, table pedestals, shelf units, and many other items (Illus. 326).

For narrow boards, you can cut the notch with a dado blade. Place the edge of the board on the saw table, and use a mitre gauge to hold it square. When the notch is longer than the maximum depth of cut of the dado blade, you can still use the table saw, but with a standard blade, by placing the board face down on the table. You will need to make two cuts. Stop the cut when the front of the blade reaches the end of the notch; remove the work from the saw. Remove the waste strip, and square up the end of the notch with a chisel. You can also make the cut with handsaws. Make the side cuts with a backsaw for short notches and with a panel saw for longer ones; then, cut the bottom of the notch with a coping saw or with a chisel. A band saw makes cutting long notches even easier.

TUSK TENONS

The tusk tenon is another joint that can be used to make knockdown projects from plywood (Illus. 327). When the tenoned member is large,

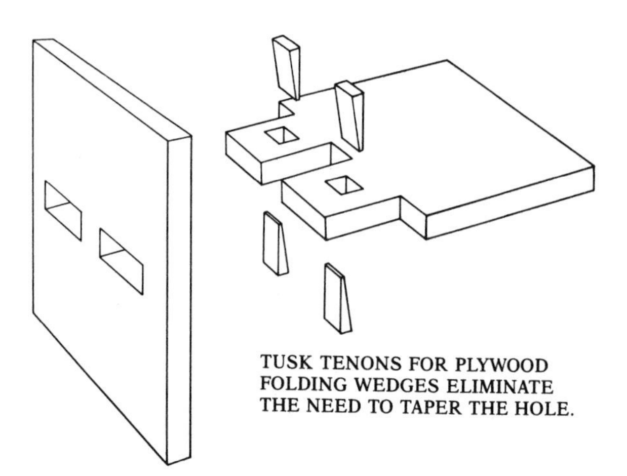

Illus. 327. Plywood tusk tenons.

divide the tenons so that you don't weaken the mortised member too much. In several ways the tusk-tenon joint is, in fact, better suited to plywood than to solid lumber. The mortise can be cut in either direction because the grain direction is not a factor. The plywood tenon will hold the wedge better because there is less chance of shear failure along the grain.

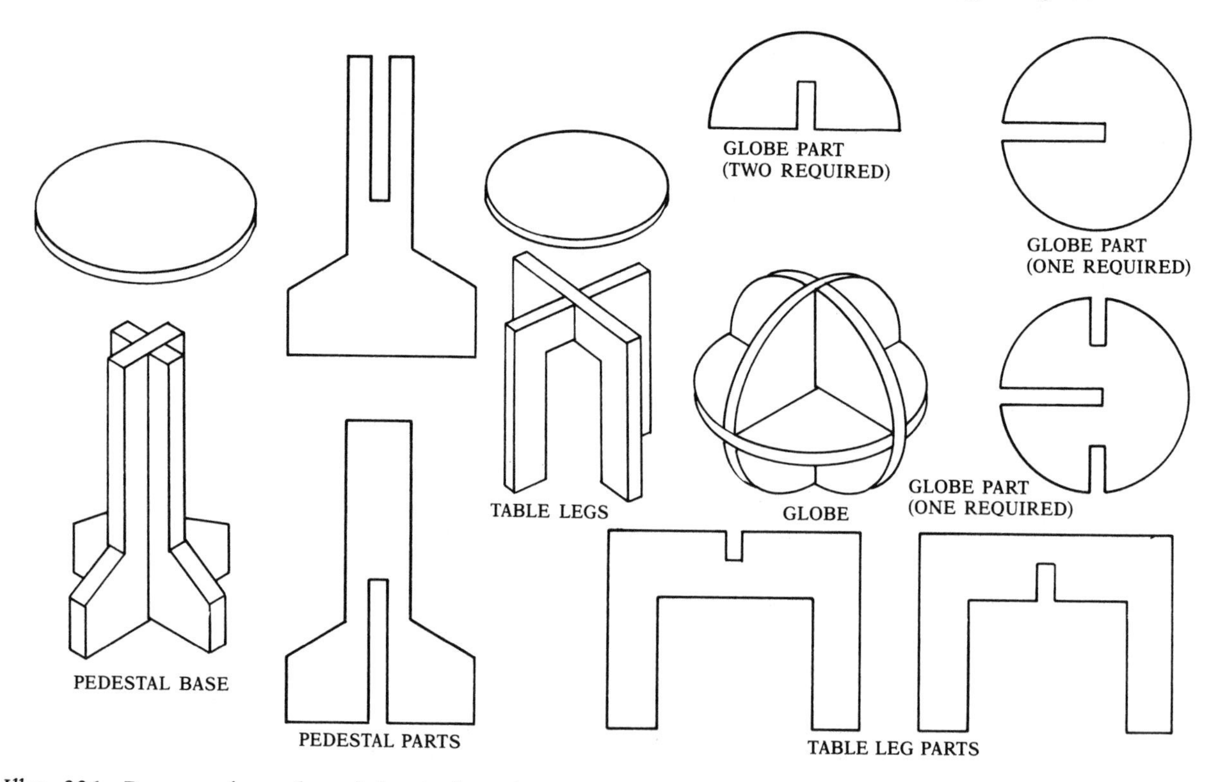

Illus. 326. Because plywood won't break along the grain as solid lumber will, the design possibilities are more varied.

RADIUS CORNERS

Another joint that is particularly well suited to plywood is the radius corner. In this joint, the plywood is actually bent around the corner (Illus. 328). Start by making a wide dado in the back face of the plywood. The depth of the dado depends on the radius; the sharper the bend, the deeper the dado needs to be. It is usually from two-thirds to three-fourths the thickness of the plywood. Then make a solid-lumber corner block shaped to the desired curve. Start with a square piece of lumber. Cut rabbets in two sides; the depth of the rabbets should equal the depth of the dado in the plywood. Now shape the corner of the block to the desired radius. After you are satisfied that the block fits the radius and the dado properly, apply the glue to the plywood and to the block. Place the block in the corner, and bend the plywood around it. Clamp until the glue sets.

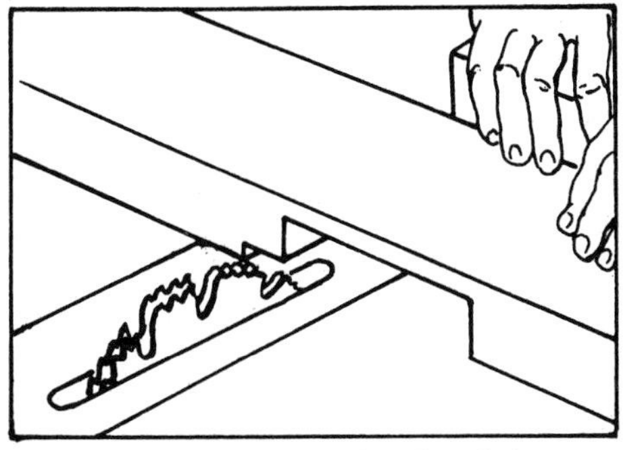

1. Cut a wide dado in plywood at bending point. Make sure that the remaining plywood is thin enough to make the bend.

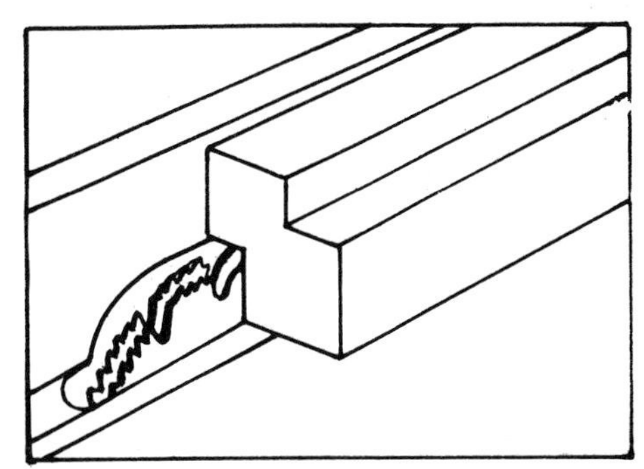

2. Cut rabbets in sides of corner block. Depth of rabbet is the same as the dado in the plywood.

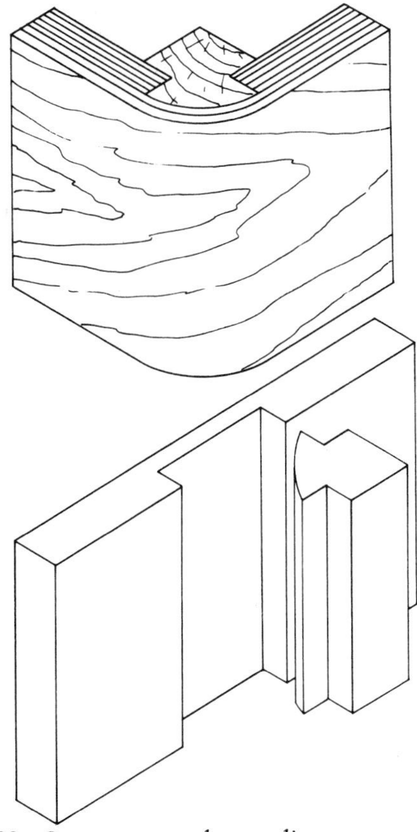

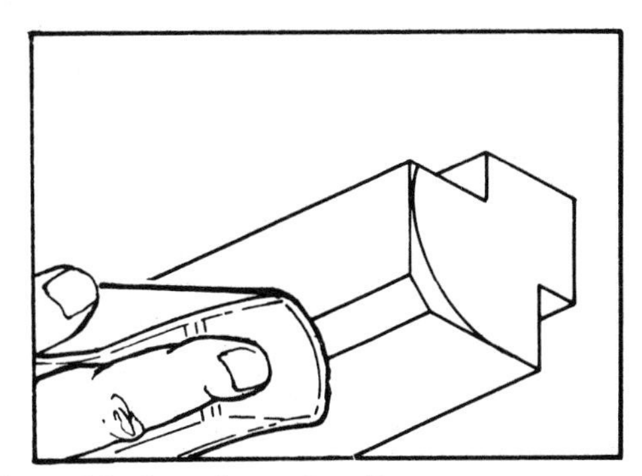

3. Shape block to desired radius.

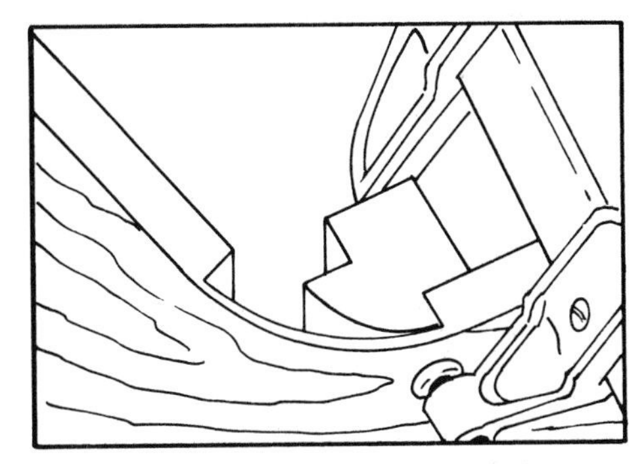

4. Apply glue and bend plywood around corner block.

Illus. 328. One way to make a radius corner step by step.

A method that is a little simpler is the kerf bent corner (Illus. 329). Make closely spaced saw kerfs on the back of the plywood in the area to be bent. The depth of the kerfs should be about two-thirds the thickness of the plywood. Tight bends will require deeper kerfs and closer spacing. Bend the plywood, then shape a corner block to fit inside the corner. Glue and clamp the corner block in place.

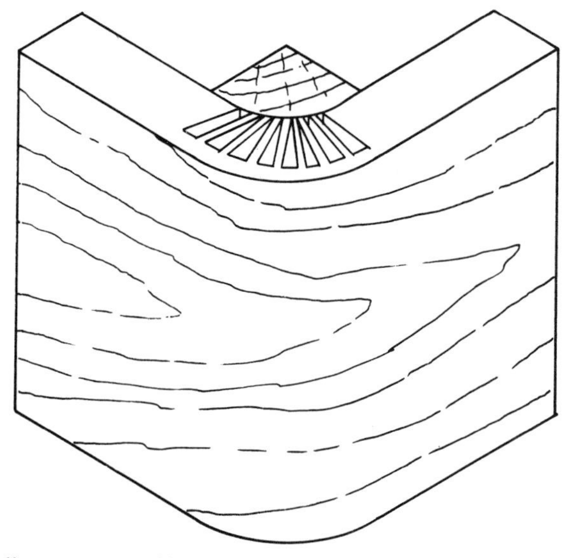

Illus. 329. Kerf bent corner.

Particleboard

Particleboard is a reconstituted wood product. It is made from small particles of wood that are bonded together with glue (Illus. 330). The glue-to-wood ratio is high, making particleboard hard and heavy. The high amount of glue rapidly dulls cutting tools, so carbide tools are recommended. Several types of particleboard are available. The type sold at most lumber yards is meant for floor underlayment and doesn't have the density or surface finish needed for cabinet work. An industrial grade is available that is denser and has a smoother finish; this type is used extensively in commercial cabinetwork. This industrial-grade particleboard is available with wood veneer, plastic laminate, or vinyl as a decorative face. When a decorative face veneer is used, you will need to take the same precautions as were described for plywood in order to prevent chipping the face while cutting joints. Particleboard is usually engineered to have less density at the core and more near the faces. This means that the joints should be designed to utilize the strength of the faces and to avoid relying on the core. Other reconstituted wood products such as wafer board and oriented strand board (OSB) are designed to have more strength than particleboard, but the joinery is similar.

When you are designing joints for particleboard, take into consideration that it is strongest under compression; the shear strength of particleboard is much less than that of solid lumber. Small projections tend to crumble, so tongues and dovetails, in particular, are not well suited to particleboard. The greatest joint strength results when the integrity of the face is preserved; reinforced butt joints are therefore the preferred joints for particleboard. Other joints such as rabbets, dadoes, and mitres are often used; but, because one face is cut away, the parts are weakened.

Particleboard edges don't glue well; the best glue bond results when faces are glued together. Screws don't hold very well in particleboard; however, they hold better in the face than in the edge. For maximum strength, specialized fasteners are needed.

Illus. 330. Particleboard is available with decorative face veneers as shown here.

JOINT REINFORCEMENT

Some type of reinforcement is needed in practically all particleboard joints (Illus. 331). Dowels are a common type of reinforcement. The dowel holes don't form a continuous break line, so face integrity is preserved, thus adding strength. Dowels can be used to reinforce all types of butt joints including T and edge butts. Dowels can also be used with mitre joints.

A recent development that can be used with dowels in any material are glue bullets, but they are most suited to use in the mass production of particleboard products. The glue bullet is a small capsule containing a premeasured amount of glue. You place the bullet in the dowel hole before inserting the dowel. Special dowels are used that have a hole in the end. When the joint is clamped, the capsule breaks open, and the glue spreads evenly throughout the dowel hole due to the special design of the dowel. The major advantage of the glue bullet is precisely that it can be used with automated equipment for mass production.

Splines can be used with particleboard also. Plate splines are preferred, of course, because the pockets don't form a continuous break line. When a standard spline is used, keep the groove away from edges, and don't make it deeper than half the thickness of the particleboard. When reinforcing a mitre with a spline, keep the spline away from the outside corner. Hardboard is the best material to use as a spline in particleboard. Since a tongue made on particleboard will crumble off, substitute hardboard splines in situations where a tongue is needed.

The latest development in splines is the liquid-plastic spline. Spline grooves are made as usual, but the joint is assembled and clamped without inserting a spline. Then a high-pressure gun is used to inject a two-component liquid polyurethane plastic. The plastic flows into the spline groove and then hardens. The resulting joint is much stronger than a normal spline because the plastic fills the groove so well that it conforms to any irregularity and soaks into the pores. At present, this is a technique that is primarily used in large production shops; but, advances in the system may make it feasible for use by both smaller shops and home woodworkers.

Specialized fasteners will hold better than nails or screws in particleboard. Standard nails and screws are, in fact, often used; but, when maximum strength is needed, use a specialized fastener. The bolt and cross-dowel fastener uses a bolt with machine threads and a metal cross dowel that is threaded to accept the bolt (Illus. 332). A hole is drilled for the bolt; then, an intersecting hole is drilled for the cross dowel. The

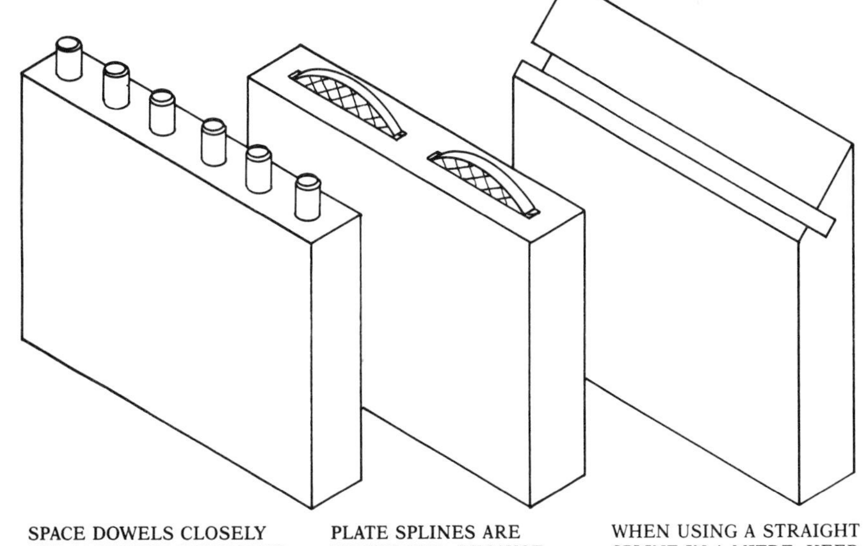

Illus. 331. Joint reinforcement for particleboard.

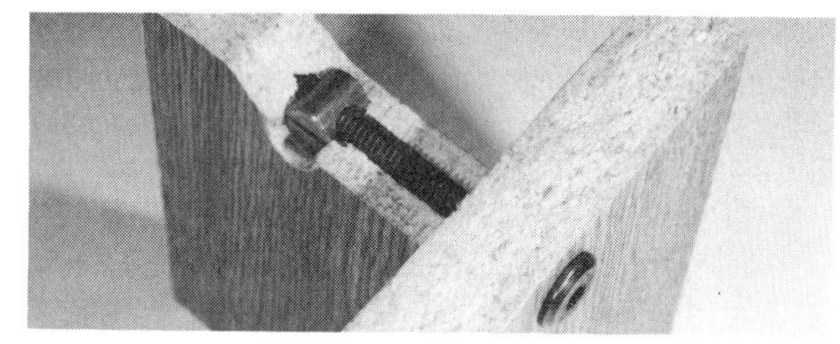

Illus. 332. The bolt and cross-dowel fastener overcomes the poor screw-holding properties of particleboard.

cross dowel is placed in its hole. The bolt is inserted and screwed into the cross dowel. The strength comes from the increased bearing surface of the cross dowel. The cross dowel also eliminates the problem of poor thread holding in the edge of particleboard. The bolt and cross dowel can be used to reinforce butt, dado, and rabbet joints. A similar type of fastener called a cam fitting uses a cross dowel that hooks into the end of the bolt. Turning the cross dowel tightens the joint by cam action.

Large, coarse threads hold better in particleboard than smaller threads, so, when a smaller thread is still required, a threaded insert can increase the holding power. Threaded inserts are made of metal and have a coarse thread on the outside with a smaller thread in the hole in the middle (Illus. 333). The threaded inserts are screwed into predrilled holes with a screwdriver or an Allen wrench. Then, smaller machine screws are used to connect the parts.

Since a screw will hold about twice as well in the particleboard face as it will in the edge, any type of reinforcement plate that places the screws on the face will help; the reinforcement can be simple bent-metal braces or knockdown fittings. Knockdown fittings are frequently used as joint reinforcements in commercial products because the product can be shipped flat and assembled after delivery. A knockdown fitting consists of two mating parts that attach to adjoining faces. When parts are assembled, a screw, cam, or clip is used to connect the two parts of the fitting.

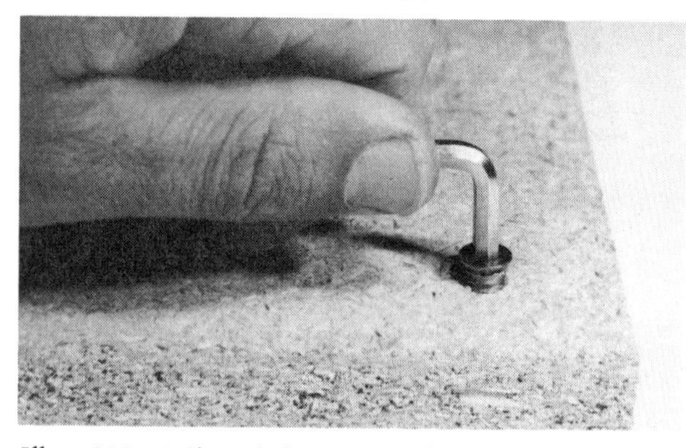

Illus. 333. A threaded insert can be used to provide greater screw holding in particleboard. They are particularly useful for attaching hardware.

A number of specialized fasteners is made to be used with the 32-mm system of building cabinets. The 32-mm system is largely used by mass production cabinetmakers. In this system, all holes are 32-mm apart, so the same boring machines can be used for dowel holes, specialized fasteners, and hardware. In mass production, for the most part, computerized boring machines drill the holes; but, anyone can use the 32-mm hardware. Use a dowelling jig to drill the holes, and space them 32-mm apart. Illus. 334 shows three types of corner brackets designed for use in the 32-mm system. They are very good for reinforcing particleboard corners because the screws are driven into the face. Special screws come with the brackets; the threads are designed particularly for added holding power in particleboard.

Solid-wood glue blocks are a good method of reinforcement when the appearance is not the

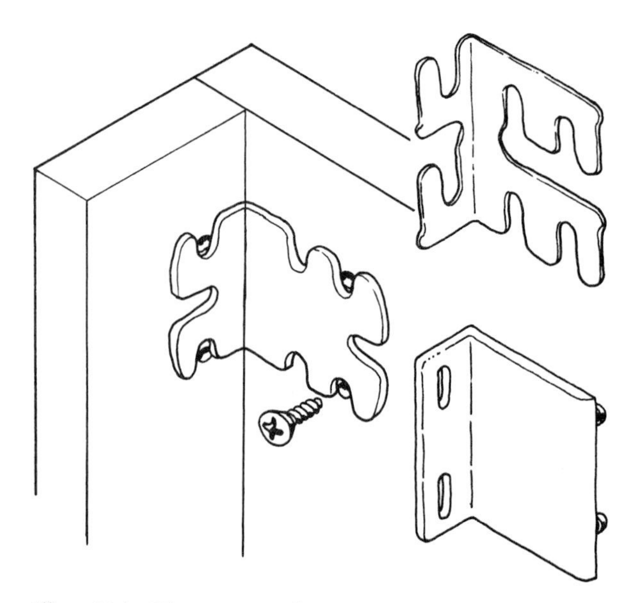

Illus. 334. These corner braces designed for the 32-mm system of cabinetmaking are a good method for reinforcing particleboard joints.

foremost consideration. Reinforcement blocks provide a good glue surface on a face and provide for face nailing or screw attachment. Whenever possible, drive the screws through the particleboard, and then screw them into the solid wood because the solid wood will hold the threads much better than the particleboard.

Solid-wood corner blocks can be used in a manner similar to that described for plywood. But, since a tongue on particleboard is not recommended, use splines, or form the tongue on the solid-wood corner block. Illus. 335 gives step-by-step directions for forming a tongue on the corner block.

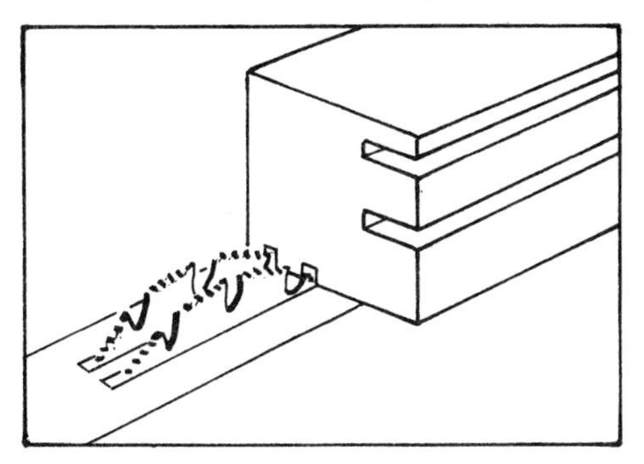

1. Make the cheek cuts for the tongues. You can use twin blades separated by a washer to cut two cheeks at a time.

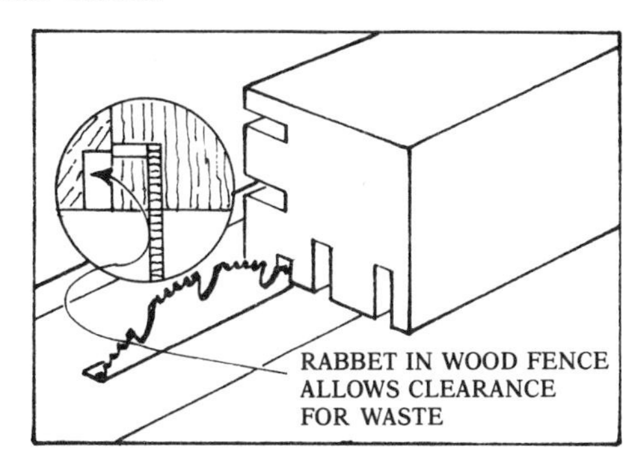

2. Cut one of the inside shoulders. Use an auxiliary fence with a rabbet at the bottom to prevent kickback of the waste.

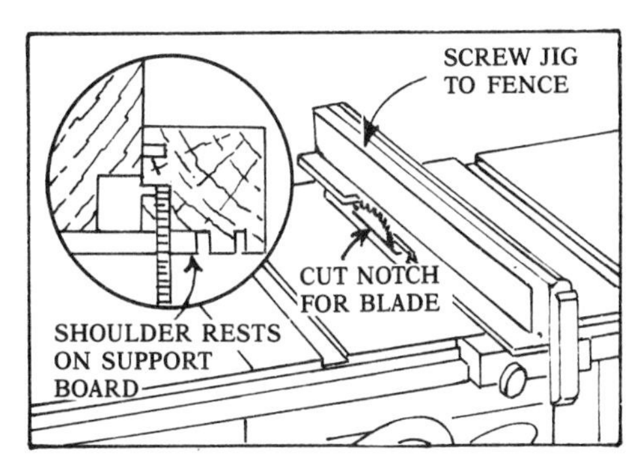

3. A special jig is needed to make the second inside shoulder. The jig supports the board where the first shoulder has been cut away.

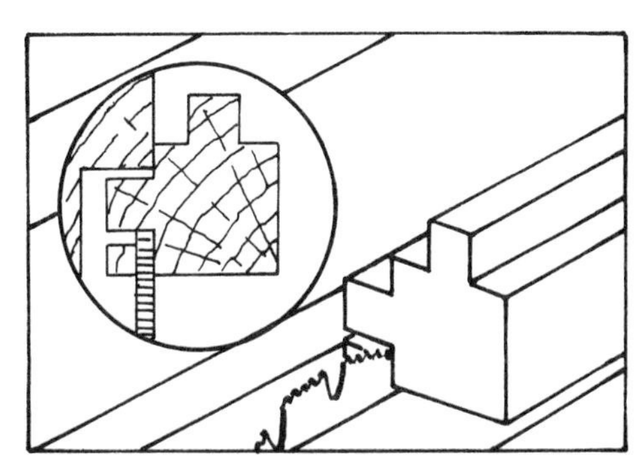

4. Cut the outside shoulders.

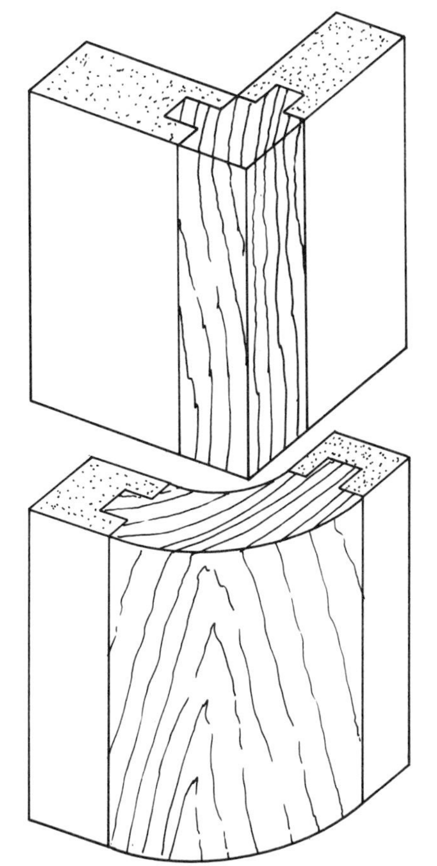

PROCEDURE FOR CUTTING TONGUES IS THE SAME. ROUND CORNERS AFTER CUTTING TONGUES.

Illus. 335. Solid-corner blocks for particleboard step by step.

13
Specialty Joints

There are many specialities within the broad scope of woodworking. Many of these specialized trades use their own specialty joints. While the range of woodworking specialties is even too large to cover in one book, I will present in this chapter a few joints from some of these specialties. I have chosen joints that have applications in more general woodworking.

Moulding Joints

The finish carpenter or joiner is usually the one concerned with applying mouldings, but all woodworkers have occasion to work with moulding. When the interior trim is applied in a building, the moulding is one of the last steps. This means that the joinery has to be sufficiently adaptable to compensate for irregularities or out-of-square conditions that exist.

THE COPED JOINT

Here is a perfect example of a joint that can be used to compensate when the moulding must meet at an out-of-square inside corner. A standard mitre could be used, of course, but if the corner is out of square, the joint will be open. The mitre also tends to gap open as the wood shrinks or as the building settles. The coped joint stays closed much better and can also compensate well for an out-of-square corner.

To make a coped joint, one moulding is cut with a square end and applied all the way into the corner (Illus. 336). Next, cut a mitre on the mating moulding. The intersection between the mitre cut and the face of the moulding serves as the cutting line for the coped cut; use a coping saw to cut along the line. The cut should be close to 90° to the face of the moulding; but, to ensure a tight joint line, angle it back a few degrees. After the coped cut is complete, place the moulding over the other one, and check the fit. Use a pocketknife or a file to make minor adjustments.

OUTSIDE CORNER MITRES

These can't be coped, so a standard mitre must be used. Since the corners in a building are seldom exactly square, the joints frequently have gaps on the first try. If the error is large, one of the parts must be recut at a different angle. Hold the joint together, and draw a line on one part using the mitre cut on the other part as a guide. This will give you the correct angle to fit the joint. When the error is small, finish carpenters often use this trick: apply glue to the joint, and nail the moulding in place. While the glue is still wet, tap the corner of the joint with a hammer, working lightly over the joint line. This will crush some of the wood fibres and cause the wood to expand. Keep tapping the joint until it closes. This will result in a slight rounding over of the corner, but that is not usually objectionable in this application. After the glue is dry, go over the joint with sandpaper to remove any projecting fibres.

MITRING CURVED MOULDINGS

This requires a special procedure. A straight 45° cut will result in a misalignment of the mouldings. For the parts to line up correctly, the mitre line must be curved (Illus. 337). You need to make a full-size drawing of the parts to get the curve. Draw the two parts in their proper relationship, but continue all of the lines so that they intersect. The point that each line crosses the same line on the other part indicates a point on the curve of the joint line. Connect all of the points with a smooth curve. Trace this curve onto a piece of cardboard to use as a marking template for the joint. Transfer the curve to the wood, and cut the joint. You can use a coping saw, band saw, or jigsaw to make the cut; or, you can make a straight cut, and then use a drum sander to shape the end of the straight piece to the correct curvature. Trace the curve onto the mating part, and use a disc sander to shape it.

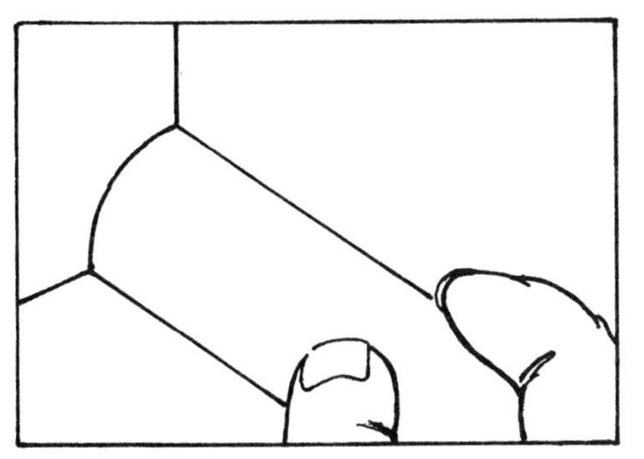

1. Apply moulding with square end all the way to corner.

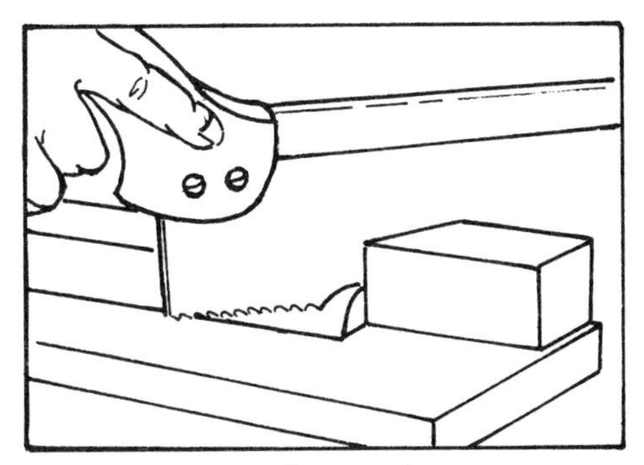

2. Cut mitre on part to be coped.

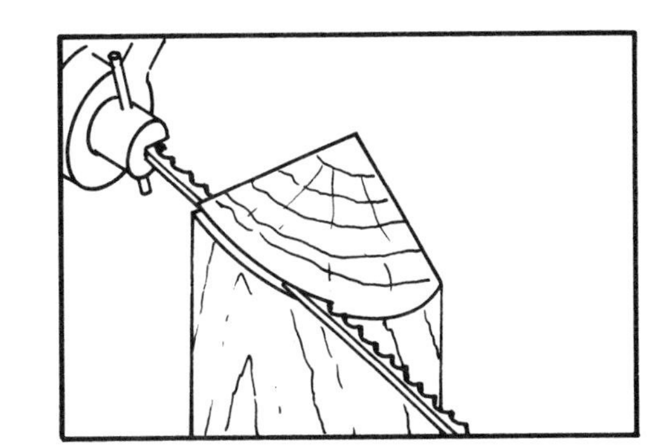

3. Use coping saw to cut on profile.

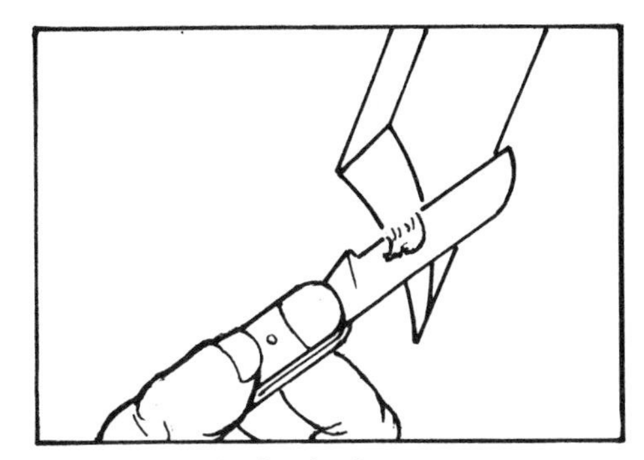

4. Use knife to make final adjustments.

Illus. 336. Coped joint step by step.

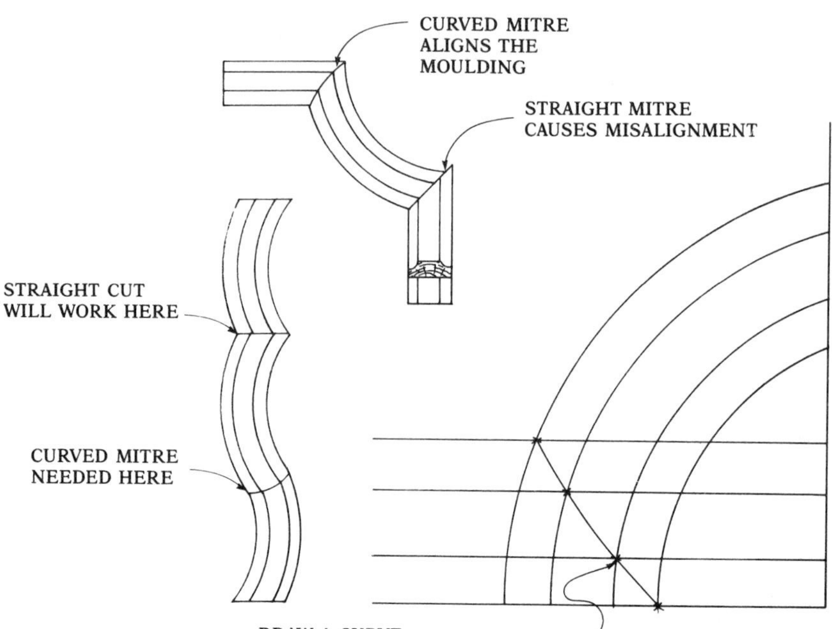

Illus. 337. A curved mitre must be used to properly align the joint when curved mouldings meet a straight piece.

When two curved mouldings meet facing the same direction, the mitre cut is straight; but when they meet curving in the opposite direction, a curved mitre is needed.

If the face of the curved moulding is flat, there won't be the problem of misaligned design elements of the moulding, but the joint still won't fit when cut at 45°. Use the same procedure for making a full-size drawing; but, instead of a curved line, you only need to make a straight line connecting the points where the edges cross. Measure the angle, and cut the parts using this measure as the mitre angle.

ODD-ANGLE MITRES

Odd-angle mitres result when mouldings meet at angles other than 90°. You can measure the angle with a protractor and divide it in two to get the mitre angle; but, there is another way that doesn't rely on a protractor (Illus. 338). It is simply the method of bisecting an angle using a compass. Trace the angle onto a piece of paper.

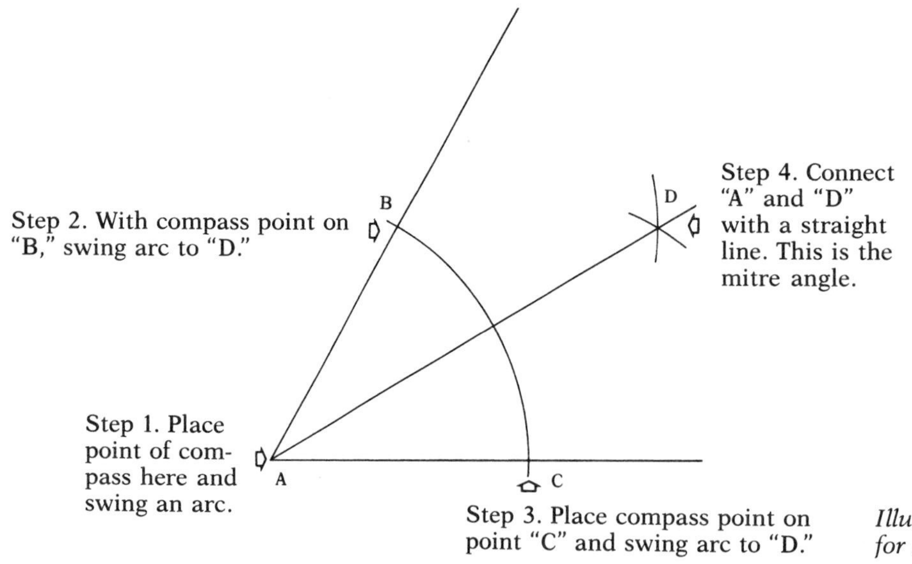

Illus. 338. Graphic method for determining mitre angles.

Place a drawing compass with the point at the corner, and swing an arc across the two legs. Next, place the point of the compass at the point where the arc intersects one of the legs. Swing another arc into the middle of the angle. Repeat this procedure on the other leg. Now draw a line between the point where the two arcs cross and the corner. You can set a sliding T-bevel directly from this line.

This same basic procedure will work when three parts meet. Place the compass at the middle point of the joint, and draw a circle. Use the points where the circle intersects the legs of each joint to swing the other arcs. When three parts meet, there will be two cuts on each joint, so the point must be on the middle line of the board.

THREE-WAY MITRES

These result when three mouldings meet at a corner. Each piece requires two mitre cuts. Make the first one as usual; then, turn the first cut face up, and make a second cut so that a point is formed (Illus. 339).

SCARF JOINTS

Scarf joints are used when a single piece of moulding isn't long enough (Illus. 340). In moulding work, the scarf angle is usually 45°. This is satisfactory because the moulding is supported by the surface to which it is applied. In the section below on splicing joints, scarf joints for other applications are discussed. The scarf joint is superior to the standard butt joint because it is less likely to open up as the boards shrink and as the building settles. A plate spline can be used to reinforce and align the scarf joint.

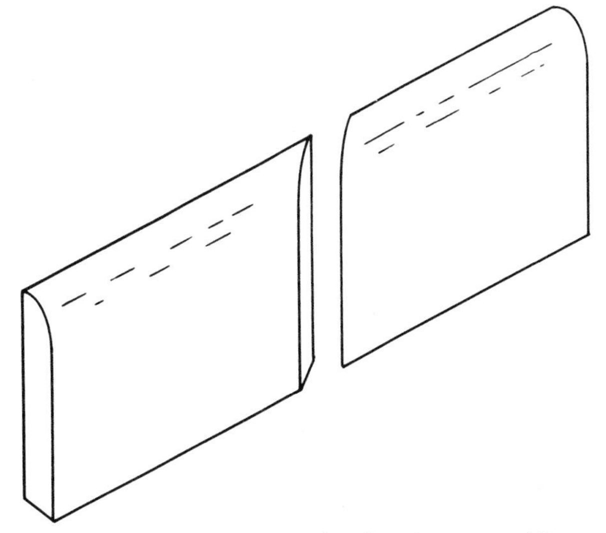

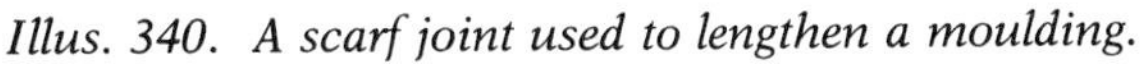

Illus. 340. A scarf joint used to lengthen a moulding.

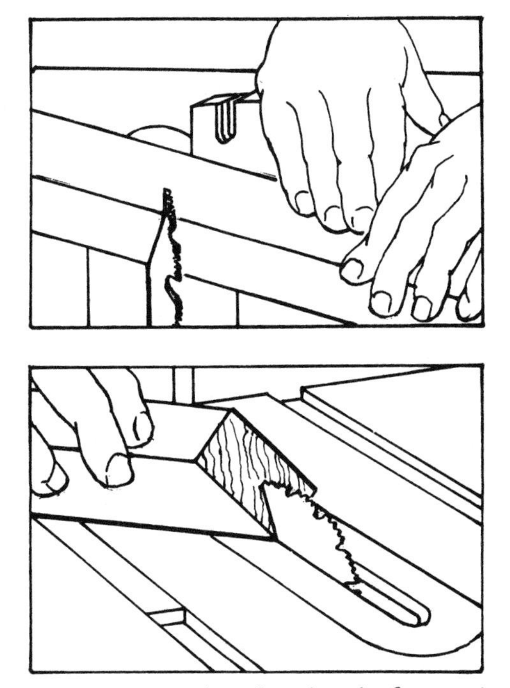

Illus. 339. To cut a three-way mitre, first make a 45° cut as usual; then, turn the board so that the first cut is face up, and make a second 45° cut.

Splicing Joints

Splicing joints are often used in millwork to make clear stock for mouldings as well as window and door parts. Defects are cut out of the lumber, and splicing joints are used to join the short, clear pieces into usable lengths. Splicing joints used for large timbers, in particular, are discussed below in the section covering timber framing.

End grain doesn't glue very well, so a simple butt joint between the ends of two boards doesn't provide much strength. The tensile strength of an end-to-end butt is only equal to about 10 percent of the strength of the surrounding wood. To get a strong glue bond, the joint must be designed to provide some long-grain contact area or mechanical locking (Illus. 341).

LAP JOINTS

Lap joints can be used to splice boards. The long-grain contact area between the two cheeks provides a good glue bond. The shoulder-to-end joint area of the lap joint is weak because it joins end grain to end grain. The lap joint will fail under bending stress at this point where the shoulder and end meet. If the stress is pure tension, however, the joint can be quite strong.

THE SCARF JOINT

This application of the scarf joint eliminates the shoulder-to-end problem because of the angle. For the contact area to approach being long grain, the joint must be fairly long. Maximum strength is reached at a slope of 1:12. A scarf joint with a 1:12 slope has a relative tensile strength of 90 percent, which means that it is only 10 percent weaker than the board itself. As a general rule of thumb, any scarf joint where strength is important should be at least ten times longer than the thickness of the board. A 1:10 slope has a relative tensile strength of 85 percent.

In most boards, anyway, the grain runs at a slight angle to the face. When it is possible, you should cut the joint so that the scarf runs essentially parallel to the grain. Of course, this isn't always practical when a particular face of the part must match with the other.

Scarf joints can be hard to align, particularly when they are clamped. Unless the joint receives

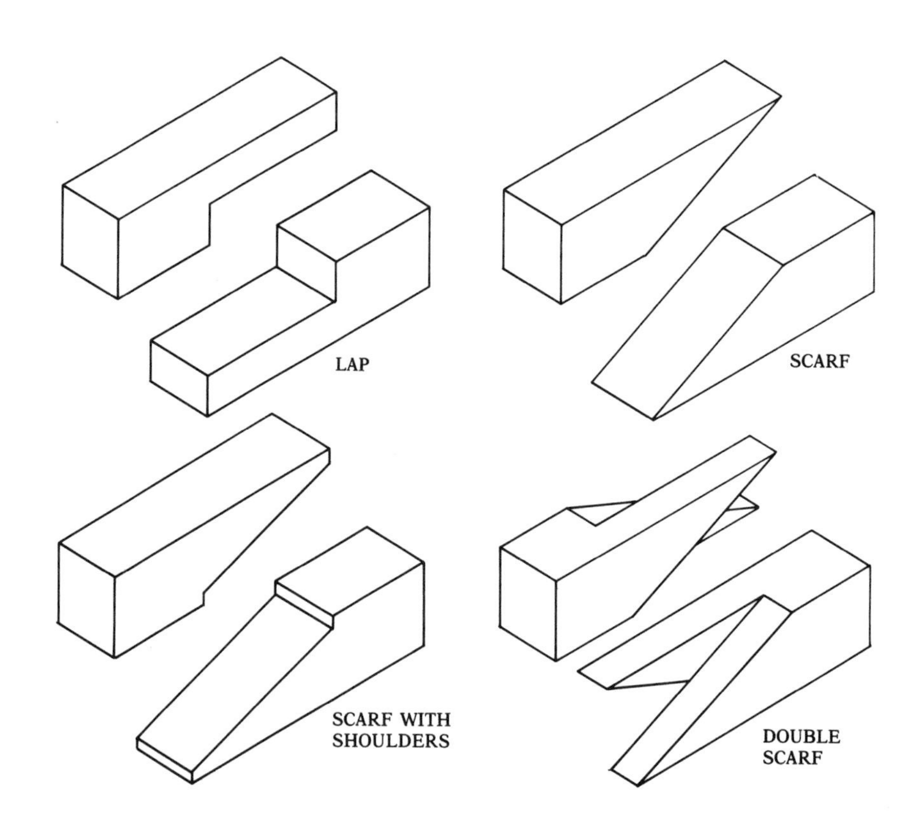

Illus. 341. Splicing joints.

even clamping pressure, much of the strength will be lost. Secure the ends of the board before clamping the joint to prevent slipping; then, apply even pressure across the joint. You can also lay out the scarf with small shoulders to be cut at the ends to help in alignment without sacrificing too much strength.

The double scarf is a variation on the scarf joint. Because of the interlocking arrangement, the double scarf has more compressive strength.

FINGER JOINTS

These are the type of splicing joint most used by industry. They have multiple angled fingers. The strength of a finger joint is actually less than that of a well-made scarf joint under tension; but, the finger joint can better withstand compression and bending, besides which it is easier to align. Industrial equipment designed to make finger joints is beyond the price range of most small shops; however, special router and shaper bits are available to make the joint. The strength of the joint depends on the slope and the pitch (spacing) of the fingers. In tests conducted by the U.S. Department of Agriculture Forest Service Forest Products Laboratory, the greatest strength was achieved with a finger pitch of 7/16" and a slope of 1:16. Since the slope and the pitch are determined by the cutter that you are using, you don't have much direct control over it at the time you cut. The only choice you really have is making your selection when you buy a cutter. Generally, the joint will be stronger if the fingers are longer.

A finger joint can be oriented on the board in two ways. Horizontal-finger joints are used where the appearance of the wide face is more important than considerations of strength. But, for structural applications, vertical-finger joints should always be used (Illus. 342).

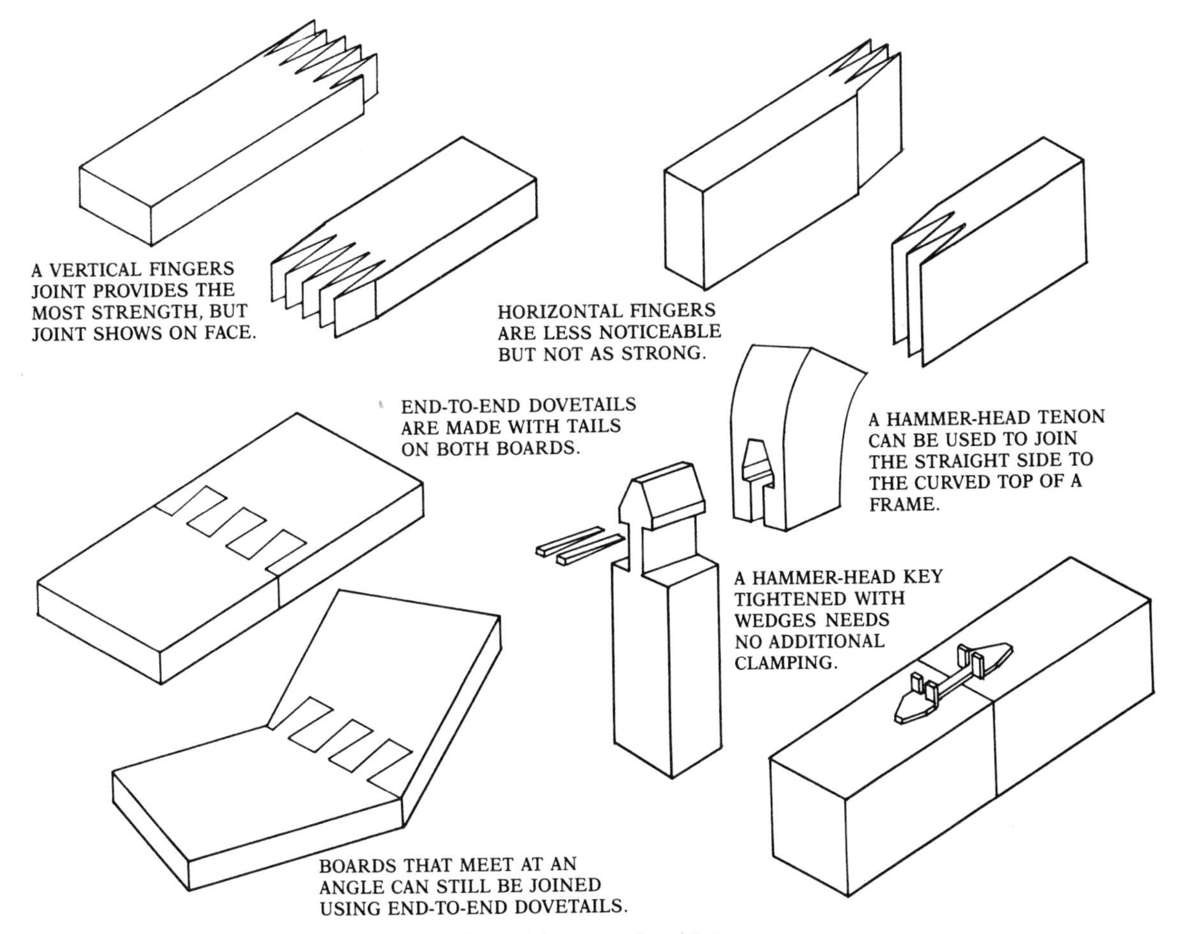

Illus. 342. Finger joints, end-to-end dovetails, and hammer-head joints.

Clamping pressure must be applied in two directions to achieve a good bond in finger joints. The clamps must be placed in such a way as to provide longitudinal pressure as well as pressure across the joint.

Finger joints can be used to join at an angle. This is very useful when you are making curved parts. If you cut a curved part out of a single piece of wood, there will be a weak short-grain section. By joining several pieces with finger joints, the grain can be aligned to avoid this short-grain weakness.

END-TO-END DOVETAILS

End-to-end dovetails introduce mechanical locking to a splicing joint. Like a finger joint, they also provide some long-grain contact area. The end-to-end dovetail is more decorative than are other splicing joints, so it can be used as part of the design of a project (Illus. 343).

The distinctive feature of end-to-end dovetails is that both parts have tails and there are no pins in the joint. The tails are laid out and cut using any of the methods described in the earlier chapters. Make the tails first on one board; then, transfer the layout to the other board, and make a mating set of tails.

Illus. 343. End-to-end dovetails introduce mechanical locking to a splicing joint.

Illus. 344. End-to-end dovetails can be cut on the Leigh dovetail jig in the half-blind mode. Both boards have tails cut on them.

The Leigh dovetail jig is particularly well adapted for making the joint (Illus. 344). Even though the joint is a through dovetail, the jig is set up for the half-blind mode. Place the first board in the front clamp, and rout with the jig set for half-blind dovetails. Remove the first part, and set the jig for half-blind pins. Place the second board in the front clamp, and rout. Because the board is placed in the front clamp rather than in the top clamp, the result will be tails instead of pins. You will need to do some trial-and-error adjusting of the depth, so make a test joint first.

End-to-end dovetails can also be used to join boards at an angle. Just as with finger joints, you can use end-to-end dovetails to align the grain in curved parts. To cut the joint at an angle, first cut the desired angle of the end of the board; then, lay out the joint. If you are using the router jig, attach angle guides to help position the work. The cutting procedure is the same as above. Since it is hard to get the spacing just right, you may want to make the parts wider than is necessary, and then rip to final width after the dovetails are made. That way you can make adjustments for the positions of the half tails on the edges.

THE HAMMER-HEAD JOINT

This joint makes a self-clamping splice. It can be used for joining either curved or straight parts. A hammer-head tenon can be cut on the end of one of the parts, or a hammer-head key can be inserted in the joint (refer to Illus. 342). Wedges driven into the joint pull it tight. Power equip-

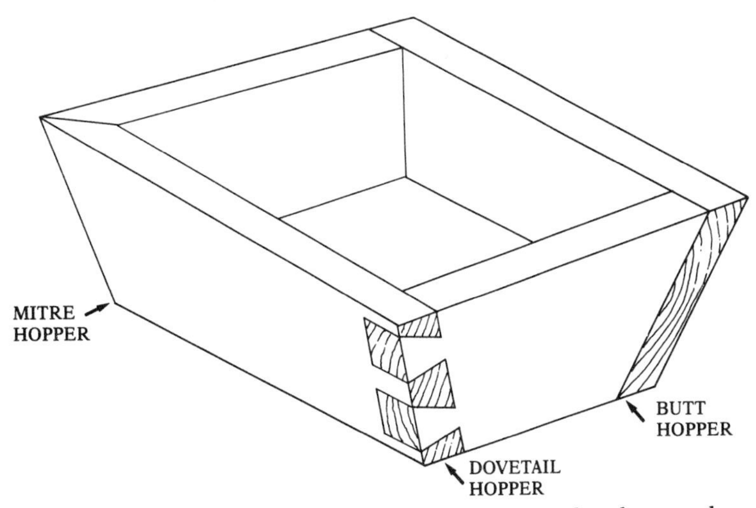

Illus. 345. Hopper joints are compound-angle joints used to make tapering four-sided objects. Butt, mitre, and dovetail joints can all be used for making hoppers.

ment can be used to rough out the joint; but, this is basically a hand-cut joint that is made by using a backsaw and chisels.

Hopper Joints

Hopper joints are needed to make four-sided objects that have a large opening at one end and taper down to a smaller opening at the other end. Although the name implies that this joint is used to make hoppers, it can also be used to make drawers that fit into odd-shaped openings, tool carriers, boxes, or whatever requires sloping sides. Hopper joints can be made using butt, mitre, or dovetail joints (Illus. 345).

When all four sides or the hopper are at equal angles, you can use the same technique as used to cut compound mitre joints. Illus. 346 gives the blade-tilt angle and mitre gauge setting to use. To make a mitre joint, set the blade tilt to the

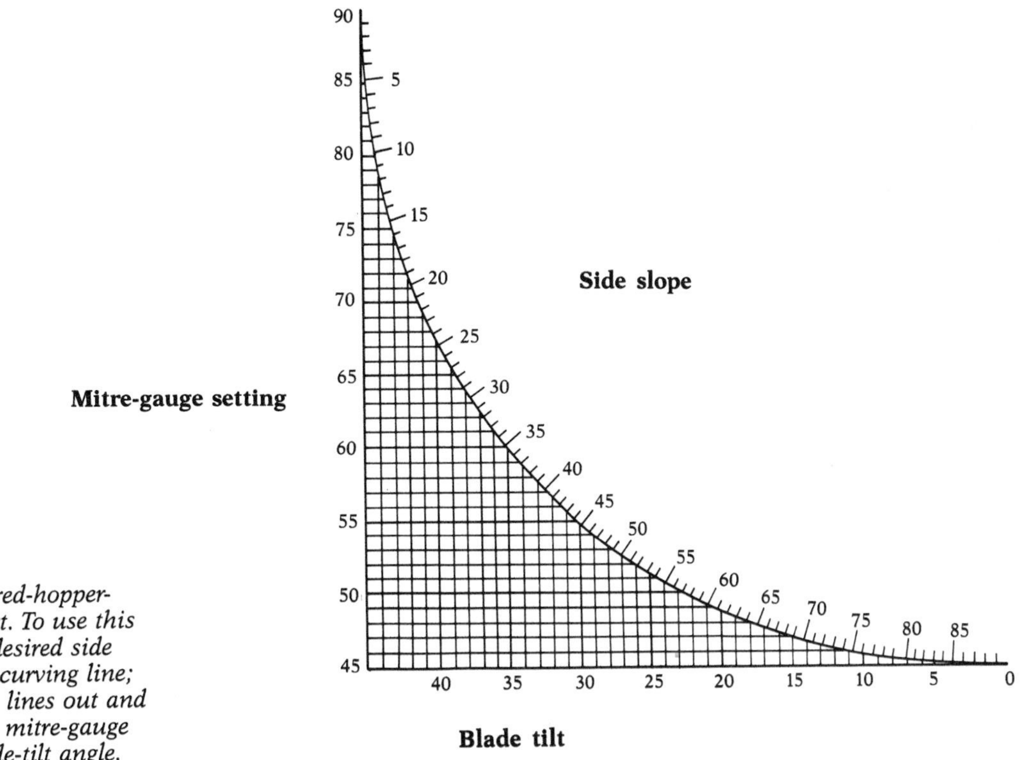

Illus. 346. Mitred-hopper-joint angle chart. To use this chart, find the desired side slope along the curving line; then, follow the lines out and down to get the mitre-gauge setting and blade-tilt angle.

angle specified, and guide the board using the mitre gauge set to the angle listed. Butt joints are made in the same way as mitre joints, but using the angles listed in the butt-hopper-joint angle chart (Illus. 347).

You can determine the blade angle and mitre gauge setting for mitred-hopper joints using a graphic method. Once you learn this method, you won't need a chart to refer to, and you can set a bevel directly from the drawing (Illus. 349).

Butt-Hopper-Joint Angle Chart

Side Slope	5°	10°	15°	20°	25°	30°	35°	40°	45°	50°	55°	60°
Mitre Gauge	85°	80.25°	75.5°	71.25°	67°	63.5°	60.25°	57.25°	54.75°	52.5°	50.75°	49°
Blade Tilt	0.5°	1.5°	3.75°	6.25°	10°	14.5°	19.5°	24.5°	30°	36°	42°	48°

Illus. 347. Butt-hopper-joint angle chart. To use this chart, find the desired side slope along the top, and read down to get the mitre-gauge angle and blade-tilt angle.

Cut the same angle on the ends of the front, back, and sides of the hopper. With the initial setup, you can only cut half of the ends. To cut the other ends, either set the mitre gauge to the same angle in the opposite direction, or reposition the mitre gauge in the opposite slot, and flip the boards over (Illus. 348). If you want the top and bottom edges to be horizontal rather than square with the angled sides, you need to rip them on an angle. Set the blade tilt to the same angle as the side slope. Alternatively, you can plane the edges to the correct angle after assembly.

Illus. 348. When cutting hopper joints, the blade and mitre gauge are both at an angle. To cut the opposite end of the board, the mitre gauge must be repositioned or reset.

Begin by drawing a horizontal line and a vertical line on a piece of paper. Next, draw a line (*BE*) intersecting the two other lines at the desired side slope. If the hopper must fit an existing angled opening, use a bevel to transfer the angle from the opening to the paper. If the specific angle isn't critical, you can just eyeball it. Next, place the point of a compass where the slope line crosses the horizontal line (*B*), and set the other end to touch the corner (*A*) between the horizontal and vertical lines. Swing an arc that crosses the slope line. At the point where the arc crosses the slope line (*C*), draw a horizontal line across to the vertical line. Connect the point (*D*) where this line crosses the vertical line with the point (*B*) where the slope line crosses the horizontal line. This is the blade-tilt angle. Set a bevel to this angle, and use it to adjust the saw.

To get the mitre-gauge angle, draw another vertical line starting at the point (*B*) where the slope line crosses the horizontal line. Place the compass point in the same hole as before (*B*), and set the other end to the point (*E*) where the slope line crosses the vertical line. Swing an arc that crosses the second vertical line. Using the point (*F*) where the arc crosses the second vertical line as a starting point, draw a horizontal line across to the first vertical line. Connect the point (*B*) where the compass point was with the point (*G*) where the second horizontal line crosses the first vertical line. This is the mitre-gauge angle. Set a bevel from the drawing, and use it to set the mitre gauge.

When the sizes of the bottom and top openings are more important than the angle of the sides,

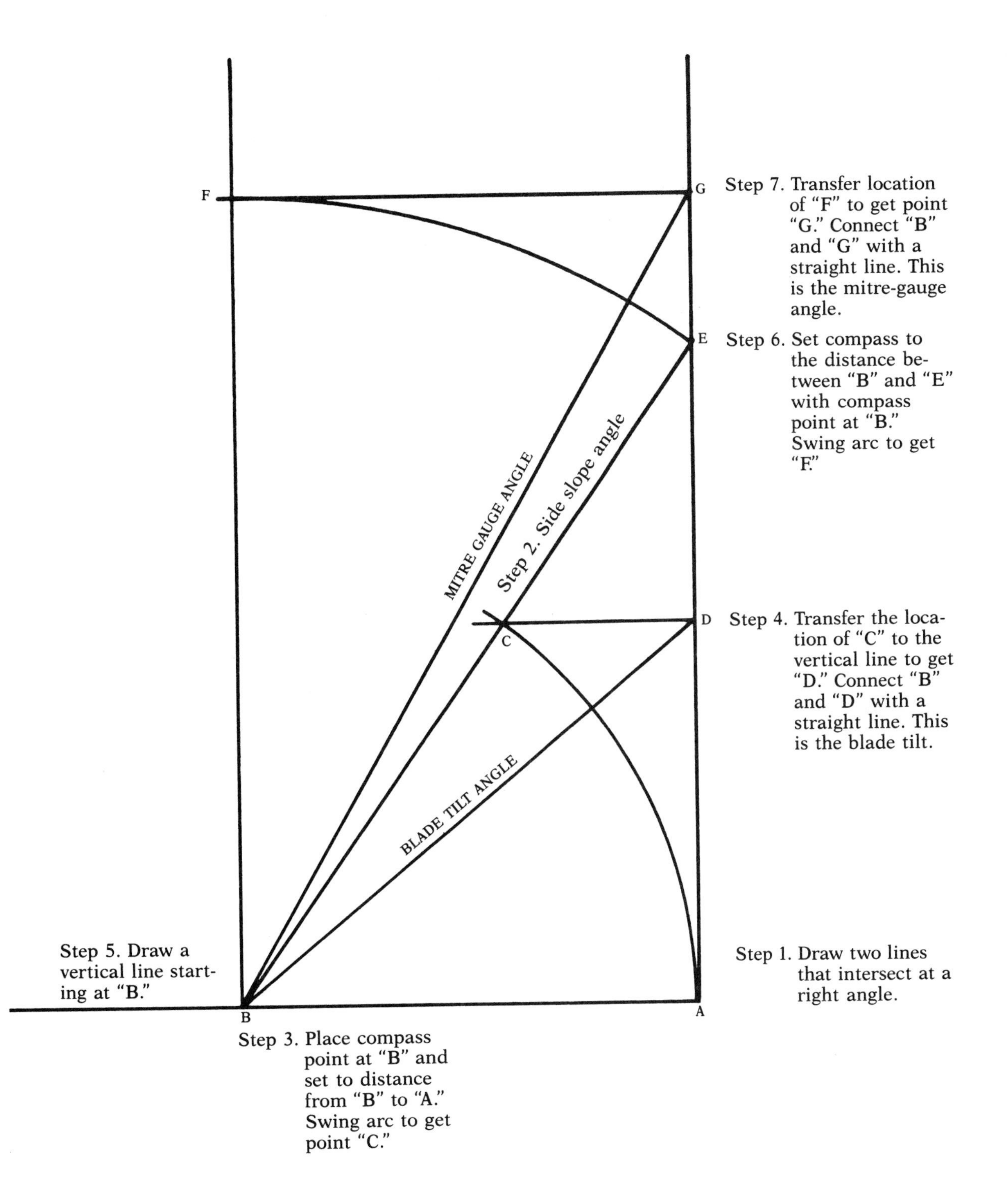

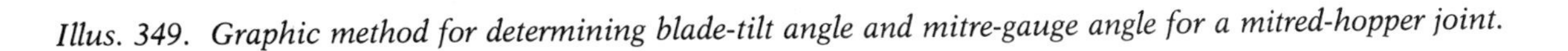

Illus. 349. Graphic method for determining blade-tilt angle and mitre-gauge angle for a mitred-hopper joint.

or when the sides need to be set at different angles, you can use the following method to make a butt hopper (Illus. 350).

First, draw a full-size front-and-side elevation of the hopper. To make the elevations, start with a middle line, and measure out to the ends of the top and bottom. Connect the ends of the lines with a straight line. This line is not the true joint angle, but it gives you the width of the parts and the edge angle. Measure the width of the front from the angled line on the side elevation. Measure the width of the side from the angled line on the front elevation. Set a sliding T-bevel to the angle on the side elevation formed between the top and front. Use the bevel to gauge the blade tilt on the table saw. Now rip the front (and the back, if it is the same angle) to width.

Draw a line down the middle of the front, and transfer the length of the top and bottom edges from the drawing. Connect the marks with a straight line. Now set the mitre gauge by lining up a straight edge with the blade and angled line on the board.

To set the blade tilt, hold a square against the beveled bottom edge of the board. Hold the other edge of the board against the mitre gauge. Tilt the blade until it lines up with the square (Illus. 351). Then, cut the end of the front to the com-

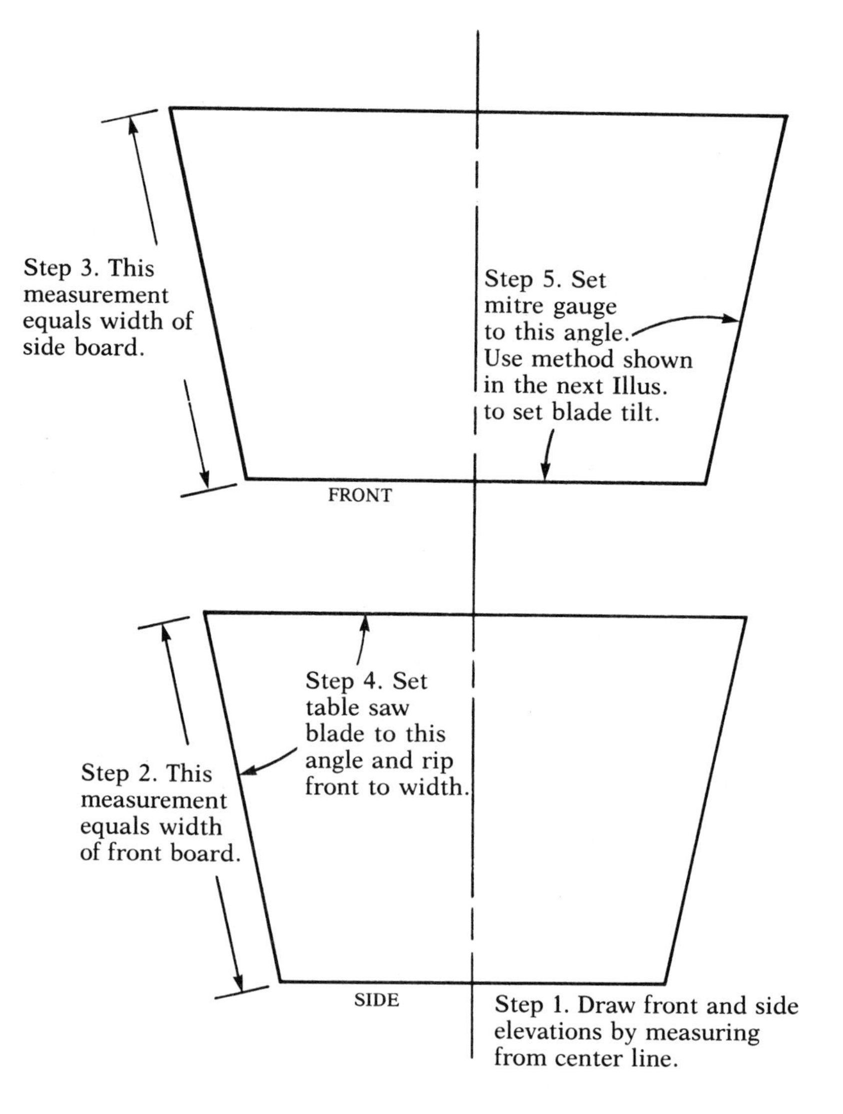

Illus. 350. Graphic method for determining butt-hopper angles.

Illus. 351. To set the blade tilt when using the graphic method for determining butt mitre angles shown in the previous illustration, hold a square against the bevelled bottom edge of the board. The mitre gauge is set to the angle previously determined on the drawing. Adjust the blade tilt to line up with the square.

pound angle formed by the blade tilt and the mitre gauge setting. If the other end of the front is at the same angle, put the mitre gauge in the other slot, and flip the board over to make the cut. If the angle is different, repeat the above procedure to set the saw.

To cut the sides, set a sliding T-bevel to the top and bottom angle on the drawing, and tilt the saw blade accordingly. Rip the sides to width. Use the same method as that for the front to transfer the side angles from the drawing and to set the mitre gauge and blade tilt.

For a strong hopper joint, use dovetails. The boards are first cut using one of the techniques described for butt joints. The length of both boards should be equal to the outside dimensions. When you are cutting the joint by hand, you can adjust the angle of the pins to align them with the joint rather than with the face of the board. Because of the angled ends, a marking gauge can't be used. Instead, use the mating board to mark the pin board for the depth of the dovetails. To get the proper pin angle, make a full-size drawing of the joint (Illus. 352). Draw a line perpendicular to the edges of the board. Next, draw two lines at 80° to the perpendicular line. Set a sliding T-bevel to the correct angle by placing it on the drawing so that the handle is aligned with the angled end and the blade is aligned with one of the 80° lines. Now mark one side of the pins on the board. Hold the handle of the bevel square against the face of the board. Because the end is angled the blade will only touch at the corner. Use a knife to mark the line; hold it square as you follow the blade of the bevel. Reset the bevel to the other 80° line, and mark the other sides of the pins.

Reset the bevel to make the lines on the front and the back faces of the board. Place the handle of the bevel on the angled end of the board, and adjust the blade to align with the edge of the board. Then, line up the blade with the marks made on the end of the board, and make the lines. Once the initial layout is done, the process is similar to making ordinary dovetails. After the pins are cut, transfer the pin layout to the tail board by placing the end of the pins against the inside face of the tail board. Use a knife to scribe around the pins. Because this joint may require more fitting than a standard dovetail, it is a good idea to cut the tails a little oversize, and then trim to fit with a chisel.

The Leigh dovetail jig can also be used to cut dovetails on a hopper joint. The pin angle can't be aligned with the grain as it can in the hand-cut version; but, this isn't a big problem when the side angle is small. When a large angle is involved, however, the joint may be weakened because of the short-grain areas resulting from

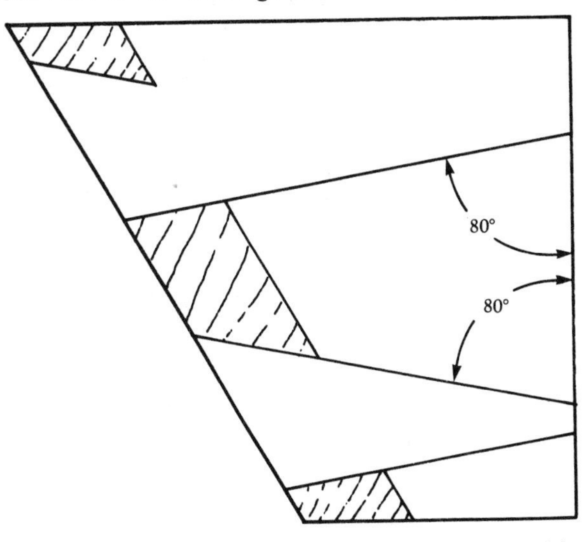

Illus. 352. Hand-cut dovetailed-hopper joints should have the dovetail angles aligned with the grain in the board as shown here.

the angle. The jig is set up in much the same way as it is for standard through dovetails (refer to Chapter 7). Make the boards ¼″ wider than normal, and don't rip the edges to the slope angle until after the dovetails are cut. Install the accessory angled side stops on the jig. Adjust the side stops so that the angled end of the board is parallel to the fingers on the jig. Set the fingers to the desired joint layout, and then proceed as you normally would.

Coopering Joints

Coopering is the craft of making barrels, casks, buckets, and similar articles from wood staves (Illus. 353). Generally, it takes at least four years of apprenticeship to become a cooper, so don't expect this brief section to tell you all there is to know; yet, with this information, you will be able to produce some simple cooperage.

The principal parts of any coopered item are the staves. The size, shape, and joint angle are all important aspects of the staves. The experienced cooper can judge all of these by eye. Traditionally, the staves are riven from a section of tree trunk. The trunk is first cut to a length a little longer than that needed for the staves. Then, it is split into quarters. The staves are then riven from the quarters along the radius. This produces the strongest, most watertight staves. For the stave to be dressed, it is clamped in a horse, and draw knives are used to shape it. The inner curvature is formed with a convex hollowing knife. The outside of the stave is shaped with a concave draw knife.

Illus. 353. The craft of coopering uses staves of wood to produce barrels, casks, buckets, and similar articles.

The familiar barrel shape is determined by the next step called listing. A side ax is used to shape the edges of the stave so that it is widest in the middle and tapers to each end.

The joint between the staves is a mitre. The mitre angle is just slightly less than 90° when many staves are used. An experienced cooper knowingly judges the angle by eye. A jointer is used to cut the mitre. Traditionally, this is a hand jointer that is a long inverted plane with legs. The stave is pushed across the plane iron.

Once the staves are shaped, the process of raising-up begins. The cooper has a set of raising-up hoops. These are not the same hoops that eventually will hold the coopered item, a cask in this example, together; instead, they are designed to hold it together as it is constructed. Other specialty hoops are used in the construction process to shape the cask end to support it as the joints for the heads are made.

Before the cask can be pulled into shape, the wood must be softened; this is done by firing. The raised-up cask is dampened and placed over a fire. When the wood is judged to be soft enough, heavy truss hoops are driven over the cask to pull it into shape.

The heads are made of four or five boards that are edge-joined with dowel-reinforced butt joints. The raising-up hoop is replaced with a chiming hoop, and the ends of the cask are chimed by cutting a bevel on the ends with an adze. Then, a toppling plane is used to square off the ends of the staves. A chive is a special plane used to smooth the inner surface in the area where the head will joint to the staves. The head fits into a dado; but, in coopering, it is called a groove. The groove is formed with a plane called a croze. The edges of the head are beveled to make a water-tight joint. The cooper's term for the bevel is basle. To install the heads, the chiming hoop is removed and the bottom head is tapped into place from the inside. A metal handle called a heading vise is used to pull the top head into place. Final shaping of the outside is done with a downright plane and a scraper called a buzz.

The hoops can be metal or wood. Metal is most common nowadays, but wooden hoops were often used in the past.

From the description above, you can see that coopering takes a lot of experience and specialized equipment; however, you can make simple coopered items using standard shop tools. To begin with, make things such as buckets or butter churns that taper in only one direction. Unless you have a tree trunk that you can use to make the staves, you won't be able to make riven staves. Commercially cut lumber can be used, but it won't be as strong; nevertheless, chances are that you are making the item mostly for decoration anyway.

The band saw or the table saw can be used to cut the staves. In the following example, I'll use a band saw to make a bucket (Illus. 354). An experienced cooper can use staves of varying size, but

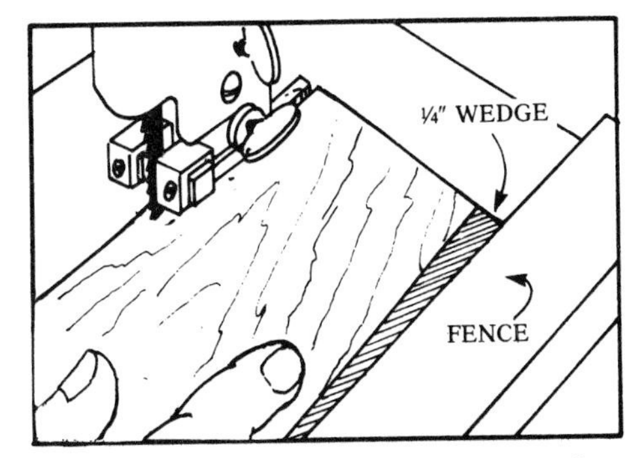

Step 1. Tilt table 10°. Use ¼" wedge against fence. Put stave inside face down.

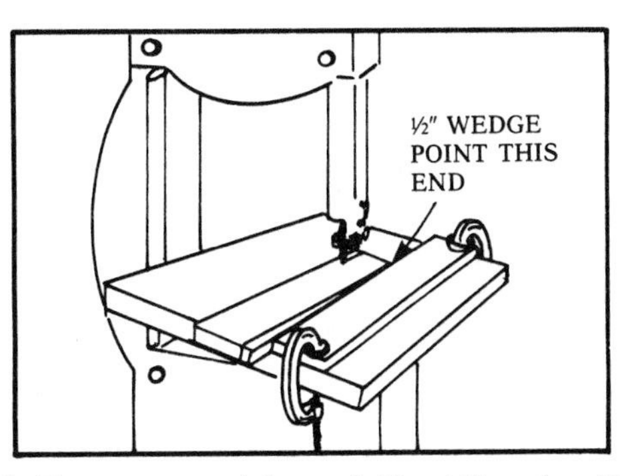

Step 2. Turn stave end for end. Use ½" wedge. Keep inside face down.

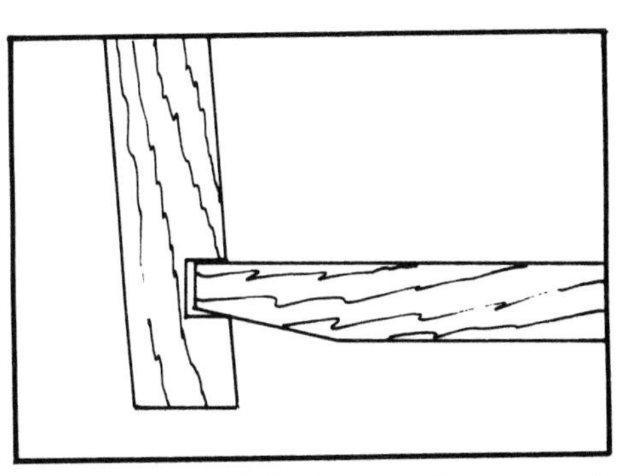

Step 3. Taper edges of the bottom for a snug fit in the dado.

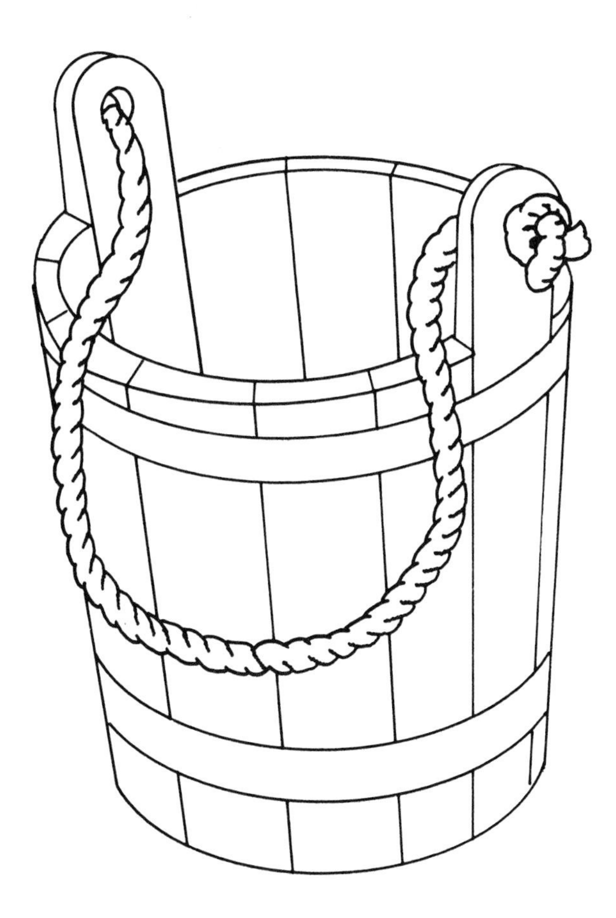

Illus. 354. Building a coopered bucket step by step.

the beginner will have better success with staves that are equal in width. This bucket will be about 11″ in diameter and 10″ high. Cut ten staves that are 3″ wide and 10″ long. The two staves to which the handle will attach are 3¼″ by 13½″, making a total of twelve staves. If you want, you can make the inside surface of the stave concave by using a draw knife, but it is okay to leave it flat.

Next, make two tapered spacers about 11″ long: one should be ¼″ at the wide end, tapering to a point at the other end; the other should be ½″ at the wide end and also taper to a point. Tilt the band-saw table to 10°. Use the saw fence or clamp a board to the table to guide the work. Make the first cut with the inside of the stave against the table and with the ¼″ tapered spacer between the edge and the fence. The wide end of the spacer should face the blade. Next, turn the stave so that the other end is facing the blade, but keep the inside face against the table. This time use the ½″-wide spacer between the fence and the stave; place it with the point facing the blade.

After all the joints have been cut, make a trial assembly. Use bungee cords or web clamps to hold the bucket together. Examine the joints, and mark any that need adjusting. Disassemble the staves, and use a plane to adjust the angle of the joints.

After the joints fit properly, cut a dado for the bottom of the bucket. Make the dado ½″ wide and 1½″ from the end of the stave. Cut a bottom out of ¾″-thick stock; you may need to glue up several smaller boards to make the width. Use a plane to taper the edges so that the bottom fits snugly in the dado.

In traditional cooperage, the hoops hold the joints tight, and no glue is used; but, the amateur may find that it is easier to glue the work together and then to apply hoops that are mostly decorative. Apply the glue to both surfaces of the joint. But, don't use any glue in the dado for the bottom. Use bungee cords or web clamps to hold the joints tight as the glue sets. After the glue is dry, use a plane to round the outside of the bucket.

You can make a rustic-looking hoop from a green sapling (Illus. 355). Remove the bark, and split the sapling in half. Tack one end to one of the staves, and wrap it around the bucket several times; then, tack the other end to a stave. Put a few more tacks into the hoop around the circumference.

For a more finished look, you can use a thin strip of wood for the hoop; the ends can be joined using the joint drawn in the lower right of Illus. 355. Begin the hoop joint by making a saw kerf halfway through the strip at a point 3″ in from each end on the inside surface. From the saw

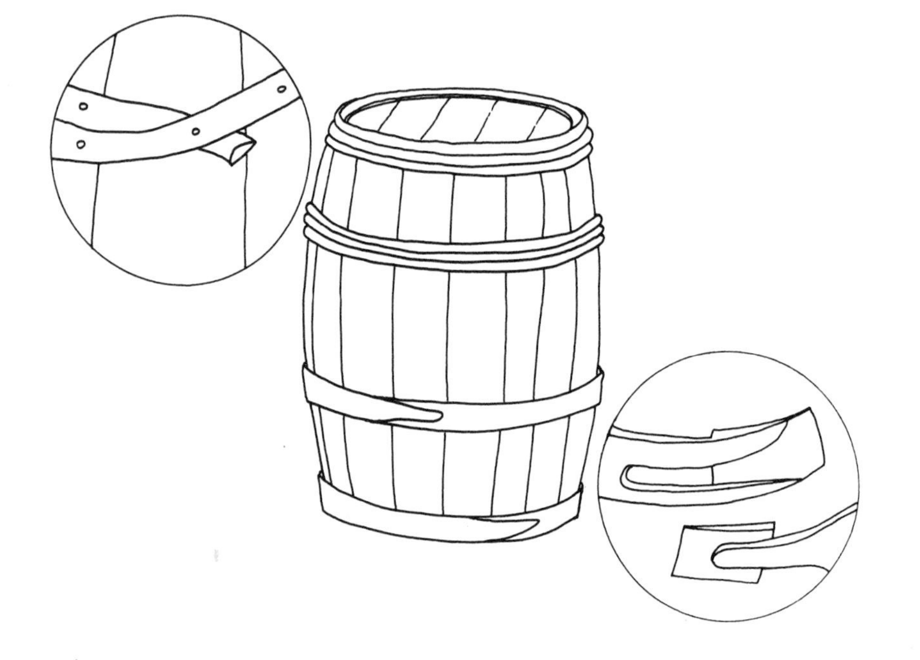

Illus. 355. The hoops at the top of this barrel are made from a split sapling. The ends are secured by tucking them under a loop and tacking in place. The bottom hoops are made from thin strips of wood. The hoop joint is described in the text.

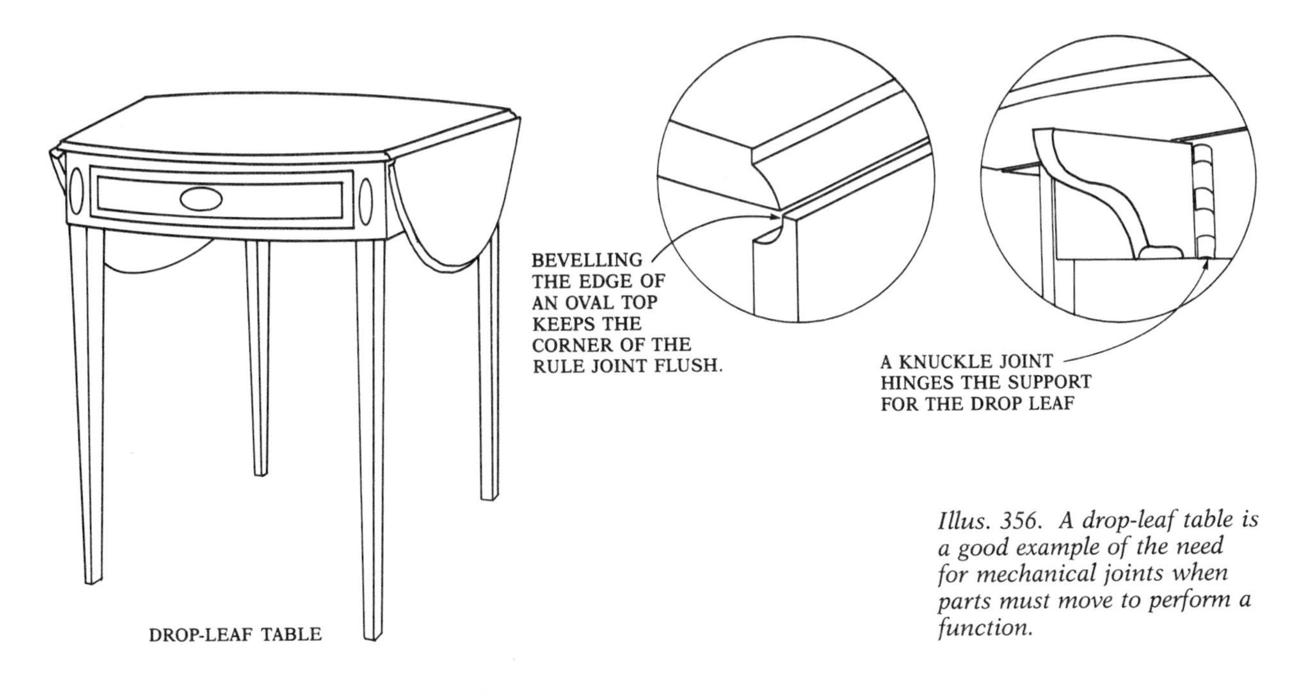

Illus. 356. A drop-leaf table is a good example of the need for mechanical joints when parts must move to perform a function.

kerf, taper the wood 3″ in both directions as shown in the illustration. The rest of this hoop joint is carved using a sharp knife. Twist the end, and slip it into the slot in the other end; work the two ends together. Then, slip the hoop onto the bucket, and fasten it with tacks. If the hoop won't bend enough, you may need to soak it in boiling water or use hot-tube bending to shape it.

Mechanical Joints

Mechanical joints are necessary when parts of the project must move to perform a function. Drop-leaf tables, secretary writing desks, and folding tables are a few examples of projects that require mechanical joints (Illus. 356).

RULE JOINTS

These are probably the most common type of mechanical joints (Illus. 357). They are used on drop-leaf tables or similar applications. The rule joint gives a neat appearance, but more importantly it provides support for the leaf when it is up, taking the stress off the hinges. Special hinges called back flaps are used. The knuckle is on the opposite side from the countersinking,

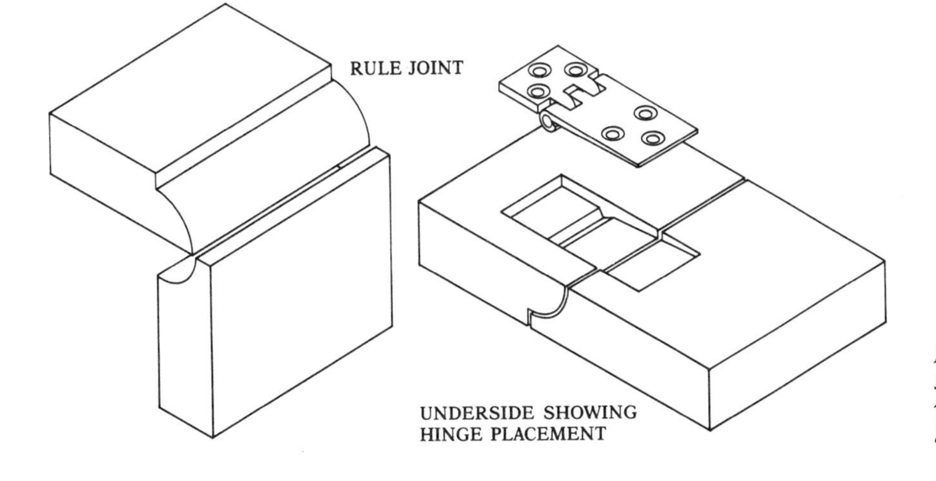

Illus. 357. Rule joints require special hinges and may be cut with shaper cutters or by hand.

and one leaf of the hinge is longer than the other. This joint is usually made with a special set of shaper cutters; but, it can be cut by hand. You can purchase a set of matched shaper cutters designed for the job, or you can use standard cutters that you may already have. You need a quarter-round cutter for the table edge and a cove cutter for the leaf. The radius of the cutters, of course, must match. Adjust the depth setting so that the shoulders will be equal on both parts.

To make the joint by hand, start with the hinge that will be used; all measurements depend on the pin location of the hinge. Set a marking gauge to the distance from the back of the hinge to the middle of the hinge pin. Mark this distance on the end of the table edge and the leaf. Next, mark the shoulder line on the end of the tabletop and the leaf. The distance between the two marks is the radius of the arc. Set the marking gauge to this distance, and make a line that intersects the first line that you made. This gives the location of the middle of the hinge pin. Use the same setting to make a mark on the leaf. Instead of curving, the area below the hinge line should follow this straight line. Set a compass to the radius of the arc, and mark the curve on both parts.

The first step in cutting the joint is to make a rabbet on the top of the tabletop and on the bottom of the leaf. The size of the rabbet is determined by the shoulder location. Next, use a plane to remove the waste on the outside of the arc on the tabletop. You can also plane away most of the waste on the leaf; but, you need to use a gouge to make the final curvature. For a perfect fit, the useful yet simple tool of a set of matched scrapers in a scratch stock can be used to do the final shaping.

Cut the gains for the hinges on the underside of the table. The hinge is positioned with the knuckle against the tabletop, so a recess must be cut for it. There does need to be some clearance in the joint also for it to operate smoothly. You can place a piece of heavy paper in the joint before attaching the hinges as one way to provide the correct clearance. Install the hinges, but with only one screw in each leaf, and check the operation. If adjustment is needed, loosen one screw and then install one in another hole to make the proper adjustment. When the fit is right, install the rest of the screws.

When a rule joint is used on an oval tabletop, the corner of the joint on the leaf will project slightly past the edge of the tabletop. This projection can catch on clothing and is prone to damage. To eliminate this problem, bevel the edge of the table: then the lower edge of the top will project out far enough to meet the top edge of the joint on the leaf. To determine the bevel angle, hold a straight edge against the edge of the table or on a full-size drawing. The straight edge should be tangent to the oval at the point where the rule joint meets the edge. Set a bevel to the angle formed between the rule joint and the straight edge. This is the bevel angle to use for the edge.

THE BEADED JOINT

This joint performs the same function as the rule joint, but it is easier to make (Illus. 358). The bead on the tabletop fits into a cove on the leaf. Downward force on the leaf is transmitted to the

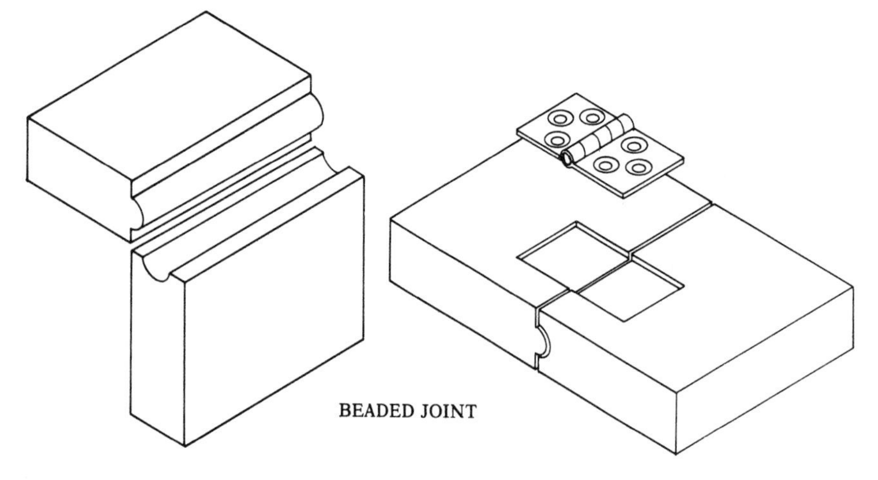

Illus. 358. The beaded joint performs the same function as the rule joint.

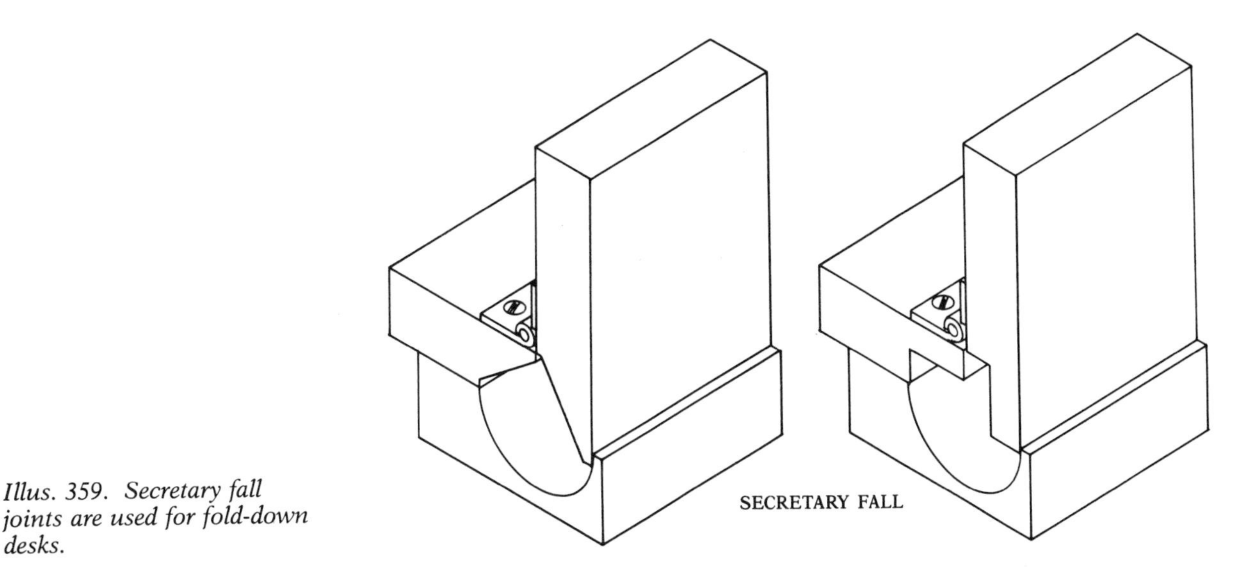

Illus. 359. Secretary fall joints are used for fold-down desks.

top through the joint, taking the strain off the hinge. Standard hinges can be used with this joint.

SECRETARY FALL JOINTS

Secretary fall joints are used for concealed writing surfaces. The surface may be disguised as a drawer or simply as a folding front. The same type of joint can be used to make a door that lifts and then slides into a pocket. Illus. 359 gives two variations of this joint. The procedure for cutting the joint is fairly self-evident and therefore does not require explanation, except for the cove in the rail. You can make the cove on a table saw. Clamp a wood fence at an angle to the blade; raise the blade to the depth of the cove, and push the rail diagonally over the blade, using the wood fence as a guide. Experiment on scrap, changing the angle of the fence until you get the correct-size cove.

FINGER JOINTS

Finger joints use the wood itself as a hinge (Illus. 360). They are frequently used on the vertical brackets that support a drop leaf. You can make this joint entirely on the table saw. First, cut the ends of the boards to 45°. Install a dado blade set to the desired width of the fingers. You can make a jig like the one described for box joints, or you can lay out the joint on the board and align the blade with the layout lines. Make an auxiliary fence for the mitre gauge. The face of the fence should be cut to 45°. Cut the joint with the 45° end of the board flat against the table and have the face of the board supported by the angled auxiliary fence on the mitre gauge. Trim the ends

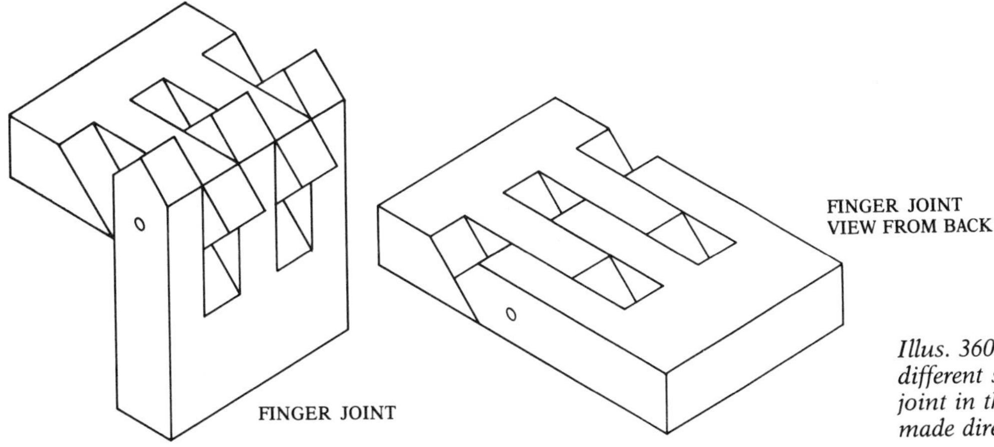

Illus. 360. Finger joints are a different sort of mechanical joint in that the hinge is made directly from the pieces.

of the fingers to a point by making another 45° cut.

Assemble the joint, and clamp both parts to a straight board. Make sure that the joint is aligned correctly; then, drill a hole for the pin. A 16d nail can be used for the pin. If the projecting ends of the fingers will interfere with the operation, they can be trimmed, and, if needed, a cove can be cut in the part that interferes with them.

KNUCKLE JOINTS

Knuckle joints essentially are a more sophisticated type of finger joint that provide a wider range of motion (Illus. 361). You can see from the illustration that the joint resembles a hinge. Knuckle joints are often used to hinge the rear legs of a side table.

The joint is strongest when the travel is limited to 90°, but it can be used for up to about 220° of travel. For best results, use a hardwood such as beech or birch to withstand the wear.

A bull-nose or rabbet plane can be used to remove the waste right up to the shoulder (Illus. 362). You can also use a chisel to remove the waste near the shoulder, and then you can finish rounding the work with a block plane. After you have shaped the knuckles, layout five equal divisions. Place an *X* on the middle and the two end divisions on one half and on the remaining two divisions on the other half. These are the sections to be cut out. Saw down to the shoulder with a backsaw while keeping the kerf in the waste. Use a chisel to remove the waste just as you would for making dovetails. You can use a gouge to shape the bottoms of the end cuts. The shapes of the bottoms of the inner cuts aren't as critical; you can simply undercut with a straight chisel to provide the necessary clearance.

Clamp the parts together against a straight board, and use the drill press to drill a hole for the pin. A 16d nail again can be used for the pin. When the joint is oriented vertically, as is often the case, place the pin so that the head is at the top to keep it from falling out. Countersink the pin hole at the top to make the head of the pin flush. A little epoxy glue in just the last segment of the knuckle will also help to keep the pin in place.

REVOLVING BRACKETS

These can be used to support the drop leaf of a table (Illus. 363). The joint is simple to make. The ends are cut at 45°, and the bracket is merely cut free from the rest of the board. You can do this with a table saw by first lowering the blade below the table. Then, place the board on the table above the blade. Clamp the work in place, and turn on the saw. Raise the blade until it cuts through the surface. You can then remove the clamp and continue the cut until the blade gets

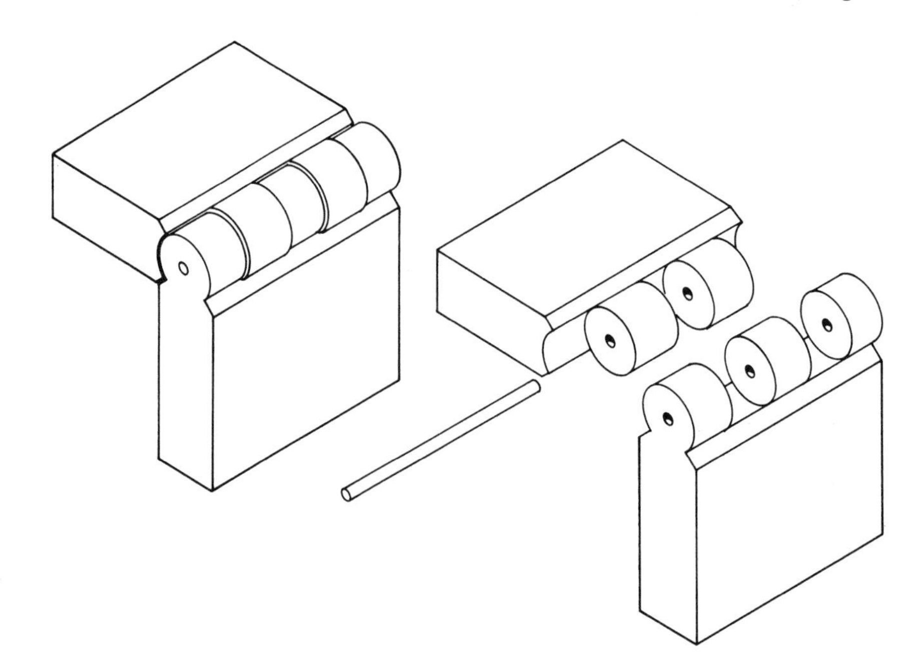

Illus. 361. The knuckle joint is a hinging finger joint that provides a wider range of motion than the simple, pointed-finger joint.

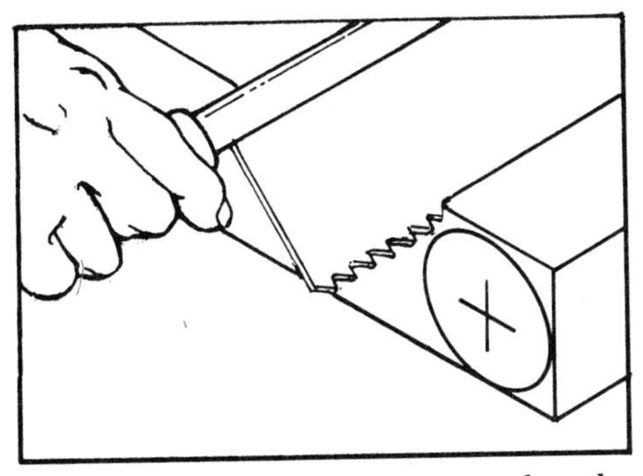

1. Lay out a circle with a diameter equal to the board thickness; then saw shoulder line.

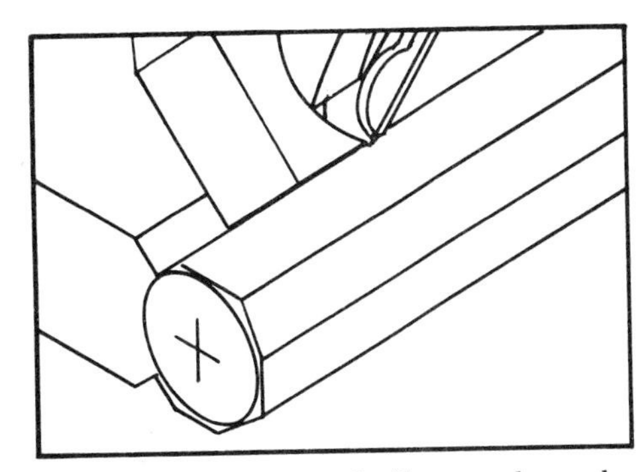

2. Plane away waste. Use a bull nose plane close to the shoulder.

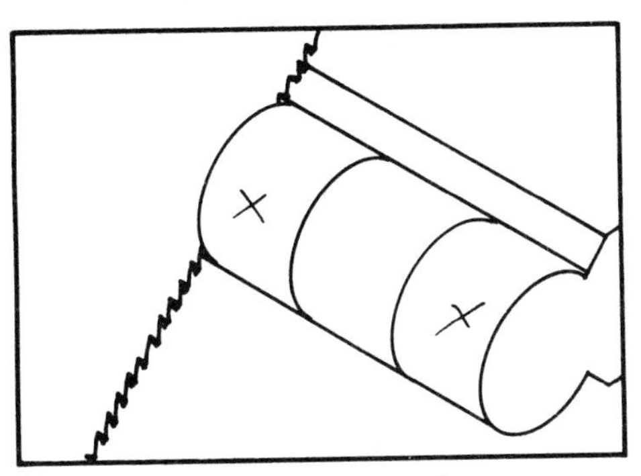

3. Lay out five equal divisions. Make sure to saw on waste side of line.

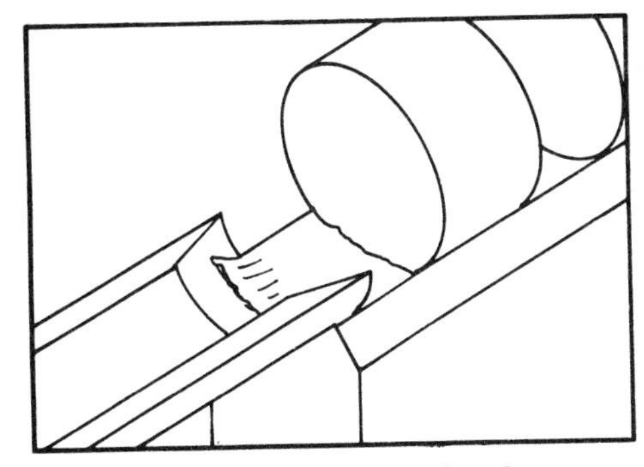

4. Use a gouge to shape bottom of end cuts.

Illus. 362. Knuckle joint step by step.

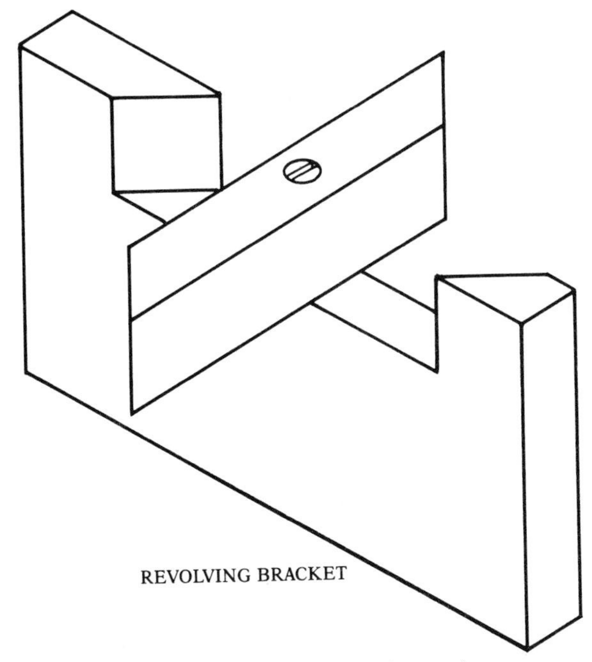

Illus. 363. Revolving brackets can be used to support the drop leaf of a table. Drill the pilot hole for the screw before cutting the bracket; then, cut the bracket free using a table saw and a handsaw.

close to the other end. Finish the cut with a handsaw. The saw kerfs will make the bracket smaller than the surrounding board. To remedy this, start with the board oversize by the width of the kerf; then, plane off the extra wood from the surrounding board after the bracket is cut. Use a long screw as the hinge pin.

THE TRIPOD-LEG JOINT

This wonderfully practical joint is found in the construction of old wooden camera tripods, but it is useful for making artists' easels or anything that requires a leg that can be adjusted for length (Illus. 364). The upper portion of the leg is about three times wider than the lower extension. Make a groove in the upper leg to the desired width of the extension leg. Then, cut a slot in the middle of the groove, ending about 3″ shy of the end; a plunge router is the easiest way to make this slot. Cut the extension leg to fit into the groove. If the upper leg is sufficiently thick, the extension leg can be flush with the back. If not, it can extend past the back of the upper leg. A metal or wooden bracket at the bottom of the upper leg keeps the extension leg in place. A car-

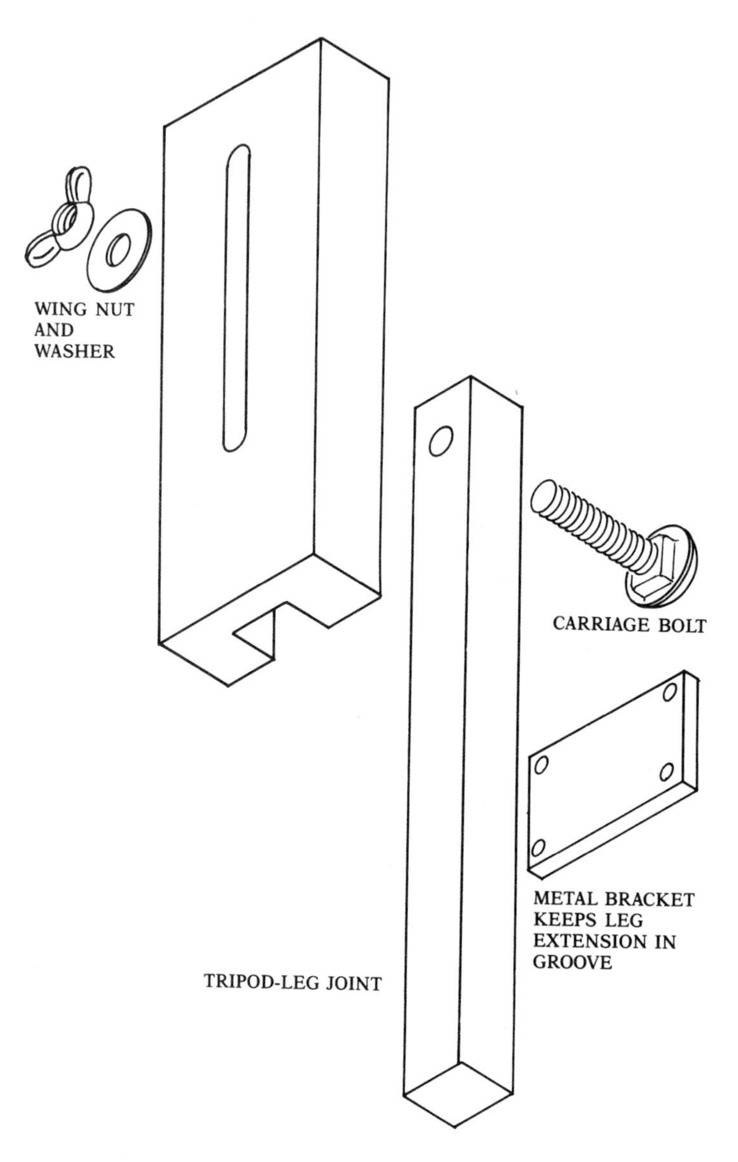

Illus. 364. The tripod-leg joint was originally used on wooden camera tripods. It can be useful whenever a leg that can be adjusted for length is required.

riage bolt near the top of the extension leg is used for adjustment by sliding along the slot where it is clamped with a wing nut and washer.

Sash Joints

Sash joinery has been a specialty trade since the very early days of making windows. Understandably, this is because the tools and techniques are very specialized. Even though you probably have no desire to make all the windows for your new house, you may find sash-making joints useful in other applications. Furniture and cabinetry with glazed doors also use sash-making joinery.

A standard window sash consists of a frame made of two stiles with rails at the top and bottom. Individual panes of glass are fitted into a framework made of muntins or sash bars (Illus. 365). The muntin-frame members are rabbeted on one side to accept the glass, and the other side is moulded to improve the appearance. It is this moulding especially that complicates the joinery (Illus. 366). In many ways, sash joinery is like panel-frame joinery; some of the terminology is even the same. The moulded edge is called sticking, and scribed or coped joints are used to accommodate the sticking. Practically all sash joints are variations on the mortise-and-tenon (Illus. 367).

Illus. 365. A standard window sash consists of a frame with two stiles and top and bottom rails. The panes of glass fit into a framework of sash bars called muntins.

Illus. 366. Special joints are needed to join muntins.

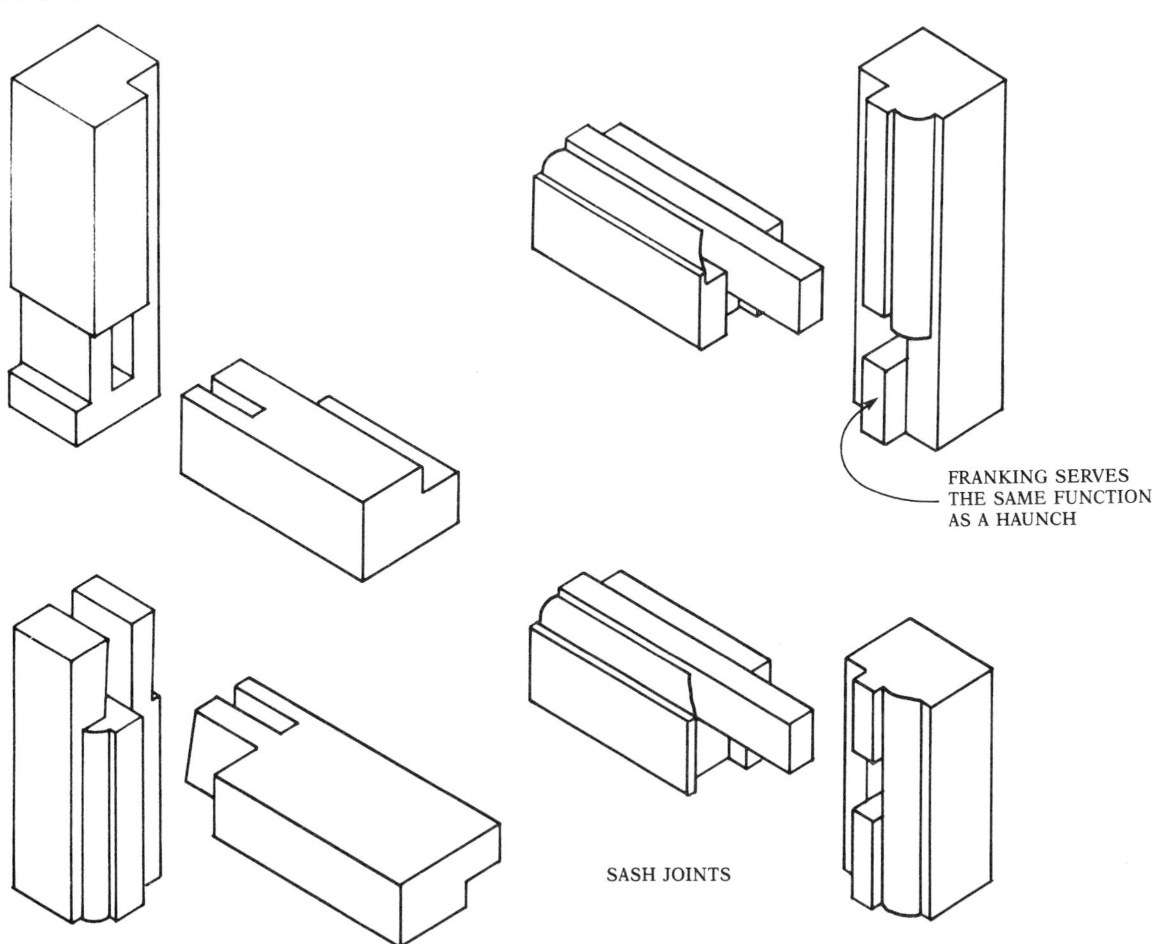

Illus. 367. Variations on the mortise-and-tenon joint are used to join the stiles and rails of a sash.

Most modern sash joinery is done by machine. Matched sets of cutters make the sticking and cope the tenon shoulders. Mortising machines chop the mortises. To make a sash with hand tools, you need a set of specialty planes and chisels. The sticking gets beat up during the process of making the joints, so usually the joints are cut before the sticking is done. Make a story stick for each part of the sash so that you can lay out the joints without repeated measurements. Be sure to number the parts so that you can assemble the sash correctly. Chop the mortises, and saw the tenon shoulders; then, use the moulding plane to plane the sticking and rabbets. The method used by eighteenth-century joiners was to plane the four edges separately, whereas nineteenth-century joiners used a kind of plane that cut the sticking and the rabbet in a single operation. Using this plane, you can make the muntins in pairs and then separate them after planing by scoring a line with a cutting gauge and snapping them apart. A sticking board helps to hold the muntins during the sticking operation. This is a board with a rabbet on the edge into which the muntin fits. A screw acts as a stop at one end, and a small blade driven into the sticking board secures the other end. A more sophisticated sticking board has various grooves and mouldings to hold the muntin more securely. Once the sticking is done, the joints can be coped or scribed.

The joints used for the stiles and rails are much the same as those described for panel-frame making. The joints between the stile and rail in handmade sashes are usually pegged; this is a perfect situation in which to use the draw-boring technique. The pegs are usually split out from the waste that was left from cutting the tenons. Make them roughly octagonal using a chisel, and point the end a little to make it easier to draw the joint tight (Illus. 368).

The muntin joints are more complex. In most sashes, the vertical muntins are continuous, while short horizontal muntins are tenoned to them. This requires a scribed joint. First, a mitre template is used to guide the chisel or saw to make a 45° cut on the sticking. On muntins there is sticking on two edges, so you need to cut a mitre on both. Use a saw to continue the cheek cut on the tenon until you reach the end of the mitre. Use an incannelled gouge that matches the radius of the sticking to pare out the waste. The waste can also be removed with a coping saw (Illus. 369). Half-lap joints can be used where sash bars meet (Illus. 370). The sticking can be mitred or coped. The coping process is the same as usual, but it must be done on both sides of the joint (Illus. 371).

Glazed doors for furniture and cabinetry require a somewhat different joinery because the parts are usually smaller and more delicate. They may also involve angles other than 90°. Illus. 372 shows a typical glazed door, for which the glazing bars are made from two parts: a middle bar and an astragal. Where the glazing bars cross, half-lap joints can be used on the center bar, but the astragals need to be mitred. When three bars meet, the middle bar must also be mitred. Strips of linen can be glued to the joints to act as reinforcement. The glass can be held in with putty just as it is in a window, but wooden fixing beads give a more finished appearance.

Illus. 368. Handmade sashes usually use pegs to secure the tenons. These pegs are usually square or octagonal rather than round.

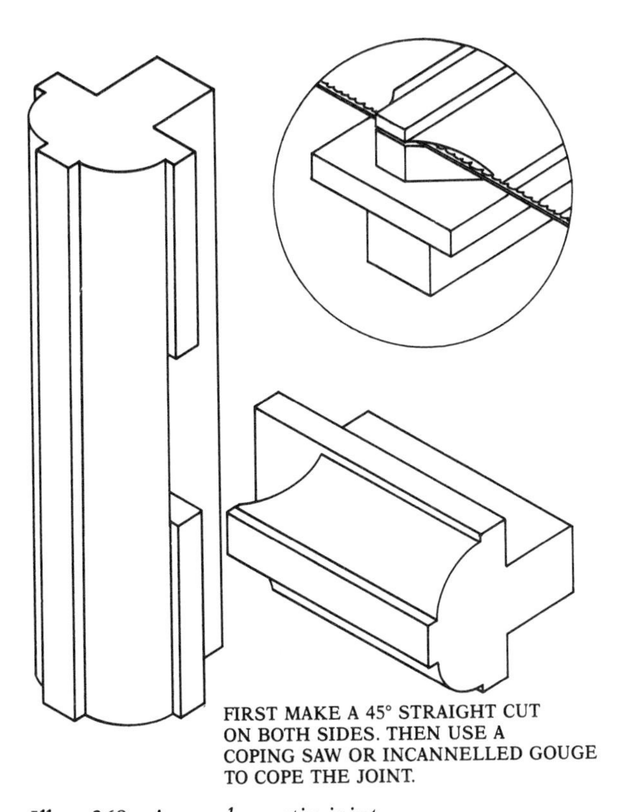

Illus. 369. A coped muntin joint.

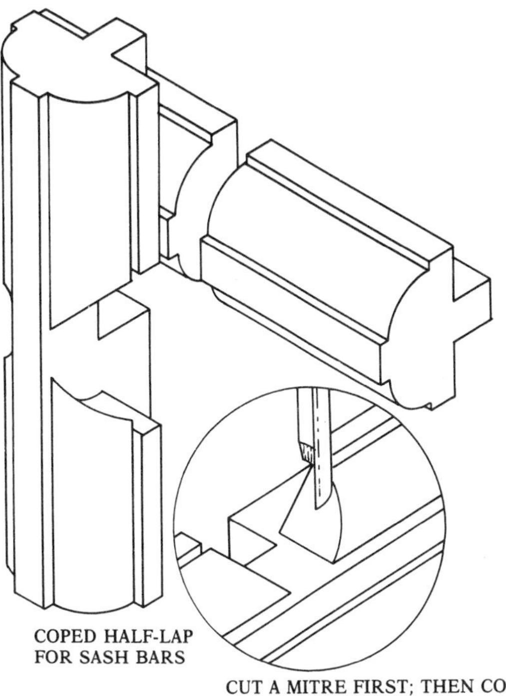

Illus. 371. Coped half-lap.

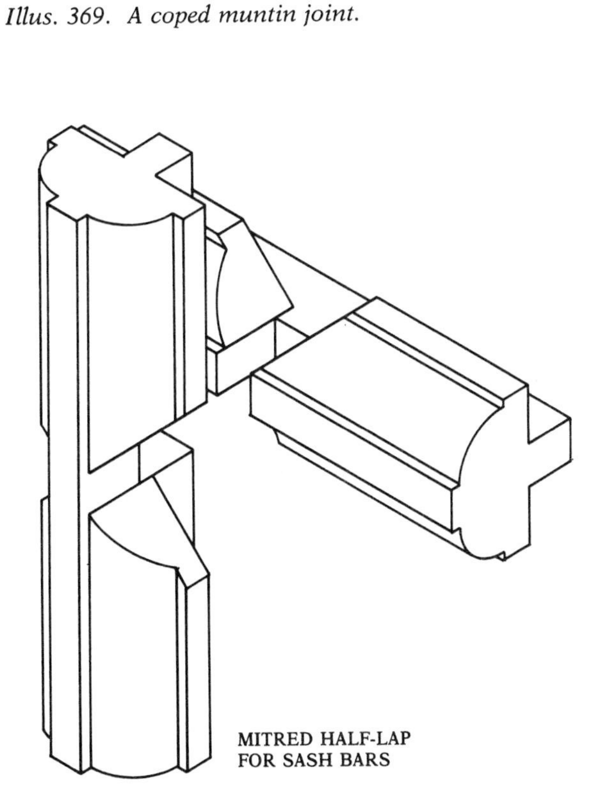

Illus. 370. A mitred half-lap.

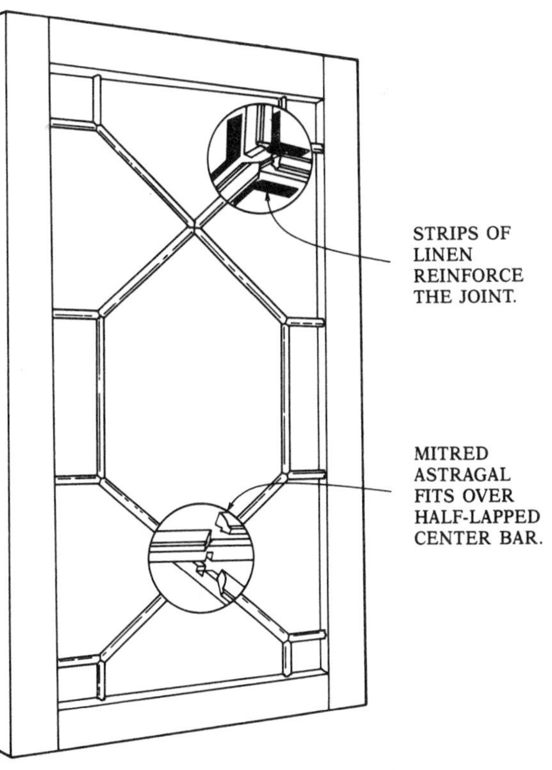

Illus. 372. A typical glazed door used on interior cabinetry.

When the glazing bars meet at odd angles, you can determine the mitre angle by making a full-size drawing. Use a compass to bisect the angle just as was described in discussing odd-angle mitres and in discussing Illus. 338 above. When you get to the point where you make a line between the corner and the point where the two arcs cross, this is the mitre line. You can set a bevel from the drawing.

When three or more bars meet, the process is the same, but to start you place the compass point at the middle of the joint rather than the corner (Illus. 373). Notice that each part requires two mitre cuts. Make the first cut just as you would a normal mitre. Then measure the length of the mitre, and make a mark in the middle. The second cut must line up with that mark.

Timber Framing

Modern house framing actually uses very simple joints. Most of the joints are butt joints reinforced with nails or metal plates. The earlier system of framing used heavy timbers and complex joints (Illus. 374). Timber framing is making a comeback because of its aesthetic appeal. In fact, some new buildings are framed using modern techniques, and then timber framing is added to the interior strictly for appearance (Illus. 375). We usually think of prefabricated buildings as a modern development, but in the timber-framing era it was actually commonplace. Because the joinery was complex, it was usually left to an expert; he would cut all of the timbers to size and cut the joints. Each joint was numbered

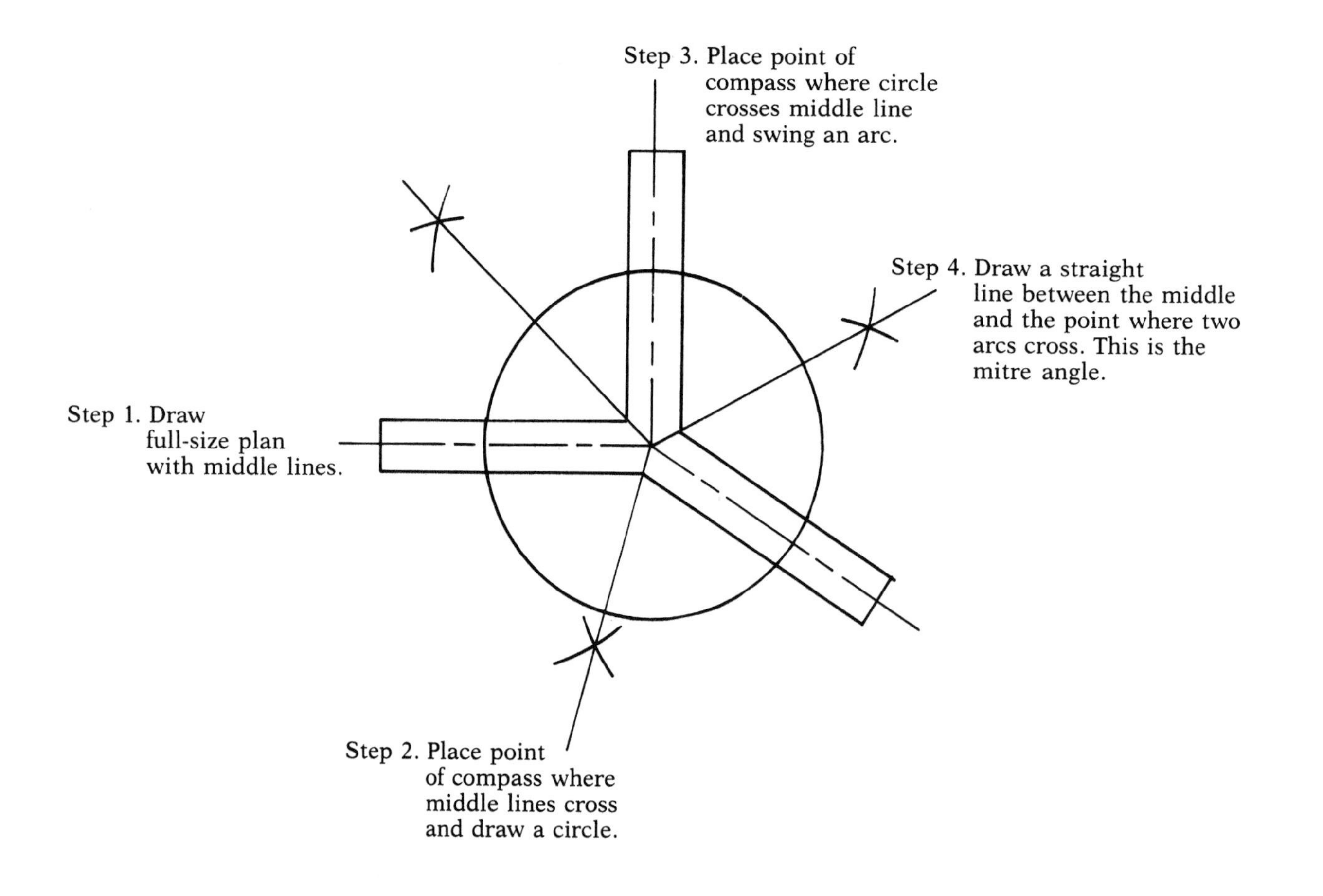

Illus. 373. Graphic method for determining three-way mitre angles.

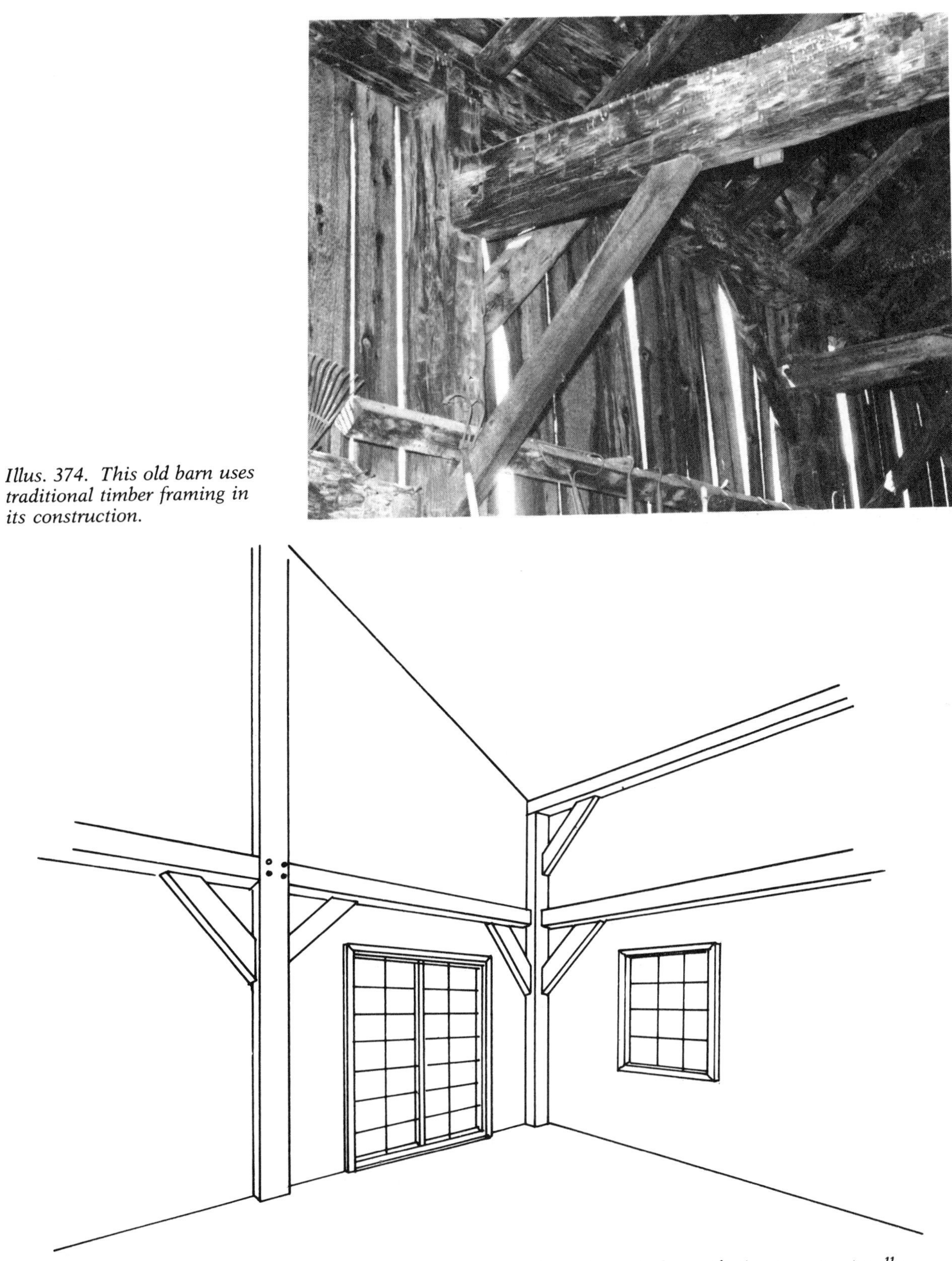

Illus. 374. This old barn uses traditional timber framing in its construction.

Illus. 375. Timber framing in modern construction is frequently used purely for aesthetics, not structurally.

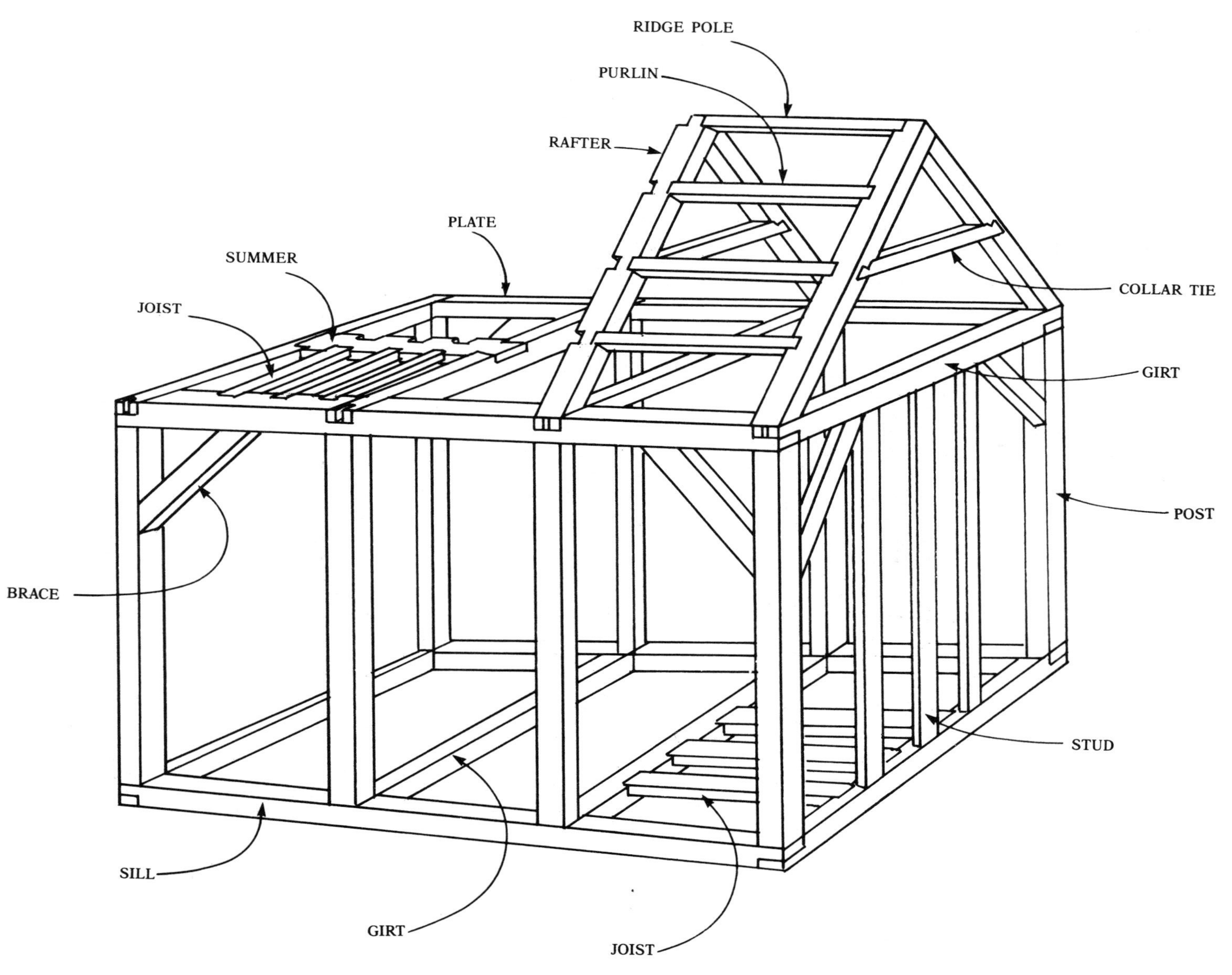

Illus. 376. Timber-framing terminology.

using Roman numerals that could be easily inscribed with a straight chisel. The completed parts were then shipped to the destination. The traditional house-raising party was used to erect the frame. The assembly process took a lot of muscle but not necessarily a lot of skill, since the joints were all cut before-hand.

At the peak of its development, timber framing reached a high degree of sophistication. Builders' manuals that give the strength of various wood species were used so that the joints could be proportioned for maximum strength. Because the joint design plays such a critical role in the overall strength of the structure, I strongly recommend that you consult a builders' manual before attempting any major timber-frame construction. Information contained in this section is intended exclusively to get you started with decorative and light-duty applications.

Each part of a timber frame has a name. Illus. 376 shows a diagram of a typical timber frame and the names of the members. Note the distinction between sill, girt, and joist, and their various occurrences in Illus. 376.

Variations on the mortise-and-tenon make up the majority of timber-framing joints. The joints can be simple or complex depending on the application. A simple barefaced mortise-and-tenon, for example, can be used to join a stud to the sill, but a more complex joint is needed where a plate and a girt meet at a corner post. Angle braces are a very necessary part of timber framing (Illus. 377). The joints involved are more complex because of the angles involved, and because a seat must be added to the joint to take most of the load. The tenons serve to hold the joint together. Splicing joints are also used in timber framing to make the long sills and plates required in large structures. Illus. 378 thru 384 show some examples of timber-framing joints.

Illus. 377. Angle braces are a necessary part of timber framing. Specialized joints are needed to give the required strength.

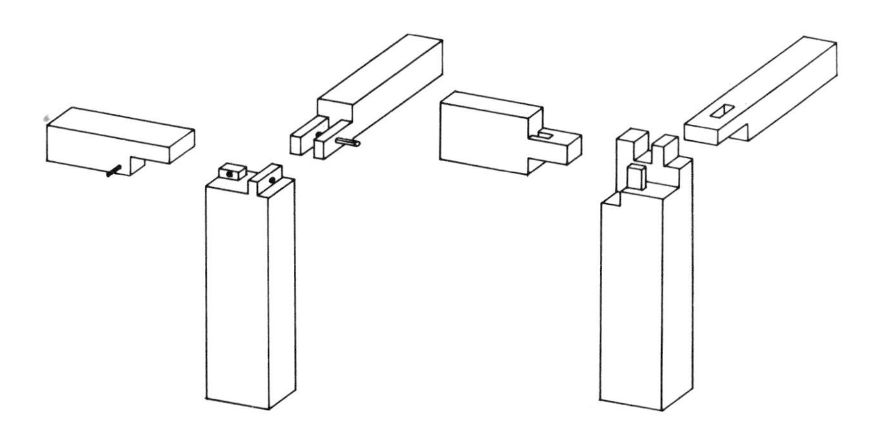

Illus. 378. Corner-post joints.

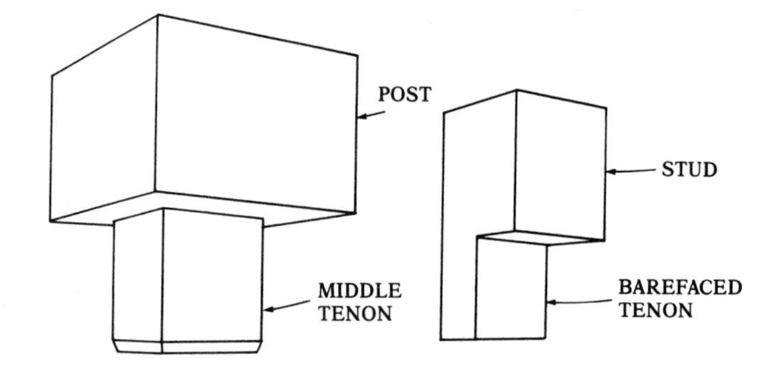

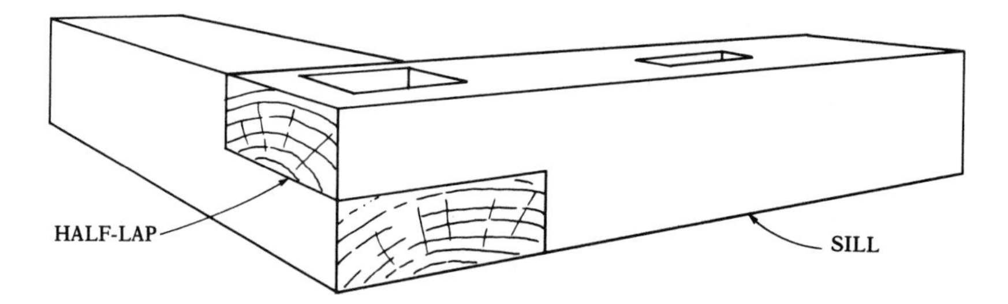

Illus. 379. Sill joints.

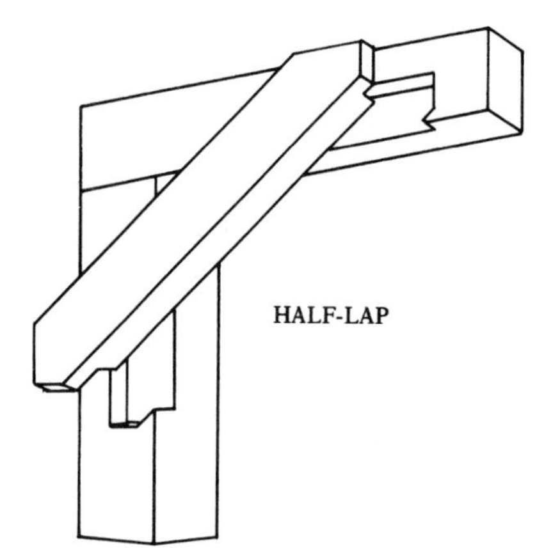

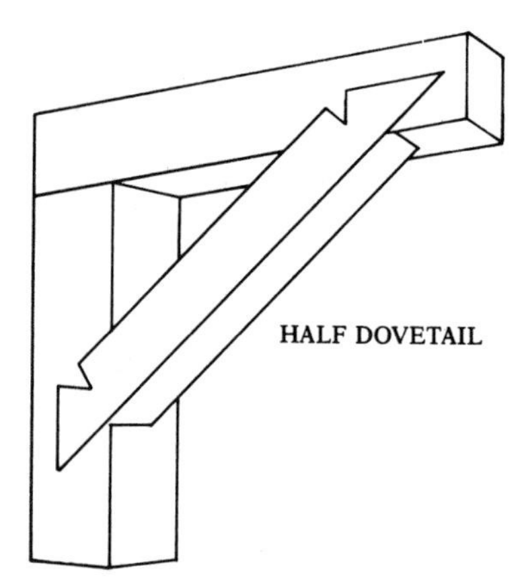

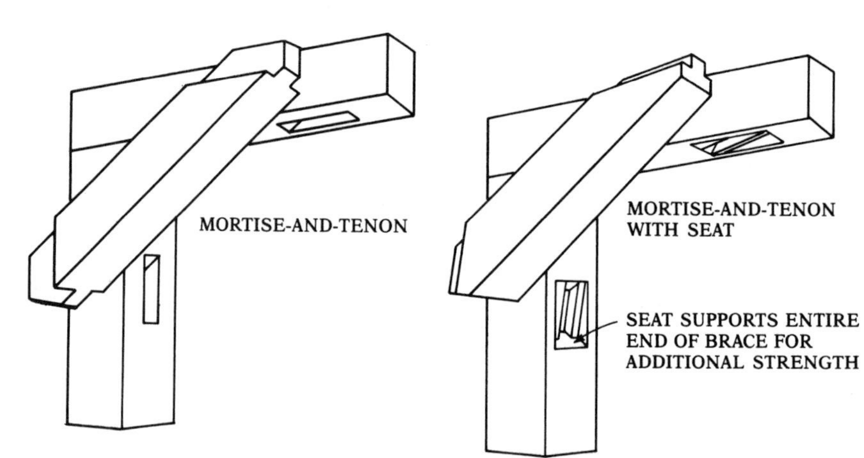

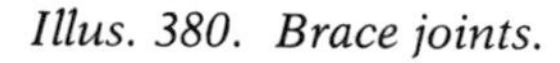

Illus. 380. Brace joints.

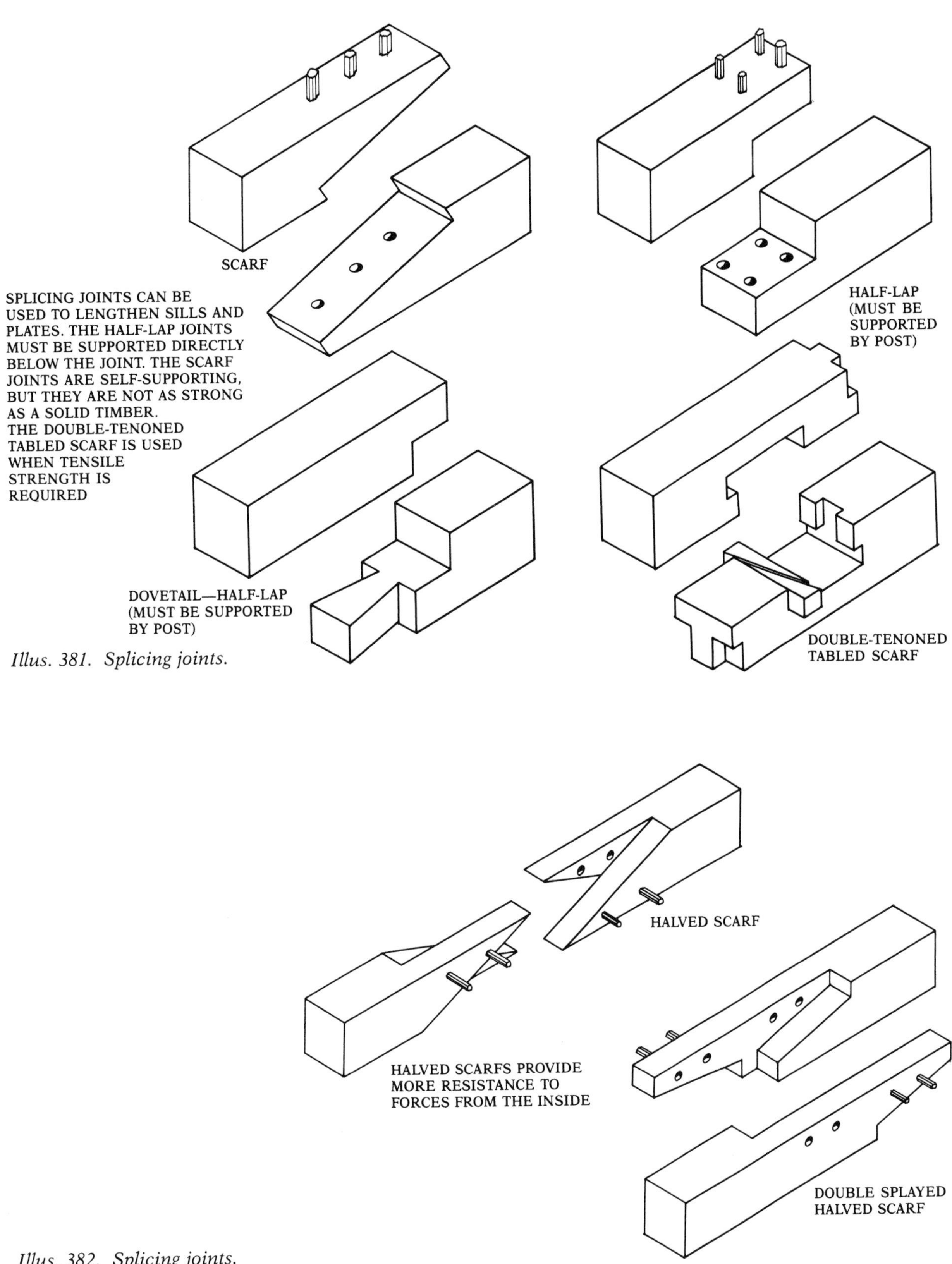

Illus. 381. Splicing joints.

Illus. 382. Splicing joints.

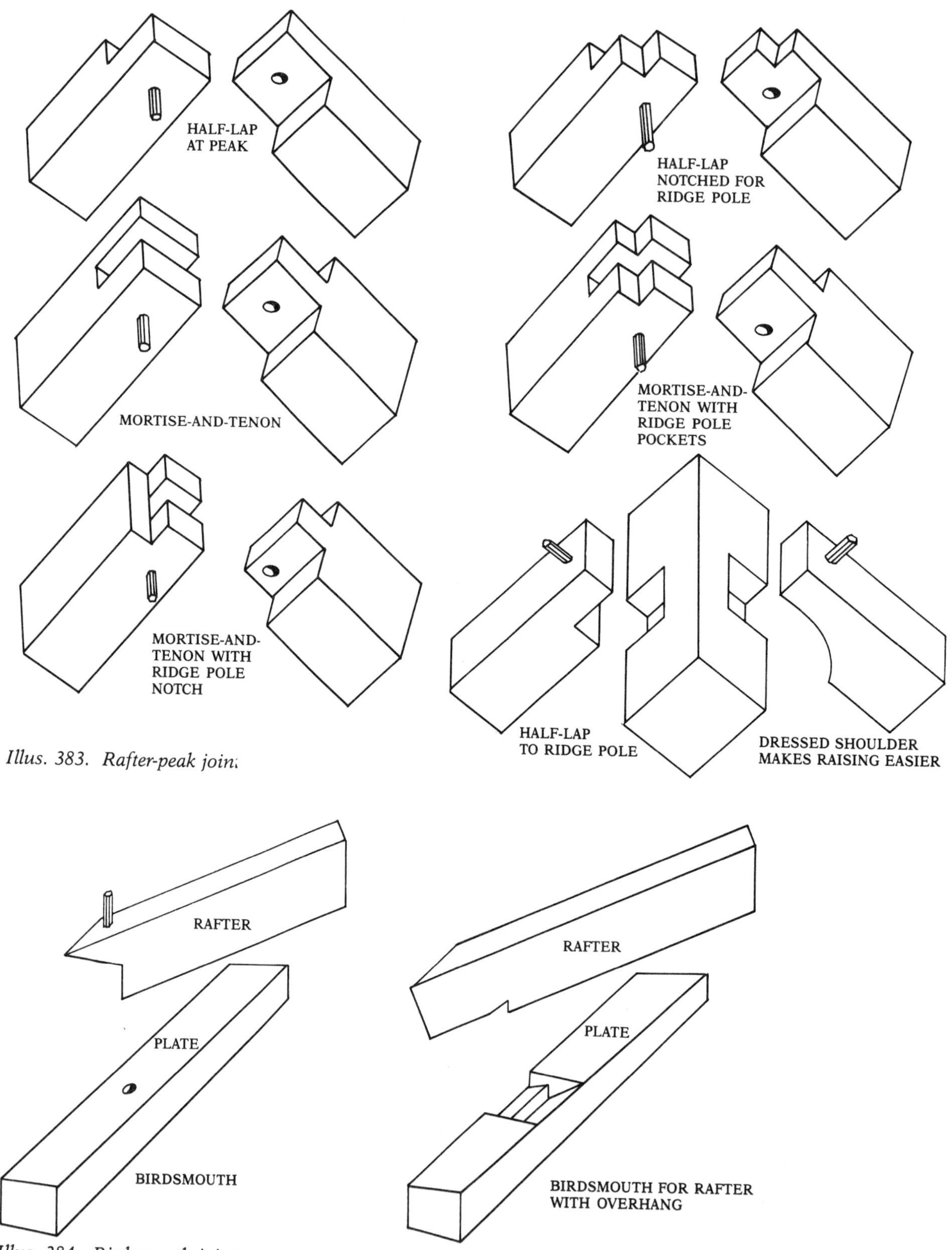

Illus. 383. Rafter-peak joint

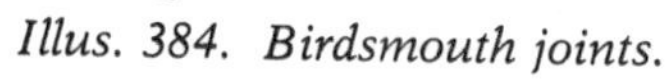

Illus. 384. Birdsmouth joints.

Because of the large size, the techniques for making the joints are different from those for making smaller joints. The rule of thumb for sizing the tenon is to make the tenon thickness larger than one-third and less than one-half the width of the mortised member. The standard, steel framing square is a useful layout tool for timber framing; the tongue is 1½" wide, and the blade is 2" wide. These two sizes are the most frequently used tenon thicknesses. Most of the waste in the mortise is removed with an auger. Special mortise-making machines are available that guide the auger. The machines are similar to large dowelling jigs; they have a depth stop, and some can be adjusted to various angles. After most of the waste is removed, large framing chisels are used to square up the mortise. A special corner chisel can be used to cut the corners square (Illus. 385).

Tenons are cut by sawing the shoulder and then splitting off the waste with a hachet or chisel. Final smoothing is done with a framing chisel.

Some joints need to be pegged for added strength; the draw-boring method is used. The pegs should be made from well-seasoned heart pine or oak. The pegs can be shaped into rough octagons with a hewing hatchet. Using a wooden mallet will allow you to drive the pegs more efficiently than if you use a steel hammer.

Illus. 385. After removing most of the waste with an auger bit, the mortise is squared up with a chisel. The special corner chisel shown speeds up the process.

Much of the timber framing that is done nowadays makes use of power equipment. In fact, some manufacturers of prefabricated timber framing have come so far as to use computer-controlled equipment to design and machine the joints.

14
Decorative Joints

Traditionally, woodworkers have tried to hide joinery details. While earlier joiners may have taken just as much pride in their craftsmanship as present-day woodworkers, many woodworkers today want to show off their joinery. In this case, the joinery becomes an integral part of the whole design rather than merely some means of fastening the parts together (Illus. 386).

Joints can be used for decorative effect in several ways; one way is to leave standard joints such as dovetails exposed as part of the design. To heighten the effect, the joint can be emphasized by using contrasting wood for different parts or by inlaying a contrasting veneer in the joint. Joints can also be emphasized by leaving parts proud or by rounding over edges. In particular instances, a small rabbet at the joint line increases visual awareness of the joint (Illus. 387). Changing the shape or spacing of the parts of the joint provides further visual interest. Some joints are designed primarily for their visual impact, with strength only a secondary consideration.

Another trend in joinery is to try to make joints biomorphic. The basic premise of the idea is that wood began as a living thing. Things relating to life or living processes are referred to as biological. Biological objects tend to be rounded

Illus. 386. Rather than hide the joinery, many modern designs use exposed decorative joints.

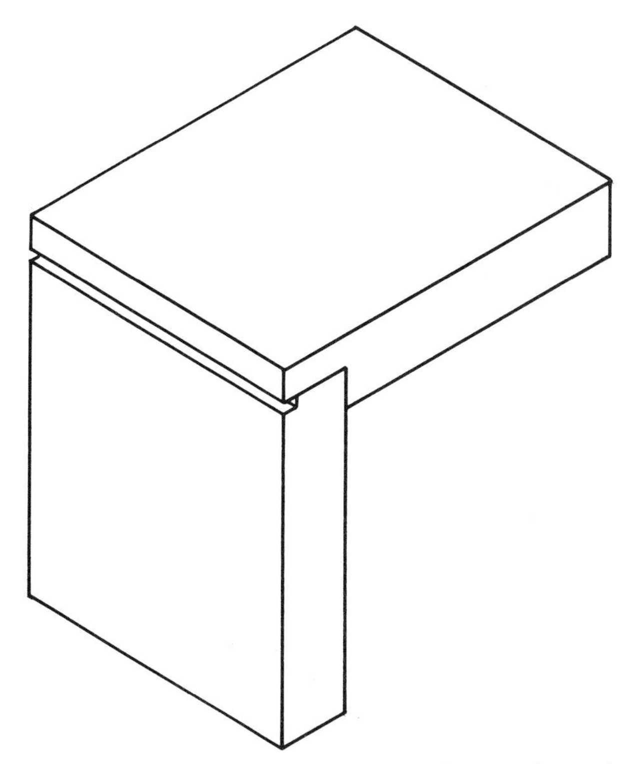

Illus. 387. A small rabbet at the joint line can be used for emphasis.

and flow in smooth curves, whereas mechanical things are square and angular. Biomorphic things suggest the forms of living organisms; biomorphic joints are designed to fit the organic nature of wood. They are rounded and flow in easy curves. The sculptured joint is one type of biomorphic joint. In this joint, the joint line is straight, but the parts are sculptured to flow into each other. Another type of biomorphic joint uses a curved joint line. The biomorphic half-lap and the curved dovetail are examples of this type of joint.

Dovetail Variations

The dovetail is one of the most decorative joints in its own right. Part of the beauty of the joint comes from the fact that it is obviously functional. Hand-cut dovetails and dovetails made on an adjustable jig can be variably spaced. You can use the variations in spacing to create a visual tension or to draw the eye to a specific point in the design. The variation can be subtle or bold depending on the requirements of the design.

COGGED DOVETAIL

This is a variation on the standard dovetail that uses dovetails of differing height (Illus. 388). Illus. 389 gives step-by-step directions for cutting a cogged dovetail by hand. The Leigh dovetail jig can be used to cut the joint with a router (Illus. 390). In this case, you can do the work more efficiently if you use two routers, since two different size bits are used to cut the same part. If you change the router bits during the operation, the depth setting may be disturbed, and then the joint fit would be affected. Set the fingers for the desired spacing. Make a test cut with each of the routers, and determine the correct gauge settings as if you were making the entire joint using that one bit. Record these settings for later reference.

Cut the tails first. The larger dovetail bit is used first. Set the depth of cut to match the thickness of the pin board. Make all of the cuts

Illus. 388. The cogged dovetail combines small and large pins and tails in a single joint.

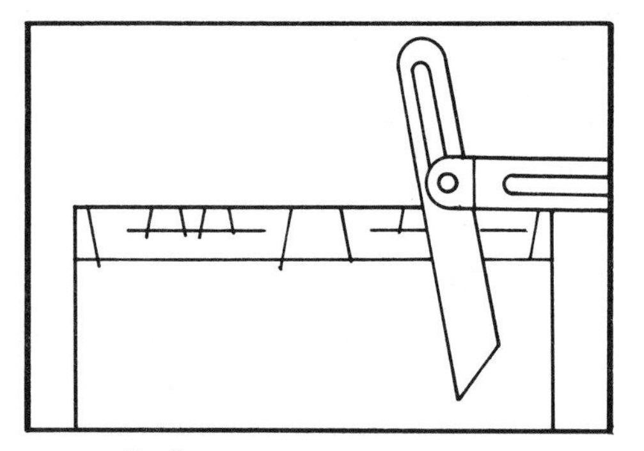

1. Lay out tails first.

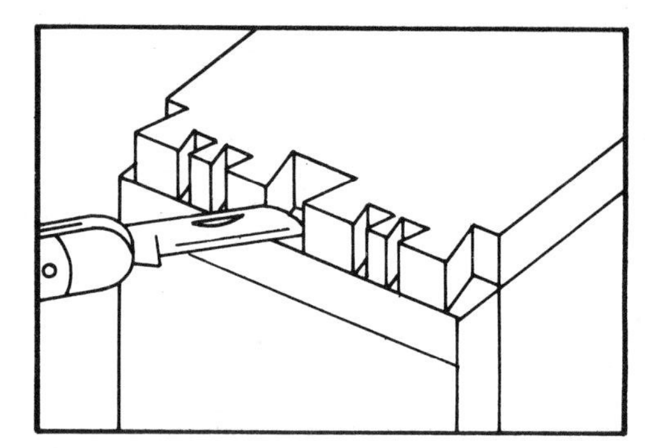

2. Cut tails; then use tail board to mark pins.

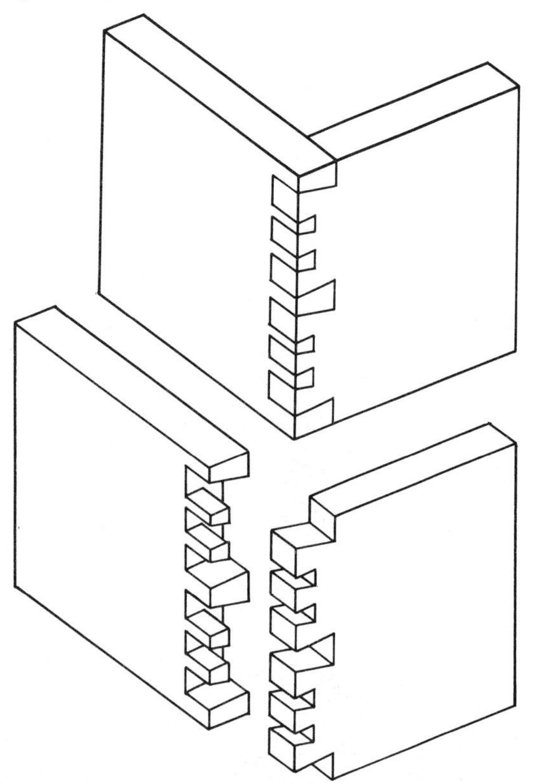

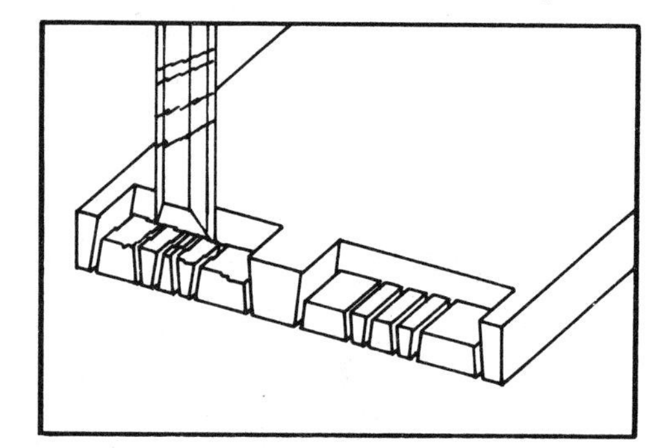

3. Chop out waste behind small pins.

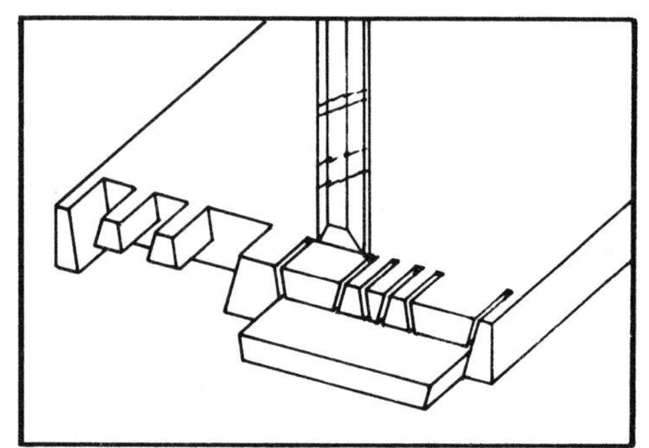

4. Support the small pins with a block while chopping the shoulders.

Illus. 389. Cogged dovetail hand technique step by step.

Illus. 390. When using the Leigh dovetail jig to cut a cogged dovetail, use the large dovetail bit first to cut the large tails.

that require the large bit, then switch to the other router with the smaller bit (Illus. 391). The depth of cut should be set to ¼″ less than the larger bit. Use the second router to make the remaining cuts, and the tail board is complete.

To cut the pins, set the gauge to the setting determined previously for the large tails (Illus. 392). Use this setting and a straight bit to cut all of the pins. Next, set the gauge to the setting for the smaller pins that you determined during the test cut using the small router bit. With the gauge in this position, use the straight bit to reduce the size of the cogged pins (Illus. 393). Next,

Illus. 391. Switch to the smaller dovetail bit, and cut a pin socket inside the large tails.

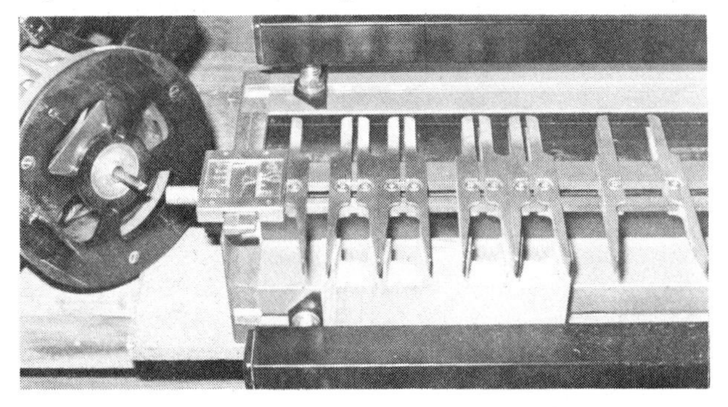

Illus. 392. First cut all of the pins using the gauge setting for the large tails.

Illus. 393. Move the gauge to the setting for the smaller tails, and trim the mating pins to size.

turn the pin board around so that the face side is against the jig. Put the finger assembly in the TD mode, and install the crosscut bar (Illus. 394). Make sure that the fingers are touching the pins so that they support the finger assembly. Adjust the crosscut bar so that it is 5⁄16″ away from the front edge of the pin board. Use this setup to guide the router while you shorten the cogged pins (Illus. 395).

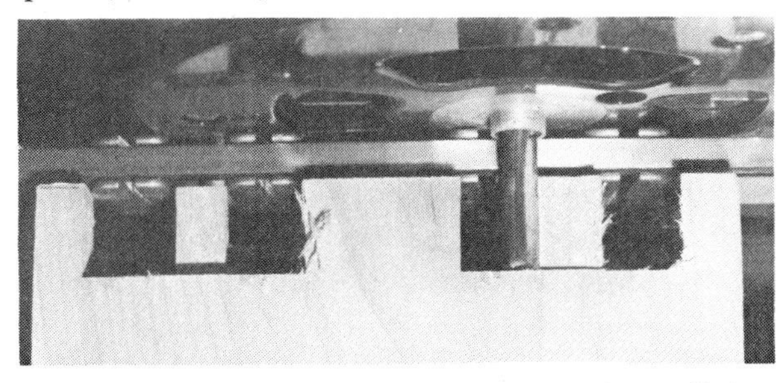

Illus. 394. Turn the pin board around, and install the crosscut bar. Adjust the bar so that it is 5⁄16″ from the front edge of the pin board; then shorten the cogged pins.

Illus. 395. The completed cogged joint is ready for assembly.

IMPOSSIBLE DOVETAILS

These only look impossible (Illus. 396). The assembled joint seems incapable of being cut or assembled, but the disassembled view reveals the joint as merely a sliding dovetail that is cut on an angle.

These joints don't have a lot of practical applications, but they make interesting conversation pieces for your front-room table. To make the most of the puzzle aspect of these joints, you will probably want to make two samples of each joint. Glue one sample together, and keep it on display. After you have perplexed your friends, bring out the unglued sample, and show them how it works. You can nevertheless incorporate these joints into some types of projects; but, you will need to design the project around the joint.

In Illus. 396, for example, the joint on the right could be used to join a leg to a table; the joint on the left can also join a table leg, if only one sliding dovetail is used.

You can cut these joints with a router, but for the best visual effect, cut them by hand. Since the illusion of impossibility is created by having the dovetail on an angle, any dovetails cut with a router will look a little distorted. You can correct the distortion—or rather, create the intended distortion—to give the properly proportioned face views when you cut them by hand. Lay out the dovetail on the flat face, then lay out the diagonal lines.

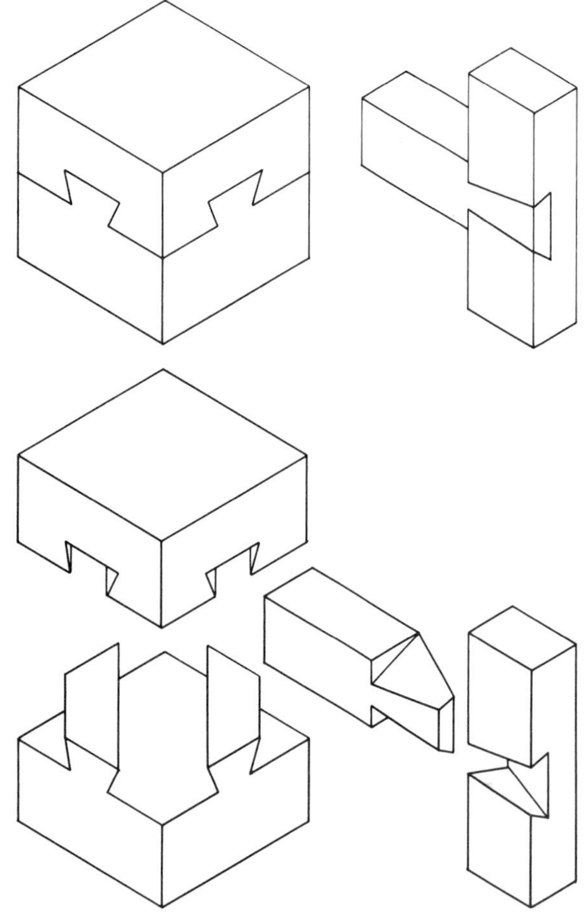

Illus. 396. Impossible dovetails look impossible until you see the exploded view. They are really sliding dovetails cut at an angle to the face.

CURVED DOVETAILS

Curved dovetails give the joint a more organic look (Illus. 397). They can be cut mostly by machine with a little hand chiselling. The curve can be on one side or both sides.

Illus. 397. A curved dovetail joint ready for assembly shows an example of having the curve on both the pin and the tail boards.

To cut a one-sided curved dovetail, first cut the pins as usual (Illus. 398). Next, lay out the curved shoulder line for the tails. Transfer the pin locations to the tail board, and cut the tails. Finally, cut a curved rabbet on the pin board.

The two-way curved dovetail is somewhat more complex (Illus. 399). Begin by making a curved rabbet on the pin board that is equal to the thickness of the tail board. Also, make a curved rabbet on the tail board, but make sure its width is equal only to the depth of the smallest pin. You can make the curved rabbet with a table saw. The curve is limited by the diameter of your dado blade. Set the dado blade to the width of the cut, and lower it below the table. Clamp an auxiliary fence to the saw table to position the middle of the end of the board over the blade, and set the rip fence to control the width of the cut. Place the board against the fences, and crank up the blade with the saw running. When the cut reaches the edges of the board, stop raising the blade and turn off the saw. Repeat the procedure for all of the rabbets.

Lay out a curved shoulder line for the pins; you can use a board with a curved rabbet to scribe the curve. Lay out the pins. The pins can be cut

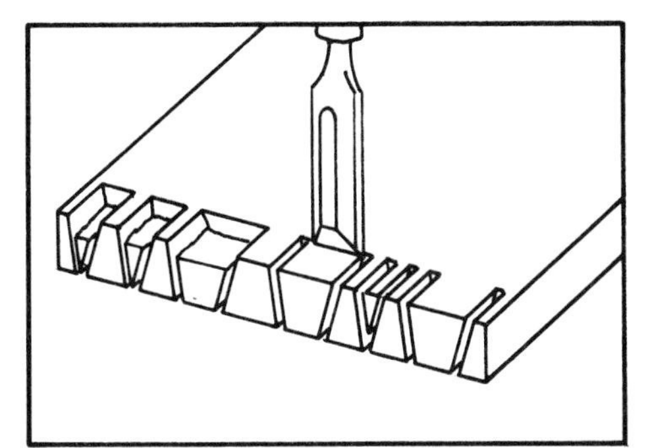

1. Cut pins as usual.

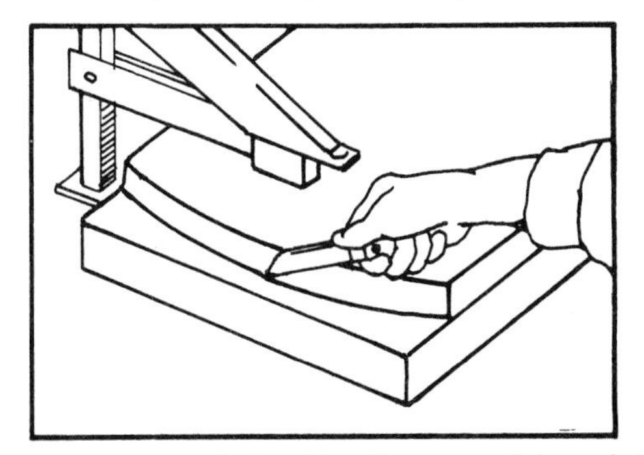

2. Lay out a curved shoulder line on tail board. Use a template.

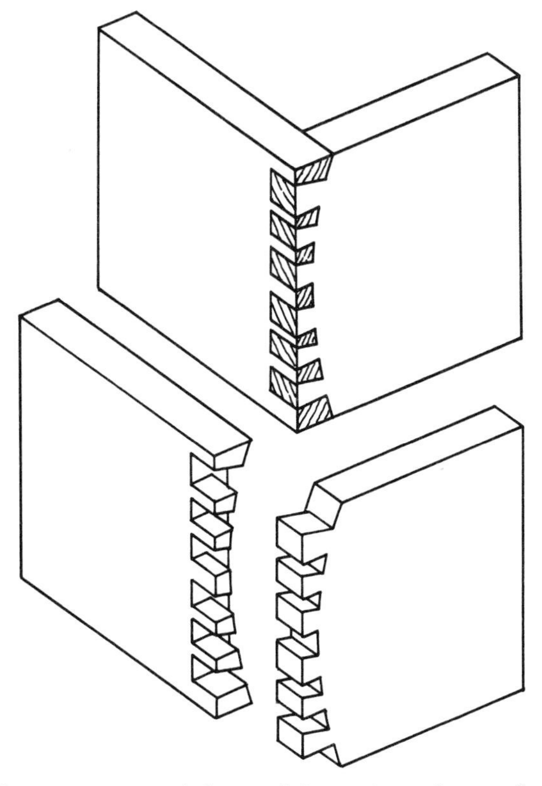

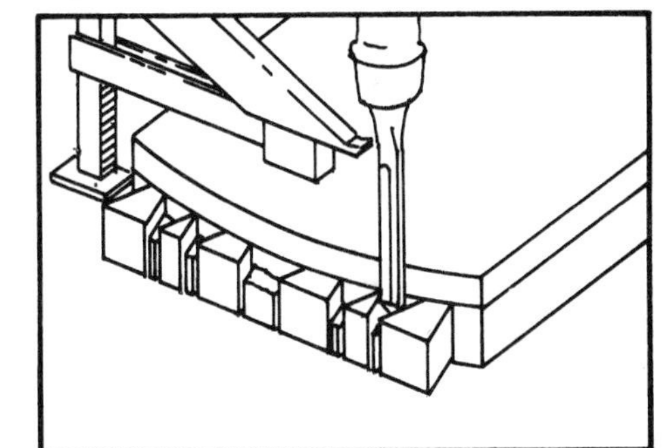

3. Cut tails. Use template to guide shoulder cut.

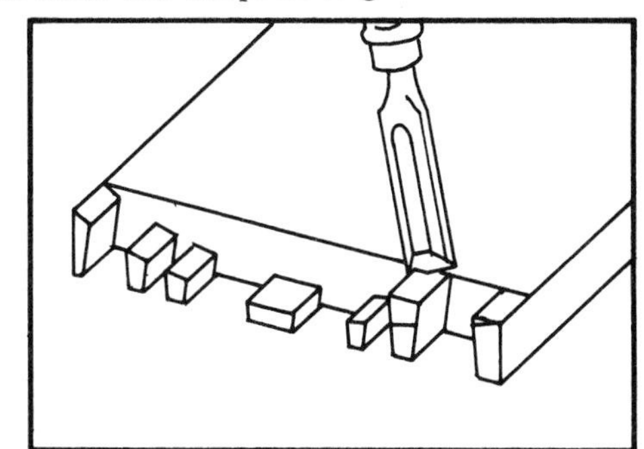

4. Cut a curved rabbet on pin board.

Illus. 398. One-sided curved dovetail step-by-step hand technique.

by hand or with a band saw or jigsaw. Use the pins to lay out the tails. The tails can also be cut on the band saw or jigsaw.

The rabbet on the tail board curves in two directions. The first curve can be cut on the table saw, but the second curved shoulder must be chiselled by hand.

OUTLINED DOVETAILS

Outlining a dovetail joint makes use of a contrasting wood to emphasize the joint (Illus. 400). There are two methods for making outlined dovetails: one uses veneer while the other uses solid wood.

To outline the joint with contrasting veneer, cut a shallow rabbet on the inside face of both parts before the joint is cut (Illus. 401). Glue a piece of the veneer into the rabbet. Next, lay out and cut the joint as usual. Glue and assemble the joint. After assembly, make a saw kerf along the joint lines. Hold the saw at a 45° angle, and stop the kerf as soon as the saw reaches the band of veneer already in place. Cut triangular pieces of veneer, orienting the grain so that it will match

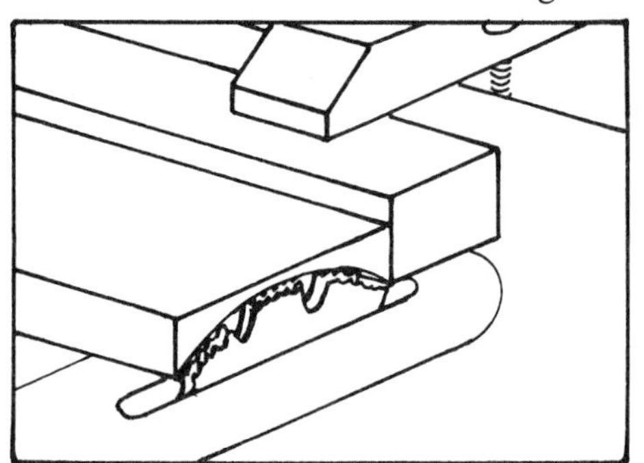

1. Cutting rabbet on table saw. Note: Fence removed for clarity.

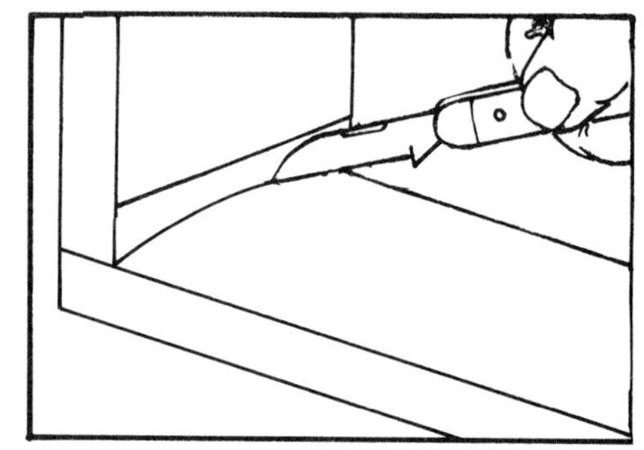

2. Using rabbeted board to scribe shoulder.

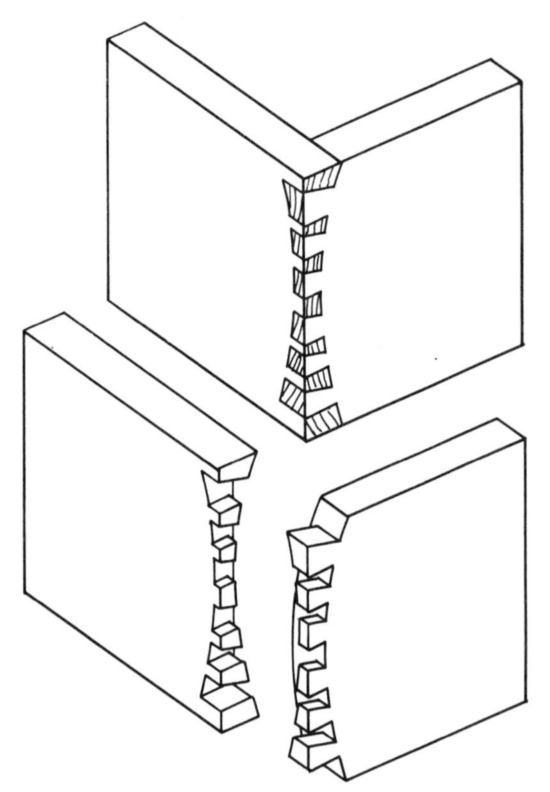

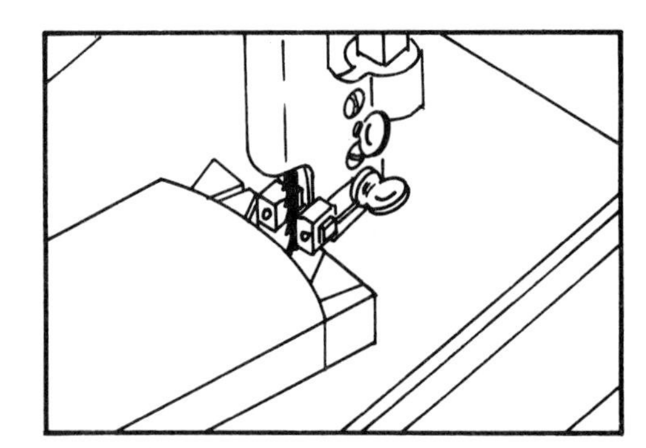

3. Cutting on band saw.

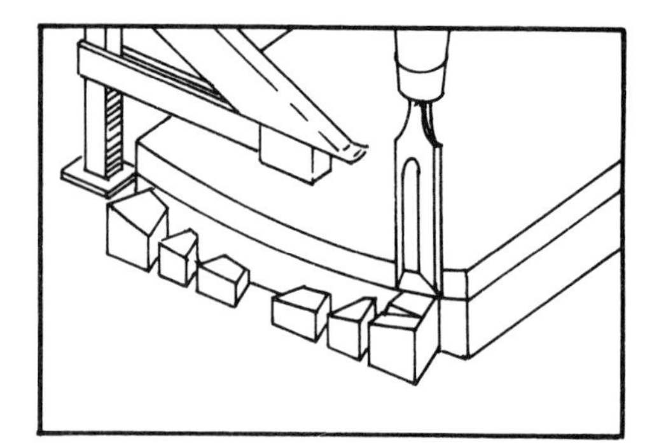

4. Chiselling tail board rabbet.

Illus. 399. Two-way curved dovetail step-by-step power-tool method.

the grain in the joint. Apply glue to the kerf but not to the veneer. Slip the veneer into the kerf. The glue will cause the veneer to swell slightly, so if the kerf is the right size, the joint will be very tight. If you can't match the kerf and veneer thickness, use a saw that makes a kerf slightly smaller than needed. Then thin the veneer by compressing it on an iron anvil with a steel hammer.

If you use a dovetail jig to cut the joint, the process is even simpler. Prepare the parts as described above by making a rabbet and gluing in a piece of contrasting veneer. When you cut the

Illus. 400. Contrasting wood can be used to outline a dovetail joint to emphasize the joint line.

1. Glue veneer in shallow rabbet.

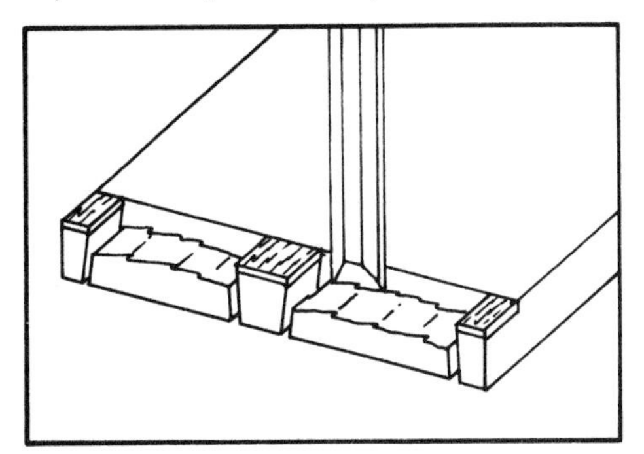

2. Cut joint as usual.

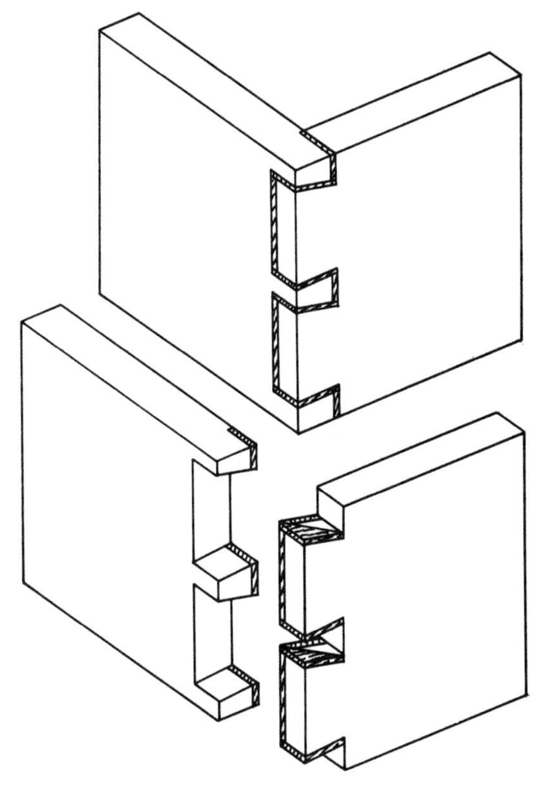

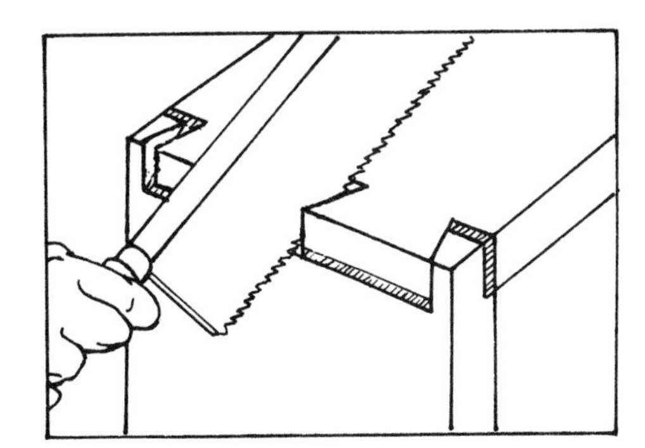

3. Saw along joint lines.

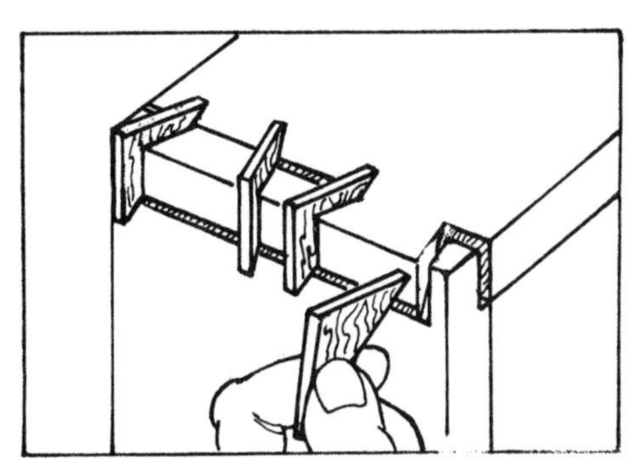

4. Insert triangular pieces of veneer.

Illus. 401. Outlined dovetail step by step.

joint, adjust the jig to make a loose fit (Illus. 402). Make a test joint and by trail and error adjust the jig until the gap between the pins and the tails is just right to accept a piece of veneer (Illus. 403). Once you have the jig set, you can make many joints rapidly.

The second method gives an even bolder appearance to half-blind dovetails (Illus. 404). This joint can be hand-cut or made with a router. To make it with a router, you need an adjustable jig (Illus. 405).

Begin by laying out a joint with large tails and pins, but use a contrasting piece of wood for the tail board instead of what will eventually be the mating part (Illus. 406). Cut and assemble this joint. After the glue is dry, saw off the excess wood on the tail board, leaving just the right amount to form the border. Next, lay out another joint with smaller pins and tails that will fit in-

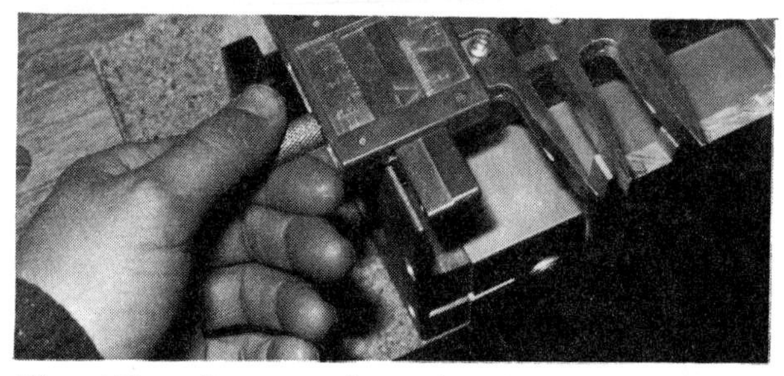

Illus. 402. Adjusting a dovetail jig for a loose fit makes it possible to insert veneer in the joint during assembly.

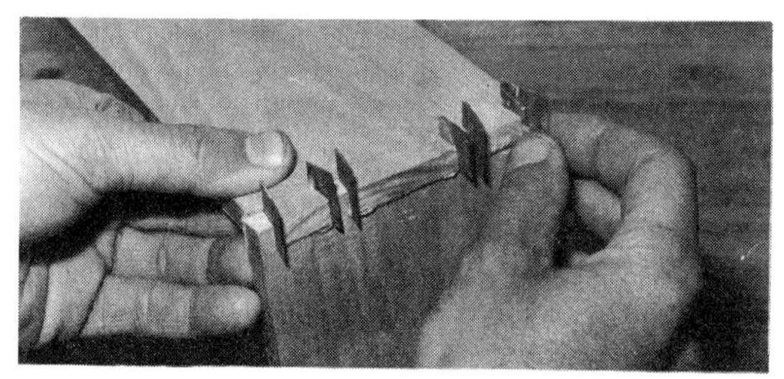

Illus. 403. As you assemble the joint, slip pieces of veneer between the pins and tails.

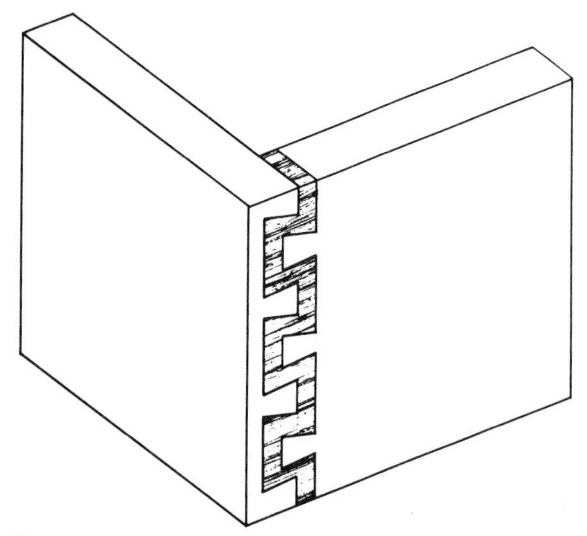

Illus. 404. For an even bolder outline effect, a solid piece of wood can be used.

Illus. 405. An adjustable router jig can be used to make the bold-outline dovetail.

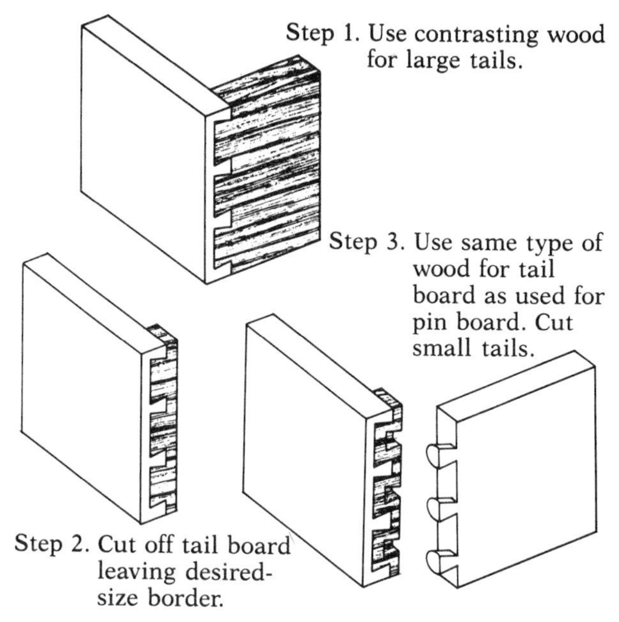

Illus. 406. Bold-outline dovetail step by step.

side the contrasting wood of the previous tail board. Cut the pins again and transfer their location to the mating tail board. Cut the tails as usual.

BUTTERFLY JOINTS

A double dovetail with a butterfly key can be used for decorative effect especially if a contrasting wood is used. The joint can add visual interest to a solid tabletop or similar project (Illus. 407). For a bold appearance, make the double dovetail keys large, about 3½″ by 1⅜″. For ¾″-thick stock, make the key ⅝″ thick and the mating mortise ½″ deep; this gives you some extra thickness in the key so that you can plane it down to be flush with the surface. The mortise can be chopped with a chisel, or you can remove most of the waste with a router and then use the chisel to finish. Make a hardboard template, and use a template-following collar on the router base (Illus. 408). Use a chisel to square up the corners of the mortise. When you are using a template-following collar, the template cutout will be larger than the finished mortise. This can make it difficult to make a template that is properly sized to fit a specific size of key. The simplest solution is to start with the template rather than the key; make the template approximately the size you want. Make a test cut with it, then use the cut to size the key accordingly to fit the finished size of the eventual mortise.

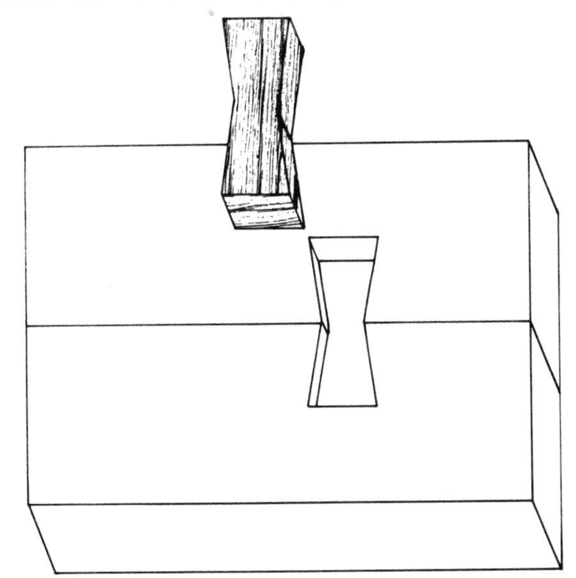

Illus. 407. Butterfly joint.

THE THREE-WAY DOVETAIL

The three-way dovetail joins three boards at a corner. The joint is very decorative because dovetails are exposed on both the front and the side (Illus. 409). First, cut a dovetail slip joint on

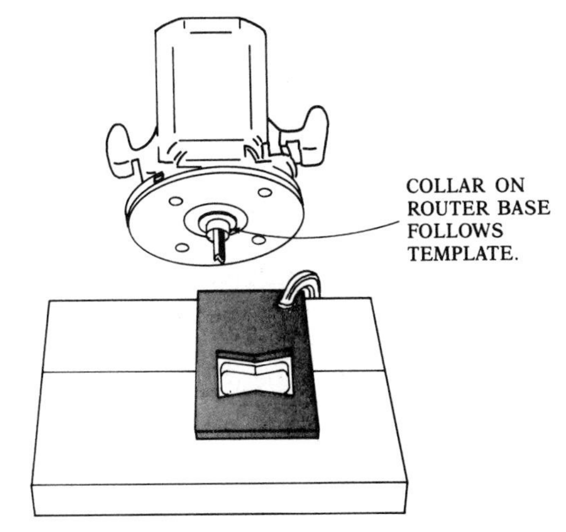

Illus. 408. A simple template can be used to cut the mortise for a butterfly key.

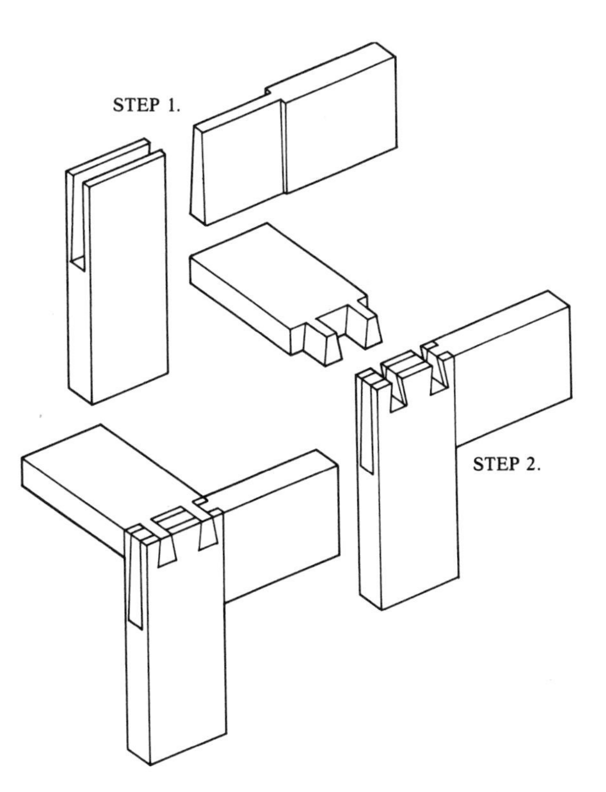

Illus. 409. The three-way dovetail joins three boards at a corner.

the two side frame members; then, glue and assemble the joint. The top rail is then attached with a second dovetail joint. Because the joint is cut after the first one is assembled, the layout and cutting do not require any special or unusual treatment and can proceed normally.

INSERTED TAILS

Inserted tails can be used to create a dramatic-looking joint (Illus. 410). The pin board is cut in the usual fashion. Then the tails that taper entirely to a point are cut from a contrasting color of wood. The tails fit into V-shaped notches cut in the tail board. To lay out the location of the V notches, place the pin board against the end of the tail board, and scribe the pin locations. Then, using a bevel set to the same angle as the pins, mark the V notch. Glue the tail inserts in place, and assemble the joint.

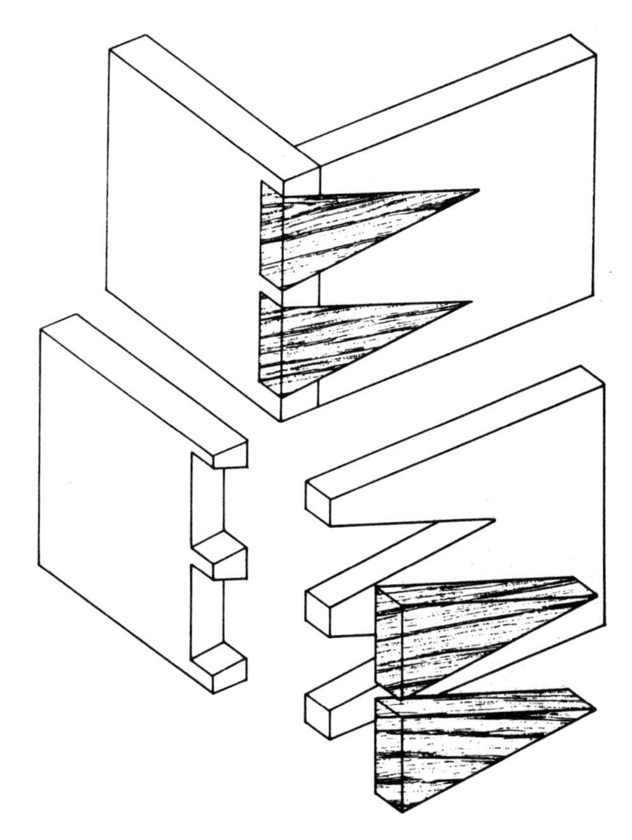

Illus. 410. Inserted tails made of contrasting wood can create a dramatic-looking joint.

Inlaid Joints

A simple butt or mitre joint can be made decorative by the addition of visible reinforcement. The reinforcement takes the form of the inlaid splines or dowels. By arranging the splines or dowels in various ways, many different effects can be achieved (Illus. 411). Usually, a contrast-

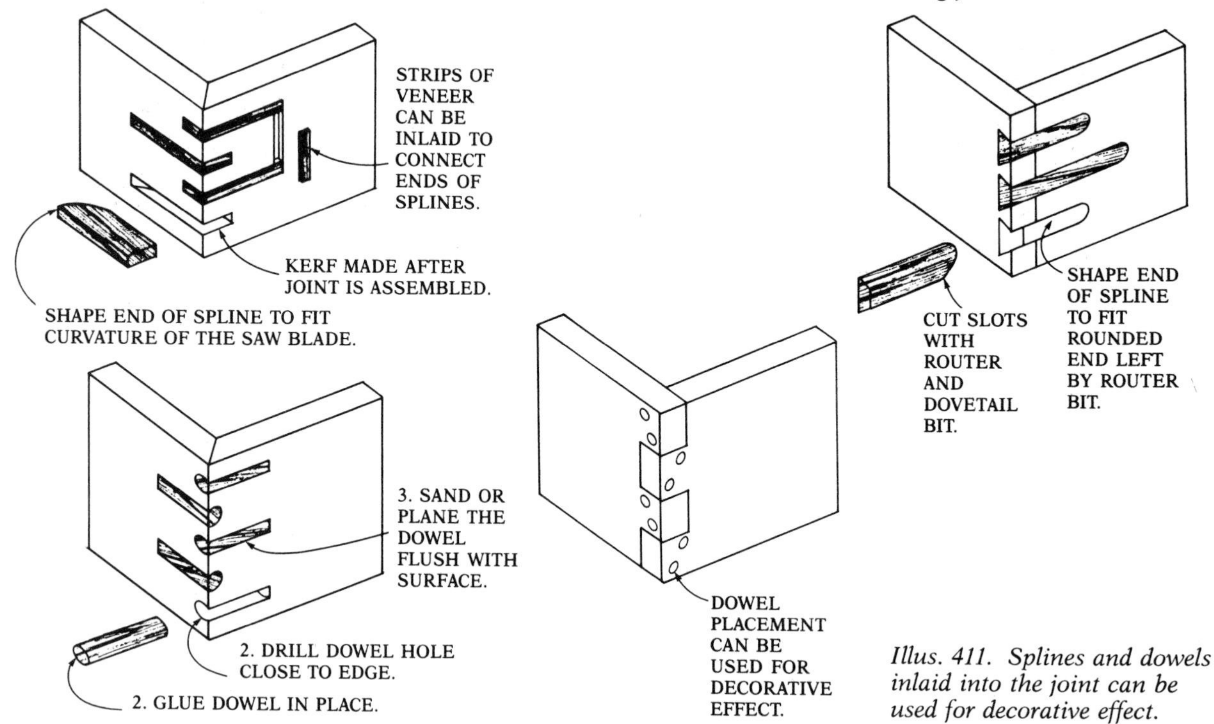

Illus. 411. Splines and dowels inlaid into the joint can be used for decorative effect.

ing color of wood is used for the splines or dowels. The grooves for the inlaid pieces can be made with a router or on the table saw. All of the grooves are made after the joint is assembled. This makes it easy to make a complex-looking joint. The ends of the splines or dowels can be joined with inlaid strips of veneer to create even more intricate designs. Dowels can also be used to decorate and reinforce other types of joints such as box joints. Once you understand the inlaid-reinforcement technique, you can use your imagination to come up with numerous other possibilities.

Built-up Joints

Joints can be built up in log-cabin fashion to create interesting interlocking-finger joints. By using contrasting woods or adding strips of veneer between the joints, you can achieve a variety of effects (Illus. 412).

Biomorphic Joints

The purpose of a biomorphic joint is to create a sculpted or curved joint that has a more organic or biological look than the standard type of joint. When the design of a project calls for an organic shape, standard joints may look out of place. Part of the idea or philosophy involved is that the shape of an object should reflect the characteristics of the material from which it is made. Since wood is an organic material that is always curved and rounded in its original form, the design of wooden objects, as this thinking goes, should use the same types of curves found in a living tree.

SCULPTURED JOINTS

Sculptured joints use traditional joinery, usually a mortise-and-tenon or a dowel-reinforced butt joint. The difference is that, after assembly, the parts are shaped into flowing curves so that the various parts seem to grow out of one another like the branches of a tree (Illus. 413). The joints are cut while the parts are still square, so the joinery is fairly standard. The difference is that transition pieces must be allowed for around the joint to permit the sculpturing after assembly. Separate transition pieces can be used; but, the best method is to use wood that is already wide enough to allow the transition area to be made. The joints will be easier to cut if you make them before any shaping is done on the boards. After

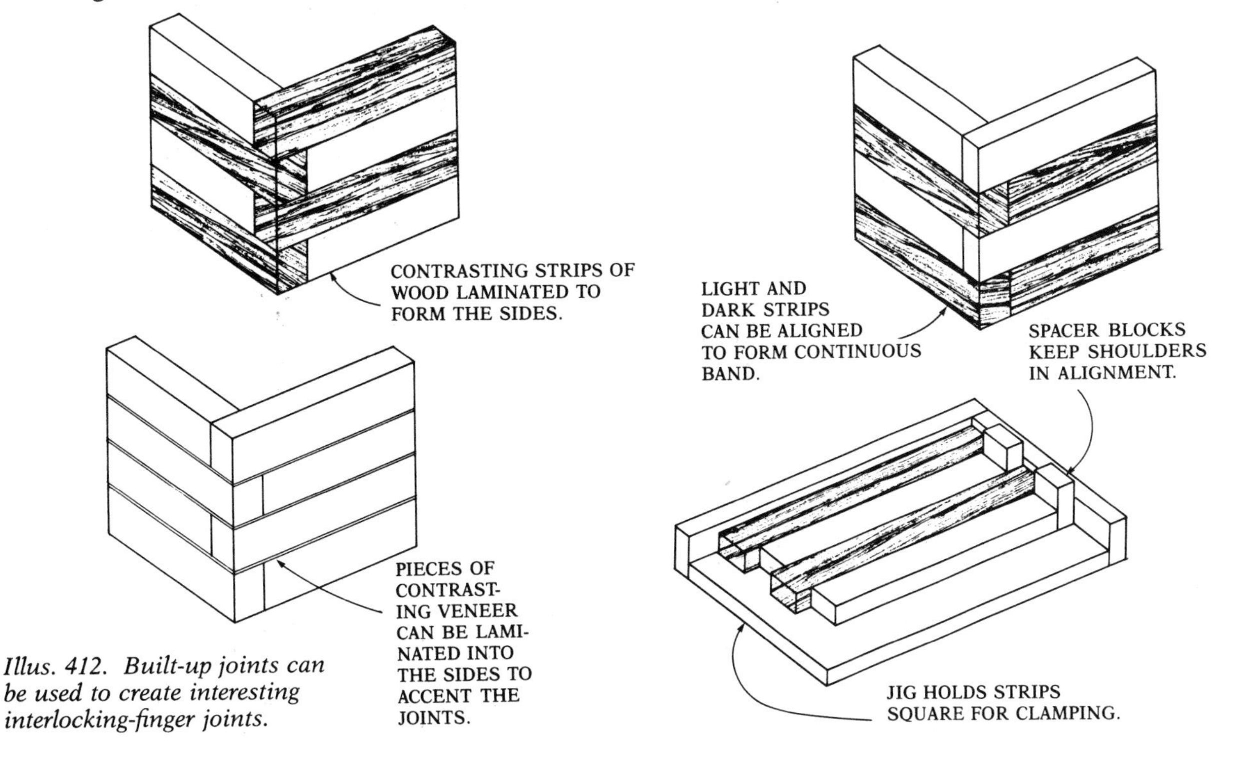

Illus. 412. Built-up joints can be used to create interesting interlocking-finger joints.

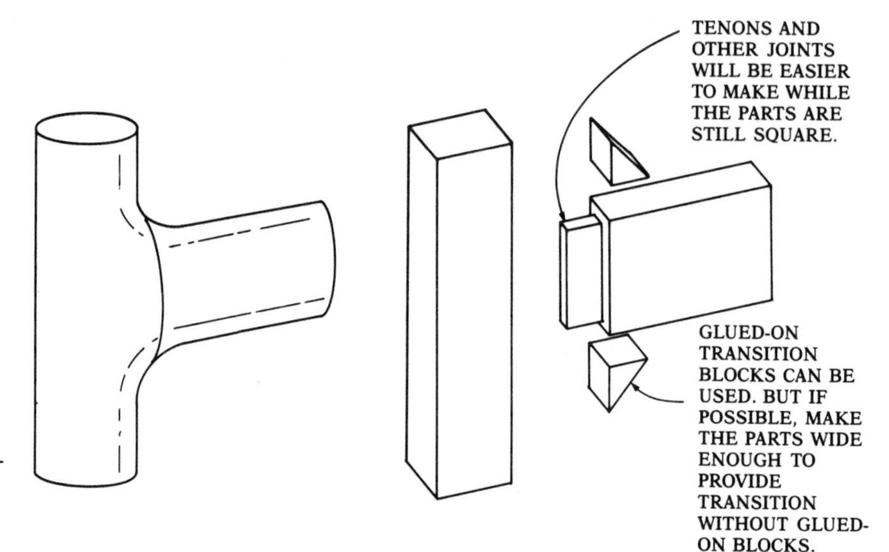

Illus. 413. A sculptured joint makes a smooth transition between parts.

the joints are cut, but before assembly, use a band saw to cut the parts to rough shape. Once the project is assembled, use a rasp, draw knife, or spoke shave to sculpt the joints.

When a great degree of curvature is needed in the transition area, short-grain problems can arise. This can lead to the transition piece splitting off later. To avoid this problem of splitting, use a mitred shoulder on the mortise-and-tenon joint. This will lengthen the grain in the transition area. There are two types of mitred shoulders: the straight shoulder and the sloped shoulder (Illus. 414).

To make the straight-shoulder type, begin by cutting a standard mortise-and-tenon joint with about a ¼″ shoulder below the tenon. The tenoned member should be longer than the finished size to allow for the mitred shoulder. Next, dry-assemble the joint, and mark the location of the bottom of the tenoned member on the edge of the mortised member. Disassemble the joint, and make a 45° line starting at this mark. Use a marking gauge to make a line 3⁄16″ from the edge of the mortised member. Where the two lines meet, make a square line out to the edge. Reassemble the joint, and mark a 45° line on the bottom of the tenoned member using the previously made line as a starting point. Then, saw away the waste, and test the fit of the joint. Make any adjustments that are needed by paring with a chisel.

The straight-shoulder type works fine when the parts meet at a corner; but, when the tenoned member meets the mortised member at a point other than the corner, the sloped shoulder must be used. The procedure is similar to the method just described for straight shoulders. Cut a standard joint first, allowing extra length for the mitred shoulder. Lay out the lower mitre as before. Then, set a bevel to intersect the mitre joint on one end and the edge of the joint at the other end. Mark this angle on both parts. Use a

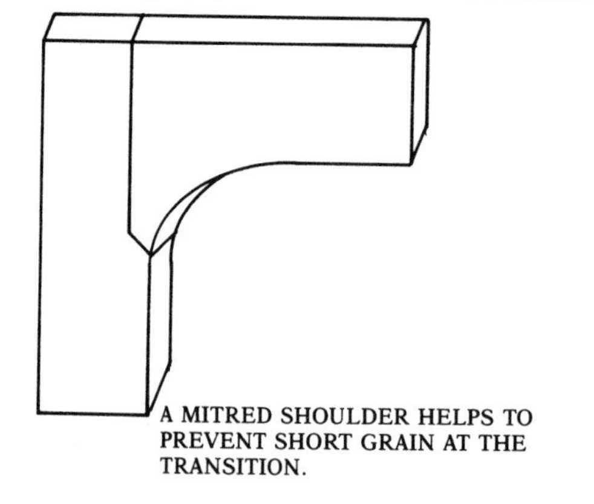

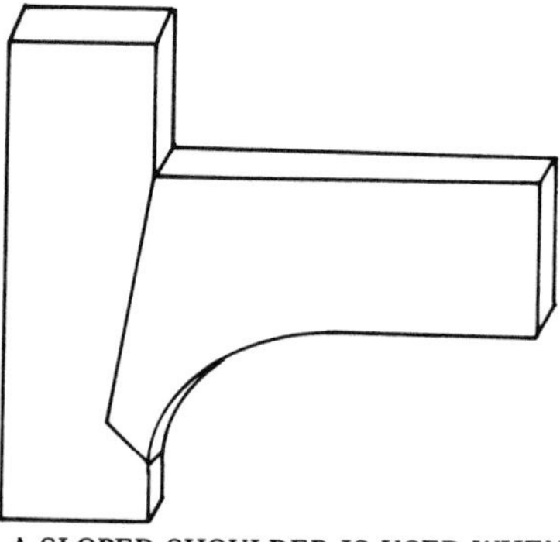

Illus. 414. To avoid short-grain problems, a straight mitred shoulder or sloped shoulder is often used at a transition point.

backsaw to make the cuts, and pare the new shoulder on the tenon to fit.

CURVED JOINT LINES

The sculptured joints described above still have straight joint lines. To give the joint an even more organic look, curved joint lines can be used (Illus. 415). Curved joints are often combined with sculpted transitions to make the entire joint a free-flowing curve. As with straight sculptured joints, the joint is easier to make if most of the work is done while the boards still have straight edges to work from. Then, you can cut the curves, and finally, you can sculpt the joint after assembly.

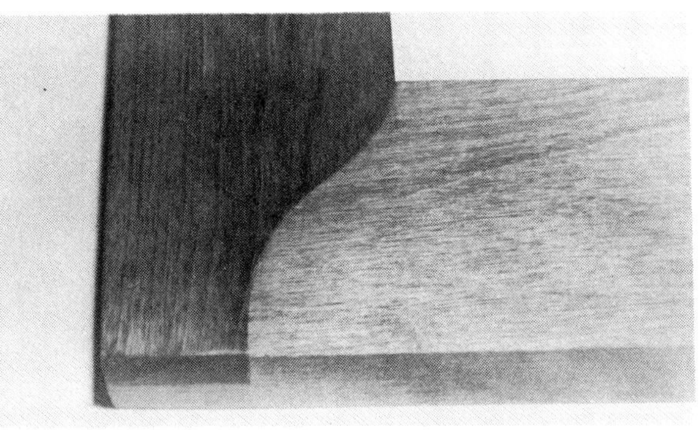

Illus. 415. Curved joint lines are another way to give the joint an organic look.

A curved half-lap joint can be cut with hand tools (Illus. 416). Cut a standard half-lap on one part, then use a coping saw to cut a curve. Place the part over the mating board, and scribe the curve with a knife. Saw away most of the waste; then, chisel to the curved shoulder.

The router is the power tool most frequently used to make curved joints. Even though you want the joint to look free flowing, it is necessary to use an accurate template to guide the router because the two parts must have identical curves for the joint to be tight (Illus. 417). There are two ways that you can follow a template with the router. One method uses a template-following collar; this fits on the router base and surrounds the bit. The template size must account for space between the bit and the outside edge of the collar. This can make template design difficult. The template-following collar can present a problem because it attaches to the router base. This can cause a lack of concentricity with the bit. If the distance between the bit and the collar isn't exactly the same all the way around, the circumference of the cut can vary depending on how the router is positioned relative to the template. The concentricity problem can be compensated for by keeping the router in the same position relative to the template throughout the cut; a better

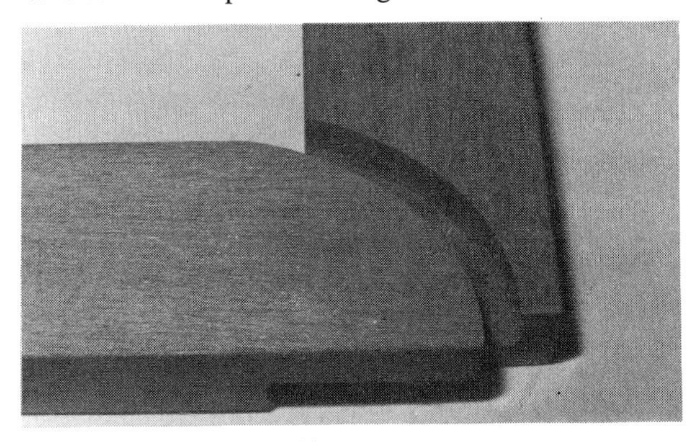

Illus. 417. Curved half-lap.

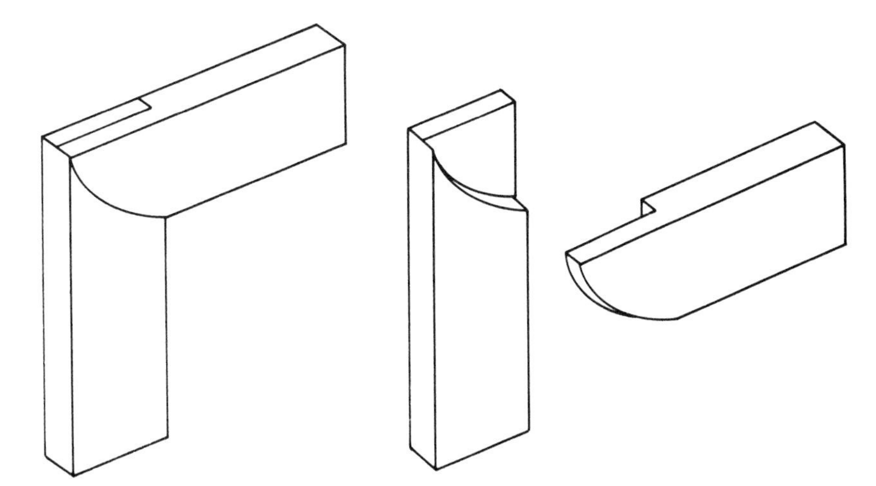

Illus. 416. The curved half-lap can be cut with hand tools.

solution is a router bit with a ball-bearing pilot mounted on the shaft. In this case, the bit position remains the same for any router-base orientation.

Two templates are needed for each joint, one positive and one negative (Illus. 418). The templates described here are for use with the bit with a shaft-mounted bearing. The templates are made from ½"-thick plywood. The extra thickness allows for depth adjustment. If thinner material is used, the bearing may not ride against the template when the bit is raised. Cut the first template on the band saw or jigsaw; sand the edges smooth. The first template can then be used to make the matching template; but first, an intermediate template must be made to account for the width of the router bit. You will need a rabbeting bit for the router that makes a rabbet exactly the same size as the template-following bit. For example, if the template-following bit is of ½" diameter, the distance from the bearing to the cutting edge on the rabbeting bit also must be ½" (Illus. 419).

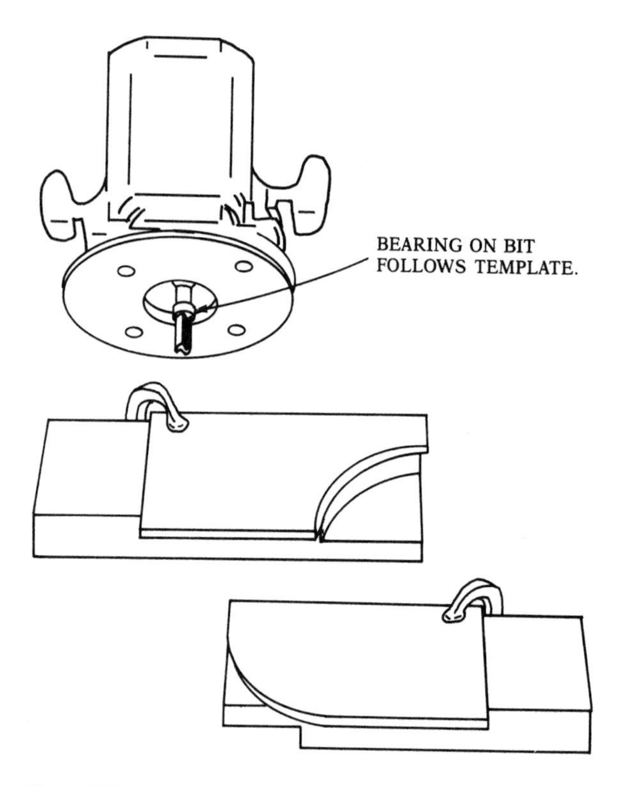

Illus. 418. A router guided by templates can produce tight-fitting curved joint lines. Both a positive and a negative template are needed to make the joint.

Rough cut the intermediate template on the band saw; then, clamp it on top of the original template. Adjust the router depth so that the bearing on the rabbeting bit will ride on the

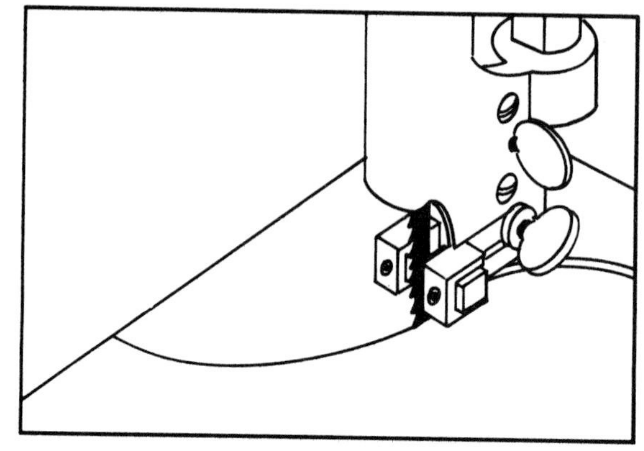

1. Cut original template on band saw.

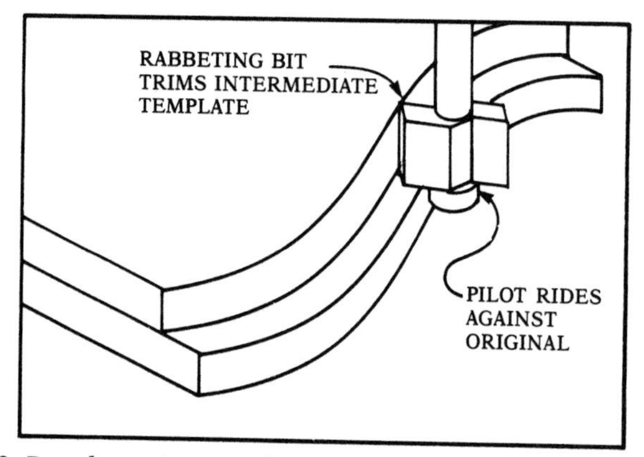

2. Rough-cut intermediate template and clamp it on top of original. Use rabbeting bit to trim.

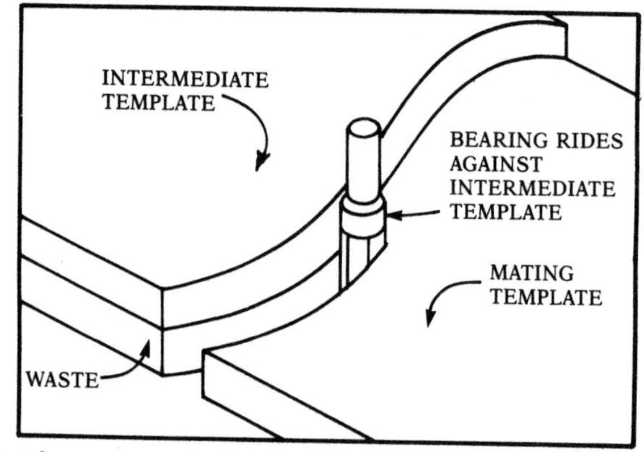

3. Clamp intermediate template on top of blank for mating template. Use a bit with a ball-bearing guide to cut.

Illus. 419. Making a curved template step by step.

original and the cutting edge will trim the intermediate template. Routing along the edge produces an intermediate template that is offset ½″ from the original.

The intermediate template can then be used to make the matching template. Clamp the intermediate template on top of the blank for the mating template, on the waste side of the cut. Use the ½″ template-following bit to make the cut. Be sure to keep the bearing against the template at all times because the good part of the cut is on the outside of the template. You should find then that you can place the mating template so it fits perfectly against the original.

With the templates completed, you are ready to make the curved half-lap joint: first cut a normal half-lap on one part; then, clamp the template in position, and rout the profile on the part. The routing will be easier if you use the band saw to cut the part to rough shape and just use the router for final trimming (Illus. 420). Next, clamp the other template to the mating part. Set the router to cut at half the board thickness. Rout the waste, and use the template to cut around the shoulder.

To cut a mortise-and-tenon with the templates, start by chopping a normal mortise or by making an open mortise. Cut the rear cheek of the tenon as usual, but leave the front cheek uncut. Now clamp the template to the front face of the tenon. Follow the template with the router to remove the waste and to form the curved shoulder. Next, clamp the other template to the front face of the mortised member. Follow the template with the router in order to cut away the waste (Illus. 421).

Illus. 420. A ball bearing on the router bit rides against the plywood template to trim the half-lap to shape.

Start with simple curves at first and then move on to more complex joints as you gain confidence in using the technique. Once you are familiar with the procedure, you can design jigs and holding fixtures that will make the job of alignment easier and that will also allow you to mass-produce the joints.

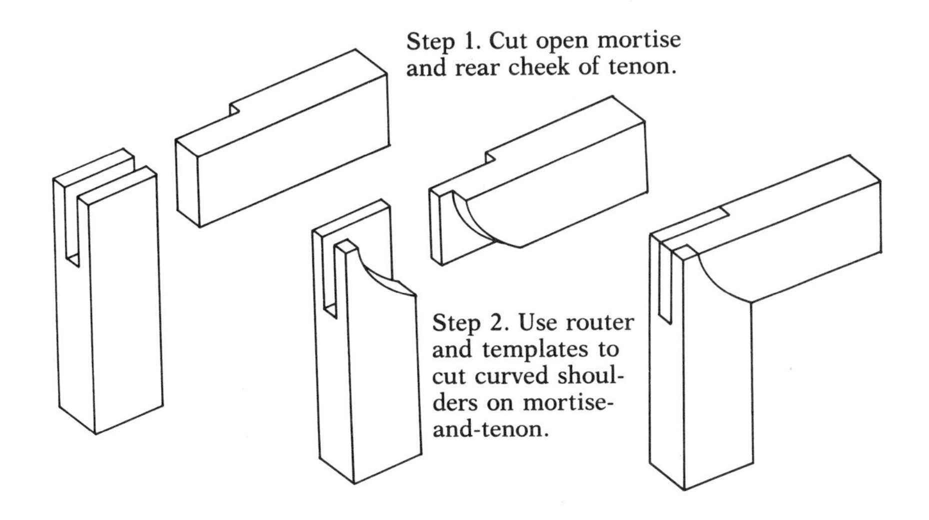

Illus. 421. Curved mortise-and-tenon step by step.

15
Joints from China and Japan

The nature of wood imposes certain requirements that must be met in a successful joint. These requirements are independent of the culture that is designing the joints. For this reason, it is interesting to compare the joints developed in China and Japan with those developed in Europe. For many years, the cultures of the East and West were isolated so that woodworking traditions developed separately. However, even though tools and techniques differ, the principle of good joint design remain the same. It is thus the nature of the wood itself that accounts for the many similarities in joints from differing woodworking traditions. Even without any cross-cultural influence, mortise-and-tenon joints, mitres, dovetails, and half-laps show up in these if not all woodworking traditions. It is the subtle design variations and ways of combining the element of the joints that differ. To the eye of an experienced woodworker from one culture, the joints used by another look familiar even though they appear superficially very different (Illus. 422). A comparison of joints from other traditions can help you to develop a clearer understanding of what makes a good joint.

While the inherent similarities can be attributed to the nature of wood, the differences seem to come from differing philosophies, differing aesthetics, and the specifically available materials. China has abundant stone that is suitable for use in buildings so that, while furniture joinery is prevalent, timber framing isn't as developed there as it is in Japan, where the stone is less suitable as a building material but where large coniferous forests have continued to provide the raw materials for timber-framed structures. In Japanese architectural tradition, the structural elements of the building are left exposed; in what is probably a cooperative rela-

Illus. 422. The Mechigai-koshikake-kama-tsugi *is a Japanese joint that at first glance appears very different from Western joints; but, if you compare it to some of the timber-framing joints in Chapter 13, you may begin to notice similarities.*

tionship, there has occurred the development of many joints whose purpose is more for aesthetic pleasure than structural strength.

Because the forests of Japan are softwood, the joinery makes use of the characteristics of softwoods to a greater extent than European joinery. Most European joints were developed for use with hardwoods and then later adapted to softwoods. One important property of softwoods is that they can be compressed as they are assembled. This is used to advantage in the Japanese mortise-and-tenon joint. Although very similar to the European version, the Japanese mortise is slightly tapered so that the tenon is compressed as it is inserted. This make a very tight joint that is less likely to loosen as the wood dries.

In China and Japan, many traditional joints are assembled without glue. This has led to the development of very sophisticated ways of wedging or locking the joints (Illus. 423).

Illus. 423. Wedges are used in a variety of ways in Japanese joinery.

Chinese Furniture Joints

A particularly distinctive aspect of Chinese furniture is that practically all visible joints appear to be mitres. To achieve the necessary strength, hidden mortise-and-tenon joints reinforce the mitres. The desk in Illus. 424 is a good example of Chinese joinery. Framed panels are used throughout; even the top writing surface is a framed panel. As evidence of how effectively the craftsman understood wood dimensional change, this desk has survived the move from China to the dry climate of an area in the western United States without a single split panel.

Illus. 424. A modern Chinese desk.

In a similar desk of Western design, the panel frame would most likely use scribed or coped mortise-and-tenon joints. Notice in this Chinese design that all of the panel frames appear to be mitred. But, a standard mitre joint would not be strong enough for this application. So, to keep the clean, simple appearance and yet strengthen the joint, a hidden mortise-and-tenon joint has been used. Illus. 425 shows one example of this type of joint. To make this joint, lay out the mitre; then, gauge the mortise location. The end of the mortise is even with the inside corner of the mitre. The mortise width is one-third the thickness of the stock; the length of the mortise is one-third the width of the stock. Use the same

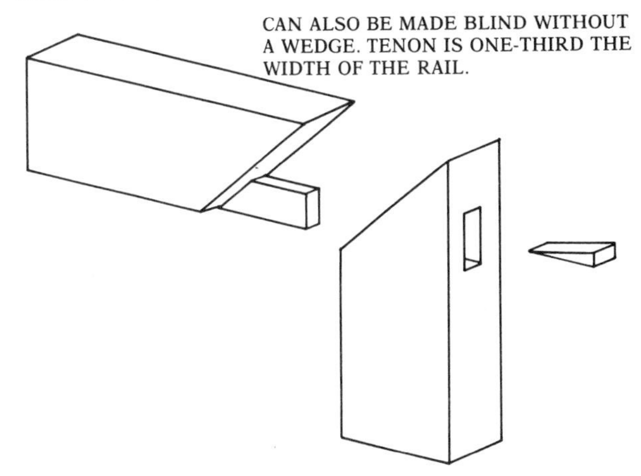

Illus. 425. Chinese method for making a mortise-and-tenon mitre.

gauge settings to lay out the tenon. Chop the mortise before cutting the mitre. The mortise tapers slightly to the outside; this allows for wedging after assembly.

To cut the tenon, make as many of the saw cuts as possible before removing any of the waste; this way the layout lines will be intact and therefore still visible. Place the board in a vise at a 45° angle. This will position the mitre line parallel with the bench top. Hold the saw parallel to the bench top, and make the side-cheek cuts. Reposition the board in the vise so that it is straight up, and make the cut for the top cheek. Finally, cut the mitre, and remove the waste.

Illus. 426 shows one method of leg attachment that is used to show a mitred face. A three-way mitre is also often used in Chinese joinery. The joint between the leg and top of the table in Illus. 427 is a good example. The joint is a variation on the mortise-and-tenon reinforcement described earlier (Illus. 428). The two side rails of the top are joined using the same technique as described above, but the layout must be adjusted to avoid interference with other parts of the joint. In this joint, the tenon thickness is one-quarter of the rail thickness. The mortise is located one-fourth of the way down from the top of the rail.

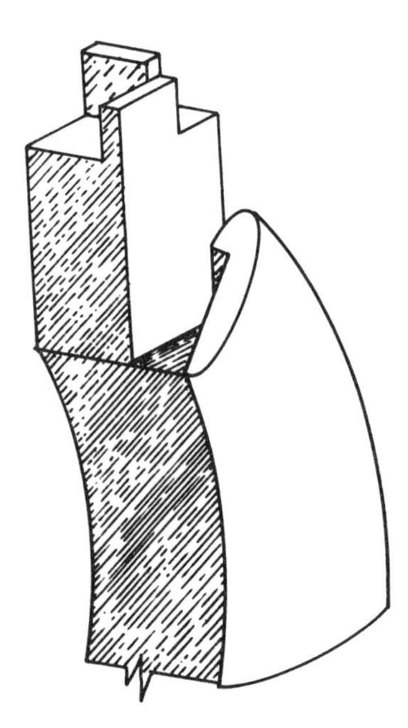

Illus. 426. This method of leg attachment combines the strength of a mortise-and-tenon with the appearance of a mitre.

Illus. 427. This three-way mitre is secured with hidden tenons.

Illus. 428. From the underside you can see clues to where the tenons are.

To lay out the joint between the leg and the top, divide the sides into five equal divisions (Illus. 429). The outside mitred section is one-fifth the stock thickness; the space between the tenon and the inside edge of the mitred section is one-fifth the stock thickness; and the tenon thickness is one-fifth the stock thickness.

When one part meets another in Chinese joinery, a mitre is almost always used. The framing around the drawers on the desk above in Illus. 424 and the stretcher between the legs of a small table are good examples (Illus. 430). Close examination of the stretcher joint shows how it is made (Illus. 431). The mitre cuts are made on the front shoulder of a mortise-and-tenon joint.

Dovetail joints are often used in Chinese furniture, but the proportions are different from those used by European woodworkers. The pins are larger than you would find ordinarily on a hand-cut dovetail of European design. The Chinese woodworkers recognized that the larger pin gave the joint greater strength. They hadn't been influenced by the European fashion that dictated the most delicate pins as a measure of fine craftsmanship.

A variation on the sliding dovetail is used in Chinese knockdown construction (Illus. 432).

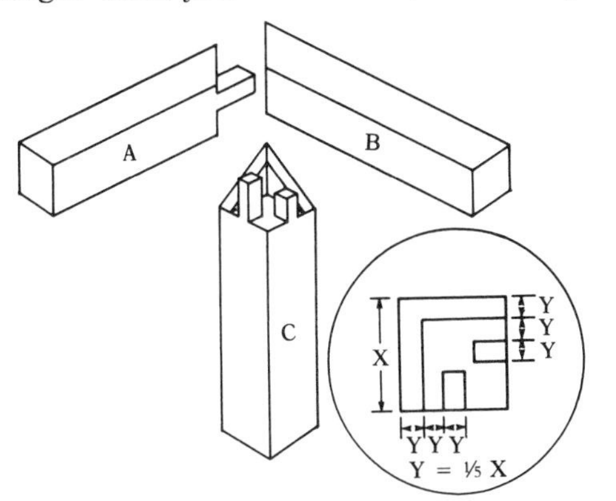

Illus. 429. Three-way mitre mortise-and-tenon joint exploded view. The layout for the tenons is based on five divisions along both inside edges.

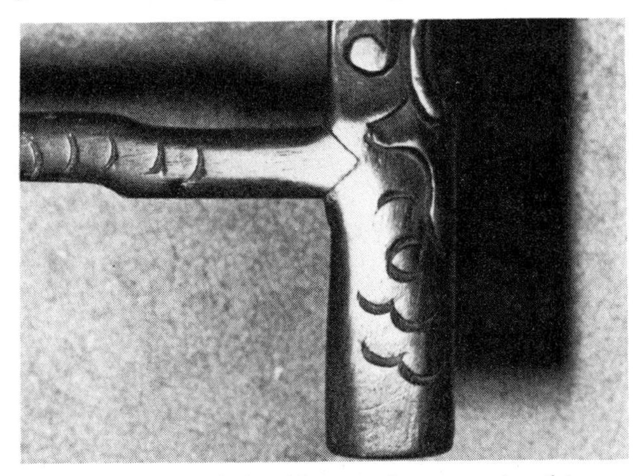

Illus. 430. Mitred shoulders on the tenon give this joint a typically Chinese look.

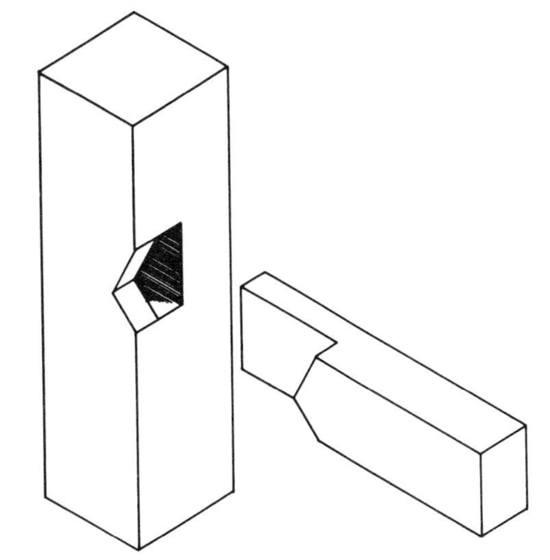

Illus. 431. Mitred shoulder tenon exploded view.

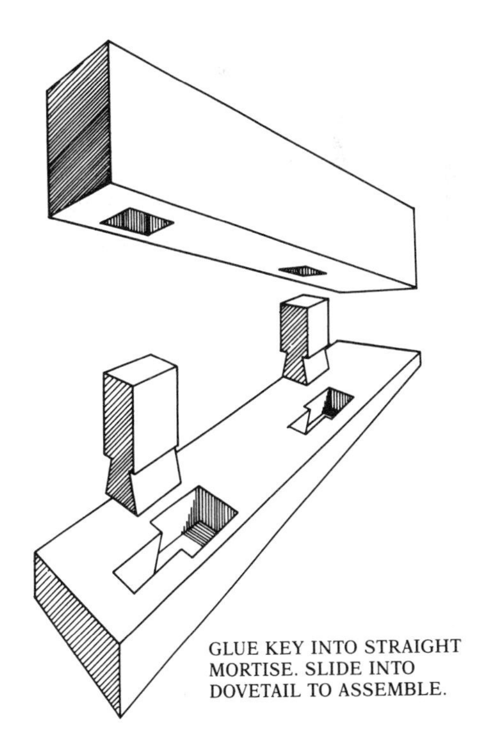

Illus. 432. Dovetailed keys glued into mortises can be used in knockdown applications.

One part is mortised normally, but the other part has a relatively complex mortise that is about twice the length of the other. One half is a normal straight-sided mortise, but the other half is dovetailed. A key that is dovetailed on one end fits into both mortises. The straight end of the key is permanently attached in the standard mortise. The dovetailed section then projects from the surface of the board. Usually several of these joints are required along the edge of the part. To assemble, the dovetailed key is placed in the straight-sided end of the remaining mortise and then it is slid into the dovetailed section, locking the parts together.

The small box in Illus. 433 shows another way the Chinese reinforce a mitre joint. Small fingers project from one side to interlock with the other (Illus. 434).

A particular splicing joint that is unique to Chinese woodworkers is used to join curved sections of a chair back. Illus. 435 shows two variations of this joint.

Illus. 433. This small box uses mitre joints reinforced with interlocking fingers.

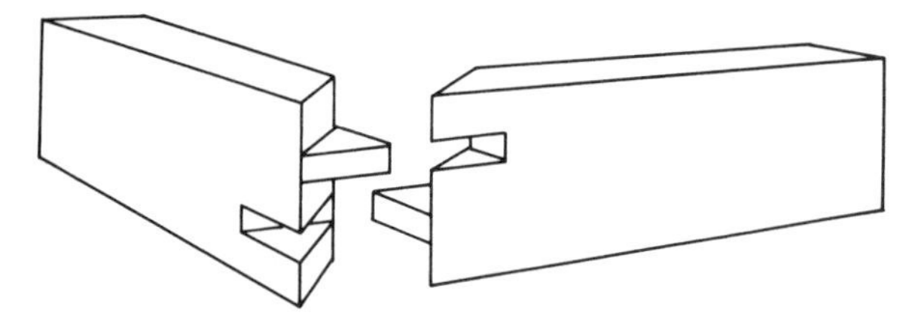

Illus. 434. Interlocking-finger mitre exploded view.

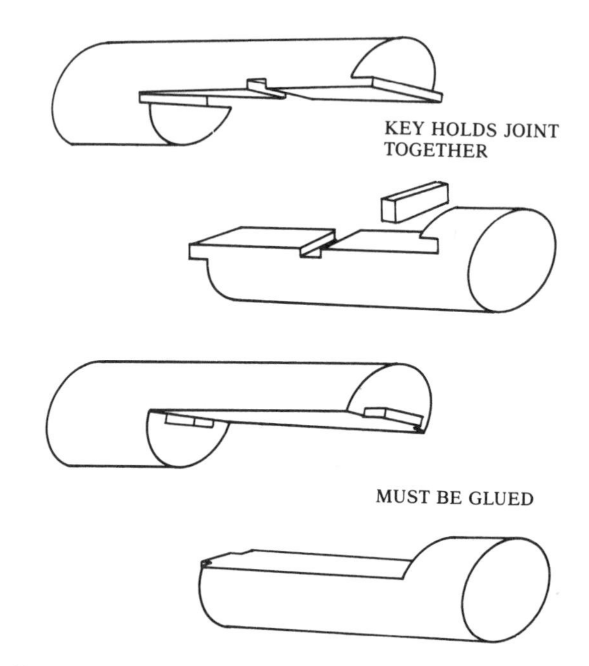

Illus. 435. These splicing joints are used to join curved sections of a chair back.

Japanese Joinery

The woodworking tradition of Japan is based on a deep reverence for the wood and for the tools used to shape it. The joinery used in the construction of a shoji illustrates how the Japanese craftsman uses joints that seem familiar to the Western woodworker but with a subtle difference. The shoji is a type of sliding door used in Japanese houses to divide the interior space (Illus. 436). There are a number of varieties of shoji. Illus. 437 shows one type and gives the Japanese names for the various parts.

A master shoji maker is called *shokunin*. The *shokunin* places a great deal of importance on both accuracy and speed in cutting the joints. The joints are not rough cut and then trimmed to fit as is often the case in Western joinery. Instead, the saw or chisel is placed right on the layout line, and the first cut is the final cut.

Through mortises are used on other types of sliding doors that are found on the exterior of the house; but, for shoji, the end of the tenon must not show. The tenon is made as long as possible for maximum strength, but a paper-thin layer of wood is left at the bottom of the mortise to hide the end grain. The ends of the mortise taper in. Because softwood is used, the tenon will compress as it is driven into the mortise, creating a very tight joint. Special chisels are used to chop the mortise and remove the waste, permitting the paper-thin bottom to be left unmarked (Illus. 438). Rather than chopping the mortise from one end to the other as is the usual Western practice, the Japanese woodworker starts in the middle and progresses outward. The groove in the face is called the *ura*. The *ura* always faces the middle of the mortise except for the last paring cuts to square the ends. To remove the waste, a hook-ended *mori-nomi* is driven into the waste then pulled up. The *sokozarai-nomi* has a right-angle edge around on the end. It is used to smooth the bottom of the mortise (Illus. 439). Rice glue is used during assembly to secure the joints.

Illus. 436. In Japanese architecture, the shoji serve the same function as interior walls, windows, and doors in a Western house.

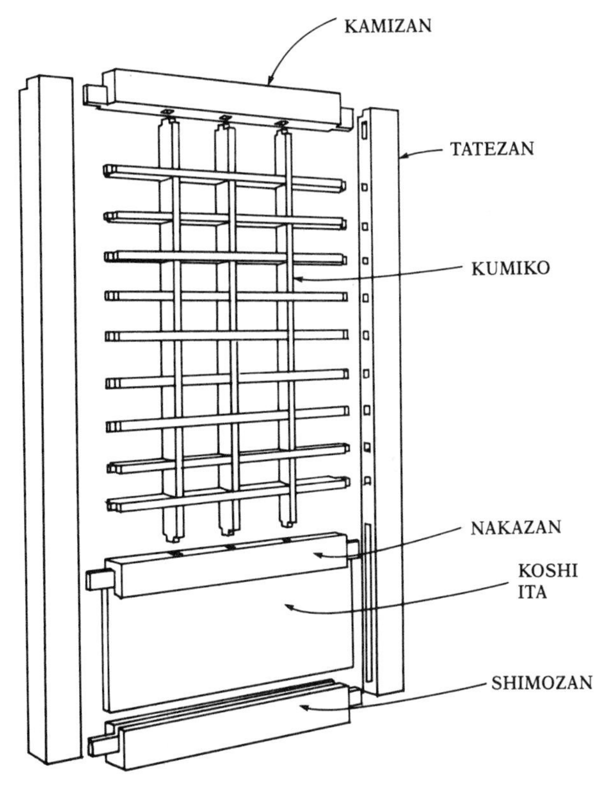

Illus. 437. Parts of a shoji.

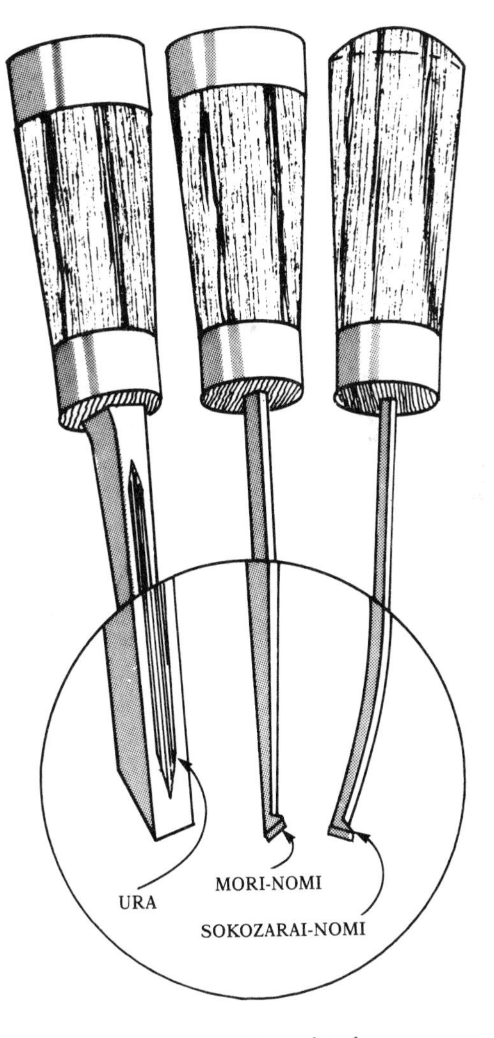

Illus. 438. Japanese mortising chisels.

The rice paper is applied to a framework made of vertical and horizontal members called *kumiko*. The *kumiko* fit into small mortises in the stiles (*tatezan*) and the rails (*kamizan*). These mortises are made in a way that is suited only to softwood. The mortises are chopped to within about ⅛" of the final depth; then, the bottom is smoothed and brought down to the final depth by tapping the wood fibres down with a square-ended steel punch.

Where the *kumiko* intersects, half-lap joints are used. The unusual feature is how the joints are arranged so that the parts are interwoven. For example, when three vertical *kumiko* are used, the horizontal *kumiko* have two notches cut on one edge and one on the other. Because the *kumiko* would snap if it were bent enough to weave in and out, the joints are arranged such that two are side by side on one edge and the third is on the opposite edge and towards the end (Illus. 440). This joint pattern is alternated so that the overall effect is a strong interwoven unit (Illus. 441).

Joints developed for use in Japanese timber-frame construction are numerous and often complex (Illus. 442 to 446).

1. Make first cut in center, *ura* facing middle.

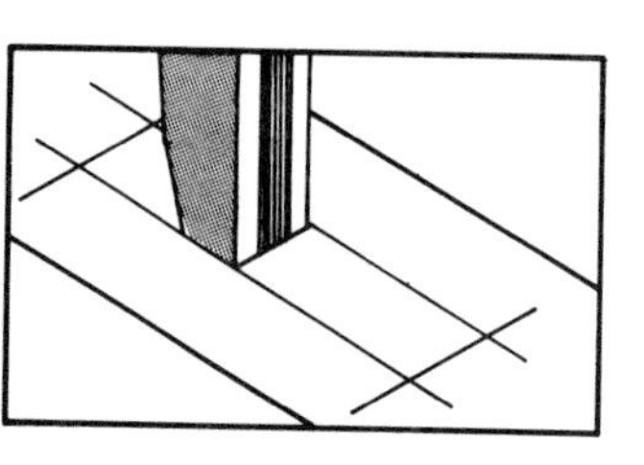

2. Reverse chisel position to make second cut. Continue this until you reach the ends.

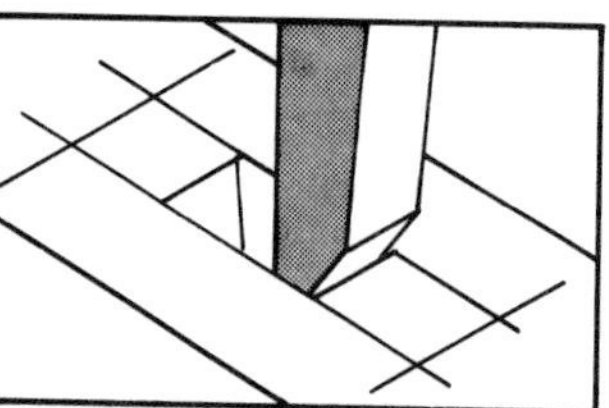

3. Turn chisel so that *ura* faces the end of the mortise and square up the ends.

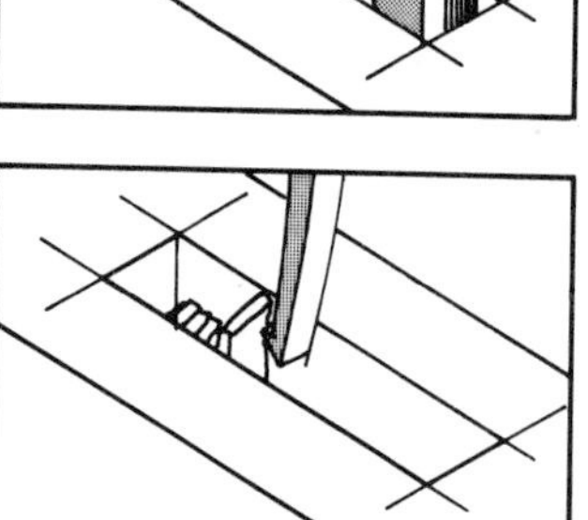

4. Drive the *morinomi* into the waste and pull out the chips.

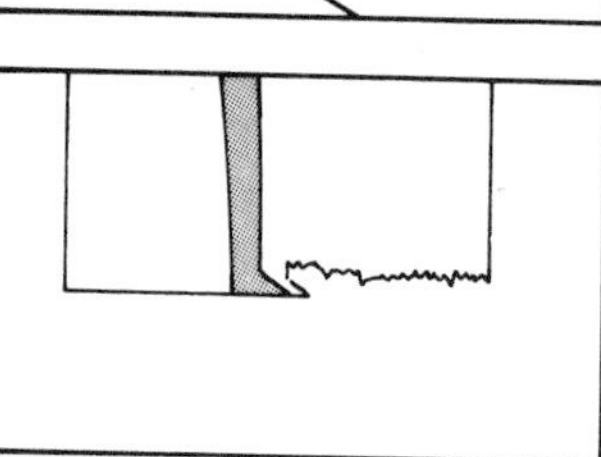

5. Smooth the bottom of the mortise using the *sokozarai-nomi*.

Illus. 439. Japanese method of mortising step by step.

Illus. 440. Half-lap joints in the kumiko *are arranged with two side by side on one edge and one on the opposite edge, so that the parts can be interwoven.*

Illus. 441. Assembling the kumiko.

Illus. 442. Japanese timber-framing joints can be complex and require a significant amount of hand work.

Some of these joints are mostly ornamental, while others are designed for great structural strength (Illus. 447 to 459). Many can be adapted for use in smaller scale work, such as furniture making. Notice how some are remarkably similar to their Western counterparts while others are unique to the Japanese woodworking tradition.

Illus. 443. A modern Japanese carpenter may use power equipment for many operations, but the traditional joinery is still used.

Illus. 445. Mortise-and-tenon joints take many forms in Japanese timber framing.

Illus. 444. The timber-frame members are usually prefabricated. Here are completed timbers awaiting assembly.

Illus. 446. Dovetails are used in Japanese timber framing to add tensile strength.

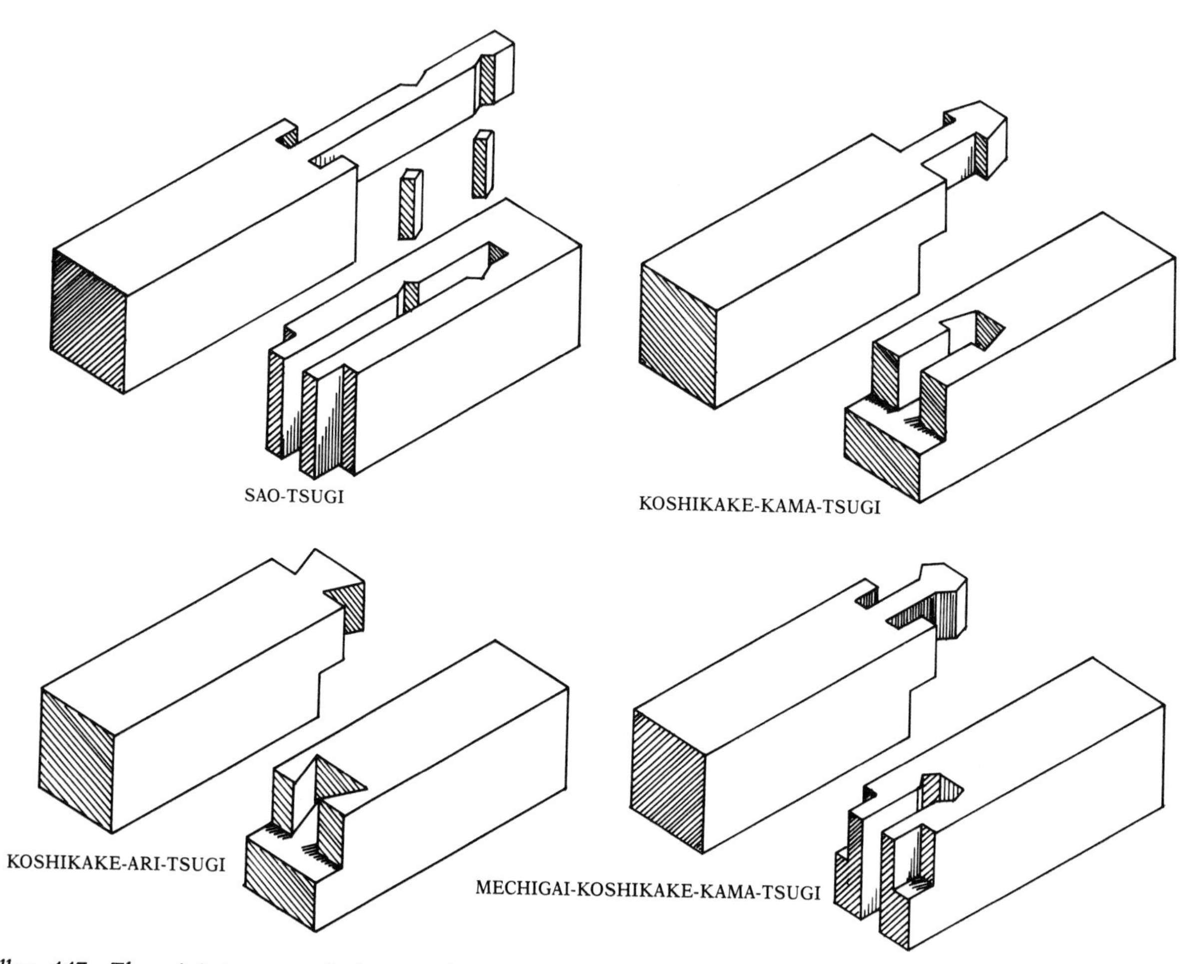

Illus. 447. These joints are used when a splice needs to resist tension.

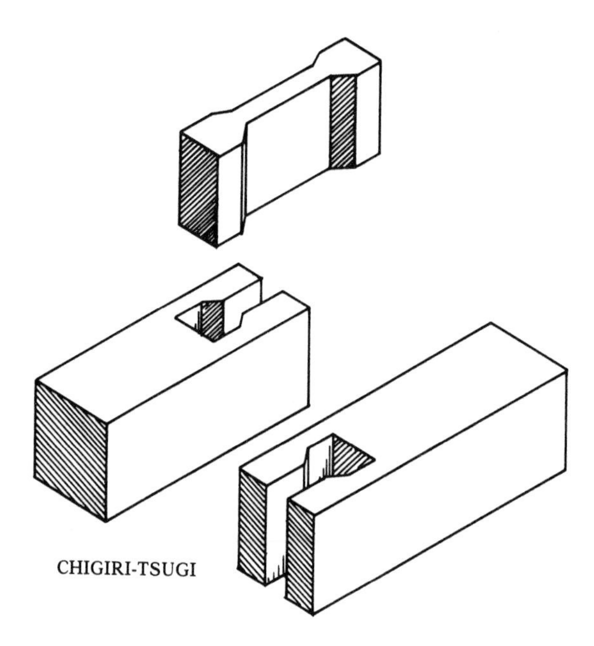

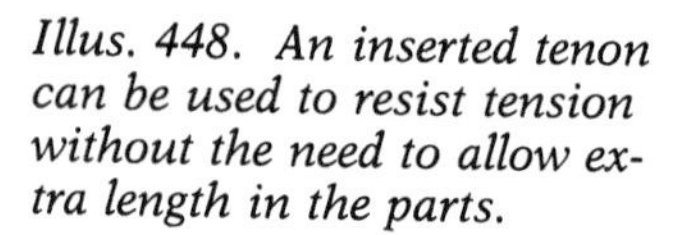

Illus. 448. An inserted tenon can be used to resist tension without the need to allow extra length in the parts.

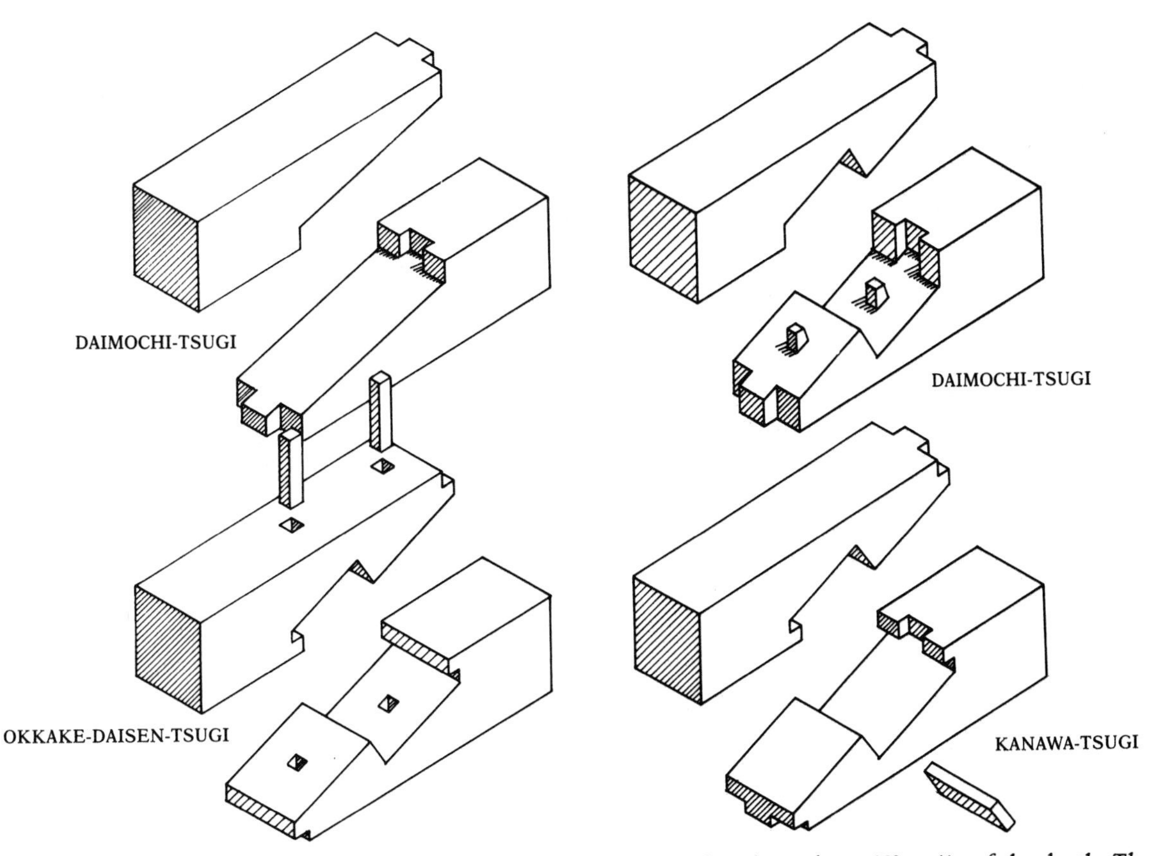

Illus. 449. These joints are similar to Western scarf joints. The scarf angle is about 40° or 1/25 of the depth. The lower section must be supported within one foot of the joint. These joints are usually used dry, but glue will greatly increase their strength.

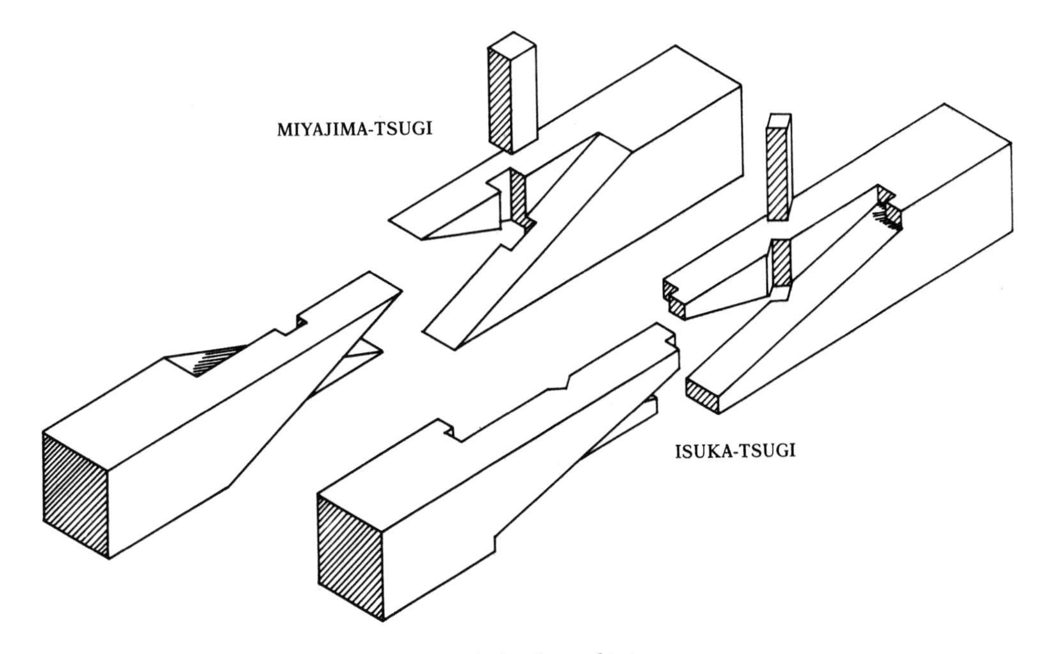

Illus. 450. These joints are very similar to Western halved-scarf joints.

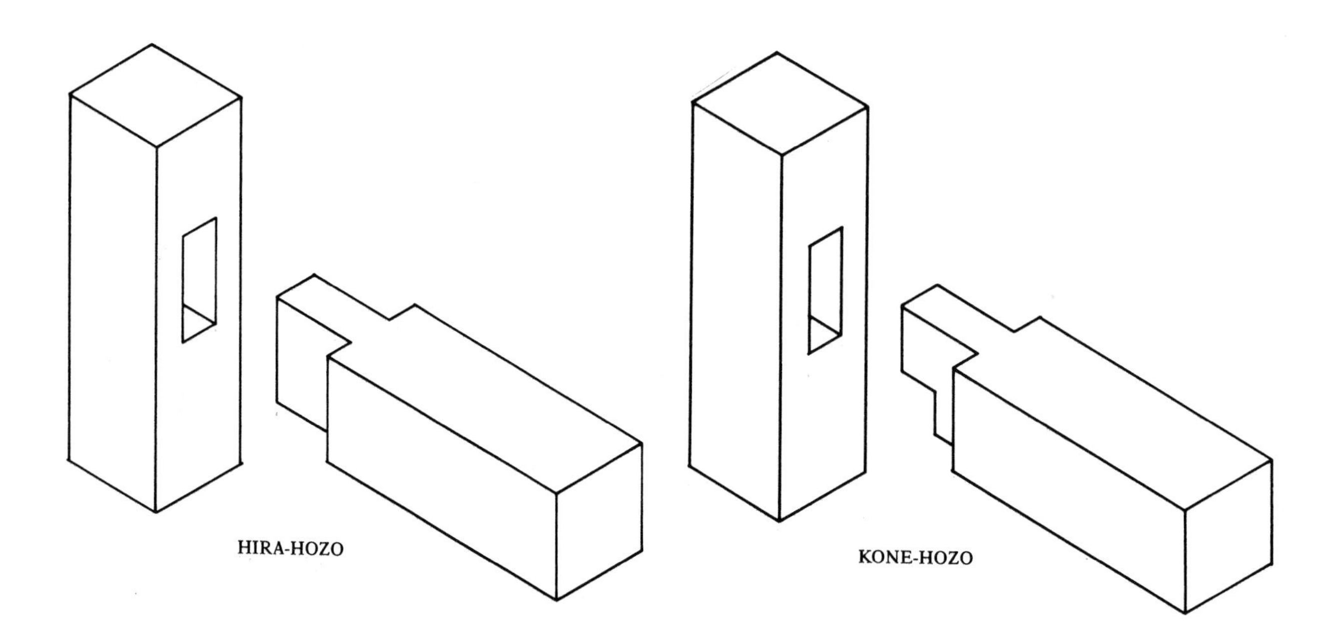

Illus. 451. Japanese mortise-and-tenon joints are very similar to their Western counterparts. The proportions are slightly different. A blind mortise is usually deeper than is customary for a Western joint, and in soft woods, the mortise is tapered for a snug fit.

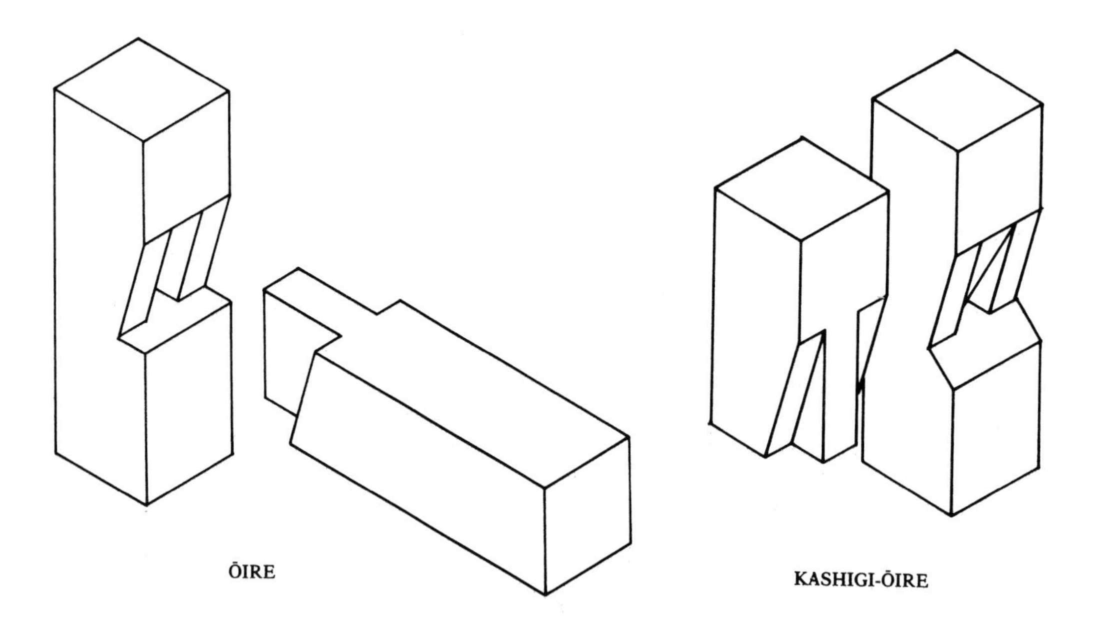

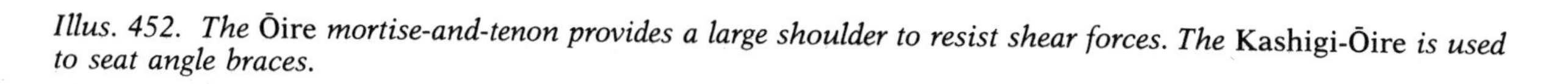

Illus. 452. The Ōire *mortise-and-tenon provides a large shoulder to resist shear forces. The* Kashigi-Ōire *is used to seat angle braces.*

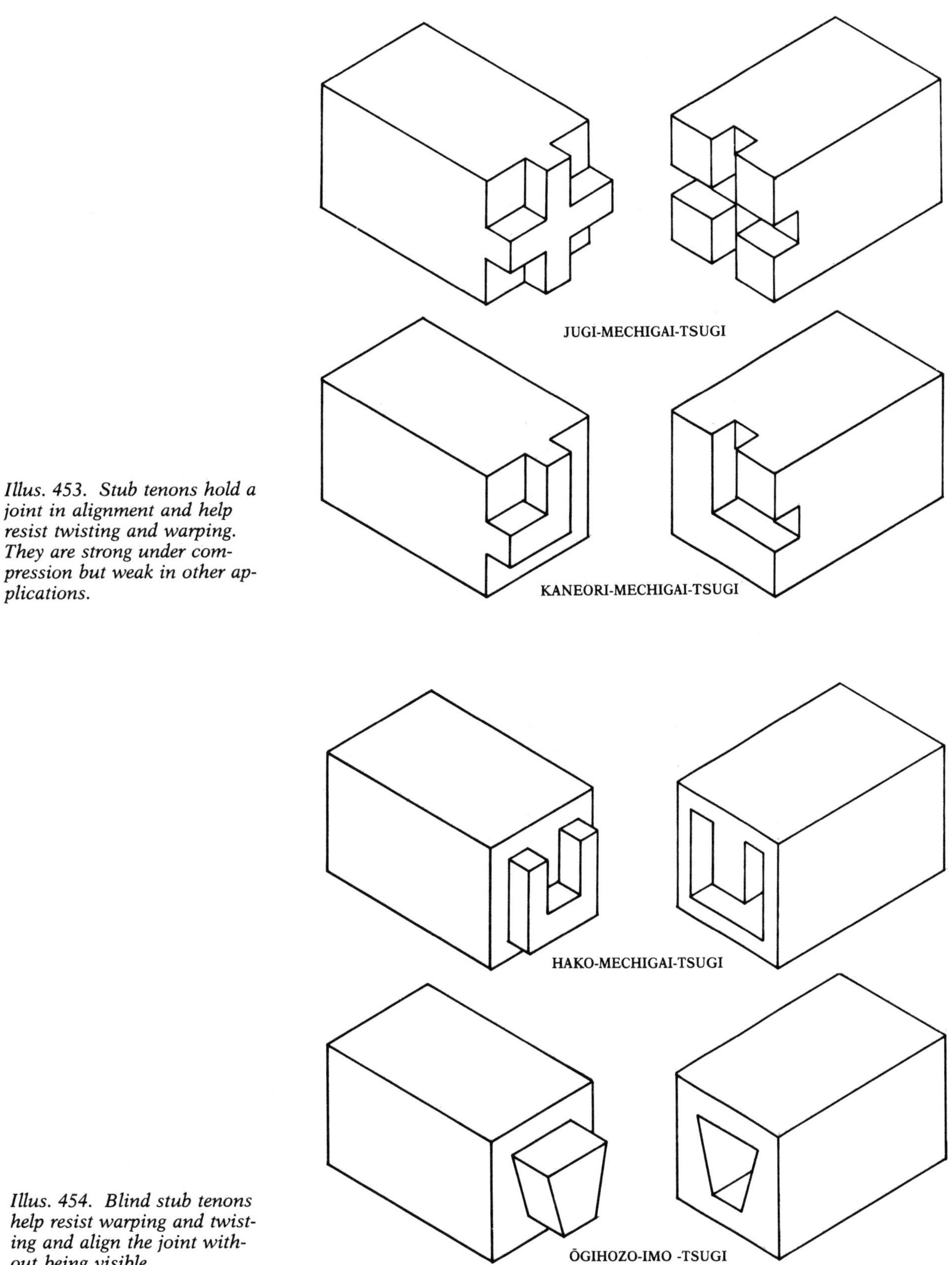

Illus. 453. Stub tenons hold a joint in alignment and help resist twisting and warping. They are strong under compression but weak in other applications.

Illus. 454. Blind stub tenons help resist warping and twisting and align the joint without being visible.

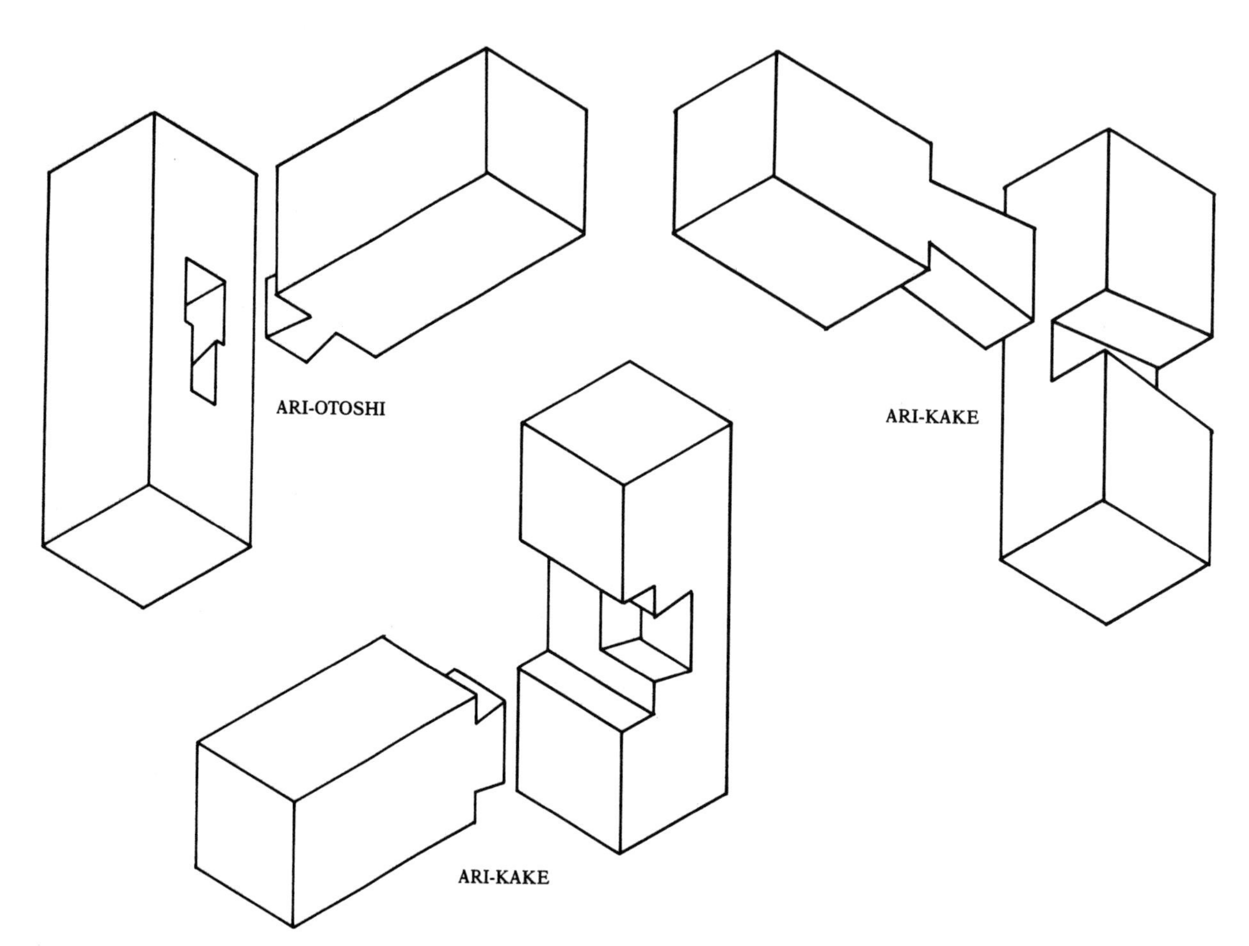

Illus. 455. Dovetailing adds tensile strength.

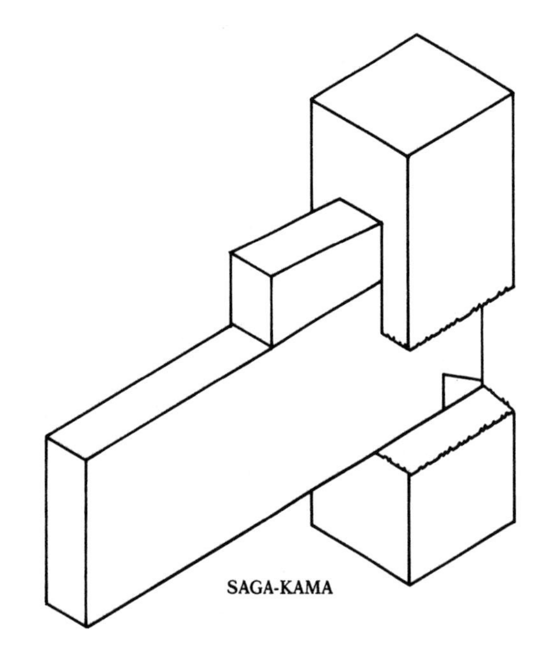

Illus. 456. The Saga-Kama *is locked by a dovetail and a wedge. The mortise is made extra long to allow the tenon to be inserted over the dovetail. The wedge fills the extra space and tightens the joint.*

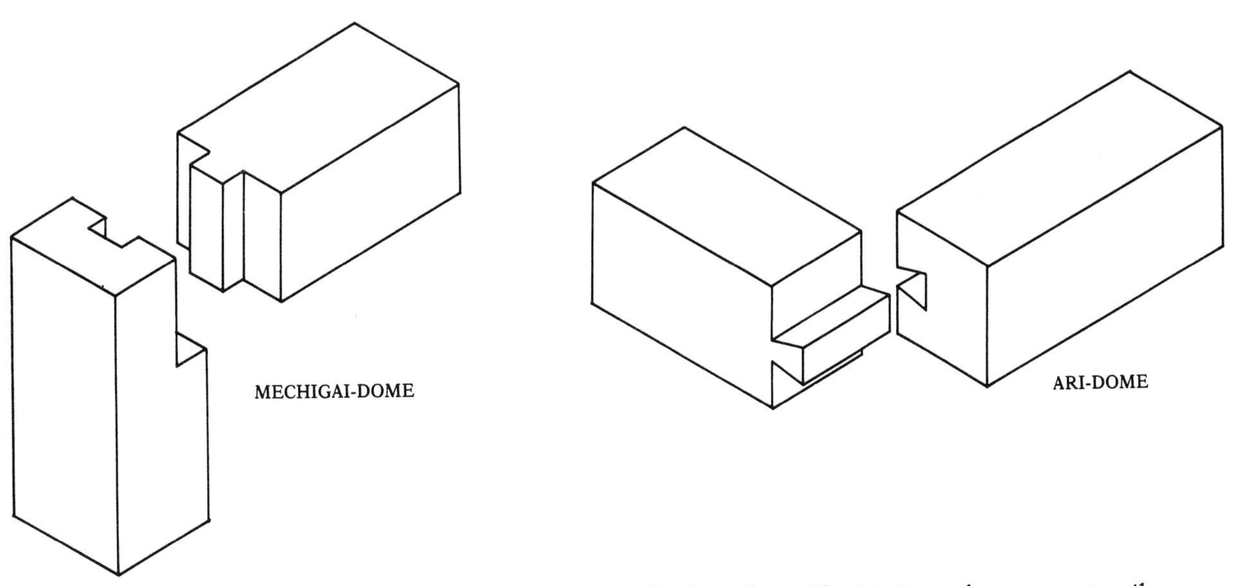

Illus. 457. The Mechigai-Dome *is designed to resist primarily shear force. The* Ari-Dome *has greater tensile strength.*

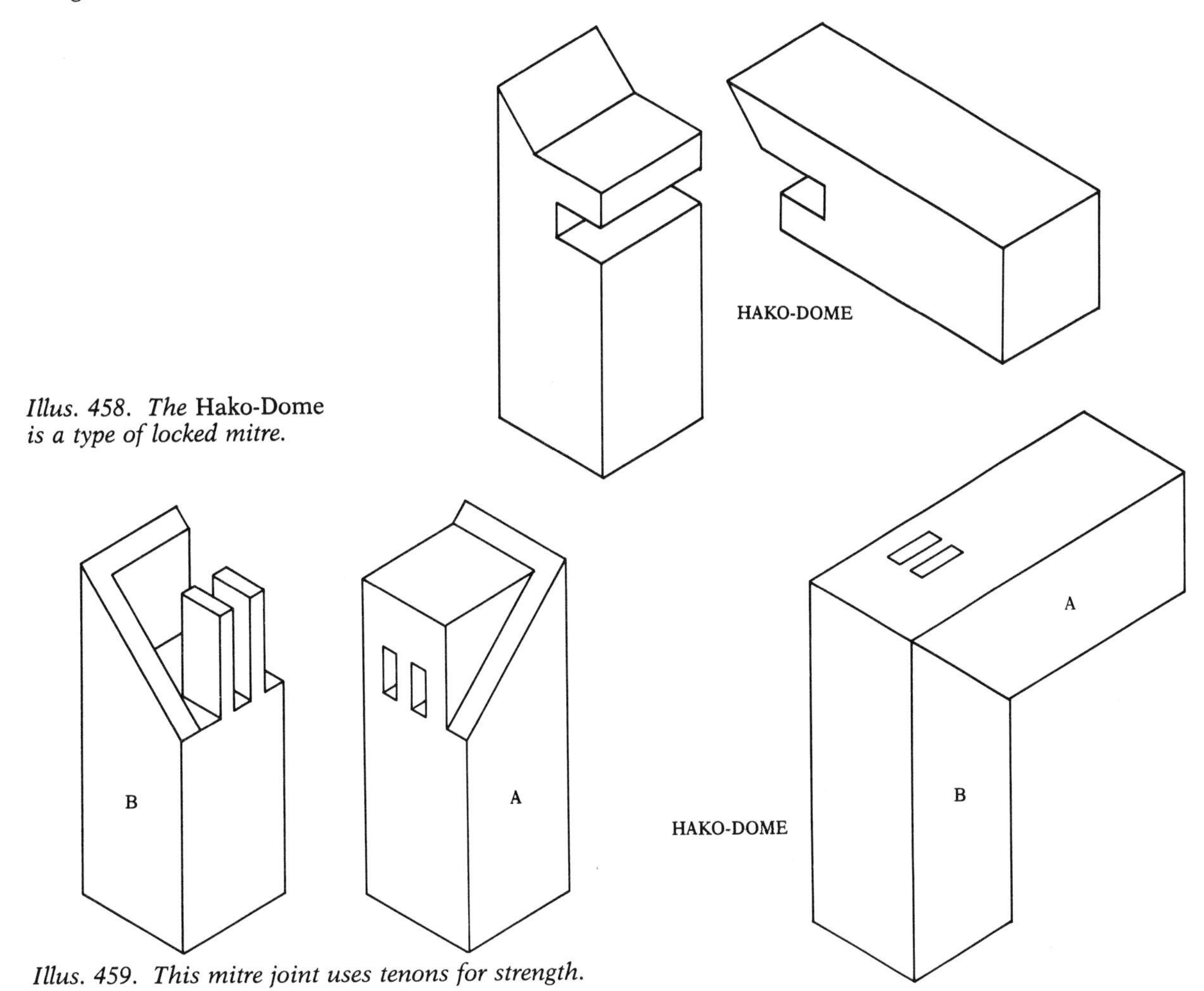

Illus. 458. The Hako-Dome *is a type of locked mitre.*

Illus. 459. This mitre joint uses tenons for strength.

METRIC EQUIVALENCY CHART

MM—MILLIMETRES CM—CENTIMETRES

INCHES TO MILLIMETRES AND CENTIMETRES

INCHES	MM	CM	INCHES	CM	INCHES	CM
⅛	3	0.3	9	22.9	30	76.2
¼	6	0.6	10	25.4	31	78.7
⅜	10	1.0	11	27.9	32	81.3
½	13	1.3	12	30.5	33	83.8
⅝	16	1.6	13	33.0	34	86.4
¾	19	1.9	14	35.6	35	88.9
⅞	22	2.2	15	38.1	36	91.4
1	25	2.5	16	40.6	37	94.0
1¼	32	3.2	17	43.2	38	96.5
1½	38	3.8	18	45.7	39	99.1
1¾	44	4.4	19	48.3	40	101.6
2	51	5.1	20	50.8	41	104.1
2½	64	6.4	21	53.3	42	106.7
3	76	7.6	22	55.9	43	109.2
3½	89	8.9	23	58.4	44	111.8
4	102	10.2	24	61.0	45	114.3
4½	114	11.4	25	63.5	46	116.8
5	127	12.7	26	66.0	47	119.4
6	152	15.2	27	68.6	48	121.9
7	178	17.8	28	71.1	49	124.5
8	203	20.3	29	73.7	50	127.0

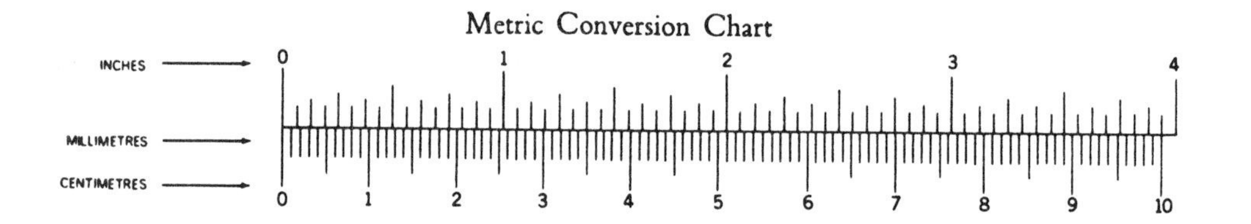

Index